Northrop Frye

AN ANNOTATED BIBLIOGRAPHY

Northrop Frye

AN ANNOTATED BIBLIOGRAPHY OF PRIMARY AND SECONDARY SOURCES

Robert D. Denham

UNIVERSITY OF TORONTO PRESS

Toronto Buffalo London

© University of Toronto Press 1987
Toronto Buffalo London
Printed in Canada

ISBN 0-8020-2630-3

Printed on acid-free paper

Canadian Cataloguing in Publication Data

Denham, Robert D.
  Northrop Frye

  Includes index.
  ISBN 0-8020-2630-3

  1. Frye, Northrop, 1912–   – Bibliography.
  I. Title.

  Z8317.83.D45 1987   016.801'95'0924   C87-094754-0

For

Jane Widdicombe

and

Louise L. Denham

Contents

PART TWO: SECONDARY SOURCES

Preface

The aim of this bibliography is to present a comprehensive, annotated account of the critical writings by and about Northrop Frye. The bibliography had its beginnings more than fifteen years ago when I first began to study Frye's criticism. John E. Grant's check-list, which had appeared in *Northrop Frye and Modern Criticism*, provided an excellent starting point. During the years that followed I continued to read Frye and to make more or less systematic notes on the critical essays and books that he kept issuing at a remarkable rate, and I also began to keep track of what other readers were saying about his work. This resulted in a preliminary check-list published thirteen years ago, *Northrop Frye: An Enumerative Bibliography*, and the several supplements that have appeared in the meantime. It is appropriate now, because of Frye's increasing reputation as a critic, to present a fully annotated account not simply of his own work but of the reaction it has received.

Daniel Pérusse suggested several years ago that if the Nobel Prize in Literature were ever to come to a Canadian it would be awarded to Frye (L400), and a recent study of 950 journals revealed that among the most frequently cited authors in the arts and humanities Frye ranked only behind Marx, Aristotle, Shakespeare, Lenin, Plato, Freud, and Barthes (P85). Frye's reputation and influence are unquestionably broad, his achievement decidedly international. This volume is intended to serve as an aid to the further study of that influence and achievement and to stand as a testimony to the large space Frye occupies in the world of critical discourse.

The bibliography is divided into two main parts. The ten sections in part 1 provide an annotated catalogue of Frye's books, essays, and reviews, as well as unpublished manuscripts, interviews, correspondence, and audio and video recordings. It also includes such things as his undergraduate

writings, editorials, short fiction, sermons, university reports, replies to
questionnaires, tributes, and other miscellaneous forms – more than one
thousand items altogether. Part 2 is an annotated list of writings about
Frye's work. It consists largely of essays and reviews – more than fifteen
hundred items. In this section I have not included the voluminous practical
applications of Frye's criticism, except in those cases where the exposition
or other use of his work is sufficiently detailed to warrant notice.

I have followed the *de rigueur* practice of classifying entries according to
their form. Some forms, however, are too few to require a separate category, so I have combined them, in section F of part 1 and section P of part
2, under the heading Miscellaneous. The primary entries are listed chrono-
logically within each section because of the inherent importance of the
diachronic perspective. The manuscripts and correspondence, however, are
catalogued according to the location of the archives in which they have
been deposited. The secondary sources are entered alphabetically by author. While this has the advantage of grouping together those essays
by readers who have written about Frye's work on more than one occasion,
it has the disadvantage of making it more difficult than a chronological
list would to determine the historical contours of the reaction his work has
received. Accordingly, I have included an appendix that lists chronologi-
cally the entry numbers in sections K and L.

The subspecies of discursive writing are more various in Frye's case than
in most, and this results in what may appear to be artificial categories or
arbitrary decisions about where to locate a given item. The dividing
line between the review and the review essay, for example, is not always
clear. Generally I have included in the latter category those reviews in
which Frye goes beyond commenting on the book under review to develop
a constructive position of his own or to expand the discussion in some
other way. I have reserved the former category for brief reviews, some of
which amount to no more than notices. In order to make it easier for
users to determine the critical reception of Frye's own books, I have abandoned this distinction in section M.

For Frye's books, I have listed in section A all of the editions, both
hardcover and paperback, and their translations. These have been given
separate entry numbers, except in those few cases where the hardcover and
paperback versions were issued simultaneously. Many of Frye's essays
were first presented as addresses at conferences and professional meetings.
The time and place of these meetings, when I have been able to discover
this information, are listed at the end of the annotation.

For secondary sources, I have given complete pagination for the articles,
reviews, and chapters of books that are not devoted entirely to Frye, but
these are followed by the page numbers within square brackets for the
material that does concern his work. For the reviews of Frye's books (section M), I have given the approximate number of words in each of the
reviews, except for the brief notices, at the end of the entry.

In part 1, reprinted essays and portions of books are listed under the entry of their original appearance. In those cases where the title of the re-printed material differs from that of the original, I have included a separate entry, without annotation though cross-referenced to the original, according to the date of the reprint. This will make it easier for users who have access only to a reprinted essay to locate its first appearance. Reprint information for those of Frye's books that are not collections of essays is entered in section A immediately following the last edition or translation of the book. The separate essays in each of Frye's collections (*BG*, *DG*, *FI*, *NFCL*, *SM*, and *StS*) are listed under 'Contents' following the entry for the collection, and each of these essays is cross-referenced to the primary entry in section C or D, where the reprint information, as well as the original date and place of publication, will be found. I have made separate entries in section D for several of Frye's papers originally presented as lectures but not published until they appeared in one of his collections.

In some cases users will have to rely on the title index to determine the original dates and places of publication of Frye's uncollected essays. 'By Liberal Things,' for example, was published under a different title in a 1960 issue of *Varsity Graduate*, with no indication that it was first published as a separate monograph in 1959. But the user can discover this and similar kinds of information by using the index and the system of cross-references.

One additional place where entries are repeated is in the section of audio and video tapes, the material cause of which would have perhaps presented Aristotle a taxonomic problem, too. Several of the tapes are interviews, so they are listed in section G as well, where they are cross-referenced to the annotations in section H.

I have tried to give enough information in the annotations to enable users to determine whether or not they would like to consult the material in question. Although I have occasionally made judgments in the annotations, my primary aim has been to provide a descriptive abstract of the subject matter or the argument of the entry. I have departed from this practice with the interviews (section G), the discontinuous form of which caused me generally to resort to a catalogue of the issues discussed or questions answered.

The primary entries form, so far as I know, a complete record of Frye's work through June 1987. I cannot, however, claim completeness – that elusive goal – for the secondary sources. There are certainly a number of accounts of Frye's work that have escaped my notice. For several dozen items, mostly reviews in foreign-language publications that are not micro-filmed, I have not been able to discover the volume number or page numbers or both. I have included these items, even though the only publication information is the author, title, and date. But I have not included several items, most of which appeared in German newspapers, from which the date of publication is missing from my photocopies. I have entered, though not annotated, about two dozen Japanese articles and reviews that

I have not seen but for which I have references. All of the Japanese titles, incidentally, have been translated and/or transliterated.

Reprint information is also, I am certain, incomplete, the few indexes that provide such data being sketchy at best. Though I have checked the requests for permission to reprint in Frye's own files, I have not consulted his publishers for this information. Still, the bibliography contains references to hundreds of publications where the user can find both primary and secondary sources reprinted. Such information can be useful when the original publication is obscure or otherwise difficult to locate. The files of press clippings on Frye are, of course, thick. While I have included some items from the popular press, especially in section P, I have not catalogued the hundreds of press notices, the large majority of which appeared in Canadian newspapers, that are of only fugitive interest.

The index, along with the cross-references, provides one of the primary keys to the bibliography, enabling users to locate information by author's surname and by title. The index also includes selected subject references.

In compiling this bibliography I have continually encountered the goodwill of scores of people who responded to my inquiries and requests. Northrop Frye gave generously of his time in replying to my questions when he had more important things to do. I record my deep thanks to him for his help over the years, for permitting me to examine his library and files, and for providing me office space during a sabbatical in Toronto. This is the place, too, to record my debt to Northrop Frye for the profound way his essays and books have helped to shape my life over the past two decades. What motivates the bibliographer is, of course, the desire to provide a useful reference work. Bibliographers are, too, I suppose, somewhat like detectives and stamp collectors: they take delight in uncovering the elusive item and in solving riddles of various kinds, and they are driven by a rage for order and completeness. Yet what goaded me on above everything else was my profound admiration for the subject himself. Perhaps this volume will stand as a symbol of gratitude for the instruction and delight Northrop Frye has given me, for his exemplary life as a teacher and critic, and for his providing occasional glimpses of that third order of experience about which he speaks so eloquently.

My debt to Jane Widdicombe, Northrop Frye's secretary for almost two decades, is considerable. She has for many years responded to all my requests promptly and with patience, care, and good faith, and has set me straight on a number of matters, including left-handedness. I express my warm thanks to her here and on the dedication page.

I also record my gratitude to the following individuals for supplying information of one kind or another or for helping me with the translations: Johan Aitken, University of Toronto; Charles Altieri, University of Washington; Roy Anker, Northwestern College; Hugh Anson-Cartwright, Toronto; David W. Atkinson, University of Lethbridge; John Ayre, Guelph,

Ont; William B. Bache, Purdue University; Pat Barclay, Victoria, BC; Sylvan
Barnet, Cambridge, Mass; Bruce Bashford, State University of New York,
Stony Brook; Ronald Bates, University of Western Ontario; Kathryn Beam,
University of Michigan Library; Munro Beattie, Carleton University; John E.
Becker, Fairleigh Dickinson University; Joy Bennett, Concordia University
Library; Deanne Bogdan, Ontario Institute for Studies in Education; Wayne
C. Booth, University of Chicago; Robert C. Brandeis, Victoria University
Library; Jamie Brown, Writers' Union of Canada; Charles Byrd, Emory &
Henry College; Harry Cargas, Webster College; Sylvia Castellanos, Emory,
Va; Jane Clark, University of Toronto Library; John Robert Colombo,
Toronto; Eugene Combs, McMaster University; L. Couette, Canadian Em-
bassy, Washington, DC; Ruth Crouse, Emory & Henry College; Peter
Cummings, Hobart College; Scott D. Denham, Harvard University; Michael
Dolzani, University of Toronto; Beatrice Donald, Simon Fraser University;
Gail Donald, CBC Radio Archives; Craig Doyle, Anansi Press; Dennis Duffy,
University of Toronto; Jan Ulrik Dyrkjob, Copenhagen University; Merle
Fabian, Canadian Embassy, Washington, DC; Sidney Feshbach, City Uni-
versity of New York; Graham Forst, Capilano College; Kathryn Gagnon,
Queen's University Archives, Kingston; F.W. Galan, University of Toronto;
Ellen Gartrell, Duke University Library; Sylvia Giroux, National Gallery
of Canada; Ann Goddard, Public Archives of Canada; Homer Goldberg,
State University of New York, Stony Brook; Branko Gorjup, Toronto; Helen
Gougeon, Toronto; John E. Grant, University of Iowa; Thomas B. Green-
slade, Kenyon College; Terry R. Griffin, Emory & Henry College; Rachel
Grover, University of Toronto Library; A.C. Hamilton, Queen's University,
Kingston; Julia Hamilton, Indiana University Press; Susan F. Harbison,
Harvard University; Anne Hart, Media Centre, University of Toronto; Cathy
Henderson, Harry Ransom Humanities Research Center, University of
Texas; A. Hill, Purdue University Library; Brian L. Horne, King's College,
London; Ben Howard, Alfred University; Carol Irving, Carleton University;
Andrew Jenkins, Toronto *Globe and Mail*; Jorgen I. Jensen, Copenhagen
University; W.T. Jewkes, Virginia Polytechnic Institute and State University;
William A. Johnsen, Michigan State University; Louise Johnston, McGill
University; Charles LeBlanc, Canadian Embassy, Beijing, China; Alvin Lee,
McMaster University; Ura M. Lloyd, Indiana University Alumni Asso-
ciation; Gary A. Lundell, University of Washington Library; Jennifer Lyn-
ton, National Gallery of Canada; Adrienne Macaulay, Columbia University
Press; Louis H. Mackey, University of Texas; Madeleine Marier, Radio
Canada International; Franca Mazzolani, Canadian Embassy, Rome; Rina
Mendelsohn, Cameri Theatre of Tel Aviv; Dido Mendl, CBC Radio Archives;
Ann Merriman, Richmond, Va; Bruce Mickleburgh, Seneca College; Ed-
ward J. Miles, University of Vermont; John Hanly Morgan, Don Mills,
Ontario; Kenji Nakamura, University of Tokyo; R. Gordon Nodwell, To-
ronto; Eizaburo Okuizumi, University of Chicago Library; E.M. Oppen-
heimer, Carleton University; Patricia Parker, University of Toronto; Edward

J. Pennington, Social Planning Council of Metropolitan Toronto; Stephano
Persichelli, Montreal; Bruce W. Powe, Toronto; Annis Pratt, University
of Wisconsin; Richard J. Preston, McMaster University; John Paul Pritchard,
University of Oklahoma; Jana Prokop, University of Toronto Library;
William Ray, Wake Forest University; Harold Remus, Wilfrid Laurier
University; Marion Richmond, Canadian Publishing Foundation; R.T.
Robertson, University of Saskatchewan; Margaret P. Robinson, Dartmouth
College; Julian Rodriguez, University of Murcia; John Rollins, Kalamazoo,
Mich; S.P. Rosenbaum, University of Toronto; Kenneth Rothwell, University of Vermont; Alexander Sackton, University of Texas; Imre Salusinszky,
Oxford University; Judith Ann Schiff, Yale University Library; Dorothy
Sedgwick, Toronto; Per Seyersted, University of Oslo; Douglas Shephard,
Arizona State University; Glenna Davis Sloan, City University of New
York; Norman Snider, Toronto; Luis F. Fernandez Sosa, Western Illinois
University; Peter Stevens, University of Windsor; Helen J. Stewart, St
Catharines, Ont.; Anand Swarup, D.A.V. College, Ambala City, India;
Richard Taberner, Oxford University Press; Shunichi Takayanagi, Sophia
University; Clara Thomas, York University; Kathy Quinn Thomas, University of Toronto; Elizabeth Thorrington, New Science Publications; Memye
Curtis Tucker, Agnes Scott College; Francesca Valente, Italian Cultural
Institute, San Francisco; David A. Wells, Queen's University, Belfast; Bruce
Whiteman, McMaster University Library; Thomas Willard, University of
Arizona; Eugene Williamson, University of Alabama; George Woodcock,
University of British Columbia; Hisaaki Yamanouchi, University of Tokyo;
Dorothy Zeist, Library of Congress; Betty Zirnite, Cornell University Press.

Special thanks are due to my editors at the University of Toronto
Press – Prudence Tracy, Lorraine Ourom, and Darlene Money – and to the
head librarians and their staffs at Emory & Henry College, the University
of Chicago, Yale University, Harvard University, the Library of Congress,
the University of North Carolina at Chapel Hill, the University of Virginia,
the University of Kentucky, York University, the University of California at
Berkeley, New York University, and the University of Toronto. For grants
that enabled me to complete this project I am indebted to the National
Endowment for the Humanities and to the Canadian Embassy. This book
has been published with the help of a grant from the Canadian Federation
for the Humanities, using funds provided by the Social Sciences and
Humanities Research Council of Canada.

Finally, my deepest thanks go to my wife, Rachel. Like Dilsey, she
endured, though at times she felt as nonplussed as the woman in the *New
Yorker* cartoon, whose husband, pounding away on his typewriter and
surrounded by reams of manuscript pages, looks up long enough to reply,
'Finish it? Why would I want to finish it?'

Chronology

1912 Herman Northrop Frye born Sherbrooke, Quebec, 14 July, to Herman
Edward Frye and Catharine Maud Howard Frye
1919 Moves to New Brunswick
1928 Graduates from Aberdeen High School in Moncton, New Brunswick,
where he enrols for a short time in a business course
1929 Enters Victoria College, University of Toronto
1933 Graduates from Victoria College. Enters Emmanuel College, University of
Toronto
1934 Spends the summer near Shaunavon in southwestern Saskatchewan on a
circuit of the United Church of Canada
1936 Graduates from Emmanuel College. Is ordained in the United Church of
Canada. Receives a Royal Society of Canada fellowship to study the
prophecies of William Blake. Enters Merton College, Oxford
1937 Marries Helen Kemp, 24 August. Appointed as lecturer in the honours
course in English literature at Victoria College
1938 Returns to Merton College, Oxford, to complete studies for the BA degree
1939 Begins tenure as member of the faculty at Victoria College
1940 Receives MA from Merton College
1943 Promoted to rank of assistant professor at Victoria College
1947 Publishes *Fearful Symmetry*. Becomes an associate professor at Victoria
College and literary editor of the *Canadian Forum*
1948 Promoted to rank of full professor at Victoria College. Becomes editor of
the *Canadian Forum*, a position held until 1954
1950 Receives a Guggenheim fellowship. Begins writing an annual survey of
Canadian poetry for the *University of Toronto Quarterly*
1951 Elected as fellow of the Royal Society of Canada
1952 Becomes chairman of English department at Victoria College

1953 Serves as chairman of the English Institute

1954 Is appointed Class of 1932 Visiting Lecturer at Princeton University

1957 Publishes *Anatomy of Criticism*. Is visiting lecturer at Harvard University

1958 Receives the Lorne Pierce Medal from the Royal Society of Canada

1959 Becomes principal of Victoria College

1963 Publishes *The Educated Imagination, The Well-Tempered Critic, Fables of Identity*, and *T.S. Eliot*

1965 Publishes *A Natural Perspective* and *The Return of Eden*

1967 Appointed to position of University Professor at the University of Toronto. Receives the Canada Council Medal. Publishes *Fools of Time* and *The Modern Century*

1968 Publishes *A Study of English Romanticism*

1969 Elected as a foreign honorary member of the American Academy of Arts and Sciences

1970 Receives the Pierre Chauveau Medal from the Royal Society of Canada. Publishes *The Stubborn Structure*

1971 Publishes *The Bush Garden* and *The Critical Path*. Receives the Canada Council's Molson Prize

1972 Elected companion of the Order of Canada

1974 Elected honorary fellow of Merton College, Oxford

1975 Becomes corresponding fellow of the British Academy

1976 Publishes *The Secular Scripture* and *Spiritus Mundi*. Becomes foreign member of the American Philosophical Association. Serves as president of the Modern Language Association

1978 Publishes *Northrop Frye on Culture and Literature*. Becomes chancellor of Victoria College. Receives Royal Bank Award

1979 Makes lecture tour of Italy, speaking to large audiences in Milan, Florence, Venice, Rome, and other cities

1980 Publishes *Creation and Recreation*

1981 Elected honorary member of the American Academy and Institute of Arts and Letters

1982 Publishes *The Great Code* and *Divisions on a Ground*

1983 Publishes *The Myth of Deliverance*

1986 Publishes *Northrop Frye on Shakespeare*

1987 Attends an international conference in Rome, Italy, 25–27 May, devoted to assessing his work. Receives Governor-General's Award. Begins fiftieth year of teaching at Victoria College

Abbreviations

Frye's Books

Date of publication is in parentheses; entry number is in square brackets.

AC   *Anatomy of Criticism: Four Essays* (1957) [A2]
BG   *The Bush Garden: Essays on the Canadian Imagination* (1971) [A13]
CP   *The Critical Path: An Essay on the Social Context of Literary Criticism* (1972) [A14]
CR   *Creation and Recreation* (1980) [A18]
DG   *Divisions on a Ground: Essays on Canadian Culture* (1982) [A20]
EI   *The Educated Imagination* (1963) [A3]
FI   *Fables of Identity: Studies in Poetic Mythology* (1963) [A4]
FS   *Fearful Symmetry: A Study of William Blake* (1947) [A1]
FT   *Fools of Time: Studies in Shakespearean Tragedy* (1967) [A9]
GC   *The Great Code: The Bible and Literature* (1982) [A19]
MC   *The Modern Century* (1967) [A10]
MD   *The Myth of Deliverance: Reflections on Shakespeare's Problem Comedies* (1983) [A21]
NFCL *Northrop Frye on Culture and Literature: A Collection of Review Essays* (1978) [A17]
NFS   *Northrop Frye on Shakespeare* (1986) [A23]
NP   *A Natural Perspective: The Development of Shakespearean Comedy and Romance* (1965) [A7]
RE   *The Return of Eden: Five Essays on Milton's Epics* (1965) [A8]
SR   *A Study of English Romanticism* (1968) [A11]
SeS   *The Secular Scripture: A Study of the Structure of Romance* (1976) [A15]
SM   *Spiritus Mundi: Essays on Literature, Myth, and Society* (1976) [A16]
StS   *The Stubborn Structure: Essays on Criticism and Society* (1970) [A12]
TSE   *T.S. Eliot* (1963) [A5]

WTC   *The Well-Tempered Critic* (1963) [A6]

Associations and Periodicals

AULLA   Australasian Universities Language and Literature Association
AUMLA   Australasian Modern Language Association
CEA   College English Association
CRNLE   Center for Research in the New Literatures in English
CRTC   Canadian Radio-television and Telecommunications
          Commission
IAUPE   International Association of University Professors of English
JSOT   *Journal for the Study of the Old Testament*
MLN   *Modern Language Notes*
NCTE   National Council of Teachers of English
PN Review *Poetry Nation Review*
UNISA   University of South Africa

Other Abbreviations

ALS   autographed letter signed
chapt   chapter
CTS   carbon typescript
ed   editor *or* edited by *or* edition
et al   and others
F   Frye
FHA   Frye's holograph annotations
gen ed general editor
MS(S)   manuscript(s)
MTS   mimeographed typescript
nd   no date
no   number
np   no place *or* no publisher
OH   original holograph
OTS   original typescript
p, pp   page, pages
PTS   photocopied typescript
rev   revised
rpt   reprint *or* reprinted
TLS   typed letter signed
TLU   typed letter unsigned
trans   translator *or* translated
Univ   University
vol   volume
w   words

Primary Sources

A

Books

A1 *Fearful Symmetry: A Study of William Blake.* Princeton, NJ: Princeton Univ
Press 1947. 462 pp. Hardcover
Widely recognized as one of the most important contributions to the study
of Blake, especially his prophetic works. F's purpose is to examine the
relationship between Blake's mature thought and the literary tradition.
Assumes that Blake is best understood when his entire canon is viewed as
a unified achievement. Shows Blake's relationship to the Western tradition
and thereby establishes him 'as a typical poet and his thinking as typically
poetic thinking.' Insists on the unity of Blake's poetic system and emphasizes the central role that the supreme figure of the artist, Orc, plays in this
system. Begins his exegesis with Blake's theory of knowledge, that of a
visionary, which sets him off from the separation of subject and object in
the 'cloven fiction' of Locke's epistemology. Argues that we must read
Blake in terms of his unitary theory of the imagination, rather than simply
in historical terms, and that by following his allegorical method we are
confronted with the 'doctrine that all symbolism in all art and all religion is
mutually intelligible among all men, and that there is such a thing as the
iconography of the imagination.' The 'grammar' of this iconography, or the
way Blake represents his vision of reality by means of his special yet
traditionally rooted symbolism, is charted throughout the final two-thirds
of the book. Here Blake is related to Spenser, Milton, and especially
the Bible. Ranges freely over Blake's entire canon, yet gives a detailed
exegesis of Blake's attacks on society in *The Marriage of Heaven and Hell*, of
his emphasis on freedom through action in *America* and *Europe*, and of
his conception of apocalypse in *The Song of Los*. Then provides major commentaries on *The Book of Urizen, The Four Zoas, Milton*, and *Jerusalem*.
Concludes by proposing a general application of the allegorical approach

used in the book – one by which the archetypal vision can provide the
context for reading all poetry.

A1a *Fearful Symmetry: A Study of William Blake*. Princeton, NJ: Princeton Univ
Press 1958. 462 pp. Paperback ed of A1, issued with third printing

A1b *Fearful Symmetry: A Study of William Blake*. Boston: Beacon Press 1962. 462
pp. Paperback rpt of A1, incorporating several minor changes. Contains
preface written for this edition (see D132). Illustrations are found throughout the text rather than being gathered in one place as in A1 and A1a.

A1c *Fearful Symmetry: A Study of William Blake*. Princeton, NJ: Princeton Univ
Press 1969. 462 pp. Another reprinting of A1 with preface added. Incorpo-
rates minor changes made in A1b. Issued in hardcover and paperback.

A1d *Agghiacciante simmetria: Uno studio su William Blake*. Trans Carla Plevano
Pezzini and Francesca Valente. Milan: Longanesi 1976. 492 pp. Contains, in
addition to the preface for A1c, another preface written in 1975 for the
Italian translation (see D236). The translation by Pezzini and Valente was
revised by Amleto Lorenzini, based on conversations with F. Stiff paper
wrappers

REPRINTED PORTIONS OF FS
Chapt 2 rpt in *Toward a New Christianity: Readings in the Death of God
Theology*, ed Thomas J.J. Altizer (New York: Harcourt, Brace & World 1967),
17–42; chapt 1 rpt in *English Literature and British Philosophy*, ed S.P. Rosenbaum (Chicago: Univ of Chicago Press 1971), 119–35; portions of chapts 5
and 12 rpt in *Modern Literary Criticism, 1900–1970*, ed Lawrence I. Lipking
and A. Walton Litz (New York: Atheneum 1972), 189–97.

A2 *Anatomy of Criticism: Four Essays*. Princeton, NJ: Princeton Univ Press 1957.
x + 383 pp. Hardcover
Sets out to develop a comprehensive system of critical terms and principles,
derived from literature itself, for understanding literature, especially the
relation of literary works to one another. The First Essay examines literature
in terms of the hero's power of action. F is able to discover five primary
modes (mythical, romantic, high mimetic, low mimetic, and ironic), each of
which has manifested itself in fictional and thematic forms. Fictional
modes, moreover, can be either tragic or comic, and thematic modes either
encyclopedic or episodic, so that there are twenty modal categories altogether. The analysis of modes illustrates that the structural principles
of narrative remain constant even though historically they have been displaced from myth toward realism. In the Second Essay, F analyses symbolic
meaning. He aims to discover the various phases or levels of symbolism
(literal, descriptive, formal, mythic, and anagogic) and combine them into a
comprehensive theory of meaning. Each of the five phases of symbolism
is shown to have its own kind of symbol, *mythos*, and *dianoia*, and each is
related to a kind of art and criticism. The last two essays are extensions
of F's interest in archetypal criticism. The Third Essay (theory of myths) is
a schematic account of the structure of archetypal imagery considered
from the perspective of both meaning (*dianoia*) and narrative (*mythos*). F

gives long analyses of the structure and characters of the basic narrative patterns (romance, comedy, tragedy, irony), each of which has six separate phases. The Fourth Essay is chiefly an effort to define the four genres (drama, *epos*, fiction, and lyric) on the basis of their predominant forms and rhythms and to differentiate the species of each. This book is widely regarded as the most significant and influential work of Anglo-American critical theory of the past fifty years.

A2a *Analyse der Literaturkritik.* Trans Edgar Lohner and Henning Clewing. Stuttgart: W. Kohlhammer Verlag 1964. 380 pp. Includes a brief foreword (p 7) by Edgar Lohner about the difficulties of translating some of F's terms. Paperback

A2b *Anatomy of Criticism: Four Essays.* New York: Atheneum 1965. 383 pp. Rpt of A2 in paperback ed. Page size slightly reduced

A2c *Anatomie de la critique.* Trans Guy Durand. Paris: Gallimard 1969. 454 pp. Stiff paper wrappers

A2d *Anatomia della critica: Quattro saggi.* Trans Paola Rosa-Clot and Sandro Stratta. Turin: Einaudi 1969. 484 pp. Vol 115 in the Piccola Biblioteca series. Index not included in this translation. Paperback

A2e *Anatomy of Criticism: Four Essays.* Princeton, NJ: Princeton Univ Press 1971. x + 383 pp. Paperback issue of A1. Page size slightly reduced

A2f *Anatomia della critica: Quattro saggi.* 2nd ed of A2d. Trans Paola Rosa-Clot and Sandro Stratta. Turin: Einaudi [1972]. 484 pp. Index not included in this translation, which was revised with the help of Amleto Lorenzini. Paperback

A2g *Anatomia criticii.* Trans Domnica Sterian and Mihai Spăriosu. Bucharest: Editura Univers 1972. 473 pp. Includes a preface by Vera Călin (see L74). Hardcover

A2h *Anatomia da crítica.* Trans Péricles Eugênio and Silva Ramos. São Paulo: Editora Cultrix [1973]. 362 pp. Index not included in this translation. Stiff paper wrappers

A2i *Anatomia de la critica: Cuatro ensayos.* Trans Edison Simons. Caracas: Monte Avila Editores 1977. 500 pp. Index only of authors and titles cited in the text. Paperback

A2j *Anatomija kritike: Četiri eseja.* Trans Giga Garčan. Zagreb: Naprijed 1979. 407 pp. Index not included in this translation. Hardcover

A2k *Hihyo no kaibo.* Trans Hiroshi Ebine, Hiroshi Izubuchi, Kenji Nakamura, and Hisaaki Yamanouchi. Tokyo: Hosei Univ Press 1980. viii + 529 + 34 pp. Includes a sketch of F's career by Hisaaki Yamanouchi, a bibliography of books by and about F, and a translators' note and acknowledgments. Hardcover

REPRINTED PORTIONS OF AC

Selections from *AC* have been reprinted in numerous places, including the following: 'The Structure of Comedy,' in *Eight Great Comedies*, ed Sylvan Barnet et al (New York: Mentor Books 1958), 461–9; 'Specific Forms of Drama,' in *The Study of Literature: A Handbook of Critical Essays and Terms*, ed

Sylvan Barnet et al (Boston: Little, Brown 1960), 139–52; excerpt in *The Comic in Theory and Practice*, ed J.J. Enck et al (New York: Appleton-Century-Crofts 1960), 87–91; 'The Forms of Fiction,' in *Discussions of the Novel*, ed Roger Sale (Boston: Heath 1960), 3–11; 'Fictional Modes' [abridged] and 'Specific Continuous Forms,' in *Approaches to the Novel*, ed Robert Scholes (San Francisco: Chandler 1961), 31–7, 41–54; 'The Mythos of Winter: Irony and Satire,' in *Modern Satire*, ed Alvin Kernan (New York: Harcourt, Brace & World 1962), 155–64; 'The Structure of Comedy,' in *Aspects of the Drama: A Handbook*, ed Sylvan Barnet et al (Boston: Little, Brown 1962), 70–80; 'Anagogic Phase: The Symbol as Monad,' in *Modern Criticism: Theory and Practice*, ed Walter Sutton and Richard Foster (New York: Odyssey Press 1963), 296–303; 'Specific Forms of Drama,' in *The Context and Craft of Drama*, ed Robert W. Corrigan and James L. Rosenberg (San Francisco: Chandler 1964), 214–27; 'Theory of Genres,' in *Perspectives on the Epic*, ed Frederick H. Candelaria and William C. Stange (Boston: Allyn & Bacon 1965), 114–20; 'The Rhythm of Recurrence: Epos,' in *The Structure of Verse: Modern Essays on Prosody*, ed H.S. Gross (Greenwich, Conn: Fawcett 1966), 168–80; 'Comic Fictional Modes,' in *The Play and the Reader*, ed Stanley Johnson et al (Englewood Cliffs, NJ: Prentice-Hall 1966), 84–7; 'The Four Forms of Prose Fiction,' in *The Theory of the Novel*, ed Philip Stevick (New York: Free Press 1967), 31–43; 'Notes on the Tragic Hero,' in *Twentieth-Century Interpretations of 'Samson Agonistes,'* ed Galbraith M. Crump (Englewood Cliffs, NJ: Prentice-Hall 1968) 107–8; 'Specific Forms of Drama,' in *Perspectives on Drama*, ed James L. Calderwood and Harold E. Toliver (New York: Oxford Univ Press 1968), 137–47; 'The Mythos of Romance: Summer,' in *Pastoral and Romance: Modern Essays in Criticism*, ed Eleanor T. Lincoln (Englewood Cliffs, NJ: Prentice-Hall 1969), 208–24; several paragraphs on satire from pp 227, 309–10 of *AC* rpt in *Twentieth-Century Interpretations of 'The Praise of Folly,'* ed Kathleen Williams (Englewood Cliffs, NJ: Prentice-Hall 1969), 106–7; 'Specific Continuous Forms (Prose Fiction),' in *The Novel: Modern Essays in Criticism*, ed Robert M. Davis (Englewood Cliffs, NJ: Prentice-Hall 1969), 30–42; 'Polemical Introduction' [abridged] and 'Tentative Conclusion,' in *Criticism: The Major Texts*, ed Walter Jackson Bate (New York: Harcourt Brace Jovanovich 1970), 609–15, 617–25; 'The Mythos of Winter: Irony and Satire,' in *Satire: Modern Essays in Criticism*, ed Ronald Paulson (Englewood Cliffs, NJ: Prentice-Hall 1971), 233–48; 'Specific Continuous Forms,' in *Nineteenth-Century Novel: Critical Essays and Documents*, ed Arnold Kettle (London: Heinemann 1972), 24–36; 'The Mythos of Summer: Romance,' in *Dramatic Romance: Plays, Theory, and Criticism*, ed Howard Felperin (New York: Harcourt Brace Jovanovich 1973), 196–208; 'The Bible as Epic' [selections from pp 315, 316, 317, 319, 320, 325, 189, 190, and 191 of *AC*], in *The Strand* [Victoria College, Univ of Toronto], 24 January 1973, 1–5; 'Mythos of Spring,' in *Dramatic Theory and Criticism*, ed Bernard Dukore (New York: Holt, Rinehart and Winston 1974), 902–5; 'Der Mythos des Frühlings: Komödie,' in *Wesen und Formen des Komischen*

im Drama (Darmstadt: Wissenschaftliche Buchgesellschaft 1975), 159–89; 'A
Menippean Satirist,' in *Peacock: The Satirical Novels*, ed Lorna Sage (London:
Macmillan 1976), 180–1; 'Theory of Archetypal Meaning: Apocalyptic and
Demonic Imagery,' in *The Bible in Its Literary Milieu*, ed John Maier and
Vincent Tollers (Grand Rapids, Mich: Eerdmans 1979), 57–66; 'Tragic
Modes,' in *Tragedy: Developments in Criticism* (London: Macmillan 1980),
157–64.

A3 *The Educated Imagination.* Toronto: Canadian Broadcasting Corp 1963. 68
pp. Hardcover and paperback
Explores generally the value and uses of literature. Posits the existence of
three levels of mind: the level of consciousness and awareness, the level
of social participation, and the level of imagination, 'which produces
the literary language of poems and plays and novels.' Investigates the
creative origins of world literature; the decisive role the imagination plays
in all arts; and the universality and timelessness of myth, metaphor,
and symbol, all of which illustrate the 'primitive effort of the imagination
to identify the human with the non-human world.' Develops a theory
of literature that places unique emphasis on the social usefulness of the
literary arts, maintaining that the study of literature encourages tolerance
in the reader by enabling him or her to see possible beliefs and to imagine
worlds other than his or her own. Offers proposals for teaching literature
that place early emphasis on poetry, the central and original literary form,
and on Greek and Latin classics and the Bible. Originally presented as
six radio talks in the Massey Lecture series of the Canadian Broadcasting
Corp (see H7).

A3a *The Educated Imagination.* Bloomington: Indiana Univ Press 1964. 156 pp.
U.S. ed of A3. Hardcover

A3b *The Educated Imagination.* Bloomington: Indiana Univ Press [1966]. 156 pp.
Paperback reprint of A3a. Midland Book 88

A3c *The Educated Imagination*, ed with an introduction by Hisaaki Yamanouchi.
Tokyo: Tsurumi shoten 1967. viii + 135 pp. This edition was prepared
for Japanese college students. Yamanouchi's introduction (i-viii) and notes
(102–35) are in Japanese; F's text is in English. Paperback

A3d *Kyôyô no tame no sôzôryoku.* Trans Toru Egawa and Masahiko Maeda.
Tokyo: Taiyosha 1969. 188 pp. This translation contains essays by Maeda
on 'The Development of Frye's Critical Theory' (153–80) and by Egawa
on 'Literature and the Myth of Identity' (129–51) (see L331 and L140).
Hardcover

A3e *Pouvoirs de l'imagination: essai.* Trans Jean Simard. Montreal: Editions HMH
1969. 168 pp. Collection Constantes, vol 22. Stiff paper wrappers

A3f *L'immaginazione coltivata.* Trans Amleto Lorenzini and Mario Manzari.
Milan: Longanesi 1974. 125 pp. Stiff paper wrappers
REPRINTED PORTIONS OF EI
'The Keys to Dreamland' and 'Verticals of Adam,' in *The Making of Modern
Poetry in Canada*, ed Louis Dudek and Michael Gnarowski (Toronto: Ryer-

son 1967), 178–97; 'The Keys to Dreamland,' in *The Norton Reader*, rev
and subsequent eds, ed Arthur Eastman (New York: Norton 1969), 624–32;
in *Quartet: A Book of Stories, Plays, Poems, and Essays*, 2nd ed, ed Harold
P. Simonson (New York: Harper & Row 1973), 809-18; in *The Writer's World*,
ed George Arms et al (New York: St Martin's 1978); in *One Hundred Major
Modern Writers: Essays for Composition*, ed Robert Atwan and William
Vesterman (Indianapolis: Bobbs-Merrill 1984), 250–60; 'The Vocation of
Eloquence' abridged as 'Of Free Speech and Vision' in *Chicago Tribune*, 28
February 1965; 'Giants in Time' in *The English Leaflet* 63 (Midwinter 1974):
10–14; and selections from chapts 1, 5, and 6 in *The Harper & Row Reader*,
ed Wayne C. Booth and Marshall W. Gregory (New York: Harper & Row
1984), 236–41.

A4 *Fables of Identity: Studies in Poetic Mythology*. New York: Harcourt, Brace &
World 1963. 265 pp. Paperback
Contents:
1   The Archetypes of Literature (see D49)
2   Myth, Fiction, and Displacement (see D120)
3   Nature and Homer (see D98)
4   New Directions from Old (see D117)
5   The Structure of Imagery in *The Faerie Queene* (see D118)
6   How True a Twain (see D130)
7   Recognition in *The Winter's Tale* (see D134)
8   Literature as Context: Milton's *Lycidas* (see D107)
9   Towards Defining an Age of Sensibility (see D82)
10 Blake after Two Centuries (see D88)
11 The Imaginative and the Imaginary (see D127)
12 Lord Byron (see D104)
13 Emily Dickinson (see D129)
14 Yeats and the Language of Symbolism (see D30)
15 The Realistic Oriole: A Study of Wallace Stevens (see D89)
16 Quest and Cycle in *Finnegans Wake* (see D85)
A selection of F's critical essays written between 1947 and 1962. The first
four essays are largely theoretical, treating topics that receive greater
elaboration in *AC*: archetypal and myth criticism, displacement, literary
conventions, and the structure of poetic imagery. The remaining twelve
essays examine writers and works 'in the central tradition of English
mythopoeic poetry ... a tradition in which the major and prevailing tendencies are Romantic, revolutionary, and Protestant.' Maintains throughout
that there is a unifying structure of imagery that is larger than purely
verbal structure. Emphasizes the received literary forms and conventions
that persist and that provide the imaginative framework that gives shape to
human experience. Observes in the introduction that the hinge of his
total argument is his conception of romanticism, 'one of the most decisive
changes in the history of culture,' a period during which 'the forms of
civilization come to be regarded as man-made rather than as God-made.'

A4a *Favole d'identità: Studi di mitologia poetica*. Trans Ciro Monti. Turin: Einaudi 1973. ix + 346 pp. Paperback

A4b *Doitsusei no guwa*. Trans Tetso Maruko et al. Tokyo: Hosei Univ Press 1983. iv + 469 + 9 pp. Includes an additional set of translators' notes (413–44) and a translator's epilogue (467–9). Hardcover

A5 *T.S. Eliot*. Edinburgh: Oliver and Boyd 1963. 106 pp. Paperback
Begins by distinguishing Eliot's genuine from his polemical literary criticism, the former stemming from the practice and study of literature and the latter from the historical myth of the decline of the modern world and the disintegration of Christianity. Sees Eliot's contribution to the science of criticism as resting in his basic principles, one of which is that literature has a simultaneous existence and order. Analyses the structure of Eliot's poems and plays and the conceptual implications of their imagery. Seeks to establish thereby the iconography of Eliot's total imaginative universe as it is represented in the early, chiefly satiric poetry and in the purgatorial vision of the later poems and plays.

A5a *T.S. Eliot*. New York: Grove 1963. 106 pp. Same text as A5. Paperback

A5b *T.S. Eliot*. New York: Barnes & Noble 1966. 106 pp. Same text as A5. Paperback

A5c *T.S. Eliot*. Edinburgh: Oliver and Boyd 1968. 106 pp. Revised ed of A5. Paperback

A5d *Eliot*. Trans Jesús Díaz. Madrid: Ediciones y Publicaciones Españolas 1969. 173 pp. Paperback

A5e *T.S. Eliot*. New York: Capricorn Books 1972. 106 pp. Same text as A5c. Paperback

A5f *T.S. Eliot: An Introduction*. Chicago: Univ of Chicago Press 1981. 109 pp. Same text as A5c. Reproduced in slightly larger format than previous editions and the bibliography of secondary sources has been brought up to date. Paperback

A5g *T.S. Eriotto*. Trans Hikaru Endo. Tokyo: Shimizukobun-do 1981. xvi + 150 + 71 pp. Includes index (i–xvi), extensive Eliot bibliography (1–71), and bibliography of works by and about F (139–50). Hardcover (boxed)

A6 *The Well-Tempered Critic*. Bloomington: Indiana Univ Press 1963. 160 pp. Hardcover.
Reformulates the traditional idea of three levels of style by placing it in a more literary and less social frame of reference. Posits the principle of three primary rhythms distinguishable in ordinary speech: verse rhythm, dominated by regular accent and often accompanied by such features as rhyme and alliteration; prose rhythm, dominated by the subject-predicate relation of the sentence; and associative rhythm, dominated by the short, irregular phrase and by primitive syntax. Sees the three kinds of rhythm as influencing one another in such a way as to produce six possible matrices for identifying style. Is able to discover, in addition to the primary form of each rhythm, secondary and tertiary forms as well, the entire schema yielding fifteen categories of rhythm, each of which is illustrated with

examples from the history of literature. Turns next to the role of language
in literature. Discovers two forms, the demotic and the hieratic, for each
of the three conventional levels of style. In the final chapter, examines the
implications which the study of style has for critical theory and for the
teaching of literature and its place in society. Connects the mimetic
(classical) and creative (romantic) traditions by seeing literature as a self-
contained universe, which includes both belief and action. Concludes
by returning to high style, which is the world of imagination raised to the
highest level, reflecting all possible worlds. Originally presented as the
Page-Barbour Lectures, University of Virginia, March 1961. An early version
of the first chapter appeared as 'The Well-Tempered Critic' in *Acta Victoriana* 85 (March 1961): I–XII (see D119).

A6a *The Well-Tempered Critic*. Bloomington: Indiana Univ Press 1965. 160 pp.
Paperback rpt of A6. Midland Book 77

A6b *Il critico ben temperato*. Trans Amleto Lorenzini and Mario Manzari. Milan:
Longanesi 1974. 141 pp. Stiff paper wrappers

A6c *Yoi hihyoka*. Trans Michiko Watanabe. Tokyo: Yashio shuppansha 1980. 151
pp. Includes afterword by Watanabe (147–51). Hardcover (boxed)

A6d *The Well-Tempered Critic*. Markham, Ont: Fitzhenry & Whiteside [1983]. 160
pp. Same text and format as A6, but slightly smaller page size. Paperback

A6e *The Well-Tempered Critic*. Bloomington: Indiana Univ Press [1983]. 160 pp.
Same text and format as A6d. U.S. ed, printed in Canada. Paperback
REPRINTED PORTIONS OF WTC
Selections from chapt 1 rpt as 'Ordinary Speech, Verse and Prose,' in *The
Canadian Century: English-Canadian Writing since Confederation*, ed A.J.M.
Smith (Toronto: Gage 1973), 238–51; chapt 1 in *Modern Canadian Essays*, ed
William H. New (Toronto: Macmillan 1976), 93–103.

A7 *A Natural Perspective: The Development of Shakespearean Comedy and Romance*.
New York: Columbia Univ Press 1965. ix + 159 pp. Hardcover
A study of Shakespeare's comedies from a 'middle distance,' treating them
as a single group unified by recurring images and structural devices.
Sees the four romances as the culmination of Shakespeare's achievement.
In the first two chapters, describes the conventional nature of the comedies,
which are operatic because their structure is analogous to music. Distinguishes the plays from Jonson's, which attempt to create the illusion
of realism. Shakespeare, however, is not interested in creating illusion but
in an audience that surrenders itself to the story for its own sake and to
its childlike and concrete conventions. Examines these conventions, as well
as the primitive and popular features of the plays. In Chapter 3, concentrates on the typical structure of the comedies, recapitulating some of
the arguments from *AC*: Renaissance comedy is based on the formula of a
New Comedy, which involves the struggle of the younger generation to
establish a new social order in the face of opposition from the older
generation, and which involves passage through three phases. In the fourth
chapter, argues that the romances are 'the inevitable and genuine culmina-

tion of the poet's achievement': they are the positive outcome of the comedies. The romances develop the theme of the cycle of nature, a movement toward rebirth and renewal that is opposed to the tragic concept of the wheel of fortune. This book is a revised version of the Bampton Lectures presented at Columbia University, November 1963.

A7a *Shakespeares Vollendung: Eine Einführung in die Welt seiner Komödien.* Trans Hellmut Haug. Munich: Nymphenburger Verlagshandlung 1966. 195 pp. Includes translator's preface, explanatory notes, and index of plays cited in the text. Paperback

A7b *A Natural Perspective: The Development of Shakespearean Comedy and Romance.* New York: Harcourt, Brace & World [1969]. ix + 159 pp. Paperback rpt of A7. Harbinger Book H701. Currently rpt as a Harvest/HBJ Book by Harcourt Brace Jovanovich.

REPRINTED PORTIONS OF NP

Chapt 4 partially rpt in *Modern Literary Criticism, 1900–1970,* ed Lawrence I. Lipking and A. Walton Litz (New York: Atheneum 1972), 241–4; brief excerpt from p 81 rpt in *Twentieth-Century Interpretations of 'Much Ado about Nothing,'* ed Walter R. Davis (Englewood Cliffs, NJ: Prentice-Hall 1969), 109–10; selections from pp 91–2 rpt as 'Integrating and Isolating Tendencies in Shakespeare's Comedies,' in *Twentieth-Century Interpretations of 'As You Like It,'* ed Jay L. Halio (Englewood Cliffs, NJ: Prentice-Hall 1968) 111–12.

A8 *The Return of Eden: Five Essays on Milton's Epics.* Toronto: Univ of Toronto Press 1965. viii + 143 pp. Hardcover

Organizes each of the five chapters around a central theme: (1) the encyclopedic nature of epic forms and the hierarchical structure of Renaissance imagery; (2) Milton's cosmology and its relation to his doctrine of good and evil; (3) the Miltonic view of reason, will, and appetite as they manifest themselves on each of the Renaissance levels of reality; (4) the themes of liberty and Milton's revolutionary art; and (5) the structure of *Paradise Regained* and its relation to *Paradise Lost.* Sees the central theme of Milton's epics as 'the return of Eden,' Eden representing the condition of freedom to which human beings aspire and which is to be found within them rather than in nature or history. The thrust of the argument throughout derives from F's understanding of *dianoia,* as seen in his treatment of such topics as the structure of Milton's imagery, his conceptual universe, and his thematic emphasis on 'the garden within.' Looking at Milton's work as a whole, however, F sees it as comprising a total cyclic action. He perceives the epics, then, not only as a vast symmetric ordering of themes but also as an equally vast narrative movement – an interior quest to recover the vision of freedom before the Fall. Chapters 1–4 were originally presented as the Centennial Lectures, Huron College, March 1963. Chapter 5 is a revised version of 'The Typology of *Paradise Regained*' (see D80).

A8a *Five Essays on Milton's Epics.* London: Routledge & Kegan Paul 1966. viii + 158 pp. Same text as A8, though printed in different format. Unlike A8, contains index. Hardcover

A8b *The Return of Eden: Five Essays on Milton's Epics.* Toronto: Univ of Toronto Press 1975. viii + 143 pp. Paperback rpt of A8. Canadian University Paperback 166

A8c Italian translation of *RE* forthcoming from Longanesi.

REPRINTED PORTIONS OF RE

'The Garden Within' and selections from 'The Story of All Things' rpt in *On Milton's Poetry*, ed Arnold Stein (Greenwich, Conn: Fawcett 1970), 228–36, 89–96; 'The Story of All Things,' in *Paradise Lost*, ed Scott Elledge (New York: Norton 1975), 405–22.

A9 *Fools of Time: Studies in Shakespearean Tragedy.* Toronto: Univ of Toronto Press 1967. viii + 121 pp. Hardcover

Outlines three chief kinds of tragic structure in Shakespeare: (1) the social tragedy, which is rooted in history and concerned with the fall of the prince or the killing of the father; (2) the tragedy of Eros, which deals with the separation of lovers, the conflict of duty and passion, or the conflict of social and personal (sexual or family) interests; and (3) the tragedy of the isolation of the spirit, in which the hero is removed from his context and forced to search for a purely personal identity. Argues that the tragedies of order (*Julius Caesar, Hamlet,* and *Macbeth*) are built around a sense of a lost world; in each a strong ruler is killed, replaced by a rebel-figure, and avenged by a nemesis-figure. In the tragedies of passion (*Romeo and Juliet, Antony and Cleopatra,* and *Troilus and Cressida*) the heroes rebel against the debased society in which they find themselves but are destroyed by the conflict between personal and social loyalties. In the tragedies of isolation (*Othello, King Lear,* and *Timon of Athens*) the hero is bitterly separated from everything that sustains life and is left to face the bleak tragic vision of absurdity and anguish. In all of the tragedies we are shown 'the impact of heroic energy on the human situation. The heroic is normally destroyed in the conflict, and the human situation goes on surviving.' This book is the original written version of the Alexander Lectures, presented at the University of Toronto, March 1966.

A9a *Fools of Time: Studies in Shakespearean Tragedy.* Toronto: Univ of Toronto Press 1973. viii + 121 pp. Paperback rpt of A9. Canadian University Paperback 137

A9b *Tempo che opprime, tempo che redime: Riflessioni sul teatro di Shakespeare.* Trans Valentina Poggi and Maria Pia De Angelis. Bologna: Il Mulino 1986. 197 pp. Part 1 (13–113) is trans by Valentina Poggi of *FT*. Published along with *MD* (see A21b). Paperback

REPRINTED PORTIONS OF FT

Part of Chapt 3 rpt as 'King Lear: The Tragedy of Isolation,' in *Shakespeare: 'King Lear': A Casebook*, ed Frank Kermode (Nashville, Tenn: Aurora 1970), 265–9; part of Chapt 1 rpt as 'A Tragedy of Order' in *Yulius Kaissar*, Theatre Program of the Cameri Theatre, Tel Aviv 1977; part of Chapt 2 in *Twentieth-Century Interpretations of 'Antony and Cleopatra,'* ed Mark Rose (Englewood Cliffs, NJ: Prentice-Hall 1976), 114–25.

A10 *The Modern Century.* Toronto: Oxford Univ Press 1967. 123 pp. With
foreword by E.T. Salmon. Hardcover
Begins by examining the dilemma of alienation and anxiety in modern
society, associated in large measure with the idea of technological progress.
Society has become enslaved by its progress-oriented machines; this
creates an alienation that may lead to 'the city of the end of things.' Chapter
2 considers the role that the arts have taken in forming the modern
imagination. They reflect the anxiety of the age, but at the same time they
are a creative and emancipating force. Argues that whereas in the past
the human problem was to relate economic to political structures, or theological to natural ones, now the problem is to relate the world of imagination to political structures. Here the artist has a chief role to play: he is
a liberating force, one who is opposed to the repression of the state and to
the false ideas of universal progress. In the last chapter, illustrates the
ways in which the arts are absorbed into society through education. As
technology increases the amount of leisure time, education will more
and more turn away from training toward the creation of myth. What is
needed is an open mythology suited to a democratic society – one in which
human beings, rather than God, are looked to as creators. Originally
presented as the Whidden Lectures at McMaster University, Hamilton,
Ont, 1967, and later broadcast by CBC Radio (see H12).

A10a *Le siècle de l'innovation: essai.* Trans François Rinfret. Montreal: Editions
HMH 1968. 162 pp. Collection Constantes, vol 18. Notes added to identify
the sources of chapter titles. Paperback

A10b *La culture face aux media: essai.* Trans François Rinfret. Tours: Maison Mame
1969. 115 pp. Same trans as A10a. Notes added to identify the sources
of chapter titles. Paperback

A10c *The Modern Century.* London: Oxford Univ Press 1969. 123 pp. Paperback
rpt of A10. Galaxy Book 282

A10d *Cultura e miti del nostro tempo.* Trans Vittorio Di Giuro. Milan: Rizzoli 1969.
120 pp. Stiff paper wrappers

A10e *Gendai bunka no hyaku nen.* Trans Hiroshi Ebine. Tokyo: Otowa shobo 1971.
152 pp. Hardcover

A10f *The Modern Century.* Ed with introduction by Toshihiko Shibata. Tokyo:
Tsurumi shoten 1971. ii + 138 pp. This ed prepared for Japanese college
students. Shibata's introduction (i–ii) and notes (112–38) are in Japanese. F's
text is in English. Paperback

A11 *A Study of English Romanticism.* New York: Random House 1968. vi + 180
pp. Studies in Language and Literature 21. Paperback
Treats the romantic movement as primarily a change in the mythological
structure brought about by various historical and cultural forces. Argues
this thesis in the first chapter, a revised and expanded version of 'The
Drunken Boat: The Revolutionary Element in Romanticism' (see D138). Sees
romanticism, first, as giving birth to a new mythological structure in
Western culture, one that has a different myth of creation from that of the

preceding ages. Human beings come to see that the creative activity
previously ascribed to God is projected from humanity and that they
themselves have created the forms of their civilization. In the second place,
romanticism splits away the scientific vision of nature from the poetic and
existential vision. It forms an open mythology of concern: new types of
belief are possible. Thus, the older cyclical myth of the Bible from fall to
reconciliation assumes a different shape. The old unfallen state becomes the
original identity between individual human beings and nature, and the
myth of alienation is changed from a fall into sin to a fall into self-conscious
awareness of the subject-object relation to nature. Third, romanticism
profoundly alters the schema of four levels of reality. This structure becomes more ambiguous and much less concretely related to the physical
world. The imagery associated with heaven and hell, for example, becomes
based upon the opposition between 'within' and 'without' rather than
upon 'up' and 'down.' In the last three chapters F illustrates how Beddoes,
Keats, and Shelley embrace the romantic myth. Beddoes's preoccupation
with death as an imaginative realm outside the world of experience,
for example, permits us to see him as a central, perhaps even potentially a
major, figure of English romanticism. He 'revolves around the heart of
Romantic imagery, at the point of identity with nature of which death is
the only visible form.' He is not, then, simply a morbid writer whose place
is somewhere on the fringes of the romantic myth. This book grew out
of a series of lectures presented to the Graduate School at Western Reserve
University, May 1966.

A11a *A Study of English Romanticism.* Chicago: Univ of Chicago Press 1982. vi +
180 pp. Paperback rpt of A11 in slightly larger format. Phoenix Book

A11b *A Study of English Romanticism.* Brighton, Suss: Harvester Press 1983. vi +
180 pp. Same as A11a. Paperback

A11c *Igirisu Romanshyugi no Shinwa.* Trans Michiko Watanabe. Tokyo: Yashio
shuppansha 1985. 245 pp
REPRINTED PORTION OF SR
Chapt 1 partially rpt as 'Romanshyugi to muishiki no shuhen,' trans Kenji
Nakamura, in *Gendai shiso* 7, no 2 (1979): 174–9.

A12 *The Stubborn Structure: Essays on Criticism and Society.* Ithaca, NY: Cornell
Univ Press 1970. xii + 316 pp. Hardcover
Contents:
1 The Instruments of Mental Production (see D161)
2 The Knowledge of Good and Evil (see D171)
3 Speculation and Concern (see D166)
4 Design as a Creative Principle in the Arts (see D160)
5 On Value Judgments (see D173)
6 Criticism, Visible and Invisible (see D147)
7 Elementary Teaching and Elemental Scholarship (see D143)
8 Varieties of Literary Utopias (see D151)
9 The Revelation to Eve (see D195)

10 The Road of Excess (see D141)

11 The Keys to the Gates (see D163)

12 The Drunken Boat: The Revolutionary Element in Romanticism (see D138)

13 Dickens and the Comedy of Humours (see D178)

14 The Problem of Spiritual Authority in the Nineteenth Century (see D150)

15 The Top of the Tower: A Study of the Imagery of Yeats (see D184)

16 Conclusion to *Literary History of Canada* (see D154)

A collection of essays and lectures composed between 1962 and 1968. The first seven essays are primarily theoretical, treating the contexts of literary criticism, especially the social context, which F insists he has not ignored. Examines such topics as social commitment and the morality of detachment, teaching and education, creative labour, and literary evaluation. The last nine essays, arranged in a more or less historical sequence, are studies in English literary history. Seeks throughout to defend literary scholarship in modern society.

A12a *The Stubborn Structure: Essays on Criticism and Society*. London: Methuen 1970. xii + 316 pp. Same as A12. Hardcover

A12b *The Stubborn Structure: Essays on Criticism and Society*. Ithaca, NY: Cornell Univ Press [1971]. xii + 316 pp. Paperback rpt of A12. Cornell Paperback 110

A12c *La estructura inflexible de la obra literaria: Ensayos sobre crítica y sociedad*. Trans Rafael Durbán Sánchez. Madrid: Taurus 1973. 411 pp. Coleccion Persiles no 60. Paperback

A12d *The Stubborn Structure: Essays on Criticism and Society*. London: Methuen 1974. xii + 316 pp. Paperback rpt of A12a

A12e *L'ostinata struttura: saggi su critica e società*. Trans Leonardo Terzo and Anna Paschetto. Rev by Amleto Lorenzini. Milan: Rizzoli 1975. 267 pp. Includes notes by translators and by Lorenzini, whose revisions of the translation were based on conversations with F. Paperback

A12f *The Stubborn Structure: Essays on Criticism and Society*. London: Methuen 1980. xii + 316 pp. Issued as Methuen Library Reprint. Same as A12a, but with different cover and dust-jacket. Hardcover

A13 *The Bush Garden: Essays on the Canadian Imagination*. Toronto: Anansi 1971. x + 256 pp. Hardcover

Contents:

1 From 'Letters in Canada,' *University of Toronto Quarterly* (see D46, D54, D60, D68, D74, D78, D86, D97, D102, and D112)

2 Canada and Its Poetry (see D18)

3 The Narrative Tradition in English-Canadian Poetry (see D24)

4 Turning New Leaves (see D69)

5 Preface to an Uncollected Anthology (see D94)

6 Silence in the Sea (see C5)

7 Canadian and Colonial Painting (see D10)

8 David Milne: An Appreciation (see D33)
9 Lawren Harris: An Introduction (see D192)
10 Conclusion to *Literary History of Canada* (see D154)
A collection of F's essays on Canadian literature and painting written over
the course of more than twenty-five years. More than half of the book
consists of a generous selection from F's reviews of Canadian poetry that
appeared in the *University of Toronto Quarterly* from 1950 to 1960. Also
included is an essay on E.J. Pratt (chapt 6) and several articles on Canadian
poetry in general. F's recurring concern is with the ways the Canadian
imagination has shaped and been shaped by its environment. The preface
is reprinted in *The Oxford Anthology of Canadian Literature*, ed Richard
Weaver and William Toye (Toronto: Oxford Univ Press 1973), 126–33; in
Vic Report, 4 June 1976, 6–7, 13; and partially reprinted as 'In Quest of
Identity and Unity' in *Globe Magazine*, 20 February 1971, 8–9, 12.

A13a *The Bush Garden: Essays on the Canadian Imagination*. Toronto: Anansi 1974.
x + 256 pp. Paperback rpt of A13

A14 *The Critical Path: An Essay on the Social Context of Literary Criticism*. Bloomington: Indiana Univ Press 1971. 174 pp. Hardcover
Treats a far-ranging body of topics, including the difference between oral
and writing cultures, Renaissance humanism, the critical theories of Sidney
and Shelley, Marxism and democracy, social contract theories and utopias,
contemporary youth culture, McLuhanism, and theories of education.
What holds these apparently unrelated topics together is the dialectical
framework of the two opposing myths of Western culture: the myth
of concern and the myth of freedom. The myth of concern is communal
and conservative; it holds to truths of coherence, issues in belief, and
values authority. The myth of freedom is individual, detached, and liberal;
it holds to truths of correspondence and stresses objectivity and tolerance.
Argues that the merging of freedom and concern produces the social
context of literature. Interprets cultural phenomena from the perspective of
these two myths.

A14a *The Critical Path: An Essay on the Social Context of Literary Criticism*. Bloomington: Indiana Univ Press 1973. 174 pp. Paperback rpt of A14. Midland
Book 158

A14b *O caminho critico: Um ensaio sobre o contexto social da crítica literária*. Trans
Antônio Arnoni Prado. São Paulo: Editora Perspectiva 1973. 169 pp.
Paperback

A14c *Hihyo no michi*. Trans Hiroichiro Doke. Tokyo: Kenkyu-sha 1974. 212 pp.
Hardcover

A14d *The Critical Path: An Essay on the Social Context of Literary Criticism*. Brighton,
Suss: Harvester Press 1983. 174 pp. Same as A14. Paperback

A14e *El camino crítico: Ensayo sobre el contexto social de la crítica literaria*. Trans
Miguel Mac-Veigh. Madrid: Taurus 1986. Contains notes added by translator. Paperback

A15 *The Secular Scripture: A Study of the Structure of Romance.* Cambridge, Mass:
Harvard Univ Press 1976. viii + 199 pp. Hardcover
Refers to this book as a 'geography lesson ... in the mythological or
imaginative universe.' Argues that in much nineteenth- and twentieth-
century literature the structure of romance has replaced the structure
derived from the Bible. The first two chapters provide general descriptions
of romance and its place in the history of literature. The next three outline
the characteristics of the heroes and heroines of romance and of the
conventional romantic narrative patterns of ascent and descent. In the final
chapter, F maintains that romance, 'the structural core of all fiction,'
ends with the isolation of the hero in his newly created identity, the search
for identity being the chief goal of the romantic quest. In this quest, the
hero seeks to assert the fabulous in the face of chaos, to return to an Eden
that no longer exists, and to create his own earth, heaven, and hell.
Romance is, thus, a secular scripture, paralleling the sacred scripture,
which has God as its hero. Originally presented as the Norton Lectures,
Harvard University, April 1975.
A15a *The Secular Scripture: A Study of the Structure of Romance.* Cambridge, Mass:
Harvard Univ Press 1978. viii + 199 pp. Paperback rpt of A15
A15b *La scrittura secolare: Studio sulla struttura del 'romance.'* Trans Amleto Loren-
zini. Bologna: Il Mulino 1978. 191 pp. Includes introduction (7–14) by
Giovanna Capone (see L78) and preface (17) by F (see D248). Paperback
A15c *La escritura profana: Un estudio sobre la estructura del romance.* Trans Edison
Simons. Barcelona: Monte Avila 1980. 235 pp. Paperback
A16 *Spiritus Mundi: Essays on Literature, Myth, and Society.* Bloomington: Indiana
Univ Press 1976. xvi + 296 pp. Hardcover
Contents:
1 The Search for Acceptable Words (see D216)
2 The University and Personal Life (see D197)
3 The Renaissance of Books (see D219)
4 The Times of the Signs (see D223)
5 Expanding Eyes (see D226)
6 Charms and Riddles (see D224)
7 Romance as Masque (see D194 and D225)
8 Spengler Revisited (see D220)
9 Agon and Logos (see D217)
10 Blake's Reading of the Book of Job (see D189)
11 The Rising of the Moon (see D157)
12 Wallace Stevens and the Variation Form (see D218)
A collection of essays written between 1969 and 1975, all but two of which
(6 and 7) were previously published. The first four essays examine, respectively, the evolution of the research degree from its philological origins
to its focus on general cultural study, social contract theories and utopias
and their relation to modern ideologies, the authority of the written word

over other forms of communication, and the ways myth has shaped
scientific concepts, which themselves originated as imaginative forms of
thought. The next four essays are studies of, respectively, literature as an
expression of structural patterns of life; the two generic 'seeds' of literature: charms and riddles; Old and New Comedy, with special reference to
Shakespeare's use of masque and antimasque; and Spengler's cyclic view
of history. The last four essays examine the work of Milton, Blake, Yeats,
and Stevens.

A16a *Spiritus Mundi: Essays on Literature, Myth, and Society.* Bloomington: Indiana
Univ Press 1983. xvi + 296 pp. Paperback rpt of A16. Midland Book 289
A16b *Spiritus Mundi: Essays on Literature, Myth, and Society.* [Markham, Ont]:
Fitzhenry & Whiteside [1983]. xvi + 296 pp. Same as A16a. Paperback
A16c Italian translation of *SM* forthcoming from Garazanti.
A17 *Northrop Frye on Culture and Literature: A Collection of Review Essays.* Ed Robert D. Denham. Chicago: Univ of Chicago Press 1978. viii + 264 pp.
Hardcover
Contents:
1 Myth as Information (see D70)
2 The Shapes of History (D29)
3 Symbolism of the Unconscious (see D109)
4 World Enough without Time (see D103)
5 Total Identification (see D27)
6 Art in a New Modulation (see D63)
7 Forming Fours (see D72)
8 Ministry of Angels (see D64)
9 The Rhythm of Growth and Decay (see D36)
10 Nature Methodized (see D113)
11 The Acceptance of Innocence (see D38)
12 The Young Boswell (see D45)
13 Long, Sequacious Notes (see D65)
14 Neoclassical Agony (see D91)
15 Interior Monologue of M. Teste (see D101)
16 Phalanx of Particulars (see D56)
17 Orwell and Marxism (see D25)
18 Novels on Several Occasions (see D43)
19 The Nightmare Life in Death (see D114)
20 Graves, Gods, and Scholars (see D83)
21 Poetry of the Tout Ensemble (see D87)
A collection of F's reviews published between 1947 and 1960, two-thirds of
which were originally published in the *Hudson Review*. The first ten reviews examine the writings of some of the central figures in twentieth-
century thought, including Spengler, Jung, Cassirer, Frazer, Toynbee,
Langer, and Eliade. The last eleven reviews are on the works of poets and
novelists, including Cervantes, Boswell, Coleridge, Wyndham Lewis,

Valéry, Pound, Orwell, Hemingway, Moravia, Charles Williams, Beckett, Robert Graves, and René Char. For the introduction to this collection by Robert D. Denham see L117.

A17a *Northrop Frye on Culture and Literature: A Collection of Review Essays.* Ed Robert D. Denham. Chicago: Univ of Chicago Press 1980. viii + 264 pp. Paperback rpt of A17. Phoneix Book 867

A18 *Creation and Recreation.* Toronto: Univ of Toronto Press 1980. 76 pp. Canadian University Paperback 254
Examines the concept of creation and the relationship between human and divine creativity. Looks especially at the way the structure and imagery of literature have been influenced by the ideas and images associated with the word 'creation.' Shows that traditionally everything in nature was associated with divine creation, but that when applied to human activity the word 'creative' disturbs or neutralizes its original sense. Artistic creation, therefore, turns out to be 'decreation.' Distinguishes between stories that look to heaven and those that look to earth. Contrasts these to the human, counter-movement of creation in literature, which F calls 'recreation.' Originally presented as the Larkin-Stuart Lectures, Toronto, January–February 1980.

A19 *The Great Code: The Bible and Literature.* New York: Harcourt Brace Jovanovich 1982. xxiii + 261 pp. Hardcover
'This book attempts a study of the Bible from the point of view of a literary critic.' F begins part 1, 'The Order of Words,' with an analysis of language, separating it into three primary uses or phases (the poetic or metaphorical, the allegorical or metonymic, and the descriptive) in order to illustrate that while the Bible is not identical with literature it is certainly similar to literature because its language is more metaphorical than metonymic. The poetic function of language combined with the existential function produces the rhetorical form of the Bible: proclamation or kerygma. Argues throughout that the Bible is best read as a unity. In the second and third chapters, examines how the metaphors and narratives of the Bible contribute to that unity. Addresses particularly the question of the literal meaning of biblical imagery and narrative. Here F's general thesis is 'that the Bible comes to us as a written book, an absence invoking a historical presence "behind" it, as Derrida would say, and that the background presence gradually shifts to the foreground, the re-creation of that reality in the reader's mind.' Shows next how the rhetorical device of typology brings coherence to the Bible. Part 2, 'The Order of Types,' reverses the sequence of topics in Part 1, beginning with a typological study of the seven phases of revelation and concluding with a 'rhetoric of religion,' which, through an account of the various levels of meaning, 'attempts to suggest some answers to questions about the direction in which we go from the "literal" meaning.' In the two middle chapters in part 2, surveys the structures of imagery and the narrative patterns of the Bible. Refers throughout to the

relation between biblical and secular knowledge, and shows how the Bible is a fundamental element in the imaginative experience of Western culture.

A19a *The Great Code: The Bible and Literature.* Toronto: Academic Press 1982. xxiii + 261 pp. Canadian ed of A19. Hardcover

A19b *The Great Code: The Bible and Literature.* London: Routledge & Kegan Paul 1982. xxiii + 261 pp. British ed of A19. Hardcover

A19c *The Great Code: The Bible and Literature*: San Diego: Harcourt Brace Jovanovich 1983. xxiii + 261 pp. Paperback ed of A19. A Harvest/HBJ Book. Slightly reduced page size

A19d *The Great Code: The Bible and Literature.* Toronto: Academic Press 1983. xxiii + 261 pp. Paperback ed of A19a. Slightly reduced page size

A19e *The Great Code: The Bible and Literature.* San Diego: Harcourt Brace Jovanovich 1983. xxiii + 261 pp. Another paperback version of A19c. Same dimensions as A19c, but type has been reduced, book is printed on thinner paper, frontispiece has been reproduced on inside front cover, and ISBN differs from that of A19c.

A19f *The Great Code: The Bible and Literature.* London: Ark Paperbacks 1983. xxi + 261 pp. Ark Paperbacks is an imprint of Routledge & Kegan Paul. A rpt of A19b, issued with different cover and title-page and with slightly reduced page size. Omits frontispiece and half-title page, resulting in repagination of the introductory matter.

A19g *Le Grand Code: La Bible et la littérature.* Trans Catherine Malamoud. Preface by Tzvetan Todorov. Paris: Editions du Seuil 1984. 339 pp. Paperback. For the preface by Todorov see L520.

A19h *Il grande codice: la Bibbia e la letteratura.* Trans Giovanni Rizzoni. Turin: Einaudi 1986. 306 pp

A19i *De Grote Code: De bijbel en de literatuur.* Trans Léon Stapper. Nijmegen: SUN 1986. 351 pp. Includes introduction by W. Bronzwaer (7–15)

A19j Japanese translation of *GC* forthcoming from Hosei Univ Press.

A19k Spanish translation of *GC* forthcoming from Taurus.

A19l Serbo-Croatian translation of *GC* forthcoming from Prosveta.

A20 *Divisions on a Ground: Essays on Canadian Culture.* Ed James Polk. Toronto: Anansi 1982. 199 pp. Hardcover
Contents:
   1 Culture as Interpenetration (see D240)
   2 Across the River and out of the Trees (see D256)
   3 National Consciousness and Canadian Culture (see D235)
   4 Sharing the Continent (see D243)
   5 Conclusion to *Literary History of Canada*, 2nd ed (see D233)
   6 Teaching the Humanities Today (see D238)
   7 Humanities in a New World (see D105)
   8 The Writer and the University (see C1)
   9 The Teacher's Source of Authority (see D251)
   10 The Definition of a University (see D210)

11 The Ethics of Change (see D191)

12 Canada: New World without Revolution (see D227)

13 The Rear-View Mirror: Notes toward a Future (see D245)

A selection of essays and addresses written between 1957 and 1980, all, except the first, previously published. The essays, although arranged under the headings of 'Writing,' 'Teaching,' and 'The Social Order,' treat a variety of literary, educational, social, and political topics, Canadian and otherwise. For the editor's preface see L404.

A21 *The Myth of Deliverance: Reflections on Shakespeare's Problem Comedies*. Toronto: Univ of Toronto Press 1983. viii + 90 pp. Paperback

A study of the structure of Shakespeare's 'problem comedies': *Measure for Measure, All's Well That Ends Well*, and *Troilus and Cressida*. Sees all three as 'romantic comedies,' similar in structure to the late romances because of the attention Shakespeare gives to the recognition scenes. Argues that each play contains one of the three elements found in comic form: the Aristotelian reversal (in *Measure for Measure*), the Platonic sublimination of Eros (in *All's Well That Ends Well*), and the ironic reversal (in *Troilus and Cressida*). Interprets the plays from the perspective of these three reversals – the reversal of action, energy, and reality, respectively – and maintains that in their connection with Shakespeare's romances they embody the myth of deliverance. Originally presented as the Tamblyn Lectures at the University of Western Ontario, London, 25–27 March 1981.

A21a *The Myth of Deliverance: Reflections on Shakespeare's Problem Comedies*. Brighton, Suss: Harvester Press 1983. viii + 90 pp. British ed of A21. Hardcover and paperback

A21b *Tempo che opprime, tempo che redime: Riflessioni sul teatro di Shakespeare*. Trans Valentina Poggi and Maria Pia De Angelis. Bologna: Il Mulino 1986. 197 pp. Part 2 (115–97) is translation, by Maria Pia De Angelis, of *MD*. Published along with *FT* (see A9b). Paperback

A22 With Sheridan Baker and George W. Perkins. *The Harper Handbook to Literature*. New York: Harper & Row 1985. ix + 563 pp. Paperback

A glossary of literary terms, along with longer entries on literary styles, periods, forms, and movements. F wrote the following entries: allegory, archetype, Bible as literature, translations of the Bible, comedy, epic, Freudian criticism, genre, Jungian criticism, lyric, mimesis, myth, plot, romance, satire, structure, symbol, and tragedy.

A23 *Northrop Frye on Shakespeare*. Ed Robert Sandler. Markham, Ont: Fitzhenry & Whiteside 1986. vii + 186 pp. Hardcover

An edited version of F's Shakespeare lectures at Victoria College, taped over a period of years and here conflated into chapters on *Romeo and Juliet, A Midsummer Night's Dream, Richard II* and *Henry IV, Hamlet, King Lear, Antony and Cleopatra, Measure for Measure, The Winter's Tale*, and *The Tempest*. The introduction stresses the thematic and poetic aspects of the plays and provides basic information on Shakespeare's time and audience. Maintains that *Hamlet* was 'the central Shakespearean play for the nineteenth and early twentieth centuries,' that *King Lear* has moved into the center in our own time, and that *Antony and Cleopatra* 'looks most like the kind of world we seem to be moving into now.' Discusses throughout the historical backgrounds of the plays, their comic and tragic conventions (including imagery, character, and plot), and their mythic roots.

A23a *Northrop Frye on Shakespeare.* Ed Robert Sandler. New Haven: Yale Univ Press 1986. vii + 186 pp. Hardcover. Issued with a different dust-jacket from that of A23

A23b Italian translation of *NFS* forthcoming from Il Mulino.

B

Books Edited

B1 John Milton. *'Paradise Lost' and Selected Poetry and Prose*. New York: Holt,
Rinehart and Winston 1951. xxxviii + 601 pp. Paperback
A Rinehart Edition, which includes 25-page introduction, chronology of
Milton's life, bibliography, and 63 pp of notes. For the introduction see D51.

B2 Pelham Edgar. *Across My Path*. Toronto: Ryerson 1952. xiv + 167 pp.
Hardcover
The autobiography of Edgar, one-time head of both the French and the
English departments of Victoria College, Toronto. Includes in addition to
standard reminiscence and anecdote a series of informal essays about
the personality and work of several Canadians, among them F himself,
who was one of Edgar's students at Victoria. F edited the unfinished
manuscript upon Edgar's death. For F's introduction see D57.

B3 William Blake. *Selected Poetry and Prose of William Blake*. New York: Random
House 1953; rpt with revised title and copyright pages and with slightly
reduced page size as Modern Library College Edition. xxx + 475 pp.
Hardcover and paperback
A Modern Library volume, which includes a 17-page introduction and
notes to Blake's work. The text reproduces selections from Keynes's edition,
with some rearrangement. For F's introduction see D66.

B4 Charles Trick Currelly. *I Brought the Ages Home*. Toronto: Ryerson 1956; rpt
1958; first paperback printing, 1967. xx + 312 pp
An account of how Currelly developed the Royal Ontario Museum of
Archaeology into one of the world's greatest collections. The form of the
book is autobiography, describing Currelly's life first as a student in
Canada, then as an excavator in Egypt before World War I, and finally as
director of the museum he created. F remarks in the introduction (see
D84) that his editorial duties were 'confined to minor re-arrangements and

to some smoothing of the reader's path.' He in fact was practically a ghost writer of the book.

B5 *Sound and Poetry: English Institute Essays, 1956.* New York: Columbia Univ Press 1957. xxvii + 156 pp. Hardcover
Includes papers presented to the 1955 and 1956 conferences of the English Institute. For F's 'Introduction: Lexis and Melos,' see D92.

B6 E.J. Pratt. *The Collected Poems of E.J. Pratt.* 2nd ed. Toronto: Macmillan 1958. xxviii + 395 pp. Hardcover
A collection of all the poems Pratt wished to preserve, including two narrative poems that did not appear in the first edition (1944). In the 'Editor's Preface,' F says he accepted the editorial duties for this volume 'purely as an act of personal homage to the poet in his seventy-fifth year.' For F's introduction see D99.

B7 Shakespeare. *The Tempest.* Pelican Shakespeare, gen ed Alfred Harbage. Baltimore: Penguin 1959; rev ed 1970. 112 pp. Paperback. Published also in Shakespeare, *The Complete Works,* gen ed Alfred Harbage [Pelican Text Revised] (Baltimore: Penguin 1969), 1369–95. Hardcover
For F's introduction, 15–26 (rev ed, 14–24), see D106.

B8 Peter F. Fisher. *The Valley of Vision: Blake as Prophet and Revolutionary.* Toronto: Univ of Toronto Press 1961. xi + 261 pp. Hardcover
Examines Blake's work 'within the historical perspective of the Enlightenment.' Written by one of F's former students, 'a critical mind of singular erudition and power.' F has added a preface (see D124) and an opening chapter to the revised manuscript that existed at the time of Fisher's death, as well as the beginning of another chapter from an unrevised manuscript.

B9 *Design for Learning: Reports Submitted to the Joint Committee of the Toronto Board of Education and the University of Toronto.* Toronto: Univ of Toronto Press 1962. x + 148 pp. Hardcover
Results of a study of the school curriculum undertaken by the joint committee indicated in the subtitle. Includes the recommendations for the curricula of grades 1–13 in English, social science, and science. For F's introduction to the report see D131.

B10 *Romanticism Reconsidered: Selected Papers of the English Institute.* New York: Columbia Univ Press 1963. ix + 144 pp. Hardcover
Consists of papers by M.H. Abrams, Lionel Trilling, René Wellek, and F, presented to the 1962 session of the English Institute, which was chaired by F. In an introductory essay, F analyses the revolutionary element in romanticism (see D138). For his foreword see D139.

B11 *Blake: A Collection of Critical Essays.* Englewood Cliffs, NJ: Prentice-Hall 1966. 183 pp. Hardcover and paperback
A representative collection of thirteen contemporary critical essays on Blake, including two by F. For F's contributions see D47 and D90, and for his introduction to the volume see D162.

B12 With James V. Logan and John E. Jordan. *Some British Romantics: A Collection of Essays*. [Columbus]: Ohio State Univ Press 1966. 343 pp. Hardcover
Fourth volume in a series on British romanticism sponsored by the Modern Language Association Committee on Research Projects. Includes, in addition to F's 'The Keys to the Gates' (see D163), essays by Vivian Mercier on Landor, Geoffrey Tillotson on Lamb, Stephen F. Fogle on Leigh Hunt, Douglas Grant on De Quincey, Kathleen Coburn on Hazlitt, Ian Jack on John Clare, John Henry Raleigh on Scott, Karl Kroeber on minor romantic narrative poetry, and William S. Ward on nineteenth-century periodical literature.

B13 *Shakespeare Series: I: King Lear, Twelfth Night, Antony and Cleopatra*, ed F.D. Hoeniger, J.A. Levin, and B.W. Jackson. Toronto: Macmillan; New York: Odyssey Press 1968. *Shakespeare Series: II: Hamlet, The Tempest, Henry IV, Part I*, ed M.B. Smith, David Galloway, and J.F. Sullivan. Toronto: Macmillan; New York: Odyssey Press 1969
These two volumes are a part of the College Classics in English series, for which F was general editor. His 'General Editor's Introduction' appears only in the Shakespeare volumes (see D179). He was, however, general editor for the following additional titles in the series: Dickens, *Great Expectations*; Bacon, *A Selection of His Works*; Bronte, *Wuthering Heights*; Chaucer, *A Selection*: Dickens, *Little Dorrit*; Hardy, *Tess of the Durbervilles*; Mill, *A Selection*; Spenser, *A Selection*; Swift, *A Selection*; Swift, *Gulliver's Travels*; Thackeray, *Vanity Fair*; and *Three Restoration Comedies*.

B14 *Literature: Uses of the Imagination*. 12 vols. New York: Harcourt Brace Jovanovich 1972–3
Vols 1–6, ed Alvin A. Lee and Hope Arnott Lee; W.T. Jewkes, gen ed: *Wish and Nightmare; Circle of Stories: One; Circle of Stories: Two; The Garden and the Wilderness; The Temple and the Ruin;* and *The Peaceable Kingdom*. Vols 7–12, ed W.T. Jewkes: *The Perilous Journey; Man the Mythmaker; A World Elsewhere: Romance; A World Enclosed: Tragedy; The Ways of the World: Satire and Irony;* and *A World Remade: Comedy*. F was supervisory editor for the series. For his monograph written for the series see C6.

B15 With Sheridan Baker and George Perkins. *The Practical Imagination: Stories, Poems, Plays*. New York: Harper & Row 1980. xxi + 1514 pp. Rev compact ed, also by Barbara Perkins, 1987. xix + 1448 pp. The material on poetry also exists as a one-volume anthology, *The Practical Imagination: An Introduction to Poetry*. New York: Harper & Row 1983. xx + 499 pp
An anthology for college literature courses. In addition to helping select the stories, poems, and plays, F wrote the introductions to the three genres, 'On Fiction,' 'On Poetry,' and 'On Drama' (see D259).

C

Separately Published Monographs

C1 *Culture and the National Will.* Ottawa: Carleton Univ for the Institute for
Canadian Studies 1957. 15 pp. Wrappers. Partially rpt as 'The Writer and
the University' in *DG*, 118–24.
On the relation of the university and culture in general to the Canada
Council Act, and on the nature of popular literature and its educational
function. Argues that the Canadian character and experience do not create
Canadian literature but are created by the Canadian writer; thus, Canadian
literature should be judged by international rather than local standards,
just as any other literature is judged. If Canadian literature is to become
popular, that is, become a 'literature which provides a simple and direct
form of imaginative experience,' it will spring from the stories, history, and
wisdom of the cultural tradition: 'the Bible, the classics, and the great heritage of our mother tongue.' Education should include popular literature
in this sense; without it students are deprived of 'one of the keys to
the whole imagination and thought of Western culture' and are unable to
judge the culture of their own time, including its mindless forms, and
to defend the freedom of academic thought and discussion. Originally
presented as a Carleton University convocation address, St James United
Church, 17 May 1957.

C2 *By Liberal Things.* Toronto: Clarke, Irwin 1959. 23 pp. Issued in both
hardcover and wrappers, the latter form of which is entitled 'An Address
by H. Northrop Frye on the Occasion of His Installation as Principal of
Victoria College.' Rpt with slight changes as 'The Principal's Address' in
Varsity Graduate 8 (January 1960): 47–61; abridged version rpt in *The Strand*
[Victoria College, Univ of Toronto] 8 (28 October 1959): [6–7].
Comments on the nature of the university and the colleges that compose
it. Seeks chiefly to define the social beginnings and ends of education,

maintaining that it is through the university that one becomes aware of the
continuity of human life, learns to develop memory through constant
application, is able to arrive at decisions based upon trained intelligence,
and comes to realize that 'education can only lead to maladjustment
in the ordinary world' of comfort and security. Presented as an address on
the occasion of F's installation as principal of Victoria College, 21 October
1959.

c3 *The Changing Pace of Canadian Education.* Montreal: Association of Alumni,
Sir George Williams Univ 1963. 10 pp. Wrappers
On the function of the modern university in a changing social context.
Bases his understanding of this function on a distinction between two levels
of reason: speculative, which has to do with our knowledge of the objective world and which depends on detachment and suspension of judgment;
and practical, which has to do with social engagement, freedom, and
choice. Argues that the practical intelligence is central to the process of
education. It cannot be directly taught, but it originates in one's overall
vision of what society should be like. This vision, much of which is left
to the student's initiative to develop, should cause dissatisfaction with ordinary social virtues, such as popularity and security, which work against
the free mind. Presented as the Second Annual Kenneth E. Norris Memorial Lecture, Sir George Williams University, 24 January 1963.

c4 *Convocation Address by Dr. H. Northrop Frye.* Downsview: York Univ 1969. 8
pp. Wrappers
Observes that there are two kinds of education: the primary kind, which
comes from society and which is education in concern or in what society
accepts; and the secondary kind, which the university gives and which
derives from reason, evidence, and the imagination. Argues that the campus radical movements, such as the one at Berkeley, are symptomatic
of a crisis in the primary kind of education, caused by a weakening of the
sense of social coherence. The way out of this crisis is 'through the
recovery of our own revolutionary and inclusive democratic tradition.' The
university itself, being neither a church nor a political party, cannot
directly restore the social vision; rather, 'the university shows us, more
clearly than any other aspect of society, why it is important to have a
social vision.' Address delivered to the graduating class at York University,
30 May 1969.

c5 *Silence in the Sea.* St John's: Memorial Univ of Newfoundland 1969. 15 pp.
Wrappers. Rpt in *BG*, 181–97; and in *E.J. Pratt*, ed David G. Pitt (Toronto:
Ryerson 1969), 124–38; portions of three paragraphs rpt in *Modern Commonwealth Literature*, ed John H. Ferres and Martin Tucker (New York: Ungar
1977), 333–4.
Speaks about E.J. Pratt 'in the context of modern poetry, and in the further
context of the relation of modern poetry to modern civilization.' Comments
on Pratt's affinity to the oral tradition of narrative poetry and to the
romantic tradition, and on the primitive and popular qualities of his verse.

Considers the contrast Pratt recognized between 'the human heroism and endurance' he saw around him and 'the moral unconsciousness of nature.' Concludes by referring to Pratt's myth-making powers, especially his 'vision of the unquenchable energy and the limitless endurance which unite the real man with real nature,' a romantic and life-giving myth rather than an ironic and fatalistic one. Presented as the first Pratt Memorial Lecture at Memorial University of Newfoundland, March 1968.

c6 *On Teaching Literature.* New York: Harcourt Brace Jovanovich 1972. 33 pp. Issued in both hardcover and wrappers. A selection, with a commentary by J[ohn] S[yrtash], rpt as 'Myth and Imagination' in *The Strand* [Victoria College, Univ of Toronto], October 1973, 8–9.
'In this essay I am trying to set down some of my views about literature as a subject of teaching and learning.' This monograph was written in connection with the twelve-volume series, *Literature: Uses of the Imagination* (see B14), of which F was the supervisory editor. Devotes separate sections to such topics as archetypes, the primacy of poetry, the four narrative patterns, myth and the imagination, literature and society, and the reality of metaphor. Incudes an outline for a secondary school curriculum in literature.

c7 *Bungaku no Genkei.* Trans Iketani Toshitada. Nagoya: Nagoya eibei gendaishi kenkyû-kai 1974. 12 pp. Wrappers
A Japanese translation of 'The Archetypes of Literature' (see D49).

c8 *Criticism as Education: The Leland B. Jacobs Lecture.* New York: School of Library Service, Columbia Univ, 1980. 29 pp. Wrappers
Argues against value-judgments as the distinguishing aspect of literary education, maintaining that the final aim of the study of literature is absorbing the verbal power of literature within oneself. Believes that neither the education of the will, as represented in Machiavelli's advice to the prince, nor the education into leisure-class virtues, as represented in Castiglione's advice to the courtier, provides the proper model. The proper model, rather, derives from the ideal of fraternity. This ideal permits one to recreate his or her sense of social context. Argues that the educational process should begin with continuity. Distinguishes between the creative continuity that comes from habitual practice and the reactionary, anxious continuity that aims to prevent all change. Maintains that the function of literature is 'to recreate the primitive conception of the word of power, the metaphor that unites subject and object.' Presented as the first Jacobs Lecture, Columbia University, 26 October 1979. The monograph includes introductions by Kay E. Vandergrift and Glenna Davis Sloan.

c9 *Il 'Cortegiano' in una società senza cortigiani.* Trans Francesca Valente and Alfredo Rizzardi. Urbino: Universita degli studi di Urbino 1979. 16 pp. Wrappers. Original English text published as 'Il Cortegiano' in *Quaderni d'italianistica* 1, no 1 (1980): 1–14 (see D258).
Places Castiglione's *The Courtier* in its historical context but believes the beauty and power of the book derive from things other than this context;

these include its genre and literary tradition, which descend from the Platonic symposium; Roman rhetorical theory; the cyropedia; and the utopia. Discusses the chief activities and qualities of the courtier as presented in Books 1–3: his role as a court functionary, his attention to sports and the fine arts, his manifesting the qualities of grace by *sprezzatura* and *disinvoltura* in everything he does, his open showmanship and ornamental social function, and his effort to make aggressiveness socially acceptable. Reviews the issue of whether the courtier is to be seen as a courtly and humanistic adviser to the prince or as his active and contemplative teacher. Locates the final value of *The Courtier* in Castiglione's having grasped the importance of the educational idea of fraternity: 'that is why his book is not only a beautiful handbook of grace but a profound vision of human destiny.' Originally presented as a lecture at Aula Atti Accademici, Venice, 23 May 1979, and at the University of Urbino, Urbino, 29 May 1979.

C10 *Something Rich and Strange: Shakespeare's Approach to Romance* (A Lecture Given by Northrop Frye for the Stratford Shakespearean Festival, July 11, 1982, Festival Theatre). [Stratford: Stratford Festival] 1982. [16 pp]. Wrappers

Discusses the dramatic structure and typical characters in four plays written near the end of Shakespeare's career: *Pericles, Cymbeline, The Winter's Tale,* and *The Tempest.* Examines especially *The Tempest,* concentrating on its action: 'the reversing of the usual conceptions of reality and illusion.'

D

Essays, Introductions, Review Articles, and Contributions to Books

D1 'Current Opera: A Housecleaning.' *Acta Victoriana* 60 (October 1935): 12–14
Begins as a review of a performance of *Madame Butterfly* but turns into a
short essay on the history and the nature of opera. Observes that opera
ideally should be completely conventionalized, that the higher forms of
opera (eg, Mozart's) appear as comedy, that opera tends to move toward
pathos and melodrama, and that Wagner shattered the opera so completely
'that it is now in a state of decadence from which it can never be rescued.'

D2 'Ballet Russe.' *Acta Victoriana* 60 (December 1935): 4–6
A review of three ballets, two by Tchaikovsky and one by Rimsky-
Korsakov. Analyses the function of rhythm, symbolism, and convention in
ballet. Concludes that this particular performance of the Ballet Russe was
too allegorical and gave 'little idea of the emotional range or intensity of its
chosen form.'

D3 'The Jooss Ballet.' *Canadian Forum* 16 (April 1936): 18–19
Ostensibly a review of four performances by the Jooss Ballet, judged by F
to be powerful and well executed, but most of his remarks discuss the
nature of ballet as a musical art. Speculates that in an age when the oratorio
is dead and the opera moribund the ballet, which requires a strongly
social sensibility, may be emerging as a 'genuinely new art-form ... becoming as expressive for the twentieth century as Elizabethan drama or
Mozartian opera was for their respective times.'

D4 'Wyndham Lewis: Anti-Spenglerian.' *Canadian Forum* 16 (June 1936): 21–2
Argues that, although Lewis seeks to analyse culture in an absolute,
detached, and anti-Spenglerian manner, 'all of Lewis' critical work is a
special application of the Spenglerian dialectic' and is 'dominated by
Spenglerian concepts.' Based primarily on the views expressed in *Time and
Western Man*, *The Art of Being Ruled*, and *The Lion and the Fox*, with glances

at *Tarr, The Apes of God, Paleface, Men without Art,* and *The Dithyrambic Spectator.*

D5 'Frederick Delius.' *Canadian Forum* 16 (August 1936): 19–20
An assessment of Delius's musical achievements. Concentrates on Delius's romanticism: its vertical or chordal conception of music, its interest in tone color, its treatment of the sonata form, its subjectivity. Sees Delius as a proponent of 'a kind of revised pagan religion,' which descended from Nietzsche's doctrine of the will-to-power, Whitman's 'ecstatic absorption in nature,' and 'the languor and sensuousness of the Swinburnian school of English poetry.'

D6 'Music and the Savage Breast.' *Canadian Forum* 18 (April 1938): 451–3
Traces the development of music from its savage and magical ancestry to the present time. Argues that although the superstitious element of music has largely disappeared its emotional impact has not, and that this emotional impact can be a powerful force for social evil. Relates music to the current forces of tyranny and social reaction, forces that can be overcome in the musical arts only through the growth of co-operative or group forms, the chief of which is musical drama. 'But there are other forces at work, trying to make this growth of co-operation lead to a more efficient, saner, and peaceful civilization.' These are the ballet and cinema, both of which could develop into significant political forces.

D7 'Men as Trees Walking.' *Canadian Forum* 18 (October 1938): 208–10
Traces the development of surrealistic painting from the chaos of early Dadaism through the stages of its two later influences: the libido, dream, and split-consciousness theories of Freud and the universal symbolic-language theory of Jung and the Cambridge anthropologists. Sees surrealism as beginning to come of age in its merger with abstract expressionism (as in the works of Chirico, Klee, Miro, and Picasso), but believes it can truly mature only as it moves beyond the patterns of private association to a more explicit, fundamental, and genuinely communal symbolism.

D8 'Canadian Art in London.' *Canadian Forum* 18 (January 1939): 304–5
A review of a Canadian exhibition at the Tate Gallery and a critique of the reviews that the exhibit received in the British press. Observes that Canadian art lacks subtlety but that it has rediscovered the obvious and embodies the virtues of good humour, life, and buoyancy. If these qualities persist, Canadian painting 'is capable of absorbing what other qualities are necessary for mature craftsmanship.'

D9 'War on the Cultural Front.' *Canadian Forum* 20 (August 1940): 144, 146
Seeks to distinguish democracy from Naziism and Communism, not on the basis of political and economic theory, but on its being rooted in a broader concept of culture. 'Democracy is in essence cultural *laissez faire*, an encouragement of private enterprise in art, scholarship and science.' Argues that regardless of who wins the war, there will be a tendency to expand political and economic systems internationally, but that what culture will need, especially literature and painting, is 'some kind of decentralizing.'

Concludes with a plea that 'in the present war it is our business to disintegrate and disorganize this world-state *whatever else happens*' because a world-state would be nothing less than a dictatorship.

D10 'Canadian and Colonial Painting.' *Canadian Forum* 20 (March 1941): 377–8. Rpt in *BG*, 199–202.
A comparison and contrast of the works of two Canadian painters, Tom Thomson and Horatio Walker. Focuses on the way in which the environment affected each artist. 'What is essential in Thomson is the imaginative instability, the emotional unrest and dissatisfaction, one feels about a country which has not been lived in: the tension between the mind and a surrounding not integrated with it.' Praises Thomson's use of colour and his sense of design and focus. Sees Walker, in contrast, as lacking an organized vision. He painted only the 'predigested picturesque' and thought the appeal of art was located in a 'queasy and maudlin nostalgia.' The earliest of F's many accounts of the effect the environment has had upon Canadian culture.

D11 'The Great Charlie.' *Canadian Forum* 21 (August 1941): 148–50
An analysis of Charlie Chaplin's achievement, especially as it appears in *Modern Times* and *The Great Dictator*. Sees cinema as the form that will come to have a 'central and dominating influence' in modern art, one that can take the lead in integrating modern art and life when it is in the hands of a genius such as Chaplin. Examines the theme of anarchy in *Modern Times* – 'an allegory of the impartial destructiveness of humor' in the tradition of Twain. Points to a number of parallelisms between *The Great Dictator* and the Christian story.

D12 'Music in Poetry.' *University of Toronto Quarterly* 11 (January 1942): 167–79
Analyses the direct and indirect influence of music on poetry. Stresses that the use of the term 'musical' to describe a poetic quality makes most sense if it is understood as counterpoint, the production of a variable number of syllables between sharp stresses that yields 'a harsh, rugged, dissonant poem,' as in Browning's work. Traces this kind of rhythm throughout the history of English literature, beginning with Lydgate, the father of 'modern musical poetry.' Includes Skelton, Wyatt, Dunbar, Donne, Herbert, Crashaw, Milton, and Blake among the musical poets; Surrey, the later Spenser, Waller, Pope, Southey, and Tennyson among the unmusical ones – those with a sentimental concept of music as the regular flow of sweet sounds. A revised form of this essay is incorporated into F's analysis of the generic rhythm of *epos* in *AC*, 251–62.

D13 'The Anatomy in Prose Fiction.' *Manitoba Arts Review* 3 (Spring 1942): 35–47
Seeks, in his first major critical essay, to distinguish among the forms of prose fiction. Determines that there are four major forms: the romance, the novel, the confession, and the Menippean satire or anatomy. Distinguishes among the four types on the basis of their differing tones, styles, mental attitudes, and forms. The significance of this essay rests primarily in the 'discovery' and analysis of the anatomy: a variety of prose satire that

emphasizes ideas, is bookish and erudite, stresses the data of culture as against those of civilization, favours the cynical and detached attitude, attacks society in general rather than the individual, and tends toward the encyclopedic farrago and the intellectual paradox. Content of this article appears in a thoroughly revised form as 'The Four Forms of Prose Fiction' (see D41), which, with further revisions, becomes a part of F's theory of genres in *AC*, 303–14.

D14 'Reflections at a Movie.' *Canadian Forum* 22 (October 1942): 212–13
Laments the lack of attention that Canadians have paid to the spoken language. But 'rhetoric and oratory are back again to stay, and the radio and movie have brought them back.' These media have also helped collapse the distance between spoken and written language. Urges Canadians to become more aware of the sounds and rhythms of their own language and thus discover something distinctly Canadian in it. Argues, finally, that the opposition between speech that follows the conventions of proper usage and normal, effective, colloquial speech should be abandoned.

D15 'A Mixed Bag.' *Canadian Forum* 22 (December 1942): 282–4
Review of *New Directions in Prose and Poetry*, 1942, no 7, ed James Laughlin. Finds the selections in the anthology 'uneven in interest' and devotes most of the review to quarrelling with the principle of selection by the editor: that lively literature is produced by the clash between tradition and experiment. 'No art of any importance can fit such a dialectic.' Observes, in what is to become a common theme throughout his work, that 'original' implies a return to origins and 'radical' a return to roots. Also disagrees with the editor's claim that literature evolves and improves. Finds the criticism in the anthology to be generally superior to the poetry and fiction. Praises the symposium on Ford Madox Ford, poems by Joure and Eberhart, a fable by Kafka, two essays by Paul Goodman, and a play by William Carlos Williams.

D16 'Music in the Movies.' *Canadian Forum* 22 (December 1942): 275–6
Argues for a more sophisticated use of music in the movies. Hollywood has so far treated music only as sound effects, but film 'demands a running musical commentary'; there should be 'a continuous use of musical symbolism ... in complete accord with the whole structure of the movie.' Observes that future directors will learn to do what Chaplin has done with music thematically and symbolically. When they do, the movies might become 'clean-cut musical drama.' For replies to this article see P111 and P168.

D17 Review of *Voices: A Critical Quarterly*, ed Ralph Gustafson, and *Genesis: Book One*, by Delmore Schwartz. *Canadian Forum* 23 (June 1943): 68–70
Devotes two-thirds of the review to reflecting on the task of the critic-as-reviewer, concluding that he or she should try to discover some middle ground between exuberant approval and querulous complaint. The middle ground is that of leisured experience: one's claim to be a critic 'rests simply on the fact that he likes reading poetry, that he finds it pleasant

and not a duty, that reading poetry is one of the best ways of entertaining himself in leisure moments.' From *Voices*, singles out the poems of E.J. Pratt, Robert Finch, Leo Kennedy, Patrick Anderson, P.K. Page, Ralph Gustafson, and F.R. Scott as deserving honourable mention. Judges the scheme of Schwartz's 'loosely cadenced' narrative poem to be 'worked out with considerable intelligence and power,' though the story itself is commonplace.

D18 'Canada and Its Poetry.' *Canadian Forum* 23 (December 1943): 207–10. Rpt in *BG*, 129–43, and in *The Making of Modern Poetry in Canada*, ed Louis Dudek and Michael Gnarowski (Toronto: Ryerson Press 1967), 86–97.
A long review of *The Book of Canadian Poetry*, ed A.J.M. Smith. Praises the anthology for its unity of tone. Its appearance 'is an important event in Canadian literature.' Devotes most of the review to determining whether or not there are any truly Canadian qualities in the country's poetry. Isolates, first of all, the 'colonial tendency,' which results from two themes: the imperial theme (basically English) and the regional (basically French). Argues that the colonial position of Canada has produced 'a frostbite at the roots of the Canadian imagination.' The result is that Canadian poets have had to overcome a number of forms of social and religious prudery. Sees the reaction to nature as the primary characteristic of the Canadian poetic imagination. Nature is first seen as 'unconsciousness, then as a kind of existence which is cruel and meaningless, then as the source of the cruelty and subconscious stampedings within the human mind.' Nature is not idealized but consistently represented as sinister and menacing.

D19 'The Nature of Satire.' *University of Toronto Quarterly* 14 (October 1944): 75–89. Rpt in *Satire: Theory and Practice*, ed Charles A. Allen and George D. Stephens (Belmont, Calif: Wadsworth 1962), 15–30; in *Satire: An Anthology*, ed Ashley Brown and John L. Kimmey (New York: Harper & Row 1977), 323–39; and in *Satura: Ein Kompendium moderner Studien zur Satire*, ed Bernhard Fabian (Hildesheim: Olms 1975), 108–22. Incorporated, with major revisions, into *AC*, 223–39.
Defines satire as a literary tone or attitude, rather than a form, that depends upon two ingredients: wit or humour and an object of attack. Satire thus lies between pure denunciation at one extreme, and pure gaiety or exuberance at the other. The sardonic vision requires that the writer and his audience agree on the undesirability of what is being attacked; thus satire asserts or defends a moral principle. The exuberant side of satire results in absurdity or grotesqueness – the 'poetic imagination in reverse gear.' Satire 'belittles and minimizes' rather than intensifying the 'imaginative impact of things.' Also observes the similarities that exist between satire, irony, and tragedy ('the sardonic vision is the seamy side of the tragic vision') and the differences between satire and comedy. This essay, exemplifying F's wittily allusive method, contains references to scores of works, from Petronius and Lucian to Walt Disney and E.J. Pratt.

D20 Review of *New Directions Annual*, 1944, n. 8, ed James Laughlin. *Canadian Forum* 24 (November 1944): 189–90

Disagrees with the theory of 'experiment' that underlies the editor's introduction. (Has lodged the same objection against the previous volume of this series. See D15.) Finds Lorca's writing to be the best part of the anthology. Discovers the influence of Kafka, Marx, Freud, and Joyce throughout. Devotes the last half of the review to the opinion that the real 'new direction' in literature is the change in techniques caused by 'the movie, the radio, the magazine, the newspaper, and their subsidiaries ... a revolution greater than anything in literature since the invention of the printing press.' Argues that the function of the serious writer today who has not been influenced by the techniques of the media is to do the same thing that all highbrow writers have done – to digest their learning and insight into an artistic form. When such digestion does not occur, as it does not in most of the pieces in this anthology, the result is a critical essay in the form of a poem or short story, not a work of art.

D21 'Water Colour Annual.' *Canadian Art* 1 (1944): 187–9
Compares the water-colours exhibited at the Art Gallery of Toronto with oil paintings. Finds the Canadian oils to be generally academic and without interest and the water-colours to be lively and interesting. Water-colours are 'a fertilizing influence in painting' because they are not painted for ex-hibition, are the products of cultivated amateurs (and thus are taken less seriously), have a greater sense of lightness and humour, are devoted more to the rhythm of design than to detail, tend toward more challenging subjects, and display a wider variety of techniques. Illustrated with repro-ductions of water-colours by Haworth, Milne, and Crawford.

D22 'A Liberal Education.' *Canadian Forum* 25 (September 1945): 134–5
Deplores the attacks on liberal education by the Tory politicians and *laissez-faire* capitalists interested only in vocational training. Argues that while the *laissez-faire* philosophy was once a liberating social force it has now become a reactionary condition. Similarly, science, which once 'had a liberal and even revolutionary cast' as opposed to the conservative attitude associated with the humanities, has become more and more a function of government and in the service of the ruling class. Observes that science can never have a great social role because its source of authority is the impersonal one of its own subject. But the source of authority in the hu-manities is personal, and no coherent social reform can occur without upholding this sense of personal authority. 'The realization that in the great works of culture there is a vision of reality which is completely human and comprehensible, and yet just a bit better than what we can get by ourselves, is the mainspring of all liberal thought.' Also argues against *laissez-faire* or progressive philosophies of education because they can lead easily into fascism. 'There is no coherent socialism except that which is attached to a liberal theory of education, and derives its ideals from that theory.'

D23 'A Liberal Education: Part II.' *Canadian Forum* 25 (October 1945): 162–4
Examines two views of education: (1) the technical and vocational ('pro-gressive') view, which encourages the adjustment of the student to the

actual environment, rather than to an ideal one, and (2) the liberal view, which assumes that the study of literature and philosophy is essential for providing the right motives for action and for causing genuine social change. Believes, however, that education that tries to fit students into either an actual or an ideal environment is misguided, for the real purpose of liberal education 'is to achieve a neurotic maladjustment in the student,' to help him or her develop a critical mind.

D24 'La tradition narrative dans la poésie canadienne-anglaise,' trans Guy Sylvestre. *Gants du Ciel* 11 (1946): 19–30. English text rpt in *Canadian Anthology*, ed Carl F. Klinck and Reginald Watters, rev ed (Toronto: Gage 1966), 523–8; and 3rd ed (Toronto: Gage 1974), 605–8; English text also rpt as 'The Narrative Tradition in English-Canadian Poetry' in *BG*, 145–55. In seeking to discover the chief feature of Canadian poetry, finds a number of similarities between the Canadian poet's reaction to his environment and that of the Old English poet to his. In both there is 'a feeling of melancholy of a thinly-settled country under a bleak northern sky, of the terrible isolation of the creative mind in such a country, of resigning oneself to hardship and loneliness as the only means of attaining, if not serenity, at least a kind of rigid calm.' Sees the form of much Canadian poetry as following the conventions of the romantic lyric, though its themes and moods are more appropriate to older forms, such as the ballad and especially the longer narrative poem. Traces this narrative tradition throughout the poems of Heavysege, Isabella Crawford, Archibald Lampman, D.C. Scott, Charles Mair, and E.J. Pratt, all of whose work is built upon the contrast betweeen the mindless forces of nature and the human values of civilized life.

D25 'Turning New Leaves.' *Canadian Forum* 26 (December 1946): 211–12. Rpt as 'Orwell and Marxism' in *NFCL*, 204–6; and in *George Orwell: The Critical Heritage*, ed Jeffrey Meyers (London: Routledge & Kegan Paul 1975), 206–8. A review of George Orwell's *Animal Farm*. Finds some excellent satiric touches in the novel, but the book as a whole does not present a very searching satire on Russian Communism. It 'completely misses the point as a satire on the Russian development of Marxism, and as expressing the disillusionment which many men of good will feel about Russia.' Comments on the causes of this disillusionment, the chief of which is that dialectical materialism, despite Marx and Engels's disclaimers, has become an exclusive and dogmatic metaphysical materialism. It has absolutized expediency into a principle and has thus become intellectually dishonest, capable of rationalizing any ruthless action. Argues that official Marxism has therefore prevented itself from giving a 'revolutionary dynamic' to the body of modern thought, and that the real reasons Marxism has become 'a kind of parody of the Catholic Church' could be the basis for a more meaningful satire on Russian Communism.

D26 'Blake on Trial Again.' *Poetry: A Magazine of Verse* 69 (January 1947): 223–8 A review of *William Blake: The Politics of Vision*, by Mark Schorer, and *The*

Portable Blake, ed Alfred Kazin. Contends that although Schorer intends his study to be sympathetic he ends up saying, in effect, that Blake's prophecies are close to madness. Schorer sees Blake as being pulled by two opposing views of art and as never achieving fulfilment in either: the acceptance of the prophetic role of the artist (as in Rilke) versus the rejection of it (as in Rimbaud), pure versus applied poetry, the poet in the ivory tower versus the poet in the market-place. Believes that Schorer's book, which does not take the customary route of isolating Blake from his own culture, raises real issues, but contends that 'the best way to approach Blake is to surrender unconditionally to Blake's own terms.' Maintains that Kazin's anthology does not replace Keynes's one-volume edition (also portable) of Blake's work. Sees Kazin's approach in his introduction as similar to Schorer's: 'often sensitive and eloquent in dealing with the lyrical poems,' his approach to the prophecies is, like Schorer's, 'simply not good enough.' Both ultimately fail because of their method: they do not engage the whole of Blake for fear that he 'is not intelligent enough to withstand exhaustive scrutiny.' On *The Portable Blake* see also E46.

D27 'Turning New Leaves.' *Canadian Forum* 26 (March 1947): 281–2. Rpt as 'Total Identification' in *NFCL*, 107–10.

A review of *The Meeting of East and West*, by F.S.C. Northrop. Believes that the value of this book lies in the information it provides about a wide range of topics – from the idea of causation in Aristotle to the role of Mexico in contemporary society – rather than in its thesis, which is that global understanding can result from a synthesis of the 'theoretic' or Western understanding of experience and the 'aesthetic' or Eastern one. Argues that a global understanding will not necessarily make for a more unified or better world and that there is no good reason for seeking a world-wide cultural federation. Suggests finally that the attempt to assimilate Western and Eastern thought is based on a misunderstanding of the highest modes of apprehension, which go beyond both the theoretic and the aesthetic to achieve a vision of 'total identification.'

D28 'Education and the Humanities.' *United Church Observer* 9 (1 August, 1947): 5, 25

Distinguishes the sciences from the humanities on the basis of their different kinds of authority: the authority that comes from the unity in the scientific disciplines themselves and the personal authority that comes from the great artists who have created the classics. Maintains that the humanities are more difficult to teach than the sciences because they require an expanded growth of the mind as a whole, which can only come from the slow development of taste and the gradual adjustment of the mind to the personal authority of the great artists.This adjustment of the mind 'begins to lead us toward the central form of our religion,' for Christianity 'is teachable too only in a limited way'; like literature and art, it 'is revealed to us in the form of a book.' Concludes by observing that in times of crisis and confusion people turn to the humanities because they lead away from ordinary life 'toward the discipline of spiritual freedom from which they derive the name of liberal.'

D29 'Toynbee and Spengler.' *Canadian Forum* 27 (August 1947): 111–13. Rpt as 'The Shapes of History' in *NFCL*, 76–83.

A review of D.C. Somervell's abridgment of the first six volumes of *A Study of History*, by Arnold J. Toynbee. Begins by comparing Toynbee's vision of history with Spengler's *Decline of the West*, the thesis of which is summarized in some detail. Finds that Toynbee's first three volumes are 'an improved version of Spengler backed up by a far greater knowledge of history' but that when Toynbee begins to criticize Spengler's theory of the organic nature of culture, which still has not been refuted, his argument begins to weaken. Toynbee's own metaphors, in fact, betray a conception of history based upon organic stages, and his view of historical change is founded more upon a theory of chance than upon an understanding of cause and effect. Toynbee's optimism about the present shape of history and his hope that the status quo can be maintained do not properly account for where the instruments of production are leading us. To explain current history will require what Toynbee can perhaps develop in subsequent volumes: a view of history based on a synthesis of Spengler and Marx.

D30 'Yeats and the Language of Symbolism.' *University of Toronto Quarterly* 17 (October 1947): 1–17. Rpt in *FI*, 218–37.

Observes that because the nineteenth century did not contain a coherent critical tradition, one that could have organized the language of symbolism, its poets turned to other symbolic systems for their poetic language. Yeats sought his symbolic language in the heroic and popular folklore of Irish mythology and in the theosophic doctrine and spiritual discipline of the occultism of his time. In his search, Yeats did not really discover a new language of symbolism; he merely fulfilled 'the romantic tradition from which he started, his final position being simply a more systematic expression of the romanticism of Nietzsche and Lawrence.' The grammar of this romantic symbolism is found in *A Vision*, which opposes the phenomenal world of consciousness to the noumenal world of subconsciousness. Concludes by comparing Yeats's symbolism with that of Blake, a poet 'who knew a greater tradition than the romantic one.' Although Yeats's vision is, from Blake's perspective, a vision of the physical world of Generation, Yeats does move from his early romanticism through the values of the tragic mask to, finally, the emancipating vision of exuberance, 'flying far above the conflicts of illusion.'

D31 'The Eternal Tramp.' *Here and Now* 1 (December 1947): 8–11

Analyses the various phases in the development of Chaplin's view of comedy, from *The Gold Rush* to *Monsieur Verdoux*. Concentrates on Chaplin's use of the conventions of comedy, especially on the character of the tramp and his relationship to society. The tramp begins as a social misfit of

the Huck Finn type (a phase that ends with *City Lights*), becomes a
character hypnotized by a mechanized society (in *Modern Times*), and represents eventually the normal human being (in *Monsieur Verdoux*), though
he is a more complex figure now and one who must be examined as an
actor in a 'religious drama'; for in this film he represents both the Antichrist
and Everyman, and in the latter role he sustains his dignity to the very
end.

D32 'Turning New Leaves.' *Canadian Forum* 27 (March 1948): 283
Review of *On the Marble Cliffs*, by Ernst Jünger, an anti-Nazi allegory
written by a former Nazi sympathizer. Sees the allegory as somewhat
veiled, though its general thesis seems 'to be that Hitler is the serpent in
the paradise of German romanticism.' Compares the book to another
allegory, Rex Warner's *The Aerodrome*, where the conflict between freedom
and tyranny is quite clear. Still, Jünger now seems prepared to affirm
'the values of the liberal, Christian and humanist traditions.' A rewarding
book for those interested in the post-Nazi conscience, though on that
subject Chaplin's *The Great Dictator* tells us all we need to know 'about the
psychology of the anti-Nazi Nazis.'

D33 'David Milne: An Appreciation.' *Here and Now* 1 (May 1948): 47–8. Rpt in
BG, 203–6.
Likens the perspective in Milne's paintings to that of Oriental or medieval
art, where 'the observer's eye seems to be at the circumference of the
picture, so that it opens inward into the mind.' Understands Milne's aim
as presenting 'pure visual experience.' Reviews Milne's Canadian landscapes (the article is accompanied by illustrations) and compares their technique with that of the Group of Seven. Prefers Milne's water-colours to
his oils but both illustrate a 'desire to paint rather than ... a desire to say
something with paint.' Milne's works set free the visual experience and he
trains his observers' minds 'to see the world in a spirit of leisure and
urbanity.'

D34 'Dr. Kinsey and the Dream Censor.' *Canadian Forum* 28 (July 1948): 85–6
Examines the question of censorship, raised by the call from some quarters
to have the Kinsey report banned. Addresses chiefly the issue of whether
or not there is any knowledge that should be restricted to professional
people and concludes that such restriction cannot be permitted in a
democracy. Maintains that the social response to the Kinsey report is the
real problem, a response that has been fostered by popular amusements
that bombard society with adolescent and titillating material. This has
created a 'maudlin erotic stupor,' and people sunk in such a stupor are
'naturally irritated by the more dry and matter-of-fact tones in which adults
discuss the workings of the sexual instinct,' as in the Kinsey report.

D35 'The Pursuit of Form.' *Canadian Art* 6 (Christmas 1948): 54–7
On the paintings of Lawren Harris. Comments on the 'deceptive serenity'
in Harris's conventionalized Northern landscapes, but sees Harris's greatest power in his abstract paintings. Distinguishes non-objective from

abstract painting. The former is to painting what mathematics is to science: it establishes a continuous series of pictorial themes to suggest an apprehension of reality, which in Harris's case is open to an indefinite number of interpretations. His 'best abstractions are a unique and major contribution to Canadian painting.'

D36 'Turning New Leaves.' *Canadian Forum* 29 (September 1949): 138–9. Rpt as 'The Rhythm of Growth and Decay' in *NFCL*, 141–6.

Review of *Faith and History*, by Reinhold Niebuhr, and *Meaning in History*, by Karl Löwith. Observes that both books agree on the three chief views of history: the classical or pessimistic view that history is an endless series of cycles, the Christian view that there is meaning in history, and the modern view founded on a theory of progress. Although both writers give more negative than positive criticism, neither 'really brings out the moral horror of a progressive view of history.' Believes that more can be said about both the cyclic and Christian views. Cites Vico, Spengler, and Toynbee as upholding a cyclic understanding of history very different from the classical one. These historians see history as a 'rotary movement of rise and fall,' a view that has an affinity both to the myth of the fall and to the organic rhythm of growth and decay in the natural world. Civilizations or cultures, then, in the Vico-Spengler idea of history 'behave more or less like natural organisms and go through much the same phases of growth, maturation and decline.'

D37 'The Function of Criticism at the Present Time.' *University of Toronto Quarterly* 19 (October 1949): 1–16. Incorporated into *AC*, 3–29. Rpt in *Our Sense of Identity: A Book of Canadian Essays*, ed Malcolm Ross (Toronto: Ryerson 1954), 247–65; and in *Modern Literary Criticism, 1900–1970*, ed Lawrence I. Lipking and A. Walton Litz (New York: Atheneum 1972), 198–208.

Argues for the autonomy of criticism as a discipline that can be developed in a systematic way independent from some non-literary conceptual framework or ideology. Seeks to separate genuine criticism from both cultivated *causerie* and the issuing of value-judgments. Believes that the principles of criticism must be derived inductively from the study of literature itself. Compares the current state of criticism to that of a naïve, primitive science because it has not yet developed these principles. Maintains that the present function of criticism is to study systematically the verbal universe of literature.

D38 'Turning New Leaves.' *Canadian Forum* 29 (December 1949): 209–11. Rpt as 'The Acceptance of Innocence' in *NFCL*, 159–64.

Begins as a review of Samuel Putnam's translation of *Don Quixote*, which is said to be a good text for the modern reader even though one might prefer Motteux's eighteenth-century translation for its vigour and wit. Comments on the difference between the eighteenth-century view of Quixote (which had a common-sense view of his folly and the hard knocks he received) and the romantic and twentieth-century views of him. Sees

Quixote not simply as a satire on chivalric romance but also as a profound social parable, for what is embodied in 'the world's first and perhaps still its greatest novel' is the relationship among ridiculousness, pathos, and dignity; the problem of private mythology; and the vision of the golden age of simplicity, equality, and the genuinely childlike acceptance of innocence.

D39 'The Argument of Comedy.' *English Institute Essays: 1948*, ed D.A. Robertson, Jr (New York: Columbia Univ Press 1949), 58–73. Incorporated into *AC*, Third Essay. Rpt in *Shakespeare: Modern Essays in Criticism*, ed Leonard F. Dean (New York: Oxford Univ Press 1957), 79–89; in *Comedy: Plays, Theory, and Criticism*, ed Marvin Felheim (New York: Harcourt, Brace and World 1962), 236–41; in *Theories of Comedy*, ed Paul Lauter (Garden City, NY: Doubleday 1964), 449–60; in *Shakespeare's 'Twelfth Night,'* ed Leonard F. Dean and James A.S. McPeak (Boston: Allyn & Bacon 1965), 93–101; in *Shakespeare's Comedies: An Anthology of Modern Criticism*, ed Laurence Lerner (Baltimore: Penguin 1967), 315–25; in *His Infinite Variety: Shakespearean Criticism since Johnson*, ed Paul N. Siegel (Philadelphia: Lippincott 1964), 120–9; and in *Essays in Shakespearean Criticism*, ed James Calderwood and Harold E. Toliver (Englewood Cliffs, NJ: Prentice-Hall 1970), 49–57.
Traces the structure of comedy from Aristophanes through the New Comedy of Menander, Plautus, Terence, and the New-Comedy conventions of Jonson and Molière to the Elizabethan comedy of Shakespeare. Says that the structure of comedy derives from Greek New Comedy, as transmitted by Plautus and Terence, in which the main theme is that of a young man falling in love with a young woman and eventually, after overcoming various blocking characters, being able to possess the object of his desire. There are two centres of interest in this kind of comedy: individual (the opponents have to surrender in the end to the hero) and social (the resolution that points toward the establishment of a new social order). Argues that tragedy is actually an implicit or incomplete comedy, since it is resolved by the resurrection that follows death. Shakespeare's comedy, however, 'begins in a world represented as a normal world, moves into the green world, goes into a metamorphosis there in which the comic resolution is achieved, and returns to the normal world,' the expression 'green world' indicating the analogies Shakespeare's comedies have to ritual, like the rebirth of spring after winter, as well as to the idealized world of dreamlike desire. Shakespeare's distinctive comic resolution, finally, 'is the detachment of the spirit' that is born from the follies of the normal world and from the pastoral lovers, dreams, and fairies of the dream world.

D40 'The Church: Its Relation to Society.' *The Living Church*, ed Harold Vaughan (Toronto: United Church Publishing House 1949), 152–72
Begins by describing the social ideology of Plato's *Republic*, which really involves three different societies: that of fourth-century Greece, that of the philosopher-kings supported by military guards, and that of the sympo-

sium that produced Socrates' vision. Plato's view of the disciplined state of the philosopher-kings is not suited to encourage the three essentials of civilized life: leisure, privacy, and freedom. Thus it needs to be complemented by a 'single informing spirit' of charity, which holds society together. Society, then, is a mixture of both power and love. But the Christian has to resist the pull of the Caesarian tendency toward the dictatorial state and 'has to follow the revolutionary ideals of liberty, equality and fraternity.' The modern form of the symposium is the university, the place where free discussion can take place. Maintains, in part two of the essay, that the chief function of the Christian church is to unify the university, the world, and the City of God. Speaks of the relationship between Protestantism, liberal democracy, and inductive science on the one hand, and Catholicism, temporal authority, and Aristotelian logic on the other. Gives a social defence of the alliance of Protestantism with liberalism, observing that the genuine freedom in liberalism should not be confused with *laissez-faire* politics. Genuine freedom, which comes chiefly from Christianity, can produce a genuine version of the City of God, and it is this kind of freedom, which shows 'faith as the emancipation and the fulfilment of reason,' that the church should uphold.

D41 'The Four Forms of Prose Fiction.' *Hudson Review* 2 (Winter 1950): 582–95. Incorporated into *AC*, Fourth Essay. Rpt in *Modern Literary Criticism, 1900–1970*, ed Lawrence I. Lipking and A. Walton Litz (New York: Atheneum 1972), 208–15.
Distinguishes among four major types of fiction (novel, romance, confession, and anatomy) on the basis of two pairs of categories: personal/intellectualized and introverted/extroverted. The first pair refers largely to characterization; the second to rhetorical technique. The novel and the anatomy are extroverted forms, the former being personal and the latter intellectualized; whereas the romance and confession are introverted forms, the former being personal and the latter intellectualized. Draws, however, upon a number of other opposing categories in defining the four forms, such as realistic vs allegorical, conservative vs revolutionary, and stable vs untameable. Provides a host of examples of works, both long and short forms, for each category and shows how the various forms combine with one another. Claims that an awareness of the four forms can help us in examining writers in terms of the conventions they choose. 'If Scott,' for example, 'has any claims to be a romancer, it is not good criticism to deal only with his defects as a novelist.' Believes that critics have been especially remiss in not taking into account the anatomy.

D42 'Levels of Meaning in Literature.' *Kenyon Review* 12 (Spring 1950): 246–62. Incorporated into *AC*, Second Essay.
A restatement of the medieval theory of four levels of meaning, similar to the taxonomy of symbolism developed in *AC*, 71–128. Outlines four levels of meaning: the literal level, where the locus of meaning is centripetal; the descriptive or 'allegorical' level, where meaning exists in the

relationship between literature and other verbal structures; the archetypal or mythical level, where meaning emerges from recurring themes and symbols; and the anagogic level, where meaning emerges from seeing literature as part of a whole. We can hardly engage in anagogic criticism 'without the help of the integrations of myth which have been made in the higher religions and incorporated in their scriptures and sacred books.'

D43 'Novels on Several Occasions.' *Hudson Review* 3 (Winter 1950–1): 611–19. Rpt in *NFCL*, 207–18; partially rpt in *Twentieth-Century Literary Criticism*, ed Dennis Poupard (Detroit: Gale Research 1983), 488; paragraphs on Hemingway rpt in *Ernest Hemingway: The Critical Reception*, ed Robert O. Stephens (np: Burt Franklin 1977), 333; and in *Hemingway: The Critical Heritage* (London: Routledge & Kegan Paul 1982), 393–5.
A review of *Across the River and into the Trees*, by Ernest Hemingway; *The Disenchanted*, by Budd Schulberg; *The House of Death*, by William Goyen; *Two Adolescents*, by Alberto Moravia; *Shadows of Ecstasy*, by Charles Williams; *The Barkeep of Blémont*, by Marcel Amyé; and *The Twenty-fifth Hour*, by C. Virgil Gheorghiu. Sees Hemingway's story as presented in bits and pieces and as technically amateurish. Praises Schulberg's writing, especially the dialogue, yet thinks the hero never gets beyond pathos. Judges Goyen's novel to be 'something of a stunt' though 'an outstandingly clever and successful one' and one that is stylistically powerful. Sees Moravia as having replaced the social vision of Austen and Trollope with 'a vision based on the sense of moral autonomy.' Williams has written an 'intellectual thriller' with more irony and less didacticism than usual. Amyé's satire is in the central tradition of fiction, a novel of 'balanced and unstampeded maturity.' Gheorghiu shows us the hopelessness of the human condition, and, although the novel is somewhat sermonic, it is 'a document of great importance.'

D44 'Tenets of Modern Culture.' *The Church and the Secular World* (A Report of the Commission on Culture presented to the Fourteenth General Council of the United Church of Canada) (Toronto: Board of Evangelism and Social Service 1950), 13–14
Outlines the principles of modern American political, economic, and religious thought. Sees the fundamental axioms of American culture as 'essentially those of eighteenth-century Deism.' Its basic ideology is *laissez-faire*, and this orientation leads to the direction not of democracy but of managerial dictatorship. Examines the five main causes of the sense of imminent apocalypse in contemporary life: fascism, Communism, *laissez-faire* utopianism, technology, and atheistic parodies of religion.

D45 'The Young Boswell,' *Hudson Review* 4 (Spring 1951): 143–6. Rpt in *NFCL*, 165–9.
A review of *Boswell's London Journal, 1762–1763*, edited by Frederick A. Pottle, which 'illustrates a significant stage in the development of a writer of genius.' Sees two remarkable things in Boswell the biographer: his ability to draw Johnson out with the cunningly asked question and his

awareness of 'the organic consistency' of Johnson's character. Observes the
various masks that Boswell projects in the *Journal*: the writer of poise and
propriety, the writer who could see through his idealized mask, and
the cold, calculating, precise recorder of life. Boswell is naïve as a subject,
but candid as an autobiographer, and he has the ability always to get
the tone right – vain and ironic at the same time. This is why his journals
are 'his letter of introduction to posterity' and why they will give him
the last word over those, from Boswell's father to Macaulay, who saw
nothing in Boswell to be admired.

D46 'Letters in Canada: 1950, Poetry.' *University of Toronto Quarterly* 20 (April
1951): 257–62. Partially rpt in *BG*, 1–3.
The first of F's annual surveys of Canadian poetry. Judges the year to be
far from a banner one, but does find 'a dignified simplicity and sincere eloquence' in James Wreford's *Of Time and the Lover* and 'a high level of
competence' in Norman Levine's *The Tight-Rope Walker*. Looks briefly at
each of the volumes in the Ryerson Poetry chap-book series, the best
of which is Dorothy Livesay's radio play, *Call My People Home*, and compli-
ments occasional flashes of competence in a half-dozen other volumes.

D47 'Poetry and Design in William Blake.' *Journal of Aesthetics and Art Criticism*
10 (September 1951): 35–42. Rpt in *Discussions of William Blake*, ed John
E. Grant (Boston: Heath 1961), 44–9; in *Blake: A Collection of Critical Essays*,
ed Northrop Frye (Englewood Cliffs, NJ: Prentice-Hall 1966), 119–26 (see
B11); and, with notes added by the editor, in *The Visionary Hand: Essays for
the Study of William Blake's Art and Aesthetics*, ed Robert N. Essick (Los
Angeles: Hennessey & Ingalls 1973), 147–59.
Argues that in order to understand Blake one must consider both his
words and his artistic designs. Shows how Blake's books differ from the
illustrated books of the day and from the hieroglyphic tradition of orna-
mentation. Observes that the poetry and the designs are independent from
each other, though they are integrally related. Comments on the various
roles that the designs play in relation to the words, such as direct illustration, parody, ironic comment, and biblical reference. Concludes by observing that the 'syncopation between design and narrative' in Blake raises
the problem of the relationship between rhythm and pattern, the study of
which yields not propositional content but a total structure of imagery
or poetic meaning. Blake's designs help us understand his poetic meaning.

D48 'A Conspectus of Dramatic Genres.' *Kenyon Review* 13 (Autumn 1951): 543–
62. Incorporated into *AC*, Fourth Essay.
An outline of the formal causes of drama, which seeks to go beyond the
traditional division of dramatic kinds into tragedy and comedy. Divides
drama into two large categories, spectacular and mimetic. A related pair of
categories, epiphany (or pure vision) and mime (or pure image), constitute
the extreme dramatic points of an imaginary vertical axis; and at the
horizontal poles of the schema lie two other dramatic forms, the 'history-
play' (or act-play) and the 'philosophy-play' (or symposium). Locates

the dramatic species around an imaginary circle that connects the four points of this mental diagram: myth play, *auto*, historical tragedy, tragedy, irony, ironic comedy, comedy, ideal comedy, farce, opera, ideal masque, morality play, and archetypal masque.

D49 'The Archetypes of Literature.' *Kenyon Review* 13 (Winter 1951): 92–110. Incorporated into *AC*, Second Essay. Rpt in *FI*, 7–20; in *Myth and Method: Modern Theories of Fiction*, ed James E. Miller (Lincoln: Univ of Nebraska Press 1960), 144–62; in *Criticism: The Major Texts*, enlarged ed, ed Walter Jackson Bate (New York: Harcourt Brace Jovanovich 1970), 601–9; in *Myth and Literature: Contemporary Theory and Practice*, ed John B. Vickery (Lincoln: Univ of Nebraska Press 1966), 87–97; in *Modern Literary Criticism, 1900–1970*, ed Lawrence I. Lipking and A. Walton Litz (New York: Atheneum 1972), 215–24; in *An Introduction to Literary Criticism*, ed Laila Gross (New York: Capricorn Books 1972), 326–40; in *Dramatic Theory and Practice*, ed Bernard F. Dukore (New York: Holt, Rinehart and Winston 1974), 897–901; in *Wspołczensa teoria badan literackick za granica*, trans A. Bejska; ed H. Markiewicz (Krakow 1976), 316 ff; in *The Avant-Garde Tradition in Literature*, ed Richard Kostelanetz (Buffalo, NY: Prometheus Books 1982), 16–27; and in two issues of *The Strand* [Victoria College, Univ of Toronto]: January 1974, 2–3, 6, with untitled preface by John Syrtash, and March 1973, with 'Preface' by J[ohn] S[yrtash]. Rpt as 'Arhetipovi Knjizevnosti,' trans Nina Živančević, in *Knjizevnost* [Belgrade] 37, nos 4–5 (April-May 1982): 465–75; and partially rpt in *Metodi di critica letteraria americana*, ed Marga Cottino-Jones (Palermo: Palumbo Editore 1973), 96–101. Rpt as a separate monograph entitled *Bungaku no Genkei*, trans Toshitada Iketani (Nagoya: Nagoya eibei gendaishi kenkyû-kai [Nagoya Society for the Study of Contemporary British and American Poetry] 1974), 12 pp (see C7). Argues that criticism needs to proceed like science, inductively from structural analysis and deductively from the assumption of the total coherence of literature and the unity of criticism. Sees the archetype as providing the missing category criticism needs. Shows how the study of the archetype can lead to an understanding of the temporal dimension of literature (its movement in time) as well as its spatial dimension (its organization as a pattern of images). The former leads to a study of the quest myth, the four phases of which (romance, comedy, tragedy, and satire) are analogous to the seasonal cycle of nature and to ritual. The latter leads to a study of how imagery is embodied hierarchically on each level of reality (human, animal, vegetable, mineral, etc) and for each phase of the quest myth. Provides a table of the phases of the quest myth and one for the structure of archetypal imagery in order to show how archetypal criticism might proceed to discover the unity of its subject matter.

D50 'Blake's Treatment of the Archetype.' *English Institute Essays, 1950*, ed Alan S. Downer (New York: Columbia Univ Press 1951), 170–96. Rpt in *Discussions of William Blake*, ed John E. Grant (Boston: Heath 1961), 6–16; in *Critics on Blake*, ed Judith O'Neill (Coral Gables: Univ of Florida Press; London:

Allen & Unwin 1970), 47–61; and in *Blake's Poetry and Designs*, ed Mary
Lynn Johnson and John E. Grant (New York: Norton 1979), 510–25.
Analyses the conception of imagery in Blake's worlds of innocence and
experience as it manifests itself individually and collectively in both categories. Looks next at the narrative structure of Blake's prophecies: its
embodiment in the Orc cycle and its source in the biblical myth of creation,
fall, and apocalypse. Argues that Blake's work consists almost solely in
the articulation of archetypes, which are elements in literature, 'whether a
character, an image, a narrative formula, or an idea, which can be assimilated to a larger unifying category.' Believes that the study of Blake's
poetry can provide a model for analysing the structure of symbols and
myths in the private mythology of other poets.

D51 'Introduction.' *Paradise Lost and Selected Poetry and Prose*, by John Milton, ed
Northrop Frye (New York: Holt, Rinehart and Winston 1951), v–xxxvi
(see B1)
In part 1 examines Milton's early poetry (1629–40), especially the *Nativity
Ode* and *Comus*, which show the ignorance and confusion from which
fallen humanity must be emancipated. Analyses the major themes of Milton's controversial prose (1640–60) in part 2. Discusses the major poetry
(1660–74) in part 3, particularly the relation of *Paradise Lost* to the epic tradition and the nature of heroism in Milton's epics. Considers finally the
techniques of Milton's verse, its music, diction, rhythm, and imagery.

D52 'The Analogy of Democracy.' *Bias* 1 (February 1952): 2–6
On the relationship of the Christian church to the idea of democracy and
to social institutions, especially government, law, and the university.
Sees in democracy a secular analogy of Christianity. Argues that the secular
vision has greater appeal than does the surrender to some Pharisaic
authority. This is because the democratic conception of culture, with its
emphasis on freedom and toleration, is really more Christian than a church
that cannot separate gospel from law.

D53 'Turning New Leaves.' *Canadian Forum* 31 (February 1952): 258–60. Rpt as
'Oxford Dictionary of Nursery Rhymes,' in *Explorations: Studies in Culture
and Communication*, ed E.S. Carpenter (Toronto: Univ of Toronto 1953),
128–30.
A review of *The Oxford Dictionary of Nursery Rhymes*, ed Iona and Peter
Opie. Samples some of the Opies' scholarship on nursery rhymes: the
attacks they have received at the hands of 'psychological neo-Puritans' and
the search, both pedantic and otherwise, for their sources and meanings.
Sees nursery rhymes as important for two reasons: they illustrate the
problems of all popular and oral literature and 'they represent the only
genuine poetic experience that many people ever get.' The child who
has not had the experience of nursery rhymes will likely be taken in by the
widespread notion in the schools that poetry is unnatural or perverse
prose.

D54 'Letters in Canada: 1951, Poetry.' *University of Toronto Quarterly* 21 (April

1952): 252–8. Partially rpt in *BG*, 4–9; material on Layton rpt in *Irving Layton: The Poet and His Critics*, ed Seymour Mayne (Toronto: McGraw-Hill Ryerson 1978), 32–3.

A survey of the Canadian poetry of the year. Reviews *The Victorian House and Other Poems*, by Philip Child, whose skill as a writer is best seen in the lyrics interspersed in the narrative of his title poem; *Counterpoint to Sleep* by Anne Wilkinson, who is sometimes too self-conscious and clever; Kay Smith's *Footnote to the Lord's Prayer and Other Poems*, which is distinctive meditative poetry, occasionally lapsing into religiosity; Charles Bruce's *The Mulgrave Road*, which is simple, unpretentious, and consistently good regional verse; *Horizontal World*, by Thomas Saunders, who is a Frost-like conversationalist at his best; Irving Layton's *The Black Huntsman*, poetry of social protest that reveals a real poet but that too often also reveals a 'noisy hot-gospeller who has no respect for poetry'; Michael Hornyansky's *The Queen of Sheba*, 'an admirable practice piece'; Theresa Thompson's *Silver Shadows*, Raymond Souster's *City Hall Street*, and Elizabeth Brewster's *East Coast* – all in the Ryerson chap-book series; a selection of the poems of Duncan Campbell Scott; and the tenth anniversary issue of *Contemporary Verse*. Mentions several other volumes in passing.

D55 'Comic Myth in Shakespeare.' *Transactions of the Royal Society of Canada* series 3, 46, section 2 (June 1952): 47–58. Incorporated into *AC*, Third Essay. Rpt in *Discussions of Shakespeare's Romantic Comedy*, ed Herbert Weil, Jr (Boston: Heath 1966), 132–42.

Distinguishes Jonsonian from Shakespearean comedy. Jonson's descends from Greek New Comedy, the form of which shows up in all popular comedy down to our own time. The action in this form of comedy consists in the obstacles thrown up before a young man who is seeking a young woman; overcoming these obstacles, usually parental, constitutes the comic resolution. Jonson's comedy emphasizes the blocking characters, those who seek to thwart the hero's triumph. The interest in Shakespeare's comedy, however, is on the resolution or final discovery. Rather than Jonsonian humours, Shakespeare presents us with a world of absurd law to be overcome, which finally occurs when we are shown a vision of what life should be like. When it reaches the form of dramatic romance it 'is far more primitive and popular' than Jonsonian, 'and is of a type found all over the world,' similar in its conventions to those of Lope de Vega, *commedia dell'arte*, Italian opera, Chinese comedies, and Japanese kabuki plays.

D56 'Phalanx of Particulars.' *Hudson Review* 4 (Winter 1952): 627–31. Rpt in *NFCL*, 197–203.

A review of *The Poetry of Ezra Pound*, by Hugh Kenner. Praises Kenner for writing the first full-length study of Pound, a poet and critic who has not yet received his proper due. Says that Kenner shows how Pound grasped 'the essential fact about poetry, that it is a structure of images and that its structural principle is the juxtaposition of images.' Sees the chief failures of the book in Kenner's not being very good at polemic, in his allusive style and clever asides, in his inability to speak directly and clearly, and, most seriously, in his mouthing of the anti-romantic clichés of the 1920s. Believes that Pound is finally not so much a shaper of the poetic vision as he is a witness to it because he lacks 'the faculty of mythopoeia.' His poetry demonstrates a dense rhetorical texture of particulars but it does not have 'an enveloping body of vision.'

D57 'Editor's Introduction.' *Across My Path*, by Pelham Edgar, ed Northrop Frye (Toronto: Ryerson 1952), vii–xi (see B2)
Reviews the state of the manuscript of Edgar's autobiography at the time of his death, the edited version of which includes, in addition to a memoir, six essays on Canadian literature, and essays on both Yeats and Hardy. Speaks of Edgar's career as a teacher and friend of Canadian poets, of his temperamental link with Shelley and his romantic sensibility and tastes, of the rhythm in his elegant prose style, and of his clear-sighted, unpretentious criticism.

D58 'Three Meanings of Symbolism.' *Yale French Studies* no 9 (1952): 11–19. Incorporated into *AC*, Second Essay.
Traces the conception of the symbol from naturalism, which stresses the sign-meaning of the word, through the central tradition of *symbolisme* to the mythopoeic tradition. The central tradition seeks to unify the image and the sign, but the theory of romantic poetry carries our conception of the symbol one step further – the symbol as archetype or myth. Such a conception implies a 'unity of imaginative experience which contains all literature.' The search for the unifying factors of such experience can be discovered in a study of the role of the imagination in the creative process, in tradition and convention, and in 'the conceptual unity of all words in the Word.' Beyond the archetypal symbol is a fourth kind, the symbol as monad, 'the unit of total poetic experience' we find in Dante and Shakespeare.

D59 'Trends in Modern Culture.' *The Heritage of Western Culture: Essays on the Origin and Development of Modern Culture*, ed Randolph C. Chalmers (Toronto: Ryerson 1952), 102–17. Part 2, 'Contemporary Deism,' rpt in *The Strand* [Victoria College, Univ of Toronto] 1973, 3–4.
Examines first the evolution of and the claims made by the three dominant political ideologies: Naziism, Communism, and democracy. Sees democracy, as it has matured, as having separated itself from *laissez-faire* economics and from utopian optimism. Its current phase of the open class society is set over against the oligarchic conspiracy of fascism and the radical-reform conspiracy of Communism. Its most immediate domestic threat is fascism. Turns next to an analysis of 'contemporary deism,' the secular state religion of America, in which 'God' is not an 'effective spiritual reality' but rather a hypothesis that unifies the moral and natural worlds. The cultural effect of deism is to emphasize in education the natural and social sciences. Liberalism, however, is the real force lying behind deism. But the liberal ideal must be expanded into an ideal of 'infinite regeneration' if

democracy is to be saved. Looks finally at the analogies that the great philosophies of the past have had to the communities out of which they sprang. In modern thought we repeatedly find images of 'a beleaguered custodian of conscious values trying to fend off something unconscious which is too strong to be defeated.' If liberty is to defeat tyranny and terrorism in the modern world, it will require a spiritual and constructive power that is a real presence.

D60 'Letters in Canada: 1952, Poetry.' *University of Toronto Quarterly* 22 (April 1953): 269–80. Partially rpt in *BG*, 10–22 and in *Masks of Poetry: Canadian Critics on Canadian Verse*, ed A.J.M. Smith (Toronto: McClelland and Stewart 1962), 97–103; material on Irving Layton rpt in *Irving Layton: The Poet and His Critics*, ed Seymour Mayne (Toronto: McGraw-Hill Ryerson 1978), 35. Devotes a large part of this annual survey to two of Canada's 'leading poets,' E.J. Pratt and Earle Birney. Reviews Pratt's narrative poem *Toward the Last Spike*, which is about the linking of the east and west by the railroad. Sees the real hero of the poem as 'society's will to take intelligible form' and the real quest as the search 'for physical and spiritual communication within that society.' Regards the theme of Birney's *Trial of a City and Other Verse* as unified and serious, and 'for virtuosity of language there has never been anything like it in Canadian poetry.' Looks also at Alfred Bailey's *Border River* (which 'puts him into the first rank of Canadian poets'); Jay Macpherson's *Nineteen Poems*; Myra Lazechko-Hass's *Viewpoint*; Ruth Cleaves Hazelton's *Mint and Willow*; Vina Bruce Chilton's *A Few More Dawns*; Tom Farley's *It Was a Plane*; Louis Dudek's *Twenty-four Poems* and *The Searching Image*; *Cerberus*, a collection by Louis Dudek, Irving Layton, and Raymond Souster; and Robert Service's *Rhymes of a Rebel*.

D61 'Characterization in Shakespearean Comedy.' *Shakespeare Quarterly* 4 (July 1953): 271–7. Incorporated into *AC*, Third Essay. Rpt as 'Die Charakterisierung in der Komödie Shakespeares' in *Wege der Shakespeare-Forschung*, trans Edith and Karl L. Klein (Darmstadt 1971), 87–99.
Distinguishes four types of characters in Shakespeare's comedies: (1) The *alazon*, or humorous blocking characters, who are impostors (in the sense that they are hypocrites or lack self-knowledge), braggarts, pedants, or cranks; (2) the *eiron*, or self-deprecating character, such as the tricky slave, scheming valet, and mischievous trickster; (3) the *bomolochus*, or buffoon, whose function is to increase the mood of festivity; and (4) the *agroikos*, one who functions in opposition to the festive buffoon, such as the miserly and snobbish malcontent. Argues that characterization in Shakespeare depends on function and that the fact that characters are stock types does not mean they are not lifelike.

D62 'Towards a Theory of Cultural History.' *University of Toronto Quarterly* 22 (July 1953): 325–41. Incorporated into *AC*, First Essay. Rpt as 'Bunkashi no riron no tame no oboegaki,' trans Hiroshi Ebine, in *Gendai hyoron shu* [*Modern Literary Criticism: A Collection*], ed Hajime Shinoda (Tokyo: Shueisha 1978), 392–415.

Classifies fictions according to the power of action possessed by the hero in relation both to other men and to his environment. This principle yields five kinds of stories: (1) myth, in which the hero's power of action is different in kind from that of other men and their environment; (2) romance, in which the hero's superiority is one of degree; (3) high mimesis, where the hero is superior in degree to other men but not to nature; (4) low mimesis, in which the hero is more or less equal to other men and not superior to his environment; and (5) irony, where the hero's power of action is inferior to that of ordinary men. Distinguishes comic and tragic forms for each of these fictional modes. Analyses also 'thematic' modes, stories in which the internal characters are subordinated to the writer and his audience. Sees the tragic, comic, and thematic modes as forming a broadly historical and cyclic pattern. Cites examples of literary works for each of the modes.

D63 'Art in a New Modulation.' *Hudson Review* 6 (Summer 1953): 313–17. Rpt in *NFCL*, 111–16.

A review of *Feeling and Form*, by Susanne K. Langer. Summarizes Langer's theory of art, the governing principles of which are semblance or illusion and symbol. The latter is the means by which art achieves its end of objectifying feeling. Thinks that the thesis is not developed as a central idea around which everything revolves, that there is too much discussion of other critics' ideas and not enough of particular works of art, that the section on literature is the least satisfactory, and that the idea of art as objectified feeling does not make art 'a permanent part of the world constructed by humanity out of reality.' Despite these reservations, the book succeeds admirably in raising and exploring new questions.

D64 'Ministry of Angels.' *Hudson Review* 6 (Autumn 1953): 442–9. Rpt in *NFCL*, 130–40. Partially rpt in *Contemporary Literary Criticism*, vol 24, ed Sharon R. Gunton (Detroit: Gale Research 1983), 443.

Review of *The Forlorn Demon*, by Allen Tate; *The True Voice of Feeling*, by Herbert Read; and *Dante's Drama of the Mind*, by Francis Fergusson. Sees the first two of these books as examples of deterministic criticism, the kind that assumes that the fundamental principles of criticism are to be found in other disciplines. Tate is a religious determinist, who, for all his astuteness and brilliance, believes that the 'profoundest view of the man of letters is to take him as a lay preacher.' Read is a psychological determinist whose main theme is Longinian *ecstasis* and whose main principle is sincerity. Fergusson comes closer than the other two in discovering his guiding principles in literature itself. His 'charming and eloquent' book on the *Purgatorio* is chiefly 'a teacher's book,' which concentrates on Dante's simplicity and on the theme of 'the liberation of his own liberal art of poetry.'

D65 'Long Sequacious Notes.' *Hudson Review* 5 (Winter 1953): 603–8. Rpt in *NFCL*, 170–7.

Review of *Inquiring Spirit: A New Presentation of Coleridge from His Published and Unpublished Prose Writings,* ed Kathleen Coburn, and *The Note-books of Matthew Arnold,* ed Howard Foster Lowry, Karl Young, and Waldo Hilary Dunn. Comments on the discontinuous, aphoristic habit of mind that reveals itself in Coleridge's writings and on his inability to discover an appropriate prose form. Still, we find in Coleridge 'the union of a great mind with a great idea.' Disagrees with Miss Coburn that the central co-ordinating principle in Coleridge's work is psychological. Says rather that 'the imagination is instrumental in Coleridge: it is the power that unifies, but not the thing to be unified ... The latter is the Logos.' Arnold's *Note-books* form 'a valuable guide' to what he read but beyond this they reveal very little about him.

D66 'Introduction.' *Selected Poetry and Prose of William Blake,* ed Northrop Frye (New York: Modern Library 1953), xiii–xxviii (see B3)
On Blake's life and work. Traces the chief influences on Blake, from Basire and Linnell to the Bible. Comments on his intellectual interests, especially his views of science and politics, on his view of the imagination, and on the mythological framework lying behind his poetry.

D67 Review of *Critics and Criticism,* by R.S. Crane et al. *Shakespeare Quarterly* 5 (January 1954): 78–80
Judges the essays in this book by the Chicago Aristotelians to be 'indispensable for the serious student of criticism.' Does not consider the neo-Aristotelian opposition between mimetic and didactic works of literature to be consistent with the function of literature according to such a Renaissance critic as Sidney, and thinks that the Aristotelians may have 'reacted too far against the rhetorical confusion of *praxis* and *lexis.*' Believes that one can look at Shakespeare as a mimetic poet without at the same time denying that part of Shakespeare's profundity is profound thought. Remarks that the essays in the book about Shakespeare's plays, for all their attention to dramatic parts as they relate to poetic wholes, are still not too far from those of the best rhetorical critics. What the Chicago critics show, finally, is 'that one's critical processes should be as flexible and as little confined to one methodology as possible.'

D68 'Letters in Canada: 1953, Poetry.' *University of Toronto Quarterly* 23 (April 1954): 253–63. Partially rpt in *BG,* 23–33.
The annual survey of Canadian poetry, which includes assessments of Patrick Anderson's *The Colour as Naked,* a collection in the pastoral idiom that shows a poet 'approaching maturity'; and Douglas LePan's *The Net and the Sword,* a series of elegiac war poems. These are the two most serious books of Canadian poetry in 1953. Reviews also Irving Layton's *Love the Conqueror Worm;* J.S. Wallace's *All My Brothers;* two anthologies, *Canadian Poems: 1850–1952* and *Twentieth-Century Canadian Poetry;* Lawrence Dakin's *The House of Orseoli;* two Ryerson chap-books, Sherwood Fox's paraphrase of Cicero's *De Amicitia* and R.A. Rashley's *Portrait and Other Poems;* Ronald Hambleton's *Object and Event;* Arthur Bourinot's *This Green Earth;* Gilean Douglas's *Now the Green World;* and Edna Jacques's *The Golden Road.*

D69 'Turning New Leaves.' *Canadian Forum* 34 (July 1954): 89, 91. Rpt in *BG*, 157–62.
Review of *Folk Songs of Canada*, ed Edith F. Fowke and Richard Johnston. Praises this collection of Canadian folk-songs as competently produced and edited and agrees with the dust-jacket blurb that it is 'a major contribution to Canadian culture.' Gives a number of examples of the kinds of songs in the collection. Observes that there is nothing particularly Canadian in the folk-song because it transcends cultural and linguistic barriers.

D70 'Myth as Information.' *Hudson Review* 7 (Summer 1954): 228–35. Incorporated into *AC*, Fourth Essay. Rpt in *NFCL*, 67–75.
Review of *The Philosophy of Symbolic Forms*, vol 1, by Ernst Cassirer. Considers the book to be historically important because it brings into systematic philosophy the study of myth, around which has been constructed 'the bulk of what is distinctive in twentieth-century thought.' Using Cassirer's idea of symbolic form, seeks to discover what the relationships are among myth, language, and literature. Argues that the assimilation of language to rational thought develops out of an ideogrammatic inner structure of ideas. There are similar inner structures, the chief of which is myth, which are constructive principles in literature and may turn out to be constructive principles in psychology, anthropology, theology, history, and political theory as well.

D71 'Content with the Form.' *University of Toronto Quarterly* 24 (October 1954): 92–7. Rpt in *Contemporary Literary Criticism*, vol 27, ed Jean Stein (Detroit: Gale Research 1984), 71–2.
Review of *The Languages of Criticism and the Structure of Poetry*, by R.S. Crane. Summarizes Crane's analysis of two principal methods in criticism: (1) the Aristotelian approach, which seeks to discover the poetic whole that is synthesized from the poet's intuition of form; and (2) the a priori approach, which proceeds to deduce certain consequences of form from some predetermined rhetorical or mythological assumption about poetry. Believes that Crane's own method promises more than it delivers; that as a way of teaching, it asks the same questions that have always been asked about literature; that the claim that the New Critics use simply an a priori method is in large measure illusory; and that the distinction between mimetic and didactic works of literature is problematic. What Crane is ultimately arguing for is intelligent and candid criticism supported by a tradition and a theory.

D72 'Forming Fours.' *Hudson Review* 6 (Winter 1954): 611–19. Rpt in *NFCL*, 117–29.
Review of *Two Essays on Analytical Psychology* and *Psychology and Alchemy*, by C.G. Jung. Outlines Jung's conception of the personality, points out that two chief differences between Jung and Freud are found in the former's concepts of individuation and the collective unconscious, and looks at the similarities between Jung's thought and the religious visionary tradition. Considers the mythopoeic counterpart to Jung's analytic psychology, which is the heroic quest in myth, folklore, and literature, to be important

for literary criticism. Just as Frazer's *The Golden Bough* embodies an archetypal ritual from which the literary critic may derive the structural principles of naïve drama, so Jung's work, especially *Symbols of Transformation*, embodies an archetypal dream with close analogies to the principles of naïve romance. Similarly in Jung's study of alchemy we also discover parallels to the mythopoeic structures and symbols of literature. Jung, therefore, provides 'a grammar of literary symbolism which for all serious students of literature is as important as it is endlessly fascinating.'

D73 'The Language of Poetry.' *Explorations: Studies in Culture and Communication*, no 4 (February 1955), 80–90. Incorporated into *AC*, Second Essay. Rpt in *Explorations in Communication*, ed Edmund Carpenter and Marshall McLuhan (Boston: Beacon Press 1960), 43–53.
Emphasizes the importance of looking at literature from the perspective of its conventions, especially its conventional or recurring images (archetypes) and its myths, produced by the union of ritual and dream. Sets up a series of related categories for archetypal criticism: narrative, which is related to rhythm, movement, recurrence, event, and ritual; and content, which is associated with precept, desire, pattern, and dream. Believes that the basis of archetypal criticism is found in primitive and popular literature and that the critic can therefore learn much from such works as Frazer's *The Golden Bough*, which is really 'an essay on the ritual content of naive drama.' Wants to emphasize, however, the different goals of anthropologists and psychologists, on the one hand, and literary critics, on the other. Illustrates how archetypal criticism can reveal the structural principles of Molière's *La Malade Imaginaire*.

D74 'Letters in Canada: 1954, Poetry.' *University of Toronto Quarterly* 24 (April 1955): 247–56. Partially rpt in *BG*, 33–44 and in *Masks of Poetry: Canadian Critics on Canadian Verse*, ed A.J.M. Smith (Toronto: McClelland and Stewart 1962), 103–5; material on Carman rpt in *Twentieth-Century Literary Criticism*, vol 7, ed Sharon K. Hall (Detroit: Gale Research 1982), 147; material on Layton rpt in *Irving Layton: The Poet and His Critics*, ed Seymour Mayne (Toronto: McGraw-Hill Ryerson 1978), 38–9.
The annual survey begins by reviewing the reprinting of work by two traditional Canadian poets: Bliss Carman, whose best poetry moves away from the Emersonian oversoul and toward the mythological, and George Herbert Clarke, an academic poet of 'melancholy moods and sonorous diction.' Reviews also the learned though spontaneous poems in A.J.M. Smith's *A Sort of Ecstasy* and the sincere and urbane verse of F.R. Scott's *Events and Signals*. Looks at several volumes by a still later generation of poets: P.K. Page's *The Metal and the Flower*; Irving Layton's *The Long Pea-Shooter* and *In the Midst of My Fever*; *Trio*, a selection of verse by Gael Turnbull, Phyllis Webb, and Eli Mandel. Glances finally at chap-books by Elizabeth Brewster, A.S. Bourinot, Anthony Frisch, and Fred Cogswell.

D75 'English Canadian Literature, 1929–1954.' *Books Abroad* 29 (Summer 1955): 270–4. Rpt in *Canadian Library Association Bulletin* 13 (1956): 107–12.
Traces the history of a distinctive Canadian literature, beginning with the

narrative poetry of E.J. Pratt in the late 1920s; the New Provinces poets
(Leo Kennedy, A.J.M. Smith, A.M. Klein, F.R. Scott, and Robert Finch) a
bit later; and in the same generation the poetry of Dorothy Livesay and
Earle Birney. Looks briefly at the work of Patrick Anderson, Douglas
LePan, Louis Dudek, and Margaret Avison during the 1940s and 1950s. In
drama, surveys the contributions of Gwen Pharis, Robertson Davies,
John Coulter, and a group of CBC Radio dramatists. In fiction, looks briefly
at the work of Desmond Pacey, Mazo de la Roche, Thomas Raddall,
Frederick Philip Grove, and Morley Callaghan (perhaps the best short-story
writer in Canadian fiction); and catalogues the work of a dozen more
writers of fiction. Sees Canadian writing in general as somewhat miscellaneous with no defining characteristics except as a type of English literature.

D76 'The Transferability of Literary Concepts.' *The Association of the Princeton
Graduate Alumni* (Report on the Fifth Conference held at the Graduate
College of Princeton University on 30–31 December 1955), 54–60
Reflects on the analogy between literature and mathematics (both proceed
by postulate and hypothesis and neither is descriptive) in order to develop
the idea 'that all understanding is in a sense metaphorical understanding,
because it is an identification made by two minds of the same concept.' For
the discussion among the participants of the conference, including F, see
60–3.

D77 'Oswald Spengler.' *Architects of Modern Thought* [1st series] (Toronto:
Canadian Broadcasting Corp 1955), 83–90
Examines Spengler's view of the organic rise, growth, decline, and fall of
cultures. Despite the attacks on *The Decline of the West*, it does project
'a vision of haunting imaginative power. Its truth is the truth of poetry or
prophecy, not of science.' Spengler's power is an imaginative power
that discerns patterns in events and that can therefore 'expand and exhilarate the mind.' The chief metaphor in *The Decline of the West* is the metaphor that cultures behave just like organisms. Compares Spengler's vision
of culture with Toynbee's, which is actually a 'tribute to the originality
and power of Spengler.' Observes that modern culture has taken Spengler's
central thesis for granted, just as it has taken for granted the central
themes of Darwin, Marx, Freud, and Einstein. Like these shapers of modern thought, he had the ability to recognize 'what's straight in front of
his nose.'

D78 'Letters in Canada: 1955, Poetry.' *University of Toronto Quarterly* 28 (April
1956): 290–304. Partially rpt in *BG*, 44–57 and in *Masks of Poetry: Canadian
Critics on Canadian Verse*, ed A.J.M. Smith (Toronto: McClelland and
Stewart 1962), 105–6; material on Roberts partially rpt in *Twentieth-Century
Literary Criticism*, vol 8, ed Sharon K. Hall (Detroit: Gale Research 1982),
319; material on Layton rpt in *Irving Layton: The Poet and His Critics*, ed
Seymour Mayne (Toronto: McGraw-Hill Ryerson 1978), 41–2.
Distinguishes two poles in poetry: the representational, which is sophisti-
cated and civilized, and the formal, which is primitive and oracular.
Two volumes in the annual survey illustrate these two tendencies respec-

tively: *The Selected Poems of Sir Charles G.D. Roberts* and *Sepass Poems*, a collection of Okanagan Indian mythical verse. Judges four volumes in 1955 to be particularly important: Wilfred Watson's *Friday's Child* and Anne Wilkinson's *The Hangman Ties the Holly*, both of which are mythical and metaphorical poetry; Miriam Waddington's *The Second Silence* and Irving Layton's *The Cold Green Element*, both of which are 'polarized between personal association and a direct reaction to experience.' Reviews also Louis Dudek's *Europe*, Raymond Souster's *For What Time Slays*, Daryl Hine's *Five Poems*, Jay Macpherson's *O Earth Return*, and Dorothy Livesay's *New Poems*. Remarks briefly about books or chap-books by G.V. Downes, Thecla Bradshaw, Alfred Purdy, Myrtle Reynolds Adams, Theresa E. and Don W. Thompson, Goodridge MacDonald, Sutherland Groom, Robert Rogers, I.B. Ezra, Arthur Bourinot, and Eugenie Perry.

D79 'An Indispensable Book.' *Virginia Quarterly Review* 32 (Spring 1956): 310–15
Review of *A History of Modern Criticism*, vols 1 and 2, by René Wellek, volumes that contain 'everything essential that could reasonably be asked for in a history of this type.' Observes that Wellek's subject is not so much the history of criticism as it is the history of critical thought, which means that he has to dismiss the empirical and appreciative criticism of Lamb as unimportant. Sees one obvious value of the book in its treatment of minor figures, but believes the biographical approach, which treats one critic's work after another, pays too little attention to the impersonal, objective factors in the history of critical thought, such as the 'archetypal analogies' or the organizing categories of thought that criticism takes over from other disciplines. The message that emerges finally from Wellek's study is that criticism has suffered mainly from basing its claims on value-judgments, which are rationalizations for critics' preferences. In genuine criticism, value-judgments are founded on the study of literature, not vice versa.

D80 'The Typology of *Paradise Regained.*' *Modern Philology* 53 (May 1956): 227–38.
Rev version rpt in *RE*, 118–42; in *Milton: Modern Essays in Criticism*, ed Arthur E. Barker (New York: Oxford Univ Press 1965), 429–46; and in *Milton's Epic Poetry*, ed C.A. Patrides (Baltimore: Penguin 1967), 301–21.
On the biblical typology underlying *Paradise Regained*, which represents the second of three main episodes in the conflict between Christ and Satan. Concentrates on an analysis of the temptation scenes in Milton's 'brief epic': (1) the banquet and the offer of money, the source of which is Spenser rather than the Bible; (2) the temptation of Parthia, or false power; (3) the temptation of Rome, or false justice; and (4) the temptation of Athens, or false wisdom. The last three are temptations to false heroic action. Seeks to locate the contexts in which to understand the temptation, whether they be the Bible, Milton's other poetry and prose, Spenser, or Greek philosophy.

D81 'La poesía anglo-canadiense,' trans Jaime Rest. *Sur*, no 240 (May-June 1956): 30–9
Discusses the influence that the environment has had on a number of

Canadian poets: Heavysege, Roberts, Carman, Mair, D.C. Scott, Crawford, Lampman, Pratt, Birney, the New Provinces poets of Montreal (Smith, F.R. Scott, Klein, and Kennedy), Page, LePan, Anderson, Dudek, and Layton.

D82 'Towards Defining an Age of Sensibility.' ELH 23 (June 1956): 144–52. Rpt in FI, 130–7; in Eighteenth-Century English Literature: Modern Essays in Criticism, ed James L. Clifford (New York: Oxford Univ Press 1959), 311–18; and in The Practice of Criticism, ed Sheldon P. Zinter et al (Chicago: Scott, Foresman 1966), 25–31.
Proposes to define the period of English literature covering roughly the last half of the eighteenth century. Bases his definition on the opposition beween two views of literature: 'the Aristotelian and the Longinian, the aesthetic and the psychological, the view of literature as product and the view of literature as process.' Locates those writers who preceded the age of sensibility on the Aristotelian side of this dichotomy and those of the post-Augustan age itself on the Longinian side. Sees in the poetry of process such features as unconscious control, irregular metre, diffusion of sense, incantation, discontinuous lyrics, and fragmentary utterance. Says that the primitive process of writing is projected toward either nature or history. If projected toward nature, the poetry of sensibility will tend toward one or the other of two additional poles, either the creative or the decaying natural process. If projected toward history, the poetry tends toward the primitive lyric, on the one hand, or toward the less primitive epic and dramatic forms on the other. Looks also at the typical conception of the poet during the age of sensibility, as well as its central technical feature, metaphor.

D83 'Graves, Gods and Scholars.' Hudson Review 9 (Summer 1956): 298–303. Rpt in NFCL, 230–6.
Review of Collected Poems, by Robert Graves. Characterizes Graves as an epigrammatic writer with thematic or mythical interests. His poetry moves from exercises in form to pure incantation. Graves reveals a poetic personality that is 'one of sturdy independence, pragmatic common sense, and a consistently quizzical attitude to systematized forms of experience, especially the religious.' Speaks of Graves's influence on contemporary British poetry and of the presence in his poems of the White Goddess – the story of Attis and Cybele. Finds Graves the mythographer to be in the tradition of Rabelais and Apuleius, erudite satirists. Graves does not present a systematic mythology but leads us rather 'towards the mythical use of poetic language.' His attitude toward myth seems akin to that of Samuel Butler, ambivalent and ironic.

D84 'Introduction.' I Brought the Ages Home, by Charles Trick Currelly, ed Northrop Frye (Toronto: Ryerson 1956), vii–x (see B4)
On Currelly's role in establishing the Royal Ontario Museum of archaeology, his lifelong efforts to broaden cultural perspectives, his commitment to

the 'impartial survey of an entire field,' his resistance to the idea of great periods in ancient history, and his deep interest in things Canadian.

D85 'Quest and Cycle in *Finnegans Wake.' James Joyce Review* 1 (February 1957): 39–47. Rpt in *FI*, 256–64.

Examines the major parallels between Blake's myth of Albion and Joyce's myth of Finnegan: they have similar views about the priority of the imagination, about the 'giant forms' of the objective and subjective worlds, about the cyclical movement of nature and history, and about the struggle between good and evil. The chief differences between the two myths are that Joyce's epic does not include the forms of what is represented by the Four Zoas in Blake, and that in Joyce the cycle contains the quest, rather than vice versa as in Blake.

D86 'Letters in Canada: 1956, Poetry.' *University of Toronto Quarterly* 26 (April 1957): 296–311. Partially rpt in *BG*, 58–70. Material on Layton rpt in *Irving Layton: The Poet and His Critics*, ed Seymour Mayne (Toronto: McGraw-Hill Ryerson 1978), 56–7.

Reviews first, in this annual survey, three selections: *First Flowering*, an anthology of high school writing; *New Voices*, a collection of Canadian university writing; and *Poets 56*, an anthology of the work of ten young writers, including Jay Macpherson, 'the only completely articulate poet of the group.' Glances at five of the Ryerson chap-books (by Ruby Nichols, Freda Newton Bunner, Marion Kathleen Henry, Leonore Pratt, and Fred Cogswell), Joe Wallace's *Hi, Sister, Hi, Brother!*, Henry Moscovitch's *The Serpent Ink*, Gael Turnbull's *Bjarni*, Dick Diespecker's *Three Windows West*, and John Sutherland's *The Poetry of E.J. Pratt*, an important piece of sustained criticism. Examines *The Selected Poems*, by Raymond Souster, 'a genuine poet whose qualities are subtlety and humour'; Louis Dudek's *The Transparent Sea*; Phyllis Webb's *Even Your Right Eye*; R.A.D. Ford's *A Window on the North*; Leonard Cohen's *Let Us Compare Mythologies*; and three volumes by Irving Layton, 'the most considerable Canadian poet of his generation.'

D87 'Poetry of the Tout Ensemble.' *Hudson Review* 10 (Spring 1957): 122–9. Rpt in *NFCL*, 237–42.

Review of *Hypnos Waking*, by René Char and *René Char's Poetry*, by Maurice Blanchot et al. Admires Char both for being 'engaged' in his life, especially in his commitment to the French Resistance, and for writing an exacting and detached poetry. Notes Char's affinities with the surrealists, Rilke, and Valéry. Comments on the principle of opposites that lie behind his imagery. In Char we do not encounter the 'dissociation of sensibility' that manifests itself in twentieth-century poetry as rhetoric at one extreme and as the ironic treatment of feeling at the other. Char's critics do not liken him to Hugo, but he is probably closer to Hugo than to any other of his French predecessors.

D88 'Blake after Two Centuries.' *University of Toronto Quarterly* 27 (October

1957): 10–27. Rpt in *FI*, 138–50 and in *English Romantic Poets: Modern Essays in Criticism*, ed Meyer H. Abrams (New York: Oxford Univ Press 1960), 55–67.

Observes that Blake seems 'to be headed for what at one time seemed his least likely fate: a genuine, permanent, and international popularity.' Defines popularity not simply as what the public wants but also as that which 'affords the key to imaginative experience for the untrained.' This means that the popular has less to do with content and conceptual structure than it has with myth and metaphor, the formal principles of fiction and poetry, respectively. The former are the basis of Blake's prophecies; the latter, of his lyrics. Looks at Blake's conception of the ordinary and visionary worlds; of apocalypse, which was for him the grammar of both poetry and painting; and of his theory of painting as 'outline,' which belongs to the tradition of hieroglyphic art. Considers finally the biblical, Protestant, radical, and romantic qualities of Blake's art, qualities that characterize at least one popular tradition in English literature.

D89 'The Realistic Oriole: A Study of Wallace Stevens.' *Hudson Review* 10 (Autumn 1957): 353–70. Rpt in *FI*, 238–55; in *Wallace Stevens: A Collection of Critical Essays*, ed Marie Borroff (Englewood Cliffs, NJ: Prentice-Hall 1963), 161–76; and in *Modern Poetry: Essays in Criticism*, ed John Hollander (New York: Oxford Univ Press 1968), 267–84. Partially rpt in *Twentieth-Century Literary Criticism*, vol 3, ed Sharon K. Hall (Detroit: Gale Research 1980), 452–3.

Observes that in Stevens's work metaphysics, poetic vision, and a theory of knowledge are related. Discusses Stevens's view of the imagination (the faculty that transforms experience) and analyses the imagery of the summer, autumn, and winter visions in his poetry. Examines Stevens's view of metaphor, which appears to be based on comparison. Metaphor, however, depends upon identity rather than likeness, and Stevens's poetry is firmly grounded in 'a world of total metaphor, where the poet's vision may be identified with anything it visualizes.' Observes finally that this kind of poetry is apocalyptic, containing a fully developed vision that goes beyond rhetorical skill and novelty and so makes Stevens 'one of our small handful of essential poets.'

D90 'Blake's Introduction to Experience.' *Huntington Library Quarterly* 21 (November 1957): 57–67. Rpt in *Blake: A Collection of Critical Essays*, ed Northrop Frye (Englewood Cliffs, NJ: Prentice-Hall 1966), 23–31 (see B11).

Examines Blake's 'Introduction' to *Songs of Experience* in order to illustrate that it, along with 'Earth's Answer,' contains the main principles of Blake's thought. The 'Introduction' embodies Blake's view of the poet's function, his understanding of the divine-man Jesus, his imaginative vision as projected both temporally and spatially, and his conception of the fallen world. Argues that this lyric, 'despite its deeply serious tone, takes on the whole the redemptive or providential view,' and that in the two poems together we have the 'generating forces' of all of Blake's symbolism.

D91 'Neo-Classical Agony.' *Hudson Review* 10 (Winter 1957–8): 592–8. Rpt in
     NFCL, 178–87 and in *Twentieth-Century Literary Criticism*, vol 9, ed Dennis
     Poupard (Detroit: Gale Research 1983), 238–40.
     Review of *Wyndham Lewis: A Portrait of the Artist as the Enemy*, by Geoffrey
     Wagner. Observes that although Wagner's book is an 'excellent study'
     it lacks a centre of gravity. Examines Lewis's prose style, which is best
     suited for satire and caricature and, because it lacks discipline, for self-
     caricature; his anti-romantic theory of the creative elite; and his fondness
     for the diatribe. Judges Lewis finally to be a clever rather than a wise
     writer, yet one who for all his solipsism and perversity has to be admired
     because of the courage of the personal descent into hell portrayed in
     such books as *The Apes of God* and *The Human Age*.

D92 'Introduction: Lexis and Melos.' *Sound and Poetry: English Institute Essays,*
     1956, ed Northrop Frye (New York: Columbia Univ Press 1957), ix–xxvii (see
     B5). Rpt in *Literatur und Musik: Ein Handbuch zur Theorie und Praxis eines*
     komparatistischen Grenzgebietes (Berlin: Eric Schmidt Verlag 1984), 169–79 and
     as 'Ongakuteki shi to rizumu,' trans Akiko Masuda and Minoru Yoshida, in
     Bulletin of Tokyo Gakuen Women's Junior College 9 (1971): 143–5.
     Seeks to define the meaning of the term 'musical' in literary criticism.
     Argues that music is a matter not of the beauty of sound but of its organi-
     zation, especially its continuity and stress accent. This means that Brown-
     ing is a musical poet and Tennyson is not. Isolates stress as the primary
     principle of poetic rhythm, thus throwing the emphasis on intensity and
     duration. Calls this principle 'accentual scansion,' meaning that the stresses
     in a line of poetry mark the measures within which a variable number of
     notes is permitted. Examines also another kind of *melos*, that 'produced by
     the rising and falling inflections and the pattern of emphasis in the spoken
     word.' Observes finally that there are at least five different kinds of
     rhythm one can observe in poetry: metrical or prosodic, accentual, seman-
     tic, mimetic, and oracular or meditative. Parts of this article appear in a
     different form in *AC*, Fourth Essay.

D93 'Notes for a Commentary on *Milton*.' *The Divine Vision: Studies in the Poetry*
     and Art of William Blake, ed Vivian de Sola Pinto (London: Gollancz 1957),
     99–137
     Analyses in detail the structure of symbolism in Blake's *Milton*, which is
     based upon his conception of four levels of vision: Eden, which represents
     the paradisal view of reality; Beulah, or lower paradise; Generation, or
     the world of experience; and Ulro, or hell. Examines Blake's conception of
     metaphor, which is based upon the principle of identity. Gives an elabo-
     rate outline of the metaphors Blake uses on seven different levels of reality
     (divine, spiritual, human, animal, vegetable, mineral, and chaotic) for
     each of the four levels of vision. Concludes with a summary of the thematic
     and narrative patterns of the poem.

D94 'Preface to an Uncollected Anthology.' *Studia Varia: Royal Society of Canada,*
     Literary and Scientific Papers, ed E.G.D. Murray (Toronto: Univ of Toronto

Press 1957), 21–36. Rpt in *BG*, 163–79 and in *Contexts of Canadian Criticism*, ed Eli Mandel (Toronto: Univ of Toronto Press; Chicago: Univ of Chicago Press 1971), 181–97. Abridged version rpt in *Canadian Anthology*, ed Carl F. Klinck and Reginald E. Watters (Toronto: Gage 1966), 515–23; 3rd ed, 1974, 595–603.

Examines the imaginative impact of the Canadian environment on its poets and the two central themes that have resulted: 'one a primarily comic theme of satire and exuberance, the other a primarily tragic theme of loneliness and terror.' Cites examples of the satiric tendency, usually critical of industrial expansion and middle-class mores, in the work of Alexander McLachlan, Isabella Crawford, Frank Scott, Raymond Souster, Louis Dudek, Miriam Waddington, Irving Layton, Frank Scott, James Reaney, and others. Sees the central comic theme of the Canadian harnessing of the environment best expressed in the work of E.J. Pratt. The central tragic theme, which is the indifference of nature to human values, is found in the poetry of Heavysege, Roberts, Campbell, Macdonald, Carman, Birney, and, again, Pratt. The qualities that characterize the Canadian poet's response to his environment are actually mythopoeic qualities.

D95 'William Blake.' *The English Romantic Poets and Essayists: A Review of Research and Criticism*, ed Carolyn Washburn Houtchens and Lawrence Huston Houtchens (New York: Modern Language Association 1957), 1–31. Chapt rev and brought up to date by Martin K. Nurmi in a new ed (New York: New York Univ Press, for the Modern Language Association; London: London Univ Press 1966), 1–35.

A bibliographic essay on five areas of Blake scholarship and criticism: bibliographies, editions, biographies, criticism, and Blake as a graphic artist. Gives the fullest treatment to a survey of Blake criticism, beginning with that of Swinburne and Yeats and continuing through a transitional period until the 1920s, when Blake studies come to full maturity in the work of S. Foster Damon and Sir Geoffrey Keynes. Separates the criticism since 1933 into two areas, one having to do with Blake's thought as a system of ideas, mainly religious and philosophical, and the other with the social and historical contexts of Blake's work. Stresses in the last half of the essay not simply what has been accomplished in Blake criticism but also what remains to be done.

D96 'The Study of English in Canada.' *Dalhousie Review* 38 (Spring 1958): 1–7
Cautions against trying to popularize the humanities unduly, thus neglecting their impersonal authority. Speaks of the importance of continuity and repetition in learning. 'The process of education is a patient cultivation of habit: its principle is continuity and its agent memory.' Argues that the book should not be replaced as the foundation of the university by the discontinuous forms of popular media. Sees the main function of English teachers as that of confronting their students with the heritage of the past and emphasizing the formal and structural principles of this heritage.

Presented originally as a lecture to a group of Canadian teachers of English
in Ottawa, 19 June 1957.

D97 'Letters in Canada: 1957, Poetry.' *University of Toronto Quarterly* 27 (July
1958): 434–50. Partially rpt in *BG*, 70–87.
Devotes the first five pages of this review to Jay Macpherson's *The Boatman*,
the one 'good book' of Canadian poetry published in 1957 and 'the most
carefully planned and unified book of poems' that has appeared since
F began his surveys in 1951. Reviews also the books of two promising
poets, Daryl Hine's *The Carnal and the Crane* and D.G. Jones's *Frost on
the Sun*; Alfred W. Purdy's *Emu, Remembered*; R.G. Everson's *Three Dozen
Poems*; eight Ryerson chap-books (by Theresa and Don W. Thompson,
Mary Elizabeth Bayer, Joan Finnigan, Hermia Harris Fraser, Fred Cogswell,
Dorothy Roberts, Elizabeth Brewster, and Goodridge MacDonald); Harry
Amoss's *Churchill and Other Poems*; Gordon LeClaire's *Carpenter's Apprentice
and Other Poems*; two magazines of verse – *Yes* and *Delta*; and several
retrospective collections, including F.R. Scott's *The Eye of the Needle*, Dorothy
Livesay's *Selected Poems 1926–1956*, and *The Selected Poems of Marjorie
Pickthall*.

D98 'Nature and Homer.' *Texas Quarterly* 1 (Summer-Autumn 1958): 192–204.
Rpt in *FI* 39–51 and in *Modern Literary Criticism, 1900–1970*, ed Lawrence
I. Lipking and A. Walton Litz (New York: Atheneum 1972), 224–31.
Examines the formal cause of literature, which is not some conception of
external nature being reflected or imitated. The relation of art to nature is
rather 'an internal relation of form to content.' Nature, life, experience,
and reality are the basis of art's content and therefore its material cause,
but its formal cause is strictly literary – the forms and conventions out
of which it is shaped. The poet's personality, experience, or sincerity are
important only insofar as they conform to a literary convention. Poets
therefore do not become original by expressing their personal experience
but by returning to origins, to the primitive and popular core of literature.
Such a conception of the formal cause of literature will, F believes, help
to remove value-judgments from criticism and to expand the idea of
literature beyond simply those works written for an elite audience.

D99 'Editor's Introduction.' *The Collected Poems of E.J. Pratt*, 2nd ed (Toronto:
Macmillan 1958), xii–xxviii (see B6)
Gives a brief account of Pratt's life and then turns to the qualities that
define his poetry: his refusal to intrude his personality into his work; his
ability to tell a good story; his flexible, unpretentious style; his patient
research; and his concrete diction. Observes that in Pratt's poetry there is a
unity of the poet, society, and nature, and examines his concept of heroism as it relates to the identity between man and nature. Notes that
the Christian archetypes in Pratt's religious views organize all of his poetry
and that 'Pratt's career has been an odd mixture of the popular and the
unfashionable.' His interest in narrative rather than lyric, in blank verse

rather than free verse, and in poetic material others had rejected place
him outside the poetic fashions of his time. Still he became a genuinely
popular poet, 'a kind of unofficial laureate.'

D100 'Poetry.' *The Arts in Canada: A Stocktaking at Mid-Century*, ed Malcolm Ross
(Toronto: Macmillan 1958), 84–90
A survey of Canadian poetry from 1943 to 1958. Observes that E.J. Pratt,
with his interest in the narrative rather than the lyrical tradition, is the
dominant influence on contemporary Canadian poetry. Divides contemporary poetry into roughly two kinds: the romantic and the academic. The
best Canadian poetry of the time is academic, though such poetry is more
and more in the tradition of the romantic lyric and it is overwhelmingly
mythopoeic. Among the 'New Provinces' group, Earle Birney is an example
of the academic poet, and F.R. Scott, the neo-romantic. The romantic
tradition has been carried on by Patrick Anderson, P.K. Page, Raymond
Souster, and Louis Dudek; and the academic tradition, by Irving Layton,
Douglas LePan, Wilfred Watson, Anne Wilkinson, James Reaney, Jay
Macpherson, and Daryl Hine.

D101 'Interior Monologue of M. Teste.' *Hudson Review* 12 (Spring 1959): 124–9.
Rpt in *NFCL*, 188–96.
A review of Paul Valéry's *The Art of Poetry*. Places Valéry in the Longinian
school of criticism because of his interest in the poetic process, the reader's
mind, and inspiration as meaning. Discusses Valéry's distinction between
inward and outward meaning and comments on the fact his theory is based
on Poe. Observes that for Valéry poetry really means *symbolisme* and that
his limited sense of structural and literary tradition means that 'we cannot
afford to take him too seriously as a critic.' *The Art of Poetry* tells us a
great deal about Valéry as a man but very little about poetry.

D102 'Letters in Canada: 1958, Poetry.' *University of Toronto Quarterly* 28 (July
1959): 345–65. Partially rpt in *BG*; material on Layton rpt in *Irving Layton:
The Poet and His Critics*, ed Seymour Mayne (Toronto: McGraw-Hill Ryerson
1978), 62–4.
Begins the annual survey with high praise for James Reaney's *A Suit of
Nettles*. Reviews also John Glassco's *The Deficit Made Flesh*, Ronald Everson's
A Lattice for Momos, Irving Layton's *A Laughter in the Mind*, Raymond
Souster's *Crepe-Hanger's Carnival*, Louis Dudek's *En Mexico* and *Laughing
Stalks*, Miriam Waddington's *The Season's Lovers*, Marya Fiamengo's *The
Quality of Halves*, Peter Miller's *Meditation at Noon*, and George Ellenbogen's
Winds of Unreason. Devotes the second half of the review to surveying
the year's chap-books, including those by Ella Julia Reynolds, Myrtle Rey-
nolds Adams, Fred Swayze, Thomas Saunders, John Heath, Violet Ander-
son, Heather Spears, Alden A. Nowlan, John Robert Colombo, Kenneth
McRobbie, and Martin Gray.

D103 'World Enough without Time.' *Hudson Review* 12 (Autumn 1959): 423–31.
Rpt in *NFCL*, 95–106.
A review of *Man and Time: Papers from the Eranos Yearbooks* and of five

books by Mircea Eliade: *Cosmos and History: The Myth of the Eternal Return, Birth and Rebirth, Patterns of Comparative Religion, The Sacred and the Profane,* and *Yoga: Immortality and Freedom.* Considers Eliade's books as 'essays toward a grammar of the symbolism of religion,' a remarkable introduction to which is *Patterns of Comparative Religion.* Examines Eliade's views on animism, the theme of death and rebirth, mythical time, the symbolism of the *rite de passage* and of yoga. Speaks of the importance that Eliade's studies have for literary criticism (the patterns of cyclical and initiatory symbolism characterize literature from its very beginning) but criticizes his general insensitivity to culture, his nostalgia for a superstitious religion, and his inability to see that poetry has recovered the sense of the sacred that science has destroyed.

D104 'George Gordon, Lord Byron.' *Major British Writers,* vol 2, enlarged ed, gen ed G.B. Harrison (New York: Harcourt, Brace & World 1959), 149–234. Introduction to Byron's poetry rpt in *FI,* 168–89.
A critical essay on Byron (pp 149–61), which includes a biographical sketch, an assessment of his work as a whole, a more detailed analysis of several major works, and an account of his influence. Sees Byron as 'neither a great poet nor a great man who wrote poetry, but something in between: a tremendous cultural force that was life and literature at once.' Relates Byron's literary heroes to their demonic and gothic prototypes. Traces the course of Byron's literary experiments until he settled upon the form best suited for his talents – the narrative satire. F edited and annotated the selection of Byron's poems included in this anthology (pp 161–234).

D105 'Humanities in a New World.' *3 Lectures: University of Toronto Installation Lectures, 1958* (Toronto: Univ of Toronto Press [1959]), 9–23. Rpt in *Four Essays* (Toronto: Univ of Toronto Press 1960), 15–29; in *Form and Idea,* 2nd ed, ed Morton Bloomfield and Edwin W. Robbins (New York: Macmillan 1961), 162–81; and in *DG* 102–17.
Defends the study of the humanities as central to education. Argues that thinking itself cannot take place without the skill that comes only from the disciplined and habitual use of language. Teaching the proper use of language, then, has a clear social function of moving students beyond jargon toward genuine thought. Similarly, modern men and women participate in society only to the extent that their imaginations have been educated through studying the classics. The human imagination presents us with a vision of what life should be like – 'a vision of the world in its human form.' A liberal education should, through the study of the humanities, provide the occasion for one to see his or her relation to this vision of life. Originally presented as a lecture on the occasion of the installation of Claude Bissell as president of the University of Toronto, 22 November 1958.

D106 'Introduction.' Shakespeare's *Tempest,* gen ed Alfred Harbage (Baltimore: Penguin 1959), 14–26; rev ed 1970. Rpt in Shakespeare, *The Complete Works* [Pelican Text Revised], gen ed Alfred Harbage (Baltimore: Penguin 1969),

1369–72 and in *Twentieth-Century Interpretations of 'The Tempest,'* ed Hallett
Smith (Englewood Cliffs, NJ: Prentice-Hall 1969), 60–7.
Analyses the characters in the play and the vision of a new social order
that is achieved at the end of the action. Examines the nature of Prospero's
magic, the theme of time, the play's connections with previous literature
and with contemporary accounts of shipwrecks, its genre (a spectacular and
operatic play), and its connections with Shakespeare's other late romances.

D107 'Literature as Context: Milton's *Lycidas.' Proceedings of the Second Congress of
the International Comparative Literature Association* (Univ of North Carolina
Studies in Comparative Literature 23 [1959]: 44–55). Rpt in *FI,* 119–26
and in *Milton's 'Lycidas': The Tradition and the Poem,* ed C.A. Patrides (New
York: Holt, Rinehart and Winston 1961), 200–11.
A study of the conventions of Milton's elegy: its relation to the pastoral
tradition, its conventional framework of ideas and images (archetypes), its
genre, and its central myth (the Adonis myth). Examines also the unity
of *Lycidas* as an autonomous poetic structure: its primary context is literature
itself.

D108 'Religion and Modern Poetry.' *Challenge and Response: Modern Ideas and
Religion,* ed Randolph C. Chalmers and John A. Irving (Toronto: Ryerson
1959), 23–36
Begins by listing several fallacies that result when readers confuse poetry
with direct statement: the intentional fallacy, the fallacy of assuming
that poetry itself is morally good or bad, the fallacy of the associative or
stock response. Observes that there is a natural alliance between the
languages of religion and poetry because they both are related to forms of
revelation – one human and the other divine. Examines the different
forms of revelation in the poetry of Wordsworth, Baudelaire, Frost, Hardy,
Lawrence, Graves, Rilke, Housman, Jeffers, Pound, Yeats, and Eliot.
Sees in Eliot's treatment of the Incarnation the use of the symbolic and
typological language of the Bible and the Church that had largely disappeared from English poetry after Milton. Argues that much of the obscurity
of modern poetry disappears when we understand the symbolism of
Christianity in such poets as Lowell, Thomas, Auden, and Yeats. It is the
'uninhibited imaginative speculation' of poets such as Yeats and Stevens,
rather than the precise language of sacramental poetry, that reminds us
most clearly 'that Scripture is poetic and not doctrinal.'

D109 'Sir James Frazer.' *Architects of Modern Thought,* 3rd and 4th series, Twelve
Talks for CBC Radio (Toronto: Canadian Broadcasting Corp 1959), 22–32.
Rpt as 'Symbolism of the Unconsicous' in *NFCL,* 84–94 and as 'Simbolizam
nesvesnog,' trans Ksenija Todorović, in *Književnost* 38 (May 1983): 765–77.
Gives a biographical sketch of Frazer and summarizes the argument of
The Golden Bough. Considers this massive book to be of more importance to
literary critics than to anthropologists because it is 'a kind of grammar of
the human imagination.' It is a study of 'unconscious symbolism on its

social side' and so complements what Freud and Jung have done for unconscious symbolism. Frazer revolutionized our understanding of religion,
affected the imagery of moern poetry, and was an architect of the modern
imagination and its symbolism.

D110   'The Principal's Address.' *Varsity Graduate* 8 (January 1960): 47–61. Rpt of
By Liberal Things (see C2).

D111   'Literature as Possession.' *Kenyon Alumni Bulletin*, January-March 1960, 5–9
Analyses three kinds of verbal rhythm – those of prose, verse, and ordinary speech. Distinguishes the characteristics of each style. Relates the
analysis of style, finally, to the making of aesthetic judgments. Originally
presented as one of the President's Lectures at Kenyon College, 23 November 1959. The ideas in this essay are developed and expanded in *WTC*.

D112   'Letters in Canada: 1959, Poetry.' *University of Toronto Quarterly* 29 (July
1960): 440–60. Partially rpt in *BG*, 107–27 and in *Masks of Poetry: Canadian
Critics on Canadian Verse*, ed A.J.M. Smith (Toronto: McClelland and Stewart
1962), 106–9; material on Layton rpt in *Irving Layton: The Poet and His
Critics*, ed Seymour Mayne (Toronto: McGraw-Hill Ryerson 1978), 99–101.
Praises the simplicity, readability, and diction of George Johnston's *The
Cruising Auk*, finds much to be admired in the 'richly suggestive intelli-
gence' contained in Ronald Bates's *The Wandering World*, and discovers in
Irving Layton's *A Red Carpet for the Sun* a continuing insistence on the
poet's stage personality as opposed to his poetic one. Reviews also Fred
Cogswell's *Descent from Eden*, Peter Miller's *Sonata for Frog and Man*, George
Walton's *The Wayward Queen*, and *Anerca*, a collection of Eskimo poems.
Glances at a dozen or so chap-books, including those by Mary Elizabeth
Bayer, Verna Loveday Harden, Florence Wyle, Douglas Lochhead, R.E.
Rashley, Alfred Purdy, Michael Collie, and Dorothy Roberts. Concludes
this last of his ten annual surveys with a statement about the principles of
book reviewing he has followed.

D113   'Nature Methodized.' *The Griffin* 9 (August 1960): 2–11. Rpt in *NFCL*,
147–55.
A review of Bonamy Dobrée's *English Literature of the Early Eighteenth
Century*. Argues that the point of literary history is not to order a mass of
documents into a coherent whole but 'to awaken and refresh our imaginative experience by showing us what unexplored riches lie within a certain
area.' Thus the literary historian should begin in the 'background' with
such things as letters, memoirs, and travel books, and then move from the
periodicals and magazines in the foreground to the intellectual issues of
the age. Praises Dobrée's book for its great volume of material and its
sense of proportion. What the book lacks, however, is 'that final unification
of material which is the mark of the completely realized history.'

D114   'The Nightmare Life in Death.' *Hudson Review* 13 (Autumn 1960): 442–9.
Rpt in *Twentieth-Century Interpretations of 'Malloy,' 'Malone Dies,' 'The
Unnamable,'* ed J.D. O'Hara (Englewood Cliffs, NJ: Prentice-Hall 1970), 26–

45; in *Samuel Beckett: The Critical Heritage*, ed Laurence Graver and Ray-
mond Federman (London: Routledge & Kegan Paul 1979), 206–14; and in
NFCL, 219–29.
A review of *Malloy, Malone Dies*, and *The Unnamable* by Samuel Beckett.
Surveys a large part of Beckett's other work, including his essay on Proust,
Waiting for Godot, Watt, Murphy, Endgame, Krapp's Last Tape, and *All That
Fall*. Identifies the central theme in Beckett's fiction as the lost paradise,
manifest in its tragic form as the failure to possess and in its comic form
as the failure to communicate. Though Beckett keeps insisting that there
can be no continuous version of the ego, he does reveal finally that the
secret of identity is to be found in art, the function of which is to restore
silence 'in a world given over to obsessive utterance.'

D115 'Push-button Gadgets May Help – But the Teacher Seems Here to Stay.'
Varsity Graduate 8 (Christmas 1960): 45–7, 82
Examines two articles about teaching machines. Believes that such machines, more properly called 'learning aids,' have the advantage of compel-
ling concentration and of immediately reinforcing correct answers. Maintains
that even though there is some basis for the fears about teaching machines,
one fear springs from a genuine problem in education – 'the problem of
breaking down mechanical responses in places where they don't belong.'

D116 'Introduction.' *The Stepsure Letters*, by Thomas McCulloch ([Toronto]:
McClelland and Stewart 1960), iii–ix
Places McCulloch's Mephibosheth Stepsure in the tradition of the industrious apprentice as he exists from Deloney's fiction through Samuel Smiles
and Benjamin Franklin to Horatio Alger. Sees *The Stepsure Letters* as
having a minor place in developing the convention of the industrious-
apprentice myth. Examines the different character-types in McCulloch's
satire, especially the comic ones who oppose Stepsure. Contrasts
McCulloch's *Letters* with the more famous satire by Haliburton in his Sam
Slick papers, fifteen years later. Concludes that although the idle and
industrious apprentice no longer exists as a central type of vice and virtue,
'vice and virtue are still what they always were' and that McCulloch's
treatment of them makes him 'the founder of a genuine Canadian humour.'

D117 'New Directions from Old.' *Myth and Mythmaking*, ed Henry A. Murray
(New York: George Braziller 1960; Boston: Beacon Press 1968), 115–31. Rpt
in *The Making of Myth*, ed Richard Ohmann (New York: Putnam 1962),
66–82; and in *FI*, 52–66.
Seeks to distinguish poetic from other kinds of thought by annotating
Aristotle's argument about the relation of poetry to action. Outlines the
differences between the poet, on the one hand, and the historian and
the philosopher, on the other. The poet gives us secondary imitations of
both actions and thoughts; he gives us, that is, myth and images. In
the second part of the essay, outlines the conventional structure of images
that poets such as Dante, Spenser, and Milton have used. Then contrasts
this poetic 'topocosm' with that of the Romantics.

D118 'The Structure of Imagery in *The Faerie Queene.' University of Toronto Quarterly* 30 (January 1961): 109–27. Rpt in *FI*, 69–87 and in *Essential Articles for the Study of Edmund Spenser*, ed A.C. Hamilton (Hamden, Conn: Archon Books 1972), 153–70; partially rpt in *Edmund Spenser's Poetry*, ed Hugh Maclean (New York: Norton 1968), 582–93 and in *Edmund Spenser*, ed Paul J. Alpers (Harmondsworth: Penguin 1969), 277–90.
Demonstrates the unity of *The Faerie Queene* by examining the structure of its imagery. Shows Spenser's use of the conventional framework of four orders of existence (death and sin, ordinary experience, upper nature, and the divine world), of the imagery of the natural cycle that is associated with romance, and of the dialectical movement in the poem between the various orders of existence. Traces the symbolism, which derives from these conventions and from the Bible, throughout the six books of the poem.

D119 'The Well-Tempered Critic.' *Acta Victoriana* 85 (March 1961): I–XII [issued as a 'Feature Supplement' to this issue of *Acta Victoriana*]
An early version of the first chapter of *WTC*. The later version is organized somewhat differently, especially in section 2 of the first chapter, and material has been added to all three sections in the book version. The argument as a whole, however, remains unchanged, even though some paragraphs are deleted from the original.

D120 'Myth, Fiction, and Displacement.' *Daedalus* 90 (Summer 1961): 587–605. Rpt in *FI*, 21–38; in *Criticism: The Major Texts*, enlarged ed, ed Walter Jackson Bate (New York: Harcourt Brace Jovanovich 1970), 625–36; in *Literary Criticism: An Introduction*, ed Lionel Trilling (New York: Harcourt, Brace, and World 1970), 574–90; and as 'Shinwa, fikushon, oyobi shinwakei haijo,' trans Koichi Aihara, in *Gendai hihyo no kozo* [*The Structure of Contemporary Literary Criticism*], ed Jiro Ari et al (Tokyo: Shicho-sha 1971), 93–110.
An exposition of the term 'myth' in current literary criticism. Sees two chief meanings to the word: the continuous linear movement of fictional plot and the spatially organized, simultaneously unified theme. Relates *mythos* to the 'recognitions' that manifest themselves in different but conventional plot structures. Illustrates how the earliest forms of myth are displaced in the direction of plausibility. Shows how myth assimilates nature to human form through analogy and identity. Believes that we need to move beyond critical naturalism to a 'criticism of causes, specifically the formal cause which holds the work together.'

D121 'Academy without Walls.' *Canadian Art* 18 (September-October 1961): 296–8. Portions rpt in *Western Humanities Review* 16 (Winter 1962): 95–96.
On the role of the artist in contemporary society and on his relation to the academy. Argues that the increase in technical resources and the possibilities of form have freed the artist to become academic and scholarly. Art has thus become absorbed into and a necessary part of the education of our time. The arts reflect society, but they also teach. In a democratic, as opposed to a mob, society, they have a revolutionary role to play in

presenting us with a 'vision of the human world that man is trying to build out of nature.' Originally presented as an address to the Canadian Conference of the Arts, May 1961.

D122 'Comment.' *Approaches to the Study of Twentieth-Century Literature* (Proceedings of the Conference in the Study of Twentieth-Century Literature, First Session) (East Lansing: Michigan State Univ Press 1961), 79–83
Comments on Fr Walter J. Ong's essay, 'Synchronic Present: The Academic Future of Modern Literature in America,' by expanding on some of Fr Ong's themes. Distinguishes between two kinds of time: *chronos* and *kairos*. Observes that *kairos* – time in which something not wholly temporal becomes manifest – is particularly appropriate to the humanities: the classics were completed in and are the heritage of the past, but they manifest themselves continuously in the present. Argues that the study of modern literature means 'not the reinforcing of the past by the present, but the reinforcing of the authority of tradition by a sense of participation in it.' Urges that the study of modern literature not be separated from the study of the entire verbal culture of the present, including verbal trash. For F's contribution to the discussion of other symposium papers, see pp 95–6, 100, 101, 122, 133, 143, 161–2, and 164–5.

D123 'The Critical Discipline.' *Canadian Universities Today: Symposium Presented to the Royal Society of Canada in 1960*, ed George Stanley and Guy Sylvestre (Toronto: Univ of Toronto Press 1961), 30–7. Rpt in *The Aims of Education* (Conference Study no 1), ed Freeman K. Stewart (Ottawa: Canadian Conference on Education 1961), 24–32.
Examines 'the relation of the liberal arts to education as a whole and to the conditions of life in Canadian society.' Argues against progressive theories that assume that education is a matter of social adjustment. Education in the university requires rather that students see a dialectic between their social and cultural environments. After acquiring information and skills in the primary grades and forming social opinions and attitudes in secondary school, students learn, or should learn in their university years the difference between what the world is and what it can become. Maintains that scholarship should always have priority in the university because only when it does can everything be subordinated to the authority of the subjects being taught and to their laws and principles. Originally presented as an address to the fellows of sections 1 and 2 of the Royal Society of Canada, June 1960.

D124 'Editor's Preface.' *The Valley of Vision: Blake as Prophet and Revolutionary*, by Peter Fisher, ed Northrop Frye (Toronto: Univ of Toronto Press 1961), v–vii (see B8)
An account of Peter Fisher's literary and philosophical interests, particularly the relation between Blake and Oriental philosophy; of the nature of Fisher's study (Blake's context rather than his sources); and of the state of the manuscript as it came to F after Fisher's accidental death.

D125 'Appearance and Reality in Education.' *Saturday Night* 77 (17 March 1962): 20–4

A slightly different version of part 3 of F's 'Introduction' to *Design for Learning* (see D131)

D126 'To the Class of '62.' *Douglas Library Notes* [Queen's University, Kingston, Ont] 11 (Summer 1962): 5–6, 11–13

Calls for an imaginative heroism and an expanded vision in a time of social and moral crisis. Maintains that the arts and sciences are the real form of human society and can therefore provide the vision to hold society together. Describes the nature of the university and the two kinds of knowledge it provides – knowledge about and knowledge of. This convocation address was given on the occasion of F's being awarded an honorary degree from Queen's University, 18 May 1962. The address borrows some paragraphs from 18 and 110.

D127 'Fellowship Lecture: The Imaginative and the Imaginary.' *American Journal of Psychiatry* 119 (October 1962): 289–98. Rpt in *FI*, pp 151–67.

Defines the imagination as the creative faculty that produces culture and civilization. 'It is the power of transforming a sub-human physical world into a world with a human shape and meaning.' Sees the imagination as polarized by sense (the pragmatic habit of mind) and vision (the pure desire to extend human perception). Traces the history of the imagination and its relationship to madness and melancholy from the Renaissance to the romantic period, drawing examples from Shakespeare, Burton, Montaigne, Cervantes, Spenser, Fletcher, Swift, Blake, and Wordsworth. Originally presented to the annual meeting of the American Psychiatric Association, Toronto, 7–11 May 1962.

D128 'Haliburton: Mask and Ego.' *Alphabet*, no 5 (December 1962), 58–63. Rpt in *On Thomas Chandler Haliburton*, ed Richard A. Davies (Ottawa: Tecumseh Press 1979), 211–15 and in *Beginnings: The Canadian Novel*, II, ed John Moss (Toronto: New Canada Publications 1980), 40–4.

An assessment of Haliburton's Sam Slick sketches. Sees Slick as a stage American or comic character, one who is kept alive today by his wit rather than his wisdom. Understands Haliburton's purpose as to make fun of his own people, the Bluenoses. The eight Sam Slick books have succeeded because Slick is a character in his own right. When they fail, it is because Slick becomes a mouthpiece for Haliburton's ego, 'and nobody's ego is worth listening to.' Still, the sketches are 'extraordinarily good,' and it is better to appreciate Haliburton as a good writer than to regret that he might have been a great one. Originally presented as a CBC Radio talk (see H3).

D129 'Emily Dickinson.' *Major Writers of America*, vol 2, gen ed, Perry Miller (New York: Harcourt, Brace & World 1962), 3–46. Rpt in *FI*, 193–217; partially rpt in *Modern American Poetry: Essays in Criticism*, ed Jerome Mazzaro (New York: McKay 1970), 18–39.

Gives a biographical sketch of Dickinson, but advises that she is 'most demanding if we look at her poems for what her imagination has created, not for what event may have suggested it.' Locates her poetry in the tradition of popular and primitive verse because of her conceptual use of language, which tends toward the proverb and the riddle, and because of her unconventional syntax, punctuation, and diction, which give her poetry an epigrammatic, oracular, and colloquial style. Examines the religious themes of her verse, especially the themes of death and immortality, and the experiences she records of the ecstatic vision. In this vision the human consciousness is represented as both the circumference and the centre of human experience.

D130 'How True a Twain.' *The Riddle of Shakespeare's Sonnets,* ed Edward Huber (London: Routledge & Kegan Paul; New York: Basic Books 1962), 25–53. Rpt in *FI*, 88–106.

Argues against the biographical approach in studying Shakespeare's sonnets. Rather than assuming that Shakespeare's life provides the key, we should 'start with the assumption that the sonnets are poetry, therefore written within a specific literary tradition and a specific literary genre.' Examines Shakespeare's use of the generic conventions of courtly love poetry and shows that the sonnets embody the entire range of love relationships, from the 'high' Platonic forms through the Petrarchan norm to the 'low' forms that parody the Petrarchan conventions. Maintains that there are three cycles lying behind the arrangement of the sonnets. Analyses the imagery Shakespeare uses throughout the poems.

D131 'Introduction.' *Design for Learning: Reports Submitted to the Joint Committee of the Toronto Board of Education and the University of Toronto,* ed Northrop Frye (Toronto: Univ of Toronto Press 1962), 3–17 (see B9). Partially rpt in *The Making of Meaning,* ed Anne E. Bertoff (Montclair, NJ: Boynton/Cook 1981), 191–6.

Introduces the reports by tracing the history of the joint committee; by attacking simplistic theories of progressive education; by outlining the idea of a spiral curriculum; by stressing the importance of students' learning the central principles in science, social science, and language; and by analysing the primary, secondary, and tertiary phases of education, which roughly correspond to the elementary, secondary, and university levels of education.

D132 'Preface to the Beacon Press Edition.' *Fearful Symmetry: A Study of William Blake,* by Northrop Frye (Boston: Beacon Press 1962), [iii–iv]

Reflects on his purpose in writing *FS*, which was to articulate Blake's 'argument.' Notes that the book reflects the influence of Frazer and perhaps Freud. Observes that there is a close connection between Blake's view of art and the theory of criticism in *AC*: 'I had not realized, before this last re-reading, how completely the somewhat unusual form and structure of my commentary was derived from my absorption in the larger critical theory implicit in Blake's view of art.'

D133 'Proposal of Toast.' *Stratford Papers on Shakespeare*, ed B.W. Jackson (Toronto: Gage 1962), 194–5
In proposing a toast to Shakespeare at the 1961 Stratford seminar, F speaks of the three aspects of his personality: the man himself, the playwright, and the person whose social vision and insight into humanity have helped us to formulate our own thoughts, visions, and speech.

D134 'Recognition in *The Winter's Tale*.' *Essays on Shakespeare and Elizabethan Drama: In Honor of Hardin Craig*, ed Richard Hosley (Columbia: Univ of Missouri Press 1962), 235–46. Rpt in *FI*, 107–18; in *Essays in Shakespearean Criticism*, ed James L. Calderwood and Harold E. Toliver (Englewood Cliffs, NJ: Prentice-Hall 1970), 357–67; and in *Shakespeare's Later Comedies*, ed D.J. Palmer (Harmondsworth: Penguin 1971), 332–45.
Calls attention to the double recognition scene in the play: the first is only reported and derives from the conventional *cognito* of New Comedy; the second is the statue scene in which Hermione is awakened. Shakespeare is more interested in the second. Observes that the controlling power of the action is identified both with the will of Apollo and with the power of nature, and that art is 'part of the regenerating power of the play.' Examines the three kinds of art mentioned in the play and concludes that at the end 'nature provides the means for the regeneration of artifice,' all of which is worked out within the dialectical framework of Renaissance cosmology and the conventional framework of the cycle of nature. Originally presented as a paper to the Modern Language Association.

D135 'Shakespeare's Experimental Comedy.' *Stratford Papers on Shakespeare*, ed B.W. Jackson (Toronto: Gage 1962), 2–14
An analysis of *Love's Labour's Lost*. Sees the play as coming from the tradition of Greek New Comedy; the *commedia dell'arte*; the comedy of wit and dialogue in Peele, Greene, and Lyly; and the Renaissance masque. Observes that the play differs from Shakespeare's other comedies in that it does not have the normal comic ending – the festivity that symbolizes the birth of a new society. Analyses the play as a comedy of humours, with the stock characters forming 'a kind of chorus to the main action.' The humour that the kings' court has to be released from is an excess of wit. Unlike the happy, green-world endings of Shakespeare's other comedies, *Love's Labour's Lost* has no suggestion that spring is to triumph over winter. Originally presented as a lecture at the Shakespeare seminar, Stratford, Ont, 1961. The printed text of the lecture is followed by a series of questions from the floor and F's responses (pp 13–14).

D136 'The Tragedies of Nature and Fortune.' *Stratford Papers on Shakespeare*, ed B.W. Jackson (Toronto: Gage 1962), 38–55
An analysis of Shakespeare's Roman plays, chiefly *Coriolanus*. Concentrates on explaining the division of moral sympathies in the play, concluding that Shakespeare intended to make 'the dramatic confict as sharp and as evenly divided as possible.' Shows how the tragedy of Coriolanus is a mixture of the heroic and the ironic and how, because he 'is a man without

a mask, or fully developed social personality ... there is nothing to mediate between his thought and his expression.' Still, the play illustrates the power of rhetoric in forming the destiny of man, even though Coriolanus's impatient sincerity ends in disaster. Originally presented as a lecture at the Shakespeare seminar, Stratford, Ont, 1961. The printed text of the lecture is followed by a series of questions from the floor and F's responses (pp 51–5).

D137 'The Developing Imagination.' *Learning in Language and Literature* (Cambridge, Mass: Harvard Univ Press 1963), 31–58
Outlines three phases of learning, each of which has a conservative and consolidating aspect and a radical or exploratory aspect. In the primary phase, the conservative power is memory, which holds content; the exploring power is sense or reason, which holds structure. In the secondary phase, the conservative and radical aspects of learning become more conceptual: they ask, respectively, why things exist and what good they are. In the tertiary phase, the conservative aspect takes on an awareness of society and its institutions, while the radical aspect becomes aware of the difference between the real and ideal forms of society. Running throughout all three phases is the imagination, which develops finally into a constructive power. Within this framework, F advances a number of familiar themes: that literature is mainly structure and that teaching it can follow a deductive pattern, that the classics and the Bible contain the structural principles of literature, and that literary education has a social function. Originally presented as the Inglis Lecture for 1962 at the Graduate School of Education, Harvard University. This lecture is quite similar to F's 'Introduction' to *Design for Learning* (see B9 and D131).

D138 'The Drunken Boat: The Revolutionary Element in Romanticism.' *Romanticism Reconsidered: Selected Papers from the English Institute*, ed Northrop Frye (New York: Columbia Univ Press 1963), 1–25 (see B10). Rpt in *StS*, 200–17 and in *Perspectives in Contemporary Criticism*, ed Sheldon Grebstein (New York: Harper & Row 1968), 345–56; abridged version rpt in *Romanticism: Points of View*, 2nd ed, ed Robert F. Gleckner and Gerald E. Enscoe (Englewood Cliffs, NJ: Prentice-Hall 1970; Detroit: Wayne State Univ Press 1975), 298–313; expanded into chapt 1 of *SR*.
Sees in romanticism 'a profound change, not primarily in belief, but in the spatial projection of reality.' Shows how the old hierarchy of existence, with its divine, human, and natural levels, was changed by the romantic poets. The metaphorical structure of their poetry tended to move 'inside and downward' instead of, as in the older model, 'outside and upward.' Sees romanticism, therefore, as primarily a revolution in poetic imagery.

D139 'Foreword.' *Romanticism Reconsidered: Selected Papers from the English Institute*, ed Northrop Frye (New York: Columbia Univ Press 1963), v–ix (see B10)
Notes that the purpose of the English Institute session 'was to examine the real degree of content the term Romanticism has.' Traces some of the central themes in papers presented at the session by M.H. Abrams, René Wellek, Lionel Trilling, and himself: the revolutionary character of roman-

ticism and the pattern it frequently displays of enthusiasm followed by
disillusion.

D140 'Literary Criticism.' *The Aims and Methods of Scholarship in Modern Languages
and Literatures*, ed James Thorpe (New York: Modern Language Association
1963), 57–69; 2nd ed 1970, 69–81. Rpt in *Bungaku kenkyu to gengogaku*,
trans Hitoshi Suwabe (Tokyo: Hokusei-do Press 1972), 121–42. This translation of 2nd ed includes a biographical sketch of F and notes to his essay,
176–82.

Distinguishes between judicial criticism, which should be restricted to
reviewing, and academic criticism, which completes the work of scholarship
and is independent of value-judgments. Argues that the critic's primary
function is to categorize, describe, identify, and explain a writer's work and
so contribute to a growing body of knowledge about it. Outlines the
function of commentary in identifying the structure of themes and images.
Following this, critics should examine the conventions, genres, and myths
of the poem in question, thus enabling them to see it as a part of the
total order of words. 'The primary axiom of critical procedure is: Go for the
structure, not for the content.'

D141 'The Road of Excess.' *Myth and Symbol: Critical Approaches and Applications*,
ed Bernice Slote (Lincoln: Univ of Nebraska Press 1963), 3–20. Rpt in
StS, 160–74; in *Romanticism and Consciousness: Essays in Criticism*, ed Harold
Bloom (New York: Norton 1970), 119–32; in *Contexts of Canadian Criticism*,
ed Eli Mandel (Toronto: Univ of Toronto Press; Chicago: Univ of Chicago
Press 1971), 125–39; and in *Modern Literary Criticism, 1900–1970*, ed
Lawrence I. Lipking and A. Walton Litz (New York: Atheneum 1972),
232–40.

Examines the connections between his study of Blake and the theory of
literature worked out in *AC*. Shows that Blake collapses the distance
between creation and criticism and that his work requires us to contemplate
it as a simultaneous unity in space rather than as a narrative movement
in time. Sees the framework of Blake's art as archetypal and mythopoeic
rather than as allegorical or ironic. Comments on Blake's being the first
Romantic to identify 'the creative imagination of the poet with the creative
power of God' and on his belief that poetic vision is, through its use of
metaphor, what humanizes reality. Originally presented as a lecture at the
joint meeting of the Midwest Modern Language Association and the
Central Renaissance Conference, University of Nebraska, April 1962.

D142 'We Are Trying to Teach a Vision of Society.' *Educational Courier* 34 (January-February 1964): 21–3

The text of an address presented at the first annual meeting of the Ontario
Curriculum Institute, 13 December 1963. Praises the institute for its goals
and argues that of Aristotle's four causes the formal (what we teach)
and the final (why we teach) are the most important for educators.

D143 'Elementary Teaching and Elemental Scholarship.' *PMLA* 79 (May 1964):
11–18. Rpt in *StS*, 90–105.

Outlines a program of literary education that places poetry at the centre of the child's verbal training and that is organized around a set of deductive critical principles in grammar, rhetoric, and literary themes and structures. Maintains that children should be taught 'the grammar of the imagination which all literature employs' – its conventional images and recurring myths. Argues that such a literary education has the practical result of enabling one to participate imaginatively in society. Originally presented as an address at the Modern Language Association annual meeting, Chicago, 29 December 1963.

D144 'Education – Protection against Futility.' *Alumni Journal* [Univ of Manitoba] 24 (Summer 1964): 4–7
The text of an address to the 85th Spring Convocation, University of Manitoba, 21 May 1964. Emphasizes that education is a lifelong experience.

D145 'Ned Pratt: The Personal Legend.' *Canadian Literature* 21 (Summer 1964): 6–9. Rpt in *Canada: A Guide to the Peaceable Kingdom*, ed William Kilbourn (Toronto: Macmillan 1970), 299–303.
Reminisces about the Canadian poet, E.J. Pratt. Recalls his life as a story-teller, editor, teacher, and writer.

D146 ' "Silence upon the Earth." ' *Canadian Poetry Magazine* 27 (August 1964): 71–3
A tribute to E.J. Pratt. Praises his generosity of spirit, his life as a teacher, his liberal values, and the quality of his poetry. This essay is similar in content and language to D145.

D147 'Criticism, Visible and Invisible.' *College English* 26 (October 1964): 3–12. Rpt in *StS*, 74–89 and in *The English Critical Tradition: An Anthology of English Literary Criticism*, vol 2, ed S. Ramaswami and V.S. Seturaman (Atlantic Highlands, NJ: Humanities Press 1979).
Argues that knowledge about literature is the central activity of criticism and that such knowledge comes about by relating literature to other things: the writer's life and time, the history of literature, and the total 'order of words.' A further context of literature, however, is its visible and invisible levels or limits. The lower level includes the active and passive approaches to verbal experience. The higher level is something that cannot be taught – 'the inner possession of literature as an imaginative force.' This is the level of Plato's *nous* (as opposed to *dianoia*), of wisdom (as opposed to knowledge), and of identity (as opposed to confrontation). Maintains throughout that evaluative criticism cannot be rightly regarded as the basis of literary study. Originally presented as an address at a conference devoted to F's work, Trinity College, Hartford, Conn, April 1964.

D148 'The Norms of Satire: A Symposium.' *Satire Newsletter* 2 (Fall 1964): 9–10
Gives a brief account of the moral norm that makes satire satiric and argues against the use of value-judgments in discussions about the effectiveness of satire.

D149 'Preface.' *The Psychoanalysis of Fire* by Gaston Bachelard, trans Alan C.M. Ross (Boston: Beacon Press 1964), v–viii

Shows the importance of Bachelard's psychological analysis of fire for the literary critic: fire is an imaginative construct, linked by analogy and identity to numerous other parts of experience. Illustrates how such an image is part of our central mythological inheritance and gives literary examples of the various 'complexes' (myths) that Bachelard examines.

D150 'The Problem of Spiritual Authority in the Nineteenth Century.' *Literary Views: Critical and Historical Essays*, ed Carroll Camden (Chicago: Univ of Chicago Press 1964), 145–58. Rpt in *StS*, 241–56; rev version rpt in *Essays in English Literature from the Renaissance to the Victorian Age Presented to A.S.P. Woodhouse*, ed Millar MacLure and Frank W. Watt (Toronto: Univ of Toronto Press 1964), 304–19; slightly abridged version rpt in *John Henry Newman*, ed Joseph W. Hoppert (St Louis: B. Herder 1968), 5–24. Traces the changing conceptions of spiritual authority advocated by Milton, Rousseau, Burke, Butler, Morris, Mill, Newman, and Arnold. Finds that the debate about spiritual authority in the nineteenth century is located between the counter-revolutionary arguments of the later Burke and the revolutionary position of Morris. Examines the chief metaphors used by nineteenth-century thinkers to construct their various theories of humanity, culture, society, and authority. Concludes that the university seems 'to come closer than any other human institution to defining the community of spiritual authority.' Originally presented as a lecture at Rice University, during the year of its centennial celebration, 1962–3.

D151 'Varieties of Literary Utopias.' *Daedalus* 94 (Spring 1965): 323–47. Rpt in *StS*, 109–34 and in *Utopias and Modern Thought*, ed Frank E. Manuel (Boston: Houghton Mifflin 1966), 25–49; rpt as 'Edebiyatta Ütopya Türleri,' trans Akşit Göktürk, in *Türk Dili* 23 (March 1971): 510–31 and as 'Spielarten der utopischen Literatur' in *Wunschtraum und Experiment: Vom Nutzen und Nachteil utopischen Denkens*, ed Frank E. Manuel (Freiburg: Romach 1970), 52–74. Sees utopias as imaginative visions of the *telos* of life, as opposed to social contract theories, which are concerned with the origins of society. Observes that utopias are speculative myths and that they describe social behaviour ritually. They become rational only after their ritual significance is explained. Believes that most writers of utopias stress either the legal structures of their society and thus come close to actual political and social theory (as in Plato and More) or the technological power of their society and thus come close to science fiction. The two kinds of utopian romances produced by technological society are the straight utopia, which presents ideal social goals, and the utopian satire or parody. Shows how utopias are rooted both in the social attitudes of the day and in imaginative literature itself; this latter means that utopias 'are less concerned with achieving ends than with visualizing possibilities.' Applies these observations to the utopias of Plato and More and relates both to the myths of the creation and the fall in Christianity. Concludes with an account of the Golden Age myth in utopian thought, 'the seed which brings it to fruition.'

D152 'A Poet and a Legend.' *Varsity Graduate* 11 (June 1965): 65–9. Rpt in *Vic Report* 7 (Summer 1979): 6–7.
Reflects on the two selves of E.J. Pratt: his congenial, absent-minded, and fun-loving self and his poetic self, which produced poems of lonely, bitter, brooding themes and moods. Sees these two selves coming together in Pratt's integrity, sincerity, and high standards.

D153 'Allegory.' *Princeton Encyclopedia of Poetry and Poetics*, ed Alex Preminger (Princeton: NJ: Princeton Univ Press 1965), 12–15; englarged ed 1974, 12–15. Selections rpt in *Topics in Literary Criticism*, ed Christopher Butler and Alastair Fowler (London: Longman 1971), items 185 and 195.
Classifies allegory as either (1) historical or political or (2) moral, religious, philosophical, or scientific, the two categories deriving from the two aspects of fiction, *mythos* and *dianoia*. Observes that allegory may be either simple or complex. Traces the history of allegorical interpretation from the classical interpretation of myth to the romantic conception of symbolism and twentieth-century techniques of reading spawned by Freud and Frazer.

D154 'Conclusion.' *Literary History of Canada*, ed Carl F. Klinck (Toronto: Univ of Toronto Press 1965), 821–49. Rpt in French in *Histoire littéraire du Canada: Littérature canadienne de langue anglaise*, trans Maurice Lebel (Quebec: Les Presses de l'Université Laval 1970), 971–1005; rpt in an edited version in both *StS*, 279–312, and *BG*, 213–51; partially rpt in *Canadian Writing Today*, ed Mordecai Richler (Baltimore: Penguin 1970), 312–22. For a rev ed of this essay see D233.
A four-part essay that (1) examines the social, cultural, historical, political, and geographical contexts of Canadian literature; (2) characterizes the Canadian imagination as forming itself out of a 'garrison mentality,' and, after the centre of Canadian life moves from the fortress to the city, becoming a revolutionary garrison; (3) places Canadian literature in the context of the myths and conventions of literature in general; and (4) analyses the effects of nature on Canadian literature, especially as it takes the form of the pastoral myth.

D155 'Foreword.' *The Prospect of Change: Proposals for Canada's Future*, ed Abraham Rotstein (Toronto: McGraw-Hill 1965), xiii–xv
Introduces the essays in this collection by arguing for a social philosophy of moderation, one that exists between the introverted resistance to change and the staid support of continuity. Examines briefly the chief social myths that appear in the anthologized essays.

D156 'Nature and Nothing.' *Essays on Shakespeare*, ed G.W. Chapman (Princeton, NJ: Princeton Univ Press 1965), 35–58
An interpretation of Shakespeare's plays based on their movement between two poles of a dialectic: nature and nothing. Nature exists on two levels, the upper level of human nature, which is the world of innocence and art, and the lower level of physical nature. 'Nothing' represents the order of annihilation and non-being, which exists below physical nature. Analyses

more than a dozen of Shakespeare's plays from the perspective of these levels of being, concentrating on the kinds of action and imagery found on each level.

D157 'The Rising of the Moon: A Study of "A Vision." ' *An Honoured Guest: Essays on W.B. Yeats,* ed Denis Donoghue and J.R. Mulryne (London: Edward Arnold 1965), 8–33. Rpt in *SM*, 245–74.

Argues that the 'associative constructs' of metaphor and mythology are, aside from whatever they may or may not tell us about the external world, the framework for the imagery of poetry. Outlines this framework, with its cyclical and dialectical patterns, in Dante, Spenser, and Blake. Then the major part of the essay examines the two chief patterns in Yeats's poetry – the historical and the cyclical – along with his archetypal imagery. Bases his interpretation of Yeats's metaphors and archetypes partially on their outline in *A Vision*, even though this work is deficient in expressing some of Yeats's most profound insights.

D158 'The Structure and Spirit of Comedy.' *Stratford Papers on Shakespeare, 1964,* ed B.W. Jackson (Toronto: Gage 1965), 1–9

Distinguishes between the two forms of literary experience that are based on the limitations of human life, with its natural and social contracts (tragedy and irony) and the two forms that are based on freeing life from these contracts (comedy and romance). Then analyses the simple form of comic structure, exemplified in the works of Beaumarchais, and the more complex form, exemplified by Shakespeare and Molière, where there is a complicated interchange between reality and illusion. Originally presented as an address at the 1964 Shakespeare Festival, Stratford, Ont.

D159 'Verse and Prose.' *Princeton Encyclopedia of Poetry and Poetics,* ed Alex Preminger (Princeton, NJ: Princeton Univ Press 1965), 885–90; enlarged ed 1974, 885–90

Discusses three kinds of rhythm in the use of language: discursive (prose), metrical (verse), and associational. Identifies examples of each kind of rhythm as it exists in its pure state and in combination with each of its neighbours. This article is a summary of the argument that appears in a more detailed and complex form in *WTC* (see A6).

D160 'Design as a Creative Principle in the Arts.' *The Hidden Harmony: Essays in Honor of Philip Wheelwright,* ed Oliver Johnson et al (New York: Odyssey Press 1966), 13–22. Rpt in *StS*, 56–65.

Argues that design, in William Morris's sense, is what makes the visual arts creative, and that the same is true of verbal design in literature. The principles of design in both visual and literary arts appear in the minor and popular forms as well as in the major and more sophisticated ones. By focusing on design rather than realistic content, writers, somewhat para-doxically, are more likely to reach a wide public. An earlier version of this essay was presented at a festival of the arts at the University of Rochester.

D161 'The Instruments of Mental Production.' *Chicago Review* 18 3–4 (1966):

30–46. Rpt in *The Knowledge Most Worth Having*, ed Wayne C. Booth (Chicago: Univ of Chicago Press 1967), 59–83 and in *StS*, 3–21.

Distinguishes between scholarship, which is responsible only to its subject, and general education, which is primarily a social rather than an intellectual matter. Argues that education results from genuine leisure – 'a product of a vision of human society that is more permanent and coherent than actual society.' Traces the concept of education from Plato through the Renaissance to the nineteenth-century humanists' views, especially the revolutionary and utopian forms of education. Maintains that mythology forms the initiatory pattern of education. The informed citizen is created at the next level by 'the mythical structure formed by the humanities and the vision of nature afforded by general science.' The third level, which has authority over the other two, is the world of art and scholarship. Originally presented as an address at the University of Chicago, 1 February 1966, as a part of the university's seventy-fifth anniversary liberal arts conference.

D162 'Introduction.' *Blake: A Collection of Critical Essays*, ed Northrop Frye (Englewood Cliffs, NJ: Prentice-Hall 1966), 1–7

Places the thirteen essays in this collection within the context of their differing critical approaches to Blake's work. Comments on the early resistance to the normality of Blake's mind and on the universal relevance of Blake's genius.

D163 'The Keys to the Gates.' *Some British Romantics: A Collection of Critical Essays*, ed Northrop Frye et al ([Columbus]: Ohio State Univ Press 1966), 3–40. Rpt in *StS*, 175–99 and in *Romanticism and Consciousness: Essays in Criticism*, ed Harold Bloom (New York: Norton 1970), 233–54.

Provides an introductory guide to the symbolism of Blake's prophecies. Gives a detailed account of this schematic symbolism: its twofold vision of innocence and experience; its single vision of death and Satan (the covering Cherub); the threefold vision of resurrection (Tharmus); and the fourfold vision of creative power (Los and Eden).

D164 'Letter to the English Institute: 1965.' *Northrop Frye in Modern Criticism*, ed Murray Krieger (New York: Columbia Univ Press 1966), 27–30. Partially rpt in *Modern Literary Criticism, 1900–1970*, ed Lawrence I. Lipking and A. Walton Litz (New York: Atheneum 1972), 244–5.

Speaks of the reason for his absence from the English Institute session devoted to his work (to permit uninhibited discussion), of the schematic nature of his critical thought, and of the systematic element and interpenetrating visions of criticism.

D165 'Reflections in a Mirror.' *Northrop Frye in Modern Criticism*, ed Murray Krieger (New York: Columbia Univ Press 1966), 133–46. Partially rpt in *Contemporary Literary Criticism*, vol 24, ed Sharon R. Gunton (Detroit: Gale Research 1983), 222–3.

Reiterates his views on the systematic nature of criticism, on education and the role of the teacher, on the separation of knowledge and experience, on value-judgments, on literary structure and convention, on displacement, on the relation between literature and social mythology, and on the goal of literary study. Also comments on the essays by Angus Fletcher (see L165), Geoffrey Hartman (see L212), and W.K. Wimsatt (see L571), included in the English Institute volume devoted to his work.

D166 'Speculation and Concern.' *The Humanities and the Understanding of Reality*, ed Thomas B. Stroup (Lexington: Univ of Kentucky Press 1966), 32–54. Rpt in *StS*, 38–55.

Argues that the essential difference between the sciences and the humanities is that 'science exhibits a method and a mental attitude, most clearly in the physical sciences, of a stabilized subject and an impartial and detached treatment of evidence,' whereas the humanities 'express in their containing forms, or myths, the nature of the human involvement with the human world,' and they give human beings a sense of responsibility for living in the world they have created. Originally presented as a lecture at the Conference on the Humanities, University of Kentucky, 22–23 October 1965.

D167 'Il mito romantico.' *Lettere Italiane* 19 (October–December 1967): 409–40. A translation by S. Rosso-Mazzinghi of 'The Romantic Myth,' chapt 1 of *SR*, 3–48. Abridged version, with the same title, rpt in *Il Romanticismo: Atti del Sesto Congresso dell' Associazione Internationale per gli Studi di Lingua e Letterature Italiana*, ed Vitore Branca and Tibor Kardos (Budapest: Akademiai Kiado 1968), 33–52.

D168 'A Meeting of Minds.' *University of Toronto Graduate* 1 (December 1967): 11–13

Comments on the importance of establishing institutes and centres in the university, such as McLuhan's Centre for Culture and Technology, as places for discovering new approaches to conventional subject matter and for countering the natural tendency of scholarship toward specialization.

D169 'Blake, William.' *The Encyclopedia of Philosophy*, ed Paul Edwards (New York: Macmillan 1967), 319–20

Provides an introduction to Blake's life and thought. Outlines his theory of the imagination, the definitive role of the Bible in his work, his anti-Lockean position, and the action of his prophetic works, which move toward 'the integration of the human and divine powers represented in Christianity by Jesus.'

D170 'Foreword.' *1984* by George Orwell (Don Mills, Ont: Bellhaven House 1967), vii–xii

Emphasizes that Orwell's book is not simply a satire on Communism but a contemporary vision of hell that reflects the perversity and folly of the human mind.

D171 'The Knowledge of Good and Evil.' *The Morality of Scholarship*, ed Max Black (Ithaca, NY: Cornell Univ Press 1967), 1–28; Tokyo: Kenkyu-sha 1980, 1–31 [English text ed for Japanese students by Ariyoshi Mizunoe]. Rpt in *StS*, 22–37.

Believes that the ideal for scholarship is the proper combination of detachment and concern. Says that detachment and objectivity are insufficient as exclusive moral goals and must thus be balanced by an engaged and committed concern not just for one's own society but for all humanity. Detachment is necessary for freedom and autonomy, and it prevents concern from degenerating into anxiety; concern is necessary for the total vision of the human situation and prevents detachment from degenerating into indifference. Originally presented as a lecture at the formal inauguration of the Society for the Humanities, Cornell University, 27 October 1966.

D172 'Literature and Myth.' *Relations of Literary Study: Essays on Interdisciplinary Study,* ed James Thorpe (New York: Modern Language Association 1967), 22–54. Rpt as 'Littérature et mythe' in *Poétique: revue de théorie et d'analyse littéraires,'* trans Jacques Ponthoreau, no 8 (1971), 489–514, and as 'Literatur und Mythe' in *Interdisziplinäre Perspektiven der Literatur,* trans Marianne Burneleit (Stuttgart: Enke 1977) 42–71.
Examines the relationships between literature and myth. Distinguishes, first, between the content of myths (studying them as accounts of what people believed really happened or as explanations of things important to the community) and the form of myths (studying them primarily as stories and relating them to other stories of the same shape). Observes that myth as a total corpus of stories has two characteristics: its origins cannot be uncovered and its stories are implausible. Myths also have two tendencies: they tend to stick together and form a mythology and they tend to identify similar characters, usually gods. Analyses the connections between mythology and poetry, and argues that for the literary critic 'the real meaning of a myth is revealed, not by its origin ... but by its later literary career, as it becomes recreated by the poets.' This career can be understood by examining the structural principles of literature itself – the conventions, genres, and archetypes (or recurring images).

D173 'On Value Judgments.' *Contemporary Literature* 9 (Summer 1968): 311–18. Rpt in *Criticism: Speculative and Analytical Essays,* ed L.S. Dembo (Madison: Univ of Wisconsin Press 1968), 37–44 [this vol is a rpt of the Summer 1968 number of *Contemporary Literature*]; rpt with minor changes as 'Contexts of Literary Evaluation' in *Problems of Literary Evaluation* (Yearbook of Comparative Criticism, vol. 2), ed Joseph P. Strelka (University Park: Pennsylvania State Univ Press 1969), 14–21; and rpt in *StS*, 66–73.
Cautions against making value-judgments either the starting point or the goal of criticism. Maintains that value-judgments always contain some social or moral prejudice; that they are historically relative, dependent upon the tastes of the age; and that, deriving from experience, they have no relation to knowledge or scholarship. Originally presented as an address to the Poetics and Literary Theory Group at the meeting of the Modern Language Association, Chicago, December 1967.

D174 'Student Protest Has Shallow Roots.' *Toronto Star,* 19 September 1968, 7
Abridged form of 'The Social Importance of Literature' (see D175).

D175 'The Social Importance of Literature.' *Educational Courier* 39 (November–

December 1968): 19–23. Abridged form appears as 'Student Protest Has Shallow Roots.' *Toronto Star*, 19 September 1968, 7.

Examines the nature of the university and of the student protest movement against some of its practices. Believes that the movement has 'shallow social roots, and does not have a very long-time career ahead of it.' Argues that genuine education is a matter of repetition, drill, and practice in those subject matters that themselves possess the final authority. Maintains that the study of literature belongs with the sciences at the centre of the educational process. It provides 'training in a constructive and imaginative vision of man's own sense of his social goal.' Says that the teaching of literature should be systematic and structured and contain a large contemporary element. Originally presented as an address to the annual meeting of the Canadian Association of School Superintendents and Inspectors, 17 September 1968.

D176 'The Myth of Light.' *artscanada* 25 (December 1968): 8

An account of the three phases of the myth of light: (1) the religious, found in the Genesis creation story and in early Greek philosophy, in which light is associated with the essence of an object; (2) the human or secular, in which light is an attribute of an object; and (3) the natural, in which light is the energy underlying form. Gives examples of the kinds of imagery associated with each phase.

D177 'Why the Youth Revolution Isn't.' *Financial Post*, 7 December 1968, 13. Excerpts from pp 45–52 of 'The Ethics of Change' (see D191). Also appears as 'Our Permanent Revolution' in *Vancouver Sun*, 14 December 1968, 5.

D178 'Dickens and the Comedy of Humours.' *Experience in the Novel*, ed Roy Harvey Pearce (New York: Columbia Univ Press 1968), 49–81. Rpt in *StS*, 218–40; in *The Victorian Novel: Modern Essays in Criticism*, ed Ian Watt (New York: Oxford Univ Press 1971), 47–69; and in *Literary Criticism: Idea and Act: The English Institute, 1939–72: Selected Essays*, ed W.K. Wimsatt, Jr (Berkeley: Univ of California Press 1974), 537–55.

Shows how Dickens's novels, unlike most nineteenth-century fiction, are written in the tradition of New Comedy, with its episodic and implausible plots and its emphasis of characterization. Elaborates Dickens's conventional handling of the New Comedy plot structure and analyses his dependence on the many kinds of 'humours' – the miser, hypocrite, parasite, pedant, braggart, and 'tagged' humours (those associated with repeated set phrases). Shows how Dickens is anarchistic in social outlook, the only institution he regards as genuine being the family, which is, for him, the key to social identity; and how his hidden world is not ironic, as in twentieth-century fiction, but romantic, the presiding genius of which is Eros.

D179 'General Editor's Introduction.' *Shakespeare Series*, 2 vols (Toronto: Macmillan; New York: Odyssey Press 1968), vii–xii in both vols

Cautions against using the biographical approach to Shakespeare's plays, and discusses briefly the main scholarly issues in the study of Shakespeare:

dating the plays, sources used, staging the plays in Shakespeare's theatre, and establishing the texts. On F's general editorship of the series see B13.

D180 'John Keats.' *Encyclopedia Americana* 16 (1968 and subsequent editions): 328–31
Gives an account, largely chronological, of Keats's short life and literary career.

D181 'Mythos and Logos.' *The School of Letters, Indiana University: Twentieth Anniversary, 1968* (Bloomington, Ind: np 1968), 27–40. Rpt in *Yearbook of Comparative Literature* 18 (1969): 5–18 and as 'Mito e logos' in *Strumenti Critica* 3 (1969): 122–43.
Addresses the issue of determinism in criticism, ie, its dependence on some other discipline, by examining the cultural context of the classic defences of poetry by Sidney and Shelley. Shows that Sidney's case for poetry depends upon a set of socially accepted values but that Shelley's case assumes that these values can be continually questioned and recreated. Argues that the critic's social function is to examine the kinds of anxieties – those directed both to the past and to the future – that lie behind the attacks on poetry resisted by Sidney and Shelley. The critic, therefore, must understand the mythical habits of mind that originate in an oral culture as well as the logical habits of mind that begin in a writing culture. Originally delivered as a lecture at the summer session of the Indiana School of Letters, Bloomington, June 1968.

D182 'Research and Graduate Education in the Humanities.' *Journal of the Proceedings and Addresses of the Twentieth Annual Conference of the Association of Graduate Schools in the Association of American Universities*, ed W. Gordon Whaley (Austin: Univ of Texas Press 1968), 37–43
Comments on the centrality of the library in humanistic research; on the relative novelty of serious critical work in the humanities, caused partially by the superstition that 'students in the humanities are custodians of values'; on the necessity, therefore, of humanists and librarians paying attention to popular literature and minor writers of the past; and on the new areas that have opened criticism to topics other than historical and biographical research, especially the interrelated areas of social mythology. For a summary of F's contribution to the discussion that followed his remarks to the conference see pp 55–6.

D183 'The University and the Heroic Vision.' *Wascana Review* 3, no 2 (1968): 83–7
Emphasizes the importance of lifelong learning, a process that results in our becoming not more conservative but more aware of 'the invisible continuities of existence.' Observes that the contemporary revolutionary movement, which is more psychological than political, will have little effect on the university, and that the real heroic vision is the educated one – an imaginative power arising from what science, religion, philosophy, and the arts have created. Originally presented as a convocation address, University of Saskatchewan.

D184 'The Top of the Tower: A Study of the Imagery of Yeats.' *Southern Review* 5

(Summer 1969): 850–71. Rpt in *StS*, 255–77 and in *William Butler Yeats: A Collection of Criticism*, ed Patrick J. Keane (New York: McGraw-Hill 1973), 119–38.

Examines Yeats's imagery within the context of the four main levels of symbolism in Western poetry – those of the Logos vision, the Eros vision, the Adonis-Dionysus vision, and the Thanatos vision. Concentrates on the ways in which Eros is embodied in Yeats's poetry, especially the sexual and the sublimated or religious Eros quest. Observes that Yeats consistently rejects the goals of the Eros vision that lead to the Logos vision, preferring the sexual, gyre-like forms of Eros that descend away from the Logos and that turn his vision of human life and history into an ironic one. Originally presented at the Sligo Conference on Yeats, Summer 1968.

D185 'The University and Personal Life.' *University of Toronto Graduate* 2 (Summer 1969): 36–52. Part 2 of 'The University and Personal Life: Student Anarchism and the Educational Contract' (see D197)

D186 'Anarchism and the Universities.' *New Society* 14 (13 November 1969): 769–71. The first half, slightly abridged, of 'The University and Personal Life: Student Anarchism and the Educational Contract' (see D185 and D197)

D187 'The Educational Contract.' *New Society* 14 (20 November 1969): 811–14. A reprinting, with slight editorial changes, of the second half of 'The Universities and Personal Life: Student Anarchism and the Educational Contract' (see D185 and D197)

D188 'America: True or False?' *Notes for a Native Land: A New Encounter with Canada*, ed Andy Wainwright (np: Oberon Press 1969), 52–5

Summarizes the political and economic ills of American society but holds out hope that the social ideals of democracy might eventually be able to overcome exploitation and imperialism.

D189 'Blake's Reading of the Book of Job.' *William Blake: Essays for S. Foster Damon*, ed Alvin H. Rosenfeld (Providence, RI: Brown Univ Press 1969), 221–34. Rpt in *SM*, 228–44.

Sees Blake's vision in the Book of Job not only as a work of creative imagination but also as a work of powerful critical analysis, the latter resulting from Blake's putting the Book of Job into a literary context, which is the Bible as a whole. Because Blake sees the story of Job as the epitome or microcosm of the entire biblical narrative, the restoration of Job to prosperity does not appear arbitrary to him. Blake's engravings indicate that he understands Job's story as a series of opposing forces, the chief of which opposes Job as an individual to Job as a social being. For Blake, the comic resolution of descent-and-return makes sense only when society itself, not just the individual, is recreated. Thus, Job can fight Satan's vision of experience with his own vision of innocence.

D190 'Contexts of Literary Evaluation.' *Problems of Literary Evaluation* (Yearbook of Comparative Criticism, vol 2) ed Joseph Strelka (University Park: Pennsylvania State Univ Press 1969), 14–21. A reprinting of 'On Value Judgments' (see D173)

D191 'The Ethics of Change: The Role of the University.' *A Symposium: The Ethics of Change* (Toronto: Canadian Broadcasting Corp 1969), 44–55. Rpt in *Middlebury News Letter* 44 (Autumn 1969): 4–6 and in *DG*, 156–66. Several paragraphs appeared as 'Why the Youth Revolution Isn't' in *Financial Post*, 7 December 1968, 13, and as 'Our Permanent Revolution' in *Vancouver Sun*, 14 December 1968, 5.

Addresses the issue of student unrest in the late 1960s by comparing it with student radicalism in the 1930s. Believes that the real radical dynamic in the contemporary world is one of 'permanent revolution ... a dialogue of society engaged in a continuous critique of its order and its assumptions,' and that just as the end of detachment is the individual so the end of committed dialogue is the community. The university, because of its continuity and its foundation in society, is of all social institutions best prepared to critique society; whereas the existential questions springing from student radicalism are to be answered, not by the university, but 'in some area of religion, however secularized.' Some of the ideas in this essay appear also in 'The Critical Path' (see D200) and in 'The University and Personal Life' (see D197). 'The Ethics of Change' was originally presented on the occasion of the inauguration of John J. Deutsch as principal and vice-chancellor of Queen's University and was later broadcast on the CBC 'Ideas' program.

D192 'Introduction.' *Lawren Harris*, ed Bess Harris and R.G.P. Colgrove (Toronto: Macmillan 1969), ix–xii. Rpt in *BG*, 207–12.

Analyses the chief qualities of Harris's paintings: the tension created by their struggle between representation and abstraction; their meditative intensity; their stylizing and simplifying of outline, issuing in symbolic design; and their social vision.

D193 'Mito e logos.' *Strumenti Critica* 3 (1969): 122–43. A translation of 'Mythos and Logos' (see D181)

D194 'Old and New Comedy.' *Shakespeare Survey* 22 (1969): 1–5. Incorporated into part 1 of 'Romance as Masque' in *SM*, 148–56; rpt in *Types of Drama*, ed Sylvan Barnet et al (Boston: Little, Brown 1972), 450–4.

Examines the characteristics of Greek New Comedy – its teleological plot, which moves toward the birth of a new society, and the Eros symbolism typical of its imagery and characterization. Shows how New Comedy develops into Shakespearean or romantic forms, realistic or displaced forms (as in Molière), the domestic novel (as in Dickens), and parody (as in Shaw and Gilbert and Sullivan). Contrasts New Comedy with the Old Comedy form of Aristophanes, which has a dialectical plot, is distinguished by the *agon* or contest, has more spectacle than New Comedy, and treats the sexual instinct more explicitly. Originally delivered as a lecture at the Thirteenth International Shakespeare Conference, Stratford-on-Avon, September 1968.

D195 'The Revelation to Eve.' *Paradise Lost: A Tercentenary Tribute*, ed Balachandra Rajan (Toronto: Univ of Toronto Press 1969), 18–47. Rpt in *StS*, 135–59.

Shows how Eve's dreams in *Paradise Lost* convey archetypal elements in Milton's work: the masculine-father principle subordinates the female to the bride and the mother-goddess principle subordinates the male to the son-lover-victim. Maintains that the father archetype is inherently conservative, while the mother archetype is revolutionary and Dionysian; that although Milton accepted the conservative myth he understood the romantic one as having claims on the imagination; and that Eve's dream stands opposed to Adam's actual role in relation to God. Argues that in his fall Adam abandons the balance between the male and the female principles. By subordinating Eve, Milton can reassert the role of the bride, which comes in the revelation of her second dream. The Christian myth, along with the great-mother myth (with its imagery of rain, vegetation, earth, and caves) and the great-father myth (with its imagery of heat, mountains, air, and sunlight), form the basic structures of myth in *Paradise Lost*.

D196 'Sign and Significance.' *Claremont Reading Conference: Thirty-Third Yearbook*, ed Malcolm P. Douglass (Claremont, Calif: Claremont Graduate School 1969), 1–8

Argues that the centrifugal forms of criticism (biographical, psychological, historical) are essential to the entire critical process but that they need to be complemented by a centripetal approach that goes byond the explication of the New Critics by relating literature to other literature. Finds this approach in archetypal criticism, which seeks to relate the individual poem to an author's entire corpus, to the conventions, genres, and images of literature in general, and to the total order of words – the 'unified, coherent and autonomous body of imaginative experience historically conditioned but not historically determined.' Comments on how such a critical approach makes educational sense. The substance and much of the wording of this essay appear in part 1 of *CP*.

D197 'The University and Personal Life: Student Anarchism and the Educational Contract.' *Higher Education: Demand and Response* (The Quail Roost Seminar), ed W.R. Niblett (London: Tavistock Publications 1969), 35–59; San Francisco: Jossey-Bass 1970, 35–51. The first half of this essay was published simultaneously in a slightly abridged version as 'Anarchism and the Universities' in *New Society* 14 (13 November 1969): 769–71 (see D186); the second half was published with slight editorial changes as 'The Educational Contract' in *New Society* 14 (20 November 1969): 811–14 (see D187). The entire essay rpt in *SM*, 27–48; and as 'The Utopian State of Mind' in *New Statesman* 77 (23 and 30 December 1977): 896–900; an abridged version appeared as 'Utopia on the Campus' in *Globe and Mail Magazine*, 13 September 1969, 5–8.

Seeks to locate the context of New Left anarchism by comparing and contrasting it with pro-Stalinist radicalism and other Communist movements and by showing its analogies both to religious movements (eg, those of the Puritans and Anabaptists) and to American revolutionary and populist movements. Observes that the categories of contemporary anar-

chism are more psychological than economic, that the outlook of the New
Left movement is entirely consistent with modern discontinuity and
hysteria, and that today's radicalism is deeply religious in its anxieties and
assertions. Places radicalism in the context of utopian and social-contract
myths and examines its preference for commitment and engagement.
Argues that the real source of social authority is 'the educational contract,'
which is based upon the fact that knowledge is continuous and structured.
Says that this fact must be emphasized when the New Left protests
against irrelevance in higher education. Several paragraphs in this essay
appear in a somewhat different form in 'The Critical Path' (see D200).
Originally presented as a lecture at the Quail Roost Seminar, Duke University, Fall 1968.

D198 'Hart House Rededicated.' *University of Toronto Graduate* 3 (April 1970):
11–14
Uses the occasion of the rededication of Hart House on its fiftieth birthday
to reflect on the nature of the university as a community, on the amount
of courage in the face of continual crises and hysterias it takes to be a student, and on the moments of detached release provided by Hart House.
Presented as an address at the Hart House student centre, University
of Toronto, 11 November 1969.

D199 'Rear View Crystal Ball.' *Canadian Forum* 50 (April-May 1970): 54–5
Recalls his association with the *Canadian Forum* over several decades and
traces the several phases through which the journal passed: a by-product
of cultural exhilaration in the 1920s, its radical political stance in the
1930s and 1940s, and its separation from the CCF in the 1950s to become an
'independent journal of opinion.' Sees the present world as not conducive
to the kind of intellectual dialogue fostered by the *Forum* but believes
that such dialogue must replace the propaganda and 'bumbling rhetoric' of
the media if we are to survive.

D200 'The Critical Path: An Essay on the Social Context of Literary Criticism.'
Daedalus 99 (Spring 1970): 268–342. Rpt in *In Search of Literary Theory*,
ed Morton W. Bloomfield (Ithaca: Cornell Univ Press 1972), 91–193; partially
rpt in *Sociology of Literature and Drama*, ed Elizabeth and Tom Burns (Baltimore: Penguin 1973), 139–58. Revised and expanded into *CP*.
Portions of parts 1 and 3 appear in a somewhat different form as 'Mythos
and Logos' (see D181). Some of the material in parts 4–6 appear, also in
different form, in 'The Ethics of Change' (see D191) and 'The University and
Personal Life' (see D197), essays that themselves came from lectures at
Berkeley, Queen's, and Duke. The final version of the essay was presented
as a paper at the Villa Serbelloni, Bellagio, Italy, September 1969.

D201 'Literature and the Law.' *Law Society of Upper Canada Gazette* 4 (June 1970):
70–7. Rpt in *The Advocate* 12 (November-December 1977): 2–8.
Illustrates, with examples from Dickens, Austen, and Emily Bronte, the
unique fascination that British novelists have had with the law and discusses the criticism of the law that begins in the nineteenth century. This

criticism recognizes that the law is a human and therefore a fallible creation and that it involves class privilege and prejudice, both social and sexual. Examines the theme of counter-violence as it is found in revolutionary traditions, especially in the literature of revenge, and observes that the Jewish and Christian heritage consists 'very largely' of legal metaphors: redeemer, devil, judgment, and testament. Points out that 'all respect for the law is a product of the social imagination, and the social imagination is what literature directly addresses.' Originally presented as an address to the Ontario branch of the Canadian Bar Association, 7 February 1970.

D202 'Communications.' *Listener* 84 (9 July 1970): 33–5. Rpt in *The Little, Brown Reader*, 2nd ed, ed Marcia Stubbs and Sylvan Barnet (Boston: Little, Brown 1980), 420–5; in *Mass Media: Forces in Our Society*, 2nd ed, ed Francis H. Voelker and Ludmila A. Voelker (New York: Harcourt Brace Jovanovich 1975), 402–6; and in *Mass Communications: Selected Readings for Librarians*, ed K.J. McGarry (Hamden, Conn: Linnet Books; np: Clive Bingley 1972), 119–24.
Illustrates the affinities between primitive oral culture and the electronic media and the close connection between the mass media and the anxieties of the centres of power. Argues against that version of McLuhanism that claims that the simultaneous or mosaic form of understanding will replace the linear form that comes from reading. Maintains instead that the opposition is not between two kinds of media but between two mental operations and that the linear, printed document is what makes criticism and community possible. Portions of this essay, originally presented as a BBC talk, transmitted 20 June 1970, appear in a somewhat different version in *CP*.

D203 'Foreword.' *Dialogue sur la traduction à propos du 'Tombeau des rois,'* by Anne Hébert and Frank Scott (Montreal: Editions HMH 1970), 9–14, trans as 'Préface' by Jean Simard, 15–21
Comments on Frank Scott's translation of Anne Hébert's poem and on their dialogue about the translation. Speaks of the translator's aim as that of capturing the 'real poetic meaning,' rather than simply the 'over-thought' or explicit, literal meaning. Believes that the dialogue between Scott and Hébert teaches much about 'the kind of craftsmanship that goes into the making of poetry.'

D204 'Myth and Poetry,' *The Concise Encyclopedia of English and American Poets and Poetry*, ed Stephen Spender and Donald Hall (London: Hutchinson 1970), 187–90
Defines myth as a story about a god and thus an episode in mythology. Traces the several stages in the development of mythology and gives three characteristics of a totally developed mythology: (1) it provides the 'outlines of a total verbal communication'; (2) it enables poets 'to make unusually full use of metaphor, of natural imagery, of an imaginative identification of human emotion and nature'; and (3) it presents in its stories abstract literary patterns that are later displaced in the direction of

realism; thus, the same stories get told over and over. Concludes that 'a fully developed literature, as a whole, is what a fully developed mythology is in earlier ages.'

D205 'Spielarten der utopischen Literatur.' *Wunschtraum und Experiment: Vom Nutzen und Nachteil utopischen Denkens,* ed Frank E. Manuel, trans Otto Kimminich (Freiburg: Romach 1970), 52–74. A translation of 'Varieties of Literary Utopias' (see D151)

D206 'In Quest of Identity and Unity.' *Globe Magazine,* 20 February 1971, 8–9, 12. A reprint of portions of F's 'Preface' to *BG*

D207 'Edebiyatta Ütopya Türleri,' *Türk Dili* 23 (March 1971): 510–31, trans (Akşit Göktürk. A translation of 'Varieties of Literary Utopias' (see D151)

D208 'Education and the Rejection of Reality.' *University of Toronto Graduate* 3 (June 1971): 49–55
Maintains that 'real' life can be discovered for the most part only through a structured, disciplined study of the arts and sciences. Such study takes us beyond the continuous illusion of life in the world. Argues for the importance of adults' returning to the university as full-time students. Claims that continuity and unity are the two important principles lying behind 'the sense of wholeness of social vision,' which is the central need of our age. Such continuity can develop when the habit of reading becomes the basis of education. Tape-recorded from an address at the first session of Reading 71 Conference, York University.

D209 'The Quality of Life in the Seventies.' *University of Toronto Graduate* 3 (June 1971): 38–48. Rpt in *The Best of Times/The Worst of Times,* ed Hugh A. Stevenson et al (Toronto: Holt, Rinehart and Winston 1972), 33–41.
Sees the late sixties, particularly the radical political movements, as 'an age of undirected revolution.' The polarizing attitudes that the media try to establish also exhibit the quality of undirected revolution, and the self-destructive tendencies of both bear a close resemblance to war. Foresees the seventies as being a time of greater introversion, which is related to the fragmenting of social vision and therefore one of the chief problems of our age. Hopes that during the seventies the arts will recover 'something of their real function of binding together the community in time as well as space.' Originally presented at the University of Toronto Alumni Association's Seminar 71.

D210 'The Definition of a University.' *Alternatives in Education* (The Ontario Institute for Studies in Education Fifth Anniversary Lectures), ed Bruce Rusk (Toronto: General 1971), 71–90. Rpt in *DG,* 139–55. Selections from six paragraphs rpt in *Orbit* 2 (June 1971): 14.
Drawing on his early educational experiences, concludes that his own schooling was a form of penal servitude. In spite of the benevolent aim of universal education, it provided almost no sense of social participation. The reasons for this were, first, that schools developed habitual and binding attitudes that produced anxiety and prevented change; and, second, that society insisted on subordinating and protecting its young people, consid-

ering them only as immature adolescents not yet ready for real society. But the permanent form of society is not what appears to us on the surface. It is rather that form of society revealed in the arts and sciences, 'the genuinely organized structures of human civilization.' By studying these structures we learn to become dissatisfied with the temporary and transient appearance of society. This is one of the chief functions of the university, and the university should not be limited to persons of a single age group. Speaks also about the limitations of the seminar as a means of instruction, the problems of student representation on curricular and administrative bodies in the university, the University of Toronto honour course, and the difficult job the university has in trying to sustain its relation to society while at the same time asserting its authority to criticize society and to develop a new social vision. Originally presented as a lecture at the Ontario Institute for Studies in Education, Toronto, 4 November 1970.

D211 'Littérature et mythe.' *Poétique: revue de théorie et d'analyse littéraires*, no 8 (1971), 489–514, trans Jacques Ponthoreau. A translation of 'Literature and Myth' (see D172)

D212 'Universities and the Deluge of Cant.' *University of Waterloo Gazette* 12 (14 June 1972): [2]. Slightly abridged version with the same title rpt in *Globe and Mail*, 4 July 1972, 7; in *The Strand* [Victoria College, Univ of Toronto], [September] 1972, 3, and in other newspapers; rpt as 'Substitutes for Thinking' in *Technocracy Digest*, no 226 (November 1972), 8–9.

Reviews the history of the anti-intellectual bloc in society that has deluged the university with substitutes for thinking from the time of the Depression through the 1960s, using such cant as 'elitist,' 'ivory tower,' and 'establishment.' Notes that the demonstrations of the 1960s were really rituals. Like all rituals, these expressed beliefs without any action. Maintains that there is no substitute for education in achieving genuine social ends; that the real authority of society is 'the authority of the arts and sciences, the authority of logical reasoning, uncooked evidence, repeatable experiments, verifiable scholarship, precise and disciplined imagination'; and that university education has a moral, as well as an intellectual and a social, dimension. Originally presented as a convocation address, given on the occasion of F's being awarded an honorary degree at the University of Waterloo, 27 May 1972.

D213 'Substitutes for Thinking.' *Technocracy Digest*, no 226 (November 1972), 8–9. Same essay as 'Universities and the Deluge of Cant' (see D212)

D214 'Pistis and Mythos.' *Annual Proceedings of the Canadian Society for the Study of Religion* (Montreal 1972), 29–33

The summary of the argument of a talk presented by F at the annual convention of the Learned Societies of Canada, McGill University, Montreal, June 1972. Discusses a number of topics having to do with the language of faith that emerged from his teaching a course on the typology and symbolism of the English Bible. Among the topics examined are: the *mythos* and imagery of the Bible, the metaphorical quality of biblical language, the difference between mythical and historical literature, and the nature of belief. The argument is an embryonic form of many of the issues treated in much more detail in *GC*.

D215 'Canadian Scene: Explorers and Observers.' *Canadian Landscape Painting 1670–1930*. Text and catalogue by R.H. Hubbard (Madison: Univ of Wisconsin, Elvehjem Art Center 1973), 1–4. Rpt in *Art News* 72 (April 1973): 68–9.

Looks at the extent to which Canadian political separation and Canadian one-dimensional geography have influenced the country's painting. Observes that the primary rhythm of English-Canadian painting has been a 'forward-thrusting rhythm,' strongly attached to Britain but 'federal' in its attitude toward Canada. Traces this rhythm through the documentary painters, Tom Thomson, the Group of Seven, and Emily Carr. Sees the modern artistic consciousness, as represented by Morrice, Milne, and Fitzgerald, to be more 'cool, detached, urbane, and limited in objectives' as well as more international. Written for the exhibition, 'The Artist and the Land: Canadian Landscape Painting, 1670–1930,' which opened at the Elvehjem Art Center, University of Wisconsin, Madison, 11 April 1973.

D216 'The Search for Acceptable Words.' *Daedalus* 102 (Spring 1973): 11–26. Rpt in *SM*, 3–26.

A brief intellectual autobiography. Outlines his own work as a critic, contrasting it both to the old philological tradition in scholarship and to the New Criticism. Reviews the history of his interest in Blake. Comments on the nature of the expository treatise, McLuhanism, the centrality of the Bible in Western culture, myth as a structural principle of literature, and the communications media.

D217 'Agon and Logos: Revolution and Revelation.' *The Prison and the Pinnacle*, ed Balachandra Rajan (Toronto: Univ of Toronto Press 1973), 135–63. Rpt in *SM*, 201–27.

Analyses Milton's *Samson Agonistes* from the perspective of its two levels of tragic action: the lower level of nemesis, in which disaster is the result of folly or wrongdoing, and the higher or Christian level, in which tragedy is part of the analogy of law. Shows how Samson is an *agonistes* in two senses: as an entertainer or actor in a Philistine carnival and as a tragic hero or defeated champion. In the reversal of the action, which Milton expresses in the 'complex imagery of light and darkness,' Samson's tragedy becomes a triumph, and thus he is made into a dramatic prototype of Christ. Maintains that Milton's revolutionary mind does not reject tragedy but tries to explain it as something having both a cause and a cure. Originally presented as a paper at the University of Western Ontario in 1971 to mark the tercentenary of the publication of *Samson Agonistes* and *Paradise Regained*.

D218 'Wallace Stevens and the Variation Form.' *Literary Theory and Structure: Essays in Honor of William K. Wimsatt*, ed Frank Brady, John Palmer, and Martin Price (New Haven: Yale Univ Press 1973), 395–414. Rpt in *SM*,

275–94 and in *English Studies Today*, 5th series, ed Sencer Tonguç (Istanbul: Malbassi 1973), 389–404.

A study of Stevens's 'variation form,' which is similar to the presentation of a musical theme in analogous but different settings. Cites Stevens's own conviction that every image in a poem restates the poet's attitude toward the subject and that every image is the image-maker's invention of reality. Lists the characteristics of the interplay between imagination and reality for Stevens. These two elements may be in opposition: the imagination may heighten reality by stressing its unreal features, it may serve as the informing principle of reality, or it may inform reality through fictions and myths. Presented originally, in a shorter version, at the IAUPE Conference in Istanbul, September 1971.

D219 'The Renaissance of Books.' *Visible Language* 8 (Summer 1974): 225–40. Rpt in *SM*, 49–65.

Places the book among the other instruments of communication in modern society. Characterizes the paperback revolution as a change in the conception of the book from a cultural monument to an intellectual tool. Examines the cultural context of this change and considers briefly the effect of radio and television on twentieth-century society. Points out that the book, because it can be reread, can thus be consulted at will as a stationary focus for the community. It is also the technological instrument that makes democracy possible, and public access to written documents is the principle that keeps democracy functioning. Originally presented as an address to the Ferguson Seminar on Publishing, College of William and Mary, Williamsburg, 15 November 1973.

D220 'The Decline of the West by Oswald Spengler.' *Daedalus* 103 (Winter 1974): 1–13. Rpt as 'Spengler Revisited' in *SM*, 179–98.

Examines the romantic framework of Spengler's argument – his theory of the organic rhythm of Western history, which has gone through two cycles of four main stages. Sees Spengler's morphological view of history as producing imaginative visions very much like those in works of literature: 'If *The Decline of the West* were nothing else, it would still be one of the world's greatest Romantic poems.' Observes that many writers, especially poets, have in practice accepted Spengler's main thesis. Separates the confusion and rhetorical stridency in Spengler's book from his genuine prophetic vision, which has the 'power to be expanded and exhilarate the mind' to a greater degree than any of his critics.

D221 *Bungaku no Genkei*, trans Iketani Toshitada. Nagoya: Nagoya eibei gendaishi kenkyû-kai 1974. 12 pp

A translation of 'The Archetypes of Literature' (see D49), issued as a separate monograph (see C7).

D222 'Introduzione.' *Il freddo verde elemento* by Irving Layton, trans Amleto Lorenzini (Turin: Einaudi 1974), v–viii. English version rpt in *Irving Layton: The Poet and His Critics*, ed Seymour Mayne (Toronto: McGraw-Hill Ryerson 1978), 251–4.

An introduction to the Italian translation of Layton's *The Cold Green Element*.
Judges Layton to be 'perhaps the most outstanding poetic personality in
contemporary Canada.' Calls attention both to the satire and moral seriousness in Layton's poetry, particularly as it comes from his critique
of bourgeois religion, politics, and culture, and to its eloquent lyricism.

D223 'The Times of the Signs: An Essay on Science and Mythology.' *On A
Disquieting Earth Five Hundred Years after Copernicus* (Ottawa: Royal Society
of Canada 1974), 59–84. Rpt in *SM*, 66–96.
Sees the opposition between the Ptolemaic and the Copernican views of
the universe as 'essentially a collision between two mythologies, two
pictures or visions, not of reality, but of man's sense of the meaning of
reality in relation to himself.' Traces the influence of the Copernican
revolution throughout English literature from Milton, Donne, and Cowley
to the last half of the nineteenth century. Concludes by examining the
opposition between the scientific world of nature and the mythological
world of art, claiming that we must continue to live in both worlds,
the former of which is technical and progressive and the latter of which is
metaphorical and recreative. Originally presented as an address to the
Royal Society of Canada, November 1973.

D224 'Charms and Riddles.' Paper presented to the New England Stylistics
Club, Northeastern University, Boston, 3 March 1975. First published in
SM, 123–47.
Classifies charms and riddles as 'generic seeds or kernels,' different from
genres of the imagination, such as metaphors and image-clusters, and
genres of structure, such as epic and drama. Illustrates through numerous
examples the associations that charm has with song, spell, magic, incantation, the recitation of powerful names, repetitive poetic devices, sinister
siren-songs, elegiac rhetoric, nightmare visions, political oratory, and myth;
and the associations that riddle, which is charm in reverse, has with
sense, reason, the linking of the visual and the conceptual in the mind,
puns, jokes, contests, comic resolutions, verbal traps, poetic ideas and
thoughts. Shows how charm and riddle are really differences in imaginative
direction, charm taking us into the mythological universe of traditional
names and mysterious powers, and riddle taking us into the world of nature, sense experience, and reason.

D225 'Romance as Masque.' Paper presented at the Symposium on Shakespeare's
Romances, University of Alabama, 16 October 1975. First published in
SM, 148–78. Rpt in slightly different form in *Shakespeare's Romances Reconsidered*, ed Carol McGinnis Kay and Henry E. Jacobs (Lincoln: Univ of Nebraska Press 1978), 11–39.
Part 1 is a revised version of 'Old and New Comedy' (see D194). Discusses
in part 2 the organizing principles of the masque, the cosmology it reflects,
and its characteristic imagery, as these are embodied in the masque and
antimasque from Jonson to Milton. Concludes that the masque is structurally similar to the polar form and the spectacle of Old Comedy. In part

3, examines the affinities of Shakespeare's comedies and romances with the masque, antimasque, Old Comedy, and New Comedy.

D226 'Expanding Eyes.' *Critical Inquiry* 2 (Winter 1975): 199–216. Rpt in *SM* 99–122.

Traces the development of his own thought, beginning with his early contact with Blake and continuing through the other chief influences upon him: Spengler, Frazer, Ruskin, Graves and Vico. Illustrates the ways in which the various imaginative visions of these thinkers contributed to the development of his own critical perspective. Comments on the importance of the descending or tragic cultural myths (those of Adonis and Hermes) and of the ascending or comic ones (those of Prometheus and Eros) on the unity in the arts, and on their experiential and social dimension. Suggests throughout that the theory of literature in *AC* has been only one aspect of the critical task.

D227 'Canada: New World without Revolution.' *Preserving the Canadian Heritage/La préservation de patrimoine canadien*, ed Keith J. Laidler (Ottawa: Royal Society of Canada 1975), 15–25. Rpt with minor editorial changes in *DG*, 167–80. Portions of the first four paragraphs rpt as 'The Root of the Problem' in *Heritage Canada* 5 (May 1979): 33.

Sees the Canadian social environment as one in which 'Cartesian consciousness' has triumphed – a consciousness that focuses not on nature but on the geometrical shapes man has imposed on nature and that has resulted in human withdrawal and in destructive social forces. Laments the revolutionary habit of mind that sees no connections with the past and that has shifted the centres of population, but sees the seeds of hope in a newly emerging social vision based upon a balance between man and nature. Believes that the Canadian heritage can be preserved only by a sharpened sense of the past and by the realization that the genuine vitality of a culture is in its arts and society's response to them. Originally presented as an address to the fourteenth Royal Society of Canada Symposium, 'Preserving the Canadian Heritage,' Ottawa, 7 October 1975.

D228 'Foreword.' *The Child as Critic* by Glenna Davis Sloan (New York: Teachers College Press, Columbia Univ 1975; rev ed 1984), xiii–xv

Emphasizes that imaginative growth occurs when the teaching of reading is approached not as a mechanical skill but as a continuously active and leisurely process, and that stories of magic and fantasy can lead us to become Prosperos rather than Calibans.

D229 'View of Canada: Never a Believer in a Happy Ending.' *Globe and Mail*, 6 April 1976, 7

Extracts from the script of 'Journey without Arrival,' a CBC telecast in the 'Images of Canada' series, in which F examines a number of recurrent Canadian themes: the absence of a definite sense of beginnings, the relation of the problem of identity to the fact that the centres of power were elsewhere, and the 'balance sheet' mentality ('Americans like to make money; Canadians like to audit it.') Sees E.J. Pratt as a 'landmark figure in

the development of the Canadian imagination' because he understood
so well its central tragic theme and helped put Canadians in possession of
their past. On 'Journey without Arrival,' see H44.

D230 'The Bush Garden: Essays on the Canadian Imagination.' *Vic Report* 4
(June 1976): 6–7, 13
A reprint of the preface to *BG*.

D231 'Preface.' *ADE and ADFL Bulletins*, September 1976, v
Introduces this special joint issue on 'Employment and the Profession' by
placing the problems that confront teachers of language and literature
in the context of the present social order, the educational system, and the
university.

D232 'The Responsibilities of the Critic.' *MLN* 91 (October 1976): 797–813
Argues that the responsibility of the critic is 'to lead us from what poets
and prophets meant, or thought they meant, to the inner structure of what
they said.' Uses Vico's vision of 'poetic wisdom' to examine the nature
of mythological or poetic structure, and Vico's cyclic conception of history
to illustrate the precedence of poetic mythology to historical or discursive
writing. Extracts three elements of mythology in the biblical tradition
that are implicit in Vico: law and wisdom (which are horizontally related to
society) and prophecy (which is vertically related). Examines the nature
of the prophetic dimension of the arts and maintains that criticism is also
related to prophecy: 'If the critic is to recognize the prophetic ... he needs
to be prophetic too: his model is John the Baptist ... whose critical moment
came with recognizing a still greater power than his own.' The critic's
chief aim is recognition. Originally presented as a lecture at Johns Hopkins
University, 20 February 1976.

D233 'Conclusion.' *Literary History of Canada: Canadian Literature in English*, 2nd
ed, 3 vols, ed Carl Klinck (Toronto: Univ of Toronto Press 1976), vol 3:
318–32. Partially rpt as 'The American Way of Life Is Slowly Being Canadianized' in *Chelsea Journal* 3 (July-August 1977): 190–3 and, in Chinese, in
Waiguo Wenxue (Foreign Literatures) [Beijing Foreign Language Institute],
no 10 (1981), 3–11, trans Xia Zukui. Rpt in the *University of Toronto Graduate*
4 (Winter 1976): 6–7; in *DG*, 71–80; and, in Hebrew, as 'Toldot Hassifrut
Hakkanadit: Sikum' in *Mimivhar Hassifrut Hakkandit/Esrim Vahamishah Sofrei
Tzameret: Antologiah*, ed Marion Richmond and Richard Weaver (Tel Aviv:
Yachdav United Publishers 1982), 69–79.
Assesses the directions in Canadian cultural history from the time that he
wrote the 'Conclusion' to the first edition of *Literary History of Canada* in
1965 (see D154). Looks favourably upon a developing spirit of nationalism
in Canada that is different from a parallel development in the United
States. Canadian identity is not determined by its cultural heroes, revolutionary and social manifestos, or a sense of cultural continuity. In effect, the
identities of Canada and the United States in recent years have begun to
change places: 'the American way of life is slowly becoming Canadianized.'

Believes that Canadian culture is moving away from its introversion, sense of inferiority, and diffidence. This movement is suggested by a growing conservative tendency in thought and professionalism in literature.

D234 'History and Myth in the Bible.' *The Literature of Fact: Selected Papers from the English Institute,* ed Angus Fletcher (New York: Columbia Univ Press 1976), 1–19

Distinguishes between imperial and biblical monotheism, noting the revolutionary character of the latter, especially its dialectical and polarizing way of thinking and its intense concentration on some future reversal of the social order. Argues that whatever kernels of historical accuracy lie behind the biblical account the significance of this account is spiritual rather than historical, and that 'the historical narrative in the Bible is not really history but a *mythos* or narrative principle on which historical incidents are strung.' Characterizes this *mythos* as the U-shaped positive cycle of *Heilsgeschichte,* which is more important than than the inverted-U-shape of *Weltgeschichte.* Believes that the narrative of the Bible should be read as poetry and that 'literary criticism of the Bible, in the sense of a criticism that takes seriously its mythical and metaphorical aspect, has barely begun.' Such a criticism, which relies on the language of imagination, can take us to the spiritual reality beyond both language and imagination. Originally presented as a lecture to the English Institute, 1 September 1975.

D235 'National Consciousness in Canadian Culture.' *Transactions of the Royal Society of Canada,* 4th series, 14 (1976): 57–69. Rpt with minor editorial changes in *DG,* 41–55; and as 'Presa di coscienza nazionale nella letteratura canadese' in *Argomenti canadesi,* ed Amleto Lorenzini (Rome: np 1978), 26–42, trans Silvia Albertazzi, rev by Amleto Lorenzini; abridged version of this Italian translation appears as 'Una letteratura divenuta maggiorenne' in *Vita,* 18 June 1979, 3.

Sees the Canadian national consciousness as descending culturally from Tory radicalism; thus, it embodies a different set of assumptions and imaginative patterns from those found in revolutionary cultural traditions, like those in the United States. Canada, too, has had a different understanding of violence; has not adhered to historical notions of linear progress, which, as in the United States, logically relate the future to the past; and has been more meditatively shocked by the natural world. Discovers in Canadian writers and artists the recurring themes of 'self conflict, of the violating of nature, of individuals uncertain of their social context' – themes that have given Canadian culture 'an extraordinary vigour and historical significance.' Originally presented as an address to the Royal Society of Canada symposium on 'The Revolutionary Tradition in Canadian and American Society,' 6 June 1976.

D236 'Preface.' *Agghiacciante simmetria: Uno studio su William Blake* (Milan: Longanesi 1976), 9–10

A preface to the Italian translation of *FS* (see A1d). Speaks of the way in which Blake helped him to develop the theories in *AC*, Blake being 'the first poet in European literature to try to redesign [the] mythological universe' of the Bible.

D237 'Summation.' *Symposium on Television Violence/Colloque sur la violence à la télévision* (Ottawa: Canadian Radio-television and Telecommunications Commission 1976), 206–15; French translation, 215–26. Portions appear as 'La violence a la télévision est un phénomène actuel que nous ne pouvons éviter' in *Le Devoir*, 11 October 1975, 13.

Places television violence within the context of human violence in general. Sees the solution to the problem to be not some form of censorship or prohibition, which are simply other forms of violence, but the raising of the whole level of society. This means that the problem of violence is an educational problem. Children should be taught the conventions of the medium. Only with educated imaginations can they develop the proper attitude of detached concern toward the violence they see on television. Originally presented at the Symposium on Television Violence, Queen's University, Kingston, Ont, 24–26 August 1975.

D238 'Presidential Address 1976.' *PMLA* 92 (May 1977): 385–91. A slightly abridged and edited version rpt as 'Teaching the Humanities Today' in *DG*, 91–101. Examines the nature of the scholarly life and its relation to advances in knowledge, and of the university as a social counter-environment. Claims that in this environment students can become free only with discipline, directed attention, and practice, much of their freedom coming from disciplined attention to the use of language. Sees the common cause that unites teaching and scholarship, as well as creation and criticism, to be a vision in which the traditions of wisdom and prophecy are identified. Originally presented at the annual meeting of the Modern Language Association, New York, December 1976.

D239 'The American Way of Life Is Slowly Being Canadianized.' *Chelsea Journal* 3 (July-August 1977): 190–3
An abridged version of the 'Conclusion' to *Literary History of Canada* (see D233).

D240 'Culture as Interpenetration.' An address presented to UNESCO's International Council of Philosophy and Humanistic Studies, Montreal, 16 September 1977. First published in *DG*, 15–25.
Examines the relations between Canadian culture and the social conditions that produced it, seeing a parallel between these underlying conditions and the argument of Pynchon's *Gravity's Rainbow*, which opposes the harshness of the natural environment to the human need to order it, and which opposes the destructive impulse to the creative one. Shows the effects that the religious and philosophical assumptions of baroque Christianity and Cartesianism have had on death-wish paranoia and destructive attitudes toward nature. Illustrates the various literary responses to the Canadian political situation and its environment from the colonial period to the twentieth century. Sees this response as moving through three

phases: the imitative and content-oriented phase, dominated by mercantilistic assumptions; the documentary phase, still dominated by content; and the phase of interpenetration and the international idiom.

D241 'A Summary of the *Options* Conference.' *University of Toronto Bulletin* 31 (24 October 1977): 6–7. Portions appear as 'Lively Culture the Answer to Canadian Unity?' *Globe and Mail*, 18 October 1977, 7.

Summarizes the main issues that came from a conference devoted to the question of Canada's future under confederation: separatism, economic nationalism, political regionalism, provincial rights, and cultural decentralization. Sees the general response of the conference to be opposed to separatism on political and economic grounds, although believes that decentralization makes more sense culturally. For the videotape of this talk see H46.

D242 'The Utopian State of Mind.' *New Statesman* 77 (23 and 30 December 1977): 896–900

A reprint of 'The University and Personal Life' (see D185).

D243 'Canadian Culture Today.' *Voices of Canada: An Introduction to Canadian Culture*, ed Judith Webster (Burlington, Vt: Association for Canadian Studies in the United States 1977), 1–4 (in English and French). Rpt, except for the first paragraph, as 'Sharing the Continent,' in *DG*, 57–70; rpt in a slightly abridged form as 'Canada's Emerging Identity' in *Toronto Star*, 28 June 1980, B1, B4.

Brings together a number of previously argued points about Canadian history, geography, identity, and culture: its east–west geographic thrust and the separation of its regions from each other, resulting in feelings of solitude; the interest of its artists in documentary landscape painting, which is an effort to humanize an alien nature; the development of the linear, unified perspective in poetry by E.J. Pratt; the fact that cultural movements are decentralized and thus different from political and economic ones; the problems that separatism creates for culture; the effects on the imagination of Canada's having had no eighteenth century; and the sense of the close relation of the people to the land throughout Canada's history. Contrasts throughout the development of the Canadian consciousness with that of the United States. Believes that Canadian culture has now developed maturity and discipline. Originally presented as an address at the Symposium on Twentieth-century Canadian Culture, Washington, DC, 2 February 1977

D244 'Haunted by Lack of Ghosts: Some Patterns in the Imagery of Canadian Poetry.' *The Canadian Imagination: Dimensions of a Literary Culture*, ed David Staines (Cambridge: Harvard Univ Press 1977), 22–45

Contrasts the Canadian sense of identity with the American, and illustrates the themes that resulted from the Canadian poets' being 'Cartesian ghosts caught in the machine that we have assumed nature to be': guilt, loneliness, alienation, and the sense of being swallowed by the leviathan. Notices, however, that more recent Canadian poets have become less rhetorical and

more imaginative and thus view the causes of human loneliness and
fragility in psychological rather than in purely external terms. Too, more
recent writers have a different sense of tradition – one in which the
past tends to manifest itself simultaneously in space rather than sequentially
in time. Illustrates his thesis by drawing examples primarily from the
writing at Atwood, Reaney, Pratt, Wilfred Watson, John Newlove, Hermia
Fraser, Susan Musgrave, A.M. Klein, Gwendolyn MacEwen, Jay Macpherson, and Alden Nowlan. Originally presented as a lecture at Harvard
University, 26 April 1976.

D245 'An Address by Dr. H. Northrop Frye, 1978 Recipient of the Royal Bank
Award, Toronto, Ontario, September 18, 1978.' Montreal: Royal Bank 1978.
16 pp. Rpt as 'The Teacher of Humanities in Twentieth-Century Canada'
in *Grad Post*, 2 November 1978, 5–7; as 'Royal Bank Award Address:
September 1978' in *CEA Critic* 42 (January 1980): 2–9; rpt in an abridged
form as 'The Rear-View Mirror' in *DG*, 181–90; and also in an abridged form
as 'Thoughts of a Canadian' in *Report on Confederation* 2 (November 1978):
30–1.
Accepts this award, given annually to those 'whose outstanding achievement is of such importance that it is contributing to human welfare and the
common good,' in the name of all teachers of the humanities. Speaks out
against futurism and other 'phoney mythologies' that fail to understand
'the burden of the past and the meaning of tradition.' Reflects on the importance of decentralizing both culture and the university: such a process
can help to overcome social anxieties and establish genuine communities
of concern. Believes that the function of liberal education is to help students
transfer their loyalties from conformity and stock response 'to the real
world of human constructive power.'

D246 'The Teacher of Humanities in Twentieth-Century Canada.' *Grad Post*, 2
November 1978, 5–7
A reprint of F's Royal Bank Award address (see D245).

D247 'Thoughts of a Canadian.' *Report on Confederation* 2 (November 1978): 30–1
An abridged form of F's Royal Bank Award address (see D245).

D248 'Prefazione all'edizione italiana.' *La scrittura secolare: Studio sulla struttura del
'romance,'* trans Amleto Lorenzini (Bologna: Il Mulino 1978), 17 (see A15b)
On the meaning of the term 'romance' as it is used throughout the book,
and on the use of the phrase 'secular scripture' to designate those stories
in which the hero represents the possibilities of human rather than divine
existence.

D249 'Presa di coscienza nazionale nella letteratura canadese.' *Argomenti canadesi*,
trans Silvia Albertazzi, ed Amleto Lorenzini (Rome: np 1978), 26–42.
Abridged version appears as 'Una letteratura divenuta maggiorenne' in
Vita, 18 June 1979, 3.
A translation of 'National Consciousness in Canadian Culture' (see D235).

D250 'The Root of the Problem.' *Heritage Canada* 5 (May 1979): 33

A reprint of portions of the first four paragraphs of 'Canada: New World without Revolution' (see D227).

D251 'The Teacher's Source of Authority.' *Curriculum Inquiry* 9 (Spring 1979): 3–11. Rpt in *DG*, 125–35.

Argues that the real source of authority in the humanities is not method, as in the sciences, nor the teacher, but the subject being taught. Speaks of the importance of practice and habit in the educational process, the end of which is recognition on two levels: the lower level of pleasure and serenity and the higher level of informing vision. Originally presented as a lecture at the annual meeting of the American Educational Research Association, Toronto, 30 March 1978.

D252 'Literature, History and Language.' *Bulletin of the Midwest Modern Language Association* 12 (Fall 1979): 1–7. Rpt with minor typographical changes as 'Literary History' in *New Literary History* 12 (Winter 1981): 219–25 and in *The Horizon of Literature*, ed Paul Hernadi (Lincoln: Univ of Nebraska Press 1982), 43–51.

Outlines Vico's understanding of the three phases of language (hiero-glyphic, hieratic, and demotic) and applies these to the use of language since Old Testament times. Shows that the three phases manifest them-selves, respectively, as the metaphoric, the metonymic (Platonic dialectic and other forms of continuous, deductive, and analogical prose), and the descriptive (post-Baconian deductive prose). In literature these three phases appear primarily as poetry, allegory, and realism, respectively. Maintains that the Bible belongs chiefly to first-phase language, and that the primary function of poetry is 'to keep recreating the first phase of lan-guage and insisting on it as a valid form of linguistic activity during the domination of the other phases.' Originally presented as a lecture at the conference on Theories of Literary History, University of Toronto, 28–31 March 1979. Appears in a more fully developed form in 'The Meaning of Recreation: Humanism in Society' (see D257) and in *GC*, chapt. 1.

D253 'Roy Daniells.' *English Studies in Canada* 5 (Winter 1979): vii–ix

A tribute to Daniells, calling attention to his scholarship, his urbanity and humour, his criticism on Canadian literature, and his poetry.

D254 'Royal Bank Award Address: September 1978.' *CEA Critic* 42 (January 1980): 2–9

A reprint of 'An Address by Dr H. Northrop Frye' (see D245).

D255 'Canada's Emerging Identity.' *Toronto Star*, 28 June 1980, B1, B4

A reprint, slightly abridged, of 'Canadian Culture Today' (see D243).

D256 'Across the River and out of the Trees.' *University of Toronto Quarterly* 50 (Fall 1980): 1–14. Rpt in *The Arts in Canada: The Last Fifty Years*, ed W.J. Keith and B.-Z. Shek (Toronto: Univ of Toronto Press 1980), 1–14 and in *DG*, 26–40.

Reviews the history of the *University of Toronto Quarterly* and praises the scholars whose writings defined its humanistic thrust. Traces the develop-

ment of Canadian literature from the 1930s to its flowering in the 1960s
and beyond, noting that the Canadian environment, rather than any political or economic factors, determined its essential character. Examines the
contributions to Canadian scholarship following the 1930s, commenting on
his own role as a reviewer in the 1950s and on the influence that intellectuals, such as Innis and McLuhan, had on his understanding of the poetic
and social imagination and of the subculture produced by the mass media.

D257 'The Meaning of Recreation: Humanism in Society.' *Iowa Review* 11 (Winter
1980): 1–9
Notes the importance of Vico's theories of history and language for the
literary critics' understanding of the Bible. Outlines Vico's three stages of
society (poetic, aristocratic, and democratic) and the three corresponding
phases of language (hieroglyphic, hieratic, and demotic). Describes the
characteristics of *langage* for each of these phases and shows how the Bible
belongs primarily to the metaphorical or hieroglyphic phase, though it
is also related to the hieratic or oratorical phase, producing kergyma or
proclamation. Sees the function of literature to be the continual recreation
in society of the first phase of language. Originally presented as a lecture
at the University of Iowa, 12 April 1979. The ideas in this essay are similar
to those in 'Literature, History and Language' (see D252) and are developed in greater detail in chapter 1 of GC.

D258 'Il Cortegiano.' *Quaderni d'italianistica* 1, no 1 (1980): 1–14
The English version of *Il 'Cortegiano' in una società senza cortigiani* (see C9).

D259 'On Fiction,' 'On Poetry,' and 'On Drama.' *The Practical Imagination: Stories,
Poems, Plays*, ed Northrop Frye, Sheridan Baker, and George Perkins
(New York: Harper & Row 1980), 2–8, 400–12, and 874–80. 'On Poetry' rpt
in *The Practical Imagination: An Introduction to Poetry*, ed Northrop Frye,
Sheridan Baker, and George Perkins (New York: Harper & Row 1983), 2–14
[this is a reprinting as a separate volume of the section on poetry in *The
Practical Imagination* (1980)].
Introductions to the three genres for a textbook anthology. 'On Fiction'
emphasizes the distinction between the temporal pattern of oral fiction and
the added spatial dimension of written fiction. Examines also point of
view and narrative meaning. 'On Poetry' provides commentaries on sound,
figurative language, and allusion. 'On Drama' treats the topics of spectacle,
dramatic roles, and illusion and irony.

D260 'Beginnings.' *Today Magazine*, 3 January 1981, 3
Gives an account of his early life – from his years in Sherbrooke and
Moncton to his appointment at Victoria College. Talks about the influence
of his parents, his interest in music, his view of childhood as a 'waiting
period,' his interest in the ministry, and his discovering his sense of place
in the university. Based on a tape-recorded interview by Susan Gabori.

D261 'Detachment Not Possible.' *Globe and Mail*, 5 January 1981, 8
Eight paragraphs from F's keynote address to the American Association for

the Advancement of Science, Toronto, January 1981. The address is published in its entirety as 'The Bridge of Language' (see D264).

D262 'Another Look at "The Two Cultures." ' *Chemical & Engineering News* 59
(19 January 1981): 9
Six paragraphs from F's keynote lecture to the American Association for
the Advancement of Science, Toronto, January 1981. The lecture is published in its entirety as 'The Bridge of Language' (see D264).

D263 'Scientists: Professional Detachment vs Social Concern.' *Perception* 4 (March-
April 1981): 18–19
Ten paragraphs from F's keynote lecture to the American Association for
the Advancement of Science, Toronto, January 1981. The lecture is published in its entirety as 'The Bridge of Language' (see D264).

D264 'The Bridge of Language.' *Science* 212 (10 April 1981): 127–32. Portions rpt
as 'Another Look at "The Two Cultures" ' (see D262), as 'Scientists:
Professional Detachment vs Social Concern' (see D263), and as 'Detachment
Not Possible' (see D261).
Argues that the elements of human culture, including literature and the
sciences, grow out of social concern, and that, as they develop, their inner
structures begin to emerge, within which their practitioners begin to
make discoveries. When tensions arise with the concerns of society, a
divided loyalty also arises. In the past, social concerns that resisted science
or censored literature were usually wrong, but there are very intense
concerns today, such as environmental pollution, which appear to be
bringing us to a common meeting point. Originally presented as the keynote lecture at the American Association for the Advancement of Science,
Toronto, January 1981.

D265 'Metaphor I.' *American Poetry Review* 10 (September-October 1981): 21–7
Chapt 3 of *GC*, published in advance of the book, 53–77.

D266 'From *The Great Code.*' *Grand Street* 1 (Autumn 1981): 158–83
A selection of passages from the introduction and from chapter 4 ('Typology
I') of *GC*, published in advance of the book. The material here omits
some passages from xi–xiii and 78–104, and some of the material appears
in the final version in a slightly different form.

D267 'Myth.' *Antaeus*, no 43 (Autumn 1981), 64–84
Chapt 2 ('Myth I') of *GC*, 31–52, published in advance of the book. The
two texts, however, show some slight differences in wording.

D268 'The Double Mirror.' *Bulletin of the American Academy of Arts and Sciences* 35
(December 1981): 32–41
Mainly about F's preoccupation with the Bible as it relates to secular
literature and criticism. Observes that because biblical language is non-
descriptive and centripetal and because its structure is non-referential, the
phrase 'word of God' refers not to some historical presence behind the
Bible but to the book itself. The literal meaning of the Bible, then, is its
mythical or metaphorical meaning. Believes that the goal to reach consensus

in the interpretation of any text is a red herring and that texts should be
seen rather as the focus of a community. Such focus can help diminish the
egocentric and evaluative elements of criticism. Concludes by speculating
on the relationship between reading and Socrates's idea of reminding
and between language and freedom; on the uses of language that go
beyond aggressive argument; and on the inclusive rhetoric of love, with its
sexual symbolism, in the Bible.

D269 'The Beginning of the Word.' *Indirections* 6 (Winter 1981): 4–14
Maintains that the function of the teacher is 'to help create the structure of
the subject in the student's mind.' Sees mass education as crippling in
so far as it seeks to produce the disciplined, obedient citizen. Argues that
the aim of education rather is to recreate the cultural tradition so that
new structures of thought and imagination will emerge and have a revolutionary impact. The teacher's function, therefore, turns out to be Socratic:
like Socrates, the teacher should work to become a transparent medium for
his subject and a corrupter of youth, leading them beyond philistinism
and indifference toward a revolutionary individual and social vision.

D270 'Literary History.' *New Literary History* 12 (Winter 1981): 219–25. The same
essay as 'Literature, History and Language' (see D252).

D271 'The Chancellor's Message.' *Acta Victoriana* 106 (Spring 1982): 9
Part of a feature on E.J. Pratt celebrating his centenary. Recalls the leisurely
rhythm of Pratt's life and the romantic and heroic themes of his poetry.

D272 'The Meeting of Past and Future in William Morris.' *Studies in Romanticism*
21 (Fall 1982): 303–18
A study of the relation between art and society in the work of William
Morris. Discovers 'that there was quite a clear connection in Morris's mind
between romance and the state of society, and that that connection was
the reverse of the usual one.' His verse romances were Parnassian; committed to narrative, movement, and continuity; and given to 'running'
forms of meter and rhyme – all in sharp contrast to the verse of Hopkins.
Observes that Ruskin provided Morris with a definition of work as a
creative act and that Morris's attention to the minor arts was increasingly
the product of a social, moral, and political vision of collective skill. His
political stance in *News from Nowhere* emphasizes the revolutionary element
of fraternity, as opposed to *laissez-faire* capitalism, which forgets about
equality, and state socialism, which forgets about freedom. Morris's view
of art illustrates the principle that, while political and economic movements
tend spatially to centralize and temporarily to move toward the future,
culture tends to decentralize and look backward to congenial periods in the
past. His vision, finally, is a pre-revolutionary one of innocence.

D273 'Introduction.' *Rolls Royce and Other Poems* by Giorgio Bassani, trans Francesca Valente (Toronto: Aya Press 1982), [7–9]
Comments on each of the twelve poems in this collection, which are
primarily poems of exile and loneliness; an occasional epiphany, however,

does present itself to Bassani, suggesting the possibility of communication
and love.

D274 'Literature as Critique of Pure Reason.' *Descant* 14 (Spring 1983): 7–21. Rpt
in *Literary Half-Yearly* 24 (July 1983): 134–49.
Analyses the concept of reason and the metaphors behind it from the active
and aggressive forms found in such philosophers as Plato and Descartes
to the receptive and balancing reason found in the Hindu mood of Tamas
and in Kant's *Vernunft*. Sees Kant's *Verstand* as a limiting category, one
that exists on a lower level than the Hindu Sattva and Kant's *Urteilskraft*.
On this higher level 'the mind is neither reflecting on itself nor motivated
by desire, but is studying that curious assimilation of nature and art that
seems to underlie so much of what we call beauty.' It is on this level
that the concepts of creation and imagination emerge, offering a critique of
pure reason: the products of the imagination can liberate the human
mind and help build a human community in the face of the irrationalism
of modern society. Originally presented as the second of the 1982 Wiegand
Lectures.

D275 'The Ouroboros.' *Ethos* 1 (Summer 1983): 12–13
Examines the symbolism of the ouroboros as a natural, occult, and alchem-
ical image. Shows how the image continues to be found in romantic and
modern literature, from its negative uses in Blake, Shelley, and Pynchon to
its positive uses in Joyce and James Merrill.

D276 'Criticism and Environment.' *Adjoining Cultures as Reflected in Literature and
Language* (Proceedings of the xvth Triennial Congress of the Fédération
Internationale des Langues et Littératures Modernes), ed John X. Evans
and Peter Horwath (Tempe: Arizona State Univ 1983), 9–21
Emphasizes the effects on Canadian society of its geographical size, the
East-West migrations of people, mercantile ambitions, Anglo-French hostil-
ities, and the rhythms of frontier life. Examines the inverse military
history of Canada and the United States and the effects of this on Canadian
social history. Distinguishes three major phases in Canadian literature:
(1) the colonial; (2) the phase beginning with confederation and marked by
a search for a distinctive Canadian identity; and (3) a less nationalistic,
later phase during which Canadian writers turned toward other countries
for their perspectives. Calls for a new, interconnected conception of
criticism, one that will merge with communications theory and take account
of all the different aspects of language – metaphorical, metonymic, meditative, ordinary, and hieratic among others.

D277 'Literary and Linguistic Scholarship in a Postliterate World.' PMLA 99
(October 1984): 990–5
Argues that the social authority of both literature and criticism is rooted in
the 'counter-logical and counter-historical movements of myth and metaphor.' Uses examples from Plato, the New Testament, and Donne to
illustrate that such movements can lead us to 'a world of recovered identity,

both as ourselves and with something not ourselves.' Presented as an address at the Modern Language Association, New York, 27 December 1983.

D278 'Myth as the Matrix of Literature.' *Georgia Review* 38 (Fall 1984): 465–76
A very similar form of the argument developed in 'The Meeting of Past and Present in William Morris' (see D272), though here F gives more attention to explaining the literary and extraliterary types of myth, showing particularly how its decentralizing tendencies distinguish it from political and economic developments and how an awareness of the mythical and metaphorical basis of literature 'seems to be a central factor in helping us to get through a profoundly revolutionary period without a loss of freedom.'

D279 'The Authority of Learning.' *The Empire Club of Canada: Addresses 1983–1984.* [Toronto]: Empire Club Foundation 1984, 196–206
Uses Orwell's *1984* to illustrate that the debasement of language leads to permanent tyranny. Goes on to argue that the teaching of language and literature has the potential for fostering and encouraging social change. This is because they represent the genuine concerns of society, and, insofar as writers remain loyal to the demands of their art, they develop a social authority that can provide visions of a new world. Comments on the way in which Canada is especially suited to study the role of language and the humanities in culture. Published with an introduction by Douglas L. Derry, pp. 194–6. Presented as a talk to the Empire Club, Toronto, 19 January 1984. For a critique of F's address see L95.

D280 'The World as Music and Idea in Wagner's *Parsifal.*' *Carleton Germanic Papers* 12 (1984): 37–49
Places *Parsifal* in the contexts of the grail legend and Wagner's other operas. Examines Wagner's use of the principal grail symbols, particularly his complex use of Christian symbolism, and the ways in which he redistributes the themes of his sources, especially Wolfram. Maintains that *Parsifal* is a drama of the renounced quest and that the primary verbal action dramatizes Schopenhauer's worlds of will and idea. Concludes by discussing the tonality, structure, and themes of the libretto, saying that the music of *Parsifal* is what leads one to a larger vision of humanity. Originally presented as an address to the Toronto Wagner Society, 27 October 1982.

D281 'Vision and Cosmos.' *Biblical Patterns in Modern Literature*, ed David H. Hirsch and Nehama Aschkenasy (Chico, Calif: Scholars Press 1985), 5–17
On the nature of authority in literature and the arts. The argument is quite similar to that of 'Romance as the Survival of Eros' (see D287), though many of the illustrations are different. Originally presented as a lecture at Bar-Ilan University, Israel, 24 May 1982.

D282 'Approaching the Lyric.' *Lyric Poetry: Beyond New Criticism*, ed Chaviva Hošek and Patricia Parker (Ithaca, NY: Cornell Univ Press 1985), 31–7
Considers the lyric from the point of view of its tendency to block our

ordinary continuous experience of space and time. Looks at the way such blocking relates to both the speaker, as in the lyric of frustrated love, and to the reader, as in the lyric of the mental traveller. Comments on other temporal and visual forms of the lyric (eg, those of mental focus and meditation). Turns next to the aural dimension of the lyric – its association with music, magic, and mystery. Concludes by remarking on the influence of Poe and the New Critics on the study of the discontinuous poem. Originally presented as an introduction to the Conference on Lyric Poetry and the New New Criticism, Victoria College, 14 October 1982.

D283 'Lacan et la parole dans sa plénitude.' *Ornicar? revue du Champ freudien* 33 (April-June 1985): 11–14
Calls attention to several 'places where, in my study of the Bible, epigrams and observations I had read in Lacan began to reverberate.' Sees points of contact between his own concerns with language and literature and what Lacan says about transformation, the *nom du père*, the *stade du miroir*, and the distinction between *connaissance* and *savoir*.

D284 'The Expanding World of Metaphor.' *Journal of the American Academy of Religion* 53 (December 1985): 585–98
A slightly revised version of 1167. Presented as a plenary address at the annual meeting of the American Academy of Religion and the Society of Biblical Literature, Chicago, 8 December 1984.

D285 'La letteratura e la arti figurative.' *Lettere Italiane* 3 (1985): 285–98, trans Francesco Guardiani
Explores the temporal and spatial contexts, and the metaphors associated with both, for studying the visual and verbal arts. Traces the prejudices against representational art from the time of the biblical religions and Plato up through the iconic art of the Middle Ages. Notes that recurring arguments about realism in art are actually a function of the cultural and social conventions of the time. Traces the resistance to conventionalized standards of beauty in art and literature during the past two centuries, and concludes by observing that a world-wide metamorphosis in the verbal and visual arts, which have turned back to the primitive and mythic, provides 'the opportunity for renewed imaginative energy and a new freedom in seeing the world.' Originally presented as a paper at the Conference of the Associazione Internazionale per gli Studi di Lingua e Letteratura Italiana, Toronto, May 1985.

D286 'Introduction.' *Art and Reality: A Casebook of Concern*, ed Robin Blaser and Robert Dunham (Vancouver: Talonbooks 1986), 1–5
Reviews some of the main themes of the papers presented at the Art and Reality Conference, Simon Fraser University, 28 April 1983. Says that the papers 'are not so much about art and reality as about art and society.' Suggests that a theory of the authority of literature and the arts in society is based on two levels of social concern – the level of coherence and agreement and the level of detachment and objectivity. Points to the role of the university in maintaining a healthy tension between these two levels

in a democracy. Such tension will help prevent the degeneration of the
first level into mob hysteria and censorship and the second level into esoteric cults.

D287 'The Survival of Eros in Poetry.' *Romanticism and Contemporary Criticism*, ed
Morris Eaves and Michael Fischer (Ithaca, NY: Cornell Univ Press 1986),
15–29
Demonstrates how the mythology of Eros was gradually assimilated into
the Christian cosmology of medieval and later poetry. Such a process
illustrates how poets are able to discover analogies between their own
concerns and the imaginative constructs of previous myths of concern and
thus make them acceptable to social and religious authority. In the romantic period, however, poets begin not so much to accommodate their
visions to the older cosmology as to turn them upside down: the cosmos
of authority is replaced by a cosmos of revolt. The dominant shaping
powers of the post-romantic cosmos remain to be seen, but the 'gods' or
muses of the modern imagination 'bear names like Anxiety, Absurdity, and
Alienation.' The changes that poets are able to effect in cosmologies and
myths of concern raise the question of 'the authority of poetry within
a culture, which is much the same thing as the question of the social
function of poetry.' Presented as a lecture at the University of New Mexico,
16 February 1983. The essay is followed by a series of 'Questions and
Answers' from the audience (see G56).

E

Reviews

E1 'Dr Edgar's Book.' *Acta Victoriana* 58 (Christmas 1933): 17–20
Distinguishes Pelham Edgar's *The Art of the Novel* from other critical works
on the novel by noting its systematic and structural approach and its
synthesis of 'interpretation through a preconceived attitude' and 'objective
recording.'

E2 'Bach Recital.' *Saturday Night*, 30 November 1935, 8
Review of a piano performance of the Bach Inventions, presented at the
Malloney Art Galleries, Toronto, 23 November 1935. Praises the range of
the performance (by Mr Guerrero), from its lightness and piquancy at
one extreme to its emotional power and elaborate beauty at the other.

E3 'Hart House Quartet.' *Saturday Night*, 7 December 1935, 23
Review of the quartet's performance of Mozart's D Minor, Beethoven's E
Minor, and the 'Moods' of Waldo Warner, performed at the Hart House
Theatre, 30 November 1935. Judges the Beethoven to have been better
played than the Mozart, and remarks that a 'satisfying balance and even
distribution of the tone' were sustained throughout the performance.

E4 'Iolanthe.' *Acta Victoriana* 60 (February 1936): 34–5
A review of the production of Gilbert and Sullivan's *Iolanthe* by the Music
Club at Victoria College. 'A very good show ... probably as well managed
as anything the Music Club has done.'

E5 'Lord Dufferin.' *Canadian Forum* 18 (April 1938): 458
A review of *Helen's Tower* by Harold Nicholson, which is a 'readable and
entertaining' account of Lord Dufferin, Nicholson's uncle and the Governor-
General of Canada during the post-Confederation period, but 'the author
is perhaps too much in sympathy with his hero to look at him objectively.'

E6 'Delicate Rhythms.' *Canadian Forum* 19 (December 1939): 295–6
A brief review of *The Red Kite*, Lloyd Frankenberg's first book of poetry.

Praises especially the earlier poems for their sound patterns, but finds that the later poems 'do not gain much in depth of tone or expressive precision.'

E7 Review of *Elementary Part-Writing*, by Leo Smith. *Canadian Forum* 19 (March 1940): 398
A brief notice about a book of rudimentary musical theory, written for students of the Toronto Conservatory.

E8 'Canadian Watercolors.' *Canadian Forum* 20 (April 1940): 14
A review of a water-colour exhibit at the Toronto Art Gallery. Finds the movement away from conventional oil painting to be refreshing. Sees humour in a number of the works, and with it a 'sense of the importance of the random impression.' Comments, finally, on the genre studies in the exhibit, 'which may mean that Canadian eyes are slowly rising from the vegetable kingdom into human life.'

E9 'Experiment.' *Canadian Forum* 20 (April 1940): 26–7
A short review of *Poets of Tomorrow*, a selection from the work of four young British writers. Finds the poetry to be technically competent and essentially didactic: 'they offer passionate criticisms of life' and have an 'intense desire for revolution.'

E10 'Poetry.' *Canadian Forum* 20 (April 1940): 29–30
Very short reviews of four volumes of poetry: *Late Blossoms* by May Rooker-Clark, *Two Sonnets for a Centenary* by Fisher Davidson, *Ode in a Winter Evening* by John A.B. McLeish, and *Poet and Salesman* by William Thow.

E11 'Poetry.' *Canadian Forum* 20 (July 1940): 125–6
A review of Oscar Williams's *The Man Coming toward You* and Paul Potts's *A Poet's Testament*. Sees the style of Williams's poetry, which owes something to Hart Crane, to be homogeneous and metaphysical, and the content to be largely a nightmare vision of contemporary culture. Finds Williams's kenning-type mannerism to be annoying, but otherwise he 'is skillful, sub-tle and often profound, though his consistently oblique diction and monot-onous rhythm make a rather crustacean cover for his sensibility.' Discovers little in Potts's poetry, which is too self-consciously left-wing, to commend it.

E12 Review of *Lava*, by Irene H. Moody. *Canadian Forum* 20 (October 1940): 222
Considers Mrs Moody's imagist verse to be didactic, topical, and 'almost entirely unsuccessful.' 'Her chief religious idea seems to be the Shavian creative-evolution one of God as the glacier and us as the terminal moraine, which, though dead as a religion, survives as a haunting and hideous myth.' Her small group of epigrams are attractive enough to recommend the book.

E13 Review of *New Poets from Old*, by Henry W. Wells. *Canadian Forum* 20 (October 1940): 221–2
Finds this book, about the influence of earlier poets upon contemporaries, to be essential reading for anyone beginning a study of modern poetry. Wells is better on the American poets, especially Aiken and Lindsay, though the book sometimes lacks shape and is filled with historical com-

monplaces. Believes that modern poets have found the poetry of 'the
darker and more awkward ages' to be particularly useful and that in this
respect modern critics have yet to catch up.

E14 Review of *Lytton Strachey: A Critical Study*, by K.R. Srinivasa. *Canadian
Forum* 20 (December 1940): 292–3
Judges the ideas of this book to be 'commonplace' and its style 'indifferent,'
but the book does cause F to reflect on the 'group of highly talented
dons' who took over the culture of Britain between the wars, Strachey
being 'one of the best of these.'

E15 Review of *Contemporary Verse: A Canadian Quarterly* vol 1, no 1. *Canadian
Forum* 21 (December 1941): 283
Briefly comments on the work of a half dozen poets, including A.J.M.
Smith, Leo Kennedy, Earle Birney, and Dorothy Livesay. Finds some of
the poems to be too facile, metallic, and prosaic but others to be witty,
satirical, musical, and imaginative.

E16 Review of *Ebb Tide*, by Doris Ferne; *The Artisan*, by Sara Carsley; and *The
Singing Gypsy*, by Mollie Morant. *Canadian Forum* 21 (December 1941):
283–4
Praises these chap-books as a service to Canadian poetry and observes that
'a contempt for minor poetry is more vulgar and more dangerous than
the merely ignorant avoidance of all poetry.' Finds something to be admired
in each of the books – the touching simplicity and the authentic imagery
in some of the verse – but criticizes their platitudinous and commonplace
lines.

E17 Review of *Our Lady Peace and Other War Poems*, by Mark van Doren, and
Poems, by John Berryman. *Canadian Forum* 22 (October 1942): 220
Criticizes that branch of modern poetry, represented by these two volumes,
which is basically an 'elegiac lament over contemporary social evils.'
Finds the tone, mood, subject, and form of these poems to be oppressive,
unvarying, and boring, in spite of the technical accomplishments of both
poets. The deprecation of war and Fascism by the cultured, liberal, intellectual poet issues only in 'hopeless complaint and constipated elegance.'

E18 Review of *First Statement: A Magazine for Young Canadian Writers*, vol 1, nos
1–3, ed John Sutherland. *Canadian Forum* 22 (November 1942): 253
Sees the credo lying behind the work of the young poets in this little
magazine as affirming the magical quality of literature and as employing
an imagist technique. The poems are somewhat naïve, self-conscious, and
overwrought, but the magazine is 'pleasant to come upon,' and it reminds
us that 'the purely creative spirit still survives in Canada.'

E19 Review of *David and Other Poems*, by Earle Birney. *Canadian Forum* 22
(December 1942): 278. Rpt in *Earle Birney*, ed Bruce Nesbitt (Toronto:
McGraw-Hill Ryerson 1974), 39–41.
Finds much to admire in this collection of fugitive pieces, especially in the
title poem – 'a touching, beautiful and sensitively written story.' Praises
the wit, humour, ironic imagery, and use of the conceit in Birney's poetry.

Sees the alliterative line and the kenning of Anglo-Saxon verse as 'the most obvious technical influence on Mr Birney's work,' an influence he sometimes has difficulty controlling.

E20 Review of *New Writing and Daylight*. *Canadian Forum* 23 (April 1943): 21–2
Judges the level of competence in this anthology of poems, stories, and essays to be high, 'somewhere between the amateur conception of writing as a means of personal expression and the professional conception of it as skilled labor.' Singles out the poetry of Day Lewis and Terence Tiller and the critical essays, most of which treat the literary reaction to the war, for special comment, and praises an essay on Stefan George by Demetrios Capetanakis as being 'worth the price of admission in itself.'

E21 Review of *A Little Anthology of Canadian Poets*, ed Ralph Gustafson. *Canadian Forum* 23 (February 1944): 263
A brief notice about this anthology of younger Canadian writers. Wishes that the editor had included a statement of his intention and his principles of selection. Observes that the work of Margaret Avison has been omitted but that most of the important younger poets are included. For Gustafson's reply to this short review, see P88.

E22 Review of *Direction*, vol 1. *Canadian Forum* 23 (March 1944): 287
A short notice about a new literary magazine produced by a group of young Canadians in the air force, the chief of whom is Raymond Souster. Most of the poems are free-verse reflections on 'the sexual loneliness of army life' and the ironies of war.

E23 Review of *Basic*, by G.M. Young. *Canadian Forum* 24 (May 1944): 47
Presents very briefly the arguments of Young's commentary on Basic English. Believes Basic English should now be judged on its actual accomplishments rather than upon the claims of what it can and cannot do.

E24 Review of *I, Jones, Soldier*, by Joseph Schull. *Canadian Forum* 24 (October 1944): 166
Finds the writing in this narrative poem about a military career to be somewhat facile and containing too much 'flaccid rhythm,' but it contains 'a very real sincerity, and much of the readability and continuity which sincerity on such a theme [the life of a soldier] is likely to give.'

E25 Review of *New Writing and Daylight*, Winter 1943–4, ed John Lehmann. *Canadian Forum* 24 (October 1944): 164–5
Finds the general theme of this collection of poems, stories, and essays by young British writers, and by foreign writers stationed in England, to be the suspension of 'the real exuberance of creative energy' by the war. Expects that, once the war is over, such energy will manifest itself again first in poetry, which 'seems to be gathering together much larger powers of synthesis': symbolism, erudition, and critical intelligence.

E26 Review of *The Phoenix and the Tortoise*, by Kenneth Rexroth. *Canadian Forum* 24 (December 1944): 214–15
Praises Rexroth's competence, assurance, and achievement, qualities that result in large measure from his training in the classics. Steeped in the

tradition of Greek and Latin, his poetry takes on a personal authority. Rexroth is especially familiar with the Hellenistic and Byzantine ages, and he seems to have been influenced by Spengler, 'the theories of unconscious symbolism in psychology and anthropology, and the Nietzsche-Lawrence conception of the limitations of reason.' Like other twentieth-century poets, he appears to be working toward some integration of these ideas.

E27 Review of *V-Letter and Other Poems*, by Karl Shapiro. *Canadian Forum* 24 (December 1944): 213–14
Judges Shapiro to be one of the best contemporary poets. Finds in his poetry 'the expression of an alert, agile, and intelligent mind, tolerant and in the best sense of the word refined.' He has an accurately modulating wit, and, although his poems are written in a war zone, he has refrained from 'composing metrical editorials.'

E28 Review of *Unit of Five*, ed Ronald Hambleton. *Canadian Forum* 25 (May 1945): 48
Sees a great deal of genuine poetry in this small collection by five young Canadians: Louis Dudek, Ronald Hambleton, P.K. Page, Raymond Souster, and James Wreford. Praises especially the work of Dudek for its 'novelty of cadence,' freshness, and direct use of imagery. Discovers a certain derivative mannerism in Hambleton's poetry, self-consciousness of technique in Page's, epigrammatic self-expression in Souster's, and romanticism in Wreford's. Claims, however, that the poems of all five deserve an 'exhaustive critical analysis': the small volume is 'full of the real thing.'

E29 Review of *Green World*, by Miriam Waddington. *Canadian Forum* 26 (September 1946): 141–2
Describes Miss Waddington's poetry as having 'a lyrical gift of great beauty and subtlety' and 'a uniform level of excellence both in technique and expressive power.' The recurring theme throughout her work is the perplexed contrast between the innocent 'green world' of imaginative experience, which carries with it a symbolic meaning similar to Marvell's, and the world of experience, represented by the 'angled city' of corruption and the imprisoned ego.

E30 'Promising Novelist.' *Canadian Forum* 26 (October 1946): 164
A review of a novel by Joyce Marshall, *Presently Tomorrow*, which is 'a breezy and ribald tale' on the one hand and a conventional rendering of an adolescent's advance toward maturity on the other. Finds the point of view to be somewhat facile and the writing filled with clichés, but sees the qualities of a real novelist in Marshall's 'sense of construction.'

E31 Review of *It's a Long Way to Heaven*, by Abner Dean. *Canadian Forum* 26 (November 1946): 190
Short notice about this collection of Dean's eerie, allegorical, and surrealistic drawings.

E32 Review of *Modern Music: The Story of Music in Our Time*, by Max Graf. *Canadian Forum* 26 (November 1946): 190

Short notice of a book of 'not much use to anyone with a serious interest in the subject.'

E33 Review of *Selected Tales*, by A.E. Coppard, and *Bottle's Path and Other Stories*, by T.F. Powys. *Canadian Forum* 26 (November 1946): 187
Recommends, in a brief review, both collections of short fiction: Coppard's fantasies and straightforward tales and Powys's whimsical stories, the latter of which 'should be read in a room full of Russian-ballet decor and orange dragons on black curtains, beside a drink served by a breastless maid in bangs.'

E34 'Russian Art.' *Canadian Forum* 26 (December 1946): 213
A short review of *The Art of Russia*, ed Helen Rubissow. Observes that Russia became 'the Eastern colony of European art' after the seventeenth century and that the great period of Russian artistic energy emerged after the revolution.

E35 Review of *The Kafka Problem*, ed Angel Flores. *Canadian Forum* 26 (February 1947): 262
A short notice about this collection of critical studies, which is 'an essential supplement to the translations of Kafka's works now appearing.'

E36 Review of *New Writing and Daylight, 1946*, ed John Lehmann, and *Poems from New Writing: 1936–46*. *Canadian Forum* 26 (February 1947): 261
Short review of Lehmann's anthologies, the second of which contains 'a fair proportion' of contemporary British poetry. Although this poetry is highly competent, passionate, and sincere, 'the total effect is one of promise rather than achievement.'

E37 Review of *Britain between West and East*, ed A.G. Weidenfeld and H. de C. Hastings. *Canadian Forum* 27 (April 1947): 22
A brief notice about a collection of essays on 'various aspects of life, thought, and interrelationships of Britain, America, and Russia,' written in the tone of an 'unattached liberalism.'

E38 Review of *I Give You My Word*, by Ivor Brown. *Canadian Forum* 27 (June 1947): 72
A very brief notice about this series of essays on rare and interesting English words.

E39 Review of *Four Cautionary Tales*, by Feng Meng-lung. *Canadian Forum* 27 (July 1947): 95
A short notice about the seventeenth-century Chinese short stories, which 'capture for us the peculiar flavor of Classical Chinese civilization, with all its subtle blending of delicacy and cruelty, of vigorous convention and subversive humor.'

E40 Review of *The Scot in History*, by Wallace Notestein. *Canadian Forum* 27 (July 1947): 96
An 'easy-going historical jog-trot,' which tries to account for the Scottish character. Believes Notestein's purpose could have been better achieved if he had written a direct cultural history.

E41 Review of *Ibsen the Norwegian: A Revaluation*, by M.C. Bradbrook. *Canadian Forum* 27 (August 1947): 120
Observes that Miss Bradbrook's 'revaluation' focuses on Ibsen as a symbolic poet, who is best understood, not by studying his ideas, but by seeing his plays in the context of his own language and environment. A 'very readable' study with 'useful hints' about the Norwegian references in the plays.

E42 Review of *Roderick Hudson*, by Henry James. *Canadian Forum* 27 (August 1947): 118–19
Recommends that the reader unfamiliar with James would do well to begin with this reissue of his first important novel: it is an overture to his later works, but it has none of the characteristics of the later works that irritate the common reader, such as James's involved syntax and 'pansyish mannerisms.'

E43 Review of *The Innocent Eye*, by Herbert Read. *Canadian Forum* 27 (August 1947): 119
Remarks that this autobiography reads 'like a prose version of Wordsworth's *Prelude*.' Read's anarchism, romanticism, and agnosticism show him to be in direct opposition to Eliot; his religious views are somewhat cloudy, and the work as a whole is 'pretty tentative.'

E44 'Canadian Poet.' *Canadian Forum* 27 (September 1947): 140–1
A review of *Edwin J. Pratt*, by Henry W. Wells and Carl F. Klinck. Believes that Klinck's biographical study of Pratt is a little too 'folksy and anecdotal' and that Wells's interpretation of Pratt's poetry misses the mark because it tries to relate Pratt's work to classical models. Argues that a more fruitful approach would be to see Pratt's long poems in the context of the narrative tradition in English poetry – not the lyrical tradition.

E45 Review of *The Cosmic Shape*, by Ross Nichols and James Kirkup. *Canadian Forum* 27 (September 1947): 143
A very brief review about a book that argues that 'Jung's theory of "archetypes" has provided a formula for gathering together the myths of all countries into a single gigantic mythical form.'

E46 Review of *The Portable Blake*, selected and arranged with an introduction by Alfred Kazin. *University of Toronto Quarterly* 17 (October 1947): 107
Recommends this collection as a classroom text, even though the serious student of Blake will prefer the Keynes edition. Questions Kazin's having omitted the original passages to which Blake's marginalia refer and his not having included *An Island in the Moon*. Finds that the introduction 'avoids the deeper aspects' of Blake's thought and follows too closely 'the enraptured-crank stereotype' of his personality. For another review of this book see D26.

E47 'The Betjeman Brand.' *Poetry: A Magazine of Verse* 71 (December 1947): 162–5. Rpt in *Poetry: A Magazine of Verse* 121 (October 1972): 48–50.
Review of *Slick but not Streamlined*, a collection of light verse by John

Betjeman. Observes that light verse does not really emerge as a separate kind of poetry until the 1800s and that Betjeman's work, having been influenced by Clough and Praed, lies squarely in the tradition of nine-teenth-century light verse. In a number of poems Betjeman manages 'to preserve a very delicate balance of tone,' which is essential for this kind of poetry, and his best effects come from his treatment of the grotesque and macabre. Still, light verse is a limited form, since it seeks only to record rather than transform experience.

E48 Review of *Canadian Accent*, ed Ralph Gustafson. *Canadian Forum* 27 (December 1947): 214
A short notice about the appearance of this 'excellent little collection of contemporary Canadian poems, stories and essays.'

E49 Review of *Say the Word*, by Ivor Brown. *Canadian Forum* 27 (December 1947): 215
A short notice about the fourth in a series of Brown's essays, 'full of recondite and often fascinating information' about words.

E50 Review of *The Flowing Summer*, by Charles Bruce. *Canadian Forum* 27 (December 1947): 215
A very brief notice about this narrative poem, which, with its illustrations, is 'almost like a child's book designed for adults.'

E51 Review of *The Story of English Literature*, by R.F. Patterson. *Canadian Forum* 27 (December 1947): 215
A short notice about a book that is simply a series of biographical sketches of English writers. Finds that Patterson has 'no critical sense' and that he can't write.

E52 Review of *Other Canadians*, ed John Sutherland. *Canadian Forum* 27 (January 1948): 239
Brief review of an anthology of younger Canadian poets. Thinks that the anthology, although of interest as a guide to the younger poets, does not call for any revaluation of their work, most of which has already been reviewed in the *Canadian Forum*.

E53 Review of *The Shadow of Cain*, by Edith Sitwell. *Canadian Forum* 27 (January 1948): 239
Brief notice about this 'beautiful and erudite poem' by one who has become a 'major poet, a necessary part of one's literary education and current reading.'

E54 'For Tory and Leftist.' *Poetry: A Magazine of Verse* 71 (March 1948): 337–8
Review of *The Georgics of Virgil*, trans C. Day Lewis. Calls the translation 'accurate and unpretentious' and one that has 'much in common with the best of the English bucolic school.' Sees the moral, imaginative, and economic principles of Virgil as a set of values that appeal both to the Tory and to the left-wing intellectual, such as Day Lewis.

E55 Review of *The Moment and Other Essays*, by Virginia Woolf. *Canadian Forum* 27 (March 1948): 284–5
Believes that Woolf's essays, unlike her vigorous and imaginative novels,

'suffer from a self-conscious delicacy of perception' and a languor of rhythm. Still, she makes many sensitive observations about the work of Congreve, Scott, Dickens, and Lawrence and is good at discovering the novelist's personal insecurity.

E56 Review of *What Maisie Knew*, by Henry James; *In a Glass Darkly*, by Sheridan Le Fanu; and *On Art and Socialism*, by William Morris. *Canadian Forum* 28 (April 1948): 22
Brief notice about these three titles having been reissued in England in the Chiltern Library series. Comments on the importance of not only keeping the classics in print but also making accessible 'the sort of charming and mellowed book one needs for pleasure.'

E57 'An Important Influence.' *Poetry: A Magazine of Verse* 72 (July 1948): 231
A brief review of *La Wallonie, 1886–1892: The Symbolist Movement in Belgium*, by Andrew Jackson Matthews. Feels that *La Wallonie*, one of the little magazines, 'illustrates the two requirements of healthy poetry which are superficially inconsistent with each other,' that it be international (the magazine helped foster late nineteenth-century French poetry) and that it be regional (its writers were sensitive to their local environment).

E58 Review of *The Book of Canadian Poetry*, 2nd ed, ed A.J.M. Smith. *Canadian Forum* 28 (November 1948): 188
Observes that Smith's selection is more a chrestomathy than an anthology because he presents the poems 'as documents in the cultural history of Canada, relates them to the development of the country and to literary movements elsewhere, and in general attaches them to various parts of their surrounding environment.' Notes that what Smith has added to the first edition helps to illustrate the peculiarly Canadian predilection for descriptive and narrative poetry.

E59 Review of *The Varsity Story*, by Morley Callaghan. *Canadian Forum* 28 (November 1948): 189
Brief review of this 'intellectual guidebock to the University of Toronto,' which is presented as half fiction, half fact. Thinks that the book, although extremely readable, does not measure up to Callaghan's other work.

E60 Review of *Arabian Oil*, by Raymond F. Mikesell and Hollis B. Chenery. *Canadian Forum* 29 (July 1949): 96
Short notice about a technical study on Middle East oil and its relation to American foreign policy.

E61 Review of *Coral and Brass*, by Holland M. Smith. *Canadian Forum* 29 (July 1949): 96
Short notice about the memoirs of General Smith's Pacific campaign.

E62 Review of *Russian Child and Russian Wife*, by Tanya Matthews. *Canadian Forum* 29 (July 1949): 96
Short notice about the nostalgic memoirs of a Russian girl set against the background of Marxist bureaucracy and tyranny.

E63 Review of *The World Is Wide Enough*, by Percy Coates. *Canadian Forum* 29 (July 1949): 96

Short notice of a well-written story of two Yorkshire hoboes who have become professional boxers.

E64 'The Theatre.' *The Daily Princetonian*, 7 May 1954, 2
Review of a production of Molière's *Tartuffe* at Princeton. Says that the play 'grasped the essential fact about Tartuffe, that he is more a parasite than a hypocrite; what is important is not the lightning changes of a party line, but the steady advance of a malignant will.'

E65 Review of *John Ruskin*, by Joan Evans. *Canadian Forum* 34 (March 1955): 285
Places Evans in the camp of those who see Ruskin as an important art critic turned moralist. Believes that Ruskin's later works on myth and science should be taken more seriously because it is their iconography that holds Ruskin together.

E66 Review of *Blake, Prophet against Empire: A Poet's Interpretation of the History of His Own Times*, by David V. Erdman. *Philological Quarterly* 34 (July 1955): 273–4
Judges this book to be the first study of Blake's social and political interests that approaches its subject with a full knowledge of Blake's prophecies. The book 'is almost a social history of England between 1760 and 1820, as seen from Blake's point of view.' Erdman perhaps exaggerates Blake's radicalism and underestimates his attacks on Deism, but the historical scholarship clarifies much about Blake's writings and his times.

E67 Review of *The Ulysses Theme*, by W.B. Stanford, and *Tragic Themes in Western Literature*, ed Cleanth Brooks. *Comparative Literature* 9 (Spring 1957): 180–2
Summarizes Stanford's analysis of Homer's Ulysses and the subsequent adaption of the Ulysses theme in the literary tradition. Judges the book to be 'remarkable not only for its thorough scholarship but for an excellent style, at once incisive and sensitive, which illuminates very sharply both the unity and the variety in the Ulysses figure as it goes down the ages.' Sees the significance of Stanford's study in its illustrating the rightful and creative function that tradition plays in literature. The treatment of Ulysses throughout the ages is an archetype, 'a theme which carries centuries of development with it.' Concludes with brief summaries of the seven essays in Brooks's anthology.

E68 'After the Invocation, a Lapse into Litany.' *Book Week*, 22 March 1964, 6, 19
A review of *The Masks of God: Occidental Mythology*, by Joseph Campbell. Finds the organization and argument of the first part of the book to be excellent, but the book becomes weaker and less interesting as Campbell drifts into a kind of history of Western religions. 'The relentless chronological sequence' of the narrative causes Campbell to include many historical events that have no mythological significance, and when he does treat mythology it is uprooted from its cultural context.

E69 'In the Earth, or in the Air?' *TLS*, 17 January 1986, 51–2
Review of Paul de Man's *The Rhetoric of Romanticism*. Finds that the central theme in these essays is the antithetical dialectic running throughout

romanticism. Praises de Man's integrity in not trying to resolve the anti-thesis in the romantic sensibility, but finds some of de Man's readings (eg, his treatment of natural vs emblematic imagery in Yeats) to be dubious. Argues that de Man's deconstructive project can really be seen as an effort to uncover the mythological bases of ideology.

F

Miscellaneous: Undergraduate Writings, Short Fiction, Editorials, Letters to Periodicals, University Reports, Replies to Questionnaires, Tributes, etc

F1 'Mercury Column.' *Acta Victoriana* 56, nos 1–6 (1931–2)
The humour column F wrote from October 1931 to April 1932. Includes jokes, limericks, puns, triolets, one-liners, etc. Page numbers for the column in the six issues are, respectively, 38–8; 38–40; 38, 40–2; 39–42; 39–43; 39–40, 43. The column in issue no 6 is unsigned.

F2 'The Bob.' *Acta Victoriana* 56, no 1 (October-November 1931): 30
Review and editorial comment on the Victoria College Bob, an annual satiric and musical show in which the sophomores ridicule the freshmen.

F3 'Debating Society.' *Acta Victoriana* 56, no 1 (October-November 1931): 31
An announcement of an upcoming debate, in which F himself represents the opposition, and of the Debate Society's activities for the year.

F4 'The Monocle: Victoria College Debating Parliament.' *Acta Victoriana* 56, no 4 (January-February 1932): 32–3
Reviews the Debating Society's program on disarmament. Summarizes the arguments presented and laments the lack of interest in debate among his fellow students.

F5 'Monocle: "Patience," "The Silver Box," and "That Trinity Debate." ' *Acta Victoriana* 56, no 5 (March 1932): 32–4
Reviews the performance of Gilbert and Sullivan's *Patience* by the Music Club at Victoria College, the Dramatic Society's performance of Galsworthy's *The Silver Box*, and the debate between Victoria and Trinity colleges about free speech.

F6 'The Case against Examinations.' *Acta Victoriana* 56, no 6 (April 1932): 27–30
Argues against the one final 'free-for-all examination which promotes in so thoroughly Darwinian a manner the survival of the misfit.'

F7 'Acta Victoriana.' *Acta Victoriana* 56 (May 1932): 21

A statement about a new editorial policy. Hopes to make *Acta Victoriana* 'a journal of recognized literary merit.' Unsigned.

F8 'Arthur Richard Cragg.' *Acta Victoriana* 57 (November 1932): 18–19
An editorial tribute to Cragg, after his election as president of the Victoria College Union the preceding year. Praises his personal qualities, intelligence, and sense of values.

F9 'Editorial in Undress.' *Acta Victoriana* 57, no 1 (November 1932): 31
Outlines the editorial policy of the magazine. Hopes it will become 'the verbal epitome of the college itself.'

F10 'On the Frosh: An Editorial.' *Acta Victoriana* 57 (November 1932): 24–6
Classifies the freshmen into three groups – the annuals, the biennials, and the perennials – and, with tongue in cheek, characterizes each group. Unsigned.

F11 'Editorial in Undress.' *Acta Victoriana* 57, no 2 (December 1932): 7
Comments on the contributions to this number of the magazine and announces a literary contest.

F12 'James Delmer Martin.' *Acta Victoriana* 57 (December 1932): 21–3
An editorial about the balance and solidity of Martin, president of the senior year at Victoria College. Unsigned.

F13 'The Question of Maturity: An Editorial.' *Acta Victoriana* 57 (December 1932): 23–5
Compares the present generation of students with those forty years earlier by looking at the concerns expressed in an issue of *Acta Victoriana* from the 1890s. Finds that today's students are more brilliant though less serious, and that they display more analytical power and impartial judgment. Unsigned.

F14 'Editorial in Undress.' *Acta Victoriana* 57, no 3 (January 1933): 29
Speaks about the contributions to this issue of the magazine, which includes an essay on the library by Helen G. Kemp.

F15 'Editorial in Undress.' *Acta Victoriana* 57 (February 1933): 7–8
Comments on the lack of good poetry submitted to the *Acta* literary contest.

F16 'The Monocle: Pinafore.' *Acta Victoriana* 57 (April 1933): 34–5
A review of the production of Gilbert and Sullivan's *Pinafore* by the Music Club at Victoria College. Thinks the performance was an unqualified flop and urges that other means for musical training and expression be developed at the college.

F17 'The Monocle: Press Cuttings.' *Acta Victoriana* 57 (April 1933): 35–6
A review of the Dramatic Society's performance of Shaw's *Press Cuttings*. Urges the Dramatic Society at Victoria College to promote its shows and to perform more plays by Shaw, 'not only the most popular, but actually the greatest, of contemporary dramatists.'

F18 'Pro Patria Mori.' *Acta Victoriana* 57 (April 1933): 31–2
An editorial on the resolution of the Oxford Debate: 'that this house will under no circumstances fight for its King and Country.' Attacks the propagandistic phrasing of the resolution.

F19 'The Pass Course: A Polemic.' *Acta Victoriana* 57 (Midsummer 1933): 5–10
     Argues that the pass course should be unconditionally abolished at Victoria
     College and that all students should be required to take the honour course.

F20 'Iolanthe.' *Acta Victoriana* 60 (December 1935): 26
     A notice of a forthcoming production of Gilbert and Sullivan's *Iolanthe* by
     the Music Club at Victoria College. Includes a brief comment on the nature
     of light opera.

F21 'The Ghost.' *Acta Victoriana* 60 (April 1963): 14–16
     A short story about a ghost who, having killed himself when his lover,
     Margaret, fell in love with another, returns to haunt his rival and to protect
     Margaret. After both efforts fail, he turns to a priest, who sets him straight
     on the nature of ghosts.

F22 'Fable ... in the Nineteenth-Century Idiom.' *Canadian Forum* 16 (June 1936):
     15
     A fable about a young man who wishes to become a writer. He is visited
     by 'seven spirits who hold the seven great secrets of writing,' but the
     spirits turn out to be the seven deadly sins. Written under the pseudonym
     Richard Poor.

F23 'Face to Face.' *Acta Victoriana* 62 (March 1938): 10–12
     A satirical sketch in which an unnamed narrator reports to his drinking
     partner the beliefs of a tribe of colour-blind South Sea islanders. Their
     main belief is the resolution of opposites into a balanced and harmonious
     synthesis. Their religious beliefs turn out to be represented by the absence
     of colour: grey.

F24 'Affable Angel.' *Acta Victoriana* 64 (January 1940): 2–4
     A fable about an angel who suddenly appears to two Londoners, is treated
     matter-of-factly by them, and, after drinking with them in a bar, soars
     away, but not before causing a Nazi plane to plunge into the Thames.

F25 'The Resurgent.' *Canadian Forum* 19 (February 1940): 357–9
     A story about a painter, Andrew Larrabin, told from the point of view of
     his sister. Larrabin believes that painting is a patriotic duty and begins
     to produce works after the manner of Soviet realism. But against this belief
     another force begins to work, a visionary and revolutionary force springing
     from his unconscious and expressing itself in conventional and symbolic
     forms. Larrabin is unable to control this obsession and it leads eventually
     to hysteria and suicide. But the sister-narrator, who tells much of the
     story by drawing upon her brother's diary, fails to understand, seeing his
     genius in his devotion to the cause of the Resurgence and his heroic
     loyalty to the state.

F26 'Gordon Webber and Canadian Abstract Art.' *Acta Victoriana* 65 (February
     1941): 39–42
     A review of Webber's paintings in the context of the work of Thomson,
     Jackson, Carr, and Harris.

F27 'Art Does Need Sociability.' *Saturday Night* 16 (August 1941): 2
     A letter to the editor replying to an article by Sir Wyly Grier, who claimed

that organizations of artists are not necessary because the great writers
did not need their friends to help them write. Argues by reference to Dante,
Shakespeare, Milton, and Sir Joshua Reynolds ('the great pioneer among
all organizers of the arts') that social relations among artists and between
artists and other people are an important ingredient in the life of art.

F28 'Prelude.' *Canadian Forum* 21 (September 1941): 185–6
A retelling of the Paris and Helen myth, which concludes, when Paris
gives Venus the apple, with a Greek version of the Fall.

F29 'Two Italian Sketches. 1939.' *Acta Victoriana* 67 (October 1942): 12–14, 23
Two vignettes from F's trip through Italy in 1939. The first juxtaposes the
ubiquitous reminders of Mussolini in the little town of San Gemignano
with descriptions of three frescos in the town cathedral. In the second
sketch, 'Venice,' F reflects on the money economy that served the city
throughout history and is reminded of *The Merchant of Venice*.

F30 'Undemocratic Censorship.' *Canadian Forum* 26 (July 1946): 76
An unsigned editorial attacking the censorship of such books as Edmund
Wilson's *Memoirs of Hecate County* and Joyce's *Ulysses*. Argues that such
censorship is undemocratic, not because it violates what the majority wants
but because 'it compels the most intelligent and cultivated section of the
public to break the law merely because it is the most intelligent and
cultivated section of the public.' Urges Parliament to consider the matter
thoroughly in order to prevent a post-war attack on certain books in
the name of somebody's moral or religious standards.

F31 'Canadian Authors Meet.' *Canadian Forum* 26 (August 1946): 101
An unsigned editorial supporting the Canadian Authors Association and
urging it to work toward forming an authors' union.

F32 'Revenge or Justice?' *Canadian Forum* 26 (November 1946): 171
An unsigned editorial that argues that the news coverage of the Nuremberg
trials appealed only to the feeling of revenge, and that the real meaning
of the trials should have been to make it an international crime to start
preventive wars and to engage in blatant forms of imperialism.

F33 'Merry Christmas.' *Canadian Forum* 26 (December 1946): 195
An unsigned editorial that observes that Christmas, having descended
from the winter solstice, has today turned into two different religious festi-
vals: one celebrates a divine as well as a human light coming into the
world while the other celebrates the triumph of nature and man.

F34 'So Many Lost Weekends.' *Canadian Forum* 26 (March 1947): 269
An unsigned editorial that questions the support of the temperance lobby-
ists by Protestant churches.

F35 'Merry Christmas?' *Canadian Forum* 27 (December 1947): 195
An unsigned editorial calling for readers of the *Forum* to affirm Christmas
and what it symbolizes, and thereby help to offset the feeling of helpless-
ness that descends upon a world of tyranny, war, starvation, and fear.

F36 'Duncan Campbell Scott.' *Canadian Forum* 27 (February 1948): 244
An unsigned editorial written in memory of Scott, who had "as varied and

comprehensive knowledge of Canada as any writer we have produced.'
Praises especially Scott's poetry.

F37 'Gandhi.' *Canadian Forum* 27 (March 1948): 267
An unsigned editorial. Finds it difficult to understand the mind of the
apostle of violence who murdered Gandhi. Discovers, however, a foreboding
strain in Gandhi's recent statements that suggest that he himself 'felt
that he had outlived his time.' Observes that it is difficult for the modern
political saint not to become an anachronism: Gandhi's followers did not
really understand his innocence and tried to make him into a god whom
they could invoke to justify any kind of action.

F38 'Canadian Dreiser.' *Canadian Forum* 28 (September 1948): 121–2. Rpt in
Frederick Philip Grove, ed Desmond Pacey (Toronto: Ryerson 1970), 186–7;
partially rpt in *Twentieth-Century Literary Criticism*, vol 4, ed Sharon K.
Hall (Detroit: Gale Research 1981), 135–6.
An unsigned editorial on the work of perhaps Canada's 'most important'
prose writer, Frederick Philip Grove. Sees Grove as 'our only example
of an artist who made his whole life a drama of the artist's fight for survival
in an indifferent society,' yet wonders how much of Grove's integrity as
a writer was 'a self-conscious pose of integrity.' Calls for the Canadian
writer to move beyond Grove's view that contemporary artistic achievement
in Canada can be nothing more than a tragic failure.

F39 'Editorial Statement.' *Canadian Forum* 28 (September 1948): 125. Rpt in
Canadian Forum 35 (October 1955): 161.
Presents the editorial aims and policy of the *Forum* as centring on two
main interests, cultural and political.

F40 'Dean of Critics.' *Canadian Forum* 28 (November 1948): 169–70
An unsigned editorial memorializing 'the greatest public figure in Canadian
literature,' Pelham Edgar. Traces briefly Edgar's achievements as a critic,
teacher, administrator, and public servant.

F41 'Merry Christmas.' *Canadian Forum* 28 (December 1948): 193–4
An unsigned editorial claiming that the persistent appeal of Christmas is
not explained by commercialism but by the desire to see life for a brief
instant annually 'as it should be and could be.'

F42 'Cardinal Mindszenty.' *Canadian Forum* 28 (March 1949): 267
An unsigned editorial that condemns the Mindszenty trial for the illegal
procedure of Mindszenty's being kidnapped by the police, the possibility of
his being tortured, and the government's using the case as a propaganda
stunt.

F43 'Culture and the Cabinet.' *Canadian Forum* 28 (March 1949): 265–6
An unsigned editorial that laments the failure of the Canadian government
to support culture and to establish a national theatre, library, and a
policy on education. Fears that the royal commission established to study
the relation of the government to the arts and sciences will go nowhere
because the government lacks a genuine interest in culture.

F44 'The Two Camps.' *Canadian Forum* 29 (April 1949): 3

An unsigned editorial on the impasse in the confrontation of communism and democracy. Argues that violations of civil liberties in the United States and Canada do nothing but aid the communist position.

F45 'On Book Reviewing.' *Here and Now* 2 (June 1949): 19–20
A response to a questionnaire on the function of book reviewing. Sees the review as belonging to the preparatory stage of criticism. The reviewer's function is first to determine the book's category and then to judge how well it delights and instructs.

F46 'Law and Disorder.' *Canadian Forum* 29 (July 1949): 75
An unsigned editorial criticizing the communist witch-hunt in the United States, which has resulted in the 'evil of intimidation, character assassination, forcible suppression of evidence and the spreading of terrorized insecurity among government employees.' Whatever steps are taken against communists need to be taken within the regular legal channels and with definite legal procedures.

F47 'To Define True Madness.' *Canadian Forum* 29 (September 1949): 125
An unsigned editorial occasioned by the charge of treason against Ezra Pound. Argues that Pound's *Cantos*, for all of their peevishness and shrill hysteria, and his political leanings should not cause his case to be considered with fear and anger, 'but simply with a desire to know what drove him mad.'

F48 'Nothing to Fear but Fear.' *Canadian Forum* 29 (November 1949): 169–70
Unsigned editorial attacking the capricious refusal of American immigration officials to grant visas to, among others, Professors Shortliffe of Queen's University and Barker Fairley of the University of Toronto.

F49 'Merry Christmas.' *Canadian Forum* 29 (December 1949): 193–4
An unsigned editorial that briefly surveys the history of Christmas and laments the panic and compulsion of its present commercialism. Believes the real meaning of Christmas is a combination of themes from both of the New Testament accounts: Matthew's with its gloom and fear of menace and Luke's with its vision of a new society.

F50 'The Ideal of Democracy.' *Varsity* [University of Toronto], 7 February 1950, 3
Examines the fundamental tenets of democracy: its essential aims, its dynamic, and its economic structure. Looks briefly at the threats to democracy by fascism and communism.

F51 'George Orwell.' *Canadian Forum* 29 (March 1950): 265–6
An unsigned editorial that reviews Orwell's literary career. Sees *1984* as Orwell's greatest novel, 'one of the greatest the twentieth century has yet produced' because of its simplicity and honesty. Observes that the book is not entirely or even chiefly a satire on Russian communism. What Orwell satirizes, rather, is the 'entrenched tyranny' of any small ruling class.

F52 'Back to Work.' *Victoria Reports* 1 (November 1951): 29
Anecdotes from F's year in the United States as a visiting lecturer at Harvard and the University of Washington.

F53 'Installation Luncheon.' *Victoria Reports* 2 (March 1952): 5–6
Report on the luncheon held in honor of Lester B. Pearson upon his
installation as chancellor of Victoria University.

F54 'New Liberties for Old.' *Canadian Forum* 32 (December 1952): 195–6
An unsigned editorial occasioned by the resignation of four journalists of
'unquestioned ability and integrity' from the staff of *Saturday Night*, the
Canadian weekly. Suggests that the magazine might be turning away from
being a forum of independent opinion and might find itself serving
instead the interests of a capitalistic monopoly.

F55 'John D. Robins.' *Canadian Forum* 32 (January 1953): 218
An unsigned editorial eulogizing Robins, a professor of English at Victoria
College, University of Toronto, longtime contributor to the *Canadian
Forum*, and 'a central figure in the cultural history of Canada.'

F56 'Regina vs the World.' *Canadian Forum* 33 (June 1953): 49–50
An unsigned editorial, occasioned by the coronation of Elizabeth II. Comments on the irony involved in the historical process in which 'institutions
grow as ideas when they decline in physical strength.' With Elizabeth I,
who had power to rule, royalty was a function of character, whereas
with Elizabeth II character is a function of royalty. Still, the queen can
serve as 'a centripetal social force' who can remind her subjects that
'in some dim and mysterious way we are all members of one body.'

F57 'From the Principal of Victoria ... Greetings.' *The Strand* [Victoria College,
Univ of Toronto] 8 (24 September 1959): 1, 3
Advice to the entering class at Victoria College on the difference between
instruction and learning, the virtues of specialization, and the way to avoid
flunking out.

F58 'Abeunt a Lot More Studia.' *Victoria Reports* 9 (November 1959): 6–8
A report on the new Victoria College library, the necessity of maintaining
the federated system within the university, the activities of the faculty,
the Armstrong Lecture by I.A. Richards, among other things.

F59 'Dialogue Begins.' *The Mike*, [October 1960], 1, 10
Claims that the first two chancellors of Victoria College, Ryerson and
Nelles, had a more profound understanding of the relationship between
the university and the church than did Matthew Arnold.

F60 'Operations Proceeding: II.' *Victoria Reports* 10 (December 1960): 7–9
A report on staff changes at Victoria College, the accomplishments of the
faculty, student dramatic and musical activities, and the resumption of
the public lecture series.

F61 'Autopsy on an Old Grad's Grievance.' *Varsity Graduate*, Spring 1961, 30–3
Replies to an article by Harold Taylor in the *Saturday Review*, in which
Taylor, who attended Victoria College at about the same time F did, laments
the absence of intellectual vitality in his student days at Victoria. F says
his experience during these years was 'bewilderingly different.' Lists a host
of examples to rebut Taylor's view of what was and was not going on at
Victoria and the other colleges at Toronto.

F62 'The Principal's Message.' *Victoria College Student Handbook* [1961], 10, 33

Defines for entering students the relation of Victoria College to the larger university and the meaning of its religious connection.

F63 'Fearful Gauntlet.' *Victoria Reports* 12 (April 1962): 7–9
A report on the year's activities by faculty and students at Victoria College.

F64 'Weather Clear, Track Fast.' *Victoria Reports* 12 (November 1962): 6–9
A report largely about staff changes at Victoria College for the 1962–3 academic year.

F65 'The Dean of Women.' *Victoria Reports* 13 (May 1963): 20–1
A tribute to the intellectual, cultural, and administrative talents of Jessie Macpherson, dean of women at Victoria College.

F66 'Victorian Era.' *Victoria Reports* 13 (May 1963): 26–7
An annual report on student achievements and activities and other Victoria College functions.

F67 'New Faces, Old Ways.' *Victoria Reports* 13 (December 1963): 5–7
An annual report on the faculty and student activities at Victoria College.

F68 'The Classics and the Man of Letters.' *Arion* 3 (Winter 1964): 49–52
Replies to a sixteen-part questionnaire on such topics as the influence of the classics on his critical work, the meaning of the classics in contemporary culture, the validity of Greek and Roman myths today, and the value of classical education and scholarship.

F69 'Foreword.' *The Living Name: A Tribute to Stefan Stykolt from Some of His Friends,* ed W.J. Stankiewicz ([Toronto]: Univ of Toronto Press 1964), vii–ix
Pays tribute to Stefan Stykolt for his work as a student at Victoria College, as editor of the *Canadian Forum,* and as a person with a large intellectual potential.

F70 A Tribute to John Crowe Ransom. *John Crowe Ransom: A Tribute from the Community of Letters,* ed D. David Long and Michael R. Burr. Supplement to *The Kenyon Collegian* 90, no 7 (1964): 15
A brief tribute to Ransom on the occasion of the celebration of his seventy-fifth year. Comments on Ransom's distinguished poetry, criticism, and teaching.

F71 'The Time of the Flood.' *Victoria Reports* 15 (December 1965): 5–6
A report on the increasing enrolment at Victoria College and on the student activities during the first part of the year.

F72 'Charles Bruce Sissons, 1879–1965.' *Proceedings of the Royal Society of Canada,* fourth series, 3 (1965): 1973–5
A biographical sketch of Sissons, a fellow of the Royal Society, and a testament to his achievement as an academic and a historian.

F73 'Edwin John Pratt, 1882–1964.' *Proceedings of the Royal Society of Canada,* fourth series, 3 (1965): 161–5
Gives a brief sketch of Pratt's life and traces his poetic career. Acknowledges Pratt as Canada's greatest poet in English, the only Canadian writer thus far 'great enough to establish a personal legend.' Comments on the qualities of Pratt's Dionysian narrative verse and pays tribute to his genuine human spirit.

F74 'New Programmes.' *Graduate Studies at the University of Toronto: Report of the*

President's Committee on the School of Graduate Studies, 1964–65. Toronto:
Univ of Toronto Press 1965, 41–2
F wrote that section of this report dealing with ways that the theological
faculties at Emmanuel, Trinity, Wycliffe, Knox, and St Michael's colleges
might form a nucleus to offer an MA and PH D program in Religious
Studies.

F75 'A New Principal for Victoria.' *Victoria Reports* 14 (December 1966): 8
A brief outline of the accomplishments of Professor J.E. Hodgetts, F's
successor as principal of Victoria College.

F76 'Writing to Order.' *Canadian Author and Bookman* 42 (Winter 1966): 15
A brief reply to a questionnaire about commissioned writing. Says that
writers should see commissions in relation to forwarding their own intellectual life and that established writers should always take commissions
seriously, making them as creative as anything else they write.

F77 With James V. Logan and John E. Jordan 'Preface.' *Some British Romantics:
A Collection of Essays.* [Columbus]: Ohio State Univ Press 1966, [iii]
Brief remarks about the relation of this volume to three other books on
English romanticism sponsored by the Modern Language Association. The
three editors speak of having given the ten contributors freedom to ap-
proach their subjects however they pleased. See B12.

F78 'The Baccalaureate Sermon.' *Victoria Reports* 17 (April 1967): 3–10
Preaching from the text 'take no thought for the morrow,' urges the
graduating class to forgo 'the expectation of identifying [their] lives with a
definite body of work achieved': a life that manifests the practical wisdom
of a social vision is to be preferred to a body of accomplishments. Such
a vision may occasionally give one a glimpse of a greater wisdom, 'a sense
of a presence which is ourselves yet infinitely bigger than ourselves,
which lives with us but which will not disappear into death when we do.'

F79 Reply to a Questionnaire on the Vietnam War. *Authors Take Sides on
Vietnam: Two Questions on the War in Vietnam Answered by the Authors of
Several Nations,* ed Cecil Woolf and John Bagguley (New York: Simon
and Schuster 1967), 35
Strongly opposes the war in Vietnam and thinks the conflict could be
resolved by 'a planned series of strategic withdrawals with the final objective of getting out of Southeast Asia and reverting to the Monroe Doctrine.'

F80 'William Blake. 1757–1827, *Adam and Eve and the Angel Raphael.* 1808.' *Man
and His World.* (np [1967]), 144
Descriptive entry for Blake's drawing, included in the International Fine
Arts Exhibition at Expo 67 in Montreal. Gives a brief interpretation of
the drawing, based on Blake's views about love and the Fall. Text is in
French and English.

F81 'Book Learning and Barricades.' *Book World,* 4 August 1968, 1
Replies to a question about student unrest. Says that its roots lie in the
post-Sputnik creation of a student proletariat and predicts that the university will soon cease to be its target because it has become merged with
other forms of social protest.

F82 'Symbols.' *Acta Victoriana* 93 (November 1968): 32–4
A sermon delivered at a dedicatory service in Victoria College Chapel.
Bases his message on the symbolic contrast between darkness and light,
between the inner dark world of our own privacy and the outer world of
light, which, according to Jesus, is the world of action, clearly visible to
others. Says that the language of symbolism is the only language that 'can
express a faith which is pure vision.' Such language points to the meaning
of the communion rite, where our ordinary associations of light and
darkness are reversed: 'we discover that it is this sunlight world that is
really the uncomprehending darkness, and the darkness where we can only
listen to the Word really a blaze of light, a golden city.'

F83 'On Editors and Critics.' In D.I.B. Smith's 'Introduction' to *Editing Eighteenth-Century Texts*, ed D.I.B. Smith (Toronto: Univ of Toronto Press
1968), 3
The third of three paragraphs from F's otherwise unpublished welcoming
remarks to the third Conference on Editorial Problems at the University of
Toronto, 27 October 1967. Notes that the educations of the critic and the
editor are parallel, and issues a caveat to both to avoid value-judgments.
See 129.

F84 'In Memoriam: Miss Jessie Macpherson, M.A. Ph.D.' *Victoria Reports* 19
(May 1969): 12, 20
A tribute to Macpherson, delivered at a memorial service in Victoria College
Chapel, 21 March 1969. Praises her lifelong battle against sentimental,
uncritical, and philistine attitudes.

F85 Congratulatory Statement. *Greetings to Dartmouth: Bicentennial Convocation
and Commencement, June 15, 1969* (Hanover, NH: Dartmouth College 1969),
19–20
A statement of congratulations and best wishes on the occasion of Dartmouth's bicentennial celebration.

F86 Reply to a Questionnaire on Horace. *Arion* 9 (Summer-Autumn 1970): 132
Maintains that interest in Horace needs to be revived, that he represents
'the authority of the humanist tradition,' and that 'his chief virtue is
the virtue of urbanity, which means primarily the virtue of being able to
live in a civilization.'

F87 'Wright Report.' *Globe and Mail*, 18 March 1972, 6
Letter to the editor criticizing the draft report of the Wright Commission,
especially its assumptions about the amount of preparation time required
for lecturing. For replies see P73, P112, P129.

F88 'Wright Report.' *Globe and Mail*, 30 March 1972, 6
Replies to J.E. Orton's letter about F's views on the report of the Wright
Commission, expressed in his letter of 18 March 1972 (see F87). For Orton's
letter see P129.

F89 'The Teaching of Literature.' *Minneapolis 72: Convention Concerns*, ed Martha
R. Ellison (Urbana, Ill: National Council of Teachers of English 1972), 21–2
Four paragraphs from F's address, 'The Social Uses of Literature' (see H31).

F90 'Northrop Frye.' *Douglas Duncan: A Memorial Portrait*, ed Alan Jarvis
(Toronto: Univ of Toronto Press 1974), 14–15

A tribute to Duncan for his selfless work in arranging for exhibits of
Canadian painting.
F91 Letter to the Editor. *Parabola* 1 (Winter 1976): 4
Expresses pleasure that this new journal devoted to myth and the quest
for meaning has been established.
F92 'From the Chancellor.' *Victoria University Handbook,* 1979
Explains the unique relation between Victoria University and the University
of Toronto, defines briefly the aim of the university, and suggests that
students should take a certain amount of social and academic initiative.
F93 'Oh, the Dear Good Days ... ' *University of Toronto Graduate* 4, no 3 (1979):
16
Recalls two memories from his student days at Victoria College: the reading
of Ned Pratt's poem, *The Truant,* and a lecture by John Robins about
King Alfred's battle with the Danes. Reports that these two events gave
him 'a sense of how real scholars in a real university react to a major crisis'
– World War II.
F94 'A Breath of Fresh Air.' *Deer Park Church Magazine,* June 1980, 1–3
A sermon delivered in Metropolitan United Church, Toronto, for the
baccalaureate service of Victoria and Emmanuel colleges, 23 March 1980.
Takes his text from the Book of Wisdom 7 in the Apocrypha, and from the
story of Nicodemus in John 3. Speaks of the way that the community of
knowledge can release one from the prison of the ego. Observes that
the speculations of both texts about the *Logos* and the objective world of
nature are full of metaphors having to do with fire, wind, and water.
Explores the implications of the metaphors as they relate to power, wisdom,
and love.
F95 'The Great Code.' *Globe and Mail,* 21 November 1981
Letter to the editor in reply to an article, 'Northrop Frye's Long-Awaited
Book' (*Globe and Mail,* 19 November 1981). Sets the record straight about the
reasons for the delay in the publication of *GC.*
F96 'How It Was.' *Studies in Romanticism* 21 (Winter 1982): 571
In reply to a questionnaire about what the study of romanticism was like
in the early days, recounts the beginnings of his interest in the Romantics,
which developed, he says, in conscious opposition to some of the vogues
of the time and 'as much out of perversity as anything else.'
F97 Letter to the Editor. PMLA 100 (March 1985): 238
A reply to Lawrence W. Hyman's critique of F's understanding of the
relationship between literature and politics (see L240). Clarifies what he
means by 'primary concern.' Agrees that we 'cannot use literary experience
directly to improve society'; we can, however, 'use it to improve experience itself.' Maintains that today the social function of literature must go
far beyond an alliance with political and religious ideologies and that
the kind of social imagination called for today is 'of a different order from
what any conceivable political action can attain to by itself.'
F98 'On Living inside Real Life.' *Vic Report* 14 (Spring 1986): 2

An editorial on the continuity and freedom of the university, which F says is not outside of 'real life' but inside it.

F99 'The Dedicated Mind.' *Vic Report* 15 (Winter 1986–7): 12–13
Excerpts from a sermon delivered at a service of thanksgiving at Metropolitan United Church, Toronto, 5 October 1986. The theme of the sermon is that knowledge, which leads to joyful wisdom, is rooted in love. For the full text of the sermon, which was delivered in connection with Victoria University's sesquicentennial celebration, see 1190.

G

Interviews and Dialogues

G1 'What Has Become of Conversation?' Audiotape in the CBC Radio Archives, Toronto. CBC reference no 820303-9 (4). Broadcast on CJBC, December 1948. 30 min
A panel discussion in 'The Varsity Story' series among Lister Sinclair (moderator), Prof Linden Smith, Anthony Wallace, James Reaney, and F. The discussion centres on defining the nature and function of conversation. F maintains that the society of conversation is a form of society as a whole.

G2 'On Education.' Unpublished typescript of a conversation between F and an unnamed interviewer, 1961. 4 pp. See I15.
Replies to questions about the nature of education and the usefulness of disciplines. Includes a seminar discussion between F and fourth-year university students on the possibility of there being a contemporary tragic hero.

G3 *University*. Montreal: National Film Board, 1961. 27 min. Black and white. 16 mm
Several minutes of this film are devoted to F's responses to questions about the purposes of education, the difficult art of thinking, and the connection between freedom and disciplined speech. The film also reproduces a portion of a discussion on *Death of a Salesman* in one of F's seminars.

G4 'Northrop Frye and Literature.' *The Gazette* [Univ of Western Ontario], 12 March 1963, 6
Responds to questions on literary and critical trends in Canada and the United States. Remarks specifically on the work of Layton, Reaney, Mailer, Salinger, and Nabokov, and on the growth of theoretical criticism. Interviewed by Tim Traynor, Jerry Wadsworth, and Pete Miller.

G5 'The Voice and the Crowd.' *Media 1* (Toronto: CBC Publications 1966), 12–18. Rpt with the subtitle 'A Dialogue on Man's Search for Salvation' in *University of Toronto Graduate* 13 (December 1966): 75–6, 78–91.

A dialogue between F and the Reverend Gregory Baum, a Roman Catholic theologian and ecumenist. They discuss the meaning of salvation, religious freedom, tyranny and martyrdom, detachment and involvement, Marxism, sin and alienation, and the situation of human beings as they are represented in modern literature. Presented originally as a CBC broadcast in 'The Human Condition' series, 7 April 1966 (see H11).

G6 'Culture, Literature, and Education.' Audiotape in the CBC Archives, Toronto. CBC reference no 670314–2. Broadcast on 14 March 1967. 19 min
An 'Ideas' series discussion between F and Murray MacQuarrie on culture, literature, and education in the modern world. The dialogue centres on the dangers of indulging in a dogmatic mythology, particularly that of politically founded religious movements such as Communism.

G7 'Northrop Frye: 10 ans avant la néo-critique.' Le Devoir, 3 June 1967, 13
Responds to questions about AC, modern criticism in general, Canadian literature, critical controversy, and mass culture. Interviewed by Naïm Kattan.

G8 'Entretien: "Je ne souhaite pas avoir de disciples. Je voudrais être utile." '
Le Monde, 25 October 1967, iv
Speaks about the relationship between literature and history, Lukács's view of genres and their connection with historical periods, and mass culture. Interviewed by Naïm Kattan.

G9 'Présentation de Northrop Frye ... ou l'anti-McLuhan.' Le Devoir, 23 November 1968, 11
Replies to sixteen questions about the relationship of literature to life, the social function of criticism, and the connection between mythology and religion, among other things. Interviewed by Naïm Kattan on the occasion of the French translation of MC.

G10 Exchange #2. Toronto: Metropolitan Educational Television Association of Toronto. Filmed by York Univ Television Centre, [1968]. 29 min. Black and white. 16 mm
Responds to questions by Roby Kidd and D.M. Smyth on teaching and criticism, political and social pundits, continuous learning, film, the imagination, leisure, and excellence.

G11 'An Interview.' Random, January 1969, 18–22
Answers a series of questions about education, ranging from the structure of the modern university to the role of the student in society. Interviewed by Bob Bossin.

G12 'The Only Genuine Revolution.' Monday Morning, February 1969, 20–6
On the aims of education, the structure of academic subjects, levels of learning, the core curriculum, the social aspect of education, the integrity of the humanities in a shoddy and brutal world, the basis of authority in the schools and their class biases, and the relationship between scholarship and teaching. Interviewed by Bruce Mickleburgh.

G13 'Educating the Imagination.' Monday Morning, March 1969, 22–8
Part 2 of G12. Responds to questions on the status, use, and levels of language; literary criticism as a discipline; the teaching of myth in the

schools, especially biblical and classical mythology; the place of grammar and rhetoric in the curriculum; film and television; classical education; the social vision in contemporary literature; the educated imagination; literary form; and literary experience. Interviewed by Bruce Mickleburgh.

G14 'Into the Wilderness: An Interview on Religion with Northrop Frye.' *Acta Victoriana* 94 (February 1970): 39–50
Replies to questions about the meaning of the word 'God,' martyrdom, the religions of Marxism and New-Left social-protest movements, the individual and social dimensions of religion, the religious nature of mythologies, and the spiritual sterility of the modern church. Interviewed by John Ayre.

G15 'There Is Really No Such Thing as Methodology.' *Orbit 1* 1 (February 1970): 4–7
Answers questions about the necessity of practice in learning, the teaching of classical and Biblical stories to children, the lecture as a means of instruction, the structure of knowledge, course requirements, educational media, creative writing classes, and the teaching of content vs process learning and method. Interviewed by Johan Aitken.

G16 'Blake's Cosmos.' Toronto, Canadian Broadcasting Corp, 1971. CBC Audiotape no 578. Released by the Center for Cassette Studies, North Hollywood, Calif, 1975. 28 min
A discussion between F and Melvyn Hill about the myth of creation and fall in Blake's cosmology and its relation to the traditional Christian cosmology that emerged with the scientific revolution; Blake's view of the artist and his role in society; and the way Blake's cosmology transcends the categories of subject and object and therefore transcends the philosophies of introversion and objectivity. Produced by Catherine Gallant as part of the CBC 'On Man and Cosmos' series.

G17 'The Limits of Dialogue.' Toronto: Canadian Broadcasting Corp, 1971. CBC Audiotape no 275. 73 min. Originally broadcast on CBC Radio on 19 February 1969. CBC reference no 740618-9 (5)
A conversation with Eli Mandel about the limits of dialogue and, therefore, about poetry, prayer, lunacy, possession, the shape of thoughts and feelings in language, and a wide range of other related topics. This dialogue has been transcribed by Robert D. Denham.

G18 'Two Heretics: Milton and Melville.' Toronto: Canadian Broadcasting Corp, 1971. CBC Audiotape no 572. Released by the Center for Cassette Studies, North Hollywood, Calif, 1975. 20 min
A discussion between F and John Teunissen about the role of Chaos in Shelley's *Prometheus Unbound* and Milton's *Paradise Lost* and about the differences between cosmic and social visions in literature. Presented as part of the CBC series, 'On Man and Cosmos,' organized by Robert Zend. The tape includes a 38-minute address by John Teunissen on Milton and Melville. The discussion between F and Teunissen has been transcribed by Robert D. Denham.

G19 *Impressions*. Toronto: Canadian Broadcasting Corp, 1973. 16 mm. 27 min.

Audiotape in the CBC Radio Archives, Toronto. CBC reference no 730902-2.
Originally broadcast on 2 September 1973
A segment in the 'Impressions' television series in which F discusses with
Ramsay Cook his youth in Moncton, NB, and the relations between the
French and English factions there; the writers and teachers who influenced
him; his studies at Oxford and his fondness for Victoria College; his view
of literature as a total imaginative structure; Margaret Atwood's *Survival*; his
desire for a post-national consciousness in Canadian literature; teaching;
his present book on the Bible, theology, and myth; and his twenty-five
years of giving a course in 'The Bible as Literature.'

G20 'A Conversation with Northrop Frye, Literary Critic.' *Harvard Magazine* 77
(July-August 1975): 52–6
Responds to questions about the literary influence of the Bible, the difference between fable and myth, the pastoral convention, the failures of
the educational system, the teaching of literature, critical value-judgments,
and the vocation of the critic. Interviewed by Justin Kaplan.

G21 'Beyond the Ivory Tower.' Toronto: Canadian Broadcasting Corp. CBC Audiotape no 863. Released by the Center for Cassette Studies, North Hollywood, Calif, 1975. 6 min
Replies to questions about the present quality of university education, the
results of flexibility in university curricula, and the directions the university seems to be moving in. Interviewed at the Learned Societies Meeting
at McGill University and presented as part of the CBC 'Ideas' program prepared by David McPherson. This tape includes interviews with three
others and an address by Robin Mathews.

G22 'The Canadian Imagination.' Toronto: Canadian Broadcasting Corp. CBC
Audiotape no 650. Released by the Center for Cassette Studies, North
Hollywood, Calif, 1975. 25 min
Responds to a series of questions about his views on Canadian literature
in *BG*. Talks about, among other things, the reason for the relatively small
number of good Canadian novelists, the absence of a myth of the West
in Canadian writing, the didactic strain and 'garrison mentality' in Canadian
letters, and the similarity between the geographical and historical situation
of Canada and Scandinavia, which accounts for Canada's rather meagre
literary output and the destructive themes in its writing. Interviewed
by David McPherson.

G23 'Northrop Frye on Evil.' Toronto: Canadian Broadcasting Corp. CBC Audiotape no 693. Released by the Center for Cassette Studies, North Hollywood, Calif, 1975. 27 min
A discussion between F and Janet Sommerville about the doctrines of good
and evil in *Paradise Lost* and in a number of other works from the time of
the ancient Hebrews to modern ironists. This dialogue has been transcribed
by Robert D. Denham.

G24 'Symmetry in the Arts.' Toronto: Canadian Broadcasting Corp. CBC Audiotape no 893. Released by the Center for Cassette Studies, North Holly-

wood, Calif, 1975. 16 min. Originally broadcast on CBC Radio, 17 November 1972. CBC reference no 721117-3
Replies to questions about the meaning of symmetry in Blake's work as it relates to his poetic rhythms, metaphors, images, and sense of design. Interviewer unnamed. The tape also includes a separate interview with Jacques Languirand on the topic of symmetry. The interview with F has been transcribed by Robert D. Denham.

G25 'Canadian Voices.' Canada Today/D'Aujourd'hui 7 (January-February 1976): 3–4. Two paragraphs rpt in Canada Today/D'Aujourd'hui 11 (November 1980): 11
Brief replies to questions from an unnamed interviewer about the differences between Canada and the United States, irony in Canadian literature, the significance of technology, economic domination, nationalism, and the Canadian Radio-television and Telecommunications Commission.

G26 'A Conversation with Northrop Frye: Education, Religion, Old Age.' Varsity [Univ of Toronto], 22 October 1976, 14–15
Answers more than forty questions about the present student generation, his own reputation, his relation to and opinion of Matthew Arnold, his interest in the Bible, and his views on religion and the United Church of Canada. Interviewed by Philip Chester.

G27 'A Literate Person Is First and Foremost an Articulate Person.' Interchange 7, no 4 (1976–7): 32–8
Replies to more than fifty questions about educational standards and illiteracy; the Ontario Curriculum Institute; the teaching of writing, grammar, and reading; the place of Canadian literature in the curriculum; the intended audiences of his own books; the social context of literature; the processes of identification and detachment in literary experience; the biblical and classical foundations of literary education; and the future role of television. Interviewed by Hugh Oliver.

G28 Interview with Don Harron. Audiotape in the CBC Archives, Toronto. Recorded on 6 February 1978 and broadcast on the CBC 'Morningside' series.
A wide-ranging, five-part interview on religion in contemporary life. F and Harron discuss myth, ritual, history, Christianity, Spengler, Eastern religions, and the prophetic tradition – among numerous other topics. This interview has been transcribed by Robert D. Denham.

G29 'Eminent Victorians: The Frye Interview.' The Strand [Victoria College, Univ of Toronto], 1 March 1978, 5–11. Partially rpt as 'Interview: Northrop Frye' in Acta Victoriana Centennial, 1878–1978 102 (Fall 1978): 53–4
Replies to questions about life at Victoria College, John Robins and E.J. Pratt, the honour course, the student ethos, teaching large classes, the loss of autonomous departments at Victoria, Canadian culture, the ways in which poets are affected by critical ideas, separatism, the Bible, anti-intellectualism, and melodrama in contemporary films. Interviewed by Bruce Reynolds.

G30 'Interview.' *Vic Report* 7 (Winter 1978–9): 3–6
Responds to questions about his role as chancellor of Victoria University,
the principle of federated colleges, his own undergraduate days at Victoria
and Emmanuel Colleges, his ordination, the social use of science, the
effects of changing economic situations on the university, the impact of
television on modern society, and his understanding of his own strengths
as a scholar and teacher. Interviewed by John Plaskett.

G31 'Sogna sui Laghi il nuovo americano.' *La Republica*, 12 May 1979,
'Cultura' section
Answers questions about his interest in Italian culture, about Canadian
identity, and about the mythologies that make up the American myth.
Comments especially on the geographical and historical differences between
the Canadian and American myths. Interviewed by Gian Piero Brunetta.

G32 'Ho cercato di rompere le croste dello storicismo.' *Tuttolibri*, 9 June 1979, 8
Replies to questions about the anti-historicism of his criticism, saying
that his approach is to place literary works in their cultural context; and
about his interpretation of Shakespeare, especially *The Tempest* and *The
Winter's Tale*. Interviewed by Claudio Grolier.

G33 'La Sapienza del Lettore.' *L'Unita* [Florence], 11 June 1979
Responds to questions on the origins of literature; on its relationship to
science, sociology, psychoanalysis, and linguistics; on the role of the reader;
and on *SeS*. Interviewed by Beppe Cottafiva.

G34 'Quattro Domande a Northrop Frye.' *alfabeta* 1 (September 1979): 14
Replies to questions about the relation between the younger generation
and the revolutionary aspect of romanticism, the return of the fantastic in
secular literature and its relation to the sacred, and the interest in romanticism resulting from the general attitudes produced by student unrest
and by television. Interviewed by Umberto Eco.

G35 'Put kritike.' *NIN* 30 (December 1979)
Defines his relationship to the New Critics, saying that his disagreement
with them stems from their neglect of the principles of genre, convention,
and structure. Agrees with the interviewer's contention that he may
have been a precursor of structuralism. Also replies to questions about the
relationship between theory and practice in literary criticism and about
his increasing interest in social and educational issues. Interviewed by Maja
Herman-Sekulič.

G36 'A Conversation with Art Cuthbert.' Toronto: Canadian Broadcasting Corp,
1979. CBC Audiotape no 1433. 47 min
A wide-ranging conversation in which F discusses Blake, his career as a
teacher, many of his critical writings, education, the Bible, culture, and the
interaction of imagination and society. Interviewed on CBC Radio's 'Anthology' on 30 September and 7 October 1978. CBC reference nos 780930-2 and
781007-6. This tape has been transcribed by Robert D. Denham.

G37 'Frye's Literary Theory in the Classroom: A Panel Discussion.' *CEA Critic* 42
(January 1980): 32–42

A discussion among Elizabeth and Gregory Cowan, David Stewart, Richard Costa, and F, based upon the twelve-volume series of textbooks, *Literature: Uses of the Imagination*, for which F was the consulting editor (see B14). F responds to questions about his reasons for editing the series, the teacher's role in using the books, the student's ability to understand large literary patterns, the nature of children's literature, ways to make children responsive to the mythic experience in stories, the meaning of 'archetype,' the crisis in literacy, and the reading process. This discussion was recorded in April 1978 at Texas A & M University.

G38 'Northrop Frye: Identita e mito.' *Canada contemporaneo* 1 (January–February 1980), 8–9, 11
Replies to questions about the ways in which he differs from other critics, his work on the Bible, Canadian literature and identity, the charge that his critical system is ahistorical or anti-historical, and the literary tendencies of the present age. Interviewed by Gilbert Reid.

G39 'Literature, Language, and Learning: Purposes and Importance of Literature in Education.' *Language Arts* 57 (April 1980): 199–206
Answers questions about the educated imagination, the power of literature, reading as recreation, stock responses, the elementary curriculum, pop culture, value-judgments, and strategies for teaching literature, among other topics. Interviewed by Bryant Fillion.

G40 'From Nationalism to Regionalism: The Maturing of Canadian Culture.' *Aurora: New Canadian Writing 1980*, ed Morris Wolfe (Toronto: Doubleday Canada, 1980), 5–15. Rpt in *The Anthology Anthology*, ed Robert Weaver (Toronto: Macmillan 1984), 62–72.
A dialogue between F and Robert Fulford on Canadian art and culture, with particular attention to the role of the government, the media, regional and mass culture, the influence of technology, and the Americanization of Canada. Originally recorded by CBC and broadcast on CBC 'Anthology,' Fall 1980.

G41 'Fearful Symmetry: Northrop Frye on Victoria, the Bible, and the Canadian Way.' *Vic Report* 9 (Summer 1981): 9–12
Responds to questions about GC, the history of his interest in the Bible, the teachers who most influenced him, changes that have occurred at Victoria College since he was a student, his opinion of McLuhan, political separatist movements in Canada, and Canadian identity. Interviewed by D.G. Bastian.

G42 '*Acta* Interview: Northrop Frye.' *Acta Victoriana* 106 (Fall 1981): 58–70
Primarily about the relationship between the humanities and the sciences, many of the questions arising from F's address to the American Association for the Advancement of Science, 'The Bridge of Language' (see D264). Interviewed by John Cargill and Angela Esterhammer.

G43 'Canadian Energy: Dialogues on Creativity: Northrop Frye.' *Descant* 12, nos 32–3 (1981): 216–26
Answers questions about teaching, writing, the creative mind, the verbal

arts, and the emerging authority of Canadian literature. Interviewed by Deborah Shackleton.

G44 Interview with Helen Gougeon. Taped for CFRB Radio, Toronto, and broadcast on 15 April 1982. 16$^1/_2$ min

Responds to questions on a wide variety of topics, including the Bible, university education, students, Canadian politics, technology, heaven, classroom teaching, and the future.

G45 'Northrop Frye and the Bible.' Audiotape in the CBC Archives, Toronto. CBC reference nos 820406-1 and 820407-1. Broadcast on 5–9 April 1982 and rebroadcast on 9–13 August 1982

A discussion between F and Robert Prowse on GC. Broadcast on the CBC 'Morningside' series.

G46 Interview with Stan Correy. Taped for the Australian Broadcasting Corp, 20 April 1982. 30 min

Answers questions primarily about GC: its relation to AC, the seven phases of revelation discussed in GC, the narrative shape of the Bible and its relation to social and political concepts, biblical imagery, explanation by translation, polysemous meaning, the unity of the Bible, and F's affinity with Joyce and Stevens. This interview has been transcribed by Robert D. Denham.

G47 'Northrop Frye on Literature and Religion.' *The Newspaper* [Univ of Toronto], 27 October 1982, 5

Replies to questions about the process of his own writing, the relationship between teaching and writing, the tension between prophecy and organized religion, his views on divinity and life after death, and the difference between the Bible and literary texts. Interviewed by Andrew Kaufman.

G48 Interview with Susan Stanberg. Washington, DC: National Public Radio, 1984. 'All Things Considered' tape no 840424. 4 min

Interview with F on the occasion of his address, 'The Social Authority of the Writer,' presented at the Library of Congress, 24 April 1984 (see I168). F responds to questions about creativity in literary criticism, the end of critical analysis, and recent directions in criticism (the Derrida school, semiotics, and linguistics). This interview has been transcribed by Robert D. Denham.

G49 'An Interview with Northrop Frye.' *Scripsi* [Univ of Melbourne] 2, no 4 (1984): 220–6

Replies to questions about the relationship of FS to AC, what he means by 'ruling-class anxieties,' the imaginative transformation of nature, the similarities between Canadian and Australian literature, the differences between American and Canadian culture, teaching and the university, the proper time to teach literary theory to students (it should be 'put off as long as possible'), and Wallace Stevens. Interviewed by Imre Salusinszky, Alan Roughley, and Vijay Mishra at the School of Criticism and Theory, Northwestern University, 7 July 1983.

G50 'Les lecteurs doivent manger le livre.' *Liberation*, 21 November 1984, 29

Responds to questions about the relation between the Bible, history, and literature in Western society; the connection between parody and contradiction in the Bible; the idea of Marxism as a religion; and the sense in which the Bible is more than a work of literature. Interviewed by Mathieu Lindon.

G51 'Music in My Life.' Audiotape in the CBC Radio Archives, Toronto. CBC reference nos [S] 850201-6 (1) and 850201-6 (2). Broadcast on 1 February 1985 Ian Alexander interviews F on the 'Arts National' series about the importance of music in his life. F talks about the influence of George Ross upon his musical training and his interest in Gilbert and Sullivan, Mozart, Clementi, and Verdi. This interview has been transcribed by Robert D. Denham.

G52 'Interview with Northrop Frye.' 23-page typescript, forthcoming in a collection of interviews by Imre Salusinszky to be published by Methuen Replies to questions about the main steps in the development of his critical theory, the difference between ideology and 'concern,' his views about Bloom and Derrida, his attraction to the poetry of Stevens, the nature of the university, his relation to Marxism, and his future critical projects. This interview was conducted in Toronto on 16 November 1985.

G53 'Northrop Frye Talks about the Role of the Humanities.' *Columns* [Univ of Toronto], Fall 1985, 6–7
Answers questions about the function of the humanities in a technological society, the development of verbal skills, and literacy.

G54 'Embarking on an Encounter with Real Life.' *Columns* [Univ of Toronto], Winter 1985/6, 4–5
Discusses the role of the media, the university, and the arts in modern Canadian society.

G55 'Acta Interview: Northrop Frye.' *Acta Victoriana* 110 (Spring 1986): 23–5
Responds to questions about popular culture, McLuhan, and the media. Interviewed by Cheryl Carter, Stephen Graebel, and Karen Vinke.

G56 'Questions and Answers.' *Romanticism and Contemporary Criticism*, ed Morris Eaves and Michael Fischer (Ithaca, NY: Cornell Univ Press 1986), 29–45
Replies to questions on original sin, metaphor, symbolism, the phases of symbolism, romanticism, Blake, literary criticism, value-judgments, deconstruction, the social context of literature, and the myth of freedom – among other things. This dialogue took place between F and members of the audience following his address, 'The Survival of Eros in Poetry' (D282), presented at the University of New Mexico, 16 February 1983.

G57 'Moncton, Mentors, and Memories: Reflections with Northrop Frye.' *Studies in Canadian Literature* 11 (Fall 1986): 246–69
Explores with F the influence of his early environment, family, and teachers on the development of his thought. Interviewed by Deanne Bogdan.

H

Sound Recordings, Films, and Videotapes

H1 'What Has Become of Conversation?' Audiotape in the CBC Radio Archives, Toronto. CBC reference no 820303-9 (4). Broadcast on 9 December 1948. 30 min
See G1.

H2 'George Bernard Shaw.' Audiotape in the CBC Radio Archives, Toronto. CBC reference no 820730-10 (3). Broadcast on 7 July 1950. 15 min
A talk on the life and career on George Bernard Shaw. This is the final of four talks in 'The Writer as Prophet' series. The first three talks – on Milton, Swift, and Blake – were apparently not recorded by CBC on discs or tape.

H3 'Thomas Chandler Haliburton's Sam Slick.' Audiotape in the CBC Radio Archives, Toronto. CBC reference no 551101. Broadcast on 1 November 1955
A talk on Haliburton's eight Sam Slick books, aired on the CBC 'Anthology' series. Published as 'Haliburton: Mask and Ego' (see D128).

H4 'Oswald Spengler.' Audiotape in the CBC Radio Archives, Toronto. CBC reference no 820427-9 (19). Broadcast on 23 November 1955
Published (see D77).

H5 'CBC Wednesday Night Programme in Honour of Pratt's 75th Birthday.' Audiotape in the E.J. Pratt Library, Victoria Univ, Univ of Toronto. Recorded on 1 April 1958. 4 min
F and several dozen other people are included in this program. F speaks about Pratt's editing *Canadian Poetry Magazine*, his erudite poetry, and the exuberance of his personal relations.

H6 *University*. Montreal: National Film Board, 1961. 27 min. Black and white. 16 mm
See G3.

H7 'The Educated Imagination.' Toronto: Canadian Broadcasting Corp, 1972

CBC Audiotapes nos 013-018. Released by the Center for Cassette Studies, North Hollywood, Calif, 1975. 177 min. Originally broadcast on CBC Radio during November and December 1962
For the published text, which is slightly expanded from the radio talks, see A3.

H8 'Shakespeare and the Modern World.' Audiotape in the CBC Radio Archives, Toronto. CBC reference no 841023-9 (12). Broadcast on 13 May 1964. 30 min
Presented as the fifth and final program in the Shakespeare series in 'The University of the Air' series. See I24.

H9 Opening Ceremonies of the E.J. Pratt Memorial Room at Victoria University. Audiotape in the E.J. Pratt Library, Victoria Univ, Univ of Toronto, and in the CBC Radio Archives, Toronto. CBC reference no 641015-4. Broadcast on 15 October 1964
F is one of the two featured speakers on the program. Talks about the scholarly, poetic, and social features of Pratt's life, his teaching, the integrity he displayed in his standards, and his courageous view of life.

H10 'George Orwell's *1984*.' Audiotape in the CBC Radio Archives, Toronto. CBC reference no 4322. Broadcast on 25 January 1965
See D170.

H11 'The Voice and the Crowd.' Audiotape in the CBC Radio Archives, Toronto. CBC reference no 660407-2. Broadcast on 7 April 1966
See G5.

H12 'The Modern Century.' Audiotapes in the CBC Radio Archives, Toronto. CBC reference nos 670131-7, 670214-1, 740618-9 (5), 670221-5, 670228-5, and 670307-3. Broadcast during January, February, and March 1967
Presented in the 'Ideas' series. For the published version of these lectures see A10.

H13 'Culture, Literature, and Education.' Audiotape in the CBC Radio Archives, Toronto. CBC reference no 670314-2. Broadcast on 14 March 1967. 19 min
See G6.

H14 'Canadian Poetry.' Audiotape in the CBC Radio Archives, Toronto. CBC reference no 670507-8. Broadcast on 7 May 1967
A program in the 'Modern Canadian Poetry' series, which concludes with a critique by F on the development of Canadian poetry. This is the audio of a television program in the 'Extension' series.

H15 'B.K. Sandwell.' Audiotape in the CBC Radio Archives, Toronto. CBC reference no 670725-12 (bb). Broadcast on 25 July 1967. 2 min
Brief comments by F in a CBC 'Tuesday Night' series, 'A Portrait of B.K. Sandwell.' F speaks about *Saturday Night*, which Sandwell edited, in the Canadian context.

H16 'The Ethics of Change.' Audiotape in the CBC Radio Archives, Toronto. CBC reference no 681211-2. Broadcast on 11 December 1968 on the 'Ideas' series. 47 min
See D191.

H17 *Exchange #2.* Toronto: Metropolitan Educational Television Association of

Toronto. Filmed by York Univ Television Centre, [1968]. 29 min. Black
and white. 16 mm
See G10.

H18 *Fearful Symmetry: Northrop Frye Looks at the World.* Toronto: Jon Slan, 1969.
27 min. Colour. 16 mm
A documentary about F that, by juxtaposing interviews with F and scenes
from contemporary life, illustrates how literature connects with experience.
Produced and directed by Jon Slan. Reviewed by Martin Knelman (see
P105).

H19 'Notes on a Maple Leaf.' Audiotape in the CBC Radio Archives, Toronto.
CBC reference no 710424-2. Broadcast on 24 April 1971
A documentary in the 'Anthology' series about the crisis in Canadian
publishing. Includes comments on this issue by F, Margaret Atwood,
Robert Fulford, and Robert Weaver.

H20 'Poets of Canada: 1920 to the Present.' Audiotape in the CBC Radio
Archives, Toronto. CBC reference no 710522-2. Broadcast on 22 May 1971
Part two of a seven-part 'Anthology' series in which writers talk abut what
makes their work Canadian. Those discussing the issue are F, Ralph
Gustafson, Phyllis Gotlieb, F.R. Scott, Leonard Cohen, George Bowering,
D.G. Jones, John Robert Colombo et al.

H21 'Poets of Canada: 1920 to the Present.' Audiotape in the CBC Radio
Archives, Toronto. CBC reference no 710529-2. Broadcast on 29 May 1971
Part three of a seven-part 'Anthology' series. F and others take an informal
look at the history of Canadian poetry during the past fifty years.

H22 'Poets of Canada: 1920 to the Present.' Audiotape in the CBC Radio
Archives, Toronto. CBC reference no 710605-4. Broadcast on 5 June 1971
Part four of a seven-part 'Anthology' series. F and others discuss the little
magazines.

H23 'Poets of Canada: 1920 to the Present.' Audiotape in the CBC Radio
Archives, Toronto. CBC reference no 710612-3. Broadcast on 12 June 1971
Part five of a seven-part 'Anthology' series. F and others discuss concrete
and experimental poetry.

H24 'Poets of Canada: 1920 to the Present.' Audiotape in the CBC Radio
Archives, Toronto. CBC reference no 710619-5. Broadcast on 19 June 1971
Part six of a seven-part 'Anthology' series. F, Margaret Atwood, Eli
Mandel, Irving Layton, and Miriam Waddington discuss F's theories of the
garrison and the wilderness in Canadian poetry.

H25 'Blake's Cosmos.' Toronto: Canadian Broadcasting Corp, 1971. CBC
Audiotape no 578. Released by the Center for Cassette Studies, North
Hollywood, Calif, 1975. 28 min
See G16.

H26 'The Limits of Dialogue.' Toronto: Canadian Broadcasting Corp, 1971.
CBC Audiotape no 275. 73 min
See G17.

H27 'Two Heretics: Milton and Melville.' Toronto: Canadian Broadcasting Corp,

1971. CBC Audiotape no 572. Released by the Center for Cassette Studies, North Hollywood, Calif, 1975. 58 min
See G18.

H28 'The Critic and the Writer.' Toronto: Canadian Broadcasting Corp, 1972. CBC Audiotape no 861. Released by the Center for Cassette Studies, North Hollywood, Calif, 1975. 17 min
Examines the *genius loci* of his undergraduate years, associated with Pelham Edgar, E.J. Pratt, and John D. Robins, and reviews the way in which the history of literature was taught at Victoria College, his interest in Blake, his interest in Canadian literature (focused by A.J.M. Smith's anthology of Canadian poetry), and the importance of teaching to his scholarly and critical interests. Recorded at the May 1972 conference of the Learned Societies, McGill University, and presented on the CBC 'Ideas' series as part of 'The Writer in Canada' program. CBC reference no 720627-6. This talk has been transcribed by Robert D. Denham.

H29 Modern Education. Audiotape in the CBC Radio Archives, Toronto. CBC reference no 720630-4. Broadcast on 30 June 1972. 8 min
Says that flexibility and subjectivity in many modern educational programs actually serve only to erode the quality of education and that many students are in school only because of the social status it affords. Recorded at the May 1972 conference of the Learned Societies, McGill University and aired in the CBC 'Ideas' series.

H30 Harold Innis. Audiotape in the CBC Radio Archives, Toronto. CBC reference no 721121-8. Broadcast on 21 November 1972. 5 min
Includes F among other friends and followers of Innis, commenting on the man and his ideas. F compares Innis to Hegel because each of them has followers on opposing sides. Says Innis thought instruments of communication play the same part that instruments of production play in Marxist theory. Aired on a program in the CBC 'Tuesday Night' series, 'Harold Innis – Portrait of a Scholar.'

H31 'The Social Uses of Literature: The Teaching Critic.' Kenosha, Wisc: Comptron Corp, 1972. Cassette no ET–10. 47 min
Distinguishes between the allegorical approach to literature, which gives to poetry a less important social function than that of other verbal structures, and the mythological approach, which gives literature the social function of making us aware of our mythological conditioning and providing us models of social vision. Examines the sources of the Western mythological structure, rooted in the Bible, and its relation to popular literature and to teaching. Recorded at the annual convention of the National Council for Teachers of English, Minneapolis, Wisc, 1972. The tape has been transcribed by Robert D. Denham. An excerpt from the conclusion of this talk appears as 'The Teaching of Literature,' in *Minneapolis 72: Convention Concerns*, ed Martha R. Ellison (Urbana, Ill: NCTE 1972), 21–2.

H32 Easter. Audiotape in the CBC Radio Archives, Toronto. CBC reference no 730418-2. Broadcast on 18 April 1973. 26 min

Speaks about the elements that came into Christianity from earlier worship of the Sun, Adonis, Attis, Isis, et al. Describes the theme of rebirth as different from the theme of resurrection. Explores the mythologies of bodily death, the eating of the killed king, deliverance, and the harrowing of hell. Aired as a program in the 'Concern' series.

H33 *Impressions*. Toronto: Canadian Broadcasting Corp, 1973. 16 mm. 27 min
See G19.

H34 Aldous Huxley. Audiotape in the CBC Radio Archives, Toronto. CBC reference nos 731204-4 and 731205-6. Broadcast on 4 and 5 December 1973. 1 min and 2 min respectively
Brief comment on Huxley in 'The Aldous Huxley and Beyond' series. Speaks about the current implications of Huxley's *Brave New World*, which is an introduction to his Dante period.

H35 CRTC. Audiotape in the CBC Radio Archives, Toronto. CBC reference no 740218-2. Broadcast on 18 February 1974. 7 min
A news report on the Canadian Radio-television and Telecommunications Commission hearings. F challenges the models offered by Laurent Picard, president of CBC, regarding the kind of appeal CBC should aim for (commercial mass appeal, mass media appeal as it is today, or specialized minority or educational appeal). Objects that there is no grim minority of highbrows. Picard defends himself.

H36 CRTC Hearings. Audiotape in the CBC Radio Archives, Toronto. CBC reference no 740220-1. Broadcast on 20 February 1974. 5 min
News report on the third day of the Canadian Radio-television and Telecommunications Commission hearings. F comments on the suggestion that the CBC's plant facilities be separated from its programming. Says this means splitting one amoeba and getting two.

H37 CRTC Hearings. Audiotape in the CBC Radio Archives, Toronto. CBC reference no 740222-4. Broadcast on 22 February 1974. $1^{1}/_{2}$ min
News report on the final day of the Canadian Radio-television and Telecommunications Commission hearings. F comments on the good briefs requesting multicultural programs and invites response to these.

H38 Easter. Audiotape in the CBC Radio Archives, Toronto. CBC reference no 740410-3. Broadcast on 10 April 1974. 9 min
In an Easter special on the 'Concern' series, recalls pre-Christian myths, the Gospel version of the Passover, the dating of Easter, etc.

H39 CRTC Hearings. Audiotape in the CBC Radio Archives, Toronto. CBC reference no 750825-6. Broadcast on 27 August 1975
F summarizes the CRTC hearings in Kingston, Ont, on violence in the media. See D237.

H40 'Beyond the Ivory Tower.' Toronto: Canadian Broadcasting Corp. CBC Audiotape no 863. Released by the Center for Cassette Studies, North Hollywood, Calif, 1975. 38 min
See G21.

H41 'The Canadian Imagination.' Toronto: Canadian Broadcasting Corp. CBC

Audiotape no 650. Released by the Center for Cassette Studies, North
Hollywood, Calif, 1975. 25 min
See G22.

H42 'Northrop Frye on Evil.' Toronto: Canadian Broadcasting Corp. CBC
Audiotape no 693. Released by the Center for Cassette Studies, North
Hollywood, Calif, 1975. 27 min
See G23.

H43 'Symmetry in the Arts.' Toronto: Canadian Broadcasting Corp. CBC
Audiotape no 893. Released by the Center for Cassette Studies, North
Hollywood, Calif, 1975. 16 min
See G24.

H44 *Journey without Arrival: A Personal Point of View from Northrop Frye*. Toronto:
Canadian Broadcasting Corp, 1976. 57 min. National Film Board serial
no 106C 0176 140
Filmed on location in various parts of Canada. Directed by Vincent Tovell.
F reflects on Canada and on the attitudes of its people. Singles out the
poetry of E.J. Pratt and the paintings of Emily Carr, Tom Thomson,
and the Group of Seven as expressing Canada's spirit, landscape, and
consciousness. First aired on CBC television on 6 April 1976. Available in
videocassette or film. Portions of the script are printed as 'View of Canada:
Never a Believer in a Happy Ending.' *Globe and Mail*, 6 April 1976, 7
(see D229).

H45 'The Future Tense.' Audiotape in CBC Radio Archives, Toronto. CBC reference no [s] 770220-14. Broadcast on 20 February 1977. $^1/_2$ min
Brief remarks on the 'Special Occasions' series. Says he believes the human
race will continue to stagger on between the darkest predictions and the
brightest.

H46 *Options*. Toronto: Media Centre, Univ of Toronto, 1977. 31 min. Colour.
Videocassette
An overview of the conference on the Future of Canadian Confederation,
October 1977. The address was published as 'A Summary of the *Options*
Conference' (see D241).

H47 Interview with Don Harron. Audiotape in the CBC Radio Archives, Toronto.
Recorded on 6 February 1978 and broadcast on the CBC 'Morningside'
series
See G28.

H48 A Conversation with Art Cuthbert. Toronto: Canadian Broadcasting Corp,
1979. CBC Audiotape no 1433. 47 min
See G36.

H49 'Reconsidering Levels of Meaning.' Emory, Va: Emory & Henry College,
1979. Audiocassettes. 100 min
The Reynolds Lectures for 1979, presented at Emory & Henry College,
15–16 March. On the phases and uses of language and on the levels of
meaning in literature, with special reference to the Bible. The arguments of

these lectures are developed more fully in GC. The lectures have been transcribed by Robert D. Denham.

H50 'From Nationalism to Regionalism: The Maturing of Canadian Culture.' Toronto: Canadian Broadcasting Corp 1980. Audiotape. Recording of a talk between F and Robert Fulford, published as G40.

H51 *The Bible and Literature: A Personal View from Northrop Frye.* Toronto: Media Centre, Univ of Toronto, 1982–3. 30 colour video progams, each 26 min long. Executive producer: Bob Rogers
Each of these programs consists of an introduction by F followed by lectures and seminar sessions. In these sessions, F answers questions based on the lectures, which are edited versions of one-hour lectures given by F in 1981–2 as part on his course on the Bible and Literature at the University of Toronto. The first fifteen programs examine the Bible through its narrative forms and imagery; the last fifteen treat the seven stages of biblical revelation. The titles of the programs are:

1 Introduction: An Approach
2 The Shape of the Bible
3 Images of Paradise: Trees and Water
4 Parody and Manifest Demonic: Trees and Water
5 Sexual Imagery: Bride and Bridegroom
6 The Great Whore and the Forgiven Harlot
7 Pastoral and Agricultural Imagery: Part One
8 Pastoral and Agricultural Imagery: Part Two
9 The World of Angels
10 Leviathan, Dragons and the Anti-Christ
11 The Hero from Across the Sea
12 The Double Mirror: Exodus and the Gospel
13 The Metaphor of Kingship
14 King, Priest, and Prophet
15 The Question of Primogeniture
16 Genesis: In the Beginning
17 Genesis: Creation and the Sexes
18 Exodus: A Revolutionary Heritage
19 Law: Ordering a Society
20 Wisdom: The Proverb
21 Wisdom: Playing Before God
22 Ecclesiastes: Vanity of Vanities
23 Job: A Test
24 Job: The Question of Tragedy
25 Job: Restored Humility
26 The Language of Proclamation: Style and Rhythm in the Bible
27 The Gospel: Rewriting the Commandments
28 Revelation: Removing the Veil
29 Revelation: After the Ego Disappears

30 Conclusion: The Language of Love

Each of these programs is accompanied by a manual that contains (1) a transcript of the entire lecture or lectures from which the material has been excerpted for use in the program and (2) a teacher's guide for the program, written by Michael Dolzani. These guides contain a synopsis of the program, an outline of the key facts presented in the video lecture, including biblical passages cited in the lecture, suggestions for supplementary reading and for discussion, and a section called 'The Teacher's Perspective,' which provides background, examples, and thematic touchstones for use by teachers. The spiral-bound manuals average about 14 pp each; there are 432 pp altogether.

H52 'Northrop Frye and the Bible.' Audiotape in the CBC Radio Archives, Toronto. CBC reference nos 820406-1 and 820407-1. Broadcast on 5–9 April 1982 and rebroadcast on 9–13 August 1982
See G45.

H53 Interview with Helen Gougeon. Taped for CFRB Radio, Toronto, and broadcast on 15 April 1982. 16$^{1}/_{2}$ min
See G44.

H54 Interview with Stan Correy. Taped for the Australian Broadcasting Corp, 20 April 1982. 30 min
See G46.

H55 Pratt Lecture. 1 cassette audiotape and 1 reel-to-reel audiotape in the E.J. Pratt Library, Victoria Univ, Univ of Toronto. 1982
A lecture on E.J. Pratt, presented 25 November 1982 at Victoria College. Speaks of the legend surrounding Pratt and discusses the themes of communication, technology, navigation and shipwreck, and evolution in his poetry.

H56 'Hard Times in the Ivory Tower.' Audiotape in the CBC Radio Archives, Toronto. Broadcast on 2–6 October 1983
A five-part documentary in the 'Ideas' series on higher education in Canada. In parts 2 and 3 F comments on the university as a social community, the importance of Victoria College to his own work, the need for clear conversation among academics, the feeling of detachment from society one gains from reading English literature, and the excitement of the learning process. A transcript of this documentary has been published by CBC, reference no 4-ID-042; for F's comments see pp 13, 24, 46, 47–8.

H57 'Inventing a Music: Macmillan and Walter in the Past and Present.' Audiotape in the CBC Radio Archives, Toronto. Broadcast on 25–26 October 1983
A two-part program in the 'Ideas' series. F comments briefly on music as a social art. A transcript of this program has been published by CBC.

H58 'Back to the Garden: A Profile of Northrop Frye.' Montreal: Radio Canada International, 1983. 33$^{1}/_{3}$ disc. Reference no E-1296. 55 min
Traces the evolution of F's thought through conversation with him and with former students, colleagues, and critics. Prepared by Cliff Arnold and produced by Ginger da Silva.

H59 Interview with Susan Stanberg. Washington, DC: National Public Radio,
1984. 'All Things Considered' tape no 840424. 4 min
See G48.

H60 'The Social Authority of the Writer.' Washington, DC: Library of Congress,
1984. Audiotape no LWO-18595 and videotape no LVR-422. 60 min
A lecture delivered at the Library of Congress, 24 April 1984. For the
manuscript of the lecture, see I168.

H61 'History and the New Age.' Audiotape in the CBC Radio Archives, Toronto.
Broadcast on 10, 17, 24, and 31 May 1984
A four-part program in the 'Ideas' series. In part 1 F distinguishes between
history and myth. A transcript of this program has been published by
CBC, reference no 4-ID-085; for F's comments see p 2.

H62 'Richard Cartwright and the Roots of Canadian Conservatism.' Audiotape
in the CBC Radio Archives, Toronto. Broadcast on 14, 21, and 28 November
1984
A three-part program in the 'Ideas' series on Upper Canadian loyalism and
its legacy. F comments briefly on Canadian political and cultural identity.
A transcript of this program has been published by CBC, reference no
4-ID-100; for F's remarks see pp 22, 26–7.

H63 *The Scholar in Society: Northrop Frye in Conversation*. Montreal: National Film
Board, 1984. 28 min. Colour. Videotape (no 116C 0184 052) and 16 mm
(no 106C 0184 052)
A documentary film in which F discusses the role of the university in
society, the relation between education in language and in the humanities,
and the proper functioning of the individual in society. Directed by
Dawn Winkler.

H64 'Music in My Life.' Audiotape in the CBC Radio Archives, Toronto. CBC
Reference nos [S] 850201-6 (1) and 850201-6 (2). Broadcast on 1 February
1985
See G51.

H65 'The Darkening Mirror: Reflections on the Bomb and Language.' Audiotape
in CBC Radio Archives, Toronto. CBC reference no 850214. Broadcast
14 February 1985. 4 min
Responds to questions about a speech by Jacques Derrida on language.

I

Manuscripts

The manuscripts below are entered according to their location. Those in the first section, which are primarily typescripts of published and unpublished material, are at the University of Toronto. I1 through I121 are located in the Special Collections of the E.J. Pratt Library at Victoria University, and I122 through I193 are located in Frye's files at Massey College. The manuscripts in the second section, which are book manuscripts, are located in the Special Collections of the E.J. Pratt Library. These are identified by their box number in the Special Collections. In section 1, untitled manuscripts are without quotation marks.

SECTION ONE
MANUSCRIPTS AT
THE UNIVERSITY OF TORONTO

Victoria University Library

I1 'Reflections at a Movie' (1942)
CTS, 2 copies, 7 pp each. Published (see D14)
I2 'The Eternal Tramp' (1947)
CTS, 2 copies, 10 pp each. Published (see D31)
I3 'Nothing to Fear but Fear' (1949)
CTS, 2 copies, 4 pp each. Published (see F48)
I4 'Regina vs the World' (1953)
CTS, 2 copies, 4 pp each. Published (see F56)
I5 'John George Diefenbaker' (1957)
a / OTS, with FHA, 2 pp
b / CTS of rev version, 2 pp

c / PTS of b, 2 pp
An honorary degree citation read on the occasion of Diefenbaker's being awarded an honorary degree, Doctoris Litterarum Sacrarum, from the University of Toronto. Unpublished.

I6 'Carleton University Convocation Address' (1957)
PTS, 11 pp. Published (see C1)

I7 'Notes for a Commentary on *Milton*' (1957)
CTS, 44 pp. Published (see D93)

I8 Address given at the senior banquet for the graduating class, Victoria College (1958)
OTS, with FHA, 4 pp
On the function of the university as a social institution that prepares students to live with freedom in a world of falsehoods and half-truths. Distinguishes between knowledge about things, which is easily forgotten, and knowledge of things, which is never forgotten. The university in this latter sense remains with students throughout life, so that in effect they all become university teachers. Unpublished.

I9 'Installation Address – Northrop Frye, Principal, Victoria College' (1959)
a / MTS, 11 pp. Published (see C2)
b / PTS, 2 copies, 11 pp each

I10 Senior Dinner Address (1960)
OTS, with FHA, 3 pp
Reviews the history of the senior dinner and develops the idea that nobody ever really leaves the university because it has defined the character and social functions of its students for the rest of their lives. This address also exists as a one-page OTS; it was delivered in September 1968. Unpublished.

I11 'The Stepsure Letters: An Introduction' (1960)
CTS, 2 copies, 12 pp each. Published (see D116)

I12 'Preserving Human Values' (1961)
MTS, with FHA, 6 pp
An address presented to the annual meeting of the Social Planning Council of Metropolitan Toronto, 27 April 1961. Says that human values can best be preserved among those with a vision of a classless society. In such a society equality would mean that everyone would have a social function, liberty would mean that people would have the power to do what they have learned to do, and fraternity would mean that the various groups in society would be united by some common knowledge or skill. Unpublished.

I13 'Academy without Walls' (1961)
a / OTS, 10 pp. Published (see D121)
b / PTS, 2 copies, 10 pp each. Photocopies from a
c / MTS, 11 pp; notation at top: 'Canada Conference of the Arts, May/61'

I14 'The Critical Discipline' (1961)
OTS, 111 pp. Published (see D123)

115 Interview (1961)
   CTS, 4 pp, numbered 14–17, plus one small slip. Unpublished (see G2).
116 Address to the Governor-General's Committee Awards Dinner, Ottawa (1962)
   OTS, 2 pp
   Speaks about the difficulties faced by the committee in selecting the best Canadian books of the year and about the importance of public recognition of good literature. Unpublished.
117 'Convocation Address, Queen's University' (1962)
   OTS, 7 pp, plus one leaf of F's holograph notes for this address
   Except for the first paragraph, published as 'To the Class of '62' (see D126).
118 'The Developing Imagination' (1962)
   CTS, 27 pp. Published (see D137)
119 Address to the Governor-General's Committee Awards Dinner, Ottawa (1963)
   OTS, 3 pp
   Remarks that the Governor-General's awards for distinguished Canadian books are based on positive rather than comparative judgments. Places Canadian writing in the context of the imaginative and social forces that unite rather than divide, and comments on how the works of the four winners fit this universalizing vision. Unpublished.
120 Address to the Ontario Curriculum Institute (1963)
   CTS, 5 pp. Published as 'We Are Trying to Teach a Vision of Society' (see D142)
121 'Convocation Address, U.B.C.' (1963)
   CTS, with FHA, 7 pp
   On the role of the university in recruiting people for 'the bigger lower-case university of the world,' which has the social function of moving students toward the discovery of their original civilized state. Unpublished.
122 'Chapter I: Introduction' [to T.S. Eliot] (1963)
   OTS, with FHA, 5 pp. Type-setter's copy. Published (see A5)
123 'The Problem of Spiritual Authority in the Nineteenth Century' (1964)
   CTS, 25 pp. Published (see D150)
124 'Shakespeare and the Modern World' (1964)
   OTS, 10 pp
   Celebrates Shakespeare's freeing and liberalizing power in modern civilization, a power that stems largely from a 'detachment that is totally involved.' Comments on Shakespeare's emancipating style, the discipline of his selective mind, his renouncing of personality, and his identity with his audience. Unpublished. Presented as a CBC Radio talk in the Shakespeare series in the 'University of the Air' series. Broadcast on 13 May 1964. Unpublished.
125 'The Rising of the Moon: A Study of "A Vision"' (1965)
   CTS, 42 pp. Published (see D157)
126 'Summary of Speech Given by Dr. Northrop Frye at Freshman Welcome, Monday, September 19th' (1966)

CTS, 2 pp. Another one-page OTS of same text, dated 'Sept. 1966'
Comments on the importance of maturity, individuality, and choice. Says
that society is no longer hostile to the university. A university education
should cause one 'to return to one's community and devote one's life
to trying to build up a real society out of it and to fight the mob spirit
wherever it is.' Unpublished.

127 Foreword to 1984 (1966)
OTS, with FHA, 5 pp. Published (see D170)

128 Abstracts of the three chapters of *The Modern Century* (1967)
a / OTS, 3 pp. Published in a Whidden Lecture brochure, McMaster University, 1967
b / CTS, 3 pp

129 Welcoming Remarks to the Conference on Editorial Problems, Toronto
(1967)
OTS, 2 pp
Develops the idea that many editors have been mischief-makers but that
they should for the most part be invisible – transparent mediums for
what they edit. Unpublished, except for one paragraph that appears in
D.I.B. Smith's 'Introduction' to *Editing Eighteenth-Century Texts* (see F83).

130 'Paper on Value Judgments presented by Dr. Frye at MLA, Chicago,
Dec. 27–29, 1967' (1967)
a / OTS, with FHA, 8 pp
b / CTS, 12 pp, dated 9 January 1968. Published as 'On Value Judgments'
(see D173)

131 'General Introduction [to Shakespeare's plays]' (1968)
OTS, with FHA, 5 pp. Published as 'General Editor's Introduction' (see D179)

132 'Literature and Society' (1968)
a / CTS, 20 pp
b / PTS of a
On the function of literature and its social relevance, set within an autobiographical context. Recalls the various influences on his intellectual
life: the nineteenth-century novelists and the realists that followed them,
Joyce, the conception of an oral literature (by way of Pelham Edgar and
J.D. Robins), Sir Walter Scott, Virginia Woolf, Empson, Graves and Riding,
surrealism, Marx, Freud, Chadwick's *The Heroic Age*, E.J. Pratt's poetry,
the Bible, Blake, Frazer, Havelock Ellis, McLuhan, et al. Recalls how
he came to develop his understanding of the nature of literature, associative
language, metaphor, myth, oral culture, and the language of concern.
Concludes by observing that he has lived through three phases in the
relationship of literature to society: that of the Victorian middle-class
reading culture, that of post-Depression fascist and Marxist ideology, and
that of the revolutionary anarchists of the 1960s. Originally presented
as a lecture at the Univ of Saskatchewan. Unpublished.

133 'Silence in the Sea' (1968)
CTS, with FHA, 20 pp. Published (see C5)

134 Convocation Address, University of Saskatchewan (1968)

a / OTS, with FHA, 6 pp

b / CTS, 9 pp. Published as 'The University and the Heroic Vision' (see D183)

135 Address to the Graduating Class, Loyola College (1968)

a / OTS, with FHA, 6 pp

b / OTS, with FHA, 9 pp

Examines the conventional statement that college graduates, having finished their studies, are now ready to go out into the world. Traces this convention from its beginnings in the movement toward universal and compulsory education through the mass education movement to the indulgent and permissive period of the 1930s and beyond. What has resulted is a proletariat student body with revolutionary impulses, yet the real target of the present student protests seems to be something other than society in general. Argues for the resuming of normal relations in the university, which is founded on the principles of practice and habit and which emphasizes tradition in the sense of continuity. Unpublished.

136 Convocation Address, Franklin and Marshall College (1968)

a / OTS, with FHA, 6 pp

b / OTS, with FHA, 10 pp

This address, given on the occasion of F's being awarded an honorary degree, 9 June 1968, is essentially the same as 134.

137 'Mythos and Logos' (1968)

CTS, 2 copies, 32 pp each. Published (see D181)

138 'The Top of the Tower' (1968)

a / OTS, with FHA, 21 pp

b / CTS, 29 pp

c / CTS, 32 pp. Published (see D184)

139 'An Address by Professor H. Northrop Frye, University Professor in the University of Toronto, to the Annual Meeting of the Canadian Association of School Superintendents and Inspectors, Tuesday, September 17, 1968' (1968)

a / CTS, with FHA, 11 pp; p 2 is a photocopy.

b / MTS, with FHA, 13 pp. Published as 'The Social Importance of Literature' (see D175)

140 Sermon (1968)

OTS, 4 pp. Published as 'Symbols' (see F82)

141 'Old and New Comedy' (1968)

a / OTS, 11 pp, type-setter's copy

b / CTS, 2 copies, 11 pp each. Published (see D194)

c / CTS, 8 pp

142 'Notes for the San Francisco Meeting' (1968)

CTS, 2 pp

Nine numbered paragraphs, which, along with 143, served as the outline for F's tape-recorded remarks at the twentieth annual conference of the

Association of Graduate Schools. These remarks were transcribed and published as 'Panel Discussion: Research and Graduate Education in the Humanities' (see D182).

143 'Notes for the San Francisco Paper' (1968)
OTS, 2 pp
Sixteen paragraphs that served as the basis for the remarks described in 142.

144 'Professor Frye' (1968)
a / OTS, with FHA, 13 pp
b / CTS, 13 pp. Published as 'Research and Graduate Education in the Humanities' (see D182)

145 Discussion at Queen's University (1968)
a / OTS, with FHA, 5 pp
b / CTS, 7 pp. Published in *The Ethics of Change* (see D191)

146 'The University and Personal Life' (1968)
a / OTS, with FHA, 19 pp, number 1–13 and 1–6
b / CTS, 31 pp. Published (see D197)

147 'The Ethics of Change: The Role of the University' (1968)
a / OTS, 18 pp. Published (see D191)
b / CTS, with FHA, 18 pp
c / PTS, 18 pp, photocopy of a

148 'Higher Education and Personal Life' (1968)
a / OTS, 2 pp
b / CTS, 4 pp
Notes on the mythological subjects of study, the nature of liberal education, and open vs closed mythologies, among other things. Unpublished.

149 'The Revelation to Eve' (1968)
a / OTS, with FHA, 24 pp
b / CTS, 2 copies, 36 pp each. Published (see D195)

150 'Sign and Significance' (1969)
CTS, 13 pp. Published (see D196)

151 Tribute to Jessie Macpherson (1969)
a / OTS, with FHA, 3 pp. Published as 'In Memoriam: Miss Jessie Macpherson, M.A., PH.D' (see F84)
b / MTS, 3 pp

152 The Critical Path (1969)
OH transcription (by Helen Frye) with FHA, of an address given at Berkeley – the first Beckman Lecture. The material in this address was incorporated into chapters 1 and 2 of *CP*.

153 Convocation Address, Acadia University (1969)
a / PTS, with FHA, 5 pp
b / OTS, 6 pp
Centres on an analysis of the causes and effects of the student unrest at Berkeley and elsewhere, and places the radical student movement in

the context of myths of concern and freedom. The myth of freedom, which lies at the heart of the university, prevents the myth of concern from becoming tyrannical. Unpublished.

154 Convocation Address, University of Western Ontario (1969)
a / OTS, with FHA, 5 pp
b / OTS, 8 pp
Warns against the totalitarian impulse, which opposes itself to the freedom and detachment that define the university. Recounts his experience at Berkeley during the demonstrations and riots, and observes that both the militant left and the militant right are actually opposed to what the university stands for. Predicts that the student demonstrations will die from exhaustion, 'because the tactics of trying to revolutionize society by harassing the university are not serious tactics.' This address was presented on the occasion of F's being awarded an honorary degree from the University of Western Ontario, 27 May 1969. Unpublished.

155 Convocation Address, York University (1969)
a / OTS, with FHA, 5 pp
b / OTS, 8 pp. Published (see C4)

156 Funeral Service for Virginia Knight (1969)
a / OTS, with FHA, 7 pp
b / CTS, 8 pp
Readings from the Book of Wisdom, Second Esdras, Psalms, Jeremiah, Zechariah, and Revelation, plus a brief meditation on the purpose of a memorial service and a eulogy for Virginia Knight. Unpublished.

157 'Tradition and Change in the Theory of Criticism' (1969)
CTS, with FHA, 17 pp
An early version of certain arguments about documentary approaches to literature, the defences of poetry by Shelley and Sidney, myth, convention, and tradition, which were expanded into CP, especially chapters 1, 4, and 5. Originally presented as an address to the eleventh triennial congress of the Fédération Internationale des Langues et Littératures Modernes, Islamabad, Pakistan, 20 September 1969. Unpublished.

158 'Rededication Service, Hart House, November 11, 1969' (1969)
a / OTS, with FHA, 5 pp
b / OTS, 7 pp. Published as 'Hart House Rededicated' (see D198)

159 'America: True or False?' (1969)
a / OTS, with FHA, 3 pp
b / CTS, 5 pp. Published (see D188)

160 'Introduction' [to Lawren Harris] (1969)
OTS, with FHA, 5 pp. Published (see D192)

161 'Preface' [to the Italian translation of FS] (1969)
OTS, with FHA, 3 pp. Published (see A1d)

162 'Rear View Crystal Ball' (1969)
OTS, with FHA, 4 pp. Published (see D199)

163 'Sermon in the Merton College Chapel, 7th June, 1970' (1970)

a / OTS, with FHA, 3 pp
b / OTS, 4 pp
On the virtue of humility, as it is presented in biblical proverbs and the Sermon on the Mount, where life is seen not as a series of accomplishments but as a series of new beginnings. Unpublished.

164 'Communications and Society' (1970)
a / MTS of recorded talk for BBC, 16 June 1970, 2 copies, 3 pp each (front and back)
b / PTS of a. Published as 'Communications' (see D202)

165 'Speech at Fourteenth Convocation, University of Windsor, October 17, 1970' (1970)
a / OTS, with FHA, 5 pp
b / OTS, 5 pp
c / CTS, 7 pp
Defines the goal of the university in terms of the meaning of 'liberal' in the phrase 'liberal education': its primary commitment is to freedom rather than concern. Freedom exists in the vision of what society might become, and this vision is provided by human intellect and imagination. Unpublished.

166 'The Definition of a University' (1970)
a / OTS, with FHA, 23 pp plus two small slips containing additions to the MS
b / CTS, 27 pp. Published (see D210)

167 'Agon and Logos: Revolution and Revelation' (1971)
a / CTS, with FHA, 35 pp
b / PTS, with FHA, 35 pp. Published (see D217)

168 'Education and the Rejection of Reality' (1971)
a / CTS of a tape-recorded address, 20 pp
b / PTS of a. Includes an introduction by Dr Norman Baird. Published without the introduction (see D208)

169 'The Quality of Life in the Seventies' (1971)
a / PTS, with FHA, 12 pp
b / OTS, 20 pp
c / PTS of b. Published (see D209)

170 'Wallace Stevens and the Variation Form' (1971)
PTS, 28 pp. Published (see D218)

171 'William Blake' (1971)
a / OTS, with FHA, 8 pp
b / CTS, 11 pp
An illustrated talk given at the Open University, 25 August 1971, and tape-recorded for the BBC Open University program. Discusses Blake's view of creation and his revolutionary conception of the human psyche. Looks at Blake's mythology as represented in *America* and *The Marriage of Heaven and Hell*. Unpublished.

172 'The Leap in the Dark' (1971)

OTS, 10 pp

An Advent sermon, preached at the Victoria College Chapel, 12 December 1971. Points to the nativity tradition in the Book of Wisdom of Solomon and in Revelation 'which remind us that the Word of God is a sword as well as an instrument of peace.' Relates this tradition to the birth of God: 'God can only be born in the context of God's wrath.' Speaks about the negative aspects of Christmas (that it is essentially a secular festival), as well as its positive aspects (that it represents a point of contact between Christianity and other faiths). The real point of contact, symbolized by Christmas, is hope. Unpublished.

173 'Notes' [to CP] (1971)
OTS, with FHA, 2 pp. Endnotes for CP. Published (see A14)

174 'Preface' [to BG] (1971)
a / OTS, with FHA, 5 pp
b / CTS, with FHA, 8 pp. Published (see A13)

175 'Stanley Llewellyn Osborne' (1971)
OTS, 4 pp
An honorary degree citation for Osborne, which recognizes his achievements both as principal of the Ontario Ladies College and as secretary of the United-Anglican Church committee to revise the hymn-book. Unpublished.

176 'Convocation Address, University of Waterloo (Engineering Convocation)' (1972)
CTS, 7 pp. Published as 'Universities and the Deluge of Cant' (see D212)

177 'Pistis and Mythos – Northrop Frye. (Summary of Argument)' (1972)
a / OTS, with FHA, 4 pp
b / MTS, 5 pp. Published (see D214)

178 The Artist and the Land: Canadian Landscape Painting (1972)
a / OTS, with FHA, 4 pp
b / PTS, entitled 'The Canadian Scene: Explorers and Observers,' 7 pp. Published (see D215)

179 Paper for the Commission to Study University Research (1972)
CTS, with FHA, 12 pp. Unpublished in this form, but slightly expanded and somewhat differently organized to become 'Research and Graduate Education in the Humanities' (see D182)

180 'The Critic and the Writer' (1972)
PTS, 9 pp. Unpublished transcript of a tape-recorded talk (see H28)

181 Draft introduction to Harcourt Brace Jovanovich anthology (1972)
CTS, 5 pp
An introduction to the twentieth-century section of a projected anthology. Speaks of the global context of twentieth-century English literature and of the antagonism between the imagination of the modern writer and what he sees in the life around him. Observes that this antagonism 'has occurred notably three times in English history, and each time has produced a great development of mythopoeic literature' – during the

Renaissance, during the romantic age, and during the period between
the two world wars. Unpublished.

182 Introduction to the Italian translation of Irving Layton's poetry (1972)

a / OTS, with FHA, 4 pp

b / OTS, 5 pp

c / CTS of b. Published (see D222)

183 'On Teaching Literature' (1972)

a / CTS, 45 pp

b / CTS, with FHA, 41 pp. Published (see C6)

184 'General Editor's Introduction' (1972)

PTS, 184 pp

A five-part introduction to a projected Harcourt Brace Jovanovich textbook
anthology of English literature. F was the general editor of this project;
other critics were to prepare introductions and make selections for the
separate periods of English literary history. Parts 1 through 3 of F's general introduction are complete; part 4 is partially complete (it includes
a one-page outline for the remainder of the section); and part 5 consists
only of a three-page outline. The project was never completed. Unpublished.

185 Replies to editor (1972)

OTS, 2 pp

Replies to editor's queries and remarks about the MS, 'On Teaching Literature' (see C6).

186 The Search for Acceptable Words (1972)

a / OTS, with FHA, 24 pp. Published (see D216)

b / CTS of a

c / Galley proofs of a, 6 pp

187 'Lester Bowles Pearson, 1897–1972' (1973)

a / OTS, with FHA, 3 pp

b / OTS, 4 pp

A memorial-service tribute to Pearson, presented in the Victoria College
Chapel, 3 January 1973. Traces the course of Pearson's life and achievement
from his undergraduate days at Victoria College to his service as prime
minister of Canada. Unpublished.

188 'Wisdom and Knowledge' (1973)

a / OTS, with FHA, 5 pp

b / OTS, 8 pp

A sermon preached at St Thomas Aquinas Chapel, University of Toronto,
7 September 1973. Bases his message on the distinction between the
kind of wisdom found in the proverbs of Ecclesiasticus and in the Sermon
on the Mount, on the one hand, and knowledge, on the other. Wisdom
is related to potentiality and to the person who has it; its basis is the
community. Knowledge is related to actuality and to the objective world;
its basis is the individual. Unpublished.

189 'Life after Death: Spengler's Vision of Decline' (1973)

a / OTS, with FHA, 18 pp
b / CTS, 27 pp. Published as 'The Decline of the West by Oswald Spengler' (see D220)
c / Galley proofs of b

190 'The Renaissance of Books' (1973)
CTS, with FHA, 25 pp. Published (see D219)

191 'The Times of the Signs' (1973)
a / OTS, with FHA, 47 pp
b / CTS, 42 pp. Published (see D223)

192 'Wedding of Patricia Russell and Andrew Binnie' (1974)
a / OTS, with FHA, 6 pp
b / CTS, 2 pp
A preamble to this wedding ceremony, plus readings from the Bible, Milton, Blake, and a benediction. Performed in the Victoria College Chapel, 2 March 1974.

193 Renaissance and Romantic Conceptions of Time (1974)
a / OTS, with FHA, 11 pp
b / CTS, 17 pp
Examines the three kinds of temporal existence according to the Christian perspective: the eternal now, or time as one clock-tick after another; the mixture of linear and cyclical movement, or time as the universal devourer; and the unfallen experience, or time as continuous renewal. Illustrates this last conception of time with the metaphor of the dance in Sir John Davies's poetry and with the idea of cultivated repetition in Spenser. Also relates the mythology of Eros to the awareness of time on a higher level. Looks at the immanent time-consciousness of the Romantics as found in Shelley and, later, in Eliot, and contrasts this view of time with the historical awareness of the realists. Presented at the Comparative Literature Colloquium on 'Time and the Poetic Self,' University of Toronto, 2 March 1974. Unpublished.

194 'Literature and Language' (1974)
OTS, 9 pp
Argues against formalizing a theory of comparative literature distinct from the theory of literature in general 'because the barriers of language within literature are, as far as structure is concerned, accidental, even meaning-less.' Suggests looking at the problem of comparative literature from the perspective of the structural study of myth and image. Discusses the centripetal and centrifugal movements in the reading process, distinguish-ing between the descriptive use of verbal structures, with their standard of the truth of correspondence, and the poetic use of language, where the relationship of words to one another, rather than to the outer world, is the important factor. Presented at the annual meeting of the Canadian Comparative Literature Association, Toronto, 31 May 1974. Unpublished.

195 'Substance and Evidence' (1974)
a / OTS, with FHA, 9 pp

b / MTS, 3 pp (front and back)
Sermon preached in the Memorial Church, Harvard University, 17 November 1974. An exegesis of Hebrews 11:1: 'faith is the substance of things hoped for, the evidence of things not seen.' Unpublished.

I96 'Charms and Riddles' (1975)
a / OTS, with FHA, 14 pp
b / CTS, 20 pp. Published in *SM*; for annotation, see D224.

I97 'Summation of the Symposium on Television Violence, Kingston, Ontario, August 24–26, 1975' (1975)
OTS, 15 pp. Published as 'Summation' (see D237)

I98 'History and Myth in the Bible' (1975)
a / OTS, with FHA, 14 pp
b / CTS, 19 pp. Published (see D234)

I99 'Canada: New World without Revolution' (1975)
a / OTS, with FHA, 14 pp
b / CTS, 10 pp. Published (see D227)

I100 'Romance and Masque' (1975)
a / CTS, 27 pp
b / PTS of a
c / OTS, with FHA, 28 pp
d / CTS, with FHA, 39 pp. Published as 'Romance as Masque' in *SM*; for annotation, see D225.

I101 'Foreword' [to *The Child as Critic*] (1975)
a / OTS, with FHA, 2 pp
b / CTS, 3 pp. Published (see D228)

I102 'The Responsibilities of the Critic' (1976)
a / CTS, 24 pp
b / PTS of a. Published (see D232)

I103 'Haunted by Lack of Ghosts' (1976)
a / OTS, with FHA, 19 pp
b / CTS, with FHA, 24 pp. Published (see D244)
c / Galley proofs of b, 12 pp

I104 'National Consciousness in Canadian Culture' (1976)
a / OTS, with FHA, 15 pp
b / OTS, with FHA, 20 pp. Published (see D235)

I105 Address at the Installation of Gordon Keyes (1976)
OTS, 3 pp
Brings greetings, as a representative of the teaching staff of Victoria College, to Gordon Keyes on the occasion of his installation as the principal of the college. Comments on the importance of teaching in the college, on Keyes's sympathies with the traditions of teaching and independent scholarship, and on the dangers of bureaucratic centralization. Unpublished.

I106 Modern Language Association Presidential Address (1976)
OTS, with FHA, 16 pp. Published (see D238)

I107 'Conclusion' [to *Literary History of Canada*] (1976)
a / OTS, 27 pp
b / CTS of a
c / PTS of a. Published (see D233)
I108 'Expanding Eyes' (1976)
CTS, with FHA, 31 pp. Published (see D226)
I109 'Notes' (1976)
a / OTS, with FHA, 23 pp
b / CTS, 35 pp
c / OTS and holograph notes, 3 pp (5 × 8 in) and 2 pp (8½ × 11 in)
Working notes for *SeS* (see A15).
I110 'Preface' [to joint issue of ADE/ADFL *Bulletin*] (1976)
a / OTS, with FHA, 2 pp
b / CTS, 3 pp. Published (see D231)
I111 'Preface' [to *SM*] (1976)
a / OTS, with FHA, 6 pp
b / CTS, with FHA, 9 pp. Published (see A16)
c / CTS of front and end matter for *SM*, 7 pp
I112 'Canadian Culture Today' (1977)
a / CTS, 15 pp
b / OTS, with FHA, 19 pp. Published (see D243)
I113 'Culture as Interpenetration' (1977)
OTS, with FHA, 15 pp. Published in *DG*; for annotation, see D240.
I114 'Summary' [of the *Options* Conference] (1977)
CTS, 13 pp. Published (see D241)
I115 'Canadian Culture' (1977)
CTS, 3 pp. Portion of a speech that contrasts Canadian culture, history, and geography with those of the United States. Unpublished.
I116 'The Teacher's Source of Authority' (1978)
a / PTS, from a tape-recording, with holograph annotations, 17 pp
b / PTS, with FHA, 17 pp plus 12 pp of 'Closing Remarks and Questions'
c / CTS, 15 pp. Published (see D251)
I117 'Kathleen Hazel Coburn' (1978)
a / OTS, 3 pp
b / CTS of a
Citation presented on the occasion of Coburn's being awarded an honorary Doctor of Letters degree by the University of Toronto. Summarizes Coburn's career, especially her Coleridge scholarship, and comments on the qualities of loyalty, devotion, and conscience throughout her life. Unpublished.
I118 'An Address by Dr. H. Northrop Frye, 1978 Recipient of the Royal Bank Award' (1978)
a / PTS, with FHA, 12 pp
b / OTS, with FHA, 16 pp
c / CTS of b

d / CTS of b, incorporating revisions

e / Photo-offset typescript of text of d, issued by the Royal Bank, 17 pp. Published (see D245)

I119 'Installation Address, Dr Northrop Frye, October 11, 1978' (1978)

a / CTS, with FHA, 7 pp

b / OTS, 8 pp

c / CTS of b

Reviews the three distinctive traditions that have given Victoria College its identity – the religious, the humanistic, and the residential. Presented on the occasion of F's being installed as chancellor of Victoria University. Unpublished.

I120 'Canadian Culture' (1978)

OTS, with FHA, 3 pp

Five paragraphs of a speech on Canadian culture. Unpublished.

I121 Victoria College Lecture (1978)

CTS, 4 pp

Places the faith vs reason conflict into a cultural context, maintaining that the issue is really not faith against reason but 'imagination against minimal reality.' Unpublished.

Massey College

I122 Literature, Language, History (1979)

CTS, 11 pp. Published (see D252)

I123 'Shakespeare's *The Tempest*' (1979)

a / OTS, with FHA, 14 pp

b / CTS, 19 pp

Distinguishes between Jonsonian and Shakespearean comedy, maintaining that the latter requires a childlike response to the familiar and conventional characteristics of the pre-Jonsonian kind of comedy. Indicates that as Shakespeare gets closer to pre-Jonsonian comedy in his last years, his plays become romances, 'the bedrock of drama, the musical, poetic, and spectacular panorama of magic and fantasy in which there is no longer tragedy or comedy, but an action passing through tragic and comic modes to a conclusion of serenity and peace.' Illustrates the comprehensive romantic structure in *The Winter's Tale* and *Measure for Measure*, both of which have a diptych form of action. Examines *The Tempest* in terms of the conventions of dramatic romance, calling attention to the complex relations between illusion and reality that result. Discusses the analogues between *The Tempest* and initiation rites, as well as its similarities to the Japanese no plays. Sees the chief recognition in the play as having to do with the triumph of art. Originally presented as a lecture in Vicenza, Italy, 18 May 1979. Unpublished.

I124 'Roy Daniells' (1979)

a / OTS, with FHA, 3 pp

b / CTS, 4 pp. Published (see D253)

I125 'Castiglione's *The Courtier*' (1979)
CTS, 24 pp; the last 2 pp are translations into Italian of the 11 quotations used in the essay. Published as *Il 'Cortegiano' in una società senza cortigiani* (see C9)

I126 'On Translation' (1979)
a / OTS, with FHA, 2 pp
b / CTS, 2 pp
On the difficulty of translating not only the rhymes, rhythms, and verbal wit of poetry but also the 'underthought' of imagery and metaphor. Points to some of the similar themes and conventions in English and Chinese poetry. Written as an introduction to W.A.C.H. Dobson's translation of Li Po's poems, as yet unpublished.

I127 'From the Chancellor' (1979)
a / OTS, with FHA, 2 pp
b / CTS, 3 pp. Published (see F92)

I128 'Criticism as Education' (1979)
a / OTS, with FHA, 14 pp
b / CTS, 21 pp. Published (see C8)

I129 'Memorial Service – Mrs. Jean Haddow, November 20, 1979' (1979)
a / OTS, 4 pp, 5 × 8 in cards
b / OTS, 3 pp
Consists of readings from 1 Cor 13, Rev 21, Ps 90, Wisd 1, 2 Esd 2, *Republic* 3, Prov 31, three prayers, and a benediction. Unpublished.

I130 'Arthur Lismer' (1979)
a / OTS, with FHA, 3 pp
b / CTS, 4 pp
About Lismer's influence in Canadian art. Gives a personal and anecdotal account of Lismer's teaching and his gallery talks, and places his achievement as a painter in the context of modern Canadian art. Written as an introduction to a book on Lismer by Norah McCullogh, as yet unpublished.

I131 'Drama' (1979)
CTS, 14 pp. Published as 'On Drama' (see D259)

I132 'Fiction' (1979)
a / OTS, with FHA, 10 pp
b / OTS, with FHA, 7 pp
c / CTS, revised version of b, 10 pp. Published as 'On Fiction' (see D259)

I133 'Poetry' (1979)
a / OTS, with FHA, 13 pp
b / CTS, 17 pp. Published as 'On Poetry' (see D259)

I134 'A Breath of Fresh Air' (1980)
a / OTS, with FHA, 5 pp
b / OTS, with FHA, 6 pp
c / CTS, 8 pp, 2 copies
d / MTS, 2 pp, entitled 'The Metropolitan Pulpit, a Breath of Fresh Air, Rev

Dr Northrop Frye, a Sermon Preached in Metropolitan United Church, Toronto, Sunday, March 23, 1980.' Published (see F94)

1135 Address at the Installation of Alvin Lee (1980)

a / OTS, 2 pp

b / OTS, 2 pp

Presented on the occasion of Lee's installation as president of McMaster University. Representing the Learned Societies of Canada, F reviews Lee's contributions to Old English scholarship and gives support to the idea that university presidents should also be scholars. Unpublished.

1136 'Across the River and out of the Trees' (1980)

CTS, 24 pp. Published (see D256)

1137 'The Beginning of the Word' (1980)

CTS, 18 pp. Published (see D269)

1138 'Creation and Recreation' (1980)

CTS, 71 pp. Published (see A18)

1139 'The Bridge of Language' (1981)

CTS, 22 pp. Published (see D264)

1140 'Baccalaureate Service, March 29, 1981' (1981)

a / OTS, 1 p

b / CTS, 1 p

A brief 'Commissioning' (9 lines) and a 'Benediction' (3 lines). Unpublished.

1141 'The Double Mirror' (1981)

a / OTS, with FHA, 10 pp

b / Word-processor printout, with FHA, 14 pp. Published (see D268)

1142 'Criticism and Environment' (1981)

Word-processor printout, with FHA, 18 pp. Published (see D276)

1143 'Shakespearean Comedy' (1981)

CTS, 26 pp

On the reversal of action in Shakespeare's problem comedies. Essentially the same material as the first chapter of *MD*, though the book version shows a great deal of revision and F has added and deleted material from the original and rearranged many of the paragraphs in the book. Originally presented as the first of the Tamblyn Lectures, University of Western Ontario, 25 March 1981.

1144 'Myth as the Matrix of Literature' (1982)

PTS, 18 pp. Published (see D278)

1145 'Vision and Cosmos' (1982)

a / OTS, with FHA, 15 pp

b / OTS, 23 pp. Published (see D281)

1146 The Chancellor's Message (1982)

a / OTS, 1 p

b / CTS, 2 pp. Published (see D271)

1147 'Lecture for the Stratford Shakespearean Festival, "Something Rich and Strange: Shakespeare's Approach to Romance," July 11, 1982' (1982)

a / PTS, 20 pp; transcribed from a tape-recording
b / OTS, with FHA, 15 pp
c / CTS, 22 pp. Published (see C10)

1148 Approaching the Lyric (1982)
CTS, with FHA, 9 pp. Published (see D282)

1149 'The World as Music and Idea in Wagner's *Parsifal*' (1982)
a / OTS, with FHA, 22 pp. Published (see D280)
b / CTS of a
c / PTS of a

1150 'General Editor's Introduction' (1982)
MTS, 6 pp
An introduction to the second volume of Harold Innis's collected papers
(see 1151), a volume dealing with 'the growth of printing and publishing
in England and other European countries through the eighteenth century,
and with the beginnings of American journalism.' Points to the importance
of Jonson, Fielding, and Milton and of periodical publication in the history
of the printed word. Comments on Innis's chief interests in the history
of publishing. Sees his work not only as a scholarly contribution but also
as a prophetic vision. Unpublished.

1151 'Introduction' (1982)
MTS, 21 pp
Introduction to *Dispersal and Concentration: Historical Aspects of Communication*, the collected papers of Harold Innis. Gives a brief history of the
Innis project. Seeks mainly 'to incorporate [Innis] into the background
and tradition of our contemporary preoccupations.' Examines Innis's
ideas on the cultural use of verbal communication, the mosaic quality
of his writing, his theory of time- and space-bound societies, his views
on the way in which law, scientific knowledge, and the arts operate
as a *tertium quid* to neutralize competing pressures in culture, and his
understanding or oral tradition. Maintain's that Innis's work, 'for all of its
often bewildering masses of detail and outmoded sources, is still an
integral part of a social vision of a scope and comprehensiveness unparalleled
in Canadian culture.' Unpublished.

1152 Introduction to Giorgio Bassani's *Rolls Royce and Other Poems* (1982)
a / OTS, with FHA, 3 pp
b / CTS, 4 pp. Published (see D273)

1153 'Literature as Critique of Pure Reason' (1982)
a / OTS, 21 pp. Published (see D274)
b / CTS of a
c / PTS of a

1154 'The Meeting of Past and Future in William Morris' (1982)
a / OTS, with FHA, 18 pp
b / OTS, 27 pp. Published (see D272)

1155 The Ouroboros (1982)
a / OTS, with FHA, 3 pp

b / CTS, 4 pp. Published (see D275)
1156 'The Myth of Deliverance' (1982)
   a / CTS, 101 pp. Published (see A21)
   b / Page proofs of a, 96 pp
1157 'Blake's Biblical Illustrations' (1983)
   a / OTS, with FHA, 26 pp
   b / CTS, 26 pp
   An exposition of the mythological background necessary for understanding
   Blake's biblical illustrations, which turn out to be less illustrations than
   imaginative reconstructions. Points to the parallels between Vico's and
   Blake's understanding of the stages of culture and language. Outlines the
   broader cosmology of Christian and classical culture with its hierarchical
   structure, and shows how Blake's own mythology, with its primary
   symbolic figures of Urizen, Orc, and Los, turns the traditional cosmology
   upside down. Looks finally at Blake's understanding of creation and
   apocalypse and at the biblical illustrations that cluster around his mythology
   of the beginning and end. Presented as a lecture at the Art Gallery of
   Ontario, 4 February 1982. Unpublished.
1158 'The Survival of Eros in Poetry' (1983)
   a / OTS, with FHA, 19 pp
   b / PTS, 22 pp. Published (see D287)
1159 'The View from Here' (1983)
   a / OTS, with FHA, 22 pp
   b / PTS of a
   Begins with autobiographical reflections on the social and educational
   changes in Canada during the past fifty years. Discusses the ways in which
   the structures of literature 'may foster and encourage certain social changes,'
   arguing that the humanities can train our imaginations and thus clarify
   our social visions. Pursues the problem of authority in culture and the
   various levels of social concern. Points to the revolutionary consciousness
   in Blake and others as an example of how an educated imagination can
   break out of its social conditioning – which is the function of education.
   Presented as a lecture to the Victoria University Alumni, 12 April 1982.
   Unpublished.
1160 'Art and Society' (1983)
   a / OTS, 5 pp. Published (see D286)
   b / CTS, 8 pp
1161 'Convocation Address – McGill University, June 9, 1983' (1983)
   a / OTS, with FHA, 4 pp
   b / CTS, 4 pp
   Given on the occasion of F's being awarded an honorary degree from
   McGill. Speaks of graduation as an organized ritual of deliverance, not
   unlike a play, which moves the graduate out of rather than into the 'real'
   world. Unpublished.
1162 'Margaret Eleanor Atwood' (1983)

a / OTS, with FHA, 3 pp
b / OTS, 4 pp
c / CTS of b
Citation given on the occasion of Atwood's being awarded an honorary
degree of Doctor of Letters from the University of Toronto, 14 June 1983.
Traces her career as a poet, novelist, and critic. Unpublished.

1163 'Repetitions of Jacob's Dream' (1983)
a / OTS, with FHA, 20 pp
b / OTS, 20 pp
c / CTS of b
Begins with a long catalogue of images of the ladder in literature and art
from antiquity to the twentieth century and shows how the image of
the ladder, in both its ideal and ironic forms, is an integral part of the
structure of authority. The ladder, moreover, is an example of how metaphor lies behind all of our verbal constructs, literary as well as philosophical, political, and religious. The real ladder to heaven, now that the
authority of the Great Chain of Being no longer holds, is 'one that can
be constructed only by the creative imagination.' Originally presented as
a talk at the National Gallery, Ottawa, 13 October 1983. Unpublished.

1164 'Funeral Service for Jean Gunn' (1983)
OTS, CTS, and PTS: 20 pp altogether, some of which are duplicates.

1165 'Literary and Linguistic Scholarship in a Postliterate World' (1983)
a / OTS, 14 pp
b / CTS of a. Published (see D277)

1166 'The Authority of Learning' (1984)
a / OTS, 14 pp
b / PTS of a. Published (see D279)

1167 'Expanding the Boundaries of Literature' (1984)
PTS, 23 pp
In part 1, examines the nature of poetic language and the role of the reader
both in seeking to recreate the original context of poetry and in experien-
cing it as a radically oral production that 'has the power to summon an
absent presence into reappearance.' In part 2, discusses metaphor as a primitive mode of identification in which human consciousness becomes
one with some aspect of nature; when civilizations begin to arise, such a
mode of identification becomes confined to the literary uses of words,
but 'one of the social functions of literature is to keep alive the metaphorical
way of thinking and using words.' Metaphor enables poets to maintain
the element of play in literature, but more important, it unites consciousness with what it is conscious of and unifies experience. In part 3, argues
that readers and critics should seek to distinguish the disinterested vision
of literature from ideology and mythological conditioning, in order, again,
to recapture some sense of a total human consciousness – a third order
of identification in which the boundaries of a subject-object world are

dissolved. Presented as an address to the Victoria University Alumni, Toronto, 10 April 1984.

1168 'The Social Authority of the Writer' (1984)

PTS, 24 pp

Except for minor changes in wording, the same as 1166. Presented as an address at the Library of Congress, Washington, DC, 24 April 1984.

1169 'Culture and Society in Ontario, 1784–1984' (1984)

PTS, with FHA, 21 pp

Explores the reasons lying behind the movement in Ontario culture from provincialism to regionalism. Sees the central social process at work in such change as 'the shift from a rural-based to an urban-based lifestyle,' but devotes most of the paper to reflecting on the more complex cultural factors that accompany the change. Locates the provincial element in the absence of a Canadian political identity and in the *Bildungsroman* tradition in Canadian literature, especially fiction, where the standards were so often external ones. Concludes that Canadian culture begins to escape from provincialism when it develops its own standards of language and starts to develop a mythology; and 'a mythology emerges when the mental landscapes of a group of writers begin to fuse with their physical environment.' Only then does a literature achieve the imaginative coherence it needs to become communicable beyond the borders of its origin. Originally presented as an address to the Ontario Historical Society, 7 September 1984.

1170 'The Koine of Myth: Myth as a Universally Intelligible Language' (1984)

PTS, 21 pp

Retraces some familiar ground in defining the various senses of myth and in characterizing our response to it as temporal and spatial, or as metaphorically aural and metaphorically visual. Sees the connection between myth and metaphor as arising out of ritual, where, in reciting the myth to make it present, the ritual centres on the visual symbol. Shows how myth as a diagrammatic formula is at work not simply in literature but in history, philosophy, and the Bible as well. Using the extended example of the ladder or stairway, devotes one long section of the essay to illustrating how narratives 'lead up to some sort of visualized emblem, myth or narrative frozen into a complex metaphor.' Cites dozens of examples of the ladder as such a visualized emblem. Distinguishes between literary metaphors and ecstatic metaphors, the latter of which extend their meaning into life through the experience of unity. Originally presented as an address to the Society for Mediterranean Studies, Victoria College, University of Toronto, 4 October 1984. Unpublished.

1171 'The Symbol as a Medium of Exchange' (1984)

PTS, 22 pp

Begins with a definition of symbol in its primitive senses as both that which needs something else to complete it (*symbolon*) and that which links

us with something not fully understood. Glances at the non-literary
meanings of symbol, but devotes most of the paper to the double context
of symbolism in literature: the completion of the symbol by its own verbal
context and the relation of the symbol to things outside this context.
Shows how these two contexts of symbolism are at work in metaphor,
drawing examples from the Bible, Shakespeare, Wyatt, among others, and
relating the two meanings of the symbol to the syntactic overthought of
poetry and to its metaphorical underthought. Examines the ways this
underthought operates in the *symbolisme* of Rilke and Mallarmé. Finally,
locates in an aphorism of Heraclitus an illustration of the exchange or
interchange between thing and meaning, being and becoming, part and
whole that occurs in symbolism. Originally presented as an address to the
Royal Society of Canada, Kingston, Ontario, 26 October 1984. Unpublished.

1172 'The Expanding World of Metaphor' (1984)
PTS, 23 pp. Published (see D284)

1173 'Cycle and Apocalypse in "Finnegans Wake" ' (1985)
Photocopy of word-processor printout, 24 pp
Shows how Vico's cyclical theory of history and Bruno's philosophy of
polarity serve as structural principles for *Finnegans Wake*. Illustrates the
archetypal polarities underlying a number of characters in the book:
the rivalry between brothers, the opposing female figures, and the conflict
lying within the individual dreamer at the core of the story (HCE/Porter).
Discusses the three cycles of dream in the novel (the individual, the
autobiographical, and the universal) and the way coincidence functions
as a principle of design for Joyce. Examines the theme of annunciation
and Joyce's balancing of the techniques of riddle and charm. Maintains
throughout that Joyce absorbed his structural principles not only from Vico
and Bruno but from Freud, Jung, Butler, Berkeley, Yeats, Blake, and the
Bible as well. Originally presented as a lecture at the University of California at Berkeley, the University of Santa Clara, and UCLA, February 1985.
Unpublished.

1174 'Literature and the Visual Arts' (1985)
PTS, 19 pp. Published as 'La letteratura e la arti figurative' (see D285)

1175 'The Bride from the Strange Land' (1985)
PTS, 19 pp
Sees three narrative themes coverging in the Book of Ruth: that of the
levirate marriage, that of the son born to a woman who is past the age
of child-bearing, and that of the bride from a strange land. Cites biblical
examples of each of these themes. Finds the use of the Ruth story in
subsequent biblical and other literature to be relatively insignificant, probably because of 'the irrepressible cheerfulness of the story,' which 'leaves
the literary imagination with very little to do.' Maintains that the significance of the Book of Ruth lies in its embodying a microcosm of the entire
narrative of exile, return, and redemption in the Bible and in its transforming the plots, themes, and imagery associated with the harvest 'into

credible and very warm human relationships.' Originally presented as a
talk at the Holy Blossom Temple, Toronto, 25 May 1985. Unpublished.
1176 'Lacan and the Full Word' (1985)
   PTS, 5 pp. Published as 'Lacan et la parole dans sa plénitude' (see D283)
1177 'The Mythical Approach to Creation' (1985)
   PTS, 25 pp
   Examines the mythical implications of the two creation stories in Genesis
   and the imagery of the cosmological ladder that they embody. Traces
   the subsequent appearance of the ladder-cosmos image in Western culture,
   both as a structure of social authority and as a conventional, though
   deconstructed, image in the work of Eliot, Yeats, Pound, and Joyce. Illustrates how the cosmic-ladder image is reconstructed in the nineteenth-
   century myth of Prometheus and Eros. Concludes by glancing at the ways
   in which the Genesis creation myths illustrate the chief post-literary,
   social functions of myth. Presented as an address to the Canadian Theological Society at the meeting of the Learned Societies of Canada, Montreal,
   4 June 1985. Unpublished.
1178 'Language as the Home of Human Life' (1985)
   PTS, 21 pp
   A three-part essay in which F (1) maintains that since language is the
   dwelling-place of being, it is important to develop the habit of using it
   critically and with the 'courage of articulateness'; (2) uses books, especially
   books of Canadian fiction, to illustrate that this manifestation of verbal
   culture follows the same rhythms and conventions as those of myth and
   folk-tale: 'they send down their roots into a specific culture and transmit
   a heritage of shared allusion to posterity'; and (3) argues that education is
   a militant enterprise that must constantly do battle against ignorance,
   prejudice, and malice, and must seek to build a public that is receptive
   to its own culture, such receptivity being 'the most accurate indication we have of the level of its civilization.' Presented as an address
   at Athabasca University, Athabasca, Alberta, 14 June 1985.
   Unpublished.
1179 Tribute to Robert Zend (1985)
   PTS, 3 pp
   A tribute to the creative, humorous genius of Robert Zend, presented at
   Harbourfront in Toronto, 16 July 1985.
1180 'The Stage Is All the World' (1985)
   PTS, 22 pp
   Examines a number of Shakespeare's uses of the 'stage' metaphor in order
   to illustrate the way the dramatist conceives of personality or the various
   roles one plays. Suggests that in both life and drama the stage is a world
   because it is 'a place where illusion is reality.' Looks especially at the
   ways the world-stage metaphor functions in *As You Like It*, *Hamlet*, *King
   Lear*, and *Antony and Cleopatra*. Presented as a lecture at Stratford, Ontario,
   July 1985. Unpublished.

1181 'Opening of Lawren Harris and Arthur Lismer Exhibitions, Art Gallery of
Ontario, September 26, 1985' (1985)
PTS, 2 pp
Contrasts the styles and personalities of the two artists. Unpublished.

1182 'The Journey as Metaphor' (1985)
PTS, 21 pp
Surveys the metaphor of the journey in the literary tradition, citing dozens
of examples from the Greek myths and the Bible to Eliot, Yeats, and
Roethke. Notes that many of the journey metaphors come from the Gos-
pels, where Jesus's teachings about the Word embody the fundamental
principle of metaphor – the principle of identity that collapses all distinc-
tions between movement and stasis, subject and object, here and there.
Presented as a lecture at the Applewood Centre, Toronto, 8 October 1985.
Unpublished.

1183 'Framework and Assumption (1985)
PTS, 19 pp
Examines the role of convention in literature, which is part of a larger
subject forming a theory of the language of myth and metaphor. Contrasts
his own views about language with those of recent linguists, Harold
Bloom, Roland Barthes, and ideological critics. Sees ideology as a secondary
or derivative social concern. Believes that criticism should pay attention
both to the horizontal dimension of its subject – the social and ideological
environment of literature – and to the vertical dimension, which carries
the reader back to literary conventions that are essentially untouched by
ideology. By studying ideological frameworks and the assumptions on
which they are based we can discover the mythological structures from
which they derive, and these are the structures 'which literature creates
directly.' Presented as a lecture at Smith College, 24 October 1985.
Unpublished.

1184 'The Dialectic of Belief and Vision' (1985)
PTS, 23 pp
Explores the question, 'What place does the creative imagination, and the
kind of response we make to a work of literature, have in the study of
religion in general, or of the text of the Bible in particular?' Argues that
theories of critical response based on either visual experience or written
structure do not do justice to our reading of literature. Proposes that with
literary texts the process involved is one of provisional acceptance – a post-
poning of commitment and belief. Maintains that faith 'is the activity of
realizing a visionary model in the mind suggested by hope' and that
the best way to understand what faith and belief mean in the twentieth
century is to understand their appropriate language, which is the mythical
and metaphorical language of the imagination. Such language is rooted
in primary concern, which is distinct from ideology or secondary concern.
Believes the chief task of the literary critic is 'to distinguish ideology
from myth, to help reconstitute a myth as a language, and to put literature

in its proper cultural place as the central link of communication between society and the vision of its primary concerns.' Presented as an address at the School of Continuing Studies, University of Toronto, 3 December 1985. Unpublished.

1185 'The Rhetoric of Romanticism. By Paul de Man. New York, 1984. iv + 327 pp.'

PTS, 12 pp. Published as 'In the Earth, or in the Air?' (E69)

1186 Tribute to Balachandra Rajan (1985)

PTS, 4 pp

Praises the calm clarity of Rajan's scholarship on Milton and the substantial assumptions on which it is based.

1187 'Crime and Sin in the Bible' (1986)

PTS, 21 pp

Examines the religious content of the word 'sin' and the social and secular content of 'crime,' the latter deriving from a legal code based on divine revelation. The deductive construct of sin and crime in Israelite culture provides the basis for a social morality unmatched in the ancient world. In the Christian reformulation of the law, however, the gap between the two conceptions began to widen. Relates the ideas of sin and crime to natural law, which is non-biblical, and to the primary and secondary concerns of society. Presented as an address to the Law Faculty, University of Toronto, 15 April 1986. Unpublished.

1188 'Proposal of Toast' (1986)

PTS, 3 pp

A toast to Barker Fairley, on the occasion of a dinner honouring him, 21 May 1986. Recalls Fairley's contributions to German studies, his interest in furthering the cause of Canadian art, and his own portrait and landscape paintings.

1189 'Memoir' (1986)

PTS, 4 pp

A eulogy to F's wife, Helen, read on the occasion of a memorial service in her honour, September 1986.

1190 Sermon (1986)

PTS, 10 pp. Excerpts published as 'The Dedicated Mind' (F99)

1191 'Natural and Revealed Communities' (1987)

PTS, 27 pp

A reconsideration of Thomas More's Utopia. Argues that the book is, at least in part, an allegory of humanistic education. Relates More's ideal society to a wide range of utopias in classical, Renaissance, and modern literature and points to the connections between Utopia and other literary genres. Concludes that More's utopia exists 'only in the "nowhereness" of the consciousness within the individual mind' – a place where 'it can do much to inform and reform the society around it.' Presented as the Thomas More Lecture in the Humanities at the College of Holy Cross, Worcester, Mass, 22 April 1987. Unpublished.

1192 'Maps and Territories' (1987)
PTS, 8 pp
Maintains that the map is an appropriate metaphor for the structure of knowledge that criticism provides for the territory of literature. Believes that too many contemporary critical maps either tell us nothing about the territory or else attempt to replace it. Argues that there are three aspects of the social training in words: (1) the study of myths and metaphors of literature, (2) the information learned from historical and other discursive forms of words, and (3) ideology. Concludes with an account of his interest in the Bible, a sacred book that, although not literature itself, is written in myth and metaphor. Presented as the opening address at the Convegno Internazionale: Ritratto di Northrop Frye, University of Rome: La Sapienza, 25 May 1987. Unpublished.

1193 'Blake's Bible' (1987)
PTS, 26 pp
An examination of the metaphorical cosmology of Blake's fourfold vision. Shows how Blake turns upside down the reigning cosmology in Western culture up to his time and how his fourfold reading of the Bible reverses traditional views: Blake 'reads forward to the end instead of constantly looking backward to the beginning.' The apocalyptic vision that results 'is the attaining of a divine and human identity whose creative powers are entirely without limits.' Presented as an address to the St James Piccadilly Blake Society, London, 2 June 1987. Unpublished.

SECTION TWO

MANUSCRIPTS AT VICTORIA UNIVERSITY LIBRARY

1194 *Fearful Symmetry* (A1)
CTS, 92 pp. Incomplete early draft of A1. Occasional sentences and phrases in this draft appear in the published version, but the draft is completely different in extent and organization from the final version. In Box 1. Contents:
i–xii = 'INTRODUCTION.' A draft of what was to become chapter 1, 'The Case against Locke.' Corrections and revisions in ink. Incomplete: pp following xii are missing.
97–122 = 'CHAPTER SEVEN / *Experiment*.' A draft of chapter 8, part 2, and chapter 6, part 5. Corrections and revisions in ink. Pencil notation at top of p 97: 'Professor Frye's MSS of Blake (Incomplete).' Chapter 7, however, is complete in this version.
123–49 = 'CHAPTER EIGHT / 'Satire and Tragedy.' Material on 'Island of the Moon,' 'Tiriel,' and 'The Book of Thel.' Corrections and revisions in ink, including holograph entries of Greek words. Chapter 8 is complete in this version.
150–76 = 'CHAPTER NINE / Revolution.' Material on 'The French Revolution,'

'America,' and 'The Marriage of Heaven and Hell.' Corrections and revisions in ink. Chapter 9 is complete in this version.

1195 *The Well-Tempered Critic* (A6)

OTS, 80 pp. Printer's type-setting copy. Proofreader's corrections in pencil; copy editor's marks in red and blue pencil. FHA in ink. Indiana Univ Press stamp indicating job number 7462 and date received, '11/20/62.' Laid in is a TLS, dated 23 January 1967, from F to Miss Lorna Fraser, Victoria College Library, noting that he is enclosing the MS of the book. In Box 1. Contents:

[1–5] = front matter

3 = preface

4–71, including 22a and 48a = text

72–4 = notes

[75] = corrections to notes

1196 *A Natural Perspective* (A7)

OTS, 124 pp. Printer's proof copy. FHA in blue ink. After proofreading, F's further additions and deletions in pencil. Note at bottom of first page: '9464 – Bottomless Dream / Columbia Univ – 007 / Copy 1–122 (typed).' Date received stamp, 10/30/64. Some changes were made to the MS after F received page proofs. In Box 1. Contents:

1–122 = text

123–4 = preface

1197 *The Return of Eden* (A8)

OTS, 111 pp. Printer's type-setting copy. FHA in pencil. Copy editor's marks in pencil. In Box 1.

1198 *Fools of Time* (A9)

OTS, 101 pp. Printer's type-setting copy. Pages 1–102 stamped with numbering machine; p 5 missing. Laid in is a letter from Miss Y. Kawa, editorial secretary, Univ of Toronto Press, noting the return of the MS to F from the Press's files. In Box 1.

1199 *A Study of English Romanticism* (A11)

OTS, 164 pp. Printer's type-setting copy. FHA in pencil. Copy editor's marks in red and blue pencil. Stamped 'setting copy' on p 1. Note, dated 31 March 1969, from Jane Welch to Miss Lorna Fraser, Victoria College Library, noting that the MS of F's latest book is enclosed. In Box 1. Contents:

[1–7] = front matter

8–157 = text; part of p 157 has been torn away and is missing.

1200 *The Critical Path* (A14)

a / CTS of early version, 129 pp

b / PTS of early version, 98 pp

c / PTS of early version, 171 pp. 2 copies

a, b, and c are in stationery box marked 'The Critical Path: Versions other than final.'

d / CTS, 2 pp + OTS, 171 pp. Title p missing. Early version

e / CTS of f, below. Final version, 199 pp

d and e are in stationery box marked 'The Critical Path 1970 pp 194.'

f / OTS, 206 pp. Printer's type-setting copy. FHA in pencil. Laid in is a TLU, dated 24 June 1971, from F to Miss Lorna Fraser, Victoria College Library, presenting the MS to the library.

a–e are in Box 2; f is in a separate file folder marked 'The Critical Path.'

1201 *The Stubborn Structure* (A12)

CTS, 491 pp. FHA in ink. Contains erratum leaf + 14 pp of front matter + 476 pp of text. In Box 3.

1202 *The Bush Garden* (A13)

332 pp as follows:

a / OTS, 1 p, with annotations. Index

b / CTS, 14 pp, with annotation + OTS, 1 p, with FHA in green ink, to be inserted on p 6 of CTS. Introduction

c / CTS, 1 p, with annotations. Acknowledgments

d / CTS of selections from 'Letters in Canada' articles, 165 pp

e / CTS of 'Canada and Its Poetry,' 19 pp (see D18)

f / CTS of 'Turning New Leaves,' 7 pp (see D69)

g / Photocopy of printed article, 'Preface to an Uncollected Anthology,' 16 pp (see D94)

h / PTS of 'Silence in the Sea,' 23 pp (see C5)

i / CTS of 'Canadian and Colonial Painting,' 4 pp (see D10)

j / PTS of 'Conclusion' to *Literary History of Canada*,' 55 pp (see D154)

k / CTS of 'David Milne' and 'Lawren Harris,' 6 pp (see D33 and D192)

a–k all contain FHA. In Box 3

1203 *The Secular Scripture* (A15)

a / Galley proof,with FHA, 83 pp. In Box 3

b / Photocopy of a. In Box 3.1

c / Indexer's photocopy of page proofs, 95 pp. In Box 3.1

1204 *Spiritus Mundi* (A16)

Type-setter's copy, with FHA, 310 pp. In Box 4. Contents:

a / Front matter, 17 pp

b / Pasted-up photocopy of offprint of 'The Search for Acceptable Words,' 16 pp (see D216)

c / Pasted-up photocopy of offprint of 'The University and Personal Life,' 17 pp (see D197)

d / Pasted-up offprint of 'The Renaissance of Books,' 16 pp (see D219)

e / Pasted-up offprint of 'The Times of the Signs,' 27 pp (see D223)

f / PTS of 'Expanding Eyes,' 31 pp (see D226)

g / OTS of 'Charms and Riddles,' 20 pp (see D224)

h / OTS of 'Romance as Masque,' 39 pp (see D194 and D225)

i / Pasted-up offprint of 'Spengler Revisited,' 20 pp (see D220)

j / OTS of 'Agon and Logos,' 35 pp (see D217)

k / OTS of 'Blake's Reading of the Book of Job,' 24 pp (see D189)

l / Pasted-up photocopy of offprint of 'The Rising of the Moon,' 26 pp (see D157) m / Pasted-up photocopy of offprint of 'Wallace Stevens and the Variation Form,' 20 pp (see D218)

o / OTS, 2 pp. Notes

1205 *The Great Code* (A19)

a / OTS, dated 27 June 1977, 335 pp

b / OTS, with FHA, + CTS, 47 pp. Note saying 'Larkin Stuart Lecture, January 30, 1980'

c / CTS of two different versions of part 1, 'Myth and Metaphor,' 223 pp

d / OTS and CTS of two different versions of MS, 187 pp

e / OTS on yellow paper, 99 pp

a–e in Box 7

f / Word-processor printout + OTS, with FHA and typed corrections, dated '80/9/26,' 393 pp. In Box 6

g / Word-processor printout + OTS, with FHA and typed corrections, dated '80/10/30,' 193 pp. In Box 6

h / Page proofs, 237 pp

i / PTS of notes, 20 pp

j / Photocopy of galley proofs of index, 18 pp

k / Word-processor printout of text + OTS of notes and index, 503 pp. Type-setter's copy

h–k in Box 8

l / Word-processor printout + OTS with FHA, 442 pp. In Box 5

1206 *The Myth of Deliverance* (A21)

a / CTS, with annotations, 101 pp

b / Photocopy of page proofs, 96 pp

1207 *Divisions on a Ground* (A20)

Type-setter's copy

a / PTS, 1 p, with annotations. Contents

b / OTS, 1 p. Section page

c / OTS of 'Culture as Interpenetration,' 15 pp (see D240)

d / PTS of 'Across the River and out of the Trees,' 24 pp (see D256)

e / PTS of 'National Consciousness and Canadian Culture,' 20 pp (see D235)

f / PTS of 'Canadian Culture Today,' 19 pp (see D243)

g / Photocopy of printed version of 'Conclusion' [to *Literary History of Canada*], 8 pp (see D233)

h / OTS, 1 p. Section page

i / PTS of 'Presidential Address 1976,' 16 pp (see D238)

j / Photocopy of printed version of 'Humanities in a New World,' 15 pp (see D105)

k / Photocopy of printed version of 'Culture and the National Will,' 13 pp (see C1)

l / PTS of 'The Teacher's Source of Authority,' 15 pp (see D251)

m / PTS, 1 p. Section page

n / PTS of 'The Definition of a University,' 28 pp (see D210)

o / PTS of 'The Ethics of Change: The Role of the University,' 18 pp (see D191)
p / PTS of 'Canada: New World without Revolution,' 10 pp (see D227)
q / PTS of 'An Address By Dr. H. Northrop Frye, 1978 Recipient of the Royal Bank Award,' 17 pp (see D245)

SECTION THREE

MANUSCRIPTS AT THE QUEEN'S UNIVERSITY ARCHIVES, QUEEN'S UNIVERSITY, KINGSTON

1208 OTS, with FHA, 6 pp. Introduction to Pelham Edgar's *Across My Path*, 1952 (see B2)
1209 OTS, 'The University and the Ethics of Change,' a talk presented at Queen's Univ, 7 November 1968 (same as 147)

J

Unpublished Correspondence

The following list includes only unpublished correspondence that has been deposited in various special collections and archives. It is arranged according to the location of the depository.

J1 Special Collections, E.J. Pratt Library, Victoria Univ, Univ of Toronto
J1a Frye Family Letters. Box 9 of the Northrop Frye Manuscripts
These letters were secured by John Ayre, F's biographer, from Rev Donald Howard, son of John Howard, F's maternal uncle. Of the fifty-six letters, fifty-one are written to Donald Howard. Fifty-four are original holographs; two are original typescripts. The bulk of the collection (thirty-three letters) are from F's mother, 'Cassie' Frye (Catharine Maud Howard). Other correspondents include Mary Howard, 'Hatty' Layhew (Harriet Howard), and 'Dolly' Garratt (Elthea Howard), all three of whom were F's maternal aunts; and Rufus Garratt, Dolly's husband. The letters date from 24 February 1929 to 29 June 1945. Of the thirty-three letters from F's mother to Donald Howard, all but three contain information about F, particularly about his school years in Moncton, NB, Toronto, and Oxford.
J1b Letters regarding the deposit of manuscripts in the Pratt Library
    1 F to Miss L[orna] Fraser, dated 23 January 1967. TLS. 1 p. In Box 1 (see 1195).
    2 F to Miss Lorna Fraser, dated 24 June 1971. TLU. 1 p. In Box 1 (see 1200).
J1c Letters in the Pelham Edgar Collection
    1 F to Pelham Edgar, dated 28 December 1936. ALS. 1 p. On F's studies at Oxford.
    2 F to Pelham Edgar, dated 10 June 1937. ALS. 2 pp. On finishing the Blake manuscript.

3 Pelham Edgar to F, dated 2 August [1938]. ALS. 3 pp. Requests information on the origins of F's interest in Blake, which Edgar wants to
   include as part of a chapter on 'Creative Criticism in Canada' in his
   memoirs.
4 F to Pelham Edgar, dated 9 August 1948. TLS. 2 pp. Reply to Edgar's
   letter of 2 August 1938. Part of this letter is quoted in Edgar's *Across
   My Path* (see B2 and P70).

J1d Letters in the E.J. Pratt Collection
   1 E.J. Pratt to F, dated 13 November 1962. TLS. 1 p. Minor news.
   2 E.J. Pratt to F, dated 18 November 1962. TLS. 1 p. On meeting former
      students and the effects of teaching.
   3 F to E.J. Pratt [Summer 1963]. TLS. 1 p. On Victoria College staff
      changes, and on his intention to dedicate his forthcoming collection
      of essays (*FI*) to Pratt.
   4 F to Margaret Ray, dated 15 May 1964. TLS. 1 p. About the purchase
      of the Pratt manuscripts and the setting up of a poetry room at the
      Victoria College Library.
   5 F to Lorna [Fraser], dated 7 April 1967. TLS, photocopy. 1 p. About the
      purchase of the Pratt manuscripts.
   6 F to Lorna Fraser, dated 19 July 1967. TLS. 1 p. About the purchase of
      the Pratt manuscripts.
   7 F to Claire [Pratt], dated 8 April 1968. TLS. 1 p
   8 [Viola Pratt] to F, dated 19 February [1967]. ALS. 2 pp. About renaming
      the library at Victoria College and negotiations for the purchase of
      the Pratt manuscripts.

J1e More than 2200 letters to and from F from 1946 to 1978, along with
     manuscripts sent to F, postcards, invitations, brochures, and other miscel-
     laneous material. There are approximately 8800 leaves altogether. Letters
     to F are OTSS or holograph. F's replies are CTSS. This material has a finding
     list, which is indexed alphabetically either by correspondent or by organi-
     zation (eg, Modern Language Association, Canada Council). F's correspon-
     dence is chiefly in response to requests to lecture, to inquiries by readers
     about his books and articles, and to manuscripts sent to him. All of the
     material has been filed in 352 archival folders placed in fourteen manuscript
     boxes.

J2 William Ready Division of Archives and Research Collections, Mills Memo-
    rial Library, McMaster Univ, Hamilton, Ont. Letters in the Macmillan
    Archives regarding F's editing of *The Collected Poems of E.J. Pratt* (see B6).
   a / F to John [Gray], dated 9 February 1958. TLS. 1 p. Expresses interest
        in accepting the invitation to edit and write an introduction to Pratt's
        poems.
   b / F to John [Gray], dated 7 March [1958]. TLS. 1 p. On the poems to be
        included in the collected edition.
   c / F to Mr [Frank A.] Upjohn, dated 15 September 1958. TLS. 1 p. On the
        typographical layout of F's introduction.

d / F to the Macmillan Co of Canada, dated 21 September 1958. TLS. 1 p. On the layout of the page proofs.

e / F to Mr [Frank A.] Upjohn, dated 25 September 1958. TLS. 1 p. Replies to an explanation about the design of the introduction.

f / F to Miss [Winnifred] Eayrs, dated 29 September 1958. TLS. 1 p. Letter accompanying returned page proofs; suggests restoring several lines omitted from Pratt's 'The Truant.'

g / F to Miss [Winnifred] Eayrs, dated 2 October [1958]. TLS. 1 p. Letter accompanying returned page proofs suggesting some typographical changes.

h / F to Miss [Winnifred] Eayrs, dated 14 October 1958. TLS. 1 p. Suggests indenting broken lines in parts of Pratt's *Brébeuf*, rather than having them flush left.

i / F to John [Gray], dated 12 November 1958. TLS. 1 p. Brief note. Accepts invitation to a bookseller's party.

J3 Queen's Univ Archives, Queen's Univ, Kingston, Ont. Letters in the Lorne Pierce Collection regarding F's editing of Pelham Edgar's *Across My Path* (B2)

a / F to Dr [Lorne] Pierce, dated 21 April 1948. TLS. 1 p. No F005.1113. In Box B017. Short note of thanks.

b / F to Dr [Lorne] Pierce [October 1948?]. TLS. 1 p. No F005.1114. In Box B017. Regarding the manuscript of Pelham Edgar's memoirs.

c / F to Dr [Lorne] Pierce, dated 30 November 1948. TLS. 1 p. No F005.1115. In Box B017. Regarding F's editing of the manuscript of Pelham Edgar's memoirs.

d / F to Dr [Lorne] Pierce [March 1949]. TLS. 1 p. No F002.1035. In Box B018. Acknowledges receipt of Edgar's letters to Miss Perry. Hopes to devote some time to the manuscript of Edgar's memoirs in the spring.

e / F to Dr [Lorne] Pierce, dated 9 November 1949. TLS. 4 pp. No F002.1036. In Box B018. On the absence of any connecting thread in Edgar's manuscript. Proposes three alternatives to simply editing the manuscript as is.

f / F to Dr [Lorne] Pierce, dated 7 June 1950. TLS. 1 p. No F002.173. In Box B019. On the projected contents of the Edgar volume.

g / Lorne Pierce to F, dated 9 June 1950. TLU (carbon). 1 p. No F002.174. In Box B019. On the progress of the Edgar memoir at Ryerson Press.

h / Frank Flemington to F, dated 10 October 1950. TLU (carbon). 1 p. No F002.175. In Box B019. On the necessity of having to cut the Edgar manuscript because of costs.

i / F to Mr [Frank] Flemington, dated 3 August 1950. ALS. 1 p. No F002.176. In Box B019. Reply to h above. Suggests several possibilities for cutting the manuscript.

j / F to L[orne] P[ierce], dated 18 August 1951. ALS. 1 p. No F005.142. In Box B020. Brief note of acknowledgment regarding Edgar's memoirs.

Mentions the essay he has written for Chalmers book to be published by Ryerson Press (see D59).

k / F to Miss Trebell, dated 2 January 1952. TLS. 1 p. No F002.152. In Box B021. Regarding Mrs Edgar's approval of any changes in the Edgar book.

l / F to Dr [Lorne] Pierce, dated 29 March [1952]. TLS. 1 p. No F002.153. In Box B021. Letter accompanying the final version of the Edgar manuscript with recommended deletions.

m /F to Mr [Frank] Flemington, dated 28 July 1952. ALS. 1 p. No F002.154. In Box B021. Comments on the bibliography in the Edgar volume and argues against an index for it.

n / F to Dr [Lorne] Pierce [October 1952]. TLS. 1 p. No F002.155. In Box B021. Replies to an inquiry about writing workshops at Victoria College.

o / F to Mr [Frank] Flemington, dated 11 October 1952. ALS. 1 p. No F002.156–7. In Box B021. Regarding an acknowledgment for the Edgar manuscript.

p / F to Lorne Pierce, dated 8 May 1958. TLS. 1 p. No F002.121. In Box B027. Acknowledges a letter from Pierce. Comments on the honour of having won the Lorne Pierce Medal.

q / F to Lorne Pierce, dated 9 February 1959. ALS. 1 p. No F002.126. In Box B028. Acknowledges letter from Pierce. Applauds his work at Ryerson Press.

r / F to Mrs Thompson, dated 6 February 1959. TLU. 1 p. No F002.127. In Box B028. Responds to a request to support the Canadian Writers' Foundation.

s / F to Lorne Pierce, dated 4 January 1960. TLS. 1 p. No F002.125. In Box B029. Sends good wishes to Pierce on his retirement and remarks on his contribution to Canadian literature.

J4 Harry Ransom Humanities Research Center, Univ of Texas, Austin. Letters to Edith Sitwell

a / F to Miss [Edith] Sitwell, dated 7 January 1948. TLS. 1 p. Thanks Sitwell for her review of FS in The Spectator (see M8.30).

b / F to Miss [Edith] Sitwell, dated 12 April 1948. TLS. 2 pp. Thanks and praises Sitwell for The Shadow of Cain; thanks her for her appreciation of FS; discusses his frustrated efforts to have FS published in England; outlines future work he wants to do on The Faerie Queene, Shakespeare's comedies, and Rabelais; remarks on the job of a critic and on the general state of contemporary criticism.

J5 Concordia University Archives, Concordia Univ, Montreal, Que. Letters in the Irving Layton Collection from F to Irving Layton

a / F to Mr [Irving] Layton, dated 18 November 1955. TLS. 1 p. Thanks Layton for sending copy of The Cold Green Element.

b / F to Mr [Irving] Layton, dated 20 February 1956. TLS. 1 p. Thanks Layton for sending copies of two books, and remarks that he would never claim his criticism of Layton's poetry is correct or adequate, only honest in intent.

c / F to Mr [Irving] Layton, dated 18 May 1956. TLS. 1 p. Thanks Layton for sending copies of *The Bull Calf*, and comments on Layton's forthcoming selected poems.

d / F to Mr [Irving] Layton, dated 1 December 1956. TLS. 1 p. Thanks Layton for sending a copy of his *Selected Poems*, and expresses regret that several of his own favourites were omitted from the collection.

e / F to Mr [Irving] Layton, dated 28 October 1958. TLS. 1 p. Thanks Layton for sending a copy of *A Laughter in the Mind*.

f / F to Irving Layton, dated 6 January 1959. TLS. 1 p. Thanks Layton for his letter about the article 'Poetry' (see D100). Is encouraged by Layton's reaction to it.

g / F to Mr [Irving] Layton, postmarked 19 September 1960. TLS. 1 p. Thanks Layton for sending a copy of an editorial.

h / F to Irving Layton, dated 14 December 1961. TLS. 1 p. Thanks Layton for sending a copy of a sonnet sequence.

i / F to Irving Layton, dated 8 February 1965. TLS. 1 p. Replies to Layton's letter about his comments on F, saying that he has never taken them personally and that he remains an admirer of Layton's best work.

j / F to Mr [Irving] Layton, dated 23 August 19??. TLS. 1 p. Comments on the writing he hopes to see emerge from Layton. Expresses regrets on not being able to attend the Writers' Conference.

k / F to Irving Layton, dated 4 November 1970. TLS. 1 p. Thanks Layton for addressing his poem 'Elephant' to him.

l / F to Irving [Layton], dated 3 March 1972. TLS. 1 p. Thanks Layton for sending a copy of the *Collected Poems*. F also comments on the introduction he is to write for the Italian translation of Layton's poetry (see D222).

m / F to Irving [Layton], dated 19 April 1973. 1 p. Thanks Layton for sending a copy of *Anvil Blood*.

n / F to Irving Layton, dated 2 August 1974. TLS with holograph note. 1 p. Thanks Layton for various pieces of correspondence.

o / F to Irving Layton, dated 26 October 1977. TLS. 1 p. Thanks Layton for sending a copy of *The Covenant*.

p / F to Irving [Layton], dated 2 December 1981. TLS. 1 p. Expresses regret on missing a reading by Layton and welcomes him to the University of Toronto as visiting poet.

q / F to Irving [Layton], dated 18 January 1983. TLS. 1 p. Thanks Layton for sending a copy of *A Wild Peculiar Joy*.

r / F to Irving [Layton], dated 23 November 1983. TLS. 1 p. Thanks Layton for sending a copy of *The Gucci Bag* and a news story. Says he would be pleased if Layton got the Nobel Prize.

J6 Public Archives of Canada. Letters in the George Johnston Papers from F to George Johnston. Reference no MG31, D95 vol 3 and F178 vol 12, file 23

a / F to George [Johnston], dated 8 December 1952. TLS. 1 p. Thanks Johnston for sending Miss [Jay] Macpherson's poems. Incidental news.

b / F to George [Johnston], dated 20 February [1953]. TLS. 1 p. Comments on Johnston's interest in Blake and on the connections, which have not yet been fully traced, between Blake and Ossian, Cowper, Chatterton, the cult of fancy and sensibility, and the Methodist movement.

c / F to George [Johnston], [1953]. TLS. 1 p. Expresses pleasure in having met Jay Macpherson. Comments on his lectureship at Princeton for 'next year,' adding that Macpherson might follow him there.

d / F to George [Johnston], dated 30 November 1953. TLS 1 p. Having learned of Johnston's accident, sends condolences. News about Jay Macpherson's attending his lectures and other incidental news. Advises Johnston against beginning a new magazine.

e / F to George [Johnston], dated 18 June 1954. TLS. 1 p. Comments chiefly on his experiences at Princeton – the students, the preceptorial system, the high morale in the humanities, etc. Looks forward to a trip to Scandinavia and to returning to Toronto, which, F says, is more intellectually stimulating than both Princeton and Harvard.

f / F to George and Jeanne [Johnston], [1955]. ALS. 1 p. Brief note of thanks. Incidental news.

g / F to George [Johnston], dated 21 January 1955. TLS. 2 pp. Remarks concerning Jay Macpherson and Daryl Hine, plus incidental news.

h / F to George [Johnston], dated 15 November 1957. TLS. 1 p. Thanks Johnston for sending some poems. Comments on a poetry reading by Jay Macpherson and on his recent lecture tour.

i / F to George [Johnston], dated 5 September 1958. TLS. 1 p. Reactions to the death of Peter Fisher, his review of Jay Macpherson's poetry, and teaching summer school at Columbia University.

j / F to George [Johnston], dated 28 October 1958. TLS. 1 p. Expresses regret at not being able to see Johnston in Ottawa. Comments on Claude Bissell's inauguration and on Johnston's forthcoming volume of poetry.

k / F to George [Johnston], dated 18 November 1959. TLS. 1 p. Incidental news, most of it relating to F's new position as principal of Victoria College.

l / F to George [Johnston], dated 14 January 1960. TLS. 1 p. Brief note of thanks for some poems Johnston had sent.

m /F to George [Johnston], dated 28 January 1960. TLS. 1 p. Comments on Johnston's poetry.

n / F to George [Johnston], dated 26 March 1962. TLS. 2 pp. Comments on some poems and a story by Johnston. Incidental news.

o / F to George [Johnston], dated 9 June 1967. TLS. 1 p. Thanks Johnston for sending a copy of his *Home Free*, and comments on the new tone in the poems of this volume.

p / F to George [Johnston], dated 14 February 1973. TLS. 1 p. Brief note of thanks to Johnston for sending a copy of *Happy Enough*.

q / F to George [Johnston], dated 17 September 1973. TLS. 1 p. Agrees to write letter for Johnston's application for a grant. Incidental news.

r / F to George [Johnston], dated 22 October 1973. TLS. 1 p. Brief letter of thanks for a holograph copy of Johnston's new poems.

s / F to George [Johnston], dated 18 August 1976. TLS. 1 p. Responds
to an invitation to attend a dinner for Munro [Beattie].

t / F to George [Johnston], [1977]. TLU. 1 p. Brief note that accompanied
a message for Munro [Beattie].

u / F to George [Johnston], dated 24 August 1978. TLS. 1 p. Incidental news.

v / F to George [Johnston], dated 30 April 1979. TLS. 1 p. Incidental news.

w / F to George [Johnston], dated 5 September 1979. TLS. 1 p. Thanks
Johnston for sending a copy of his occasional poems, *Taking a Grip*.
Comments on his own work on 'the Bible book.'

x / F to George [Johnston], dated 24 January 1980. TLS. 1 p. Thanks
Johnston for his contribution to the CEA *Critic* issue devoted to F.

y / F to George [Johnston], dated 6 June 1980. TLS. 1 p. Thanks Johnston
for the poem he wrote in honour of F.

J7 Thomas Fisher Rare Book Library, Univ of Toronto Library

J7a Letters to A.J.M. Smith

1 F to Art, undated. TLS. 1 p. On the kind of poetry that has been recently
submitted to the *Canadian Forum*. Comments on the symbolism in E.J.
Pratt's *The Truant* ('his best poem yet').

2 F to Art, undated. TLS. 1 p. Thanks Smith for sending copies of two
articles, says he is pondering a series of articles on Canadian culture,
and requests Smith to send more poetry for the *Canadian Forum*, which
has begun to publish Avison, Wreford, and Layton.

3 F to Art, dated 30 July 1964. TLS. 1 p. Thanks Smith for the generous
review of *The Well-Tempered Critic* (see M22.19).

J7b Letters to Earle Birney

1 F to Earle, dated 15 March 1947. TLS. 1 p. Mostly incidental news about
F's role as literary editor of the *Canadian Forum*.

2 F to Earle, dated 15 August 1947. ALS. 1 p. Comments on the poems
Birney has sent to the *Canadian Forum*, on Birney's forthcoming book,
and on the 'attractive job' Princeton did with *Fearful Symmetry*. Plus
incidental news. Includes holograph note by Birney on his poems having
been rejected by Frye.

3 F to Earle, undated but with Birney's holograph annotation '[1954
August (?)].' ALS. 1 p. Responds to Birney's having taken exception to
F's review of an anthology edited by Birney.

4 F to Earle, dated 31 October 1960. TLS. 1 p. About a visit to Vancouver,
where F is to lecture.

5 F to Esther [Birney] and Earle, dated 23 November 1960. TLS. 1 p. Note
of thanks to the Birneys for making his visit to Vancouver a pleasant
one.

J7c Letters to W.A. Deacon

1 F to Mr Deacon, dated 18 August 1965. TLS. 1 p. About a recommenda-
tion F wrote to support Deacon's application for a Centennial grant.

2 F to Mr Deacon, dated 4 October 1965. TLS. 1 p. Responds to an inquiry
about Deacon's application to the Canada Council for a grant.

J8 Rare Books and Special Collections, McGill Univ Libraries, Montreal, Que

1   F to [Lawrence M.] Lande, dated 30 September [1954?]. TLS. 1 p.
    Thanks Lande for sending him a copy of his book on Job and commends
    him for including Blake's plates in the book and for isolating the Book
    of Job as a work of art in its own right. This letter is tipped in to a
    copy of *FS* in the Blake Collection.

J9 Department of Rare Books and Special Collections, Univ of Michigan
    Library, Ann Arbor, Mich
    1   F to Clarence D. Thorpe, postmarked 21 January 1957. TLS. 1 p.
        A postcard in the Clarence D. Thorpe Literary Papers. Agrees to serve
        as editor for a collection of essays on British romanticism.
    2   F to Joe Lee Davis, postmarked 29 November 1961. TLS. 1 p. A postcard
        in the Joe Lee Davis Papers. Grants permission to use passages from *AC*.

J10 Manuscripts and Archives, Yale Univ Library, New Haven, Conn
    The library's description of the unindexed William Kurtz Wimsatt Papers
    indicates that 'there are occasional notes from ... Northrop Frye' in Wim-
    satt's correspondence.

Secondary Sources

K

Books and Collections of Essays

K1 Ayre, John. *Northrop Frye: A Critical Biography*. Don Mills, Ont: General
Publishing Co, forthcoming
Gives a portrait of F and his work based upon family letters, archival
correspondence, interviews and correspondence with F himself, talks with
childhood and college friends, colleagues, students, and editors.

K2 Bates, Ronald. *Northrop Frye*. Toronto: McClelland and Stewart 1971. 62 pp.
Canadian Writers Series, no 10
Designed to be 'an introduction to, and not a full exposition of, the
extemely sophisticated and complex vision of criticism and literature' in
F's work published before 1970. Devotes separate chapters to *FS*; *AC*; *WTC*
and *EI*; *NP*, *FT*, and *RE*; and F's criticism on Canadian literature. Aims
'to present a skeletal outline of the total system' of F's work. Observes
that though the systematic mind still lies behind F's writing since *AC*,
his method of presentation, chiefly by way of the public lecture, tends
more and more toward 'what Bacon called Aphorisms as contrasted with
Methods.' Includes a selected bibliography.
Reviews:
Noel-Bentley, Peter C. 'The Function of Criticism at the Present Time.'
  Journal of Canadian Fiction 1 (Summer 1972): 78–80
Thomas, Clara. 'Four Critical Problems.' *Canadian Literature* 56 (Spring
  1973): 103–7 [105–6]

K3 Cook, David. *Northrop Frye: A Vision of the New World*. New York:
St Martin's 1985. 122 pp
Is concerned primarily 'with Frye as a social critic and, in particular, with
Frye's defense of liberalism and his critique of technology.' Concentrates
on the ways in which F's response to the Western intellectual tradition has
been shaped by his North American and Canadian experience – a response

that has produced, like Blake's *America: A Prophecy*, a vision of the New
World. Looks at the relationship between F's view of the imagination and
the natural world, the individual, and society, noting especially the way
a humanized technology mediates among these three orders. Devotes
a separate chapter to F's understanding of the Canadian identity. Remarks
that his treatment of F is 'closer to that of a caricature than that of a
photograph' and that his study has an imaginative and fictional dimension
to it.
Reviews:
Cook, Ramsay. *University of Toronto Quarterly* 56 (Fall 1986): 157–9
Ellaschuk, Lorne. *Books in Canada* 15 (March 1986): 20
Woodcock, George. 'Political Frye.' *Canadian Literature* 110 (Fall 1986):
 153–6
K4 Cook, Eleanor et al, eds. *Centre and Labyrinth: Essays in Honour of Northrop
Frye*. Toronto: Univ of Toronto Press in association with Victoria Univ
1983. x + 346 pp
A group of essays presented to F in honour of his seventieth year.
Contents:
Paul Ricoeur, '*Anatomy of Criticism* and the Order of Paradigms' (see L425)
Francis Sparshott, 'The Riddle of *Katharsis*' (see L484)
Patricia Parker, 'Anagogic Metaphor: Breaking down the Wall of Partition'
 (see L391)
Michael Dolzani, 'The Infernal Method: Northrop Frye and Contemporary
 Criticism' (see L124)
John Freccero, 'Manfred's Wounds and the Poetics of the *Purgatorio*'
James Nohrnberg, '*Paradise Regained* by One Greater Man: Milton's Wisdom
 Epic as a "Fable of Identity" '
Thomas Willard, 'Alchemy and the Bible'
James Carscallen, 'Three Jokers: The Shape of Alice Munro's Stories'
David Staines, 'The Holistic Vision of Hugh of Saint Victor' (see L489)
Julian Patrick, '*The Tempest*' as Supplement'
Helen Vendler, 'The Golden Theme: Keat's Ode *To Autumn*'
Milton Wilson, 'Bodies in Motion: Wordsworth's Myths of Natural
 Philosophy'
Geoffrey Hartman, 'Reading Aright: Keat's *Ode to Psyche*' (see L213)
Eleanor Cook, 'Riddles, Charms, and Fictions in Wallace Stevens'
W. David Shaw, 'Poetic Truth in a Scientific Age: The Victorian Perspective'
Jennifer Levine, 'Reading *Ulysses*'
Eli Mandel, 'Northrop Frye and the Canadian Literary Tradition' (see L337)
James Reaney, 'Some Critics Are Music Teachers' (see L419)
Harold Bloom, 'Reading Freud: Transference, Taboo, and Truth'
Angus Fletcher, 'The Image of Lost Direction'
Reviews:
Buitenhuis, Peter. 'Honor for a Literary Colossus.' *Globe and Mail*, 25 June
 1983, 17

Denham, Robert D. *American Review of Canadian Studies* 14 (Spring 1984):
    107–9
Egawa, Toru. *Eibungaku kenkyu* [*Studies in English Literature*] 61 (December
    1984): 387–90
Forst, Graham. 'Word-Centred.' *Canadian Literature* 102 (Fall 84): 69–71
Galan, F.W. *World Literature Today* 57 (1983): 695
Kastan, David Scott. 'The Triumph of Comedy.' *TLS*, 17 February 1984, 163
O'Hara, Dan. *Criticism* 26 (Winter 1984): 92–5
K5 Denham, Robert D. *Northrop Frye and Critical Method*. University Park:
    Pennsylvania State Univ Press 1978. xiv + 262 pp
    An effort to examine the whole of F's critical system by placing his argu-
    ments in the context of his total view of literature and criticism. Looks
    at F's work in terms of the problems he is addressing, the nature of his
    subject matter, the principles and concepts implied by his critical language,
    and his mode of reasoning. Assumes that *AC* is the chief work to be
    accounted for, so devotes the first four chapters to tracing the arguments
    of the theories presented there. In chapter 5, examines F's ideas about
    critical and literary autonomy, the scientific nature of criticism, value-
    judgments, and the social function of the critic. In chapter 6, analyses
    several examples of F's practical, historical, and social criticism. In the
    final chapter, points to some of the powers and limitations of F's work.
    Includes twenty-four diagrams.
    Reviews:
    Anonymous. *Annotated Bibliography of New Publications in the Performing
        Arts*, no 39 (Spring 1980), 47
    – *Choice* 16 (July–August 1979): 663
    Barfoot, C.C. 'Current Literature: 1978.' *English Studies* 60 (December 1979):
        790
    Bilan, R.P. 'Frye's Web.' *Canadian Forum* 59 (June–July 1979): 39–40
    Bronzwaer, W. et al. *Dutch Quarterly Review of Anglo-American Letters* 13
        (1983–4): 306
    Conner, Frederick. *Journal of Aesthetics and Art Criticism* 38 (Fall 1979):
        97–8
    Coulling, Sidney. 'A Careful Analysis of Influential Criticism.' *Roanoke
        Times* [Va], 22 April 1979, E4
    Fischer, Michael. *Clio* 9 (Spring 1980): 478–80
    Harris, Wendell V. *National Forum* 60 (Fall 1980): 52–4
    Hawkes, Terence. 'New Books in Review.' *Yale Review* 69 (Summer 1980):
        560–76 [574–6]
    Leighton, Betty. 'Frye, Bellow, Mailer, Conrad and Company.' *Winston-
        Salem Journal* [NC], 11 March 1979, C3
    Rajan, Tilottama. 'In Search of System.' *University of Toronto Quarterly* 51
        (Fall 1981): 93–102 [93–5]
    Schwartz, Sanford. 'Reconsidering Frye.' *Modern Philology* 78 (February
        1981): 289–95

Segal, Robert. 'Methodology.' *Journal of the American Academy of Religion*
   51 (June 1983): 334
Spector, Robert D. *World Literature Today* 53 (Summer 1979): 562
Steig, Michael. 'Frye, Freud and Theory.' *Canadian Literature* 83 (Winter
   1979): 190–4

K6 Dyrkjob, Jan Ulrik. *Northrop Fryes litteraturteori.* Copenhagen: Berlingske
   Verlag 1979. 240 pp
   Gives a critical account of F's theory of literature and, using this theory
   as a starting point, seeks to discover the relation between the vision we
   encounter in poetry and the utopian vision necessary for revolutionary
   political change. Sees the most important ideological assumptions in F's
   theory as the English left-wing Protestant tradition, the romantic
   emphasis on human creativity, and nineteenth-century cultural liberalism.
   Uses a Marxist understanding of culture, society, and poetry as the starting point for his critique of F's theory of literature and for the development
   of his own point of view.

K7 Kogan, Pauline. *Northrop Frye: The High Priest of Clerical Obscurantism*
   (Literature and Ideology Monographs no 1). Montreal: Progressive Books
   and Periodicals 1969. 98 pp. Rpt in *Ideological Forum*, nos 3, 4, and 5
   (Montreal: The Internationalists nd); rpt with minor changes in *Alive Magazine: Literature and Ideology*, no 43 (1975), 22–31
   A diatribe that purports to examine F's theories of knowledge, literature,
   and interpretation, and his views on Blake, Jung, and writers and critics in
   the class struggle. Seeks to show that F is a reactionary, obscurantist critic.

K8 Krieger, Murray, ed. *Northrop Frye in Modern Criticism: Selected Papers from
   the English Institute.* New York: Columbia Univ Press 1966. x + 203 pp
   Papers presented at the 1965 session of the English Institute devoted
   to Frye's work. One of the first formal efforts to assess F's theories and his
   place in modern criticism.
   Contents:
   Murray Krieger, 'Foreword'
   Murray Krieger, 'Northrop Frye and Contemporary Criticism: Ariel and
      the Spirit of Gravity' (see L282)
   Northrop Frye, 'Letter to the English Institute' (see D164)
   Angus Fletcher, 'Utopian History and *Anatomy of Criticism*' (see L165)
   W.K. Wimsatt, 'Northrop Frye: Criticism as Myth' (see L571)
   Geoffrey Hartman, 'Ghostlier Demarcations' (see L212)
   Northrop Frye, 'Reflections in a Mirror' (see D165)
   John E. Grant, 'A Checklist of Writings by and about Northrop Frye'
      (see O6)
   Reviews:
   Anonymous. *Yale Review* 56 (Spring 1967): VI, XII
   Blissett, William. *University of Toronto Quarterly* 36 (July 1967): 414
   Cox, R. Gordon. *British Journal of Aesthetics* 8 (January 1968): 76–9
   Griffin, L.W. *Library Journal* 91 (1 September 1966): 3951–2

Hamilton, Alice. *Dalhousie Review* 47 (Spring 1967): 105–7
Harvey, W.J. 'Not Enough Muddle.' *Listener* 77 (5 January 1967): 32
L[emon], L[ee] T. *Prairie Schooner* 41 (Fall 1967): 356
Lane, Lauriat. *Fiddlehead*, Summer 1967, 83
Lodge, David. 'Current Critical Theory.' *Critical Quarterly* 9 (Spring 1967): 81–9 [81–4]
Ricks, Christopher. *Listener* 79 (9 May 1968): 610–11
Rodway, Allan. *Notes & Queries* 212 (July 1967): 272–4
Von Hendy, Andrew. *Criticism* 9 (Fall 1967): 393–5

L

Essays and Parts of Books

L1 Abbey, Lloyd. 'The Organic Aesthetic.' *Canadian Literature* 46 (Autumn 1970): 103–4
Replies to an essay by George Bowering (L67), who attacks what he calls the 'Northrop Frye school' of poetry. Argues that F and Bowering hold different theories about the relationship between poetry and experience, and suggests that F would see Bowering's theory of organic form for what it really is – a convention.

L2 Abdulla, Adnan. *Catharsis in Literature* (Bloomington: Indiana Univ Press 1985), 97–100
Examines F's statements about catharsis in *AC* and finds that he is 'the first critic in the history of literary theory to associate catharsis with ecstasis' and that his defence of catharsis as both intellectual and emotional exuberance 'is perhaps the most passionate throughout the ages.'

L3 Ackland, Michael. 'Blake's System and the Critics.' *AUMLA* 54 (1980): 149–70
A critique of *FS* and three other books on Blake, which are faulted for ignoring the integrity of the individual poem and for often being less comprehensible than the works they interpret.

L4 Adams, Hazard. 'Criticism: Whence and Whither?' *American Scholar* 28 (Spring 1959): 226, 228, 232, 234, 238 [232, 238]
Praises *AC* for its systematic conceptual universe and for its particular insights. Believes F's theory cannot be dismissed without dismissing along with it the virtues of his system, and chides Robert Martin Adams for criticizing the systematic character of F's work, arguing that Adams's critique (M1.4) is based upon a mistrust of philosophy.

L5 — 'Frye, Northrop.' *Encyclopedia of World Literature in the 20th Century*, vol 4, ed Frederick Ungar and Lina Mainiero (New York: Ungar 1975) 126–7

A short account of F's chief contributions to literary study from *FS* through *StS*.

L6 — *The Interests of Criticism: An Introduction to Literary Theory* (New York: Harcourt, Brace & World 1969), 122–31

Discusses F's argument about the nature of criticism, as outlined in the Polemical Introduction to *AC*, and the chief theoretical concepts upon which *AC* is based, including imitation, myth, ritual, symbol, and archetype. Maintains that F has produced the most influential body of critical theory since the New Critics. Takes issue, however, with F's view on value-judgments.

L7 — 'The Literary Concept of Myth.' *Philosophy of the Literary Symbolic* (Tallahassee: Univ Presses of Florida 1983), 263–86

A detailed account of F's theory of symbolism, 'the most comprehensive theoretical effort to gather the strands of romantic and postromantic literary theory together.' Discusses F's idea of symbolic forms in relation to the concept of imitation, his understanding of anagogy, his use of the analogy between literary and mathematical languages, the relation between his view of literary symbolism and his more general interests, and his conception of the myths of freedom and concern.

L8 — 'Northrop Frye.' *Critical Theory since Plato* (New York: Harcourt Brace Jovanovich 1971), 1117–18

An account of F's theory of symbolism. Serves as an introduction to the Second Essay of *AC*, which is rpt in Adams's anthology. A number of references to F are scattered throughout the book: see pp 2, 6, 8–10, 67, 116, 400, 445, 721, 942, 993, 1079, 1167, 1200.

L9 Adkins, Curtis P. 'The Hero in T'ang *Ch'uan-ch'i* Tales.' *Critical Essays on Chinese Fiction*, ed Winston L.Y. Yang and Curtis P. Adkins (Hong Kong: Chinese Univ Press 1980), 17–46 [18–21]

Uses F's conception of the archetype as both a recurring symbol and a narrative pattern to examine the quest myth in the T'ang *ch'uan-ch'i* tales.

L10 Ahmad, Iqbal. 'Imagination and Image in Frye's Criticism.' *English Quarterly* 3 (Summer 1970): 15–24

Argues that for F imaginative energy creates imaginative reality, the images of which are found in the patterns or archetypes of literature: the original writer does not repeat the archetype but recreates it. Believes that F's theory of the imagination helps the reader to understand literature but cannot be used to evaluate specific works.

L11 Aichele, George, Jr. 'Modern Comic Theories.' *Theology as Comedy: Critical and Theoretical Implications* (Lanham, Md: Univ Press of America 1980), 17–42 [26–8, 31–2]

Categorizes F's theory of comedy as 'light,' because, like the theories of Bergson and Langer, it views comedy as socially creative, edifying, preservative, and culturally powerful. Opposes this view to the 'dark' or negative theories of comedy in such writers as Baudelaire and Camus.

L12 Aitken, Johan L. *English and Ethics: Some Ideas for Teachers of Literature*

(Profiles in Practical Education no 10). Toronto: Ontario Institute for Studies in Education 1976. 34 pp
A manual, significantly shaped by F's insights, on the coalition between ethics and literary study.

L13 — 'Northrop Frye and Educational Theory: Some Implications for Teaching.' *Teacher Education* 10 (April 1977): 50–9
Examines F's understanding of several key objectives or priorities in education: contemplation, communication, free speech, and social vision. Argues that teachers need an educational theory and that F's, as presented in *On Teaching Literature* (c6) and other essays, can help them to grow. This essay is an abridged version of chapt 1, part 3, of 'Children's Literature in the Light of Northrop Frye's Theory' (N2).

L14 — 'The Tale's the Thing: Northrop Frye's Theory Applied to the Teaching of Tales in the Elementary School.' *Interchange* 7, no 2 (1976–7): 63–72
Shows how F's theories of literature apply to the tales children relish, and how they help teachers make connections and perceive hidden likenesses.

L15 — 'Teaching *The Great Code*.' Paper presented at the annual meeting of the South Atlantic Modern Language Association, Atlanta, Ga, 10 November 1984. 10 pp. Photoduplicated typescript
Recounts her experience of teaching F's GC, supplemented by his videotaped lectures on the Bible (H51), to students in the University of Toronto School for Continuing Studies.

L16 — 'The Shape of Myth.' *Indirections* 6 (Winter 1981): 28–39
Using F's proposal that mythology should serve as the basis of education, shows how teachers can examine biblical and classical myths with children.

L17 — et al. *Wavelengths 31*. Np: Dent (Canada) 1970; *Wavelengths 32*, ibid 1971; *Wavelengths 33*, ibid
A series of textbooks, based upon F's conceptual framework of literary modes, for children in the elementary grades.

L18 Allen, James Lovic. 'The Road to Byzantium: Archetypal Criticism and Yeats.' *Journal of Aesthetics and Art Criticism* 32 (Fall 1973): 53–64 [55–8]
Claims that F's archetypal categories are 'too highly schematized and theoretical' to be of use in the practical criticism of Yeats's work. Analyses F's archetypal framework in *AC* and in an essay on Yeats's imagery (D184). Concludes that Yeats's neo-Platonic imagination required 'only two main categories of images and archetypes, not the three or four postulated by Northrop Frye.'

L19 Altieri, Charles. 'Northrop Frye and the Problem of Spiritual Authority.' *PMLA* 87 (1972): 964–75
Analyses F's definition of man, a definition established by the study of origins and expressed both in a society's 'myths of concern' and in its imaginative creations. Man's *telos*, or the underlying structure and imagery of his desire, is seen as a principle of mediation, not unlike what one finds in Sartre, Lukács, and Ricoeur. Argues that this principle can become

a model for both moral action and literary criticism, and it can be used
to resist the relativisim of such structuralist critics as Foucault and Derrida.

L20 — 'Some Uses of Frye's Literary Theory.' *CEA Critic* 42 (January 1980):
10–19
Testifies to the mediating values of F's literary theory in three areas. First,
sees F's definition of both the centripetal and the centrifugal functions
of literature, his dialectical understanding of literature as both temporal
and spatial, and his attention to both the authorial and the dramatic
aspects of texts as being more descriptively adequate than theories that
emphasize only one of the poles in these oppositions. Second, believes that
F's focus on the structure of the desires that inform actions helps to
define the acts and identities of critics. Third, F's unwillingness to reduce
literature to irony and criticism to description, on the one hand, or to
deconstructive play, on the other, forces the critic to confront his ultimate
problem: how to relate literature to *praxis* and existential reality.

L21 Anastasjew, N. 'Literaturkritik in den USA heute.' *Kunst und Literatur* 32,
no 2 (1984): 223–34
Sees F as the ancestor of the current evils that beset criticism because of
his assumption that criticism builds on an internally governed structure of
ideas that are relatively independent of art.

L22 Anonymous. 'Canadian Culture in the 1960's.' *TLS*, 28 August 1969, 941–3
[942]
Sees F as the 'most eloquent' and 'brilliant' representative of Canada,
'almost universally admired,' a 'virtuoso performer ... unlikely to have any
successors, not only because of his erudition, but because he has elegantly
side-stepped the central critical debate of our time on the relation between
literature and society.'

L23 — 'Northrop Frye Challenges Validity of Sacred versus Secular Scripture.'
Harvard Gazette, 11 April 1975, 3
Reports on the first of F's Charles Eliot Norton lectures (A15), delivered
7 April 1975, and entitled 'The Word and the World of Man.'

L24 — 'Our Man in Washington.' *Arts Bulletin*, April 1977, 14
Summarizes F's address at the Symposium on Canadian Culture, Washington, DC, 2 February 1977 (D243).

L25 — 'Secular Scripture: Romance Offers Polarized Reality, Says Northrop
Frye.' *Harvard Gazette*, 18 April 1975, 4
Reports on the second and third of F's Charles Eliot Norton lectures (A15),
entitled 'The Context of Romance' and 'Our Lady of Pain: Heroes and
Heroines of Romance.'

L26 — 'Sons of New Critic.' *TLS*, 25 November 1965, 1078
A brief judgment about F's contribution to American literary criticism in
the 1950s and 1960s. Characterizes F's *AC* as a tolerant 'new eclecticism,'
exciting and suggestive, and observes that it has nourished a number
of recent essays in practical criticism.

L27 Aranguren, Jose Luis L. 'Los Generos Literarios.' *Triunfo*, 10 November
1973. 1300 w
Places F's theory of genres in the discussion of genre that preceded it,
and gives a summary of F's theory of modes, symbols, and *mythoi*.
L28 Atwood, Margaret. 'Northrop Frye Observed.' *Second Words: Selected Critical
Prose* (Toronto: Anansi 1982), 398–406
A memoir by one of F's former students. Recounts the experience of being
in F's classes at Victoria College and reflects on the 'delicate question' of
his influence on her writing and her life.
L29 Ayre, John. 'The Alphabet of Forms: The Development of Northrop Frye's
Archetypal Criticism.' Paper presented at Brock Univ, 14 February 1986.
Unpublished typescript. 10 pp
Gives an account of the influences on F's intellectual development: Greek
myths, the Bible, serial movies, juvenile novels, Blake, Spengler, Frazer,
Jung, Renaissance mythological handbooks, Austin Farrer, et al.
L30 — 'The Mythological Universe of Northrop Frye.' *Saturday Night* 88 (May
1973): 19–24
On F's educational background and career as a teacher and administrator.
L31 Barry, Jackson K. 'Form or Formula: Comic Structure in Northrop Frye
and Susanne Langer.' *Educational Theatre Journal* 16 (1964): 333–40
Argues that F's theory of comic form leads one outside of particular
dramatic works and thus fails to describe or evaluate them accurately. Says
that F's archetypal criticism looks through a work of art to a myth beyond
it that contains the artistic meaning and form; the meaning is then read
back into the work itself. Concludes that such a method 'can both equalize
and transcend the specific works it operates on.'
L32 Bashford, Bruce. 'Literary History in Northrop Frye's *Anatomy of Criticism*.'
Connecticut Review 8 (October 1974): 48–55
Seeks to answer the question, What kind of literary history is presented
in the first essay of *AC*? Argues that F is writing a 'formal' rather than a
conventionally descriptive literary history; that is, the principles of F's
theory of modes are the deductive consequence of the basic categories with
which he begins. F is not a philosophical historian. Rather his theory of
modes represents the scale of thematic and fictional possibilities. Concludes
by comparing F's kind of literary history with Aristotle's.
L33 — 'Northrop Frye: Thoughts on Disputed Questions.' Unpublished typescript. 9 pp
Seeks to answer two questions about F's work: 'in what sense is criticism
a "science" for him? and what is the explanatory power of archetypal criticism?' Argues that the discovery of a co-ordinating principle is the fundamental step F takes in establishing a systematic criticism and that this
principle for F is found in the archetypes of the anagogic phase of symbolism. Finds that by using archetypes to identify the controlling form of a
literary work F relies on a conventional kind of explanation: he explains by
identifying the type of thing the form is.

L34 — 'Oscar Wilde and Subjectivist Criticism.' *English Literature in Transition: 1880–1920* 21 (1978): 218–34
Compares Wilde's subjectivist theory of criticism with F's view that literary works determine their own significance. Finds a resemblance, on the level of principle, between both critics' understanding of a comprehensive human desire. Sees a difference, however, between F's view of apocalyptic reality, where all men become one man, and Wilde's view, in which human beings maintain their separate identities. Comments also on the two critics' different views of literary education and their different approaches to practical criticism.

L35 Bašić, Sonja. 'Northrop Frye kao mitski i arhetipski kritičar.' *Umjetnost riječi: časopis za nauku o književnosti* 14 (1970): 353–84
Examines the development of F's mythopoeic criticism in relation to the New Criticism, neo-Aristotelianism, and structuralism. Looks also at F's precursors (Frazer, Jung, Jacobe, Bodkin, and Murray) in order to illustrate how the archetypal tradition found its synthesis in *AC*. In the absence of a translation (in 1970) of *AC* for the Yugoslav reader, gives a comprehensive overview and summary of *AC*. Notes that F rejects the New Critics' approach by insisting that criticism concern itself with moral, social, and educational matters.

L36 Bassett, Sharon. 'The Uncanny Critic of Brasenose: Walter Pater and Modernism.' *Victorian Newsletter* 58 (Fall 1980): 10–14
Sees a similarity between Pater's *Greek Studies*, with its 'transhistorical psychology,' and F's ethical criticism.

L37 Bate, Walter Jackson. 'Northrop Frye.' *Criticism: The Major Texts*. Enlarged ed (New York: Harcourt Brace Jovanovich 1970), 597–601, 609, 615–17
An overview of F's work from his early study on Blake to his later writings in cultural and social criticism. Sees F as 'the most controversial and probably the most influential critic writing in English since the 1950's.' Reprints, in addition to two of F's essays, the introduction and conclusion to *AC*, and gives a brief summary of the argument of that book. Says that essentialism, or the desire to return to the fundamental, is F's greatest strength.

L38 Bates, Ronald. 'Northrop Frye, Teacher.' *CEA Critic* 42 (November 1979): 29–36
Recollections of F as a person, scholar, and teacher. Comments especially on the absence in F of narrow professionalism and on his genuine humanism.

L39 Belliveau, John Edward. 'Three Scholars.' *Atlantic Advocate* 69 (October 1978): 40, 43–7 [40, 45–7]
On the lives and contributions of three of the most famous citizens of Moncton, NB: astronomer Simon Newcomb, Justice Ivan Cleveland Rand, and F. Sketches F's contributions as a literary critic, comments on the impressions he made as a high school student upon the author, and traces his career from Moncton to Toronto.

L40 Belsey, Catherine. 'Northrop Frye.' *Critical Practice* (London: Methuen 1980), 21–9
Places F's criticism in the context of the New Criticism. Argues that his formalism rests upon a concept of human nature and culture in which desire is the fundamental category, and that his theory of literature transcends history and ideology. Sees F's assumptions, finally, as quite similar to the idealist-empiricist assumptions of the New Critics.

L41 Belyea, Barbara. 'Butterfly in the Bush Garden: "Mythopoeic" Criticism of Contemporary Poetry Written in Canada.' *Dalhousie Review* 56 (Summer 1976): 336–45
Argues that the variety of Canadian poetry contradicts the claims of recent literary critics (Reaney, Jones, Atwood) who have made F's mythopoeic approach a *parti pris,* and that there is not a Canadian national literature 'definable by a number of dominant archetypes contributing to a coherent mythic evolution in a search for cultural identity.'

L42 Bentley, Allen. 'Vic, Canada's Letters, and Northrop Frye.' *Acta Victoriana* 79 (November 1954): 11–13
On Frye's contribution to the criticism of Canadian literature.

L43 Bentley, G.E., Jr, and Martin K. Nurmi. *A Blake Bibliography: Annotated Lists of Works, Studies, and Blakeana* (Minneapolis: Univ of Minnesota Press 1964), 25–6
An assessment of F's contribution to Blake criticism. Maintain that with *FS* 'Blake criticism came of age, for here at last was a book that overcame most of the major obstacles to understanding his thought and art. Frye brought to bear on Blake a criticism which was not merely a collection of critical perceptions, analyses of ideas, histories of traditions and the like, but a unified critical method of the kind needed to understand a unified mind and sensibility like Blake's.' Give a brief account of the central argument of *FS.*

L44 Berger, Harry, Jr. 'The Renaissance Imagination: Second World and Green World.' *Centennial Review* 9 (Winter 1965): 36–78 [47–50]
On F's conception of the 'green world' versus the 'normal world' in Elizabethan comedy.

L45 Berry, Ralph. 'Shakespearean Comedy and Northrop Frye.' *Essays in Criticism* 22 (January 1972): 33–40
Aims to refute F's thesis in *NP* that Shakespearean comedies embody typical patterns. Objects especially to F's claim that the normal action of comedy moves from irrational law to festivity. Concludes that F's theory of comedy applies to only a few Shakespearean plays and that to use his theoretical framework, therefore, is to over-simplify the complexity of these plays.

L46 — *Shakespeare's Comedies: Explorations in Form* (Princeton, NJ: Princeton Univ Press 1972), 3–5
Argues against F's method of building a theoretical model or meta-form

for studying Shakespeare's comedies: 'one cannot accumulate data from certain plays, use them to construct a "genre" model that implies a more than cognate relationship with "genus," and then deploy the "genre" pattern as a triumphant interpretation of a recalcitrant specimen.' Says that such a procedure distorts the individual comedies.

L47 Bialostosky, Don H. 'Literary "Romanticism and Modernism" in Robert Langbaum's *The Poetry of Experience* and Northrop Frye's *Anatomy of Criticism*.' *Cahiers roumains d'études littéraires* 1 (1982): 110–17
Examines the terms F uses in his account of the relation between romanticism and modernism and compares them with Langbaum's treatment of the relation. Looks especially at F's definition of romanticism in his theory of modes in *AC*, where the conventions of the 'low mimetic' mode are distinguished from the ironic mode of modernism. Argues that F is an idealist in his method but that he does not go far enough: 'he fails to distinguish radically enough between his conceptual modes and the historical eras to which he applies them' and to be aware of 'the problematic relation between forms and actual experience.' Sees F's enterprise, however, as a more worthy and 'higher' one than Langbaum's because it asks the more universal questions.

L48 Birney, Earle. 'Epilogue.' *Earle Birney*, ed Bruce Nesbitt (Toronto: McGraw-Hill Ryerson 1974), 213
Claims that in a review of his *David and Other Poems* (E19), F misunderstood the prosody.

L49 Bissell, Claude. *Halfway up Parnassus: A Personal Account of the University of Toronto, 1932–1971* (Toronto: Univ of Toronto Press 1974), 75–6
On the unofficial literary coterie in the early 1940s at Toronto, which included Earle Birney, A.J.M. Smith, E.J. Pratt, Pelham Edgar, and F. See also pp 15, 50, 80, 180, 190.

L50 Black, Max. 'Foreword.' *The Morality of Scholarship*, ed Max Black (Ithaca, NY: Cornell Univ Press 1967), v–xi [ix–x]
A brief observation about some of the qualities of F's essay, 'The Knowledge of Good and Evil' (D171), included in this anthology: its construction of a general conceptual framework, its metaphysics, and its attention to the social side of morality.

L51 Blazina, S. 'Romanzi di sogno.' *Alfabeta* 41 (1982): 7–8
Considers the novels of Svevo, Berto, Ottievi, and Malerba in light of both *AC* and Starobinski's *L'oeil vivant*.

L52 Bleich, David. 'The Subjective Paradigm in Science, Psychology, and Criticism.' *New Literary History* 7 (Winter 1976): 313–34 [331]
About F's pursuit of *dianoia*, the knowledge *about* literature, as opposed to *nous*, the knowledge *of* literature, which is experiental and subjective.

L53 Bliss, Frank W., and Earl R. MacCormac. 'Two Poles of Metaphor: Frye and Beardsley.' *Journal of Aesthetic Education* 11 (January 1977): 33–49
An analysis of F's and Beardsley's theories of metaphor, which stand as

polar opposites. 'Frye attempts to protect metaphor from losing its tension and decaying into ordinary language. He wants metaphor to retain its suggestiveness and its absurd juxtaposition to referents. At the other extreme, Beardsley wants to ground metaphor in the literal ... Neither presents a theory of metaphor that can account for the variety of metaphoric uses one finds in literature.'

L54 Bloom, Harold. 'Interview.' Forthcoming in a collection of interviews by Imre Salusinszky to be published by Methuen. Typescript. 24 pp
Speaks about his differences with F on the romantic tradition, value-judgments, and the social function of criticism, but says that F is his 'authentic precursor' and refers to him as 'a kind of Miltonic figure ... the largest and most crucial literary critic in the English language' since Pater and Wilde.

L55 — A Map of Misreading (New York: Oxford Univ Press, 1975), 30
Argues that F's myths of freedom and concern are a Low Church version of Eliot's Anglo-Catholic myth of tradition and the individual talent, but that such understanding of the relation of the individual to tradition is a fiction. Believes that we now need a theory of literary history that highlights the interplay of repetition and discontinuity rather than simply the theory of continuity he sees in F's work.

L56 Blyth, Molly. 'James Reaney's Poetic in The Red Heart.' Essays on Canadian Writing 2 (1975): 2–8
Argues that The Red Heart reveals the influence of F's theories, but not to the extent suggested by Alvin Lee's James Reaney (L296). The Red Heart reveals rather a 'mythology which is the daemonic, post-lapsarian counter-part' to F's vision of innocence.

L57 Bogdan, Deanne. 'From Stubborn Structure to Double Mirror: The Evolution of Northrop Frye's Theory of Literary Response in The Great Code.' Paper presented at the annual meeting of the South Atlantic Modern Language Association, Atlanta, Ga, 10 November 1984. 18 pp. Photoduplicated typescript
Examines 'the role of the reader in The Great Code and ... what Frye's conception of poetic response in it can tell us about his theory of literature.' Discovers that in GC F has shifted from his earlier positions on both response and creation. His earlier associations of temporality with centrifu-gal meaning and spatiality with centripetal meaning have been modified, so that he now encourages a direct, participating response no longer separated from the critical response.

L58 — 'Is It Relevant and Does It Work? Reconsidering Literature Taught as Rhetoric.' Journal of Aesthetic Education 16 (Winter 1982): 27–39
Argues that F's apology for poetry can help counter the Platonic fallacies about the relationship between art and life. F, like Sidney and Shelley, justifies the extrinsic value of literature on the basis of its aesthetic integrity.

L59 — ' "Let Them Eat Cake." ' English Journal 70 (November 1981): 33–40
Outlines F's conception of the centrifugal fallacy in criticism (seeing literary

meaning as referring to some extra-literary truth) and the centripetal fallacy (seeing literary meaning as aesthetically self-referential). Discovers that the first fallacy lies behind a great deal of thinking in those current educational theories that seek to make literature relevant (eg, the Language and Learning Movement) and that the second fallacy appears in educational theories that want to make literary form affect emotional response or morality. Argues that both fallacies base the value of art on something that it is not.

L60 — 'Literary Response as Dialectic: Modes and Levels of Engagement and Detachment.' Paper presented at the University of Murcia, 22 April 1985. Forthcoming in *Cuadernos de Filología Inglesa*
An expanded version of 'Response to Literature' (L63). Uses F's concepts and some of his language to analyse and classify the different kinds of literary response.

L61 — 'Northrop Frye and the Defence of Literature.' *English Studies in Canada* 8 (June 1982): 203–14
Examines F's work as a 'defence of literature' in the tradition of Sidney and Shelley. Believes F's system resolves the philosophical problem of the Platonic paradox or Socratic dilemma: the poet as a licensed liar. Sees F's contribution to the question of the value of literature in his broad conception of the dialectic between poetic creation and response: in this framework literature can successfully delight without injuring its seriousness and instruct without destroying its integrity. Concludes that F resembles Plato himself, in that the true artist becomes the wise man and the ultimate art-form becomes the ongoing process of the dialectical action between literature and life.

L62 — 'Pygmalion as Pedagogue: Subjectivist Bias in the Teaching of Literature.' *English Education* 16 (May 1984): 67–75
Argues against the simplistic separation of subjective and objective responses to literature. Calls upon F's conception of the social value of literature to argue that the response to literature should be to its structure as well as its content and that such an approach to literature can lead to valuable practical and pedagogical results.

L63 — 'Response to Literature.' Paper presented at the 1984 International Federation of Teachers of English Conference, East Lansing, Mich. 5 pp. Photoduplicated
Draws upon F's theory of literary value to argue that aesthetic response should be properly conceived as a dialectic of engagement and detachment.

L64 Booth, Wayne C. 'The Use of Criticism in the Teaching of English.' *College English* 27 (October 1965): 1–13 [5–13]
Sees no evidence for F's claim that there is a total order of literature and an ideal science of criticism. 'One way to test my misgivings would be to take the five most respectful readers of the *Anatomy* and give them a work not mentioned by Mr. Frye and ask them to decide whether it is comedy, romance, tragedy, or irony or some combination, and then to

describe the archetypes they detect. The chaotic results can be predicted.'
As an alternative to F's approach, proposes a more inductive method
based on literary response.

L65 Borklund, Elmer. 'Frye, (Herman) Northrop.' *Contemporary Literary Critics*
(London: St James Press; New York: St Martin's Press 1977), 212–18.
2nd ed ([London]: Macmillan 1982), 228–34
A summary of F's critical views, analysed from the perspective of Aristotle's
four causes. The second edition does not change the text but brings the
bibliography up to date.

L66 Bové, Paul A. *Destructive Poetics: Heidegger and Modern American Poetry*
(New York: Columbia Univ Press 1980), ix, 49, 109–10
Sees F's archetypal criticism as 'only the completion of the New Critical
impulse to stabilize literary conventions to produce meaning.' Claims
that for F literature is 'hermetic and nonrelational.' Observes a
parallel between F's theory of modes and Cleanth Brooks's interpretation
of Yeats.

L67 Bowering, George. 'Why James Reaney Is a Better Poet (1) Than Any
Northrop Frye Poet (2) Than He Used To Be.' *Canadian Literature* 36 (Spring
1968): 40–9. Rpt in Bowering, *A Way with Words* (np: Oberon Press 1982),
24–36.
A critique of what Bowering calls the 'Frye school' of Canadian poets –
poets who are over-conscious about myth and critical theory in constructing
their verse. Objects to F's stressing that literature is made out of other
literature. Claims that for F and for the poets influenced by him poetry is
without moral content or experiential reference and criticism nothing more
than a game.

L68 Boys, Mary C. 'Principles and Pedagogy in Biblical Study.' *Religious Education* 77 (September–October 1982): 487–507 [489–90]
Argues for the necessity of reading the Bible as, among other things, a
work of literature that transcends time, using F's concepts of the non-linear
and imaginative nature of literature to reinforce the claim.

L69 Brienza, Susan D., and Peggy A. Knapp. 'Imagination Lost and Found:
Beckett's Fiction and Frye's *Anatomy*.' MLN 95 (May 1980): 980–94
Seek to determine whether F's theory of fictional modes is adequate to
account for Beckett's 'Imagination Dead Imagine,' 'Ping,' and 'The Lost
Ones.' Discover that these 'stories' are displaced myths and that F's criteria
for the ironic and satiric *mythoi* do define many of the characteristics of
Beckett's fiction written in the 1960s.

L70 Brooke-Rose, Christine. 'Historical Genres/Theoretical Genres.' *New Literary
History* 8 (Autumn 1976): 145–59 [145–9]. Rpt in Brooke-Rose, *A Rhetoric
of the Unreal: Studies in Narrative and Structure, Especially of the Fantastic*
(Cambridge Univ Press 1981), 55–71.
On F's theory of modes and the criticism of this theory by Todorov (L517).
'Frye's theory of modes is a theory of historical modes, not theoretical
modes. Inasmuch as Frye tells us explicitly that it is historical (and even

cyclical), Todorov's criticism is unjustified. Inasmuch as Frye calls his critical work theoretical, Todorov is right.'

L71 Buitenhuis, Peter. 'Northrop Frye's *Iliad*: the Alexander Lectures 1965–66.' *Varsity Graduate* 12 (June 1966): 2, 4–6, 8, 10, 98–100
A detailed and thorough summary of F's lectures on Shakespearean tragedy, published as *NP*.

L72 Bush, Douglas. 'Literature, the Academy, and the Public.' *Daedalus* 107 (Fall 1978): 165–74 [168]
An essay on the increasing isolation of critical thought from the reading public. Includes a short survey of literary criticism in this century, one phase of which is archetypal criticism. Salutes F as its 'chief contemporary theorist' and praises his 'range of active knowledge, inexhaustible fertility of ideas, and taxonomic genius,' yet believes that his 'purely verbal universe' has no ethical or aesthetic foundation and is connected only tenuously with life.

L73 Cahill, P. Joseph. 'Literary Criticism, Religious Literature, and Theology.' *Studies in Religion / Sciences réligieuses* 12 (Winter 1983): 51–62
Draws upon F's conceptions of the literary universe and literary conventions in arguing that the centre of theological discourse is religious literature.

L74 Călin, Vera. 'Prefata.' *Anatomia criticii*, trans Domnica Sterian and Mihai Spariosu (Bucharest: Editura Univers 1972), v–xiv (see A2g)
Contrasts F's aesthetic approach to myth with sociological, psychological, and anthropological approaches. Places F's work in the context of archetypal criticism, drawing especially upon the arguments developed in *FI* and *AC*. Gives an overview of F's understanding of the historical modes of literature and of its *mythoi*, symbols, genres, and archetypes.

L75 Calvino, Italo. 'La letteratura come proiezione del desiderio.' *Libri Nuovi*, August 1969, 5
Sees the principles of ritual and dream as informing the entire structure of *AC*. Because ritual is the technical or institutional use of myth, the city, to take one example, can be seen as a symbol of the projection of human terror, revealed in such mythic constructs as the city of Cain, the labyrinth, or the modern metropolis. But because dream is the projection of desire and the rejection of present institutions, the city can also symbolize the city of God, the New Jerusalem, and the court of the king. Sees the most innovative sections of *AC* as those that treat comedy, romance, and irony. Concludes by contrasting F's criticism with structuralism, seeing the latter as austere and reductive and the former as a game of mirrors in which individual works of literature reflect the encyclopedia of human civilization.

L76 Cameron, Barry A. 'Tercentenary Celebrations of *Paradise Lost*.' *Seventeenth-Century News* 26 (Spring 1968): 17
A report on F's untitled lecture delivered to a conference of Milton scholars, October 1968, at the University of Western Ontario, and later published as 'The Revelation to Eve' (D195).

L77 Cantrell, Carol Helmstetter. 'John Hawkes's *Second Skin*: The Dead Reckon-
ing of a Northrop Frye Romance.' *Rocky Mountain Review* 35 (1981): 281–90
Using principles from *SeS*, shows how the 'conventions of romance illuminate every aspect' of Hawkes's novel.

L78 Capone, Giovanna. 'Introduzione all'edizione italiana.' In F's *La scrittura
secolare: Studio sulla struttura del 'romance,'* trans Amleto Lorenzini (Bologna:
Il Mulino 1978), 7–14 (see A15b)
Introduces Italian readers to F's central preoccupations and key terms,
especially as they relate to romance, which Capone sees as a recurrent
theme throughout F's criticism.

L79 — *Canada: Il Villaggio della Terra* (Bologna: Pàtron Editore 1978), 21–2
Gives a brief account of F's major works in the context of three other
masters of Canadian culture: Pratt, Innis, and McLuhan. Points to the
critique of McLuhan's theories in *SM*.

L80 Carpenter, E.S. Letter to Marshall McLuhan, 20 January 1961. *From Cliché
to Archetype* (New York: Viking Press 1970), 18
Says that F and Robert Graves arrange the symbols of myths to create
'content,' pigeon-hole it to come up with archetypes, 'direct their attention
towards a most important problem and, like a hedgehog, build humour-
less, water-tight systems ... , that, instead of answering the problem
or even illuminating it, block access to it.'

L81 Casey, John. 'A "Science" of Criticism: Northrop Frye.' *The Language of
Criticism* (London: Methuen 1966), 140–51
Claims that the central problem of F's work is his attempt to establish a
science of criticism. Argues that F's theory is not scientific in the sense that
Karl Popper uses the term: there are no principles that permit it to be dis-
confirmed, and archetypal categories do not explain literature as scientific
categories explain the natural world.

L82 Cavell, Richard A. 'Canadian Literature in Italy.' *Canadian Literature* 87
(Winter 1980): 153–6
Comments on the great respect F has in Italy and refers to his 1979 lecture
tour there.

L83 Cavell, Stanley. 'Pursuits of Happiness: A Reading of *The Lady Eve*.' *New
Literary History* 10 (Spring 1979): 581–601
Argues that Preston Sturges's film, *The Lady Eve*, 'is an inheritor of the
preoccupations and discoveries of Shakespearean romantic comedy, espe-
cially as that work has been studied by, first among others, Northrop
Frye.'

L84 Celati, Gianni. 'Archetipologia sistematica: Per una iniziazione all'opera
di Northrop Frye.' *Lingua e Stile* [Bologna] 4 (1969): 23–41
Maintains that F attempts a Coleridgian reconciliation of imitation and
inspiration, the two principal methods of studying occidental literature.
Gives a summary account of F's use of the Aristotelian terminology.
Reviews the five phases of symbolism F develops in the Second Essay of
AC and the structure of archetypal imagery and myths of the Third Essay.

Claims that F's most important contribution derives from his method of synthesis, a method that goes beyond considering the literary symbol simply for its psychological or existential content. 'The critical model elaborated by Frye ... presents perhaps several partial difficulties, rendered less evident by an unusual stylistic force. But its great advantage is that it does not close its door to other critical methods, equally based on systematic demands or – what is more important – on an effective and extensive *field work.'*

L85 Ceserani, Remo. 'Northrop Frye utopico pianificatore della città letterarià.' *Strumenti Critici* 1, no 4 (October 1967): 431–6
Introduces F to Italian readers. Calls attention to F's detractors (mentioning John Fraser) as well as those who exalt him, and reviews the several essays in the English Institute volume devoted to F (κ8). Contrasts F's elaborate rhetorical world, with its labyrinths and recurring designs, to the 'more sober and rigorous construction' of Auerbach. Summarizes F's remarks on *Cymbeline* in *NP*, concluding that although F does not take us into the particularities of the play he does invite us to discover its musical structure as well as its links with tradition; and herein lies F's importance as a critic.

L86 Charney, Maurice. *Comedy High and Low: An Introduction to the Experience of Comedy* (New York: Oxford Univ Press 1978), 181
Notes the strong influence on Frye of Francis M. Cornford's ritual theory of comedy.

L87 Cixous, Hélène. 'Une science de la littérature.' *Le Monde* (Supplement to no 7086), 25 October 1967, iv
A summary of F's 'science of literature' as developed in *AC*. Outlines the theoretical bases of F's system, including his theories of genre, archetype, and myth. 'Frye demonstrates that the revolutions in the history of literature are always revolutions of literary form, "modulations" of literary convention. He recommends, then, for those who want to understand the changes in sensibility (romanticism, for example), to begin by studying the history of imagery: it is in the image of the world projected by men that is the "imaginary dwelling" into which they enter when they begin to read – the image of another world which is ours.'

L88 Clark, J. Wilson. 'The Line of National Subjugation in Canadian Literature.' *Literature & Ideology* 7 (1970): 81–8
Says F is one of the dominant critical figures who writes from a willing posture of Canadian subjugation to United States economics, politics, and culture. Cites F's 'Conclusion' to *Literary History of Canada* (D154) as an example of this posture.

L89 — 'Two Lines in Canadian Literary History.' *Literature & Ideology* 15 (1973): 27–36
Maintains that literary historians such as F, who insist that the physical environment has been the primary force shaping the Canadian imagination, explain Quebec's separatism in terms of isolation – the garrison mentality

induced by a vast countryside. Compares this view with Margaret
Atwood's.

L90 Clark, Richard C. 'Bibliographical Spectrum and Review Article: Is There
a Canadian Literature?' *Review of National Literatures: Canada* 7 (1967): 133–64
[154–6]
On Frye's 'Conclusion' to *Literary History of Canada* (D154).

L91 Clark, Walter H., Jr. Review of René Wellek, *Discriminations: Further
Concepts of Criticism. Journal of Aesthetics and Art Criticism* 30 (1972): 389–91
[390–1]
Takes issue with Wellek's attack on F's criticism as an elaborate and fanciful
fiction that totally disregards the literary text. Maintains that the significant
thing about F's system 'is not so much the term "mythology" but rather
the fact that he is proposing a means of identifying, sorting and relating
works of literature according to type ... It is as genre, or taxonomy, that
Frye's system is of greatest theoretical interest.'

L92 Cleary, Thomas R. 'Fielding: Style for an Age of Sensibility.' *Transactions
of the Samuel Johnson Society of the Northwest*, vol 6 (Calgary, Alta: Samuel
Johnson Society of the Northwest 1973), 91–6
Examines F's description of Fielding as a 'product' novelist of the eighteenth
century, opposed to such 'process' novelists as Sterne. Concludes that
F's distinction, which appears in 'Towards Defining an Age of Sensibility'
(D82), may be false.

L93 Colwell, C. Carter. *A Student's Guide to Literature* (New York: Washington
Square Press 1968), 7–8, 14, 46–7
An introductory manual on the elements and forms of literature, which
includes brief summaries of F's theories of plot, character, and comic form.
Diagrams F's four plots, comments on his two pairs of contrasting charac-
ter types, and seeks to reconcile his theory of comedy with Susanne
Langer's.

L94 Conville, Richard. 'Northrop Frye and Speech Criticism: An Introduction.'
Quarterly Journal of Speech 56 (December 1970): 417–25
An interpretation of F's writings as a contribution to speech criticism.
Argues that F's four *mythoi* – romance, comedy, tragedy, and irony – are
structural principles not only of literary texts but of speech texts as well.
Concludes that F's theory of myth has two important implications for
speech criticism: it treats speech events as *specific* communication behaviour
to be studied in its own right and as *general* communication activity with
its own rules for producing rhetorical artefacts.

L95 Corbeil, Carol. 'Assessment of Orwell Leads to Clash of the Titans.' *Globe
and Mail*, 26 January 1984, E1
A critique of F's address, 'The Authority of Learning' (D279), which Corbeil
sees as a somewhat reactionary defence of humanism. Believes McLuhan
is more enlightening than F about the reasons for the erosion of interest
in language and literature.

L96 Crane, R.S. *The Languages of Criticism and the Structure of Poetry* (Toronto:
Univ of Toronto Press 1953), 137–8 and passim

An analysis of F's place in contemporary criticism. Groups F with other critics (such as Bodkin, Burke, Trilling, and Chase) whose chief interest is in establishing analogies between poetic meanings and other kinds of discourse. Since F thinks of poetry as symbolic language, his approach can be called 'semantic.'

L97 Crews, Frederick. 'Anaesthetic Criticism.' *New York Review of Books* 14 (26 February 1970): 31–5, and 14 (12 March 1970). Rpt with slight changes in *Psychoanalysis and Literary Process*, ed Frederick Crews (Cambridge, Mass: Winthrop 1970), 1–24.

A polemic directed against the prevalent tendency to renounce 'methods that would plainly reveal literary determinants.' Sees F as one of the chief promulgators of the doctrine that critics should not stray outside literature in developing their fundamental principles. Says this notion is 'intellectually indefensible.' Establishes his own Freudian critical framework in opposition to F's.

L98 Culler, Jonathan. 'A Critic against the Christians.' *TLS*, 23 November 1984, 1327–8

In an essay on Empson, attacks F for promoting a dogmatic religious ideology and for making literature a substitute for religion.

L99 — *Structuralist Poetics* (Ithaca, NY: Cornell Univ Press 1975), 119–22, 136, 222, 235–7

Finds the status of F's categories 'curiously indeterminate' and their relationship to literary experience and poetics obscure, but does think that the structuralists could benefit from the kind of study of plot and character F has developed.

L100 Cummings, P.M. 'Northrop Frye and the Necessary Hybrid: Criticism as Aesthetic Humanism.' *The Quest for Imagination: Essays in Twentieth-Century Aesthetic Criticism*, ed O.B. Hardison, Jr (Cleveland: Press of Case Western Reserve Univ 1971), 255–76. Partially rpt in *Contemporary Literary Criticism*, vol. 24, ed Sharon R. Gunton (Detroit: Gale Research 1983), 225–6.

An analysis of two apparently opposing tendencies in F's work, one deriving from the disinterested philosophy of aesthetic literary criticism and the other from the socially conscious philosophy of humanistic criticism. Argues that F is able to synthesize the aesthetic and humanistic claims not by imposing them on literature from without but by discovering them within the imaginative dimension of literature itself. In the course of his argument, presents an account of F's chief assumptions, his critical language, and his method.

L101 Czarnecki, Mark. 'The Gospel According to Frye.' *Maclean's*, 5 April 1982, 40–4. Rpt in an abridged form as 'The Vision of Northrop Frye' in *Reader's Digest* [Montreal] 121 (October 1982): 55–8; adapted by Daniel Pérusse and rpt as 'Le Testament d'un génie ou l'homme biblionique' in *L'Actualité* 10 (February 1985): 8, 11.

Cover story, occasioned by the publication of GC, about F's reputation as a critic. Comments on the influence of Blake on F, gives a number of biographical anecdotes, traces his academic career, glances at his major

books, and observes that 'although his works have secured him an exalted
niche in the pantheon of contemporary thinkers, the memory of Frye as
a teacher is what Frye the man hopes will linger on.'

L102 Dauster, Frank. 'Frye y Fergusson: Hacia una teoría del teatro.' *Texto Crítico*
15 (October–December 1979): 128–32
Examines the similarities and differences between F's theory of comedy
and tragedy and that of Francis Fergusson. Concludes that for all of their
differences, they both, through their intuitions about drama, provide
insights into the fundamental nature of the human mind.

L103 Davey, Frank. 'Northrop Frye.' *From There to Here: A Guide to English-*
Canadian Literature since 1960 (Erin, Ont: Press Porcépic 1974), 106–12
A summary of F's intellectual career. Gives special attention to F as a
critic of Canadian literature and seeks to correct three misconceptions
about him – that he is an apologist for the symbolist and gnostic
traditions, that he is a Platonist, and that his theories of literature require
the contemporary writer consciously to incorporate mythology into
his writing.

L104 — 'Surviving the Paraphrase.' *Canadian Literature* 70 (Autumn 1976): 5–13
[1, 6–9, 12]
Of F's place in the tradition of thematic criticism, which is said to have
dominated Canadian letters.

L105 David, Jack. 'Northrop Frye ... A Hatchet Job.' *Waves* 2 (Spring 1974):
26–30
Claims that modern science refutes F's assumption about the total coherence of criticism, that F's own practice denies his belief about the separation
of literature and criticism, and that contemporary sensibility refutes his
rejection of evaluation.

L106 Davie, Donald. *Articulate Energy: An Inquiry into the Syntax of English Poetry*
(London: Routledge & Kegan Paul 1955), 130–41, 161–5
A brief look at some of F's early views, later incorporated into *AC* on poetic
syntax and rhetoric. Remarks that F's statement about the relationship
among rhetoric, grammar, and logic is 'exceptionally subtle and intelligent,'
but takes issue with F's claim that logic and grammar move into the area
of rhetoric, and philosophy and history into the area of poetry only when
they shed their distinctive syntax. Argues, in opposition to F, that poetic
meaning comes not simply from a self-contained configuration of poetic
imagery but also from the relation of syntax to things outside the realm
of language.

L107 Davis, Kenneth W. 'Demystifying Literature: Northrop Frye in the Classroom.' *English Education* 3 (Spring 1972): 203–9
A study of F's efforts to demystify literature and of his contributions to the
methods of teaching it.

L108 Davis, Robert Con. 'Depth Psychology and "The Scene of Writing":
Jung and Freud.' *Contemporary Literary Criticism: Modernism through Post-*
structuralism, ed Robert Con Davis (New York: Longmans 1986), 218–19

Looks briefly at F's version of archetypal cricitism in the context of New
Critical assumptions about literature and history.

L109 Dean, John. *Restless Wanderers: Shakespeare and the Pattern of Romance*
(Salzburg: Institut für Anglistik und Amerikanistik 1979), 106–8
Outlines F's concept of romance as myth.

L110 DeMaria, Robert, Jr. 'The Ideal Reader: A Critical Fiction.' *PMLA* 93
(May 1978): 463–74 [468–70]
On F's conception of the reader in literature. 'Frye's ideal reader enters
literature ... [He] is a hero embarked on a quest ... Literature, as Frye's
reader encounters it in the first stage of his quest, is a "structure of
experience," and criticism, which is what the reader undertakes in the
second phase, is a "structure of knowledge." The end of criticism, however,
and the goal of the reader's quest, is again a kind of experience ... both
literary and living, not only personal but also social and universal.'

L111 Dembo, L.S. 'Introduction and Perspective.' *Contemporary Literature* 9
(Summer 1968): 277–89 [277, 279–81]. Rpt in *Criticism: Speculative and
Analytical Essays*, ed L.S. Dembo (Madison: Univ of Wisconsin Press 1968).
An introduction to some of the issues raised in F's essay, 'On Value
Judgments' (see D173), which appears in the 1968 Summer issue of
Contemporary Literature. Contrasts F's assumptions about the separation of
knowledge and value from those of Murray Krieger, whose essay, 'Literary
Analysis and Evaluation,' appears in the same issue of the journal.

L112 Denham, Robert D. 'An Anatomy of Frye's Influence.' *American Review of
Canadian Studies* 14 (Spring 1984): 1–19
Assesses the place of F in the contemporary critical scene: his relation to
the structuralists and post-structuralists, his influence on Blake and Shakespearean studies, and the assimilation of his ideas into disciplines other
than criticism. Speculates on the reasons for F's continuing influence.

L113 — 'Anti-anaesthetics: or, The Turn of the Freudian Crews.' *Centrum: Papers
of the Minnesota Center for Advanced Studies in Language, Style, and Literary
Theory* 1, no 2 (1973): 105–22 [112–17]
Takes issue, in part 2 of the essay, with Frederick Crews's attack on F (L97)
as one of the chief promulgators of the doctrine that critics should not
stray outside literature in developing their fundamental principles. Argues
that Crews misrepresents F's position.

L114 — 'Common Cause: Notes on Frye's View of Education.' *CEA Critic* 42
(November 1979): 23–8
Discusses the close alignment between the critical and pedagogical aspects
of F's work. Examines especially F's myths of freedom and concern as
the context for his view of the educational contract.

L115 — 'Frye and the Social Context of Criticism.' *South Atlantic Bulletin* 39
(November 1974): 63–72
Seeks to correct the popular conception of F as an exclusively formal
theorist. Examines F's views on the social function of criticism, the role of
literature in society, and the ethical ends of art.

L116 — 'Frye's Theory of Symbols.' *Canadian Literature* 66 (Autumn 1975): 63–79
An analysis of F's theory of meaning. Examines the several ways 'symbol,'
mythos, and *dianoia* are used in the Second Essay of *AC*, as well as the
influence of Blake on F's theory of symbolic phases.

L117 — 'Introduction.' *Northrop Frye on Culture and Literature: A Collection of
Review Essays*, ed Robert D. Denham (Chicago: Univ of Chicago Press 1978),
1–64. Partially rpt in *Contemporary Literary Criticism*, vol 24, ed Sharon R.
Gunton (Detroit: Gale Research 1983), 227–9.
Gives an overview of F's work and attempts to show how the essays in the
collection are a part of the continuous vision that characterizes his work.
Also examines F's views on the social context of criticism, his idea of
the imagination, his theory of literary symbolism, his understanding of
literary history, his practical criticism, and his views on identity as a
principle of literary structure.

L118 — 'The No-Man's Land of Competing Patterns.' *Critical Inquiry* 4 (Autumn
1977): 194–202 [197–201]
Takes issue with James Kincaid's use (L274) of F's theory of myths to
support his argument about narrative coherence. Maintains that Kincaid
misunderstands F's intention.

L119 — 'Northrop Frye and Rhetorical Criticism.' *Xavier University Studies* 11
(Spring 1972): 1–11
An analysis of F's ideas about the relationship between rhetoric and literary
theory. Examines the meaning and function of the chief categories in the
Fourth Essay of *AC* – F's 'Theory of Genres' – and shows the relations that
obtain between the principles of F's poetics and his theory of rhetoric.

L120 — 'Science, Criticism, and Frye's Metaphysical Universe.' *South Carolina
Review* 7 (April 1975): 3–18
On the two meanings of the word 'scientific' in F's work. Argues that his
grand critical framework is more like a metaphysical than a scientific
theory.

L121 Djwa, Sandra. '*The Canadian Forum*: Literary Catalyst.' *Studies in Canadian
Literature* 1 (Winter 1976): 1–25 [22–5]
Argues that F's attention to Canadian poetry in the *Forum*, especially his
review essay 'Canada and Its Poetry' (D18) provided 'the critical framework
for much of the present writing and study of Canadian poetry.'

L122 — 'The Where of Here: Margaret Atwood and the Canadian Tradition.'
The Art of Margaret Atwood: Essays in Criticism, ed Arnold E. Davidson and
Cathy N. Davidson (Toronto: Anansi 1981), 15–34 [16–22]
Outlines F's influence on Atwood's work.

L123 Dolzani, Michael. 'Controversial Aspects of *The Great Code*.' Paper presented
at the annual meeting of the South Atlantic Modern Language Association,
Atlanta, Ga, 10 November 1984. 13 pp. Photoduplicated typescript
Seeks to counter the two principal criticisms of *GC* – 'that it is over-unified
and under-historical' – by arguing that *GC* insists boldly on 'the mythical,

metaphorical, typological, and kerygmatic transfiguration of language
and perception and the illusory nature of most "normal" ego-centered
experience.' Believes that most critics of GC have a limited understanding
of the way poetic language works and a 'natural' understanding of time
and history.

L124 — 'The Infernal Method: Northrop Frye and Contemporary Criticism.'
Centre and Labyrinth: Essays in Honour of Northrop Frye, ed Eleanor Cook
et al (Toronto: Univ of Toronto Press 1983), 59–68
Sees F's fondness for anatomy and satire as performing a subversive or
deconstructive role in his criticism, causing him to be sceptical about all
intellectual systems. Argues that F's work has the detachment necessary to
interpenetrate with other critical perspectives. F's grand vision of the
constructive power of the imagination, which allows space for the social
context of criticism, liberates him from both subjectivism and formalism.

L125 Dommergues, Pierre. 'Northrop Frye et la critique américaine.' *Le Monde*
(Supplement to no 7086), 25 October 1967, iv–v
Places F against the background of the several strands of the New Criticism
(Ransom, Tate, Warren, Empson, Crane, Wimsatt, and Burke). Says that
in view of the multiplicity of today's individual approaches and critical
coteries, F is to be especially credited with having aimed at a detached,
'scientific' synthesis. Also calls attention to some of F's 'disciples': Ihab
Hassan, Harold Bloom, Hazard Adams, and Angus Fletcher.

L126 Doty, William G. 'Northrop Frye's Myth.' *Mythography: A Study of Myths
and Rituals* (University: Univ of Alabama Press 1986), 179–81
Briefly summarizes F's view of myth and his typology of the four pre-
generic phases of literature. Believes that taxonomic frameworks, such as
F's, provide a good beginning point for literary criticism and a possible
way 'of explicating the interrelations of our literary traditions,' so long
as they are not taken as exhausting the meaning of a work.

L127 Douglas, Crerar. 'A Theological Problem in Northrop Frye's Analysis
of *The Winter's Tale*.' *Christianity & Literature* 24 (Winter 1975): 9–35
'Careful examination of Frye's approach to this play' reveals that whereas
he depends upon Christian theology, his method does not sufficiently
acknowledge his debt to Christianity. By focusing upon the cyclical model,
he omits 'the importance of linear time,' but more important, he dichoto-
mizes Christian grace (superior to the natural order) and another kind
of grace (the same as nature); F is reading a later concept, associated with
Blake, into Renaissance criticism. Although he tries to fit everything into
his system, he errs in excluding theology from criticism.

L128 Douglas, Wallace. 'The Meanings of "Myth" in Modern Criticism.' *Modern
Philology* 50 (May 1953): 232–42 [232–3]. Rpt in *Myth and Literature: Contem-
porary Theory and Practice*, ed John B. Vickery (Lincoln: Univ of Nebraska
Press 1966), 119–28 [120].
A brief look at F's concept of myth as presented in an early essay. Says

that F, like the Cambridge Hellenists, is more interested in the ritual that explains the myth than in the myth itself. Observes that F discovers signs of fertility rites in literature and that he reduces literary patterns to these rites.

L129 Dragland, Stan. 'Afterword: Reaney's Relevance.' *Essays on Canadian Writing* 24–5 (Winter-Spring 1982–3): 211–35. Rpt in *Approaches to the Work of James Reaney*, ed Stan Dragland (Downsview, Ont: ECW Press 1983), 211–35.
Comments throughout on the ways in which F's myth of coherence has influenced Reaney.

L130 Dudek, Louis. 'Academic Sofa.' *Canadian Forum* 58 (June–July 1978): 26–7
Brief remarks about F's essay 'Haunted by Lack of Ghosts' (D244).

L131 — 'Frye Again (but Don't Miss Souster).' *Delta* 5 (October 1958): 26–7
Claims that F 'tries to reduce the whole spirit and meaning of art to a factor of his system of classification, a mere product of "type" and "form," having nothing to do with the author's mind, heart, or convictions.' As a result, F, 'the Great White Whale of Canadian criticism,' devalues the poet as an individual commenting on reality.

L132 — 'The Psychology of Literature.' *Canadian Literature* 72 (Spring 1977): 5–20 [5–11]. Rpt in Dudek, *Selected Essays and Criticism* (Ottawa: Tecumseh 1978), 362–80.
Examines F's view of the psychological foundations of archetypes, which is seen as an oracular, visionary, religious view and against which Dudek places his own understanding of the psychology of literature.

L133 Dyrkjøb, Jan Ulrik. 'Magtens sprog og kaerlighedens sprog: nogle teologiske perspektiver i Northrop Fryes forfatterskab.' *På fortaellingens graense*, ed Hans Hauge and Kjeld Holm. (*Kredsen* 50, no 1–2 [1983]: 1–35)
On the theological implications of F's writings. Argues that the entire body of F's work had direct and indirect implications not only for biblical criticism but for theology as a whole. Gives special attention to *GC*.

L134 Eagleton, Terry. *Literary Theory: An Introduction* (Minneapolis: Univ of Minnesota Press 1983), 91–6
Sees *AC* as a transition between New Critical formalism and structuralism. Says that F's system is more rigorously closed to history than that of the New Critics and that it conceives of literature not as a means for yielding knowledge about reality but as 'a kind of collective utopian dreaming.' Judges F to be an anti-humanist because of his emphasis upon classifying things scientifically; at the same time, says F is a Christian humanist 'who offers literature as a displaced version of religion' and whose Arnoldian vision of a classless society is simply an affirmation of 'his own middle-class liberal values.'

L135 Eastman, Arthur M. *A Short History of Shakespearean Criticism* (New York: Random House 1968), 370–82
Maintains that the extravagant power of horizontal analogy in F's criticism is not balanced by the power of vertical generalization. Isolates and

summarizes the central concepts in each of the four chapters of *NP*. Sees F's value as a Shakespearean critic in his 'definition and rationalization of the Shakespearean comic and romantic structure' (the three main parts of the action, the roles of the clown and *idiotes*, and metamorphoses at the end of the plays) and in his exploration of the romances in depth. On the other hand, echoes Reuben Brower's view (M15.14) that F's Shakespearean criticism is both circular and reductive.

L136 Ebine, Hiroshi. 'Northrop Frye and the Novel.' *Eigo bungaku sekai* [*The English Literary World*] 11 (February 1969): 18–21
In Japanese.

L137 Edwards, Paul. 'The Farm and the Wilderness in Tutuola's *The Palm-Wine Drunkard*.' *Journal of Commonwealth Literature* 9 (August 1974): 56–65
Argues that one finds in Tutuola's novel the structure of apocalyptic and demonic imagery F discusses in *AC*.

L138 Edwards, Philip. 'The Abandoned Cave.' *Shakespeare and the Confines of Art* (London: Methuen 1968), 48–70
Summarizes F's arguments in *NP* about Shakespeare's comedies, which he then uses to interpret *A Midsummer Night's Dream*, *As You Like It*, and *Twelfth Night*.

L139 Efron, Arthur. 'Could You Kindly Direct Me to the Office of Civil Disobedience?' *Paunch* 24 (October 1965): 5–17 [14–15]
Sees F's work as one of the trends in current criticism that reveals 'innoculatory [sic] variations on the one-dimensional.' F is one-dimensional in his reliance on myth, especially the myth of the Bible, as the foundation of programs of literary education.

L140 Egawa, Toru. 'Literature and the Myth of Identity.' *Kyôyô no tame no sôzôryoku* [*The Educated Imagination*], trans Toru Egawa and Masahiko Maeda (Tokyo: Taiyosha 1969), 129–51 (A3d)
In Japanese.

L141 Ellis, Frank M. 'Northrop Frye's Theory of Comedy.' Paper presented at the annual meeting of the Northeast American Society for Eighteenth-Century Studies, Philadelphia, 11 October 1986. Photoduplicated typescript. 14 pp
Reviews F's theory of the dramatic structure of comedy: it is based upon the conventions of New Comedy, in which the blocking of a young man's desire for a young woman is eventually overcome. Shows how this theory is adequate to explain the action of plays in which there are no women, such as *Captivi* and *Volpone*, because the structural principles, in which desire figures importantly, remain the same.

L142 Ellis, Katherine. 'The Function of Northrop Frye at the Present Time.' *College English* 31 (March 1970): 541–7. Rpt as 'Arnold's Other Axiom,' in *The Politics of Literature: Dissenting Essays on the Teaching of English*, ed Louis Kampf and Paul Lauter (New York: Pantheon 1972), 160–73.
Uses a quotation from F as a text for championing new methods for teaching and learning about the imaginative products of culture. Believes

that F's notions about the possibility of an Arnoldian classless culture
are essentially mistaken. Suggests a Marxist model for regenerating education and ridding it of the New Critical tendencies said to be represented
by F's approach.

L143 Ellison, Fred P. 'Soledade-Persephone: A Cyclical Myth in *A Bagaceira.*'
Woman as Myth and Metaphor in Latin American Literature, ed Carmelo Virgillo
and Naomi Lindstrom (Columbia: Univ of Missouri Press 1985), 27–41
Calls upon F's theories in *AC* to argue that one of the characters in
A Bagaceira (Soledade) is an embodiment of the Persephone archetype.

L144 Ellmann, Richard. 'Dissent and the Academy.' *New York Review of Books*
10 (15 February 1968): 6, 8, 10 [8]
Explains F's views on the social context of criticism as they appeared in his
essay, 'Speculation and Concern' (D166). Defends F's theory of education –
one based on a dialectic of detachment and concern – against the criticisms
of Louis Kampf.

L145 Engelborghs, Maurits. 'Frye en de mythekritiek.' *Dietsche Warande & Belfort*
112 (1967): 303–6
An introductory account of F's criticism. Looks at F's work largely by way
of the essays in the English Institute volume devoted to him: *Northrop
Frye in Modern Criticism* (K8).

L146 Evans, John X. 'Introduction.' *Adjoining Cultures as Reflected in Literature
and Language,* ed John X. Evans (Tempe: Arizona State Univ 1983), 3–4
Gives a summary of F's paper 'Criticism and Environment,' presented at
the fifteenth triennial congress of the Fédération Internationales des Langues et Littératures Modernes, 3 September 1982 (D276).

L147 Feder, Herbert. 'Northrop Frye's Aestheticism and Moral Development.'
Interchange 11, no 1 (1980–1): 76–90
Argues that in spite of F's aestheticism and his rejection of value-judgments
in criticism, his work does have a moral and religious dimension, and
that 'there is in Frye a veiled didacticism which, because it is concerned
with such "extra-literary" questions as truth values, religious vision,
and morality, makes the critic an important figure when one considers
the place of literature in moral development and moral education.'

L148 Feder, Lilian. 'Myth, Poetry, and Critical Theory.' *Literary Criticism and
Myth* (Yearbook of Comparative Criticism, vol 9), ed Joseph P. Strelka
(University Park: Pennsylvania State Univ Press 1980), 51–71 [53–5]
An evaluation of F's contribution to archetypal criticism. Judges F to be
most fruitful when his insights 'grow out of the familiar attributes of the
gods and heroic figures and the narrative contents of traditional myths,'
but finds that his theory of the monomyth obscures more than it eluci-
dates.

L149 Fekete, John A. 'Modernity in the Literary Institution: Strategic Anti-
Foundational Moves.' *The Structural Allegory: Reconstructive Encounters with
the New French Thought,* ed John Fekete (Minneapolis: Univ of Minnesota
Press 1984), 228–47 [230, 238–9]

Considers briefly the place F's work has occupied in North American criticism over the past several decades. F's emphasis on conventional literary patterns has helped reorient criticism away from the pole of subjectivity and toward the interrelations of literature and other verbal disciplines. At the same time, F's idealism became isolated from critical theory and method, and it legitimized the formalism of the New Critics.

L150 — 'Northrop Frye: Parameters of Mythological Structuralism.' *Telos* 27 (Spring 1976): 40–60
A Marxist critique of F's work, which intends to show that 'Frye's theory embodies aesthetic capitulation to the commotive forms of domination' and that 'it proposes a view of culture structurally articulated to preclude radical historical praxis.'

L151 — 'Northrop Frye: A Critical Theory of Capitulation.' *The Critical Twilight: Explorations in Ideology of Anglo-American Literary Theory from Eliot to McLuhan* (London: Routledge & Kegan Paul 1977), 107–31
A slightly expanded version of L150.

L152 Felperin, Howard. 'Romance and Romanticism.' *Critical Inquiry* 6 (Summer 1980): 691–706
Outlines F's theory of romance and romanticism and then argues that *The Tempest* cannot be read as a naïve romance in F's sense; rather, it shows an ironic sophistication in relation to romance, which is what makes it modern.

L153 — 'Romance and Romanticism: Some Reflections on *The Tempest* and *Heart of Darkness*, Or When Is Romance No Longer Romance?' *Shakespeare's Romances Reconsidered*, ed Carol McGinnis Kay and Henry E. Jacobs (Lincoln: Univ of Nebraska Press 1978), 60–76 [61–4, 68–9]
Summarizes F's views on romance and romanticism, the former being a displacement 'from the original unity of a putative mythic source.' Believes F's idea that romance tries to recapture the 'pristine mythic shape' does not properly account for the problematic and ironic view of romance we find in such plays as Shakespeare's *The Tempest*.

L154 — *Shakespearean Romance* (Princeton, NJ: Princeton Univ Press 1972), 314–16
Calls F the Prospero of modern students of romance and 'the foremost theorist of the romantic imagination since Coleridge.' Summarizes F's approach to Shakespearean comedy and romance: his view from the 'middle distance,' his grouping of the plays, and his understanding of displacement. Says that F abandons the problem of history, that his view of Shakespearean romance has 'a regressive and primitivist cast,' and that he retreats 'into an insulated and synchronic world of myth,' thus neglecting questions of mimesis, truth, and nature.

L155 Fennell, William O. 'Theology and Frye: Some Implications of *The Great Code*.' *Toronto Journal of Theology* 1 (Spring 1985): 113–21
Thinks that F makes too radical a separation between the language of the Bible and faith and that it is better to see a dialectical relationship 'between a myth's visionary insight and linguistic power to convey meaning, on

the one hand, and faith's understanding of reality on the other.' Sets
against F's 'spiritualizing' and 'idealizing' of the Bible a more realistic and
historical kind of understanding. Cannot accept F's identifying God with
the literal words of Scripture, and finds his interpretation of the phases
of revelation to be essentially secular.

L156 Finholt, Richard. 'Northrop Frye's Theory of Countervailing Tendencies:
A New Look at the Mode and Myth Essays.' *Genre* 13 (Summer 1980):
203–57
Sees the chief principle in the first two essays of *AC* to be the tension
created by the tendency in literature to move in two directions, toward
desire and the ideal world of myth and toward reality and the world
of plausibility. Argues that the 'plausibility tendency' in literature underlies
the theory of modes and that the 'mythic tendency' underlies the theory
of myths. Presents a revised form of the theory of modes, which is used to
outline 'the inner logic of the mythic cycle.' Seeks in the process to clarify
some of F's terms and treats some of the implications of his two theories,
especially those related to a theory of reading.

L157 Fischer, Michael. 'The Imagination as a Sanction of Value: Northrop Frye
and the Uses of Literature.' *Centennial Review* 21 (Spring 1977): 105–17.
Extensively rev version, 'The Imagination as a Sanction of Value: Northrop
Frye and the Usefulness of Literature,' in Fischer, *Does Deconstruction
Make Any Difference? Poststructuralism and the Defense of Poetry in Modern
Criticism* (Bloomington: Indiana Univ Press 1985), 14–31.
Studies F's understanding of the importance of literature to life. 'Frye's
attempt to vindicate the usefulness of literature without at the same time
arguing for its truth marks the attenuation as well as the continuation
of [the] Romantic viewpoint ... He ultimately answers arguments that minimize literature's ethical and social value by removing any grounds which
would permit a rational and objective discussion of such a question.'

L158 Fite, David. *Harold Bloom: The Rhetoric of Romantic Vision* (Amherst: Univ
of Massachusetts Press 1985), 15–17 and passim
Outlines F's influence on the development of Bloom's early theories of
romanticism and comments on their differing views of the literary tradition:
F sees it as an ideal order, Bloom as a competition.

L159 Flanagan, Joseph. 'Literary Criticism of the Bible.' *Trinification of the World:
A Festschrift in Honor of Frederick E. Crowe*, ed Thomas A. Dunne and
Jean-Marie Laporte (Toronto: Regis College Press 1978), 210–40
Begins with a summary of the theories of modes, myths, genres, and
symbols in *AC*. Seeks to show how the four theories interrelate by using
them to interpret the Bible, concluding that F's interpretive scheme 'seems
to offer a rich context for theological interpretations.'

L160 Fleming, W.G. 'Contribution of Northrop Frye.' *Ontario's Educative Society*,
vol 3: *Schools, Pupils, and Teachers* (Toronto: Univ of Toronto Press 1971),
23–5

Gives a brief summary of F's views on the aims of education, drawn primarily from 'The Critical Discipline' (D123).

L161 — *Ontario's Educative Society*, vol 5: *Supporting Institutions and Services* (Toronto: Univ of Toronto Press 1971), 179
Comments on F's 'distinctly anti-progressive ideas' as presented in his introduction to *Design for Learning* (D131).

L162 Fletcher, Angus. *Allegory: The Theory of a Symbolic Mode* (Ithaca, NY: Cornell Univ Press 1964), passim
A work that both depends on and expands F's idea of allegory. Fletcher's notes frequently provide commentary on some of F's fundamental concepts. See index, 409.

L163 — 'Foreword.' *The Literature of Fact: Selected Papers from the English Institute*, ed Angus Fletcher (New York: Columbia Univ Press 1976), vii–xxiv [xi–xii, xvi–xvii]
Summarizes F's essay in this collection, 'History and Myth in the Bible' (D234), and points to the paradoxical implications in his reading of the Bible from the perspective of anagogy and revelation.

L164 — 'Northrop Frye: The Critical Passion.' *Critical Inquiry* 1 (June 1975): 741–56
Treats a number of diverse topics: F's style, the function of 'desire' in his criticism, his general theory of outline and the nature of the literary canon, and his conceptions of the archetype, history, and myths of freedom and concern. Also looks at the way Harold Bloom has 'advanced upon Frye,' even though this advance is 'in Frye's direction.' Concludes by remarking on the absence of a developed phenomenology in F.

L165 — 'Utopian History and the *Anatomy of Criticism*.' *Northrop Frye in Modern Criticism* (Selected Papers from the English Institute [1965]), ed Murray Krieger (New York: Columbia Univ Press 1966), 31–73. Partially rpt in *Contemporary Literary Criticism*, vol 24, ed Sharon R. Gunton (Detroit: Gale Research 1983), 219–22.
Aims to counter the complaint of various critics who hold that there is an unresolved conflict between F's theory of archetypes and the fluid texture of history. Shows that historical observations are basic to *AC* and that F employs a type of utopian historiography to connect his visions of past and future. Suggests also that part of F's power derives from his revitalizing the flow of romantic sensibility and vision that the post-Eliot critical tradition had slighted.

L166 Fletcher, John. 'The Criticism of Comparison: The Approach through Comparative Literature and Intellectual History.' *Contemporary Criticism* (Stratford-on-Avon Studies 12), ed Malcolm Bradbury and David Palmer (London: Edward Arnold 1970), 107–29 [122–3]
Looks briefly at F's work in the context of a general theory of literature. Remarks that *AC* 'represents the best kind of comparatist criticism, ranging widely for its examples and illumining the known with a fresh dimension.'

L167 Forsyth, R.A. ' "Europe," "Africa" and the Problem of Spiritual Authority.' *Southern Review* [Australia] 3, no 4 (1969): 294–323
Finds that F's idea of 'the drunken boat' (see D138) is clearly present in the works of T.H. Huxley, Freud, Marx, Schopenhauer, and Nietzsche.

L168 Fortier, D'Iberville. 'I rapporti tra l'Italia e il Canada.' *Canadiana: Aspetti della storia e della letteratura canadese,* ed Luca Codignola (Venice: Marsilio Editions 1978), 11–19 [17]
Looks briefly at how F's criticism reflects the history of Canada.

L169 Foulke, Robert D. 'Criticism and the Curriculum: Part II.' *College English* 26 (October 1964): 30–7
Presents a curricular model that has its roots in *AC.* Outlines four critical approaches for teaching literature – the formalistic, the synoptic, the analogical, and the generic – each of which has its parallel in F's work. Argues that together these approaches could become the basis for structuring a college program in literary studies.

L170 Foulke, Robert D., and Paul Smith. *An Anatomy of Literature.* New York: Harcourt Brace Jovanovich 1972
A textbook anthology organized on the basis of F's four narrative patterns. The general introduction (pp 1–41), as well as extensive critical material throughout the book, relies heavily upon the principles of *AC.*

L171 Fowler, Alastair. *Kinds of Literature: An Introduction to the Theory of Genres and Modes* (Cambridge, Mass: Harvard Univ Press 1982), 118–20, 150–1, 241–3
Comments on F's systems of generic classification throughout, especially on his taxonomies of prose fiction, myths, and modes.

L172 — 'The Life and Death of Literary Forms.' *New Literary History* 2 (Winter 1971): 199–216 [201–3, 208–11]
Argues that literary forms are born and die, that the historical duration of literary works need not coincide with the duration of the forms they use. In the course of developing his argument, glances at several of F's contentions about form, mode, and genre, taking issue especially with F's theory of modes. 'Not only does [Frye] ignore many elements of generic transformation altogether; but even the historical changes he does discuss have really had a more fluctuating tendency than he suggests.'

L173 Francis, Wynne. 'Irving Layton.' *Canadian Writers and Their Works* (Poetry Series, vol 5), ed Robert Lecker et al (Toronto: ECW Press 1985), 141–234 [154–7, 209–10]
Traces F's reviews of Layton's poetry during the early 1950s and Layton's one-sided quarrel with F.

L174 Fraser, John. 'Mr. Frye and Evaluation.' *Cambridge Quarterly* 2 (Spring 1967): 97–116. Rpt in Fraser, *The Name of Action: Critical Essays* (Cambridge: Cambridge Univ Press 1984), 152–69.
An attack on F's critical position, particularly his ideas about evaluation as they are presented in 'Criticism, Visible and Invisible' (D147). Concludes

that F 'is probably doing more to bring discredit upon literary studies than anyone else now writing.'

L175 Furstenberg, Rochelle. *Jerusalem Post Magazine*, 27 May 1982, 18
A review of F's paper, 'Vision and Cosmos' (D281), along with the rest of the conference at which the paper was presented.

L176 Fussell, Paul. *The Great War and Modern Memory* (New York: Oxford Univ Press 1975), 311–14 and passim
Summarizes F's cyclical theory of modes and then uses the ironic mode with its demonic imagery to characterize the literary response of a number of writers to World War I.

L177 Gabin, Rosalind J. 'From Theory of Genres to Theory of Language: Rhetoric's Relation to Literary Criticism.' *Dieciocho* 8 (Spring 1985): 63–9 [64, 66–7]
Argues that *AC* is an 'outstanding example' of a modern critical work that moves away from a New Critical conception of poetics toward extra-textual concerns. F thus helps to usher in what has become widespread in literary discussion in the 1980s – a collapsing of sharp distinctions between poetics and rhetoric.

L178 — 'Northrop Frye: Modern Utopian.' *Classical and Modern Literature* 3, no 3 (1983): 151–64
Locates a number of differences between F and Plato, but argues that the 'Republican' structure of *AC*, 'with its commitment to unity, remains its informing element' and makes it fundamentally Platonic. Shows how the principle of unity informs much of F's criticism, both literary and social, and concludes that the Platonic utopian vision of wholeness in F's work is what makes it 'unpalatable' for the contemporary critical sensibility that wants to de-hellenize criticism by deconstructing all unified structures of meaning and knowledge.

L179 Gardner, John. 'The Idea of Moral Criticism.' *Western Humanities Review* 31 (Spring 1977): 97–109 [99–111]
Says that, like the New Critics, F claims 'that what counts in literature is not what it says, what it affirms and promulgates, but only how well it works as a self-contained, organic whole busy doing whatever it does.' Such a position abandons the primary function of art, which is affirmation.

L180 Gellrich, Jesse. 'The Structure of Allegory.' *The Existential Coordinates of the Human Condition: Poetic – Epic – Tragic: The Literary Genre*, ed Anna-Teresa Tymieniecka (Dordrecht: Reidel 1984), 505–19
Glances briefly at F's symbolic concept of genre, which is seen as a means of opening up the New Critical tendency to derive meaning solely from the surface texture of literature.

L181 Gerhart, Mary. 'The Question of Belief in Literary Criticism.' *Creativity and Method: Essays in Honor of Bernard Lonergan, SJ*, ed Matthew Lamb (Milwaukee: Marquette Univ Press 1981), 385–8
Sees F's work as representing a second stage of reflection on the question of the role of belief in literary criticism, following the first stage repre-

sented by I.A. Richards and preceding the present stage of neo-Kantians and hermeneutical critics. Summarizes F's view on the issue: he seems to argue for a 'categorical exclusion of the question of belief on the assumption that it is a threat to imagination,' but in fact he is always raising questions about meaning, verification, and commitment.

L182 Girard, René. 'Lévi-Strauss, Frye, Derrida, and Shakespearean Criticism.' *Diacritics* 3 (Fall 1973): 34–8
Uses F's discussion of *pharmakos* to lend support to his own argument about 'differentiation' in myth and ritual.

L183 Goicoechea, David. 'The Redemptive Future in Northrop Frye's Typological Repetition.' Paper presented at Brock Univ, 14 February 1986. Unpublished typescript. 13 pp
Argues that F's concept of typology in *GC* is 'a mode of thought and a figure of speech that has a double movement': the spatial, which lifts biblical literature upward toward the level of anagogy and away from literal, historical meaning; and the horizontal or temporal, which through the authority of myth and metaphor 'lets the past interpenetrate with the present by way of the future.' Uses Kierkegaard's idea of repetition ('retaking') to illustrate how F's typological readings transcend the literal, ethical, and allegorical meanings of ordinary spatial and temporal understanding.

L184 Goldberg, Homer. 'Center and Periphery: Implications of Frye's "Order of Words." ' Paper read at the annual meeting of the Modern Language Association, Chicago, 27 December 1971. 12 pp. Photoduplicated
Defines some underlying premises F shares with a broad strain of modern criticism and explores the consequences of these premises for the way we view his theory. Sees F as continuing the tradition of the New Critics because of his dialectical opposition of two orders of language: discursive and poetic discourse. Comments on the set of values that is implicit in F's bias toward the mythic and paradigmatic.

L185 Golden, Leon. 'Aristotle, Frye, and the Theory of Tragedy.' *Comparative Literature* 27 (Winter 1975): 47–58
Assesses our current understanding of the nature of tragedy based on the contributions of Aristotle and F, and then suggests a method by which their theoretical statements can lead to a fuller understanding of the potentialities and boundaries of tragedy. Draws from both the first and third essays of *AC* (theory of modes and theory of myths) in analysing F's theory of tragedy.

L186 Goldie, Terry. 'Louis Dudek.' *Canadian Writers and Their Works* (Poetry Series, vol 5), ed Robert Lecker et al (Toronto: ECW Press 1985), 73–139 [118–20]
Traces Dudek's negative reaction, throughout a series of his essays, to F's view of literature and the imagination.

L187 Goodheart, Eugene. 'The Failure of Criticism.' *New Literary History* 7 (Winter 1976): 377–92 [384–6]. Rpt in Goodheart, *The Failure of Criticism* (Cambridge: Harvard Univ Press 1978), 17–20.

Examines F's work in relation to the humanist tradition and concludes that despite F's talk in *CP* about the myths of concern and belief, his critical system is too detached and too impersonal. F removes 'the problem of humanism from the area of will and choice,' and thus avoids 'the question of the impact of culture on society.' Maintains that F's commitment is not to literature but to system-building.

L188 Gottfried, Rudolf B. 'Edmund Spenser and the NCTE.' *College English* 33 (October 1971): 76–9
A rebuttal to an article by Carol Ohmann, 'Northrop Frye and the MLA' (L374). Seeks to defend his views about F's interpretation of Spenser, which he had set forth in 'Our New Poet: Archetypal Criticism and *The Faerie Queene*' (L189) and which had been criticized by Ohmann.

L189 — 'Our New Poet: Archetypal Criticism and *The Faerie Queene*.' *PMLA* 83 (October 1968): 1362–77 [1362–9, 1377]
A critique of archetypal interpretations of Spenser's work by F and A.C. Hamilton. Argues that when the principles of *AC* are applied to *The Faerie Queene* they dangerously misrepresent its structure and meaning. F's description of the poem as a romance in six books, covering many of the six phases that make up the archetypal plot of that genre, is arbitrary. Archetypal criticism overlooks Spenser's intention and, thus, reduces his work to something it is not.

L190 Gould, Eric. 'The Gap Between Myth and Literature.' *Dalhousie Review* 58 (Winter 1978–9): 723–36 [723–6]
Notes the 'accuracy for literary scholarship' in the relationships F has discovered between literature and the myths of human experience. Says, however, that F 'mistakes for form religious content and has few suggestions as to how mythic thought itself ... actually operates.'

L191 — *Mythical Intentions in Modern Literature* (Princeton, NJ: Princeton Univ Press 1981), 25–8, 31
Sees F's theories of myth and archetype as 'applied Jungianism.' Is dubious about F's claim that criticism is an 'objective totality' and that the appeal of myth is to a 'total form.' Understands F's theory of myth to be basically an allegorical one: F locates archetypes 'with a certain authoritarian, even if, at times, a highly subtle flair for allegorical commentary.' Believes F's theory is 'suggestive,' but that it does not adequately confront the problems of interpretation.

L192 Grady, Wayne. 'The Educated Imagination of Northrop Frye.' *Saturday Night* 96 (October 1981): 19–24, 26, 28
A feature article occasioned by F's completing *GC* and framed by an account of his delivering the Tamblyn Lectures at the University of Western Ontario. Traces F's career from his early years to his faculty appointment at Victoria College. Notes the chief intellectual influences on his work, his impact on Canadian culture, and the relation between *GC* and his other books. Records several anecdotes from the lecture tour to Western Ontario.

L193 Graff, Gerald. *Literature against Itself: Literary Ideas in Modern Society*
(Chicago: Univ of Chicago Press 1979), 81–5, 189–91
Argues that the values and meanings of culture 'do not for Frye rest on
any prior objective beliefs about the way things are.' Criticizes his theory
of literature because he does not grant literature any mimetic relation
to the world and so has no authoritative grounds for carrying out its
functions of humanizing, ordering, and making sense of experience.

L194 — 'Northrop Frye and the Visionary Imagination.' *Poetic Statement and
Critical Dogma* (Evanston: Northwestern Univ Press 1970), 73–8
An analysis of the disjunction in F's work between fact and value, between
the objective world and the world of myth, imagination, and desire.
Maintains that 'Frye's writings reflect evidence of the vacillation, ambiva-
lence, and evasiveness ... found to be characteristic of anti-propositional
theorists in general. Frye wishes to emancipate the imagination from
all empirical and objective considerations, yet he also aims at what he calls
"the educated imagination," and he insists that literature "refine our
sensibilities." But the concept of "refinement" is meaningless apart from
some sort of appeal to reality and the reality principle.'

L195 Gray, Bennison. *The Phenomenon of Literature* (The Hague: Mouton 1975),
1–14, 431–49
On F's theories of literature and interpretation.

L196 Grebstein, Sheldon. 'The Mythopoeic Critic.' *Perspectives in Contemporary
Criticism*, ed Sheldon Grebstein (New York: Harper & Row 1968), 311–20
[317–19]
A brief account of myth criticism, serving as an introduction to essays by
five myth critics. Places F's work in the context of myth criticism in general.
'The mythopoeic perspective has been most impressively represented by
Northrop Frye's *Anatomy of Criticism*, which stands as the *Poetics* of the
entire mythopoeic movement.'

L197 Grob, Alan. 'The Uses of Northrop Frye: "Sunday Morning" and the
Romantic Topocosm.' *Studies in Romanticism* 22 (Winter 1983): 587–615
Applies F's concept of topocosm (the four-tiered structure of poetic imagery)
to several romantic poems and to Stevens's 'Sunday Morning' to illustrate
the 'functional unity' of the concept. Believes that the structures in this
part of F's system are less determinate than he thinks and are sometimes
subverted in 'Sunday Morning,' but still finds them to be useful tools
for the 'eclectic *bricoleur*.'

L198 Grolier, Claudio. 'Frye, un piano regolatore per la foresta letteraria.'
Tuttolibri, 9 June 1979, 8
Provides a profile of F's work. Points to the importance of understanding
how the word 'anatomy' functions in his criticism. Surveys some of the
key terms in his typology of literature, remarks on the difference between
F's view of archetypes and Jung's, and observes that in F's later work
he tackles two great themes – the sacred and the secular scriptures. Notes

that F's work has been criticized for not paying enough attention to the
verbal quality of individual works of literature, for the rigidity and lack
of coherence in his theories, and (from the Marxists) for his failure to confront the social element of history.

L199 Gross, Lalia. 'Frye.' *An Introduction to Literary Criticism*, ed Lalia Gross
(New York: Capricorn Books 1972), 324–6
A summary of F's position, serving as an introduction to 'The Archetypes
of Literature' (D49), which is rpt in Gross's anthology. Treats briefly the
content of *AC*, F's theory of archetypes, and his Aristotelian debt.

L200 Grossman, Marshall. 'The Vicissitudes of the Subject in Frye's *Anatomy
of Criticism.' Texas Studies in Language and Literature* 24 (Fall 1982): 313–27
Argues that *AC* reflects the issues of the subject and of the priority of language to the subject, even though F does not explicitly develop these
issues. Sees thought as the mediating category in *AC* between self and
other; literature, which imitates thought, is able to communicate certain
intuitions and make them shareable, but it also mediates between subject
and object. Observes that the social import of F's work is embodied in
his concept of civilization, which is the synthesis of desire (psychological
subjectivity) and experience (thought turned toward the physical world).

L201 Gunton, Sharon R., ed. '(Herman) Northrop Frye.' *Contemporary Literary
Criticism*, vol 24 (Detroit: Gale Research 1983), 207–33
Reprints selections from the following critical accounts of F's work: John
Garrett, 'Turning New Leaves' (M8.18); Frank Kermode, 'Northrop Frye'
(M1.53); M.H. Abrams, 'Anatomy of Criticism' (M1.1); John Holloway,
'The Critical Zodiac of Northrop Frye' (L233); Frank Kermode, 'Deep Frye'
(M15.24); W.K. Wimsatt, 'Criticism as Myth' (L571); Geoffrey H. Hartman,
'Ghostlier Demarcations' (L212); Angus Fletcher, 'Utopian History and
the *Anatomy of Criticism*' (L165); Frye, 'Reflections in a Mirror' (D165); Mur-
ray Krieger, 'Northrop Frye and Contemporary Criticism' (L282); Peter
Cummings, 'Northrop Frye and the Necessary Hybrid' (L100); Harold
Bloom, 'Northrop Frye Exalting the Designs of Romance' (M18.11); Robert
D. Denham, 'Introduction' to *Northrop Frye on Culture and Literature* (L117);
Frank Lentricchia, 'The Place of Northrop Frye's *Anatomy of Criticism*'
(L300); and Francis Sparshott, 'Critical Discussion: *The Great Code*' (M10.111).

L202 Gurewitch, Morton. *Comedy: The Irrational Vision* (Ithaca, NY: Cornell Univ
Press 1975), 17–19, 43–4
On F's theory of comedy as it is developed in 'The Argument of Comedy'
(D39), *NP*, and *AC*.

L203 Gwynn, Frederick L. 'Sequence and Change in the College English Curric-
ulum.' *College English* 26 (October 1964): 1–2
An account of the Trinity Conference on college English curricula, to which
F delivered the keynote address (April 1964). Comments briefly on several
of F's writings in educational theory and on his address to the conference,
'Criticism, Visible and Invisible' (D147).

L204 Hagopian, John V. Review of *In Search of Literary Theory*, ed Morton W.
Bloomfield. *College English* 35 (October 1973): 72–7 [74–6]
Finds F's contribution to this collection, 'The Critical Path: An Essay on the
Social Context of Literary Criticism' (D200), to be the most valuable of the
six essays. Still, because F is concerned only with nomothetic forms he
'ultimately fails to help us find a viable theory of literature.' Comments
on F's recommendations for the appropriate contexts of literary study and
on the opposition he sets up between the myths of concern and freedom –
an opposition that gives a new 'twist' to the theory of archetypal criticism.

L205 Hamilton, A.C. 'Northrop Frye: The Visionary Critic.' *CEA Critic* 42
(November 1979): 2–6
Sees F's visionary criticism as having three major characteristics, each
of which results from his standing at the centre of literature: (1) it forms a
continuous whole; (2) it possesses *integritas, consonantia*, and *claritas*; and
(3) it is creative. (This essay received the Robert A. Miller Memorial Prize
as the best article to appear in a CEA publication during 1979.)

L206 Hamilton, Patricia W. 'Too Good to Miss.' *English Journal* 72 (February
1983): 91–2
Seeks to show how AC is helpful to English teachers 'in dispelling some
of the mystery of literature and in establishing the relevance of its character
and conflicts to our students, their understanding of the progress of
civilization, and their appreciation of literature.''

L207 Hanes, V.G. 'Northrop Frye's Theory of Literature and Marxism.' *Horizons:
The Marxist Quarterly* 24 (Winter 1968): 62–78. Rpt in *Man and the Arts:
A Marxist Approach*, by Arnold Kettle and V.G. Hanes (New York: American
Institute for Marxist Studies 1968), 17–33.
An effort to counter F's approach to Marxism and his objections to Marxist
literary theory and criticism, as these are presented in AC and MC.
Analyses F's four objections to Marxist critical theory: that it holds a quasi-
organic theory of history, that it sees only one kind of literary meaning,
that it does violence to poetic autonomy and the imagination, and that it
brings an extra-critical framework to literature. Believes that 'Frye has read
little Marxist theory of any kind' and that, by stressing literary autonomy
and the importance of poetic form, he misses the significant relations
between literature and society stressed by Marxist critical theory.

L208 Hapgood, Robert. 'Shakespeare and the Ritualists.' *Shakespeare Survey* 15
(1962): 111–26 [118]
Brief comment about F's recognizing ritual qualities and seasonal analogies
in Shakespeare's comedies.

L209 Hardin, Richard F. ' "Ritual" in Recent Criticism: The Elusive Sense of
Community.'' *PMLA* 98 (October 1983): 846–62 [846–7, 849–50]
Argues that recent studies in the nature of ritual call into question the
assumption of F and others that myth originates in ritual or is a displaced
form of it.

L210 Hart, Thomas R. 'The Literary Criticism of Jorge Luis Borges.' *MLN* 78

(December 1963): 489–503 [501–3]. Rpt in *Velocities of Change: Critical Essays from MLN*, ed Richard Macksey (Baltimore: Johns Hopkins Univ Press 1974), 277–91 [289–91].
Concludes his essay by calling attention to some interesting parallels between Borges's criticism and F's.

L211 Hartman, Geoffrey. 'The Culture of Criticism.' PMLA 99 (May 1984): 371–97 [379, 387–9]
In an account of the relations among scholarship, criticism, and culture, see F's work as having been influenced by two ideals: 'Arnold's cultural evangelism' and 'the intelligibility and teachability of science.' The latter places F among those who seek a methodological antirelativism.

L212 — 'Ghostlier Demarcations.' *Northrop Frye in Modern Criticism*, ed Murray Krieger (New York: Columbia Univ Press 1966), 109–31. Rpt in Hartman, *Beyond Formalism: Literary Essays 1958–1970* (New Haven: Yale Univ Press 1970), 24–41; partially rpt in *Contemporary Literary Criticism*, vol 24, ed Sharon R. Gunton (Detroit: Gale Research 1983), 216–19.
Suggests that F's power as a critic may be due to his universalism, his unlimited reach. 'Certainly no literary thinker, systematic or not, has attained so global a point of view of literature.' Goes on to compare F's achievement with that of Eliade in comparative religion and Malraux in the history of art. Links F to the movement to democratize criticism and observes that his great achievement is the recovery of the intrinsic role of romance in the human imagination.

L213 — 'Reading Aright: Keats's "Ode to Psyche." ' *Centre and Labyrinth: Essays in Honour of Northrop Frye*, ed Eleanor Cook et al (Toronto: Univ of Toronto Press 1983), 210–26 [210–11]
Observes that F offers a contemporary justification of romance, which rejects accommodation, while at the same time presenting this justification in a highly accommodated form of prose. This contradiction is fruitful because it reminds us of just how much language resists the total form of romance. To retain romance we have to lose ourselves in its language, which is 'the road not taken by Frye.'

L214 — 'The Sacred Jungle 3: Frye, Burke, and Some Conclusions.' *Criticism in the Wilderness: The Study of Literature Today* (New Haven: Yale Univ Press 1980), 86–114 [87–90, 95, 113]
Sees F as going beyond the tradition of Arnold and Eliot in wanting criticism to be creative. F understands 'creative,' however, to mean nothing more than producing allegorical interpretations. Even though Frye 'completes Arnold by returning to Blake' and 'corrects Eliot by arguing that what is important in religion can be communicated,' his encyclopedic system of allegory and archetypes actually accommodates and so weakens the power of literature.

L215 — 'Structuralism: The Anglo-American Adventure.' *Yale French Studies* 36–7 (1966): 148–68. Rpt in Hartman, *Beyond Formalism: Literary Essays 1958–1970* (New Haven: Yale Univ Press 1970), 3–23 [9–17].

Examines British and American myth criticism as a form of literary criticism.
Looks at F's place in this movement, characterizing his work as 'an
attempt to value positively the influence of technology on culture, and
especially on the appreciation of art.' Looks also at F's distinction between
criticism and interpretation and his ideas of spatial form and archetype.
Maintains that F's literary theory tends to ignore the discontinuity of myth;
thus, 'he omits a vital aspect of mythic thought.'

L216 — 'Toward Literary History.' *Daedalus* 99 (Spring 1970): 355–83 [359–62].
Rpt in Hartman, *Beyond Formalism: Literary Essays 1958–1970* (New Haven:
Yale Univ Press 1970), 356–86 [361–4]; and in *In Search of Literary Theory*,
ed Morton W. Bloomfield (Ithaca, NY: Cornell Univ Press 1972),
197–235 [203–7].
Sees F as one of the four significant twentieth-century theorists who have
expanded the idea of literary form. F removes the elitism of art by his
analogy between primitive myths and the formal principles of all art.
He democratizes literature; yet 'he fails to bring together the form of art
and the form of its historical consciousness – which is the ideal of the
science we seek.'

L217 — 'War in Heaven.' *Diacritics* 3 (Spring 1973): 26–32. Rpt in Hartman,
The Fate of Reading (Chicago: Univ of Chicago Press 1975), 41–56.
A review of Harold Bloom's *The Anxiety of Influence*. Examines Bloom's
implicit critique of the 'sky-gods' of contemporary scholarship on romanticism: W.J. Bate, Meyer Abrams, and especially F. Comments on F's view
of cultural assimilation and on the difference between his and Bloom's view
of displacement.

L218 Hassan, Ihab. 'Beyond a Theory of Literature: Intimations of Apocalypse?'
Comparative Literature Studies 1, no 4 (1964): 261–71 [267–9]. Rpt in *Comparative Literature: Matter and Method*, ed A. Owen Aldridge (Urbana: Univ of
Illinois Press 1969), 25–35 [31–3].
A brief glance at *WTC*. Sees F's later work as less architectonic than his
earlier writings, yet remains disturbed that F still insists on a separation of
art from life and still considers criticism not as the experience of literature
but as an area of knowledge.

L219 Hastings, William T. 'New Critics of Shakespeare: An Analysis of the
Technical Analysis of Shakespeare.' *Shakespeare Quarterly* 1 (July 1950):
163–76 [167]
A short account of F's essay, 'The Argument of Comedy' (D39). Believes
that F's interpretation of the symbolism of Shakespeare is forced and
that his view of Lyly and Greene is 'incorrect.' Also objects to F's statements
that tragedy is an 'implicit or uncompleted comedy,' and that 'comedy
contains potential tragedy within itself.'

L220 Hawkes, Terence. 'Comedy, Orality, and Duplicity: *A Midsummer Night's
Dream* and *Twelfth Night*.' *Shakespearean Comedy*, ed Maurice Charney
(*New York Literary Forum* 1) (New York 1978), 155–63

Links F's 'structuralist' view and C.L. Barber and M. Bakhtin's 'Festival-Carnival' view of Shakespearean comedy to an 'orality' approach to the two plays.

L221 Hawkins, Sherman. 'The Two Worlds of Shakespearean Comedy.' *Shakespeare Studies* 3, ed J. Leeds Barroll (Cincinnati: Univ of Cincinnati 1967), 62–80
Uses F's 'green world theory' as a basis for examining Shakespearean comedy. Finds that it fits only four of the plays, and proposes a 'closed world theory' to account for the remaining plays.

L222 Hays, Richard B. 'Northrop Frye: *Mythos* and *Dianoia*.' *The Faith of Jesus Christ: An Investigation of the Narrative Substructure of Galatians 3:1–4:11.* Chico, Calif: Scholars Press 1983
Uses F's adaptation of Aristotle's *mythos* and *dianoia* as a 'conceptual foundation for the claim that there is an organic continuity between a [biblical] story and a non-narrative explication of the story's meaning.'

L223 Herman-Sekulič, Maja. 'Anatomija frajeve kritike.' *Sovremenik* 1–2 (January–February 1980): 70–86
Notes that for F myth is the fundamental structural element of literature. Examines, especially, the Third Essay of *AC*, illustrating F's use of displacement. Says F's approach frees him from the 'fetters of history' and from value-judgments. Observes that while F's mythopoeic theory permits him to move freely within the total order of words, it also leads him toward schematization. Notes that the seeking of similarities in works of literature leads to the creation of a monomyth.

L224 Hernadi, Paul. 'Entertaining Commitments: A Reception Theory of Literary Genres.' *Poetics* 10 (June 1981): 195–211
Seeks to amplify F's theory of myths into an aesthetics of reception.

L225 — 'The Erotics of Retrospection: Historytelling, Audience Response, and the Strategies of Desire.' *New Literary History* 12 (Winter 1981): 243–52
Reworks F's map of genres in order to ask whether history gives rise to literary genres or whether generic patterns arise from the human imagination.

L226 — *Interpreting Events: Tragicomedies of History on the Modern Stage* (Ithaca, NY: Cornell Univ Press 1985), 44–7
Notes that his use of the terms *comedy, satire, tragedy,* and *romance* owes much to F, but points to several basic differences between their taxonomies of generic types.

L227 — 'Northrop Frye.' *Beyond Genre: New Directions in Literary Classification* (Ithaca, NY: Cornell Univ Press 1972), 131–51 and passim
An examination of F's archetypal approach to literary classification. Devotes half a chapter to F's taxonomy of imaginative patterns (*mythoi*), literary modes, and radicals of presentation. Points out that F's theory of literature employs several principles of generic classification instead of subordinating one to another and that these principles 'help us to see literary works

within a polycentric conceptual framework.' Concludes with a discussion
of the genre theory of two writers influenced by F, Robert Scholes and
Carl H. Klaus.

L228 — 'Order without Borders: Recent Genre Theory in English-Speaking
Countries.' *Theories of Literary Genre* (Yearbook of Comparative Criticism,
vol 8), ed Joseph P. Strelka (University Park: Pennsylvania State Univ
Press 1978), 192–208 [202–7]
A summary of F's pre-generic and generic categories. Concludes that 'a
great deal of effort in the literary theory of the coming decades is likely
to be directed toward correlating some of Frye's genre concepts with those
of other major critics, ancient and modern.'

L229 Hirsch, E.D., Jr. *The Aims of Interpretation* (Chicago: Univ of Chicago Press
1976), 95–6, 126
About F's position on value-judgments and the social context of criticism.

L230 — 'Literary Evaluation as Knowledge.' *Contemporary Literature* 9 (Summer
1968): 319–31 [319–20]
Disagrees with F's position in 'On Value Judgments' (see D173) that
evaluation is not the proper function of the critic. Calls F's position 'separatist,' as opposed to the 'anti-separatist' position in Murray Krieger's
'Literary Analysis and Evaluation' (L280).

L231 Hochman, Barbara. *Character in Literature* (Ithaca, NY: Cornell Univ Press
1985), 45, 76–7, 94–6, 124, 133, 162
Draws throughout on F's conception of the archetypal forms of character
in romance and comedy.

L232 Holland, Norman. *The Dynamics of Literary Response* (New York: Oxford
Univ Press 1968), 331–3 and passim
Looks briefly at F's work in relation to various models for teaching literature. Contends that his analogical method, with its rich aura of allusion
and association, can help in effecting a richer response to literature.

L233 Holloway, John. 'The Critical Zodiac of Northrop Frye.' *Colours of Clarity:
Essays on Contemporary Literature and Education* (London: Routledge & Kegan
Paul 1964), 153–60. Partially rpt in *Contemporary Literary Criticism*, vol 24,
ed Sharon R. Gunton (Detroit: Gale Research 1983), 211–12.
Sees *AC* more as a work of metaphysics than as a work of 'scientific' critical
theory. Looks at the logic of F's arguments, concluding that *AC* is neither
inductive nor deductive but a series of dogmatic assertions. Is attracted,
however, by the quality of F's mind and the power of his radically new
point of view. Suggests that the real life of *AC* is that it is 'driving toward
some hitherto neglected great thing,' which is the capacity of great literature to locate archetypes and create myths.

L234 Hopper, Stanley Romaine. ' "Le Cri de Merlin!" or Interpretation and the
Metalogical.' *Anagogic Qualities of Literature* (Yearbook of Comparative
Criticism, vol 4), ed Joseph P. Strelka (University Park: Pennsylvania State
Univ Press 1971), 9–35 [7, 31, 35]
On F's theory of anagogy.

L235 Hough, Graham. 'Myth and Archetype II.' *An Essay on Criticism* (New
York: Norton 1966), 148–56 and passim
An exposition and critique of the principles of F's system. Summarizes
the central terms of F's critical language and indicates some of the powers
and limitations of his overall method. Concludes that *AC* is not so much a
treatise providing us with usable critical tools as it is a work of imaginative
literature in its own right: 'Frye has written his own compendious *Golden
Bough* ... It is itself poetry.' Maintains, however, that the broad outlines
of F's theory, when properly understood, will become a part of our normal
critical apparatus.

L236 Howard, Ben. 'Fancy, Imagination, and Northrop Frye.' *Thoth* 9 (Winter
1968): 25–36
On F's view of the imagination. Provides a summary of F's theory of
literature as a whole, arguing that the theory determines the concept of
the imagination, rather than vice versa. Then compares F's position with
Coleridge's, observing that Coleridge's distinction between Imagination
and Fancy has no place in F's system because in this system no radically
new forms are allowed.

L237 Hughes, Peter. 'Vico and Literary History.' *Yale Italian Studies* 1 (Winter
1977): 83–90 [85–6]
Compares Vico's *Scienza Nuova* with *AC*. Both are 'anatomies' or visions
of the world in terms of single intellectual patterns; both 'democratize and
liberate guarded hierarchies of meaning and value'; both are fascinated
'with changes from the hieratic to the demotic.' The two anatomies differ,
however, in their treatment of myth, Vico's being much more 'intensely
civil and political' in its treatment of texts.

L238 Hume, Kathryn. 'Fantasy, Modes, and Genres.' *Fantasy and Mimesis* (New
York: Methuen 1984), 150–9
Uses F's theories of myths and modes to develop a matrix for classifying
the presence of fantasy in literary works.

L239 Hunt, Peter. 'Irving Layton, Pseudo-Prophet – a Reappraisal.' *Canadian
Poetry: Studies, Documents, Reviews* 1 (Fall–Winter 1977): 1–26 [16–21]
Compares the views of F and Layton on value, the social function of the
artist, and Christianity, and finds them both wanting. Characterizes F
as a positivist, gnostic, Nietzschean secular humanist, and says he has
no objective values to which to appeal.

L240 Hyman, Lawrence W. 'Literature and Politics.' PMLA 100 (March 1985):
237–8
A letter to the editor questioning F's understanding, in 'Literary and
Linguistic Scholarship in a Postliterate World' (see D277), of the relation
between literature and the various forms of primary and secondary concern.
Believes F is mistaken in thinking that the study of literature can improve
society. Argues that such improvement comes about only through political
action, and that if we draw meaning from literature to support political
positions we do not do justice to the literary experience.

L241 — 'Moral Attitudes and the Literary Experience.' *Journal of Aesthetics and Art Criticism* 38 (Winter 1979): 159–65
Argues against the separation of moral values and literary experience, using F as an example of the amoral interpreter of literature. Cites F's views on centripetal meaning in *AC* and his arguments in *NP* about the separation of literature from life as typical of the modern emphasis on literary autonomy.

L242 Inglis, Fred. 'Professor Northrop Frye and the Academic Study of Literature.' *Centennial Review* 9 (Summer 1965): 319–31
An analysis of two essays by F (D49 and D98) that embody certain ideas of literary scholarship that are 'misdirecting our attention.' Attacks the 'system' of F's criticism, maintaining that it loses touch with literature and offers no help in understanding. Also objects to F's position on value-judgments, proposing instead that the study of literature would be better off if it followed the lead of a critic like Leavis.

L243 Izubuchi, Hiroshi. '*Anatomy of Criticism* and Its Environs.' *Eigo bungaku sekai* [*The English Literary World*] 11 (February 1969): 2–6
In Japanese.

L244 — 'Beyond Mytho-archetypal Criticism: The Case of Northrop Frye.' *Eigo seinen* [*The Rising Generation*] 117 (October 1971): 44–6
In Japanese. Places F's thought and method in the context of various 'structural' ways of looking at intellectual phenomena, such as those of Frazer, Jung, and Japanese folklore theorists (Yanagita Kunio, Origuchi Shinobu). Considers F's theory to be similar to a mathematical theory of functions – one that can predict future types or genres – and sees his method as basically post- or de-mythological. Hopes that in the future Oriental literature can be included in a more comprehensive literary theory.

L245 Jackel, David. 'Northrop Frye and the Continentalist Tradition.' *Dalhousie Review* 56 (Summer 1976): 221–39
Examines four main features of F's Canadian criticism: his interest in universals rather than particulars, his preference for the persuasive metaphor rather than the logical argument, his separation of Canadian writers from the European tradition, and his insistence on the conditioning effect of the environment on the imagination. Then argues that these features do not sufficiently account for the Canadian literary tradition.

L246 Jameson, Frederic. 'Criticism in History.' *Weapons of Civilization*, ed Norman Rudich (Palo Alto, Calif: Ramparts 1976), 38–40
Argues that despite F's use of the Freudian concept of displacement, the driving force behind his critical system is the idea of historical *identity*: his identification of myth patterns in modern texts aims at reinforcing our sense of the affinity between the cultural present of capitalism and the distant mythical past of tribal societies, and at awakening our sense of the continuity between our psychic life and that of primitive peoples. Ideology, therefore, leaves its mark on F's myth criticism, because it proposes

an unbroken continuity between the social relations and narrative forms
of primitive society and the cultural objects of our own.

L247 — 'Magical Narratives: Romance as Genre.' *New Literary History* 7 (Autumn
1975): 135–63 [138–42, 153–7]. Rev version rpt in Jameson, *The Political
Unconscious: Narrative as a Socially Symbolic Act* (Ithaca, NY: Cornell Univ
Press 1981), 103–50.
On F's theory of romance as wish-fulfilment or utopian fancy. Jameson
is sceptical of 'the importance assigned to the hero in Frye's account of the
romance paradigm' and believes that this account needs to be complemented by historical understanding.

L248 — 'On Interpretation: Literature as a Socially Symbolic Act.' *The Political
Unconscious: Narrative as a Socially Symbolic Act* (Ithaca, NY: Cornell Univ
Press 1981), 17–102 [68–75]
Sees F's greatness 'in his willingness to raise the issue of community and
to draw basic, essentially social, interpretive consequences from the
nature of religion as collective representation.' Finds the socio-political
dimension in F's criticism located in the mythical and archetypal phases
of his theory of symbols, where desire and society are informing principles.
Observes, however, that in F's anagogic phase, with its figure of Blake's
absolute man, he moves away from social or collective principles toward
the purely individual and personal, and he does so by reversing the
moral and anagogical levels of interpretation in medieval exegesis. This
movement, according to Jameson, is regrettable because the sense of
community disappears.

L249 Janoff, Bruce. 'Black Humor: Beyond Satire.' *Ohio Review* 14 (Fall 1972):
5–20 [16–19]
Outlines F's theory of the relationship between irony and tragedy and uses
this theory to analyse works by Barth, Heller, Pynchon, Hawkes, and
Donleavy.

L250 Jarrett, James. 'Response of Northrop Frye.' *Higher Education: Demand and
Response* (The Quail Roost Seminar), ed W.R. Niblett (London: Tavistock
Publications 1969; Jossey-Bass 1970), 52–5
A response to F's paper, 'The University and Personal Life' (D197). Offers
a perspective on student radicalism different from F's.

L251 Jauss, Hans Robert. 'Levels of Identification of Hero and Audience.' *New
Literary History* 4 (Winter 1974): 283–317 [283–4, 296]
Uses F's five-step typology of the hero for developing his own system
for understanding character. Jauss's system, however, is one based upon
'modalities of reception rather than forms of expression.'

L252 Jensen, Jørgen I. 'Litteraturkritiske udfordringer til teologien: Bibelske
formproblemer.' *Fønix* 4 (1977): 254–82. Rpt as 'Literaturkritische Heraus-
forderungen an die Theologie: Biblische Formprobleme.' *Evangelische Theologie* 41 (September–October 1981): 377–401
Shows that F's use of the Bible as a world of symbols and myths appealing

to the imagination is indispensable for theology. While scholarship is often divided between historical criticism and systematic theology, F considers the Bible as a total vision. He charts systematically the poetic structures of the Bible, an approach that must now be used in discussions about the language of theology.

L253 Jewkes, W.T. 'Mental Flight: Northrop Frye and the Teaching of Literature.' *Journal of General Education* 27 (Winter 1976): 281–98
Asks whether or not F's ideas are 'useful, not just to scholars in general but to teachers in particular, at every level of instruction, who must each day strive to find ways of opening up the minds of their students to the values of literary study.' Concludes that F's work is practically valuable because it identifies the proper adversary, provides a proper notion of the object of literary study, offers a practical methodology, and gives a sense of relevance.

L254 — 'Structure, Relevance, and the Teaching of Literature.' *CEA Critic* 42 (November 1979): 37–43
Argues that F's concept of structure can help rescue literary studies from the disarray they have been in during the past two decades. Summarizes F's views on the larger contexts of literary studies and on their fundamental structural forms: archetype and metaphor. Believes that F's approach to literature can 'have a direct and powerful relevance' for students, because it raises issues directly related to both their personal lives and their understanding of society. Additionally, it can educate their imaginations.

L255 Johansen, Jørgen Dines. 'Retorisk genreteori.' *Novelleteori efter 1945: En studie i litteraer taxonomi* (Copenhagen: Munksgaard 1970), 15–20
Mainly concerned with the definition of the short story and its status in criticism, especially with the terminology of literary scholarship used to discuss it. Discusses the genre theories of F, Käte Hamburger, and Emil Staiger, but rejects them all as incoherent or unprofitable.

L256 Johnsen, William A. 'The Sparagmos of Myth Is the Naked Lunch of Mode: Modern Literature as the Age of Frye and Borges.' *boundary 2*, 8 (Winter 1980): 297–311
Analyses F's theory of the relation of modern literature to the tradition. Outlines his conception of the mood of identification, which transforms nature into culture and helps us overcome (sublimate) the finitude of the world and our alienation. Seeks to determine the deep forces lying behind the contradiction in F's theory of modes, where human power in the natural world is seen as diminishing, and his theory of the imagination, where one can ultimately fulfil the dream of literature by entering the world of anagogic identity. Discovers a deeper logic in the structuralist concept of differentiation, which is said to underlie F's oppositions and to provide the motive for myth and metaphor: F shows that 'modern literature criticizes western culture as a sacrificial or differentiating system now turning back on itself.'

L257 Johnston, George. 'Northrop Frye: Some Recollections and Observations.'
      CEA Critic 42 (January 1980): 21–5
      Reminisces about F as a student, teacher, and critical intelligence. Indicates
      the debt that he owes to F as a critic and as a person. Comments on his
      authority, humanity, wit, loyalties, and influence.

L258 Jones, D.G. 'Myth, Frye, and Canadian Writers.' *Canadian Literature* 55
      (Winter 1973): 7–22
      Argues that the basic conception of poetic imagination articulated in F's
      critical theory is 'not peculiar or opposed to the main development of
      Canadian literature or the Canadian writer's imaginative convictions.'
      Shows how a number of Canadian poets give evidence to what F
      has argued, namely, that poetry gives shapes to the myths men live.

L259 Jones, Dafydd Glyn. 'Golwg ar y mathan llenyddol.' *Efryd. Anthron.*
      39 (1976): 58–74
      Discusses the concept of 'types' in contemporary literature, examining the
      views of F and R.M. Jones.

L260 Jones, Joel M. 'The Presence of the Past in the Heartland: *Raintree County*
      Revisited.' *MidAmerica* 4 (1977): 112–21
      Shows that Lockridge's novel exemplifies F's five modes – from the mythic
      to the ironic – and so is more than a historical novel.

L261 Josipovici, Gabriel. *The World and the Book* (London: Macmillan 1971;
      Stanford, Calif: Stanford Univ Press 1971), 264–5, 266–9, 289–93, 302–5
      Claims that F, more than anyone else, 'has helped to bring us back to an
      understanding of the role of literary convention and tradition.' Objects,
      however, to F's use of the concept 'myth' as he applies it to modern writers,
      for it does not account for the unique play of the relations between the
      world of literature and the moderns' sense of unique self. F 'fails to account
      for the tension that exists in each writer between the awareness of possi-
      bility and the necessity of choice, and which is resolved in the exploration,
      through art itself, of the dialectic between *langue* and *parole*, desire and
      reality.'

L262 Kawasaki, Toshihiko. 'Criticism in America: Twentieth Century.' *History of
      English and American Literature* 12, ed Hideo Kano et al (Tokyo: Taishukan
      shoten 1971), 305–8
      In Japanese.

L263 — 'The Ruby and the Planetarium: The Formalism of Northrop Frye.'
      Eigo bungaku sekai [*The English Literary World*] 9 (December 1974): 2–6
      In Japanese.

L264 Kawasaki, Toshihiko, et al. *Perspectives on Contemporary Criticism* (Tokyo:
      Gakusei-sha 1974), 92–111 and passim
      In Japanese.

L265 K[eith], W.J. 'Northrop Frye and the Bible: A Review Symposium.' *Univer-
      sity of Toronto Quarterly* 52 (Winter 1982–3): 127
      An introduction to the symposium essays on *GC* by Louis Dudek (M10.39),

David L. Jeffrey (M10.62), Emero Stiegman (M10.113), and George Woodcock (M10.132).

L266   Kennedy, Beverly. 'Northrop Frye's Theory of Genres and Sir Thomas
       Malory's "Hoole Book." ' *The Spirit of the Court: Selected Proceedings of the
       Fourth Congress of the International Courtly Literature Society (Toronto 1983)*,
       ed Glyn S. Burgess et al (Dover, NH: Burgess 1985), 224–33
       Examines *Morte d'Arthur* 'in the context established by Frye's literary
       theory, especially his theory of genres.'

L267   Kermode, Frank. Reply to a questionnaire. *American Scholar* 34 (Summer
       1965): 484
       A response to the question: 'To what book published in the past ten years
       do you find yourself going back – or thinking back – most often?' Ker-
       mode's reply: 'Northrop Frye's *Anatomy of Criticism*, I think, would be
       my choice because of the amount of positive thinking I had to do in order
       to resist it. Frye offers you the choice of thinking him entirely right or
       entirely wrong. I choose the second alternative, but pay my respects to
       the best mind in the business except for William Empson's.'

L268   — 'Spenser and the Allegorists.' *Proceedings of the British Academy: 1962*
       (London: Published for the British Academy by Oxford Univ Press 1963),
       261–79. Rpt in Kermode, *Shakespeare, Spenser, Donne* (New York: Viking
       Press 1971), 12–32.
       Criticizes the mythic-archetypal approach to *The Faerie Queene*. Objects to
       F's emphasizing radical myths and literary types at the expense of historical
       context and to his reducing Spenser's poem to a biblical quest-romance.
       Myths 'are, of course, to be found in the poem, and at the present moment
       they confer prestige; but much damage may be done in the process of
       isolating them in all their primitive glory.'

L269   Kernan, Alvin B. *The Imaginary Library: An Essay on Literature and Society*
       (Princeton, NJ: Princeton Univ Press 1982), 25
       Describes and then rejects F's view that 'literature originates in a mysterious
       quality of mind itself.'

L270   Kessler, Martin. 'A Methodological Setting for Rhetorical Criticism.' *Art and
       Meaning: Rhetoric in Biblical Literature*, ed David J.A. Clines et al (Sheffield,
       Eng: JSOT Press 1982), 1–19 [5–7]
       In a survey of rhetorical approaches to biblical literature, glances at F's
       classification of genres in *AC* and comments on his view of the Bible as a
       single archetypal structure. Concludes that F's understanding of rhetorical
       criticism 'is difficult to relate to what this method is understood to mean
       by biblical scholars.'

L271   Ketterer, David. 'New Worlds for Old: The Apocalyptic Imagination,
       Science Fiction, and American Literature.' *Mosaic* 5 (Fall 1971): 37–57 [43–5].
       Rpt in Ketterer, *New Worlds for Old* (Garden City, NY: Doubleday 1974),
       3–19 [10–11].
       A brief look at F's use of the word 'apocalypse,' against which Ketterer

develops his own, somewhat broader definition of the apocalyptic
imagination.

L272 Kilbourn, Elizabeth. 'The Arts Conference.' *Canadian Forum* 41 (June 1961):
52–3
An account of F's speech to the Canadian Conference on the Arts, 4 May
1961. F 'spoke with that olympian splendor which marks him as Canada's
first social philosopher and critic ... His discussion of the arts as the
means of giving the imagination its proper central place in society was
majestic in conception.' F's speech was published as 'Academy without
Walls' (D121).

L273 Kilian, Crawford. 'The Cheerful Inferno of James de Mille.' *Journal of
Canadian Fiction* 1, no 3 (1972): 61–7
Argues that critics have misunderstood de Mille's *A Strange Manuscript
Found in a Copper Cylinder*, but that its structure and intent become clear
if it is considered to be what F calls the Menippean satire or anatomy.

L274 Kincaid, James R. 'Coherent Readers, Incoherent Texts.' *Critical Inquiry*
3 (Summer 1977): 781–802
Argues that F's generic distinctions 'are made only to show how they are
not observed.' Thinks that all of F's narrative patterns can be found in a
novel such as *Wuthering Heights* but that, because there is no way of co-
ordinating them, generic incoherence becomes the structural principle of
such novels. For a response to this essay, see L118.

L275 Kiniry, Malcolm. 'Recent Books on Shakespearean Comedy.' *Shakespearean
Comedy*, ed Maurice Charney (New York: New York Literary Forum
1980), 281
Reviews eight books. F's influence on the criticism of Shakespearean
comedy is shown to be continuing throughout the 1970s. On the influence
of F's Shakespearean criticism, see also Charney's 'Preface,' ix.

L276 Knutson, Harold C. *Molière: An Archetypal Approach* (Toronto: Univ of
Toronto Press 1976), 4–5, 8–10, 15–16, 75–6, 118–20, 135–6, 144–6
On F's theories of comedy and romance.

L277 Korpan, Barbara D. 'Literary Evolution as Style: The "Intrinsic Historicity"
of Northrop Frye and Juri Tynianov.' *Pacific Coast Philology* 2 (April 1967):
47–52
Attacks the New Critics for the view that a poem can be treated as a
separate entity without reference to anything outside itself, but singles out
F as 'the one literary critical mind at work in the western world with the
tradition of the New Criticism who ... goes beyond it in both scope
and depth.' In its treatment of literature as a particular order of words that
has its own history yet that can be related to 'extra-literary' orders, F's
theory resembles in crucial points the criticism of one of the most advanced
of the Russian formalists, Juri Tynianov.

L278 Kostelanetz, Richard. 'The Literature Professors' Literature Professor.'
Michigan Quarterly Review 17 (Fall 1978): 425–42

Surveys F's status and influence as a critic and teacher. Gives a brief account of his life, academic and otherwise, and provides several anecdotes coming from his visit with F in Toronto. Comments on F as a public lecturer and on his writing and reading habits.

L279 Krieger, Murray. 'The Critical Legacy of Matthew Arnold; or, The Strange Brotherhood of T.S. Eliot, I.A. Richards, and Northrop Frye.' *Southern Review* 5 (April 1969): 457–74. Rpt in Krieger, *Poetic Presence and Illusion: Essays in Critical History and Theory* (Baltimore: Johns Hopkins Univ Press 1979), 92–107.

Traces the influential notions of Arnold on twentieth-century critics, including F. Sees the separation of the worlds of nature and freedom, of science and language, as F's chief Arnoldian debt. Arnold also anticipates F's concept of culture – those forms that man shapes in response to dream and desire. F resolves the difficulty, present in Eliot and Richards, of the separation of poetry and ideas: he does so by broadening the concept of poetry to include all symbolic projections of human desire.

L280 — 'Literary Analysis and Evaluation – and the Ambidextrous Critic.' *Contemporary Literature* 9 (Summer 1968): 290–310 [293–9]. Rpt in *Criticism: Speculative and Analytical Essays*, ed L.S. Dembo (Madison: Univ of Wisconsin Press 1968), 16–36 [19–24].

Sees a similarity between E.D. Hirsch's attempt to cut off interpretation from criticism and F's effort to divorce evaluation from the function of criticism. Observes that F's separation of criticism, as an objective discipline moving toward becoming a science, from both subjective experience and value-judgments about art results from his prior definition 'of criticism as the systematic construct of a total hypothesis,' which is little concerned with the particular effects of individual works.

L281 — 'The Mirror as Window in Recent Literary Theory: Contextualism and Its Alternatives.' *A Window to Criticism: Shakespeare's Sonnets and Recent Poetics* (Princeton, NJ: Princeton Univ Press 1964), 28–70 [42–9]. Part of this chapter, including the section on F, appeared originally in a slightly different form in 'After the New Criticism.' *Massachusetts Review* 4 (1962): 190–5.

Pays tribute to F's influence and to the inclusiveness of his system, yet finds his theory finally inadequate because of its inability to treat the uniqueness of individual literary works. Actually sees two Northrop Fryes: the inclusive F who wants to synthesize all approaches into one and the partisan F who argues specifically for myth criticism. F's principles can be applied with special insight to the work of poets like Blake and Yeats, but 'the more modest practitioners among us non-Blakeans, who do not see Blake or Yeats as the archetype of all poets, cannot adapt this mystical assumption about the transcendent, all-responsible, all-responsive unity of the sanctified body of literature.'

L282 — 'Northrop Frye and Contemporary Criticism: Ariel and the Spirit of

Gravity.' *Northrop Frye in Modern Criticism*, ed Murray Krieger (New York: Columbia Univ Press 1966), 1–30. Rpt in Krieger, *The Play and Place of Criticism* (Baltimore: Johns Hopkins Univ Press, 1967), 220–37; partially rpt in *Contemporary Literary Criticism*, vol 26, ed Sharon R. Gunton (Detroit: Gale Research 1983), 223–5.

An introductory essay to the English Institute volume devoted to F's work. Comments both on the theoretical situation upon which *AC* made its impact and on the aftermath of that impact. Observes that F 'has had an influence – indeed an absolute hold – on a generation of developing literary critics greater and more exclusive than that of any one theorist in recent critical history.' Argues that it is the opposition of the lunar to the sublunary that characterizes F's relation to the dominant critical tradition.

L283 — *Theory of Criticism: A Tradition and Its Systems* (Baltimore: Johns Hopkins Univ Press 1976), 56–7, 109–10, 142–4

On F's criticism as a corrective to the anti-romantic assumptions of Eliot, his concept of existential projection, and his distinction between nature and freedom. Sees this latter opposition as descending from the lineage of Kant, Goethe, Schiller, Arnold, and Richards.

L284 Kuhns, Richard. 'Professor Frye's Criticism.' *Journal of Philosophy* 56 (10 September 1959): 745–55

Outlines F's main assumptions and evaluates his contribution to critical theory. Spends some time discussing F's analogies between criticism and natural science, on the one hand, and between literature and mathematics, on the other. Takes issue with his theory of literary interpretation, especially as it relates to the problem of intention; and concludes that criticism is not as neat a discipline as the formal symmetry of F's work tends to suggest.

L285 Kuipers, Jelte. 'Pro and Contra Frye.' *Collage*, 3 October 1969, 5–8

A close look at the argument of F's essay, 'Anarchism and the Universities' (see D186). Concludes that F's views are basically incorrect, because 'he has failed to look deeply enough into the new radicalism and also because he has chosen the wrong myths to describe what he does see.'

L286 Lagerroth, Erland. *Svensk berättarkonst*. Lund: C.W.K. Gleerup [1968]

Uses F's theories of imagery and *mythos* to interpret Strindberg's *Röda rummet*.

L287 Landry, Marcia. 'Tercentenary Celebrations of *Paradise Lost*.' *Seventeenth-Century News* 26 (Summer 1968): 33

Gives an abstract of F's lecture, 'The Revelation to Eve,' presented at the University of Pittsburgh in celebration of the tercentenary of *Paradise Lost*, and later published (D195).

L288 Lane, Lauriat, Jr. 'Literary Criticism and Scholarship.' *Literary History of Canada: Canadian Literature in English* 3, 2nd ed, ed Carl F. Klinck (Toronto: Univ of Toronto Press 1976), 32–62 [58–62] consideration of 'the special yet exemplary role' F has played in Canadian ɲolarship and criticism since 1950. Also gives attention to some of the things that have been written about F's work.

L289 Langbaum, Robert. 'The Function of Criticism Once More.' *Yale Review* 54 (Winter 1965): 205–18. Rpt in Langbaum, *The Modern Spirit: Essays on the Continuity of Nineteenth- and Twentieth-Century Literature* (New York: Oxford Univ Press 1970), 3–17 [7–8].
F is seen as completing the thought of Coleridge and Arnold. Comments briefly on F's conception of the critic as the one who holds the key to all forms of verbal discourse.

L290 Langman, F.H. 'Anatomizing Northrop Frye.' *British Journal of Aesthetics* 18 (Spring 1978): 104–19
Examines F's claim that all literature can be seen as a simultaneous whole. Argues that there is no a priori reason to accept and no empirical evidence to support his assumption of universally communicable symbols. Claims that F's theory of the archetype confuses recurring images, which may be universal, with symbols, which are not. Argues further that F's terms derive from a dated and dubious psychology and anthropology. Concludes that his theory lacks both coherence and autonomy.

L291 Lapp, John. 'La critique des Mythes et l'interprétation de Racine.' *Racine: Mythes et Réalités* (*Actes du Colloque Racine*, Univ of Western Ontario, March 1974). (London, Ont: Univ of Western Ontario, Société d'Etude du XVIIᵉ siècle 1976), 71–85
Applies modern myth theory, especially F's, in interpreting selected plays by Racine.

L292 Lavin, Albert A. 'The Position Paper: Some Meanings and Uses of Myth.' *The Uses of Myth*, ed Paul A. Olson (Urbana, Ill: National Council of Teachers of English 1968), 17–27 [18–19, 22–3]
A brief summary of F's approach to myth, which is seen as one of the three representative modern approaches. 'Frye has made myth the servant of poetry by constructing an architectonic view of literature, standing back, as it were, from the results of earlier twentieth-century criticism and gaining a perspective on its main currents, synthesizing the various "armed visions" and reconciling the divisions between aesthetic and moral criticism. Perhaps Frye has stated best the place of literature and literary criticism in the city of man.'

L293 Layton, Irving. *Engagements: The Prose of Irving Layton*, ed Seymour Mayne (Toronto: McClelland and Stewart 1972), xiii, 58, 59, 109, 157, 159, 165–70, 172–4
Maintains that F can be 'safely ignored by poets and novelists.' Claims that F separates literature from life and that his science of criticism is abstract and outdated.

L294 — On Frye. Audiotape in CBC Archives, Toronto. CBC reference no 721028-1. Broadcast on 28 October 1972. 3 min
In an interview on the 'This Is Robert Fulford' series, talks about his early

criticism of F and his present admiration for him. Says that in many
ways he 'mythologized' F, making him a sinister figure. But 'all along I
had a huge suspicion of the overwhelming intellectual integrity and worth
of Frye. But precisely because he was such a tremendous intellect and
such a tremendous influence I had to fight him.'

L295 LeCoat, Gerard G. 'Literary and Musical Syntax of the Eighteenth Century.'
Intertextuality: New Perspectives in Criticism, ed Jeanine Parisier Plottel and
Hanna Charney (New York: New York Literary Forum 1978), 159–76
Seeks to demonstrate that the two recurrent literary ideologies F opposes
in 'Towards Defining an Age of Sensibility' (D82), the Longinian and
the Aristotelian, can be applied not just to the literature of the eighteenth
century but to its music as well. What F says of Pope, for example, can
also be said of Bach, his contemporary.

L296 Lee, Alvin A. *James Reaney* (New York: Twayne 1968), 21–4, 131–2
About the influence of F on Reaney.

L297 — 'Old English Poetry, Mediaeval Exegesis and Modern Criticism.' *Studies
in the Literary Imagination* 8 (Spring 1975): 47–73
Includes a detailed description of F's theory of symbols. Compares F's
theory of the levels of literary meaning with the medieval theory and then
applies both to Old English poetry. Sees F's theory of symbols ('Ethical
Criticism' in *AC*) as 'a brilliant essay that does for modern interpretative
criticism what the medieval theory of levels of meaning ... did for medieval
exegesis.'

L298 — 'Towards a Language of Love and Freedom: Frye Deciphers the Great
Code.' Paper presented at a symposium and panel discussion on *GC* at
Emmanuel College, Univ of Toronto, 1 October 1982. 24 pp. Photoduplicated
Examines F's use of the principle of polysemous meaning in *GC* and the
way it might be used in the second volume of this work. Compares the four
phases of symbolism in *AC* and the medieval four levels of meaning in
order to see how they are treated in *GC*. Thinks F has left out some of the
vital aspects of the medieval schema. Concludes by suggesting the impact
GC might have: the book 'could and should have a very powerful creative
influence on a world badly in need of a new language of love and
freedom.'

L299 Lemon, Lee T. *The Partial Critics* (New York: Oxford Univ Press 1965),
199–203
Gives a brief account of F's view of the archetype.

L300 Lentricchia, Frank. 'The Historicity of Frye's *Anatomy*.' *Salmagundi* 40
(Winter 1978): 97–121. Rev and expanded version appears as 'The Place of
Northrop Frye's *Anatomy of Criticism*' in Lentricchia, *After the New Criticism*
(Chicago: Univ of Chicago Press 1980), 3–26; partially rpt in *Contemporary
Literary Criticism* vol 24, ed Sharon R. Gunton (Detroit: Gale Research
1983), 229–31.
Examines the ways in which F's poetics pushes beyond the New Criticism

while at the same time standing as still another example of the Symbolist theory of poetry. Discusses F's attack on subjectivity and the romantic conception of the self; his mythic idea of the unconscious self, 'a kind of communal subject'; the way in which desire functions in his poetics; and the extreme form of his idealist aesthetics, one that despairs about the possibilities of historical life.

L301 Lenz, Günter. 'Von der Erkenntnis der literarischen Struktur zur Struktur der Literarwissenshaftlichen Erkenntnis: Metakritische Bemerkungen zu R.S. Crane und Northrop Frye.' *Jahrbuch für Amerikastudien* 17 (1972): 100–27
A critical analysis of the ideas of Crane and F. Shows the relationship between the methodological status of their ideas and the basic objectives of both German hermeneutics and ideological criticism in the humanities and social sciences. Remarks that F's recent work develops a conception of criticism that relates his archetypal approach to the social concerns of freedom and happiness.

L302 Levin, Harry. 'The Primacy of Shakespeare.' *Shakespeare Quarterly* 26 (Spring 1975): 99–112 [99, 100, 111–12]
The introduction and conclusion to this essay on Shakespeare's greatness are developed in opposition to F's remarks about value-judgments. Observes that *AC* draws more illustrations from Shakespeare than from any other writer.

L303 — *Why Literary Criticism Is Not an Exact Science* (Cambridge, Mass: Harvard Univ Press, 1967), 22–7. Rpt in Levin, *Grounds for Comparison* (Cambridge, Mass: Harvard Univ Press 1972), 40–56 [52–6].
A lecture, given at Churchill College, Cambridge, in 1967, which raises questions about the scientific aspects of the work of I.A. Richards, René Wellek, and F. Briefly reviews some of the principles of F's work. Concludes that *AC* is schematically over-ingenuous, a book we may set on our shelves beside Yeats's *Vision*.

L304 Levine, George. 'Realism Reconsidered.' *The Theory of the Novel: New Essays*, ed John Halperin (New York: Oxford Univ Press 1974), 231–56 [237–9, 254–5]
Levine's outline about the nature of realism draws upon the arguments of F's 'Myth, Fiction, and Displacement' (D120), an essay that has 'provoked (in both senses) much of [Levine's] recent thinking on the subject.'

L305 Levy, Maurice. 'Approaches du Texte Fantastique.' *Caliban* 16 (1979): 3–15
Finds that F's generic classifications (among those of others) are inadequate to account for fantastic literature.

L306 Lindrop, Gerald. 'Generating the Universe through Analogy.' *PN Review* 3 (1977): 41–5
Maintains that F's eminence as a critic rests not upon his taxonomies and technical innovations but upon his gifts as a master rhetorician in the service of a Platonic vision of literature. *AC* 'is not so much a classification derived from Literature itself, as a gesture of homage, to the demiurge

of Plato's *Timaeus*, who generated our universe 'through analogy ... from four "natures" or elements.' Sees the chief quality in F's 'rapid, associative and non-logical' criticism to be its fastening upon similarities between literary works. F does not yield particular critical insights; rather he is 'a myth-maker in his own right, a prophet whose vision of a transcendent unity in literature carries with it something of a religious exaltation.' Observes that the religious aspect of F's vision is becoming more explicit as time passes, so that F may be fulfilling the prophecies of Matthew Arnold. Comments on the similarity between F's work and Harold Bloom's.

L307 Lipking, Lawrence I. 'Northrop Frye: Introduction.' *Modern Literary Criticism, 1900–1970*, ed Lawrence I. Lipking and A. Walton Litz (New York: Atheneum 1972), 180–8
An introduction to F's work, serving as the preface to a generous selection of his writings. Discusses F's relation to other twentieth-century critics, the schema and method of *AC*, the visionary aspects of F's works, his doctrines of autonomy, archetypes, and value-judgments, and the practical implications of his theory. Calls F an 'indispensable critic,' linking him with Pound, Eliot, and Richards, as the major critics of the century.

L308 Litz, A. Walton. 'Literary Criticism.' *Harvard Guide to Contemporary American Writing*, ed Daniel Hoffman (Cambridge: Belknap Press of Harvard Univ Press 1979), 51–83 [64–7]
On literary criticism in America since 1945. Sees *AC* as a prologue to what has happened in criticism since 1957. Remarks that F's structuralism is an effort to see relations *between* literary works, that his chief object of study is the archetype, that he believes in a totally intelligible structure of poetic knowledge, and that his lack of interest in discrimination or critical differences 'is a profound interruption of the Anglo-American critical tradition' with its emphasis on value-judgments. Observes that F is the first major Anglo-American critic who is not a practising artist and that this 'signals a decisive turn toward the continental model.'

L309 Lohner, Edgar. 'Vorwort.' *Analyse der Literaturkritik* (Stuttgart: W. Kohlhammer Verlag 1964), 7 (A2a)
A brief note about the difficulty of translating F's work into German, a difficulty caused mainly by F's coining new terms – what he calls his 'terminological buccaneering.' Says that because F is attempting a completely new method of literary criticism, it is necessary for him not only to create new descriptive terms but also to give new meanings to well-known concepts.

L310 Lyons, Charles R. *Shakespeare and the Ambiguity of Love's Triumph* (The Hague: Mouton 1971), passim
Elaborates a number of F's ideas, which are then used to interpret Shakespeare's comedies.

L311 MacAdam, Alfred J. 'Northrop Frye's Theory of Genres and the New Literature of Latin America.' *Revista Canadiense de Estudios Hispanicos*

3 (Spring 1979): 287–90
Maintains that F's assumption about the existence of literary tradition, which includes readers as well as writers, and his concept of the 'radical of presentation' of literary genres can be used to clarify the forms of contemporary Latin American literature and its reaction, particularly in the satiric novel, to cultural dependence.

L312 — 'Rereading *Resurreição.' Luso-Brazilian Review* 9, no 2 (1972): 47–57
Uses F's theory of satire to argue that the faults many critics see in Machado de Assis's *Resurreição* do not really apply if it is seen as an anatomy rather than a novel.

L313 McCallum, Pamela. 'Indeterminacy, Irreducibility and Authority in Modern Literary Theory.' *Ariel* 13 (January 1982): 73–84 [78–9]
Observes that for all of the similar motifs in the work of F and Geoffrey Hartman (the romance quest, wandering in the wilderness, the desire for epiphany, the interest in Arnold), their orientations are fundamentally different: F sees the text as a vision of possibilities and literary studies as teleological; Hartman sees the text as a wilderness and literary studies as creative.

L314 McCanles, Michael. 'Mythos and Dianoia: A Dialectical Methodology of Literary Form.' *Literary Monographs* 4, ed Eric Rothstein (Madison: Univ of Wisconsin Press 1971), 1–88
Expands upon F's fundamental distinction between *mythos* and *dianoia* in order to develop a method for examining the dialectical structures of literature.

L315 McConnell, Frank. 'Northrop Frye and *Anatomy of Criticism.' Sewanee Review* 92 (Fall 1984): 622–9
An autobiographical account of the influence that F's work has had upon the author – from the time he first encountered *AC* in the classroom of William Wimsatt up through the publication of *GC*. Recalls that the chief effect of *AC* was 'the reach, the expanse, the sheer joy' implicit in the book, that what F chiefly taught was 'that we have the right to know, and to employ, all available information about the structure of human consciousness,' and that the exhilarating end of F's enterprise was that it showed the function of criticism to be 'simply the full exercise of the moral intelligence.' Maintains that the value of F's work is that it keeps the proper, human balance between New Critical formalism and poststructuralism. Finds analogies between *AC* and Schleiermacher's claim that any text could be sacred, sees F as anticipating the best of reader-response criticism, and discovers a similarity between *AC* and the ways in which the work of both Descartes and Chomsky encourage an encounter between objective intellectual structures and the individual human mind. Observes finally that *GC* 'completes and harmonizes' F's whole life as a critic, because this book shows that the Bible 'can be read as a model of all our reading, teaching us how to read the rest of the world.'

L316 — *Storytelling and Mythmaking: Images from Film and Literature* (New York: Oxford Univ Press 1979), 7–9
On F's contribution to the discovery that the stories of the world constitute a 'single, complicated but uniform structure.' Briefly outlines F's theory of myths.

L317 MacCormac, Earl R. *A Cognitive Theory of Metaphor* (Cambridge: MIT Press 1985), 40–1, 194–9
Examines the semantic implications of F's diaphoric understanding of metaphor, arguing that one cannot separate, as F's theory of criticism tends to do, the iconic from the semantic meaning of metaphor.

L318 MacCulloch, Clare. *The Neglected Genre: The Short Story in Canada* (Guelph: Alive 1973), 75–81
Examines how F's major generalizations about Canadian literature might be related to the Canadian short story, especially F's 'garrison mentality' theory and his views on the tragic themes that emerge from the Canadian writer's confronting a hostile environment.

L319 MacDonald, R.D. 'Frye's *Modern Century* Reconsidered.' *Studies in Canadian Literature* 4 (Winter 1979): 95–108
Gives a detailed account of each chapter of *MC*. Argues against such readers of the book as Howard Mumford Jones and George Grant, who claim, respectively, that F presents too negative a vision of modern life and that F's non-evaluative view of the humanities makes them irrelevant. Maintains that F's response to the modern century is not simply negative; rather it is concerned 'with art in relation to man's condition.' Illustrates that F's vision is comic, in that it provides an exit from the twentieth-century nightmare of alienation, anxiety, and absurdity by way of an almost religious faith 'in the elusive divinity of man.'

L320 McDougall, Robert L. 'The Dodo and the Cruising Auk: Class in Canadian Literature.' *Canadian Literature* 18 (Autumn 1963): 6–20. Rpt in *Contexts of Canadian Criticism*, ed Eli Mandel (Chicago: Univ of Chicago Press 1971), 216–31 [219–20].
A review and assessment of F's "La tradition narrative dans la poésie canadienne-anglaise" (D24). 'Professor Frye's feeling ... for our literature seems to me so absolutely right (his accounting for what he finds is another matter, for I think he is misleading when he says that the northern environment is the cause) that I have only to go on from where he leaves off.'

L321 McFadden, George. 'Twentieth-Century Theorists: Mauron, Cornford, Frye.' *Discovering the Comic* (Princeton: NJ: Princeton Univ Press 1982), 152–73 [159–73]
Points to the similarities between F's theory of comedy and those of Freud, Bergson, and Cornford. Examines F's views on comic structure and character types as presented in *AC* and points to his strong emphasis on the social aspect of comedy. Concludes that F's theory is fundamentally

romantic, stemming from his belief that comedy points toward an ideal, imaginative order of man and nature that reverses the 'natural perspective' of irony and realism.

L322 McGregor, Gaile. *The Wacousta Syndrome: Explorations in the Canadian Landscape* (Toronto: Univ of Toronto Press 1985), 357–8, 404–5, and passim
Argues that the allegorizing tendency in F's criticism makes myth, from the Canadian perspective, both 'serious *and* playful.'

L323 McLuhan, Marshall. *From Cliché to Archetype* (New York: Viking Press 1970), 7–10, 15, 18, 36, 85–7, 128–9
Seems to argue that as technical clichés are abandoned, having reached a certain stage of use, they become archetypes, which are old forms for new clichés. Refers throughout the book, most of the time disparagingly, to F's view of archetype and to his inattention to non-verbal and non-literary forms of culture.

L324 MacLulich, T.D. 'Canadian Exploration as Literature.' *Canadian Literature* 81 (Summer 1979): 72–85
Argues that exploration literature can be analysed in terms of what Hayden White, following F, calls 'emplotment,' the shaping of the historical record into one of F's four narrative patterns. Shows that there are three basic forms of exploration accounts (Quest, Odyssey, and Ordeal) and that while they 'do not correspond directly to F's typology of narrative forms ... they can be related to an overlapping, but less inclusive, set of fictional categories' (Romance, Novel, Tragedy).

L325 — 'What Was Canadian Literature? Taking Stock of the Canlit Industry.' *Essays on Canadian Writing* 30 (Winter 1984–5): 17–34 [26–7]
Finds in F's well-known essays on Canadian literature a corollary to George Grant's lament that Canada has only imitated U.S. culture and society. Notes, however, that in *MC*, F's assessment of Canadian literature takes another direction: it finds itself immersed in an international style.

L326 MacLure, Millar. 'Literary Scholarship.' *Literary History of Canada: Canadian Literature in English*, ed Carl F. Klinck (Toronto: Univ of Toronto Press 1965), 540 (2nd ed, vol 2, 1976), 61
A listing of some of F's major and minor works, along with brief remarks on his style and method. 'We are too close to Frye to assess his ultimate influence in the intellectual life of the Western academy; his work as scholar-administrator and as lecturer-at-large in the cause of the humanities is spread very widely at present and demonstrates one continuity in Canadian intellectual life, for it significantly recalls ... the careers of those missionaries of culture who created the constituencies of the Canadian universities.'

L327 Macpherson, Jay. 'Educated Doodle: Some Notes on *One-Man Masque.'* *Essays on Canadian Writing* 24–5 (Winter–Spring 1982–3): 65–99. Rpt in *Approaches to the Work of James Reaney*, ed Stan Dragland (Downsview, Ont: ECW Press 1983), 65–99.
Shows how Reaney's *Masque* imaginatively exploits the grammars of poetic

myth in *FS* and *AC*, especially the principles of the romance narrative pattern. Also illustrates F's influence on Reaney's staging and his cast of characters.

L328 McQueen, Marian. 'Ernst Jünger's *Auf den Marmorklippen* and Northrop Frye's Theory of Romance.' *Carleton Germanic Papers* 6 (1978): 37–56
Argues that Jünger's work conforms to F's view of romance, particularly to the description of the plot structure and imagery of romance F gives in *AC*. Distinguishes between F's different uses of romance (as mode, as *mythos*, and as genre) and applies these to Jünger's short 'novel,' a book that F himself reviewed in the *Canadian Forum* in 1948 (D32).

L329 Mackey, Louis. 'Anatomical Curiosities: Northrop Frye's Theory of Criticism.' *Texas Studies in Language and Literature* 23 (Fall 1981): 442–69
Analyses the extent to which *AC* is itself an 'anatomy,' a form of prose fiction, and therefore a part of the conceptual universe that his book constructs. Takes F's own definition of the anatomy as well as a number of his critical principles, and uses these to argue that F's work finally collapses the distinction between literature and criticism and thus becomes itself a kind of ironic fiction: it is 'both truth-telling science and fictive artifice.' Concludes that *AC*, although 'a failed redemption myth,' is nevertheless 'a necessary failure' – necessary because there is no human solution to the problems inherent in language; and that *AC* holds out the possibility of an authentic experience of the problems of language.

L330 — 'Poetry, History, Truth, and Redemption.' *Literature and History*, ed Leonard Schulze and Walter Wetzels (Lanham, Md: Univ Press of America 1983), 65–83 [68–75]
Examines the question of truth in history and poetry in the context of F's work, among others'. Maintains that just as the writing of history follows the traditional modes of narrative emplotment (as Hayden White suggests, using F's categories), so the path of philosophy can be similarly traced along the sequences of F's historical modes.

L331 Maeda, Masahiko. 'The Development of Frye's Literary Theory.' *Kyôyô no tame no sôzôryoku* [*The Educated Imagination*] (Tokyo: Taiyosha 1969), 153–80 (see A3d)
In Japanese. Treats the influence of Blake on F, the context of his criticism, his practical criticism, and the powers and limitations of his work.

L332 Magnet, Joseph. 'On the Nature of Critical Reasoning.' *College English* 37 (April 1976): 733–47 [740–1]
Sees F's criticism as leading to 'a rigid separation of literature from all other forms of thought and action.' Says that F accomplishes this by two moves: he first establishes literature as autonomous, and he then selects, in Arnoldian fashion and on the basis of 'informed good taste,' works from the literary tradition that are personally meaningful. Claims that interpretation is thereby sacrificed.

L333 Mandel, Eli. *Another Time* (Erin, Ont: Press Porcépic 1977), 157–8
Traces the development of F's literary and cultural criticism and relates it

to the concerns of writing in Canada. Recognizes three different positions on Canadian writing in F's work: nationalism, internationalism, and regionalism.

L334 — *Criticism: The Silent Speaking Words* (Toronto: Canadian Broadcasting Corp 1966), 8–9, 38–49

An explanation and expansion of many of F's major postulates. Claims that no other critical theory 'is as interesting, as comprehensive, as relevant, or as free from objection as Frye's.' Devotes special attention to F's ideas about education and culture; to his position on poetic language, literary convention, metaphor, myth, and the imagination; and to some of the logical and empirical objections to his critical views.

L335 — 'Double Vision.' *In Their Words: Interviews with Fourteen Canadian Writers* (Toronto: Anansi 1984), 106–23 [116–18]

In an interview with Bruce Meyer and Brian O'Riordan, comments on F's relation to a group of Canadian mythopoeic writers. Says that F did not influence the movement but commented on it and gave it validity.

L336 — 'Introduction.' *Contexts of Canadian Criticism: A Collection of Critical Essays,* ed Eli Mandel (Chicago: Univ of Chicago Press; Toronto: Univ of Toronto Press 1971), 3–25 [4, 7, 12, 17–20, 23]

Includes a number of remarks about the central role F has played in Canadian criticism.

L337 — 'Northrop Frye and the Canadian Literary Tradition.' *Centre and Labyrinth: Essays in Honour of Northrop Frye,* ed Eleanor Cook et al (Toronto: Univ of Toronto Press 1983), 284–97

Examines F's romantic reading of a Canadian literary tradition while at the same time looking at the problems this reading poses in defining a national literature. F's writings on the Canadian tradition take 'us through history and literature – wedding a Laurentian theory of Canadian history with a romantic myth of a descent to the interior, through cultural history – ranging across the folk-culture theories of nation to modernist internationalism.' F's real contribution is 'to have shown the precise points where local creation becomes part of the civilized discourse he speaks of as criticism and creativity.'

L338 — 'Toward a Theory of Cultural Revolution: The Criticism of Northrop Frye.' *Canadian Literature* 1 (Summer 1959): 58–67

Argues that a fussiness over the technical details of F's work has more often than not obscured the theme or informing principle of his criticism, which is the relationship of criticism to culture. Shows that F is a defender of the popular and an opponent of the provincial in both art and criticism. Observes a parallel between the concerns of F and Arnold, and discusses the central importance of Blake for F's entire critical scheme. F shows 'that criticism can supply the conceptual framework for a theory of culture.'

L339 Margolis, Joseph. 'Critics and Literature.' *British Journal of Aesthetics* 11 (Autumn 1971): 370–84 [378–80]

A criticism of F's analogy between the principles of taxonomy in biology and criticism. Claims F's proposals for literary classification cannot be tested. Also comments on F's theory of value and his aesthetic point of view, claiming that the former is naive and the latter not at all inductive or scientific.

L340 Marshall, Tom. *Harsh and Lovely Land: The Major Canadian Poets and the Making of a Canadian Tradition* (Vancouver: Univ of British Columbia Press 1979), 112–14
Comments briefly on F's influence on the poetry of James Reaney and Jay Macpherson.

L341 Martin, Tom. 'Comedy and the Infinite Finite.' *University of Dayton Review* 8 (Winter 1971): 15–23 [19–20]
Summarizes F's view of comedy and compares it with the comic theories of Fr William Lynch, Nathan Scott, and Peter Berger.

L342 Martins, Heitor. 'A anatomia de Serafim Ponte Grande.' *Supplemento Literário do Estado de São Paulo*, 15 February 1969; and '*A pista inexistente de Serafim Ponte Grande*,' ibid, 26 April 1969
Sees Oswald de Andrae's work as a Menippean satire in F's sense, rather than a novel, but goes on to criticize the work as lacking a central aesthetic aim.

L343 Mathews, Robin. *Canadian Literature: Surrender or Revolution*, ed Gail Dexter (Toronto: Steel Rail Educational Publishing 1978), 119–20, 136–7, 170–1
A critique of F's views on evaluation and on Canadian literature ('one of the worst – certainly one of the most arrogant – critics of Canadian literature'). Believes that F's cultural views 'guarantee our quiet colonialism by promulgating a kind of anaemic resignation.'

L344 — 'Bush League, "Bush Garden." ' *Last Post* 2 (December–January 1971–2): 47–9
Attacks F for being a colonialist. Claims that F denies Canadian existence and cultural achievement, postulates 'a phony garrison mentality and experience' in Canadian literature, and 'vulgarizes the aspirations of the reasonable Quebecois separatists.'

L345 Mazzeo, Joseph Anthony. *Varieties of Interpretation* (Notre Dame: Univ of Notre Dame Press 1978), 87–8
Brief account of F's concept of allegory, which Mazzeo finds has been adapted 'to uses quite foreign to its origins.'

L346 Meletinskii, Eleazar M. *Poetika Mifa* (Moscow: Nauka 1976), 120–1, 161
Criticizes F for differentiating literature from myth too simply, leading to 'one-sidedness.'

L347 Mendelson, Michael. 'George MacDonald's *Lilith* and the Conventions of Ascent.' *Studies in Scottish Literature* 20 (1985): 197–218
Bases his interpretation of MacDonald's work on F's definition of the romance of ascent, developed in *SeS*.

L348 Merrill, Robert. 'The Generic Approach in Recent Criticism of Shakespeare's

Comedies and Romances: A Review-Essay.' *Texas Studies in Language and Literature* 20 (Fall 1978): 474–87

Sees the development of the generic approach to Shakespearean comedy as beginning with *AC* and *NP*, books that 'constitute a major departure from earlier Shakespearean criticism.' Maintains that what Shakespearean critics C.L. Barber, Robert G. Hunter, Peter G. Phialas, Larry Champion, Thomas McFarland, David Young, Ralph Berry, and Alexander Leggatt have in common is that they all respond to or clarify an aspect of F's theory about comic form. This is especially true of Barber, whose *Shakespeare's Festive Comedy* 'documents F's remarks about the sources of Shakespearean comedy.'

L349 Meynell, Hugo. 'Northrop Frye's Idea of a Science of Criticism.' *British Journal of Aesthetics* 21 (Spring 1981): 118–29

Argues, in opposition to F.H. Langman (see L290) that F's conception of a science of criticism has merit. Examines in turn the problem of value-judgments, the cultural significance of criticism, the limitations of mere scholarship and the history of taste, the nature and desirability of a science of criticism, and the need for autonomy in criticism. Concludes that F's account of the middle three topics is essentially correct, that of the last is partly correct, and that of the first is radically incorrect but easily remediable.

L350 Mezei, Arpad. 'Critique of Literary Criticism.' *Onion* [Toronto] 3 (August–September 1978): 12–13

Maintains that the kind of systematic analysis of literature F proposes in *AC* does 'not exhaust the task of literary interpretation.'

L351 Milić, Novica. 'Antinomije kritike.' *Književnost* 71 (March 1981): 565–77

Examines the historical development of literary criticism in the twentieth century, stressing its polarization into two fundamental schools of thought, the subjective or 'internal' and the objective or 'external.' Says that it was not until F had formulated his mythopoeic approach that transcending such dualism was made possible. Observes that F's archetypal criticism is synthetic: it excludes nothing and includes everything. Its methodology allows the critic to investigate literature both as a whole and as a single work; it leads directly to the heart of the matter while retaining an open stance toward other methods. Maintains that F's method is superior to other methods only insofar as it clearly reveals the uniqueness of literature as language, capable of 'unifying diversity,' and as it acknowledges its own relative nature.

L352 Mitchell, Beverly. 'Association and Allusion in *The Double Hook*.' *Journal of Canadian Fiction* 2, no 1 (1973): 63–9

Uses F's theories of imagery, allusion, character, and displacement to help explain some of the elusive elements in this novel by Sheila Watson.

L353 Mitchell, W.J.T. 'Dangerous Blake.' *Studies in Romanticism* 21 (Fall 1982): 410–16

Sees F as the father of the third phase in the critical study of Blake, which has placed Blake firmly in the central tradition of English poetry and has demonstrated that his work is poetry rather than religion or prophecy. Believes, however, that the emerging fourth phase of Blake criticism will take issue with F's claim that such things as madness and obscenity have no critical meaning when applied to Blake.

L354 Moisan, Clément. *L'âge de la littérature canadienne* (Montreal: Editions HMH 1969), 91–4
On the contribution of 'the foremost and the best representative of the new criticism in Canada.' See also pp 21, 42, 47, 53, 64, 87, 102, 106.

L355 Morley, Patricia A. *The Comedians* (Toronto: Clarke, Irwin 1977), passim
Uses F's definition of comic narrative to examine the fiction of Hugh Hood and Rudy Wiebe.

L356 Mugerauer, Robert. 'The Form of Northrop Frye's Literary Universe: An Expanding Circle.' *Mosaic* 12 (1979): 135–47
Seeks to engage the *form* of F's thought as it is represented in his analysis of the phases of symbolism. Gives an outline of the argument behind each of the five phases, notes the characteristic images and metaphors of each phase, and argues that the logical and formal aspects of the theory of phases form a unity that can be represented as an expanding circle. Concludes that the form and content of F's theory of symbolism do form a unity, 'not to be found entirely in his literal assertions or his supporting "logical" arguments but in the very presentation of his thought.'

L357 Mugridge, Ian. 'Myth-Making and History.' *International History Review* 5, no 3 (1983): 318–21
Calls upon F's discussion in *GC* of the difference between *Weltgeschichte* and *Heilsgeschichte* to elucidate the difference between history and myth.

L358 Nakamura, Kenji. 'In Search of the Archetype: N. Frye and J.L. Borges.' *Gendai shiso* [*Revue de la pensée d'aujourd'hui*] 7 (April 1979): 98–102
In Japanese.

L359 — 'Northrop Frye: Criticism as Knowledge.' *The Bulletin* [College of General Education, Osaka Univ] 18 (March 1970): 81–103
In Japanese.

L360 — 'Northrop Frye: A Tribute on the Occasion of His Visit to Japan.' *Nihon dokusho shimbun* [*The Japan Review of Books*] 1911 (20 June 1977)
In Japanese.

L361 — 'Northrop Frye Revisited.' *Gakuto* 74 (May 1977): 12–15
In Japanese.

L362 — 'On the Stratification of the Critical Mind: A Supplementary Note on Northrop Frye.' *Eigo bungaku sekai* [*The English Literary World*] 5 (August 1970): 12–15
In Japanese.

L363 Nakanori, Koshi. 'Northrop Frye's Criticism of Comedy.' *Eigo bungaku sekai* [*The English Literary World*] 11 (February 1969): 10–13

In Japanese.

L364 Nassar, Eugene Paul. 'Literary Tone and the Rape of Illusion,' *Renascence*
18 (Winter 1966): 73–80
Argues against F's views on classification and value-judgments, maintaining
that the proper function of criticism is to specify or 'articulate the unique
tone of a work.'

L365 Natoli, Joseph. *Twentieth-Century Blake Criticism: Northrop Frye to the Present*
(New York: Garland 1982), ix
Selects FS as the starting point of this bibliography because F's book
'represents the first attempt to treat Blake's work as a coherent whole
susceptible to a literary exegesis.'

L366 Nelson, Cary. 'Reading Criticism.' *PMLA* 91 (October 1976): 801–15 [802–4,
810, 812–13]
Explores the nature of critical activity itself by looking at statements about
criticism made by F and others. Questions both the organic conception
of 'literary career' and the notion of a scholar as a disinterested historian.

L367 Nelson, Thomas A. *Shakespeare's Comic Theory: A Study of Art and Artifice in
the Last Plays* (The Hague: Mouton 1972), 25–6
Outlines F's understanding of the larger symbolic actions in Shakespeare's
comedies and, following F and Francis Fergusson, bases his own interpretation of Shakespeare upon his 'total concept of comedy,' especially the
recurring patterns in his comic action and his treatment of character.

L368 Nevo, Ruth. 'Shakespeare's Comic Remedies.' *Shakespearean Comedy*, ed
Maurice Charney (New York: New York Literary Forum 1980), 3–15
Draws throughout on F's taxonomies and analyses of the conventions of
Shakespearean comedy.

L369 Nilsen, Helge Normann. 'Yeats's "The Two Trees": The Symbolism of the
Poem and Its Relation to Northrop Frye's Theory of Apocalyptic and
Demonic Imagery.' *Orbis Litterarum* 24 (1969): 72–6
Expands F's statement in *AC* about Yeats's poem into a brief interpretation
based on apocalyptic and demonic visions.

L370 Nizzero, Gianni. 'Frye: della Fede alla Speranza nella "Tempesta" di
Shakespeare.' *Il Giornale di Vicenza*, 22 June 1979
Gives a detailed summary of F's lecture on *The Tempest*, presented in
Vicenza, 18 May 1979 (see I123).

L371 Nozick, Robert. *Philosophical Explanations* (Cambridge: Harvard Univ Press
1981), 623
Sees *AC* as going beyond the mere classification of literary forms because,
in spite of F's non-evaluative stance, he is responding to literary values
as values.

L372 O'Hara, Daniel. 'Against Nature: On Northrop Frye and Critical Romance.'
The Romance of Interpretation: Visionary Criticism from Pater to de Man (New
York: Columbia Univ Press 1985), 147–204
Sees in F's early work a dialectical opposition between a nihilistic view of
nature, taking the form of a demonic feminine will, and an idealistic

view of art, taking the form of an apocalyptic vision of freedom. Discovers
in *GC*, however, a different thrust: here the reader becomes the Apocalyptic Bride in the quest for a sublime identity. Argues that F's theoretical
system functions in the same way that Yeats's *A Vision* does: it is 'an
obsessive quest for a prophetic literary identity' that takes the form of a
critical romance. The romance of F's career takes three phases: the agon
of *FS*, the pathos of *AC* and F's subsequent practical and social criticism,
and the anagnorisis of *SeS* and *GC*. F, therefore, has institutionalized
criticism as a form of romance, which is an antithetical version of
Nietzsche's quest for identity.

L373 — 'Revisionary Madness: The Prospects of American Literary Theory at
the Present Time.' *Critical Inquiry* 9 (June 1983): 726–42
Looks at the interpretive practices of Emerson and F as viable ways of
doing criticism in an age of 'revisionary madness,' represented by the recent
opposition to literary theory. Sees in F's essay 'The Imaginative and the
Imaginary' (D127) an argument for authentic creativity in literature and
a defence of the imagination as a means for making more enlightened and
freer human beings. F provides a rational, affirmative, and moral model
of doing criticism.

L374 Ohmann, Carol. 'Northrop Frye and the MLA.' *College English* 32 (December
1970): 291–300
A response to the MLA's awarding a prize to Rudolf B. Gottfried for an
essay in which he attacks F's archetypal criticism of Spenser (see L189).
Argues that Gottfried's essay is largely dependent on misunderstandings
of F's texts, on over-emphasizing points that are minor to F, and on
irrelevant argument. Goes on to say that the MLA's commendation of Gottfried's essay shows that the prevailing ethos of the organization is one
that supports 'professional specialization pursued apart from rather than
integrated with the nature of society in which it flourishes or at least
occurs.'

L375 — 'Reply to Rudolf B. Gottfried.' *College English* 33 (October 1971): 79–83
A response to Gottfried's 'Edmund Spenser and the NCTE' (L188), which
itself was a reply to Ohmann's essay, 'Northrop Frye and the MLA' (L374).
Reiterates the points of her defence of F and speaks out once more against
the separation of scholarly and critical activity from matters of social and
political relevance.

L376 Olafson, Frederick A. *The Dialectic of Action: A Philosophical Interpretation of
History and the Humanities* (Chicago: Univ of Chicago Press 1979), 61–7
Argues, in the context of a discussion of universals in literature and historical understanding, that F's theory of generic plot structures indicates
certain repeatable patterns of action that are plotted along normative or
moral co-ordinates.

L377 Olendorf, Donna. 'Frye, (Herman) Northrop 1912–.' *Contemporary Authors*
(New Revision Series) 8, ed Ann Evory and Linda Metzger (Detroit:
Gale Research 1983), 182–5

Lists biographical data about Frye, his career, and his writings, and
provides some 'sidelights' to his work, mainly by way of reaction to it
from reviewers.

L1378 Olson, Paul A. 'Introduction: On Myth and Education.' *The Uses of Myth*,
ed Paul A. Olson (Urbana, Ill: National Council of Teachers of English
1968), 1–15 [8–13]
An account of the examination of F's theory of myth by a Dartmouth
Seminar Study Group. Looks especially at F's ideas about the monomyth,
which Olson claims are based on shaky psychological and anthropological
grounds and 'constitute a potentially disastrous oversimplification of the
business of literary education.'

L1379 Olwig, Kenneth. 'Place, Society and the Individual in the Authorship of
St. St. Blicher.' *Omking Blicher 1974: Udgivet af Blicher-Selkabet* (Copenhagen:
Gyldendal 1974), 65–115 [esp. 87–108]
On the social patterns in Blicher's *Røverstuen* and *Hosekræmmeven*, which
are classified as comedy and tragedy respectively on the basis of F's
definitions.

L1380 Ong, Walter J., Jr. 'Evolution, Myth, and Poetic Vision.' *Comparative
Literature Studies* 3, no 1 (1966): 1–20 [2–5]. Rpt in *Comparative Literature:
Matter and Method*, ed A. Owen Aldridge (Urbana: Univ of Illinois Press
1969), 308–27 [309–12].
Comments on F's cyclic theory of archetypes in the course of exploring the
basic issue between poetry and evolutionism, namely, the need in poetry,
as in all art, for repetition. Remarks that F's classification of archetypes
is based on the natural cycle of the year: this is 'something on the whole
both real and powerful,' a cycle that touches not only poetic themes,
imagery, and characters but also verbal and visual rhythm.

L1381 Ostendorf, Bernhard. 'Northrop Frye.' *Der Mythos in der Neuen Welt: Eine
Untersuchung zum amerikanischen Myth Criticism* (Frankfurt am Main: Thesen
Verlag 1971), 140–1
A critique of practically the whole of F's critical theory. Sees *AC* as regres-
sing to the 'dogmas of pre-established mythology,' as 'two-dimensional'
and fossilized. Claims that because of F's inattentiveness to historical
perspective and his neglect of temporal reality, his criticism cannot account
for the uniqueness of literature. Because Frye stands too far back from
literature, his theory is abstract, reductive, medieval.

L1382 Osumi, Hideo. 'The Notion "Archetype": Northrop Frye and German
Hermeneutics.' *Eigo bungaku sekai* [*The English Literary World*] 11 (February
1969): 22–5
In Japanese.

L1383 Pacey, Desmond. 'The Course of Canadian Criticism.' *Literary History of
Canada: Canadian Literature in English* 3, 2nd ed, ed Carl F. Klinck (Toronto:
Univ of Toronto Press 1976), 16–31 [24–8]
On the role F has played in the criticism of Canadian literature.

L1384 — *Essays in Canadian Criticism: 1938–68* (Toronto: Ryerson 1969), 202–5, 211

An account of the influence of F upon a group of Canadian poets, including James Reaney and Jay Macpherson. Sees Canadian criticism coming of
age in F's 'brilliantly creative' work, but objects to the implication by the
so-called 'Frye school of poets' that 'poetry is now being led by criticism,
rather than vice versa.'

L385 Paley, Morton D. *The Continuing City: William Blake's 'Jerusalem'* (Oxford:
Clarendon Press 1983), 24–7 and passim
Comments on the central position that F's exposition of *Jerusalem* has had
in understanding the poem – particularly F's brilliant demonstration of
the poem's coherence.

L386 Pálsson, Hermann, and Paul Edwards. 'Introduction.' *Göngu-Hrolf's Saga*
(Toronto: Univ of Toronto Press 1980), 7–11
Examine the structure of this Icelandic saga in light of F's observations
about the structure of romance. Find that the 'narrative conforms in essentials to Frye's pattern for romance fiction.'

L387 Pandeya, S.M. 'Sociology and Criticism: Social Context and Literary Theory
in America.' *Twentieth Century American Criticism: Interdisciplinary
Approaches*, ed Rajnath (New Delhi: Arnold-Heinemann 1977), 146–54
Examines F's views on advertising and propaganda (along with those of
Irving Babbit and T.S. Eliot) and the effect that these forces have had upon
his literary theory, especially as it is developed in *CP*.

L388 — 'Theory of Styles: A Note on the Ideas of T.S. Eliot, Northrop Frye and
Mammata.' *Essays and Studies: Festschrift in Honour of Prof K. Viswanatham*,
ed G.V.L.N. Sarma (Machilipatnam, India: Triveni 1977), 95–101
Finds a correspondence between the theories of style developed by Eliot,
F, and the Sanskrit critic, Mammata. Points out that Eliot's 'ordonnance,'
'words,' and 'relevant intensity' are similar to F's categories of 'melos,'
'opsis,' and 'mood,' which in turn correspond to Mammata's categories,
especially *sabdaarthau* (word and sense) and *sagunau* (relevant intensity).

L389 Paolucci, Anne and Henry. 'Canada's "Two Solitudes": Foci of a National
Eclipse.' *Review of National Literatures 7*, ed Anne Paolucci (New York:
Griffon House 1976), 38–66 [51–3]
Examine F's critique of A.J.M. Smith's theory of Canadian poetry. Although
F's essay 'Canada and Its Poetry' (D18) hailed Smith's *Book of Canadian
Poetry* as an important event, he 'wholly rejected Smith's notion that delib-
erate cultivation or critical acceptance of a cosmopolitan attitude is an
adequate alternative for the extremes of colonialism.'

L390 Parker, Brian. 'Is There a Canadian Drama?' *The Canadian Imagination:
Dimensions of a Literary Culture*, ed David Staines (Cambridge: Harvard Univ
Press 1977), 161–2
On F's view of Canadian art as being committed to a modern international
style.

L391 Parker, Patricia. 'Anagogic Metaphor: Breaking Down the Wall of Partition.'
Centre and Labyrinth: Essays in Honour of Northrop Frye, ed Eleanor Cook et
al (Toronto: Univ of Toronto Press 1983), 38–58

Explores the connection between anagogic or copular metaphor, as defined by F in *AC*, and the breaking down of walls of partition in Shakespeare and Emily Bronte.

L392 Parks, Henry B. 'Tolkien and the Critical Approach to Story.' *Tolkien: New Critical Perspectives*, ed Neil D. Isaacs and Rose Zimbardo (Lexington: Univ Press of Kentucky 1981), 133–49 [136–45]
Compares and contrasts Tolkien's understanding of the concept of story with F's.

L393 Parrinder, Patrick. *Science Fiction: Its Criticism and Teaching* (London: Methuen 1980), 49–50, 54
Asks whether science fiction can be described as romance, in F's sense of the genre.

L394 Pautasso, Sergio. 'Northrop Frye critico e moralista.' *Le frontiere della critica* (Milan: Rizzoli 1972), 99–107
Places F in the camp of such critics as Barthes, who believe that criticism is a totally independent activity and that critical and creative language have equal status. Observes, too, that for F the critical act is also a cognitive act. Believes that F's genius lies in his gift for synthesis; he is not primarily a formalist critic in the mode of the Chicago school (with whom he does have some major affinities) but a theoretician in the great rhetorical tradition of the past. He is also a humanistic critic, one who goes beyond the utopian literary order and studies the mythology of our time. By affirming literature as an essential cognitive order of words, F offers an alternative to the practical disorder in which we live.

L395 Payne, Michael. 'La Critique Engagée: Literature and Politics.' CEA *Critic* 35 (January 1972) 4–8
Argues that F's most recent work (eg, *CP*) advocates a revolutionary criticism of all that forms the consciousness of the reader and his world. Thus, F is part of the movement in contemporary criticism that is steadily moving toward commitment and engagement.

L396 Pedersen, Bertel. 'Northrop Frye: mod en kritik uden vaegge.' *Kritik: Tidsskrift for Literatur, Forskning, Undervisning* [Copenhagen] 9 (1969): 52–73
Gives a fairly complete survey of F's position and calls for the translation of *AC* into Danish.

L397 Pemberton, R.E.K. Letter to the Editor. *Canadian Forum* 25 (December 1945): 215
A response to F's essay 'A Liberal Education' (D22, D23). Suggests that F's concept of the educated man is inadequate and needs to be balanced by a greater attention to history and the sciences.

L398 Pérez Gállego, Cándido. *Morfonovelistica: Hacia una sociología del hecho novelístico* (Madrid: Fundamentos 1973), 45–69, 115–34
Following Chomsky, F, et al, Pérez Gállego seeks a model of reality in the syntax of the novel.

L399 Perosa, Sergio. 'Il più grande romanzo del mondo? Nessun dubbio: è la Bibbia.' *Corriere della sera*, 22 July 1979, 8
Contrasts the work of F and Eliot, pointing primarily to their different literary tastes. Provides a brief list of the most influential of F's books translated into Italian. Points to the similarities between F and Aristotle and to the differences between F and the linguistic structuralists. Comments briefly on F's interest in the sacred as well as the secular scripture (romance).

L400 Pérusse, Daniel. 'La littérature selon Northrop Frye.' *L'actualité* 6 (November 1981): 32[a], 34, 36
Suggests that if the Nobel Prize comes to a Canadian, it will come to F. Gives a brief sketch of his career.

L401 Petrocelli, Domenico. 'La letteratura come sogno totale dell'uomo.' *Il Tempo* [Rome], 5 June 1979, 13. Appears also as 'Northrop Frye "riscopre" l'Italia' in *Oggitalia*, June 1979.
Reports on F's successful 1979 tour of Italy, gives a brief but comprehensive biography of F, and lists all of the Italian translations of his books. Observes that F's criticism of genre does not have the same classificatory function as that of Croce or the same empirical categorizing function as that of Praz. F's genres rather are identified with the fundamental structures of reality recreated by literature.

L402 Poirier, Richard. 'What Is English Studies, and If You Know What That Is, What Is English Literature?' *Partisan Review* 37, no 1 (1970): 41–58 [52–3].
Rpt in *ADE Bulletin* 25 (May 1970): 3–13 [9–10]; and in Poirier, *The Performing Self: Compositions and Decompositions in the Languages of Contemporary Life* (New York: Oxford Univ Press 1971), 65–85 [78–80].
Commends F for being a 'liberating critic,' yet has reservations about the detachment implied by his position. Sees F's spatialization of literature as continuing the tradition of Eliot and the New Critics. 'Frye leaves even less room than do the adherents of [Brooks and Warren] for measuring or even allowing an unmeasured response to the activity that is reading and writing, the energy generated in a reader by some corresponding expenditure in the writer.'

L403 Polansky, Steve. 'A Family Romance – Northrop Frye and Harold Bloom: A Study of Critical Influence.' *boundary 2*, 9 (Winter 1981): 227–45
Compares and contrasts the critical theories of F and Bloom, examining similarities and differences in their styles, their commitment to schematic constructs, the degree to which their stances are prescriptive, their practical criticism, their indebtedness to Freud, and their understanding of tradition, influence, creation, and the imagination.

L404 Polk, James. 'Editor's Preface.' *Divisions on a Ground: Essays on Canadian Culture*, by Northrop Frye (Toronto: Anansi 1982), 9–12 (see A20)
Calls attention to the arrangement of the reprinted essays and speeches, to the steadiness over the years of F's views on Canadian literature and

on education, and to his practical and social concerns.

L405 Polletta, Gregory. *Issues in Contemporary Criticism* (Boston: Little, Brown 1973), 6–13, 15–17, 320–1
An introduction to some of the central terms and doctrines of F's work. Shows how F's criticism is formalistic but also how it is substantially different from both the New Criticism and structuralism.

L406 Powe, Bruce W. 'Fear of Fryeing: Northrop Frye and the Theory of Myth Criticism.' *Antigonish Review* 49 (Spring 1982): 123–44. Rpt in Powe, *A Climate Charged* (Oakville, Ont: Mosaic Press 1984), 34–54.
Questions the value of F's work outside of academic circles. Claims that his detached, theoretical commentary eradicates the human and moral dimension of art and that he ignores the particularity of literature. What is valuable in F 'is the comprehensiveness of his concepts, his subtle synthesis of ideas, and the richness ... in his prose,' but what F neglects is the 'practical and public' function of criticism.

L407 — 'McLuhan and Frye, Either/Or.' *A Climate Charged* (Oakville, Ont: Mosaic Press 1984), 55–8
Compares and contrasts the intentions, methods of thinking, and writing strategies of F and Marshall McLuhan.

L408 Pratt, Annis. 'Archetypal Approaches to the New Feminist Criticism.' *Bucknell Review* 21 (Spring 1973): 3–14
Argues that the insights of F, along with those of Jung and Joseph Campbell, 'if turned upside down to admit of women as human participants in the quest for identity and rebirth experience, are helpful in the elucidation of the psycho-mythological development of the female hero.'

L409 — 'Spinning among Fields: Jung, Frye, Lévi-Strauss and Feminist Archetypal Theory.' *Feminist Archetypal Theory: Interdisciplinary Re-visions of Jungian Thought*, ed Estella Lauter and Carol Schreier Rupprecht (Knoxville: Univ of Tennessee Press 1985), 93–136 [106–18]
Argues that although F's analysis of archetypes is often gynophobic, his 'method, principally the description of archetypal categories as they structure literary form, is a tool that feminist critics can appropriate profitably and use for their own purposes.'

L410 Prawer, S.S. *Comparative Literary Studies: An Introduction* (London: Duckworth 1973), 57, 111, 122, 145–6
Comments on F's work in comparative literature: his treatment of tradition, theme, periods, and his 'placing' of texts beside one another for mutual illumination.

L411 Price, Hereward T. 'A Survey of Shakespeare Scholarship in 1953.' *Shakespeare Quarterly* 5 (Spring 1954): 109–28 [122–3]
A brief account of F's essay, 'Characterization in Shakespearean Comedy' (D61). Summarizes F's argument about typical comic structures and characters and their appearance in Shakespeare.

L412 Raimondi, Ezio. 'La critica simbolica.' *MLN* 84 (January 1969): 1–15 [11–15].

Trans by Catherine and Richard Macksey and rpt as 'Symbolic Criticism' in *Velocities of Change: Critical Essays for MLN*, ed Richard Macksey (Baltimore: Johns Hopkins Univ Press 1974), 117–37 [128–31].

A summary account of F's theory of myths. 'Like an enchanted forest in the hands of an extraordinarily clever magician who never tires of discovering analogies, mysterious figures, surprising deviations and oppositions, Frye's criticism may appear from time to time to be a sort of embryology in the manner of Blake or Spengler, a gnostic odyssey, a taxonomy of the imagination, an apocalypse of Kierkegaardian "repetition," an Aristotelian utopia transplanted into symbolism, for which the last chapter of *Finnegans Wake* might serve as emblem.'

L413 Ratajczak, Dobrochina. 'Przestrzenie narodowej tragedii.' *Pamietnik Literacki* 72, no 2 (1981): 63–4

Comments briefly on F's idea of 'the phase of decline,' which lies behind the archetype of tragedy.

L414 Raval, Suresh. 'Criticism as Science: Richards and Frye.' *Metacriticism* (Athens: Univ of Georgia Press 1981), 144–52 [149–52]

Says that F's effort to treat literature as objective and autonomous is based upon metahistorical conceptions of reality that are not susceptible to logical proofs and that F's own perceptions of value (eg, his belief in the significance of romance) are 'not reducible to objectively available facts.'

L415 Reaney, James. 'The Canadian Poet's Predicament.' *Masks of Poetry: Canadian Critics on Canadian Verse*, ed A.J.M. Smith (McClelland and Stewart 1962), 110–22 [111–12, 117–18]

Draws upon F's article 'La tradition narrative dans la poésie canadienne-anglaise' (D24).

L416 — 'Editorial.' *Alphabet* 1 (September 1960): [2]–4

Discusses the various forces leading to the creation of the journal *Alphabet*, including the influence of F. Recalling an earlier time in Toronto, Reaney remarks: 'Those were the months when young men and women sat up all night reading *Fearful Symmetry* which had just come out.'

L417 — 'The Identifier Effect.' *CEA Critic* 42 (January 1980): 26–31

A personal account of F's influence as a teacher and writer on Reaney himself and on other Canadians.

L418 — 'Search for an Undiscovered Alphabet.' *Canadian Art* 22 (September–October 1965): 38–41

Discusses briefly F's understanding of Blake's pictographs and the distinction, in F's article, 'David Milne: An Appreciation' (D33), between the observer's eye in Western and Eastern painting.

L419 — 'Some Critics Are Music Teachers.' *Centre and Labyrinth: Essays in Honour of Northrop Frye*, ed Eleanor Cook et al (Toronto: Univ of Toronto Press 1983), 298–308

Offers some suggestions, based upon F's formal remarks on drama, for the staging of plays.

L420 Rebhorn, Wayne A. 'After Frye: A Review-Article on the Interpretation
of Shakespearean Comedy and Romance.' *Texas Studies in Language and Literature* 21 (Winter 1979): 553–82
Seeks to determine the impact made by F's work, and to a lesser extent
that of C.L. Barber, on the criticism of Shakespearean comedy and romance
since the early 1960s and to discover whether any progress has been
made in the interpretation of these plays since the appearance of *NP*.
Sketches the main outline of F's theory, the reasons for its centrality in the
modern criticism of the comedies, and its relationship to Barber's views.
Examines the work of dozens of Shakespearean critics, showing how their
work depends on, complements, qualifies, or deepens F's. Concludes that
F's criticism of the comedies provides the starting point for almost all
subsequent criticism.

L421 Reichert, John. 'More than Kin and Less than Kind: The Limits of Genre
Theory.' *Theories of Literary Genre* (Yearbook of Comparative Criticism,
vol 8, ed Joseph P. Strelka (University Park: Pennsylvania State Univ Press
1978), 57–79 [57–60, 70, 75]
Finds F's remarks about the power of genres to explain literary works to be
tautological, but sees the strength of his genre theory in its commitment
'to diversity, to a recognition of a plurality of possible literary forms and
aims.'

L422 — Review of *In Search of Literary Theory*, ed Morton Bloomfield. *Western
Humanities Review* 27 (1973): 213–15 [214–15]
Brief remarks about F's essay 'The Critical Path' (D200). Testifies to F's
'hypostatizing prowess.'

L423 Rhodes, Carolyn. 'Experiment as Heroic Quest in Zelazny's "For a Breath
I Tarry." ' *The Scope of the Fantastic: Culture, Biography, Children's Literature*,
ed Robert A. Collins and Howard D. Pearce III (Westport, Conn: Green-
wood 1985), 191–7
Argues that Zelazny's short story exemplifies two of the categories F finds
in the universal quest myth: the spring and birth phase and the summer
and marriage or triumph phase.

L424 Riccomini, Donald R. 'Northrop Frye and Structuralism: Identity and
Difference.' *University of Toronto Quarterly* 49 (Fall 1979): 33–47
Places F's criticism alongside structuralism in order to determine their
similarities and differences. Sees their similarities in that both (1) derive
their systems from a model (mythic and linguistic, respectively) and
proceed by the method of analogy to the model; (2) depend upon a system
of synchronic conventions (*mythos* and *langue*, respectively); (3) subscribe
to a theory of the impersonality of the artist; and (4) believe that texts
move from external references to internal self-reference and interconnection
(from the literal to the anagogic and from *vraisemblance* to metatextuality,
respectively). Sees their differences in that (1) while F gives privileged
status to literary language, the structuralists see it as only one code among

many; (2) whereas the structuralists bracket out diachronic issues, F reconciles diachrony and synchrony; and (3) F's work finally does rest upon a logocentric centre, a version of the Christian mythological order that rejects the signifier in favour of the signified and gives his system its authority. Believes that even though structuralism seeks to avoid the notion of a privileged centre and a metaphysics of presence, it does in fact, as Derrida recognizes, rest upon a hidden centre – the belief in the unity of the sign.

L425 Ricoeur, Paul. '*Anatomy of Criticism* or the Order of Paradigms.' *Centre and Labyrinth: Essays in Honour of Northrop Frye*, ed Eleanor Cook et al (Toronto: Univ of Toronto Press 1983), 1–13
Sees F's system as based on a kind of narrative understanding, dependent upon both tradition and innovation ('sedimentation and change'), which has epistemological precedence to the semiotic rationality of the French structuralists. Reviews F's theory of modes and symbols, the latter of which is seen as providing the hermeneutical key to the former. Together they justify F's view of the imaginative mode of language and thereby serve to differentiate it from the mimetic and the religious modes. Asks whether or not F's theory can account for the phenomena of schism, deviance, and the death of paradigms that are so frequently announced in modern criticism.

L426 Riddell, John. ' "This Northern Mouth": Ideas of Myth and Regionalism in Modern Canadian Poetry.' *Laurentian University Review* 8 (November 1975): 68–83 [80–2]
Uses F's method to trace a developing Canadian mythology through the recurring metaphors in the poetry of Pratt, Newlove, Purdy, and others.

L427 Righter, William. 'Myth and Interpretation.' *New Literary History* 3 (Winter 1972): 319–44 [333–42]
An essay on some of the problems raised by myth criticism. Analyses two aspects of F's work: 'the role of myth in the establishing and ordering of literature as a systematic body of knowledge providing the ground of interpretation, and the functioning of this sort of ordering in the interpretation of particular literary works.' Concludes, in the first place, that the criteria F uses to differentiate such things as the phases of a *mythos* are constantly changing, and, in the second place, that F in effect reverses the critical process, using literary works as 'explanations' for his own mythic schema, rather than vice versa.

L428 Robel, Gerald. 'The Concept of Unity and Its Normative Tendency.' *Recovering Literature* 1, no 1 (Spring 1972): 42–53 [44–6, 51–3]
Argues that there is often no real distinction between F's 'so-called' descriptive and evaluative terms. 'Frye's implicit normative referend is the "collective unconscious" of archetype – a kind of historical "consensus." ' Claims that because F's system demands formal unity he forces works of fiction into conventional patterns so as to make them fit a homogeneous

tradition: 'this itself is a process of "civilizing" literature, of making it conform in some way at least to a former category, the normative consensus of archetype.'

L429 Roberts, Jeanne Addison. 'American Criticism of Shakespeare's Comedies.' *Shakespeare Studies* 9 (1976): 1–10 [3–4]
Maintains that F's 'The Argument of Comedy' (D39) is 'the single most influential work on modern American criticism of the comedies.'

L430 — 'Shakespeare's Forests and Trees.' *Southern Humanities Review* 11 (Spring 1977): 108–25 [108–16]
On F's view of the 'green world' in Shakespeare. 'Frye is suggesting a redemptive quality in the forest or a reflection of the hero's world of desire.'

L431 Robertson, P.J.M. 'Criticism and Creativity VI: George Orwell and Northrop Frye.' *Queen's Quarterly* 92 (Summer 1985): 374–84
Compares Orwell's theory of literary value with F's: Orwell's criticism is centred on social and individual values whereas F's tends to lead 'away from being and values into analysis of form and structure.'

L432 — 'Northrop Frye and Evaluation.' *Queen's Quarterly* 90 (Spring 1983): 151–6
Examines F's views on evaluation, as presented in *GC* and *AC*, and finds them wanting. Believes that in equating criticism with speculative literary theory F displaces its traditional sense of judgment. Shows that F's work is itself packed with value-judgments.

L433 Robertson, R.T. 'Another Preface to an Uncollected Anthology: Canadian Criticism in a Commonwealth Context.' *Ariel* 4 (July 1973): 70–81 [74–5, 79–80]
Proposes to expand the model of F's 'Preface to an Uncollected Anthology' (D94) so as to develop a more formal framework for an anthology of Commonwealth criticism.

L434 Robinson, Brian. 'Northrop Frye: critique fameux, critique faillible.' *Revue de l'Université d'Ottawa* 42 (1972): 608–14
Claims that F's theory is based on principles that are suspect and that a detached analysis will reveal its faults. After giving a descriptive summary of the theory, outlines his three chief objections. Claims, first, that F's view of literature as opposed to life is not a view taken by most writers and readers across the centuries. This leads F to misrepresent writers, the French symbolist poets being a case in point. Second, his theory of value-judgments is untenable. And, third, one gains little from F for analysing particular works. F sees bridges between works of literature, but he cannot help penetrate their originality, which is their *raison d'être*. 'How can literature lead to regeneration if it doesn't speak to men in the context of their lives, but offers them an evasion in a closed universe?'

L435 Rockas, Leo. 'The Structure of Frye's *Anatomy*.' *College English* 28 (April 1967): 501–7
A summary of *AC*, with special attention to the organization of the book. Outlines the structure of each of the 'Essays' in *AC* and points to the relationship among them.

L436 Rodríguez, Julían. 'El estudio científico de la literatura a través del mito de la búsqueda según los críticos anglo-norteamericanos especialmente Northrop Frye.' *Anales de Filología Inglesa* 1 (1985): 33–51
Argues that F is the first to map out systematically the coherent order of literature. Shows how F's understanding of the loss and regaining of identity (the quest myth) is the central narrative pattern in this order. Analyses his understanding of the four *mythoi* of this large pattern, the thematic structures, and the corresponding orders of imagery. Maintains, finally, that the creative experience of the reader can also be understood as participating in the quest myth.

L437 — 'Preliminary Notes to Northrop Frye's Theory concerning the Relationship of Myth to Literature.' *Revista Canaria de Estudios Ingleses* 9 (November 1984): 123–8
Sees the myth of the loss and recapturing of identity as central to F's understanding of literature. This myth arises out of man's relation to his environment and points toward his place in society. The function of criticism for F is to understand this central myth and to elaborate the social importance of literature.

L438 Rodway, Allan. 'Generic Criticism: The Approach through Type, Mode, and Kind.' *Contemporary Criticism* (Stratford-on-Avon Studies 12), ed Malcolm Bradbury and David Palmer (London: Edward Arnold 1970), 83–105 [85–96]. Rpt in Rodway, *The Truths of Fiction* (New York: Schocken 1971), 18–40 [20–30].
An analysis of F's concept of 'mode' and its connection with the genre theories of other critics. Believes that the principles F sets down in the First Essay of *AC* are 'useful as well as beautiful,' yet their usefulness is more evident in analogical or metacriticism than in intrinsic criticism. Suggests that F's concept of mode needs to be expanded to include a psychological dimension.

L439 Romano, Carlin. 'Mighty Like a Metaphor.' *Village Voice Literary Supplement* 3 (December 1981): 9–10 [9]
Glances briefly at F's attention to metaphor in *GC*.

L440 Rosmarin, Adena. *The Power of Genre* (Minneapolis: Univ of Minnesota Press 1985), 31–3
Comments briefly on Tzvetan Todorov's critique (L517) of F's deductive procedure for defining genres.

L441 Ross, Malcolm. 'Critical Theories: Some Trends.' *Literary History of Canada: Canadian Literature in English* 3, 2nd ed, ed Carl F. Klinck (Toronto: Univ of Toronto Press 1976), 160–75 [160–8]
Argues that F, more than anyone else, has put into perspective the question of Canadian cultural identity. 'In Frye's thought, "the Canadian question" rises not only to the question of the social relevance of art, but to questions about the religious and mythic reach of art.'

L442 Ross-Bryant, Lynn. 'Archetypal Literary Criticism.' *Imagination and the Life of the Spirit* (Chico, Calif: Scholars Press 1981), 167–72
Gives an overview of F's theory of myth and its relation to ritual and the

natural cycle, and compares F's theory of romance to Joseph Campbell's theory of the monomyth. Observes that the function of literature for F parallels the function of religion.

L443 Rothwell, Kenneth S. 'Northrop Frye's *Anatomy* Again: A Reply to Mr. James Schroeter.' *College English* 35 (February 1974): 595–600
A polemical response to Schroeter's essay, 'The Unseen Center: A Critique of Northrop Frye' (L463).

L444 — 'Programmed Learning: A Back Door to Empiricism in English Studies.' *College English* 23 (January 1962): 245–50
Explores the possibilities of putting F's discoveries about literary structure into programmed-learning devices so as to make more 'scientific' the study of literature.

L445 — 'A Review Article: Northrop Frye in the Schools.' *Exercise Exchange* 18 (Fall 1973): 22–7
Reviews the twelve-volume textbook series, *Literature: Uses of the Imagination* (B14), for which F was supervisory editor. Gives an overview of eleven of the twelve volumes, praises the depth and breadth of the selections, and shows how the entire series follows the pattern of F's typological criticism. Glances in addition at Robert Foulke and Paul Smith's *An Anatomy of Literature* (L170), a college anthology that also is based upon F's theory of myths and genres.

L446 Rueckert, William. 'Literary Criticism and History: The Endless Dialectic.' *New Literary History* 6 (Spring 1975): 491–512 [497–9, 501–11]
An argument for the importance of dialectic and theory in literary criticism. F (along with Edmund Wilson and Kenneth Burke) is celebrated for being a true dialectician – for following the logic of his own system. Examines also F's attitude toward history, observing that everything he has written since *AC* confirms his 'acute historical consciousness.' Says F is an exemplary critical intelligence, a 'critical mediator dedicated, as all educationalists are, to the continuous and varied applications of his own system in a sustained attempt to shape and alter human history.'

L447 Ruland, Vernon, SJ. 'Northrop Frye.' *Horizons of Criticism: An Assessment of Religious-Literary Options* (Chicago: American Library Association 1975), 121–6 and passim
Gives a summary of *FS*, the Second Essay of *AC*, and several essays in *FI*, and then judges F's work against his own view of criticism – 'an orthocultural, psycho-mythic, religious criticism in the inclusive sense.'

L448 Ruthven, K.K. *Critical Assumptions* (Cambridge: Cambridge Univ Press 1979), 160, 202
Sees F as a deutero-creator (the metacritic as artist) in *AC*. Concludes the book by observing that although F has 'mapped out the only comprehensive "placement" theory of value,' he has done more than any other critic to convince us 'that the supreme critical act is not evaluation but recognition.'

L449 — *Myth* (London: Methuen 1976), 76, 80–1

Discusses briefly the place of *AC* ('a work of synoptic finality') among modern theories of myth criticism.

L450 Rutten, Pierre Van. 'Northrop Frye et la littérature.' *Zagadnienia Rodzajów Literackich* 24, no 2 (1981): 61–80
Sees F's work as rehabilitating the humanistic dimension of criticism at a time when literary study is too technical. Comments on F's attention to the central role of teaching, on his global perspective, and on the synchronic and diachronic unity in his work. Gives a detailed analysis of the theories in *AC*. Observes that F's fundamental principles are implicit in the 'vertical optic' of his critical theory, in which desire moves humanity from earth to sky. Believes that F's work contains too many sub-categories and that it avoids the unique in literature. Says that F's greatest merits are that he gives meaning to literature and revalorizes its study and teaching.

L451 Ryan, J.S. 'Myth Criticism as a Discipline.' *Westerly* 2 (June 1973): 49–58 [56–7]
Claims that F's myth criticism is a 'retreat from literature' to 'imaginative metaphysics' and that his achievement 'claims our attention more for its beauty than its truth.'

L452 S., J.D. 'Northrop Frye and Reactionary Criticism.' *Literature and Ideology* 2 (Summer 1969): 104–10
Essentially a review of Pauline Kogan's *Northrop Frye: The High Priest of Clerical Obscurantism* (K7). Agrees with Kogan that F represents the bourgeois idealistic critic, one who must be banished if the disintegration of culture and education is to be stayed.

L453 Sábík, Vincent. 'Northrop Frye: Anatómia literárnej kritiky.' *Romboid* [Bratislava] 4 (1968): 49–53
Quotes with approval Wellek's assessment of *AC* as the most important critical study since Arnold. Is critical, however, of Wellek and Walter Sutton for not considering F's 'dialectical synthesism' in its totality. Praises F for his 'impressive erudition, neo-Aristotelian synopsis and extraordinary historical sense.'

L454 Said, Edward. *Beginnings* (New York: Basic Books 1974), 375–7
Contrasts F's 'monumental edifice' of critical theory, based upon the metaphor of a 'center,' with the decentred methodology of Derrida, Foucault, and Deleuze.

L455 Sanders, Norman. 'An Overview of Critical Approaches to the Romances.' *Shakespeare's Romances Reconsidered*, ed Carol M. Kay and Henry E. Jacobs (Lincoln: Univ of Nebraska Press 1978), 1–10 [9]
Briefly comments on F's approach to Shakespeare's romances. Observes that these plays 'lie at the center of his critical position about literature as a whole'; they take us beyond history and tragedy to a higher order of reality that all men desire.

L456 — 'Year's Contributions to Shakespeare Studies: Critical Studies.' *Shakespeare Survey* 24, ed Kenneth Muir (Cambridge: At the Univ Press 1971), 148

Brief account of F's argument in 'Old and New Comedy' (D194), 'a typically witty and civilized essay.'

L457 Sastry, Srinivasa K. 'An Application of Northrop Frye's Myth and Archetype to E.M. Forster's *A Passage to India.*' *Literature East and West* 19, no 1 (1975): 187–94

Argues that Forster connects the human dimension to the religious one, producing F's 'mythical mode of narrator.' Forster thus creates an archetypal vision of the free human society, which, according to F, is the central myth of art.

L458 Saunders, D. 'Whatever Happened to the Wedding Feast? A Critical Look at Northrop Frye's System of Archetypal Comic Narrative and Its Application to Some Recent French Examples.' *Proceedings and Papers of the Sixteenth Congress of the Australasian Universities Language and Literature Association Held 21–27 August 1974 at the University of Adelaide, South Australia*, ed H. Bevan et al. AULLA 16 (1974): 158–68

Examines F's analysis of the archetypal narrative patterns of comedy in *AC* and then applies the scheme developed there to plays by Giraudoux, Ionesco, Arrabal, and Beckett. Distinguishes F's idea of the archetype as narrative structure from Bachelard and Durand's psychological-anthropological view. Summarizes F's account of the typical narrative pattern, characters, and phases of comedy. Is convinced that F's system 'offers both a useful working hypothesis and critical tool' for the analysis of modern comic narratives.

L459 Schafer, Roy. *A New Language for Psychoanalysis* (New Haven: Yale Univ Press 1976), 22–56

Chapter 3, 'The Psychoanalytical Vision of Reality,' draws upon F's pregeneric *mythoi* to examine the comic, romantic, tragic, and ironic features in the vision of reality embodied in psychoanalytic thought and practice.

L460 Scholes, Robert. *Structuralism in Literature: An Introduction* (New Haven: Yale Univ Press 1974), 118–27

A critique of F's theories of modes and forms. Believes that F's classification of heroic powers of action is unsystematic and inconsistent; that because F is unwilling to discuss the historical relationships of specific literary types, his theory of the forms of prose fiction is weak; and that his theory of genres is not well integrated into his theory of modes.

L461 — 'Towards a Poetics of Fiction: An Approach through Genre.' *Novel: A Forum on Fiction* 2 (Winter 1969): 101–11

An essay showing many connections to F's concept of genre. Acknowledges 'Frye's clever discussions of fictional genres and modes,' but sees his own analysis as superior to F's because it is 'more aware of specific and historical generic considerations.'

L462 Schroeter, James. 'Reply to Kenneth S. Rothwell.' *College English* 35 (February 1974): 601–2

A response to Rothwell's 'Northrop Frye's *Anatomy* Again' (L443). Seeks to defend the thesis of his earlier article (L463).

L463 — 'The Unseen Center: A Critique of Northrop Frye.' *College English* 33 (February 1972): 543–57
An indictment of F's work as irresponsible and as causing 'ludicrous misconceptions' among his followers. Says F's visionary idealism is based on 'an extreme denial of historicity and process,' on an 'abuse of scientific jargon,' and on the erection of a critical universe that takes its authority from the fairy-tale world of myth.

L464 Schuman, Samuel. 'Out of the Fryeing Pan and into the Pyre: Comedy, Myth, and *The Wizard of Oz.' Journal of Popular Culture* 7 (Fall 1973): 302–4
Argues 'that it is precisely to children's literature that we might turn for a confirmation of Frye's theories,' particularly his theory of comedy.

L465 Schwartz, Daniel R. 'Two Major Voices of the 1950s: Northrop Frye's *Anatomy of Criticism* and Eric Auerbach's *Mimesis.' The Humanistic Heritage: Critical Theories of the English Novel from James to Hillis Miller* (Philadelphia: Univ of Pennsylvania Press 1986), 118–50
Gives an overview of F's approach to literature, seeks to test the usefulness of this approach by picking out the passages in *AC* where F refers to Conrad's *Lord Jim*, and concludes that F's work raises the following problems: it is too abstract and too inattentive to the formal complexities of literature, it does not explain the origin of ideal paradigms, it ignores the temporal, historic dimension of both literature and life, it neglects the creative process, it fails to account for individuality in art, and it too ambitiously creates a new critical vocabulary. Concludes by contrasting F's work with Auerbach's.

L466 Selden, Raman. 'Objectivity and Theory in Literary Criticism.' *Essays in Criticism* 23 (July 1973): 283–97 [292–4]
Discusses F's analogy between criticism and the natural sciences as a useful polemical instrument but one that produces 'damaging effects on Frye's approach to the thorny problem of values.' Objects to the sharp dichotomy F makes between subjective experience and objective fact.

L467 Shaffer, E.S. 'Editor's Introduction: The "Great Code" Deciphered: Literary and Bibical Hermeneutics.' *Comparative Criticism* 5 (Cambridge: Cambridge Univ Press 1983), xix–xxiv [xix–xxiii]
Places F in the context of hermeneutics, particularly as it descends from Dilthey and Szondi. Argues that F is a hermeneutic critic because of his concern in *SeS* and *GC* with 'the authority of the interpretive community,' a concern that goes beyond structuralism.

L468 Shattuck, Roger. 'Contract and Credentials: The Humanities in Higher Education.' *Content and Context: Essays on College Education*, ed Carl Kaysen (New York: McGraw-Hill 1973), 65–120 [75–6, 86–7]
Discusses briefly F's view of the educational contract as it is developed in 'The University and Personal Life' (D197).

L469 Shibata, Toshihiko. 'Shakespeare Criticism: Northrop Frye.' *History of English and American Literature* 12, ed Hideo Kano et al (Tokyo: Taishukan shoten 1971), 346–50

In Japanese.

L470 — 'Tragedy Criticism as the Ideal Type.' *Eigo bungaku sekai* [*The English Literary World*] 11 (February 1969): 14–17
In Japanese.

L471 Shibles, Warren. 'Northrop Frye on Metaphor.' *An Analysis of Metaphor in Light of W.M. Urban's Theories* (The Hague: Mouton 1971), 145–50
A summary of F's theory of metaphor and his discussion of analogy and identity. Outlines what F means by literal, descriptive, formal, and archetypal metaphor. Raises questions about F's concept of metaphorical identity, seeing it as mystical and supernatural, and says that F's concept of an archetype 'might be thought of merely as a universe of discourse.'

L472 Simons, Louise. 'Authority and *Jane Eyre*: A New Generic Approach.' CEA *Critic* 48 (Fall 1985): 45–53
Faults F for devaluing women in his genre theories, yet thinks that his archetypal approach, if revised to give equal treatment to women, can be useful in interpreting *Jane Eyre*.

L473 Sitter, John. 'Flight from History in Mid-Eighteenth-Century Poetry (and Twentieth-Century Criticism).' *The Humanist as Citizen*, ed John Agresto and Peter Riesenberg (np: National Humanities Center 1981), 94–116 [109–12]
Sees a parallel between the 'avoidance of particular external referents in mid-eighteenth-century poetry' and the synchronic, autonomous nature of literature emphasized by F.

L474 Slan, Jon. 'Writing in Canada: Innis, McLuhan, and Frye: Frontiers of Canadian Criticism.' *Canadian Dimension* 8 (August 1972): 43–6
Sees F as using a critical method directed toward the forms and structures of communication that exist in a society as part of its social mythology. Points out that there is a social direction in all of F's work and that it is especially manifest in *CP*. 'What is important about Frye's work is not the truth value of his literary system of social vision, but the integrity of the imaginative response which lies behind the vision. His total work is both a demonstration and celebration of man's struggle against dehumanization, and he has the courage to confront the present without distaste, the past without nostalgia, and the future without fear.'

L475 Sloan, Glenna Davis. *The Child as Critic: Teaching Literature in the Elementary School* (New York: Teachers College Press, Columbia Univ 1975; rev ed, 1984)
An approach, based upon F's work, to literary education in the elementary school. Argues that literary study has to be set within a framework of literary theory. Her elaboration of F's own theory is chiefly in chapters 2–4. The book is based in part upon Sloan's earlier study, 'The Practice of Literary Criticism in the Elementary School' (N31).

L476 — 'Introduction' to Teacher's Manuals for *Literature: Uses of the Imagination* (New York: Harcourt Brace Jovanovich 1973), 1–23
This introduction appears in each of the teacher's manuals of this twelve-volume series (see B14).

A summary and adaptation of many of F's ideas about the function of literature, narrative forms, and structures of imagery.

L477 Slopen, Beverley. 'Climate, Distance Shape Canada's Writers.' *Publishers Weekly* 215 (5 March 1979): 66
Brief account of F's place in Canadian letters and his views on Canadian writers.

L478 Smith, A.J.M. *Towards a View of Canadian Letters* (Vancouver: Univ of British Columbia Press 1973), 202–4
An assessment of F's contribution to *Literary History of Canada* (D154), which Smith sees as 'accomplished with brilliant success' – though he takes issue with F's statements about evaluation.

L479 Smith, Barbara Herrnstein. 'Contingencies of Value.' *Critical Inquiry* 10 (September 1983): 1–35 [5–8]
Examines F's role in the debate about the proper place of evaluation of literary study during the past fifty years.

L480 Smith, Hallett. 'Myth, Symbol, and Poetry.' *Shakespeare's Romances: A Study of Some Ways of the Imagination* (San Marino, Calif: Huntington Library 1972), 197–209 [199–206]
Criticizes F's reading of Shakespeare's late plays as embodiments of the Proserpina myth, which F sees 'as the most pervasive and fundamental [myth]' in the romances. Claims that F's approach distorts the romances, is reductive, and opposes the facts of the plays.

L481 Smith, Paul. 'Criticism and the Curriculum: Part I.' *College English* 26 (October 1964): 23–30
A proposal for revising the English curriculum. Much of what Smith recommends is rooted in the principles underlying F's own theory, especially the notion of a conceptual order or total coherence in the discipline of criticism.

L482 Sosa, Luis F. Fernández. 'Northrop Frye y unos puemas anagógicos de Lezama Lima.' *Hispania* 61 (December 1978): 877–87
Looks at Lima's poetry from the perspective of the transvaluation implicit in F's concept of the anagogic vision.

L483 Sparshott, Francis. 'Frye in Place.' *Canadian Literature* 83 (Winter 1979): 143–55
Considers F's place in Canadian cultural history and assesses his importance as a critic in general. Sees his importance in the English-speaking world as having redeemed critical theory from the errors of the 'new criticism' by insisting on first principles, and says that even though he has been eclipsed by structuralism in the past decade, he should not have been because he anticipated most of what is important in the recent critical movements. The significance of F in the context of Canadian culture generally is that 'he is without doubt or qualification, a world figure.' More specifically, his significance in Canadian letters has taken two forms: his annual reviews of Canadian poetry in the 1950s and his influence on a younger generation of critics and poets. Speaks of F's role in Canada's

public life; of the relation between his critical theory and his educational
views; of his roots in eastern Canada. Maintains that F's critical theories
are those of a builder rather than a debater. Discovers in F two different
accounts of what literature is: the monistic view, rooted in Blake, Spengler,
and Frazer, of literature as a unified imaginative order, and the pluralistic
view of several different literatures elaborating the central mythology
of culture. Sees the real talent of F's literary imagination as his social
criticism.

L484 — 'The Riddle of *Katharsis*.' *Centre and Labyrinth: Essays in Honour of
Northrop Frye*, ed Eleanor Cook et al (Toronto: Univ of Toronto Press 1983),
14–37
Finds that F's solution to the problem of *katharsis*, like Aristotle's, frustrates
our attempts to understand how the emotional and imaginative transformation in our experience of literature works. Neither critic provides 'a
straightforward and satisfying answer.' Says that F's analysis of the structure of tragedy does not provide an adequate account of either the experience of ordinary playgoers or of the dynamics of social experience.

L485 — *The Structure of Aesthetics* (Toronto: Univ of Toronto Press 1963), passim
Makes frequent references to F's criticism and quotes F on a number of
topics, including aesthetic theories, the nature of criticism, beauty and sub-
limity, Blake, archetypes and anagogy, and genre theory.

L486 Spears, Monroe K. 'The Newer Criticism.' *Shenandoah* 21 (Spring 1970):
110–37. Rpt in Spears, *Dionysus and the City* (New York: Oxford Univ Press
1970), 197–228.
A study of the ways F and Frank Kermode have complemented the New
Criticism. Examines F's debt to Blake and analyses some of the basic
assumptions of *AC*, saying that F's attempt to formulate a progressive and
cumulative science of criticism is 'an outrage to common sense, as is his
postulate that the critic should have nothing to do with evaluation.' Also
says that F 'is a complete irrationalist, whose only articles of faith are
the occult "tradition" and the Imagination.'

L487 Sporn, Paul. 'Empirical Criticism: A Summary and Some Problems.' *Poetic
Theory / Poetic Practice* (Papers of the Midwest Modern Language Asso-
ciation 1), ed Robert Scholes (Iowa City, Iowa: Midwest Modern Language
Association 1969), 16–31 [18–19]
Examines F's argument for a scientific criticism along with arguments of
those making similar claims. Reviews some of the objections raised against
F's view that criticism can become inductive, systematic, and progressive.

L488 Sproxton, Birk E. 'E.J. Pratt as Psychologist, 1919–1920.' *Canadian Notes &
Queries* 14 (November 1974): 7–9
Suggests that F's 'Introduction' to Pratt's *Collected Poems* (D99) 'may have
underestimated the importance of psychology to Pratt's poetic career.'

L489 Staines, David. 'The Holistic Vision of Hugh of Saint Victor.' *Centre and
Labyrinth: Essays in Honour of Northrop Frye*, ed Eleanor Cook et al (Toronto:
Univ of Toronto Press 1983), 147–61

Explores the writings of Hugh of Saint Victor as 'an analogue to and a possible source of Frye's critical vision.'

L490 St Andrews, B.A. 'The Canadian Connection: Frye / Atwood.' *World Literature Today* 60 (Winter 1986): 47–9
Traces the influence of F on both the criticism and fiction of Margaret Atwood, particularly F's account of the way the Canadian sensibility has been shaped by its encounter with the environment.

L491 Steele, James. 'The Literary Criticism of Margaret Atwood.' *Our Own House*, ed Paul Cappon (Toronto: McClelland and Stewart 1978), 73–81 [77–80]
Argues that Atwood's criticism follows the idealism and liberalism in F's critical theory even though on the surface she appears to be a crusader for radical change. Sees Atwood as blending together F's archetypal categories and the psychological categories of Eric Berne, both of which are said to be 'static, ahistorical, abstract and one-dimensional categories of understanding.'

L492 Stendahl, Krister. 'The Bible as a Classic and the Bible as Holy Scripture.' *Journal of Biblical Literature* 103 (March 1984): 3–10 [3, 7–8]
Believes that the kind of literary interpretation of the Bible F provides in GC 'yields significant insights and opens the senses that have been numbed by overly familiar ways of reading,' but that the literary approach ultimately fails because it is the normative element in the Bible, which requires serious attention to original intentions, that makes it into a special kind of classic.

L493 Stephens, Robert O. 'Cable's The *Grandissimes* and the Comedy of Manners.' *American Literature* 51 (January 1980): 507–19
Maintains that F's 'analysis of the comedy of manners is useful for noting the conventions of the genre as they apply to' Cable's work.

L494 Stevens, Peter. 'The Writing of the Decade: Criticism.' *Canadian Literature* 41 (Summer 1969): 131–8 [133–5]. Rpt as 'Criticism,' in *The Sixties: Canadian Writers and Writing of the Decade*, ed George Woodcock (Victoria: Univ of British Columbia 1972), 131–8 [133–5].
A summary of F's work. Thinks F's best criticism of an individual author is *NP*. Finds *EI* tainted by 'cultural snobbery,' and says that F's generalizations in *MC*, however provocative, show his lack of comprehension about certain elements of modern culture.

L495 Stevenson, Sarah A. 'Comedy and Tragedy in *Markurells i Wadköping*.' *Edda* 3 (1974): 191–200
Uses F's structural approach to interpret Hjalmar Bergman's novel.

L496 Stevick, Philip. 'Novel and Anatomy: Notes toward an Amplification of Frye.' *Criticism* 10 (Spring 1968): 153–65
A commentary on F's schema for classifying forms of prose fiction. Calls this taxonomy 'the single most significant and influential event in the criticism of prose fiction in the last twenty years.' Is bothered that such an influential reorientation has received so little attention. Analyses and

seeks to amplify F's account of prose forms, especially the novel and the anatomy.

L497 Stingle, Richard. ' "All the Old Levels": Reaney and Frye.' *Essays on Canadian Writing* 24–5 (Winter–Spring 1982–3): 32–62. Rpt in *Approaches to the Work of James Reaney*, ed Stan Dragland (Downsview, Ont: ECW Press 1983), 32–62.

Examines the influence of F upon James Reaney as a student at Victoria College, as a teacher, and as a writer. Contends that Reaney gained especially from F a 'new Romantic interpretation of Christian mythology' and an understanding of the spatial and temporal structure of literary modes. Analyses these structures as they appear in Reaney's *A Suit of Nettles* and *Gyroscope*.

L498 Street, Douglas O. 'An Educational Process for the Imagination: A Retrospective Review of Frye for the Schools.' *CEA Critic* 42 (January 1980): 43–8

An analysis of *Literature: Uses of the Imagination*, a twelve-volume series of textbooks for which F was the consulting editor (B14), and *An Anatomy of Literature*, a college anthology, edited by Robert Foulke and Paul Smith, organized around F's mythopoetic concepts of nature and literature (L170). Outlines the principles upon which the series is based, beginning with the introductory volumes that, along with the final four volumes, illustrate the relationship between the seasonal cycles and their literary counterparts (romance, tragedy, irony, and comedy), and continuing through the volumes that focus upon biblical and classical materials. Believes the series to be 'a product of the highest quality' but questions whether average students and teachers will be able 'to cope with the wealth and complexity' of the material.

L499 Strelka, Joseph P. 'Preface.' *Anagogic Qualities of Literature* (Yearbook of Comparative Criticism, vol 4), ed Joseph P. Strelka (University Park: Pennsylvania State Univ Press 1971), 1–5 [4, 6]

On F's view of anagogy.

L500 — 'Vergleichende Literaturkritik und literarische Symbolik.' *Vergleichende Literaturkritik* (Bern: Francke Verlag 1970), 5–34 [6–13, 21–3]

On F's theory of comparative literature from the point of view of polysemous meaning, his precise formulation of the theoretical problems of comparative literature, and his theory of value-judgments.

L501 Stuewe, Paul. 'Beyond Survival.' *Books in Canada* 12 (February 1983): 7–10

Maintains that F's influential theories of Canadian literature result in thematic criticism of two varieties, sub-literary and meta-literary. The former means that literature must be discussed in non-literary conceptual terms, and the latter that it contains a number of national themes waiting to be identified. These assumptions, as they have been applied by F and his followers (eg, D.G. Jones and Margaret Atwood) have produced 'results that are typically arbitrary and banal.'

L502 Sullivan, Rosemary. 'Northrop Frye: Canadian Mythographer.' *Journal of Commonwealth Literature* 18, no 1 (1983): 1–13

Seeks to determine what Canadian writers have learned from F. Gives
a resumé of his theories and locates his 'interpretive commitment' in the
poetry of Blake: it is rooted in a romantic and idealistic account of human
experience and is a modern version of the 'myth of nostalgia for a lost
unity.' Examines the influence of F's understanding of popular culture
and his theory of narrative as it appears in the works of Margaret Atwood
and Jay Macpherson. Looks also at F's views on Canadian literature and
the way they have influenced Atwood. Finds that Atwood's ironically
displaced use of myth in *Surfacing* leaves the reader 'with the feeling that
the potential of the novel is unrealized,' that Macpherson's poems, which
adhere to F's theories, remain in a distant and self-contained poetic
world, and that F's ideas about Canadian literature are 'profoundly unsa-
tisfying' because they are based upon metaphor rather than upon historical
and cultural analysis.

L503 Surette, Leon. 'Here Is Us: The Topocentrism of Canadian Literary Criticism.' *Canadian Poetry* 10 (Spring–Summer 1982): 44–57
Says that for F Canadian literature is characterized by a 'disharmony
between its inherited European culture and its North American environment.' Places this kind of topocentric criticism in opposition to that of
other Canadian critics (eg, D.G. Jones and R.T. Harrison), who do not
assume a mystical discontinuity between the Canadian imagination and
its European roots.

L504 Sutherland, John. 'Critics on the Defensive.' *Northern Review* 2 (October–
November 1947): 18–23 [20–21]
A critique of F's views on Canadian poetry. Questions whether the qualities
of Canadian poetry F isolates 'are the peculiar possessions of Canadians,'
apparently a reference to F's 'Canada and Its Poetry,' a review of A.J.M.
Smith's *The Book of Canadian Poetry* (D18).

L505 — 'Old Dog Trait – An Extended Analysis.' *Contemporary Verse* 29 (Fall
1949): 17–23
Summarizes and critiques the argument of F's 'Canada and Its Poetry'
(D18). Thinks that the virtue of the essay is 'that it supplies us with the first
precise definition of the native tradition [in Canadian poetry] in a rounded
sense,' but that F's theory does not apply to younger Canadian poets in
the same way it applies to Pratt. Objects, too, that F does not say what the
limitations of the native tradition are and that he devotes little attention
to the issue of poetic technique. Believes that the vigor and vitality of
Canadian poetry is just as important a native quality as the one F isolates,
its 'evocation of stark terror.'

L506 Sutton, Walter. *Modern American Criticism* (Englewood Cliffs, NJ: Prentice-
Hall 1963), 249–59
Reviews the central claims of each of the book's four essays, as well as the
introduction and conclusion. Notes F's affinities with Arnold, and comments on his concern to create a new language for criticism. *AC* 'presents
a coherent discussion remarkable for its treatment of the literary work as

a verbal complex of many meanings.'

L507 Suvin, Darko. *Metamorphoses of Science Fiction: On the Poetics and History of a Literary Genre* (New Haven: Yale Univ Press 1979), 31–5
Considers the usefulness of F's theory of myth as a basis for science-fiction criticism. Finds that F 'has rendered a signal service to poetics by his formal hypothesis,' but that his historical premises are unpersuasive and his several definitions of myth are semantically slippery.

L508 Swinden, Patrick. *An Introduction to Shakespeare's Comedies* (London: Macmillan 1973), 162–4
Gives a brief account of F's symbolic and generic reading of *The Winter's Tale*. Believes there are dangers in F's approach: by making everything fit the pattern, he overlooks important details.

L509 Takayanagi, Shunichi. 'A Chart of Modern Literary Criticism.' *Sophia* 30 (1981): 213–22
In Japanese. Glances briefly at F's theological background and his place in the contemporary developments of literary criticism.

L510 — 'Poetry and Myth.' *Sophia* 26 (Autumn 1977): 3–22 [13–19]. Rpt in Takayanagi's *Seishinshi no naka no Eibungaku* [*English Literature in the Context of Intellectual History*] (Tokyo: Nansosha 1977), 197–216
In Japanese. Examines three of F's books (*AC*, *SM*, and *SeS*) in the context of post-war literary criticism, concentrating on the problem of critical theory, criticism as an independent discipline, and the Arnoldian idea of literature as replacing the Bible in Western culture.

L511 Teeuwissen, W. John. 'The *Anatomy of Criticism* as Parody of Science.' *Southern Humanities Review* 14 (Winter 1980): 31–42
Looks at four possible ways in which *AC* might be considered 'scientific': as science itself, as a formal imitation of science, as a parody of science, and as a total vision of culture that subsumes both science and criticism. Sees *AC* with its emphasis on process rather than pure form, to be a kind of ironic form of science. Despite the similarities of its methods to those of physics and biology, it remains a parody of science; but in a romantic age it is perhaps the closest we can come to a poetics of experiment and theory.

L512 Thomas, Clara. 'Towards Freedom: The Work of Margaret Laurence and Northrop Frye.' *Essays on Canadian Writing* 30 (Winter 1984–5): 81–95
Points to the similarities between the careers of F and Laurence: both have church-centred, Canadian Protestant backgrounds and both 'share two basic literary sources for their work, the Bible and Milton.' Finds in Laurence's fiction the same basic narrative pattern from creation to apocalypse that F finds in the Bible. 'Margaret Laurence and Northrop Frye move towards the same goal and ... they move from an identical and enduring belief in the kernel of aspiration, of possibility in every human being.'

L513 — 'Towards Freedom: The Work of Northrop Frye.' *CEA Critic* 42 (November 1979): 7–11
Outlines the important role played by F in helping criticism of Canadian

literature to come of age. Sees this as having been accomplished through his teaching of those who later became teachers, his contributions to the 'Letters in Canada' surveys in the *University of Toronto Quarterly* (1950–9), and his 'Conclusion' to *Literary History of Canada* (D154). Notes the influence that the themes and metaphors F uses to talk about Canadian literature and culture have had in the works of such critics as Douglas Jones, Margaret Atwood, Dick Harrison, and James Reaney.

L514 Thomas, Greg, and Ian Clark. 'The Garrison Mentality and the Canadian West: The British Canadian Response to Two Landscapes: The Fur Trade Post and the Ontarian Prairie Homestead.' *Prairie Forum* 4, no 1 (1979): 83–104
    Applies F's idea of the garrison mentality to the settlements built by two groups during the eighteenth and nineteenth centuries: the fur traders and the British-Canadian farm settlers in Western Canada.

L515 Thompson, Ewa M. 'Structuralism: Some Possibilities and Limitations.' *Southern Humanities Review* 7 (Summer 1973): 247–60 [248–9, 256–7]
    A brief look at F's work in the context of the structuralist movement.

L516 Tillyard, E.M.W. *Shakespeare's Early Comedies* (New York: Barnes & Noble; London: Chatto & Windus 1965), 27–31
    Sees F's approach to Shakespeare's comedies in *AC* as representing, along with the work of Janet Spens and C.L. Barber, the anthropological approach. Does not find F's theory of comedy to be convincing.

L517 Todorov, Tzvetan. 'Critique de Frye' and 'Frye et les principes structuralistes.' *Introduction à la littérature fantastique* (Paris: Editions du Seuil 1970), 13–27; *The Fantastic: A Structural Approach to a Literary Genre*, trans Richard Howard (Cleveland: Press of Case Western Reserve Univ 1973), 8–23
    Argues that F's 'modes' are abstract, theoretical genres, and thus not altogether satisfactory. Believes that an adequate modal and generic theory must give more emphasis than F does to the practical, empirical order – that it should work back and forth between the historical and the theoretical.

L518 — 'Meaning in Literature: A Survey.' *Poetics* 1 (1971): 8–15 [11, 14–15]
    Finds F's four levels of medieval exegesis to be inadequate: 'The four meanings are postulated in advance, and any utterance appears to be as ambiguous as any other.' Also speaks of the similarity between the language of F, on the one hand, and that of the Russian formalists and Czech structuralists, on the other: both speak of the same distinctive features in poetic discourse: 'linguistic signs stop being transparent instruments of communication or understanding and they acquire an importance in themselves.'

L519 — 'The Notion of Literature.' *New Literary History* 5 (Autumn 1973): 5–16 [12–14]
    Examines F's distinction between the literary and non-literary uses of language as a basis for defining literature. Finds that F combines two defi-

nitions of literature (opaqueness and fictionality) and that his discussion
has not proceeded 'beyond the stage of vagueness and imprecision.'

L520 — 'Préface' to *Le Grand Code: La Bible et la littérature*, trans Catherine
Malamoud (Paris: Editions du Seuil 1984), 5–20 (A19g)
Serves as a preface to F's literary theory rather than to *GC* and is more
an evaluation than an introduction. Points to F's New Critical roots; to the
similarities and differences between his work and that of the structuralists;
to his views on value-judgments; and to his social and cultural criticism,
especially in *CP*. Believes that F has difficulty deciding whether criticism
should treat literature as an aesthetic object or as part of a culture's
social mythology.

L521 Trousdale, M.S. 'Semiotics and Shakespeare's Comedies.' *Shakespearean
Comedy*, ed Maurice Charney (New York: New York Literary Forum 1980),
245–55
Seeks to illustrate that certain principles in F's theory of comedy can be
translated into semiotic and linguistic terms and that the conventions of
the comedies can be transformed, like the elements of syntax, into other
structures, the elements of the entire system of the comedies being defined
by their differences.

L522 Tucker, Memye Curtis. 'Archetypes and the Analysis of Popular Culture.'
Paper presented at the annual meeting of the Popular Culture Association,
Toronto, 29 March 1984, 11 pp. Unpublished typescript
Uses F's theory of archetypes as a means for understanding the conventions
in a wide range of phenomena in popular culture, including songs,
television shows, fashions, advertisements, and political campaigns.

L523 — 'The Machine as Metaphor in the Critical Theory of Northrop Frye.'
Paper presented at Interface '81: The Fifth Annual Humanities and
Technology Conference, Marietta, Ga, 23 October 1981, 12 pp.
Unpublished typescript
Discusses the symbolism in F's use of the machine as metaphor (life and
death, freedom and bondage, etc.) as a way of illustrating the function
of literature in our time.

L524 — 'Northrop Frye: The Uses of Criticism.' *CEA Critic* 42 (November 1979):
12–17
Recommends that further study of F needs to see his work in its own literary context: the literature he himself has absorbed; the schematic structure
of his thought; the influence of religion, Blake, and the Bible in his writings; and the visual and rhythmic texture of his style. Testifies to the
influence F as a critic and a person has had upon her own work, both
inside and outside the academy.

L525 — 'Northrop Frye's Prophetic Fiction.' Paper presented at the annual
meeting of the South Atlantic Modern Language Association, Atlanta,
Ga, 6 November 1980, 19 pp. Unpublished typescript
Sees the six short stories that F wrote in the 1930s and 1940s as foreshad-
owing the forms described in his later critical writing and as expressing
a revolutionary critical vision. Discovers that the genre of most of these

stories is the Menippean satire and that the primary influence behind them
was Richard Garnett's *The Twilight of the Gods*.

L526 — 'Notes toward an Anatomy of Popular Culture.' Paper presented at
the annual meeting of the South Atlantic Modern Language Association,
Atlanta, Ga, 11 November 1982, 12 pp. Unpublished typescript
Categorizes aspects of popular culture by the archetypal patterns they
express or invoke in order 'to show relationships between highly disparate
phenomena, to suggest the reasons for certain psychological effects,' and
'to clarify the context of popular culture.'

L527 — 'Shakespearean Comedy, *The Great Code*, and the Myth of Deliverance.'
Paper presented at the annual meeting of the South Atlantic Modern
Language Association, Atlanta, Ga, 10 November 1984, 11 pp. Photoduplicated typescript
Sees the myth of deliverance – the narrative pattern leading through death
to new life – as fundamental to Shakespearean comedy, the Bible, and
F's thought. Examines the 'three ways in which the myth of deliverance
functions in Frye's writings: as a descriptive category in his critical system;
as a structure of metaphor and narrative in his writing; and as the content
of his exhortation.'

L528 — 'To Plausibility and Back: Some Uses of Science and Technology in
Popular Culture.' Paper presented at Interface '84: Eighth Annual Humanities and Technology Conference, Marietta, Ga, 26 October 1984. 12 pp.
Unpublished typescript
Uses some observations about plausibility and implausibility in F's theory
of modes to comment on the various ways popular culture uses, often
in a confused way, science and technology.

L529 Underhill, Frank. 'The Academy without Walls.' *Canadian Art* 18 (1961):
299–300
A reply to F's essay, 'Academy without Walls' (D121).

L530 Via, Dan O. *The Parables: Their Literary and Existential Dimension* (Philadelphia: Fortress Press 1967), 70–109 and passim
Uses F's *AC*, especially his theories of modes and myths, to help argue
that the parables of Jesus are genuine aesthetic objects.

L531 Vickers, Brian. *Towards Greek Tragedy: Drama, Myth, Society* (London:
Longman 1973), 29–30, 169–70
On F's concepts of tragedy and myth.

L532 Vickery, John B. 'Literary Criticism and Myth: Anglo-American Critics.'
Literary Criticism and Myth (Yearbook of Comparative Criticism, vol 9),
ed Joseph P. Strelka (University Park: Pennsylvania State Univ Press 1980),
210–37 [218–20]
On the claim of F, among other claimants, that the identification of myth
and literature is not necessary for myth criticism and that myth does
not assert true or false propositions.

L533 Von Hendy, Andrew. 'A Poetics for Demogorgon: Northrop Frye and
Contemporary Criticism.' *Criticism* 8 (Fall 1966): 318–35
An exposition of the romantic assumptions underlying F's poetics. Seeks

to uncover the 'modern' or romantic complex of ideas that provide the
framework for F's literary theory. Discovers a number of these, many of
which are conflicting, or at least potentially contradictory. F's theory, with
its dialectical opposites and its flair for irony, is a reflection of the deep
tensions within nineteenth-century poetics.

L534 Wagner, Geoffrey. 'American Literary Criticism: The Continuing Heresy.'
Southern Review [Australia] 3, no 1 (1968): 82–9
Cites F as one of the American critics who illustrate the superiority of
American to British criticism.

L535 Ware, Martin. 'Review Article: The Canadian Critic's Bible.' *Dalhousie
Review* 55 (Spring 1975): 170–83 [177–81]
Comments on F's understanding of evaluative criticism and on his entire
effort to prepare the foundation for a 'complete cosmology of the literary
universe.' These comments come in a review of A.J.M. Smith's *Towards
a View of Canadian Letters*.

L536 Warning, Ranier. *Funktion und Struktur: Die Ambivalenzen des geistlichen
Spiels* (Munich: Wilhelm Fink 1974), especially 15–25
Broadly adopts the structuralist criticism of F. Sees the medieval drama
as a late expression of archetypal myth associated with religious cult and
Heilsgeschichte.

L537 Wasiolek, Edward. 'Wanted: A New Contextualism.' *Critical Inquiry* 1
(March 1975): 623–39 [623–7]
A critique of F's notions of autonomy and polysemous meaning as being
too narrow and exclusive. Even though F has sought to expand the context
of criticism from the New Critical emphasis on the work itself, Wasiolek
sees him as still within the tradition of the New Criticism because of
his insistence that the conceptual framework of criticism is derivable from
literature itself.

L538 Wasson, Richard. 'From Priest to Prometheus: Culture and Criticism in the
Post-Modern Period.' *Journal of Modern Literature* 3 (July 1974): 1188–1202
[1201–2]
On several models of culture that characterized the criticism of the sixties.
Selects F's work because it provides 'the best working model for literary
critics.' Singles out for special comment F's views on culture, on the
imaginative possibilities of desire, and on 'educating the imagination.'

L539 Watkins, Evan. 'Conflict and Consensus in the History of Recent Criticism.'
New Literary History 12 (Winter 1981): 345–64 [351–5, 357–8]
Sees F's program of literary study as equivocal. On the one hand, he
insists that criticism can be an autonomous, coherent body of principles,
yet one that can 'co-ordinate a multiplicity of specific inquiries within
a coherent framework.' On the other hand, he insists that criticism perform
the central role in democratizing culture. Still, F's emphasis upon 'context'
helped to prepare American criticism for the shock waves of European
thought.

L540 — 'Criticism and Method: Hirsch, Frye, Barthes.' *Soundings* 57 (Summer

1975): 257–80. Rpt in a shorter and somewhat different version in Watkins, *The Critical Act: Criticism and Community* (New Haven: Yale Univ Press 1978), 56–94.

Examines some of the hypothetical bases of F's criticism. Sees the archetype as both a dialectical and a taxonomic principle. Believes that F's work suffers because of the incompatibility of the two: 'The concept of the archetype ... projects an identity which is to efface the necessity for judgment by providing the possibility of a self-regulating system.' Finds Wimsatt's and Todorov's critiques of F's system to be 'cogent' and 'devastating.'

L541 Weber, Samuel. 'The Responsibility of the Critic: A Response.' *MLN* 91 (October 1976): 814–16

A reply to F's essay, 'The Responsibilities of the Critic' (D232). Argues that the critic's responsibility is to the truth of the text.

L542 Webster, Grant. 'American Literary Criticism: A Bibliographical Essay.' *American Studies International* 20 (Autumn 1981): 3–44 [10–12]

Comments on F's work in the context of myth criticism. Gives a brief overview of *AC*. Points to F's influence upon practical criticism, and mentions some of the negative reactions his work has occasioned. F 'is not the Aquinas of a new organized church, but resembles much more the Blake with whom he began in that his system is a personal one.'

L543 — 'The Missionary Criticism of Northrop Frye.' *Southern Review* [Australia] 2, no 2 (1966): 164–9

Argues that F converts his descriptive account of literature into a normative one and thus brings into his criticism the norms he objects to in his plea for objective scholarship. Contends that F is really a religious critic who 'wants to lead us from the imaginative structures of literature to critical faith and mythic doctrine.'

L544 Wegener, Mark. 'Literary Criticism and Biblical Religious Language: Insights from Northrop Frye.' *Currents in Theology and Mission* 12 (April 1985): 100–5

Summarizes F's presuppositions about the Bible and outlines the central categories he uses in discussing it: its language, plot, images, and typological structure. Contrasts F's approach with that of historical and structural critics. Says that the strength of F's theory is that it 'offers the possibility of pushing religious language to its ultimate' and thus may be able to put the authority of the Bible on a firmer foundation.

L545 Weimann, Robert. 'Literarische Wertung und historische Tradition: Zu ihrer Aporie im Werk von Northrop Frye.' *Zeitschrift für Anglistik und Amerikanistik* 21 (1973): 341–59

Argues that the meaning and influence of F's work cannot be understood simply in terms of his originality and breadth. One has to look at it in the wider context of the crisis of consciousness in twentieth-century formal criticism. In seeking to provide a new humanistic role for the critic, F has abandoned the traditional evaluator's role and has rejected both Eliot's belief in classical absolutes and the New Critics' pure aestheticism. Yet his neutrality is at odds with his effort to restore the romantic's reputation, a dilemma that comes through clearly in his most recent writings. The real separation in F's work is between aesthetics and critical knowledge, on the one hand, and value, history, and action, on the other.

L546 — 'Literaturkritik als historisch-mythologisches System: Northrop Frye und die Krise der Literaturgeschichte.' *Literaturgeschichte und Mythologie: Methodologische und historische Studien.* 3rd ed (Berlin und Weimar: Aufbau-Verlag 1974), 342–63 and passim. (Some paragraphs from this chapter appeared previously in 'Northrop Frye und das Ende des New Criticism,' L547.)

Argues that F, like the historians of ideas, abstracts from the living stream of history by sacrificing literary history to mythology. Sees Frye as divorcing the cognitive and evaluative aspects of literary scholarship by remaining at the level of myth and symbol.

L547 — 'Northrop Frye und das Ende des New Criticism.' *Sinn und Form: Beiträge zur Literatur* 17 (1965): 621–30

Places F's work in the context of the New Criticism. Sees F as participating in the final stages of this movement, now being replaced by newer critical voices. 'An objective view of the most recent trends in literary criticism in the United States leaves no doubt that Frye's dependence on the New Critics is itself already history and resulted from the ideological influence of the recent past.'

L548 — *Structure and Society in Literary History: Studies in the History and Theory of Literary History* (Charlottesville: Univ Press of Virginia 1976), 15–16, 142–5

Says F's neo-romantic criticism has failed 'in working out a new historical vocation for criticism. Frye's advocacy of the romantic tradition cannot revive the revolutionary and prophetic functions of literature in the present.'

L549 Wellek, René. 'American Criticism of the Last Ten Years.' *Yearbook of Comparative and General Literature* 20 (1971): 5–14 [8–9]. Rpt as 'Of the Last Ten Years' in *Amerikanische Literatur in 20 Jahrhundert,* ed Alfred Weber and Dietmar Haack (Göttingen: Vanderhoeck & Ruprecht 1972), 13–28; and as 'American Criticism of the Sixties' in Wellek, *The Attack on Literature and Other Essays* (Chapel Hill: Univ of North Carolina Press 1982), 104–18 [108–10].

An account of F's status as the most influential myth critic. Says F's 'most attractive writings' are his books on Shakespeare and Milton. Considers briefly the work of his 'more or less orthodox followers': Angus Fletcher, Harold Bloom, Robert Scholes, and Robert Kellogg.

L550 — 'Philosophy and Postwar American Criticism.' *Concepts of Criticism* (New Haven: Yale Univ Press 1963), 316–43 [337–8]. Rpt in *Comparative Literature: Matter and Method,* ed E. Owen Aldridge (Urbana: Univ of Illinois Press 1969), 9–23 [20].

A brief account of F's place in contemporary criticism. Sees him as a 'sensitive reader and ingenious theorist,' yet concludes that his criticism has 'over-reached itself' and that his speculations are 'completely uncontrollable.'

L551 — 'The Poet as Critic, the Critic as Poet, the Poet-Critic.' *Discriminations: Further Concepts of Criticism* (New Haven: Yale Univ Press 1970), 253–74 [257–8]
Calls F a 'creative' or 'fictional' critic who builds a 'dream universe.' Claims that he 'spins his fancies in total disregard of the text and even builds fictional universes … His criticism is an elaborate fiction which loses all relation to knowledge, science, and concept.'

L552 Welsh, Andrew. *Roots of the Lyric: Primitive Poetry and Modern Poetics* (Princeton, NJ: Princeton Univ Press 1978), 18–22
On F's theory of the 'radicals' of lyric poetry: *melos*, *opsis*, and *lexis*.

L553 Westbrook, Max. 'Riders of Judgment: An Exercise in Ontological Criticism.' *Western American Literature* 12 (May 1977): 41–51 [41–2]
Argues that the practice of an archetypal criticism based upon F's theory needs more philosophical awareness if it is to get beyond thematic studies that match one version of an archetype with another.

L554 Weston, Elizabeth. *Survey: A Short History of Canadian Literature* (Toronto: Methuen 1973), 146–7
An account of the influence of F's theory of myths on Canadian poetry.

L555 Whatley, Janet. '*La Double Inconstance*: Marivaux and the Comedy of Manipulation.' *Eighteenth-Century Studies* 10 (Spring 1977): 335–50
Applies F's theory of comedy in interpreting the novelty of Marivaux's comic vision in *La Double Inconstance*.

L556 Wheeler, Richard P. *Shakespeare's Development and the Problem Comedies: Turn and Counter-Turn* (Berkeley: Univ of California Press 1981), 22–5, 45–9
On F's effort to divorce biographical from critical considerations and on his interpretation of *All's Well That Ends Well* in 'The Argument of Comedy' (D39).

L557 White, David. 'Northrop Frye: Value and System.' *Criticism* 15 (Summer 1973): 189–211
Looks at some of the philosophical problems in F's work. Surveys a number of the criticisms directed against him (by Whalley, Spears, Casey, Hallie, Abrams, Wellek, Kermode, Adams, Holloway, et al), but finds most of them beside the point because of their emphasis on the 'purely ideational development of critical knowledge.' Would like *AC* to be extended at some future date to include an anatomy of critical experience.

L558 White, Hayden. 'The Fictions of Factual Representation.' *The Literature of Fact: Selected Papers from the English Institute*, ed Angus Fletcher (New York: Columbia Univ Press 1976), 21–44 [31]
Comments on the usefulness of F's concepts of archetype and displacement for understanding history and the philosophy of history.

L559 — 'Getting out of History.' *Diacritics* 12 (Fall 1982): 2–13. Rpt in *Contemporary Literary Criticism: Modernism through Post-structuralism*, ed Robert Con Davis (New York: Longman 1986), 146–60 [148–9]

Sees Frederic Jameson's work as an effort to compose a Marxist version of
F's *AC*. Glances briefly at Jameson's appropriation of F.

L560 — 'The Historical Text as Literary Artifact.' *Clio* 3 (June 1974): 277–303
[278–81]. Rpt in *The Writing of History: Literary Form and Historical Understanding*, ed Robert H. Canary and Henry Kozicki (Madison: Univ of
Wisconsin Press 1978), 41–62 [45–7].
Analyses F's distinction among myth, history, and fiction. Argues, in
opposition to F, that history is no less history because of its fictional
elements, particularly the kinds of plot structures its writers use.

L561 — 'Interpretation in History.' *New Literary History* 4 (Winter 1973): 281–314
[290–6]
An analysis of F's conception of historiography. Points out that although
F is aware of the important differences between poetry and history he
is also sensitive to the ways they resemble each other. Extends F's ideas to
argue that interpretation in history depends on these resemblances: the
patterns of meaning, the story forms, the pre-generic plot structures, the
conceptualized myths that historians built into their narratives. Believes
that F's distinctions are a useful 'way of identifying the specifically "fictive"
element' in historical accounts of the world.

L562 — *Metahistory* (Baltimore: Johns Hopkins Univ Press 1973), 7–11, 231–3
Draws upon F's theory of myths in order to identify four different modes
of emplotment. Uses the modes as part of his framework for analysing
the work of nineteenth-century historians.

L563 — 'The Structure of Historical Narrative.' *Clio* 1 (June 1972): 5–20
In examining the relationship between story and different kinds of narrative
history, uses F's concept of plot, or pre-generic narrative patterns.

L564 Wiebe, Donald. 'The "Centripetal Theology" of *The Great Code*.' *Toronto
Journal of Theology* 1 (Spring 1985): 122–7
Sees F's argument about the predominantly centripetal patterns of thought
in the Bible as a metatheology that should be of great interest to theologians. His metatheology is implicit in his understanding of the nature and
function of Biblical language, which focuses on the life of the individual
and community rather than upon physical, historical, or metaphysical
issues. Believes that looking for the meaning of God within the context
of language and myth 'may be the only adequate way for doing theology
today.'

L565 Wienold, Götz. *Formulierungstheorie – Poetik – Strukturelle Literaturgeschichte*
(Frankfurt am Main: Athenäum 1971), 27, 29
Comments on the opposition in F's work between genetic literary forms
(archetypes, rituals, myths, oracles) and the social, engaged, communicative
function of literature.

L566 Wilders, John. 'Shakespeare: His Comedies.' *English Drama to 1710*, ed
Christopher Ricks (London: Barrie & Jenkins 1971), 200–214 [202–6]
Observes that the 'most relevant theories of [Shakespearean] comedy'
are those of F and Susanne Langer, which emphasize the structure of

the plays. Summarizes F's view of comic structure.

L567 Willard, Abbie. *Wallace Stevens: The Poet and His Critics* (Chicago: American
Library Association 1978), 204–5, 214
Gives abstracts of F's two essays on Stevens, 'The Realistic Oriole' (D89)
and 'Wallace Stevens and the Variation Form' (D218). Observes that in the
first essay F's approach to Stevens by way of metaphor, though interesting, fails to account for the tension in Stevens's tropes. Sees the second
essay as an accurate account of the interplay between reality and imagination in Stevens's poetry.

L568 W[illeford], W[illiam]. 'Myth Criticism.' *Princeton Encyclopedia of Poetry and
Poetics*. Enlarged ed, ed Alex Preminger (Princeton, NJ: Princeton Univ
Press 1974), 955–8 [956–7]
Gives a brief account of the contribution of F, among others, to myth
criticism. Summarizes the four essays of *AC*. Sees F's 'immense appeal'
as lying, first, in the heuristic strength of his viewpoint and, second, in
its 'insistence on the derivation of literature from myth, not simply as
"poetry" but as a fundamental way of apprehending the world.'

L569 Williamson, Eugene. 'Plato's *Eidos* and the Archetypes of Jung and Frye.'
Interpretations 16 (Fall 1985): 94–104
Examines the similarities and differences among Plato's theory of ideas,
Jung's archetype-as-such, and F's literary archetypes. Concludes that
the three differ widely in the range of their reference, F's being the most
limited; that F's archetypes have no metaphysical sanction; and that F
has paid little attention to the similarities between his conception of the
archetype and Jung's, apparently because he wants to preserve the autonomy of criticism.

L570 Wimsatt, W.K., Jr. 'The Horses of Wrath: Recent Critical Lessons.' *Essays
in Criticism* 12 (January 1962): 1–17 [5–8]. Rpt in an expanded form in
Wimsatt, *Hateful Contraries: Studies in Literature and Criticism* (Lexington:
Univ of Kentucky Press 1966), 3–48 [17–20].
A survey of recent critical trends in which F comes under discussion as
one of the mythopoeic critics. Objects to F's separation of criticism and
evaluation and to his proliferation of critical categories.

L571 — 'Northrop Frye: Criticism as Myth.' *Northrop Frye in Modern Criticism*,
ed Murray Krieger (New York: Columbia Univ Press 1966), 75–107. Rpt in
Wimsatt, *Day of the Leopards: Essays in Defense of Poems* (New Haven: Yale
Univ Press 1976), 74–96; partially rpt in *Contemporary Literary Criticism*,
vol 24, ed Sharon R. Gunton (Detroit: Gale Research, 1983), 214–16.
A dissenting view about F's criticism. Objects that F's shifting categories
lead to inconsistency, that his centring on the literary relations between
works of art separates art from the rest of life, and that his archetypal
interests cheat the individual work of its uniqueness.

L572 Wimsatt, W.K., Jr, and Cleanth Brooks. 'Myth and Archetype.' *Literary
Criticism: A Short History* (New York: Knopf 1957), 709–11, 714
A brief analysis of one of F's early essays, 'The Archetypes of Literature'

(D49). Discuss F's assimilation of poetry and myth and his effort to make criticism like a social science.

L573 Wimsatt, W.K., Jr, and Monroe Beardsley. 'The Concept of Meter.' PMLA 74 (1959). Rpt in Wimsatt, *Hateful Contraries: Studies in Literature and Criticism* (Lexington: Univ of Kentucky Press 1966), 108–45 [112–14, 122, 128–9].
An examination of F's concept of metre, as presented in the Fourth Essay of *AC*. Take issue with F's musical theory of metrics and to his idea that the four-stress metre is the inherent pattern in English verse.

L574 Wollheim, Richard. *Art and Its Objects: An Introduction to Aesthetics* (New York: Harper & Row 1968), 59–61
An account of F's concept of the 'radical of presentation' as one of the essential defining characteristics of genre. Reviews what F means by saying that the interpretation of generic conventions depends upon the conditions established between the poet and his public. Believes that F's argument is one 'of extreme ingenuity' and that the radical of presentation strongly suggests that generic classification is intrinsic to literary understanding.

L575 Woodcock, George. 'Art versus Culture.' *Queen's Quarterly* 88 (Winter 1981): 672–8 [673–4]
A review of *The Arts in Canada*, which is keynoted by F's essay, 'Across the River and out of the Trees' (D256). Refers to F's rejection of the equating of political and cultural values and uses his attack on strident nationalist rhetoric as a touchstone for analysing the politics of culture.

L576 — 'Away from Lost Worlds: Notes on the Development of a Canadian Literature.' *Odysseus Ever Returning: Essays on Canadian Writers and Writing* (Toronto: McClelland and Stewart 1970), 1–11 [2, 9]. Rpt in *Readings in Commonwealth Literature*, ed William Walsh (Oxford: Clarendon Press 1973), 209–20 [210, 218].
On F's influence on the poetry of James Reaney, Jay Macpherson, and Eli Mandel. On F's influence as a critic, see *Odysseus Ever Returning*, pp 134, 141, 143, 151.

L577 — 'Diana's Priest in the Bush Garden.' *boundary 2*, 3 (Fall 1974): 185–96. Rpt in Woodcock, *The World of Canadian Writing: Critiques and Recollections* (Vancouver: Douglas & McIntyre 1980), 222–34.
Claims that F's isolation from the world of letters is a result of his loyalty to the academy and his creation of critical works that are themselves autonomous structures of the imagination. But despite his withdrawal, F has gained considerable fame outside the academic world because he is a 'public' critic of Canadian literature and a creative critic. This latter is especially linked to his interest in Frazer, whose work is similar.

L578 — 'Frye, Northrop.' *Oxford Companion to Canadian Literature*, gen ed William Toye (Toronto: Oxford Univ Press 1983), 282–4
Gives a biographical sketch and reviews the several roles F has played both inside and outside the university: teacher, scholar, administrator, reviewer, lecturer, and public critic. Glances at F's critiques of Canadian literature and culture, and reviews his major works: *FS*, *AC*, and *GC*.

'These works are without doubt Frye's masterpieces, monumentally self-contained and self-consistent in their systematization of literary and cultural history.'

L579 — 'Frye, Northrop.' *Supplement to the Oxford Companion to Canadian History and Literature*, ed William Toye (Toronto: Oxford Univ Press 1973), 107–8
A short survey of F's main achievements as editor, literary theorist, lecturer, and practical critic. 'Canada's most significant critic.'

L580 — 'The Lure of the Primitive.' *American Scholar* 45 (Summer 1976): 387–404 [397–8]
Studies the renewed interest in the primitive as represented in F's lecture, 'Sir James Frazer' (D109), which illustrates that F seeks 'manifestations of myth that are appropriate to the literary traditions he is discussing.'

L581 — 'Romanticism: Studies and Speculations.' *Sewanee Review* 88 (Spring 1980): 298–307 [300–1]
Sees in F's work the 'logical conclusions of Wilde's doctrine of the critic as artist' – a movement away from the intention of the creative persona toward the structure of a critical vision as important in itself.

L582 Workman, Mark E. 'The Role of Mythology in Modern Literature.' *Journal of the Folklore Institute* 18 (January–April 1981): 35–48
Applies F's analysis of mythic structures and images to works by Joyce, Hesse, Polanski, Hamsun, and Pynchon in an effort to account for the presence of myth in modern literature.

L583 Yamanouchi, Hisaaki. 'Frye's Criticism in England.' *Eigo bungaku sekai* [*The English Literary World*] 11 (February 1969): 7–9
In Japanese.

L584 — 'Introduction.' *Hihyo no kaibo*, trans Hiroshi Ebine et al (Tokyo: Hosei Univ Press 1980), 515–27 (A2k)
In Japanese.

L585 Yamoto, Sadamoto. 'Myth and Archetype.' *Eigo seinen* [*The Rising Generation*] 117 (October 1971): 42–4
In Japanese.

L586 — 'Northrop Frye: Schemata of Myth Criticism.' *Eigo seinen* [*The Rising Generation*] 116 (September–November 1970): 9–10, 17–19, 22–3. Incorporated into Yamoto, *Literary Criticism as Teaching* (Tokyo: Kenkyu-sha 1974).
In Japanese.

L587 Youngren, William. 'What Is Literary Theory?' *Hudson Review* 26 (Autumn 1973): 562–71 [563–4]
Brief remarks on F's essay 'The Critical Path' (D200), which is found to be well-written and entertaining, even though it tends to celebrate its own terminology.

L588 Zis, Avner Iakovlevich. 'Marksisto-leninskaia teoriaa iskusstva i ee burzhuaznye kritiki.' *Voprosy filosofii* 12 (1980): 148–59. Rpt as 'The Marxist-Leninist Theory of Art and Its Bourgeois Critics.' *Soviet Studies in Philosophy* 20 (Summer 1981): 83–104 [92–3].
Maintains that although Marxist aesthetics does not deny the importance

of myth in the history of culture, 'to reduce all creation in art to myth-making, as is done, for example, by Northrop Frye, leads away from an understanding of the objective foundations of artistic creation' and away from the social content of art. Myth, rather, is best understood in terms of Lenin's theory of reflection.

M

Reviews

M1 **Anatomy of Criticism** (*AC*) [A2]

M1.1 Abrams, Meyer H. 'Anatomy of Criticism.' *University of Toronto Quarterly* 28 (January 1959): 190–6. Partially rpt in *Contemporary Literary Criticism*, vol 24, ed Sharon R. Gunton (Detroit: Gale Research 1983), 209–11. 3350 w
Sees F's book in the tradition of Kames, Coleridge, Richards, and others who have reformulated 'literary theory from first principles, in order to accommodate existing materials to new concepts.' In F's case the new concepts come from psychology, anthropological theories of myth and ritual, and medieval symbology. Raises questions about F's synoptic systems of classification (are the forms he discovers artefacts of his own conceptual scheme?), his wanting to purge value-judgments from criticism, and his use of the medieval scheme of levels of meaning. Says that the archetypal level of interpretation presents the most troublesome problems:

the patterns F discovers by his method of analogy are neither provable
nor disprovable. Judges *AC* to be resourceful wit-criticism, more metaphysical than scientific.

M1.2 Adams, Hazard. 'Criticism: Whence and Whither?' *American Scholar* 28
(Spring 1959): 226, 228, 232, 234, 238 [232, 238]. 700 w
Praises *AC* for returning criticism to literature while at the same time
insisting on theory. Sees the book as completing the critical work of the
1930s and 1940s.

M1.3 — *Journal of Aesthetics and Art Criticism* 16 (June 1958): 533–4. 1000 w
Examines primarily the principal assumptions in the 'Polemical
Introduction.'

M1.4 Adams, Robert Martin. 'Dreadful Symmetry.' *Hudson Review* 10 (Winter
1957–8): 614–19. 2400 w
Believes that *AC* is 'a brilliantly suggestive and encyclopedically erudite
book,' 'a stimulating and agile production,' but remains sceptical about its
usefulness. Thinks that literary criticism does not need the kind of conceptual universe F proposes. F's search for conceptual unity leads to 'exagge-
rated, strained, and confused interpretations of literary fact,' it ignores
questions of value, and it disregards the rules of literary evidence.

M1.5 Akasofu, Tetsuji. *Tokyo University Newspaper* 2357 (14 July 1980)
Review of the Japanese translation (A2k). In Japanese.

M1.6 Anderson, G.L. *Seventeenth-Century News* 16 (Summer 1958): 17–18. 660 w
Applauds *AC* as a 'monumental work' ('Aristotle's *Poetics*, new style').
Praises its judicious understanding of modern criticism, its style, its going
beyond the bounds of Western literature, and its removing matters of
taste from the structure of criticism.

M1.7 Anonymous. *The Asahi*, 28 July 1980, Book Review section.
Review of the Japanese translation (A2k). In Japanese.

M1.8 — *Bulletin critique du livre français* 291 (March 1970): 251
Brief review of the French translation (A2c).

M1.9 — *Burgenländisches Volksblatt* [Eisenstadt], 6 February 1965
Brief review of the German translation (A2a).

M1.10 — *Freiheit* [Ramat-Gan, Israel], 25 September 1964
Brief notice of the German translation (A2a).

M1.11 — 'Literary Dissection.' *TLS* 2920 (14 February 1958): 1–2. 1300 w
Summarizes the central arguments of each section of the book. Finds *AC*
an impressive and stimulating contribution to the issues of critical theory.
Believes, however, that the book remains on too abstract a level, the
theory becoming almost an end in itself, and that F 'makes too little allow-
ance for the pervasive part played by judgments of value in all critical
perception.'

M1.12 — *Neuer Bücherdienst* [Vienna] 1 (March 1965)
Brief notice of the German translation (A2a).

M1.13 — *Südwestfunk* [Baden Baden], 2 September 1965. 400 w
Transcription of a radio review of the German translation (A2a). Says that

the specialized terminology and complex taxonomies make the book unnecessarily difficult, yet it deserves 'our undivided attention because it contains nothing less than a comprehensive poetics of world literature.'

M1.14 — *Theatergemeinde Bochum E.V. Bochum* 8 (1965–6)
Brief notice of the German translation (A2a)

M1.15 — *Welt der Bücher* [Freiburg] 6 (1966). 575 w
Review of the German translation (A2a). Claims that F's criticism has no practical value and that it is carried to theoretical extremes. Worries that F has bracketed out the question of literary experience.

M1.16 — *Zeitschrift für denkende junge Menschen* [Vienna] 9/10 (1965)
Brief notice of the German translation (A2a).

M1.17 B., O. *National-Zeitung* [Basel] 519 (9 November 1964). 450 w
Review of the German translation (A2a). Calls attention to the separation in *AC* between the direct experience of literature and the critical knowledge of that experience, and to the way F's terminology expresses this knowledge.

M1.18 Bannon, Barbara. *Publishers Weekly* 189 (3 January 1966): 72
Brief notice about the appearance of the Atheneum edition (A2b).

M1.19 Baum, Paull F. *South Atlantic Quarterly* 57 (Winter 1958): 140–1. 480 w
Gives an overview of the subject matter of *AC* and describes F's pluralistic aim. The 'best things in the book … are his observations along the way on individual artists and individual works.'

M1.20 Beaujean, Marion. *Buchanzeiger für Öffentliche Büchereien* [Reutlingen], June 1966
Brief notice of the German translation (A2a).

M1.21 — *Bücherei and Bildung* [Reutlingen] 6 (1966). 230 w
Review of the German translation (A2a). Distinguishes F's systematic method from the typical approach of the professional German reviewers.

M1.22 B[eebe], M[aurice]. *Modern Fiction Studies* 3 (Winter 1957–8): 366. 75 w
Comments briefly on F's theory of prose fiction in *AC*, which 'does a better job of separating fiction from other types of literature than most critics do.'

M1.23 Blankenberg, Lutz. *Die Büchkommentare* [Berlin] 4 (November 1964)
Brief notice of the German translation (A2a).

M1.24 Bloom, Harold. *Yale Review* 47 (September 1957): 130–3. 1260 w
Identifies F's critical forbears as Ruskin, Blake, and the Platonic tradition. 'The major value in Frye's *Anatomy* is constructive; a Poetics which is complete, sane, and honestly discursive … The minor value is descriptive, and equally relevant: a clear introduction to the structural principles of literature is now available.' Compares *AC* to Tovey's account of the structural principles of music, though unlike Tovey, F 'has had to work alone.' Summarizes the book's four essays. Believes, finally, that in his synoptic aim F tries too hard to be a reconciler, thus denying the 'real differences between almost all fashionable criticism and his own theories.'

M1.25 Burke, Fidelian. *Literature East & West* 5 (Summer 1958): 13–14. 950 w
Summarizes briefly the four essays of *AC*. Sees the book essentially as a

study of genre – 'a highly articulated schematization, by turns brilliant and baffling.' Despite the richness and diversity of F's treatment, he has a 'rather cavalier approach to terminology,' tends to argue in a priori fashion, and confuses historical and theoretical interpretation.

M1.26 Burke, Kenneth. 'The Encyclopaedic, Two Kinds of.' *Poetry* 91 (February 1958): 320–8 [324–8]. 1300 w
Isolates F's conceptions of mode, symbol, and archetype for special commentary. Finds F's special vocabulary somewhat discomfiting, though at the same time it reveals an exceptional personality. Observes that F's taxonomies are more 'like a sliding scale than a fixed system of differentiation.'

M1.27 Busch, Günther. 'Anatomie der Literaturkritik.' *Neues Forum* 14 (February 1967): 186–7. 1350 w
Review of the German translation (A2a). Compares and contrasts *AC* with the work of Ernst Robert Curtius: their methods, the conceptual-theoretical and the philological-historical respectively, are quite different, but they both assume a connection between critical ideas across national borders and epochs. Warns that F sometimes over-complicates his ideas and terminology, that he pays too little attention to historical phenomena, and that his view of the autonomy of criticism is suspect. But praises the book for its conceptual power and enlightening perceptions.

M1.28 Cardwell, Guy. *Key Reporter* 23 (July 1958): 7. 110 w
Believes *AC* is one of the half dozen volumes of literary criticism that will be read a half century later.

M1.29 Carrier, Giles. 'La critique est-elle une science?' *Etudes Françaises* [Montreal] 6 (May 1970): 221–6. 1750 w
Review of the French translation (A2c). Places F's critical project in the context of other recent efforts in literary theory, from Eliot and Pound to Bachelard, Wellek, and Warren. Sees Aristotle as F's primary influence. Summarizes each of the four essays in the book. Remarks that throughout F displays a flexible and novel method, specifically different from that of the other human sciences.

M1.30 Celati, Gianni. 'Anatomie e sistematiche letterarie.' *Libri Nuovi*, August 1969, 5. 1600 w
Review of the Italian translation (A2d). Argues that F's method inevitably becomes involved with the model of literary myth and ritual that his criticism begins with. Sees the method as too exclusive and not altogether different from the deductive approaches F dismisses as remnants of nineteenth-century determinism.

M1.31 Chvojka, Erwin. *Neue Wege* [Vienna] 222 (1967)
Brief review of the German translation (A2a).

M1.32 Clapp, Edwin R. *Western Humanities Review* 13 (Winter 1959): 109–12. 2150 w
Contrasts *AC* with Wimsatt and Brooks's *Literary Criticism: A Short History*. Finds F's 'inexhaustible schematism' to be esoteric and arbitrary, though his

illustrations are ingenious and fertile and his insights authentic. Still,
wishes his argument were less dense.

M1.33 Corke, Hillary. 'Sweeping the Interpreter's House.' *Encounter* 10 (February
1958): 79–82. 1500 w
Judges *AC* to be 'one of the turning points of which no art or science can
expect to boast more than two or three or four in a century.' Praises
the book for its prose and for its heroic effort to provide criticism with a
proper vocabulary for its categories.

M1.34 Daiches, David. *Modern Philology* 56 (August 1958): 69–72. 2360 w
Gives a fairly detailed overview of F's approach and 'habit of mind' and
summarizes the central principles of the book's four essays. Finds the book
to be brilliant because of its originality, learning, and wit, and provocative
because of its 'challenge to all modern ways of thinking about criticism.'
Judges F's method to be inevitably reductive but *AC* 'is the rare kind of
book that the reader must come to terms with, even if it takes him the
rest of his life.'

M1.35 Demetz, Peter. 'Heilsam durch milde Gifte: Zu Northrop Fryes Kritischer
Poetik.' *Die Zeit*, 18 September 1964, 7. 1500 w
Review of the German translation (A2a). Contrasts F's concerns with those
of German criticism, where the emphasis is upon the Hegelianism of
Adorno and Lukács, existentialism, and the non-formal concerns of Staiger.
Calls F a 'Romantic' theorist: he says that everything is potentially identical
with everything else, and herein lies the danger of his criticism becoming
borderless. Even more problematic are F's views on value-judgments. Still,
his book contains some powerful correctives for German criticism and
his phenomenology of comedy is unsurpassed for the insights it provides.

M1.36 Dorsch, T.S. *Year's Work in English Studies* 37 (1960): 12. 350 w
Chiefly a summary of the book's content.

M1.37 Douglas, Wallace. *College English* 19 (March 1958): 279–80. 600 w
Looks primarily at F's assumptions about criticism set down in the 'Polemical Introduction.' Is puzzled by F's analysis of literary quality and says
that the archetypal approach seems only to yield 'reductive generalities.'

M1.38 Friedman, Melvin J. *Books Abroad* 32 (Autumn 1958): 451–2. 350 w
Says that F's method is like Arnold's in that it wanders freely about its
subject. Applauds F's effort to raise literary criticism to a structure of
thought in its own right and to clarify the subject of genre.

M1.39 Frise, Dr. 'Kulturelles Wort.' Broadcast on Hessischer Rundfunk [Frankfurt]
on 10 February 1965. 7-p typescript. 550 w
Review of the German translation (A2a). Argues that F's strength is not in
his scientism but in his comparative experiments. Worries, however,
that *AC* has little to do with history and society.

M1.40 Grenzmann, Wilhelm. 'Der Zustand der Literaturkritik.' *Echo der Zeit*
[Recklinghausen] 18 April 1969. 1400 w
Review of the German translation (A2a). Sees F's book as helping to cure
the poor health of literary criticism by leading literary scholarship one

step further. Says that his method is unparalleled in Germany or anywhere else in Europe. Summarizes the basic arguments of the four chapters in the book. Claims that *AC* 'will be seen in America as one of the greatest literary accomplishments in recent years.'

M1.41 Hallie, Philip. 'The Master Builder.' *Partisan Review* 31 (Fall 1964): 650–1. 2600 w

Examines primarily the system in *AC*, which is found to be 'made up of inpenetrable paradox, profound incoherence, and a bold but ultimately arbitrary disregard for the facts of literary experience.'

M1.42 Herman-Sekulič, Maja. 'Jedno dugo iščekivanje.' *Kultura* [Belgrade] 45–6 (1979): 271–4. 1280 w

Review of the Serbo-Croatian translation (A2j). Provides a synoptic overview of the attempts on the part of the contemporary critics to 'place' F within the context of Western literary thought. What emerges is that F's critical approach subsumes and transcends all the existing theories, while it creates its own unique system – a system that is often dismissed as too closed or intellectually claustrophobic. Points out, however, the open-endedness of F's desire to escape the narrow confines of the contemporary critical tendencies, mainly those of the New Critics. Welcomes 'the long awaited' translation of *AC* into Croatian. Apart from the few minor semantic objections, praises the translation for its accuracy and aesthetic quality.

M1.43 Hochmuth, Marie. *Quarterly Journal of Speech* 43 (October 1957): 312–14 [313]. 700 w

Looks chiefly at F's conception of rhetorical criticism. Finds his treatment of rhetoric is 'fairly innocent' of the rich store of classical rhetoric theory and that his terminology lacks precision.

M1.44 Hugelmann, Hans. *Die Neue Bücherei* [Munich], February 1965

Brief review of the German translation (A2a).

M1.45 Isoya, Takashi. *Nihon dokusho shimbun* [*The Japan Review of Books*], 28 July 1980

Review of the Japanese translation (A2k). In Japanese.

M1.46 K., P. *Slovenské Diradlo* 2 (1968). 800 w

Review of the German translation (A2a). In Czechoslovakian. Places F's work alongside that of critics such as Ingarden and Staiger, who have used the methods of other disciplines. Just as Ingarden has used Husserl's phenomenology and Staiger has used Heidegger's existential ontology, so F's work is connected with psychology, mythology, and anthropology. Says that the positive aspect of F's method is in its effort to renew the severed connections between creativity and knowledge, art and science, myth and concept, and to build a system of criticism based upon the historical integration of mythological, scientific, and philosophical thought. Judges F's model to be an important one, similar in scope to the models of Ermatiger, Petsch, Lukács, Kayser, and Staiger.

M1.47 Ka. *Marburger Blätter* 99 (1965). 120 w

Brief review of the German translation (A2a).

M1.48 Karita, Motoshi. *Eibungaku kenkyu* [*Studies in English Literature*] 35, no 1 (1958): 121–5
Review of the English edition. In Japanese. Examines F's distinction between novel and romance. Thinks that one cannot separate literature and life as simply as F does.

M1.49 Kattan, Naïm. 'Enfin en français, "L'Anatomie de la critique." ' *Le Devoir*, 21 March 1970, p 16. 1450 w
Review of the French transation (A2c). Chiefly a summary of F's principles. Reacts against F's systematizing of literature, the power of which is said to reside in its paradoxes and its relation to life.

M1.50 Kawasaki, Toshihiko. *Eigo seinen* [*The Rising Generation*] 126 (December 1980): 35
Review of the Japanese translation (A2k). In Japanese.

M1.51 Kermode, Frank. *Review of English Studies* 10 (August 1959): 317–23. Rpt in *Puzzles and Epiphanies: Essays and Reviews, 1958–1961* (London: Routledge & Kegan Paul 1962), 64–73; partially rpt in *Contemporary Literary Criticism*, vol 24, ed Sharon R. Gunton (Detroit: Gale Research 1983), 208–9. 3500 w
Judges *AC* to be an extraordinary book and predicts for it a long life because of its style and the great intelligence lying behind it. But it does 'fall short of greatness in its kind' because it will not affect the development of literature itself and because it does not convey the 'personal presence of any of the thousands of works discussed.' Outlines the principles of the 'Polemical Introduction' and gives a detailed summary of each of the book's four essays. Argues that *AC* embodies a 'Symbolist' doctrine: it emphasizes the autonomy of verbal structures and the importance of literal meaning, it sees literary form as spatial, it is based on an organic primitivism, it always points downward to pre-conscious ritual, and it is fascinated with ornamental design. Refers to *AC* 'as a work of criticism that has turned into literature, for it is centripetal, autonomous and ethical without ... being useful.'

M1.52 Kochan, Detlef C. *Mitteilungen des Deutschen Germanisten-Verbandes* 4 (December 1965). 310 w
Review of the German translation (A2a). Finds that the book is difficult at the beginning but that it rounds itself out into a unified whole. 'A stimulating yet at the same time a problematic book.'

M1.53 Konrad, Gustav. *Welt und Wort* [Munich] 5 (1965). 320 w
Review of the German translation (A2a). Speaks of F's general theoretical method. Observes that his chief aim is 'to break down the partitions between critical approaches.'

M1.54 Kumar, Anita S. *Osmania Journal of English Studies* 3 (1963): 83–5. 500 w
Sees F as a syncretist, who, like no other contemporary critic, 'has tried to rehabilitate literary criticism as an independent "activity," ' related intimately to larger human perspectives. Thinks F's work is unlike that of the

abstract myth critics (eg, Richard Chase) in that *AC* is 'concretely practical.' Finds that the theory of genres is the weakest part of the book because it occasionally lapses into generalizations and question-begging.

M1.55 Laszlo, Barlay. *Helikon* [Budapest] 4 (1966) 1200 w
Review of the German translation (A2a). In Romanian. Says that it is unfortunate that F limits his inquiry mostly to Anglo-American literature. Believes F has a carefully disguised connection with the logical positivism of Carnap, Wittgenstein, and Morris. Struggles primarily to understand F's position on the social function of literature, which is said to be generally weak. Remarks that F's view on archetypes is stimulating, even though it squeezes 'the living reality of literature' into arbitrary categories. Thinks F pays too little attention to modern literature and avoids the issue of the development of new archetypes. Observes that for Marxists, F's important contribution is that he does not lose sight of the social content of literature.

M1.56 McDowell, Frederick P.W. 'After the New Criticism.' *Western Review* 22 (Summer 1958): 309–14. 2900 w
Believes that *AC* 'may become as seminal for the next decade as the pronouncements of Eliot, Pound, and Richards were for the 1920's and 1930's, and the Brooks and Warren textbooks and Ransom's *The New Criticism* for the 1930's and 1940's.' Gives an overview of each of the book's four essays, and comments especially on F's theory of symbols in order to illustrate the provocative quality of his discourse as well as its defects. Believes that F is sometimes over-ingenious in his categorizing and that literature has a broader foundation than the symbolic one F proposes. In 'general purport,' however, F's ideas are tenable. Cites as especially important F's theory of prose fiction, his views on aestheticism vs moralism in art, his understanding of the relation between music and literature, and his theory of tragedy. *AC* is 'destined ... to become a book constantly referred to.' It is 'of permanent value to the critic and to the student of literature.'

M1.57 Mandel, E.W. 'Frye's Anatomy of Criticism.' *Canadian Forum* 38 (September 1958): 128–9. 2200 w
Maintains that *AC* is primarily a defence or justification of criticism as a systematic and coherent body of knowledge and that two central themes run throughout the book: 'The centrality of the arts in civilization' and the conventionality or 'formality' of art. Sees *AC* as a work of 'utmost importance' for a period in which there is resistance to teaching criticism as a civilizing art; it is a seminal work because of its insistence that there can be a body of intelligible knowledge derived from the form of literature.

M1.58 Marin, Antonio Gomez. 'Northrop Frye: "Anatomia de la Critica." ' *Triunfo* 32 (3 December 1977): 56. 1040 w
Review of the Spanish translation (A2i). Summarizes F's central theses. Says that 'the assertion of Frye consists above all in convincing us by a long metaphysical detour that the sociological foundation of criticism is nothing but an ideological trap that hides the designs of change and

innovation.' Criticizes F's conception of the liberal arts because it rules out materialist and sociological thought.

M1.59 Me. *Allgemeine Deutsche Lehrerzeitung* [Frankfurt] 11 (1 December 1964)
Brief review of the German translation (A2a).

M1.60 Mercier, Vivian. 'A Synoptic View of Criticism.' *Commonweal* 66 (20 September 1957): 618–19. 1100 w
Looks primarily at the principal topics in each of the book's four essays. *AC* is 'overpowering in the originality of its main concepts, and dazzling in the brilliance of its applications of them. Here is a book fundamental enough to be entitled *Principia Critica*.'

M1.61 Muntean, George. *Revista de istorie si teorie literară* 22, no 3 (1973): 484–6. 1200 w
Review of the Romanian translation (A2g). Gives a brief account of F's career and places his work in the context of the theories of Jung, Bodkin, Fergusson, and Wheelwright. Summarizes the principles underlying F's approach, and comments on the translation.

M1.62 Niedermayer, F. 'Gericht über die Richter: Klassiker und Theoretiker der literarischen Kritik.' *Deutsche Tagespost* [Würzburg] 11–12 February 1966. 110 w
Review of the German translation (A2a). Brief remarks on *AC* as a revolutionary book and on F as participating in the New Critical movement in the United States.

M1.63 Pritchard, J.P. 'Critical Art Is Analyzed.' *Oklahoman,* 22 September 1957. 160 w
Comments briefly on F's purpose. F 'considerably clarifies the roily current of contemporary literary criticism.'

M1.64 Raditsa, Leo F. 'Anatomy of Criticism.' *The Griffin* 6 (August 1957): 18–23. 1900 w
Discusses the inclusive perspective that enables F to get beyond prejudice and view literature as a totality. Shows how F's critical system is self-referential. Discovers the roots of the ideas in *AC* in F's study of Blake. Observes that the principles of theme and narrative are elaborated throughout the book. Maintains that *AC* demonstrates how the art of criticism arrives at 'a world beyond the anxious projections of prejudice and class.' 'One cannot express the riches of [its] pages.'

M1.65 Sackton, Alexander. *Criticism* 1 (Winter 1959): 72–5. 1200 w
Gives a concise account of F's aims, methods, and central ideas. Sees the book's strengths as inseparable from its weaknesses: the breadth of F's enterprise and his expansive classifications mean that he can pay little attention to particular literary works and to the reading experience. Remarks also that F's emphasis on archetypal criticism may indicate that F wants to avoid the issue of contemporary taste.

M1.66 Saeki, Shoichi. *Shukan dokushojin* [*The Bookmen's Weekly*] 1346 (8 September 1980)

Review of the Japanese translation (A2k). In Japanese.

M1.67 Shimada, Taro. *The Yomiuri*, 28 July 1980, Book Review section
Review of the Japanese translation (A2k). In Japanese.

M1.68 St, G. *Schleswiger Nachrichten*, 6 March 1965. 210 w
Review of the German translation (A2a). Sees the book as 'a revolutionary contribution for breaking down critical ideologies.'

M1.69 Stobie, Margaret. 'Mr. Fry[e] Stands Well Back.' *Winnipeg Free Press*, 26 July 1958, 43. 960 w
Finds herself disagreeing with much of the book, including F's position on value-judgments, his dependence on Frazer and Jung in organizing his materials, and his position on the potential identity of everything in the literary universe. Says that the book lacks a 'principle of proportion' and that he has made his position neither convincing nor clear.

M1.70 Sutton, Walter. *Symposium* 12 (Spring-Fall 1958): 211–15. 1850 w
Provides a succinct summary of the four essays. Says that F sometimes forces his theories beyond the evidence and that his terminology is often slippery. Still, F 'presents a remarkably developed and coherent discussion which is impressive in its comprehensiveness, its wealth of critical insights, and its treatment of the literary work as a verbal complex of manifold meaning.'

M1.71 Takahashi, Yasunari, 'Towards a Regeneration of Criticism.' *Hon to hihyo* [*The Editors' Monthly*] 71 (September 1980); 12–18
Review of the Japanese translation (A2k). In Japanese.

M1.72 Takamatsu, Yuichi. *Asahi Journal* 21 (8 August 1980): 65–6
Review of the Japanese translation (A2k). In Japanese.

M1.73 Takayanagi, Shunichi. *Sophia* 7 (1958): 97–101. Rpt in Takayanagi's *Seishinshi no naka no Eibungaku* [*English Literature in the Context of Intellectual History*] (Tokyo: Nansosha 1977), 170–4.
In Japanese. Calls attention to F's effort to establish a scientific criticism and to his structuralist approach, emphasizes the importance of the anagogic level of meaning, and concludes that literary criticism should vigorously pursue the problem of *existence*.

M1.74 Unami, Akira. *Tosho shimbun* [*The Book Weekly*] 30 August 1980
Review of the Japanese translation (A2k). In Japanese.

M1.75 Vance, Thomas. 'The Juggler.' *Nation* 188 (17 January 1959): 57–8. 900 w
Sees the wit and learning in AC as related to the ironic tradition of Rabelais, Swift, Sterne, and Joyce and to the more serious tradition of Dante, Spenser, Milton, and Blake. Believes F's 'originality lies in his largeness of perspective.' The book is sometimes extravagant, but its value outweighs F's elaborate flights. When F 'seems to be splitting hairs, he is sometimes actually splitting atoms, and releasing a new measure of imaginative energy.'

M1.76 Warren, Fabian. 'Dichtung literarisch betrachtet.' *Oberösterreichische Nachrichten* [Linz], 12 September 1964
Brief notice about the German translation (A2a).

M1.77 Whalley, George. 'Fry[e]'s Anatomy of Criticism.' *Tamarack Review* 8
(Summer 1958): 92–8, 100–1. 3550 W
Provides a succinct summary of the book's four essays. Finds 'continuous
evidence of sustained and original thinking, of fine perception, and controlled insight.' Believes that the strength of *AC* is in its views on a wide
range of writing and its taxonomic schema. Has doubts, however, about
its usefulness as a poetics because of its conceptions of language, mimesis,
and value-judgments, and because its views on desire and repugnance
are based on a 'psychological determinism [that] ... fails to give an adequate
account of anagogic myth as we encounter it in literature.' Also, F too
often seeks refuge in irony.

M1.78 —*Modern Language Review* 54 (January 1959), 107–9
A shorter version of the assessment developed in M1.77.

M1.79 Wutz, H. *Stimmen der Zeit* [Munich] 4 (1966). 640 W
Review of the German translation (A2a). Comments on F's synoptic and
speculative approach. 'With sharp insights and a versatile intelligence, Frye
circles around the phenomenon of literature like a detective,' yet F's
vision is not defined well enough and his examples are of little help to
German readers.

M2 The Bush Garden (*BG*) [A13]

M2.1 Adams, Rick. 'Northrop Frye: Essays on the Canadian Imagination.'
It Needs to Be Said 1, no 1 (February 1974): 2. 1000 W
Argues that F uses his doctrine of literary form to dismiss the works of
poets he dislikes and to protect his theory from poetry that challenges the
autonomy of literature. Says F has contributed to our understanding of
the relationship of myth to literature but worries that his mythical heroes
are Spenser, Blake, and Milton rather than the creators of a new mythology
of social realism: Marx, Freud, Toynbee, Einstein, and Lawrence.

M2.2 Anonymous. *Association for Canadian Studies in the United States Newsletter* 2
(Spring 1972): 100
Brief notice.

M2.3 — *Quill & Quire* 37 (19 March 1971), 8
Brief notice of publication.

M2.4 Aspinall, Dawn. 'New Books, 1971.' *Canadian Dimension* 8 (January 1972),
55
Brief notice.

M2.5 Barbour, Douglas. 'Canada and Its Culture.' *Edmonton Journal*, 7 May 1971,
66. 530 W
Says the book is refreshing because it eschews theory in favor of practical
criticism and because of its 'free and generous response' to Canadian
poetry. 'What may surprise many readers is the sureness of Frye's taste
when he is dealing with contemporary works.'

M2.6 Buitenhuis, Peter. 'Visions in Mythic Second Sight.' *Globe Magazine* [Toronto], 3 April 1971, 15. 800 w
Points especially to F's treatment of the mixture of the primitive and the civilized, which constitutes so much of Canadian literature. Observes that F's emphasis upon detachment, form, and organization may suggest why there are no Canadian masterpieces: a colonial culture acts to repress passion and engagement. Believes the strength of *BG* lies in F's 'delineating the moral landscape in which the Canadian artist has worked up to now.'

M2.7 Colombo, John Robert. 'Polished Performance by a Canadian Essayist.' *Toronto Star* (Book Section), 20 May 1971, 65. 800 w
Judges the book to be a perceptive account of the Canadian *poetic* imagination. Notes that F says little about Canadian fiction and non-fiction and that he discusses Canadian poetry mainly in terms of the Canadian environment rather than in terms of other literature. F 'resembles nobody so much as a poetic Midas – everything he touches turns to metaphor.'

M2.8 Conron, Brandon. 'A Bountiful Choice of Critics.' *Literary Half-yearly* 13 (July 1972): 44–55 [54–5]
Brief notice.

M2.9 Davies, Bryn. *Wascana Review* 6, no 2 (1972): 76–8. 1350 w
Questions whether or not F's mythopoeic conception of literature is adequate to account for Canadian poetry. Believes F's separation of poets into those who write out of experience and those who add a mythical dimension is an abstract separation that strait-jackets the variety of Canadian poetry. Contrasts Canadian and Australian poetry to illustrate that the Australian writers have created a satisfying mythology out of their own experience of isolation – unlike what Canadian poets, according to F, have done. Believes that Canadian poets create and communicate their own mythology rather than trying to resurrect an old one.

M2.10 Dobbs, Kildare. Typed transcript of review on 'CBC Anthology,' 7 April 1971, 5 pp. 1850 w
Comments especially on F's poetry reviews written for the *University of Toronto Quarterly* during the 1950s. F's running engagement with the poetry of Irving Layton is an example of 'perhaps the most extraordinary thing' about *BG* – 'an existential record of the response over ten formative years of a great critic to a poet with the promise of greatness in him.' Glances at F's views on the question of Canadian identity. Distinguishes between the theoretical orientation of *AC* and the practical criticism of *BG*. The recorded version of this transcript is in the CBC Radio Archives, Toronto. CBC reference no 740410.

M2.11 Downes, G.V. *Malahat Review* 22 (April 1972): 123–5. 150 w
Comments briefly on F's 'perceptive, fresh, and witty' reviews of Canadian poetry in the 1950s.

M2.12 Dragland, S.L. *Queen's Quarterly* 79 (Summer 1972): 264–5. 1000 w
Sees the 'sureness' in F's account of Canadian literature as resulting from his wide knowledge and from his assimilating that knowledge into a

broad framework of myth. Glances briefly at the chief topics F treats in this collection.

M2.13 Dudek, Louis. 'The Misuses on Imagination: A Rib-Roasting of Some Recent Canadian Critics.' *Tamarack Review* 60 (October 1973): 51–67 [51–7]. 2560 w

Analyses F's essays on Canadian literature *vis-à-vis* his critical theory, especially his ideas on literary evaluation. Looks particularly at F's judgments about the work of Irving Layton, Jay Macpherson, and Raymond Souster. Concludes, 'that the perceptions and evaluations in these essays are of the kind predictably implicit in the theory of myths.'

M2.14 Gibson, Dorothy. 'Canadian Imagination as Our Poets, Painters See It.' *Financial Post*, 25 September 1971, 40. 350 w

Comments on F's treatment of the themes of man vs nature and city vs country as the backdrop against which Canadian poetry is written.

M2.15 Gross, Konrad. *Die Neueren Sprachen* 73 (August 1974): 371–2. 450 w

Sees the relevance of the volume as lying in F's importance as a critic, not in what he says about Canadian literature. Observes that F pays more attention to the lyric than to other genres. Thinks his 'Conclusion' to *Literary History of Canada* is the most substantial essay in the book. Says that even though F's categorizing may sometimes seem mechanical, it has helped collapse the distance between taxonomy and evaluation.

M2.16 James, Geoffrey. 'Probing the Garrison.' *Time* [Canadian edition], 26 April 1971, 10. 750 w

Singles out for comment F's tendency not to rank Canadian writers and his views on those things that hamper the development of a Canadian literary tradition: the psychological and physical threats in the Canadian environment that produce the 'garrison mentality.'

M2.17 Kattan, Naïm. 'Northrop Frye et la littérature canadienne.' *Le Devoir*, 21 August 1971, 13. 1000 w

Gives a summary account of F's reviews on Canadian poetry and the theory of Canadian literature he develops in his 'Conclusion' to *Literary History of Canada*. Says that because of his wide perspective, F tends sometimes to make judgments a little too quickly about the relationship between English and French Canadian culture.

M2.18 McPherson, David. 'The Canadian Imagination.' Toronto: Canadian Broadcasting Corp. CBC Audiotape no 650
See G22.

M2.19 Morley, Patricia. 'Canada's Quest for the Peaceable Kingdom.' *Ottawa Journal*, 17 April 1971. 550 w

Remarks that for F the distinctive feature of the Canadian tradition is 'a search for the reconciliation of man with man and of man with nature.' Notes the distinction F makes between unity, a political matter, and identity, a cultural and imaginative matter.

M2.20 Ross, Malcolm. 'Northrop Frye.' *University of Toronto Quarterly* 41 (Winter 1972): 170–3 [172–3]. 600 w

Sees the 'perceptive and lively critiques' in F's poetry reviews as the most important feature of the pieces collected in *BG*, for in these reviews F makes value-judgments. Thinks that F's own myth of the 'garrison mentality' is as 'usable and perishable' as the myth of the American frontier. Wishes F's theory of criticism (as distinct from his book reviewing) would make room for value-judgments, for F 'has done more than any man now living to advance and ennoble the cause of humane studies in our time.'

M2.21 Stevens, Peter. 'Frye-ing Canadian Culture.' *Windsor Star*, 5 June 1971, 14. 650 w
Judges the book to be an 'intelligent, perceptive, and provocative analysis of the quality of the Canadian imagination,' but thinks that F pays too little attention to recent developments in Canadian literature and that he is unsympathetic to popular culture.

M2.22 Texmo, Dell. 'Frye's Insights Go beyond Canada's Space and Cold.' *London Free Press* [Ontario], 17 April 1971, 7M. 900 w
Notes primarily what F praises and blames in his reviews of Canadian poetry.

M2.23 Wahl, C. 'Alternate Selection.' *Canadian Reader* 12, no 3 (22 March 1971): 5–6. 850 w
Believes *BG* 'shows the maturing of both Canadian literature and its most important critic.' Summarizes the thematic trends F discovers in Canadian culture and mythology.

M2.24 Weaver, Robert. 'Canadian Intellectuals? Well, besides McLuhan there's Northrop Frye.' *Maclean's* 84 (April 1971): 86, 88. 1000 w
After opening with a biographical sketch, examines the contribution F made to understanding Canadian poetry in his fugitive reviews for the *University of Toronto Quarterly*. Refers to F's 'Conclusion' to *Literary History of Canada* as 'a stunning piece of work, so well written, so well informed, and so broad in its sympathies and commitments.'

M2.25 Woodcock, George. 'Criticism and Other Arts.' *Canadian Literature* 49 (Summer 1971): 3–7. 1050 w
A slightly revised version of 'Northrop Frye Myth Dispelled' (see M2.26).

M2.26 — 'Northrop Frye Myth Dispelled: The Genial Public Critic.' *Victoria Daily Times*, 29 May 1971, 10. 1050 w
Distinguishes between F's academic criticism and his public criticism, of which *BG* is an example. The public critic is a person of taste who evaluates literature and shows how it is absorbed into society. In *BG*, 'Frye shows himself as good a field critic as he is a theoretical one.'

M3 **Creation and Recreation** (*CR*) [A18]

M3.1 Anonymous. *Christian Century* 98 (April 22, 1981): 458
Brief notice.

M3.2 — *Malahat Review* 58 (April 1981): 136

Brief notice.

M3.3 Brown, Daniel A. *Horizons* [Villanova Univ] 8 (Fall 1981): 433–4. 450 w
Notes the similarities between F's view of creation and those of H. Richard
Niebuhr and Gregory Baum.

M3.4 Cahill, P. Joseph. *Studies in Religion / Sciences religieuses* 10 (1981): 235–6.
600 w
Gives a brief summary of F's thesis about creation and recreation, which
places the reader in a central hermeneutical role. Says that F 'in a paragraph
can throw more light on the Christian Bible than one usually finds in
several issues of technical journals.'

M3.5 Drew, Philip. *Modern Language Review* 78 (October 1983): 880–1. 700 w
Comments chiefly on the paradoxes in F's arguments about myths of creation. Thinks F is 'most helpful when he is writing straightforwardly
about literature, most evasive when he is writing oracularly about mythologies.' Sees this book as an isthmus connecting *AC* with F's large critical
project on the Bible.

M3.6 G., J.W. 'Word and Spirit – Beyond Professed Belief.' *Prairie Messenger*
[Saskatchewan], 1 March 1981. 300 w
Gives a brief summary of F's ideas on professed belief vs charity and
action, and on the mythologies of creation.

M3.7 Hair, Donald. 'Begin at the Beginning.' *Brick* 11 (Winter 1981): 38–9
Compares F's understanding of creation, in which human beings become
the transformers and shapers of all things, to that of contemporary physics,
which has undermined the Newtonian view of creation.

M3.8 Harris, Randy. 'Creation and Recreation.' *Our Books Atlantic* 4, no 1 (9
January 1981). 700 w
Says that F is self-indulgent and that *CR* is sloppily edited. Despite F's self-
conscious oracular pose, his saving grace is the wit with which he writes.

M3.9 Hornbeck, Paul. 'Making Book on Fall '80.' *Quill & Quire* 46 (July 1980): 10
Brief notice.

M3.10 Jeffrey, David. 'Creation & Recreation.' *Canadian Literature* 91 (Winter 1981):
111–17. 3250 w
Complains throughout that in this book F 'is not a particularly fruitful or
reliable reader of texts.' Prefers C.S. Lewis's view of creation to F's.
Says that in his commentary on the Bible F does not show 'a very good
grasp of his subject.' Dislikes F's polemical approach to the biblical text.
Sees F moving away from interpretation toward a position in which the
critic is 'competitor and ultimately successor to the artist.' Says F confounds
myth and religion rather than connecting them. Thinks finally that *CR* is
really autobiographical dogma.

M3.11 McCombie, Frank. *Notes & Queries* 29 (June 1982): 282. 600 w
Believes that Blake serves F's purposes too neatly, that the message of the
book has been tailored to fit the medium of the lecture, that F's 'view of
the problems of biblical theology [are] a great deal too simple for the needs

of the study Professor Frye projects,' and that F's conclusion is not much more than 'a plea for the syncretic approach to ecumenism and – almost by the way – to literature.'

M3.12 Mellard, James M. *Modern Fiction Studies* 27 (Summer 1981): 392. 420 w
Summarizes the three essays of the book, the last of which shows that Frye encompasses 'the current passion for "reader response" criticism.' Observes that the book is hortative and sermonic.

M3.13 Miller, Peter. 'Creating Past and Future.' *Whig-Standard Magazine* [Kingston, Ont], 21 February 1981, 18. 570 w
A brief summary of F's central thesis about creation myths. CR 'transcends literary criticism per se and will be of interest to all readers with any interest whatever in philosophical problems.'

M3.14 Ross, Malcolm. *University of Toronto Quarterly* 50 (Summer 1981), 95–7. 1100 w
Summarizes F's central thesis about creation mythology. Understands F's quest as 'a quest for *pure act*, nameless, beyond personality, beyond and before the tentative transcience of myth.' It is an aspect of a religious quest. F's effort is, however, hampered by his 'repression, or dismissal, or avoidance of the pertinent insights of Christian theology and the rapt knowledge of the mystics.'

M3.15 Spector, R.D. *World Literature Today* 56 (Winter 1982): 190. 160 w
Notes that F applies 'the latest theories of structuralism, deconstruction and reader-responsiveness' to argue about the relationship between myth and art.

M3.16 Stuewe, Paul. 'Criticism.' *Quill & Quire* 46 (December 1980): 29
Praises F's illuminating literary insights but is distracted by his unsupported philosophical generalizations and by the chatty tone of the lectures, which 'does not translate well onto the printed page.'

M3.17 Tolomeo, Diane. *English Studies in Canada* 8 (June 1982): 245–8. 1480 w
Thinks the book is a 'frustrating disappointment.' Says F is somewhat self-indulgent, raises complex issues only to dismiss them quickly, and is irresponsible in a translation of Gen. 3:22–3. Believes that the second chapter 'contains the most interesting and stimulating ideas in the book,' even though these ideas are not particularly new. Thinks the secular theology of the third chapter will be offensive to some readers.

M4 The Critical Path (CP) [A14]

M4.1 Bromwich, David. 'The Linear Canadian.' *Nation* 213 (20 September 1971): 247–8. 850 w
Believes that the two thrusts of the book – the first, a popular defence of culture, and the second, weighty speculations about the ontology of literature – sometimes get in each other's way. Paraphrases F's argument about the myths of freedom and concern. Comments on the price paid by F's original, diagrammatic manner of thought: 'clarity of outline is

bought at the expense of detail.' Still, the virtues of the book are its 'immense learning gracefully used, an excellent prose style, and the sanity of a good liberal without quotation marks.'

M4.2 Cargas, Harry. *St Louis Post-Dispatch*, 17 February 1972, 3C
Brief note.

M4.3 Cushman, Keith. *Library Journal* 96 (15 May 1971), 1713. 175 w
Believes that F sometimes tries to fit everything too neatly into the frame-work of his myths of freedom and concern. 'Nevertheless, the fact remains that Frye is the most provocative and important literary critic of the present day.'

M4.4 Davis, Robert Gorham. 'The Problematic State of Literature.' *New Leader* 54 (17 May 1971): 7–8. 250 w
Sees *CP* as 'a thorough-going attempt to redefine literature in the face of [the] threatened destruction within and without,' but thinks F's effort is not very successful because of the loose way in which he defines myth.

M4.5 E[rdman], D[avid] V. *English Language Notes* 10, Supplement to no 1 (September 1971): 12
Brief notice that points to 'the spirit of Romantic vision,' which is every-where in the book.

M4.6 Fulford, Robert. 'It's Enormously Liberating to Read Our Leading Essayist.' *Toronto Star*, 24 December 1971, 33. 1200 w
Finds that the density of *CP* makes it difficult to paraphrase, but does see it as a kind of intellectual autobiography: it 'details the ways [Frye] relates literature to life' and 'describes Frye's own growth in response to the ideas he has encountered.'

M4.7 Jayne, Edward. *Kritikon Litterarum* 1 (1972): 316–20. 2350 w
Sees the core of F's argument as his struggle to connect myth with the reality principle. His answer is a critical path that avoids the excesses of both scepticism and dogmatism and that leads to a synthesis of freedom and concern. Believes F's position is weakened by his paying too little attention to the reality principle. Thinks that F's critique of Marxism is a critique of a straw man and that the neo-Marxist accounts of politics and culture are more adequate than F's critical path when it comes to explaining the phenomena of modern life. Judges F's book to be finally a reactionary work, 'a defense of Burkean conservatism in [its] asking for the preservation of existing institutions to protect the freedom of both the artist and critic.'

M4.8 Kastan, David Scott. 'The Triumph of Comedy.' *TLS*, 17 February 1984, 163. 520 w
Finds F's dialectical argument to be 'an attractive expression of the romantic theory of imagination that seeks not to evade the world but to appropriate it, humanizing by its projections the inhospitable and inhuman environ-ment in which we live.'

M4.9 L[evin], H[arry]. *Comparative Literature* 24 (Winter 1972): 72–3. 820 w
Believes that the book's 'most original contributions lie in its *obiter dicta*, its

unexpected linkages and discursive insights.' Points to F's interest
throughout in relating criticism to its historical and social substructure, and
cites a number of illustrations of this interest. F's book 'reminds us that
the best defense of poetry is a demonstration of its bearing on the other
aspects of life.'

M4.10 Levine, George. 'Our Culture and Our Convictions.' *Partisan Review* 39,
no 1 (1972): 63–79 [66–74]. 2050 w
Places *CP* in the context of other reconsiderations of the liberal tradition.
Finds that F 'transcendentalizes Arnold's position': he goes beyond
Arnold's disinterestedness to a kind of Platonic, visionary contemplation,
one in which literature 'becomes the one true church of the human skeptic.'
This transcendentalizing of Arnold is what injures F's position, 'for it
lacks a sense of the reality of human motives and activities.' F sees the
price of liberalism and "is prepared to suffer the martyrdom of defending
it,' even though the disinterested contemplation of the modern intellectual
is a problematic position to defend.

M4.11 Lordi, Robert J. *Steinbeck Quarterly* 8 (Summer-Fall 1975): 110–12. 870 w
Summarizes the central themes in each of the book's seven sections.

M4.12 Noel-Bentley, Peter C. 'The Function of Criticism at the Present Time.'
Journal of Canadian Fiction 1 (Summer 1972): 78–80. 2200 w
Shows how *CP* is a further stage in the development of F's work. Sees the
full implications of F's argument emerging in his discussion of open and
closed mythologies. Praises the book for bracing his spirits, enlarging
his vision, and giving him strength as a teacher.

M4.13 Rudnick, Hans. *Clio* 2 (October 1972): 72–6. 1700 w
Summarizes F's major themes and explicates the dialectical method he uses
in arguing for a tension between the myths of freedom and concern.
Points to F's attacks on the humanists for their 'submission to rhetoric,
encyclopaedic learning, and aristocratic elitism.' Claims that F has 'found a
viable myth-related vocabulary that can capture the undercurrent meanings
of literature which analytic language cannot name,' but is bothered by
F's having abandoned judgment and evaluation as part of the critic's task.

M4.14 Spector, Robert. *Books Abroad* 46 (Spring 1972): 306. 370 w
Gives a brief account of F's understanding of the function of the critic, and
observes that the critical path, for F, leads to a balancing of the myths of
freedom and concern.

M4.15 Whittaker, Ted. 'Grammar of Identity.' *Books in Canada* 1 (November 1971):
30. 320 w
Observes that in F's explication of the social function of the imagination all
of the products of culture fit into his myths of freedom and concern.

M5 **Divisions on a Ground** (*DG*) [A20]

M5.1 Abeel, Daphne. 'Stimulating Look across a Dotted Line.' *Christian Science
Monitor* 74 (13 August 1982): B7
Brief review.

M5.2 Adachi, Ken. 'His Playful Wit Enlivens Frye's Swirling Ideas.' *Toronto Star*,
26 June 1982, F10. 800 w
Reviews a selection of F's ideas on Canadian culture and calls attention to
F's wit, eloquence, and inquiring intelligence.
M5.3 Anonymous. *Canadian Studies 1983*. Toronto: Canadian Book Publishers'
Council and Association of Canadian Publishers, 1983. 14
Brief notice.
M5.4 — *Choice* 20 (December 1982): 581
Brief notice.
M5.5 Bates, Ronald. 'On the Value of Real Education.' *London Free Press* [Ontario],
5 February 1983, B9. 660 w
See *DG* as an 'excellent exemplification' of one of F's central theses, that
learning is a lifelong process. Cites several of F's warnings about university
education becoming oriented toward productivity rather than possession.
M5.6 Beardsley, Doug. 'Frye's Fresh Insights into Canadian Culture.' *Victoria
Times Colonist* [BC], 6 August 1983, C11. 1300 w
Points particularly to F's views on the role of the writer in Canada, the
cultural differences between Canada and the United States, the function of
the university, and the effect of technology. Praises F's clear and fluid
style, and thinks the book deserves to reach a wide, popular audience.
M5.7 Brown, Russell. 'Mythic Patterns.' *Canadian Forum* 62 (December-January
1982–3): 39. 1250 w
Observes that in the essays on Canadian literature in *DG*, F primarily fills
in the details of critical maps already charted. These essays differ, however, from F's previous work in that he has a new estimate of the worth of
Canadian literature, he looks more closely at its historical development,
and he examines Canadian culture in a more detailed comparative context.
Notes that F's ideas on teaching and on the social context of literature
cannot really be separated, and that F's own unifying myth is that of the
university as utopia.
M5.8 Buri, S.G. *Arts Manitoba* 2 (Winter 1983): 57–9. 1750 w
Says the book is 'sprinkled with a good amount of wit, wisdom, insight,
and information,' though it is 'of interest mainly to devotees of [F's]
oeuvre.' Finds F's essays on education to be 'pleasantly journalistic' and
his criticism of Canadian literature dependent upon a quite rigid methodology. Believes the chief failure in F's critical enterprise to be his denigration
of evaluation. Judges F's 'Conclusion' to *Literary History of Canada* to be
his most cogent exposition of Canadian literary matters.
M5.9 Cairns, A.T.J. *Canadian Book Review Annual, 1982*, ed Dean Tudor and Ann
Tudor (Toronto: Simon & Pierre 1983), 227–8. 390 w
Says *DG* contradicts the view of F as a detached, ivory-tower intellectual.
Praises the book for its 'sheer *readability*' and observes that F's mind is
remarkably up-to-date.
M5.10 Cameron, Barry. 'Frye Talking.' *Canadian Literature* 101 (Summer 1984):
113–14. 1200 w
Points to the conceptual motifs of the book and gives a brief summary of

the argument of each essay. Sees the repetitiveness of F's central themes as a rhetorical weakness. Believes there is a disparity between F's general theory of literature and his pronouncements on Canadian literature: his role in both the creation and the study of Canadian literature has been relatively minor.

M5.11 Czarnecki, Mark. 'Reflections of a Radical Tory.' *Maclean's* 95 (21 June 1982): 49–50. 450 w
Finds that, politically, the combination of prophecy and wisdom in F produces 'a classic specimen of the "Tory radical." ' Sees F's caveat about withdrawing from nature to be 'not a random whiff of bucolic romanti-cism ... but the articulation of a passionately felt organic unity embracing ecological, economic and spiritual values.' These essays show that F 'has long since abandoned the ivory tower of academe for that no man's land between wisdom and prophecy where the visionary is king.'

M5.12 Davidson, Cathy N. *American Review of Canadian Studies* 12 (Fall 1982): 127–8. 830 w
Points to the personal touches in the book, which give glimpses of F the man and F the teacher; its practical thrust, and its optimistic tone – all of which reveal 'not the brilliant theorist of archetypes in literature but Canada's own archetypal Wise Old Man.'

M5.13 Delaney, Paul. 'The Letter and the Spirit.' *Saturday Night* 97 (May 1982): 55–6 [56]. 450 w
Does not find F's thoughts about Canadian culture adequate for the 1970s and 1980s. Canadian culture has moved beyond the themes F used to discuss it earlier in his career (the garrison mentality, the Calvinist fear of sensuality, the menace of the northern wilderness), and F gives few hints as to what would replace the themes he formerly developed.

M5.14 Dickason, Olive Patricia. *Journal of Educational Thought* 17 (April 1983): 65–6. 770 w
Comments primarily on the theme of national awareness raised in F's essays. Says that F remains 'intelligently optimistic' and 'fresh in the midst of our national proclivity for tortured self-examination.'

M5.15 Evans, J.A.S. *Affaires Universitaires*, November 1982, 16. 225 w
Brief notice. Calls attention to one of the essays in *DG*, 'Teaching the Humanities Today' (see D238).

M5.16 Forst, Graham. *World Literature Written in English* 22 (1983): 293–6. 1600 w
Reviews the central themes in each of the book's three sections. Sees *DG* as quintessentially a 'teaching book' and observes that the voice that runs throughout is 'a Prospero voice that "abjures rough magic" and sets the reader's spirit free.'

M5.17 Garebian, Keith. 'The Great Coda.' *Books in Canada* 11 (November 1982): 19–21. 1060 w
Summarizes F's understanding of the growth of Canadian culture from colonial days to the present. 'Paradoxically, by moving away from cultural nationalism, Frye becomes most acutely perceptive of [Canadian] national

culture.' Calls attention to F's epigrammatic wit and his broadly humanistic intent. F's 'intellectual virtues are moral ones: prudence, sympathy, idealism, patience, and, most of all, wisdom with charity.'

M5.18 Goldfarb, Sheldon. 'Reflections on Canadian Culture.' *Winnipeg Free Press*, 5 March 1983, 46. 630 w
Summarizes F's arguments about the opposition in Canadian life between nature and culture. Points to the conservative and radical dialectic at work throughout the essays in *DG*.

M5.19 Gould, Allan M. 'Northrop Frye Work Lauded.' *Standard Freeholder* [Cornwall, Ont], 19 March 1983. 530 w
Comments briefly on the wit and wisdom found in this collection of essays.

M5.20 Kane, Sean. *University of Toronto Quarterly* 52 (Summer 1983): 471–3. 1150 w
Observes that the metaphors of tension and interpenetration run throughout this collection. Notes F's revaluation of his earlier accounts of the Canadian imagination, points to the similarity between F's vision of continuity and expansion and that of Cassirer, comments on F's 'cautiously progressive and optimistic' tone, and alerts the reader to the 'excesses in Frye's defence of individual creativity.' 'We could wish for no better interpreter of the charged gaps and spaces of our cultural memory.'

M5.21 Kreisel, Henry. 'Touching the Cultural Pulse.' *Edmonton Journal*, 11 July 1982, C5. 750 w
Comments primarily on F's view of the foundations and development of Canadian culture. F's strength is in 'the nobility of his vision and his power to articulate it.'

M5.22 Marshall, Tom. 'Our Cultural Conscience.' *Whig-Standard Magazine* [Kingston, Ont], 25 September 1982, 20. 820 w
Concludes that *DG* is 'a valuable book for anyone who wishes to explore the social vision that complements Northrop Frye's vision of literature.' Singles out for special comment F's definition of the university and his essays on the state of the ecology.

M5.23 Morley, Patricia. 'Vintage Northrop Frye: Worlds out of Words.' *Quill & Quire* 48 (May 1982): 35. 350 w
Says that F is condescending in his attitudes about Canadian culture, the result perhaps of 'the colonial attitudes that prevailed among Ontario intellectuals up to and beyond the 1960s.'

M5.24 Moss, John. *Globe and Mail*, 14 August 1982, Entertainment section, 11. 800 w
Praises *DG* for the wisdom of F's social and cultural insights, as well as 'the lovely cast of his prose, the eloquence and concrete beauty of his allusions and anecdotes, his perfect metaphors, and disarmingly human affectations.'

M5.25 Solecki, Sam. 'Criticism and the Anxiety of Identity.' *Queen's Quarterly* 90 (Winter 1983): 1026–33 [1026–9]. 1450 w
Places the essays in *DG* in the context of F's critical theory in general and

his Canadian literary criticism in particular. Finds the book both disappointing and rewarding: disappointing because the essays give one a sense
of *déjà vu* and rewarding because it is a book by a major critic who writes
forcefully and lucidly. Summarizes F's seminal ideas about Canadian
literature, which are repeated and, to a lesser extent, developed in *DG*.

M5.26 Stevens, Peter. 'Canadian Culture-Frye-d.' *Windsor Star*, 17 July 1982.
700 W
Surveys F's central theses about the relationship between society, education, and culture. Sees F's strength in his ability to arrange his material
into a coherent pattern, and his weakness in his failure sometimes to qualify
his large generalizations. *DG* 'offers a stimulating summary of F's thoughts
on Canadian culture without becoming too inwardly parochial.'

M5.27 Williams, Haydn M. 'Canadian Punditry.' CRNLE *Reviews* 2 (December
1983): 86 750 W
Characterizes the position F develops in these essays as 'Liberal conservatism' and 'Christian-humanist.' Comments especially on his controversial
views on higher education and on his 'Conclusion' to *Literary History of
Canada* (D233).

M5.28 Woodman, Ross. 'From the Belly of the Whale: Frye's "Personal Encounter." ' *Canadian Poetry* 10 (Spring-Summer 1982): 124–31 [128–31]. 1800 W
In his continuing exploration of Canadian culture, F, while still affirming
the strength of regionalism, now maintains that Canadian culture has
moved beyond provincialism toward maturity. Like Arnold, F has seen that
a larger vision is necessary to get beyond regionalism. His essays on
Canadian topics are an integral part of his more cosmic concerns.

M6 **The Educated Imagination** (*EI*) [A3]

M6.1 Anonymous. *Booklist* 61 (1 October 1964): 121–2
Brief notice.

M6.2 — *Choice* 1 (January 1965): 473
Brief review, summarizing the main argument.

M6.3 —'Explains Uses of Literature.' *Indiana Alumni Magazine* 27 (December
1964): 37. 200 W
Comments briefly on F's theory of literature, one that 'places unique
emphasis upon the social utility of literary arts.'

M6.4 —'L'imagination de Northrop Frye.' *Sept Jours*, 13 December 1969, 10. 230 W
A brief review of the French translation (A3e). Is concerned chiefly with
questioning F's view of language.

M6.5 — *Michigan Quarterly Review* 4 (1965): 72
Brief notice.

M6.6 — *Scholarly Books in America* 6 (January 1965): 43
Brief notice.

M6.7 — *Teaching Aids News* 5 (15 February 1965)
Brief notice.

M6.8 — 'L'uomo "creativo." ' *Il Giornale di Vicenza*, 30 March 1974. 240 w
Review of the Italian translation (A3f). Points to F's view of literature
as the chief component in education and his understanding of creativity as 'the indispensable condition in maintaining the freedom
of society itself.'

M6.9 Aronson, Simon. 'Package of Ideas.' *Chicago Maroon Literary Review* 2
(23 October 1964): 1, 7. 1000 w
Sees the scope of the book as its most impressive quality. Summarizes in
some detail F's exposition of the different levels of language, his understanding of the imagination, and his concept of mythology. Believes
that when F begins to relate the imagination to society, his previously
established distinctions about levels of experience begin to collapse.
Still, the book is 'a collection of original, significant, and thought-
provoking ideas.'

M6.10 Baker, Sheridan. *College English* 26 (January 1965): 330–1. 210 w
Brief review that sees *EI* as a 'practical, clear, colloquial, persuasive, and
brief' version of *AC*.

M6.11 Bannon, Barbara. *Publishers Weekly* 190 (8 August 1966): 62
Brief notice.

M6.12 Bizier, Gilles. *Culture* [Montreal] 3 (1970): 361–2. 290 w
Review of the French translation (A3e). Sees the book as a 'mediocre
justification' of the use of the imagination and a 'tissue of contradictions'
that 'only leads us down a false trail.'

M6.13 Blissett, William. 'Literary Studies.' *University of Toronto Quarterly* 33
(July 1964): 401–8. 450 w
Observes that F's views on the imagination and education are inseparable.
Sees the book as containing a program for educating the imagination
toward freedom and citizenry. Reviewed along with five of F's other books.

M6.14 Bonenfant, Jean-Charles. *University of Toronto Quarterly* 39 (July 1970): 422
Brief note about the appearance of the French translation (A3e).

M6.15 Camillus, Sister M. *The Globe* [Briar Cliff College, Sioux City, Iowa] 21
(14 March 1968): 3. 260 w
Comments briefly on the role that literature plays, according to F, in
developing the imagination.

M6.16 Carena, Carlo. 'Alla scuola di un critico ben temperato.' *La Stampa*, 14 June
1974. 550 w
Review of the Italian translation (A3f). Calls attention to the relation of *EI*
to *AC*. Summarizes F's views on the function of the imagination (to identify
the human and non-human worlds), the connections among literary
works, metaphor, and the liberating power of poetry in helping us to
overcome ordinary expression.

M6.17 Carruth, Hayden. 'People in a Myth.' *Hudson Review* 18 (Winter 1965–6):
607–12. 1150 w
Begins by examining F's work in the context of the New Criticism. Thinks
that F's ideas in the early part of the book are pernicious because they

divorce literature from moral content and moral application. Reviewed along with *NP*, to which Carruth devotes most of his attention.

M6.18 Co., F. 'Frye.' *Avanti*, 17 March 1974
Brief note about the Italian translation (A3f).

M6.19 Cook, Eleanor, and Ramsay Cook. *Canadian Annual Review for 1963*, ed John Saywell (Toronto: Univ of Toronto Press 1964), 457.
Brief note. Reviewed along with *FI*, *WTC*, and *TSE*.

M6.20 Dorsch, T.S. *Year's Work in English Studies* 45 (1964): 17–18. 100 w
Short review, summarizing Frye's beliefs about the study of literature.

M6.21 Dudek, Louis. 'Northrop Frye's Untenable Position.' *Delta* 22 (October 1963): 23–7. 1600 w
Says that despite the 'positive humanistic affirmations about literature' F makes, almost everything else he says in the book is contrary to what Dudek practices and believes. F's position is untenable because it relegates the content of literature to convention and because the central myth F finds in literature is a veiled, dogmatic version of Christianity.

M6.22 Griffith, William S. *Adult Leadership* 13 (1965): 262. 1060 w
Summarizes F's views on the nature and function of literature. Believes that the book holds little appeal for adult educators because F has not 'addressed himself to the problem of improvement of the teaching of literature and of insuring that the imagination would be used for moral purposes.'

M6.23 Kattan, Naïm. 'Pouvoirs de l'imagination de Northrop Frye.' *Le Devoir*, 3 January 1970, 9
Brief review of the French translation (A2e).

M6.24 Kibel, Alvin C. 'The Imagination Goes to College.' *Partisan Review* 32 (Summer 1965): 461–4, 466. 1500 w
Quarrels with F's analogizing literature to mathematics. F's system leaves no room for relating literature to social, political, or religious life. For F, literature is 'an exercise of the spirit uncontaminated by matter, which demonstrates the hypothetical freedom of repudiation and desire from historical complication.'

M6.25 Kitching, Jessie. *Publishers Weekly* 186 (7 September 1964): 64
Brief notice.

M6.26 Kloski, Anelle. 'Literature and Society.' *Humanist* 25 (May-June 1965): 137. 300 w
Gives an abstract of F's central thesis about the social function of literature. Thinks that in F's effort 'heroically to encompass the two worlds of traditional literature and of "action," ' he may betray both.

M6.27 L[azarus], A[rnold]. *Quartet* [West Lafayette, Ind] 2 (Spring 1965): 30–1. 530 w
Does not believe that criticism can be the science that F proposes in this 'germinal book.' Thinks that F's hierarchy of literary modes cannot be taught in the order that he suggests. F's 'literary criticism remains more convincing than his pedagogy.'

M6.28 Libaire, Beatrice B. *Library Journal* 89 (15 October 1964): 3960
Brief notice.

M6.29 McGrath, Joan. *Canadian Book Review Annual, 1983,* ed Dean Tudor and
Ann Tudor (Toronto: Simon & Pierre 1984), 272. 280 w
Brief review on the occasion of the eighteenth printing of this volume.
'Never can an introduction to a theory of literature and literary education
have been more persuasive, or more enjoyable.'

M6.30 Mackenzie, Manfred. *Southern Review* [Australia] 1, no 3 (1965): 85–8.
1300 w
Sees *EI* as a demythologized version of *AC*, adopting the same touchstone
method used in that book in its most apocalyptic moments. Traces the
roots of *EI* also to F's study of Blake. F's 'theory is in fact a broad, but still
direct, allegorization of Blake.' Describes F as an apocalyptic monist, in
that he sees literature as a giant form, and as a humanist, in that he takes
an aesthetic view of religious belief in art.

M6.31 Major, André. 'Un essai de Frye.' *Le Devoir*, 15 November 1969, 10. 600 w
Review of the French translation (A3e). Summarizes F's answers to the
questions: what is the function of literature? why do people write? why do
they read?

M6.32 Mandel, Eli W. 'The Language of Humanity: Three Books by Northrop
Frye.' *Tamarack Review* 29 (Autumn 1963): 82–9. 3400 w
Says *EI* is 'calculated to show how criticism moves from its practical or
technical concern with literature to its theoretical concern with a structure
of ideas or "co-ordinating principles" which give it coherence, and ultimately social significance, as a discipline.' Places *EI* in the context of F's
other works, especially *AC*: 'as an introduction to Frye's theories, one
wonders how it could be bettered.' Believes that the difficult part of F's
argument is his account of how the imagination and society interact,
a question *WTC* seems consciously intent to answer. Reviewed along with
TSE and *WTC*.

M6.33 M[ickleburgh], B[ruce]. *Educational Courier* 34 (May-June 1964): 57–9.
1680 w
Examines the book primarily from the perspective of its significance
for teaching. Thinks that it could 'set in motion a transformation that
would make the teaching of literature' much more effective than is
now the case and could 'help us to find a new orientation in
professional development work.' Most of the review consists of
citations of particular points F makes about language and
teaching.

M6.34 Picchi, Mario. 'Freschi di Stampa.' *L'Espresso*, 24 March 1974, 61. 50 w
Brief review of the Italian translation (A3f). Says that F ignores Bachelard,
but he gives us 'a brilliant series of comparisons and syntheses.'

M6.35 Pierce, James. *English Journal* 54 (April 1965): 343–4. 810 w
Emphasizes those parts of F's argument that have to do with the conventional structure of literature. Says that 'few have the sense of the totality

of literature that Frye possesses' and thinks that the book would be ideal
for curriculum planning in English departments.

M6.36 S[hoben], E[dward] J[oseph], [Jr]. 'Book Notes.' *Teachers College Record* 66
(January 1965): 384–5. 270 W
Gives a brief summary of F's views on the imagination as that faculty that
seeks to identify the human with the non-human world. 'If [*EI*] falls
short of providing a persuasive rationale, it contributes valuably to the
discussion' of the role of literary study in an age dominated by science.

M6.37 Sussex, R.T. *AUMLA* 24 (November 1965): 317–18. 920 W
Summarizes F's main points. Thinks this is a wise book and, unlike some
of F's other writing, it has a 'direct human touch.' It 'might well be
daily Bible-reading for any student in the humanities.' Has a reservation,
however, about F's assumption that the imagination always creates what is
true.

M6.38 Unterecker, John. 'Literary Criticism.' *New York Times Book Review*, part 2
[Paperbacks], 26 February 1967, 28
Brief notice.

M7 Fables of Identity (*FI*) [A4]

M7.1 Alter, Robert. 'Programmed Profundity.' *Book Week*, 19 July 1964, 8. 810 W
Thinks that F has 'a real gift for generalizing' but that his insights into
literature come in spite of rather than because of his archetypal scheme.
This scheme is 'not so much a scientific description as a poetic creation,' so
much so that the appeal of F's book is that of a carefully balanced and
complete work of art. Judges his essays on Blake (D88) and on the age of
sensibility (D82) to be of the most lasting value.

M7.2 Anonymous. *Booklist* 60 (15 January 1964): 434, 436
Brief notice.

M7.3 Beattie, Munro. 'Nature-Inspired Myths Framework of Literature.' *Ottawa
Citizen*, 21 March 1964, 28. 580 W
Summarizes F's approach to the study of literature by way of the conven-
tions of myth, and outlines the book's contents. 'It is a spellbinding web
Frye weaves, with astonishing range of illustration, comprehensiveness of
types and themes of literature, and touches of art.'

M7.4 Blissett, William. 'Literary Studies.' *University of Toronto Quarterly* 33 (July
1964): 401–8. 260 W
Says *FI* is the most considerable of the six books F published within the
year, more accessible to the non-specialist than *AC*. Refers briefly to
the writers to whom F applies his concepts of myth, archetype, and displacement. Reviewed along with *TSE*, *WTC*, *EI*, *Learning in Language
and Literature* (D137) and *Romanticism Reconsidered* (B10).

M7.5 Carruth, Hayden. 'Poetic Mythology.' *Poetry* 104 (September 1964): 369–74
[372]. 150 W
Brief comment on the book as a 'somewhat simplified view of Frye's theory

and practice.' It is less adequate than *AC*, 'but for readers who wish a quick dunking and who are willing to put up with the atrocious writing of the early essays, *Fables of Identity* will be useful.'

M7.6 Co., F. 'Frye.' *Avanti*, 17 March 1974. 250 w
Brief note about the Italian translation (A4a).

M7.7 Cook, Eleanor, and Ramsay Cook. *Canadian Annual Review for 1963*, ed John Saywell (Toronto: Univ of Toronto Press 1964), 457
Brief note. Reviewed along with *EI*, *TSE*, and *WTC*.

M7.8 Donoghue, Denis. 'The Well-Tempered Klavier.' *Hudson Review* 18 (Spring 1964): 138–42. 2300 w
Complains throughout that in devoting so much attention to the system of literary conventions F slights the particularities of poetic texture and the differences among literary works. Believes F's method works well for what it attempts to do: it just does not do enough to provide readers the feeling of poetry. Believes, also, that F twists literary facts to fit his schematic theses, citing his essay on Stevens's poetry as an example. Still, though Stevens's poetry is ten per cent structure and ninety per cent texture, readers of Stevens will owe a great deal to mapmakers such as F.

M7.9 Fraser, G.S. 'Mythmanship.' *New York Review of Books* 1 (6 February 1964): 18–19. 1320 w
Argues primarily that drama and prose fiction are artistic advances upon the primitive concept of myth because they involve human beings choosing and reacting to the concrete world around them. This is the element left out of F's 'very original critical synthesis' – the element of reality.

M7.10 Fuson, Ben W. *Library Journal* 89 (1 February 1964): 631–2
Brief notice.

M7.11 Hallie, Philip. 'The Master Builder.' *Partisan Review* 31 (Fall 1964): 650–1, 653–8. 2600 w
Says *FI* is an important book, but devotes most of this review to criticizing the fundamental principles of F's entire critical system.

M7.12 Price, Martin. 'Open and Shut: New Critical Essays.' *Yale Review* 53 (Summer 1964): 592–9 [592–4]. 1200 w
Praises F's brilliance as a critic and the liberation provided by his work, but resists his system-building because it 'may shrink up our perception of diversity and novelty.'

M7.13 Reaney, James. 'Frye's Magnet.' *Tamarack Review* 33 (Autumn 1964): 72–8. 2500 w
Devotes most of this review to illustrating how F's account of literary design works to good effect in arranging one's literary experience. Examines several sets of the designs (the four *mythoi*, epiphanies) in F's map of literature, and seeks to show that F's method functions as a magnet, drawing to itself the iron filings that in the reading process tend otherwise to get lost. Praises the book also for its texture, wit, and power.

M7.14 Saltina, Vittorio. 'Un mito per ogni stagione.' *L'Espresso* 20, no 44 (3 November 1974): 87. 520 w

Review of the Italian translation (A4a). Emphasizes the difference between
F and the French structuralists. Says the importance of *FI* is that it puts
the theory expounded in *AC* into practice. Outlines F's understanding of
archetypal form. Agrees with F that archetypal analysis is the premiss
on which aesthetic criticism is founded, but questions his linking the *mythoi*
of comedy, romance, tragedy, and irony with the four seasons.

M7.15 Skelton, Robin. 'The House That Frye Built.' *Canadian Literature* 24 (Spring
1965): 63–6. 1500 W
Sees *FI* as a work of metacriticism, which means that everything in it is in
the service of its unifying vision. Believes F is overly concerned to create a
structure for this vision, a structure that pleases in the same way that
poems please. Thus F can overlook facts and change the meanings of terms
to suit his own purposes. The result is over-simplification, dogma, and
sometimes absurdity. Still, *FI* is a 'challenging, enlivening book.' One
emerges from it 'having had a totally new and strange experience of the
meaning of literature, the nature of mythology, and the function of
criticism.'

M7.16 Swayze, Walter E. 'A Rich Experience.' *Winnipeg Free Press*, 30 May 1964
[Modern Living section], 4
Gives an overview of the central ideas of the first part of *FI*. Objects to F's
frequent blurring of distinctions and failing to explain, but claims his
daring achievement evaporates all local complaints.

M8 **Fearful Symmetry** (*FS*) [A1]

M8.1 Ames, Alfred. 'Escaping Selfhood.' *Poetry* 71 (1947): 101–3. 500 W
Reviews briefly a half dozen twentieth-century books on Blake but claims
that none of them 'should be permitted to jostle *Fearful Symmetry* aside.'
Praises F's ability to illuminate the grammar of Blake's large poetic vision.
Glances at F's understanding of Blake as a visionary proclaiming the
Word of God and at the difference between Shakespeare, whose plays
have a surface, and Blake, whose prophetic works do not.

M8.2 Anonymous. 'The Challenge of William Blake.' *Newsweek*, 5 May 1947, 102.
200 W
Brief notice. Calls *FS* 'a praiseworthy and lucid study.'

M8.3 — 'Elucidation of Blake.' *TLS*, 10 January 1948, 25. 1150 W
Briefly surveys the history of Blake criticism from Gilchrist to Middleton
Murry, seeing most of the interpreters as reading into Blake their own
ideas. But F 'comes nearer than any other to a complete systematic analysis
and interpretation from within.' Believes that F has 'triumphantly carried
out a task ... which cannot help being immense.': uncovering the structure
of Blake's total vision and relating it to the structure of ideas in Western
culture. But the greatness of the book depends finally on whether or
not most readers will be able, after studying *FS*, to read Blake with the

same appreciation that they get from writers, such as Shakespeare and
Homer, whose work is founded on less difficult myths.

M8.4 — *New Yorker* 86 (26 April 1947): 86
Brief notice.

M8.5 — 'Sanity of Genius Found in Blake by Toronto Don.' *Toronto Star*, 17 May
1947, 9. 675 w
Primarily a summary of F's purpose. Says the book is 'scholarly enough for
the most exacting specialist and lucid enough for the average serious
reader.'

M8.6 Belitt, Ben. 'Auguries of Energy.' *Virginia Quarterly Review* 23 (1947):
628–30. 900 w
Calls attention to F's emphasis on Blake's theory of knowledge and to his
making clear Blake's characteristic activity 'of *renaming* the myth in order
to set it free.' Judges the final effect of F's study to be two-fold: (1) he
illuminates the symmetry of Blake's massive iconography of the imagination, and (2) he recovers for the reader each element of the poetic process
itself. Concludes with a summary of Blake's sweeping critique of eighteenth-century rationalism and materialism.

M8.7 Bentley, G.E., Jr, and Martin K. Nurmi. *A Blake Bibliography: Annotated Lists
of Works, Studies, and Blakeana* (Minneapolis: Univ of Minnesota Press
1964), 25–6, 269. 450 w
Judges FS to be 'the single most important study of Blake to appear thus
far,' largely because of F's unified critical method. Says that F's main
argument is that Blake is a traditional rather than an eccentric poet, one
working within the conventions of archetypal symbolism. In a separate
annotation to FS on p 269, the authors remark: 'A magisterial analysis of
Blake's poetry and thought, remarkable alike for its brilliance and its
complexity. It is and probably will remain the most important single work
of Blake criticism.'

M8.8 Bostetter, Edward E. 'Without Contraries Is No Progression.' *Interim* 3 no 1
(1947): 9–16. 3700 w
Says that FS rescues Blake from the cultists by showing him to be a
visionary rather than a mystic. Notes that F's interest is in relating Blake to
the philosophical and religious currents of the age and in placing him in
the context of the mythopoeic traditions from the Renaissance on. Summarizes F's treatment of the Orc symbolism to illustrate his method. Believes
that his effort to squeeze all the possible meanings out of the symbol
sometimes destroys its identity and that 'in the piling of symbol on symbol
he bewilders and exhausts' his readers.

M8.9 Briosi, Sandro. *Uomini e Libri* 58 (April 1976): 75. 275 w
Review of the Italian translation (A1d). Points to the connection between
FS and AC and summarizes F's understanding of Blake's poetic and
religious archetypes, his treatment of the Orc cycle, and his synthetic
reading of *Milton* and *Jerusalem*.

M8.10 C., S.C. 'In Consideration of William Blake.' *Christian Science Monitor*, 27 September 1947, 17. 520 w

Does not believe that F's exposition, though presented 'with force and conviction,' will convince any readers except perhaps the most robust and energetic that Blake's work is of aesthetic importance.

M8.11 Davies, Blodwen. 'I Give You the End of a Golden String.' *The Beacon* 36 (February 1948): 314–19. 2800 w

Says FS is evidence that Blake was one of the enlightened, who sensed a unity among humankind – a genius who expressed the spiritual nature of humanity. Reviews primarily the nature of the imagination as found in Blake's work and its relation to his understanding of beauty and of sin. FS 'is a great imaginative act, a piece of prophetic criticism which can, in the hands of imaginative readers, break open the bondage of the cocoon and free the winged future of a transformed society.'

M8.12 Deacon, William Arthur. 'Masterly Interpretation of William Blake's Poems.' *Globe and Mail*, 17 May 1947, 12. 850 w

Calls FS 'a notable achievement,' a book that 'has enriched the whole literary world by rescuing the major works of a great poet from misunderstanding and obscurity.' Singles out for special comment F's treatment of Blake's epistemology and his views on imagination and civilization.

M8.13 E[rdman], D[avid] E. *ELH*, 15 (March 1948), 10. 300 w

Points to F's analogical and anagogical method of studying Blake, to his slighting of history in explaining Blake's work, and to his interpretation of Blake's idea of Mental Fight.

M8.14 F[lewelling], R[alph] T[yler]. 'Blake Redivivus.' *Personalist* 29 (Spring 1948): 215–17. 950 w

Judges FS to be 'perhaps the most outstanding attempt ever made to bring William Blake's greatness home to the common reader.' Cites primarily F's attention to the attacks by Blake on materialism, external regimentation, and conformity.

M8.15 Frankenberg, Lloyd. 'Forms for Freedom.' *Saturday Review of Literature* 30 (19 July 1947): 19. 1100 w

Comments on F's completely identifying himself with Blake's vision and on the way he opens up Blake's world. Thinks that F handles the material in the book unsystematically and that the piecemeal approach always proves Blake to be superior. Believes that Blake's chief failure was his choice of symbols, even though beneath his symbolism 'lies a real and magnificent play of ideas.' Says that F himself frequently fails in not being able to organize and explain these ideas.

M8.16 G., W. 'William Blake.' *Queen's Quarterly* 54 (Autumn 1947): 395–7. 1040 w

Comments on F's placing of Blake in the contexts of his own age, the tradition of English literature and the Bible, and the arts of painting and music. F 'has gladdened the hearts of those who have long read Blake, and he has opened the way for others.'

M8.17 Gardiner, C. Harold. 'Poetry, Criticism, Short Stories.' *America* 78
       (15 November 1947): xviii
       Brief notice.

M8.18 Garrett, John. 'Turning New Leaves.' *Canadian Forum* 27 (July 1947): 90.
       Partially rpt in *Contemporary Literary Criticism*, vol 24, ed Sharon R. Gunton
       (Detroit: Gale Research 1983), 207–8. 950 w
       For the study of Blake, F 'has tackled the most difficult problem of all: the
       exposition of Blake's esoteric and complicated symbolism.' Gives a brief
       overview of the themes F treats. Criticizes the exclusiveness of Blake's
       doctrine of imaginative vision, but praises F for his 'unravelling the baffling
       symbolism and prophetic message' of Blake.

M8.19 Hallie, Philip. 'The Master Builder.' *Partisan Review* 31 (Fall 1964): 650–1.
       2600 w
       Sees *FS* as an important book, but devotes most of this review to a critique
       of F's system in *AC*.

M8.20 Hamilton, Kenneth. *Dalhousie Review* 27 (October 1947): 381–3. 1320 w
       Thinks F starts at the proper place (Blake's theory of knowledge) and that
       F's account of the unity of Blake's symbolism is 'rightly stressed and
       scrupulously presented.' F's original contribution is his account of Blake's
       imaginative vision and his uncompromising method. Wishes that F had
       made some evaluation of Blake's complete system – 'a critical examination
       of his thought on its intrinsic merits.'

M8.21 Hughes, Josephine Nichols. *The Thomist* 11 (April 1948): 257–9. 1000 w
       Points to F's partisanship and 'his strong conviction that Blake's thought
       cannot be explained wholly in the light of his sources' as two things
       that make *FS* a valuable work for the critical reader. Is distressed, however,
       that F accepts so uncritically Blake's Calvinistic myth of the Fall and his
       'monstrous concept of God and creation.' Points to the beliefs in Blake's
       work that make him an astoundingly perceptive and seminal artist, but
       thinks that F fails in not discriminating between Blake's genuine perceptions
       and his absurd and antinomian excesses.

M8.22 Keynes, Geoffrey. 'The Poetic Vision.' *Time and Tide* 28 (27 December 1947):
       1394. 1100 w
       Points to F's purpose (to establish Blake as a typical poet) and to his
       method (discursive, analytic commentary). *FS* is a book of 'eloquence and
       insight' that will 'carry our understanding of Blake's message well into
       the inland of our consciousness.'

M8.23 Lees, Gene. 'Afterthoughts.' *Downbeat*, 22 December 1960, 4. 670 w
       Recommends *FS* to 'all jazzmen and critics and intelligent admirers of the
       art,' because the book 'opens up such magnificent vistas of meaning,
       and clarifies so much about the relationship of man to art [and] to God.'

M8.24 McLuhan, Herbert Marshall. 'Inside Blake and Hollywood.' *Sewanee Review*
       55 (October-December 1947): 710–13. 1450 w
       Thinks F's work supplants all previous studies of Blake, because F is able

to abandon the linear perspective and, by putting himself inside Blake, 'speak of current issues as we might suppose Blake would have spoken.' F's exegesis is essential because the emphasis upon the intellectual rather than the artistic allegory in Blake's work means that to read about Blake is more satisfactory than reading Blake himself.

M8.25 Margoliouth, H.M. *Review of English Studies* 24 (October 1948): 334–5. 700 w
Sees *FS* as 'a massive achievement,' one that 'provides a solid foundation for all further work on the subject.' Summarizes the topics dealt with in each of the book's twelve chapters, points to several 'superficial faults,' and questions F's interpretation of the Seven Eyes of God.

M8.26 Marnau, Fred. 'William Blake.' *New English Review* 16 (February 1948): 190, 192. 380 w
Calls *FS* a 'profound book,' which not only does justice to Blake but also provides a defence of poetry itself.

M8.27 Morley, Edith J. *Year's Work in English Studies* 28 (1947): 219–20. 320 w
Calls *FS* a 'success in indicating the path that must be followed' to discover the meaning of Blake's visionary prophecies.

M8.28 Randall, Helen W. 'Blake as Teacher and Critic.' *University of Toronto Quarterly* 17 (January 1948): 204–7. 1550 w
Calls attention especially to F's treatment of Blake's epistemology and his visionary theory of art. F's 'brilliant exposition of the developing diagrammatic forms of the Prophecies and of the whole formal pattern of the engraved canon is a super piece of symbolical and anagogical interpretation.' Is not convinced, however, that the method for reading Blake can be applied, as F urges, to reading all literature.

M8.29 Sandwell, B.K. 'Student of Pelham Edgar's Writes Epoch-Marking Volume on Blake.' *Saturday Night* 62 (19 July 1947): 17. 1050 w
Uses a generous selection of quotations from *FS* to illustrate that the book is not simply about Blake's work but about the entire enterprise of poetry and its place in society. Comments on F's understanding of the mythopoeic tradition in English literature. *FS* 'is a blazing light thrown upon the thinking and feeling and consequently upon the bewilderment and anguish' of our own age. It is therefore 'proof of the essentially prophetic character of all great poetry.'

M8.30 Sitwell, Edith. 'William Blake.' *Spectator* 179 (10 October 1947): 466. 1300 w
'To say [*FS*] is a magnificent, extraordinary book is to praise it as it should be praised, but in doing so one gives little idea of the huge scope of the book and of its fiery understanding.' Quotes a number of passages from *FS* to show how F illuminates Blake's creative thought. For F's response to this review see J4a and J4b.

M8.31 Thomas, Ivo. *Blackfriar's* 29 (August 1948): 395–6. 500 w
Judges F to have covered Blake's relation to English literature with 'thoroughness and objectivity.' Comments briefly on F's analysis of Blake's epistemology and his conception of identity.

M8.32 Wasser, Henry. *Modern Language Quarterly* 9 (June 1948): 248–9. 540 w

Sees F as having rectified two failures in much Blake criticism: the failure
to see the historical context of Blake's poetry and the neglect of Blake's
fundamental ethical impulse.

M8.33 Weinberg, A.M. 'Songs and Prophecies.' *UNISA English Studies* 8 (November
1970): 34–5 [35]. 700 w
Reviews F's thesis that Blake is a conscious artist and his central claim that
all of Blake's works must be viewed as part of a unified canon expressing
a coherent mythology based mainly on the Bible. F's 'argument is extremely
lucid,' but the book is flawed by F's failure to analyse Blake's poetic
texture.

M8.34 Wellek, René. *MLN* 64 (January 1949): 62–3. 450 w
Judges *FS* to be 'one of the major achievements of modern Blake scholarship,' but faults F for failing 'in the actual critical task of evaluation and
even analysis of poetry as poetry.' Believes that something is wrong with
F's mythopoeic conception of poetry because, even if Blake's work is
symbolically coherent, it cannot be defended as poetry.

M8.35 White, Helen C. *JEGP* 49 (January 1950): 124–7. 2030 w
Judges F's analysis of Blake's ideas and his basic myth to be lucid and
coherent. But more than that, the book is 'a very warm and sympathetic
affirmation of the value and significance of the message of Blake and of the
importance of Blake as a prophet.' F's distinctive contribution is in treating
Blake's mythmaking in the context of the viable mythmaking in Blake's
own time. Believes the book could have been even better had F paid more
attention to Blake the artist.

M9 **Fools of Time** (*FT*) [A9]

M9.1 Anonymous. *Booklist* 64 (1 October 1967): 165
Brief notice.

M9.2 — *Choice* 4 (December 1967): 1113
Brief notice.

M9.3 — *Humanities Association Review* 25 (Spring 1974): 185–6. 360 w
Outlines F's analysis of the three kinds of Shakespearean tragedy. Judges
the division to be 'persuasively argued.' 'An indispensable text for the
student of Shakespeare.'

M9.4 — 'Shakespeare in Three Parts.' *TLS*, 25 July 1968, 778. 750 w
Sees the structure of the book as 'an intellectual stream of consciousness,'
which presents in lieu of detailed analyses 'a kind of fluid myth-map of
Shakespeare's historical and tragical plays, drawn up in a series of cool and
choice epigrams, definitions, generalizations, and off-hand profundities.'
Thinks *NP* is a much more convincing example of archetypal criticism than
FT.

M9.5 — *Times Educational Supplement*, 13 September 1968, 490
Brief notice.

M9.6 Engelborghs, Maurits. 'Recent Kritisch Werk.' *De zeven Kunsten* 8 (19 September 1967): 4

M9.7 Ferguson, W. Craig. *Queen's Quarterly* 74 (Winter 1967): 773–4. 450 w
Finds that F's deductive method necessarily limits and distorts Shakespeare, who is too large to fit the Procrustean bed of F's categories. Even though the tragedies do not quite fit F's theories, his experimental approach can be a stimulating starting-point for discussion and argument.

M9.8 Foakes, R.A. *English* 17 (Autumn 1968): 99–102 [100]. 225 w
Brief comments on F's scheme for classifying Shakespeare's tragedies, which is sometimes helpful in drawing analogies between the plays.

M9.9 Frye, Roland Mushat. *Shakespeare Quarterly* 29 (Winter 1969): 101. 380 w
Maintains that F is primarily interested in assimilating the conventions of Shakespeare's tragedies into his a priori categories. Finds F's study of archetypal characters more helpful than his analysis of the three kinds of tragedies. Even if one rejects F's underlying system, 'it seems impossible to read Northrop Frye without being enriched by him.'

M9.10 Fuhara, Fusaaki. *Eigo seinen [The Rising Generation]* 113 (March 1968): 186–7
In Japanese. Brief review that agrees generally with F's theory of tragedy, but points to some cases that do not fit.

M9.11 Hamilton, Alice. 'According to Frye.' *Winnipeg Free Press*, 15 July 1967 [Leisure Magazine section], 15
Believes that Frye is too much bound by his nineteenth-century, non-historical approach to Shakespeare. 'The book, on the whole, is hasty and disorganized, opinion not being justified by evidence.'

M9.12 — *Dalhousie Review* 47 (Summer 1967): 279, 281. 680 w
Outlines the way F uses his primary categories. Believes F's idea of 'conflict in time' reveals little that is new, and that the book as a whole 'bears the signs of hasty writing, opinion, confusion, contradiction, and unfounded statements.'

M9.13 Hibbard, G.R. *Shakespeare Survey* 22 (1969): 156–7. 300 w
Finds the book disappointing because no real argument ever emerges. 'Frye attempts to pull too many different approaches together.'

M9.14 Hoy, Cyrus. *Studies in English Literature* 8 (Spring 1968): 365–8. 1000 w
Argues that the book contains more wit than judgment. F's schematizations are ingenious and endlessly fascinating, but they tell us more about F than about Shakespeare's tragedies. His 'contrivance is dazzling ... but very much an end in itself.'

M9.15 Kattan, Naïm, 'Shakespeare est-il tragique?' *Le Devoir*, 21 October 1967, 13. 1200 w
Summarizes F's argument about the three kinds of Shakespearean tragedy and their relation to melodrama, dream, and Christianity. Finds the book to be 'not only a brilliant illustration of his theories and his method, but equally a penetrating and original analysis of Shakespeare's tragic plays.'

M9.16 Kermode, Frank. 'Reading Shakespeare's Mind.' *New York Review of Books* 9
(12 October 1967): 14–17. 1240 w
Says that 'this remarkable book ... seems to prove that Frye's systems are
mnemotechnical in character, a way of making fruitful connections between disparate activities of an extraordinary mind.' Gives an overview of
F's tripartite division of Shakespeare's tragedies. Finds the account of
Christianity and tragedy to be an example of F's pre-eminence, which
'depends upon the self-consciously fictive power of his schemes as well as
upon their power to make him speak more than they know.' *NP* is a
successful work of art because it helps us to make sense of the world.

M9.17 Kernan, Alvin B. 'Exegetes and Paracletes.' *Yale Review* 57 (Winter 1968):
296–8. 1000 w
Gives a sketch of F's schematic approach to Shakespeare. Observes that F's
readings may seem completely indifferent to 'facts.' But despite this, or
perhaps because of it, he is an authentic and prophetic critical voice. 'Out
of his visionary selection and manipulation of details emerges as true a
picture as we are ever likely to get of Shakespearian tragedy.'

M9.18 Markels, Julian. *Wascana Review* 3, no 1 (1968): 95–8. 1650 w
Says that 'this rewarding book ... is ... an intense moral experience.'
Discusses F's comprehensive and flexible method, which is designed not to
do complete justice to Shakespeare's individual plays but to provide a
vision: 'What Frye gives us, like his master Blake, is not so much a method
as a practice, not so much a system as a vision, not so much a theory as
a poem.'

M9.19 Martin, Augustine. *Studies* [Dublin] 59 (Summer 1970): 211–14 [211–12].
500 w
Judges F's critical framework to be unsound: it fails 'to give a coherent
context for the succession of valuable perceptions thrown up by the lectures
almost in its despite.' Finds the book to be wilfully digressive, obscure,
and incoherent.

M9.20 Nathanson, Leonard. *Shakespeare Studies*, 5, ed J. Leeds Barroll (Dubuque,
Iowa: William C. Brown 1970), 329–31. 1120 w
Gives a full summary of the central arguments of each of the three chapters.
Says the book's strength lies in the interrelations among the tragedies
that F is able to uncover and in his fitting of these into 'the larger order of
literary works.'

M9.21 Palmer, D.J. *Review of English Studies* 20 (August 1969): 386. 500 w
Points to the book's primary insight – the experience of being in time and
the heroic struggle against the irony of such experience. Says 'the book's
most valuable quality is one that pervades the whole, namely the impulse
to "get at" the fundamental issues': F keeps the important questions
always in view.

M9.22 Ricks, Christopher. 'Dead for a Docket.' *Listener* 79 (9 May 1968): 610-11.
1440 w

Mainly a critique of F's method. Claims that nothing important issues from the categories F sets up and very little is illuminated from the comparisons he points to.

M9.23 Shibata, Toshihiko. *Eibungaku kenkyu* [*Studies in English Literature*] 45, no 1 (1968): 79–83
In Japanese. Points to the difficulty of theorizing about Shakespeare's tragedies. Has reservations about F's excluding 'life' from literary criticism.

M9.24 Smith, Marion B. *University of Toronto Quarterly* 37 (July 1968): 400–3. 1060 w
Says F's archetypal frame of reference 'illuminates his materials far more often than it distorts them.' Cites examples of F's insights, especially from his chapter on the tragedies of passion. Sees the chief difficulty with the book in the limitations imposed by its original form, the public lecture, which leads to a distortion of emphasis and unargued assumptions.

M9.25 Uhlig, Claus. *Anglia* 89, no 3 (1971): 385–6. 750 w
Thinks that although F throws 'occasional sidelights on the plays discussed,' his schematic framework distorts Shakespeare and tends to ignore the evidence of the texts. 'Critical brilliance, stimulating though it may be, is no compensation for lack of scholarly exactitude.' Criticizes F for ignoring previous research and for using Shakespeare's plays 'primarily as a pretext for rather unrestrained speculation.'

M10 **The Great Code** (*GC*) [A19]

M10.1 Adachi, Ken. 'Canadian Books: A Vintage Season.' *Toronto Star*, 12 September 1981, F10
Brief note.

M10.2 Ages, Arnold. 'In the Beginning Was the Word.' *Montreal Gazette*, 13 March 1982, D8. 825 w. Similar, slightly briefer reviews by Ages appear as 'Frye Probes Bible and Literature,' *The Spectator* [Hamilton, Ont], 27 February 1982, 50, and as 'Northrop Frye Offers a New Vision of the Bible,' *Calgary Herald*, 27 March 1982, F8.
Reviews F's critique of the historical, theological, and purely literary approaches to the Bible and comments on the tools F uses in his own structural analysis.

M10.3 Alexander, Howard. *Quaker Life* 25 (January-February 1984): 32
Brief review.

M10.4 Alter, Robert. *Blake: An Illustrated Quarterly* 17 (Summer 1983): 20–2. 1850 w
Maintains that F's view of the Bible is 'misleading and sometimes dead wrong' because his archetypal method leads him away from the 'differential structures of specific literary texts,' and his attention to typology causes him to distort the referentiality of the Bible. Claims that F misreads the imagery of Psalm 1, the David and Michal story, Genesis 1, and the Book of Job.

M10.5 — *Books in Canada* 11 (August-September 1982): 41–2

Brief note.

M10.6 — *Chatelaine* 55 (May 1982): 6
Brief review.

M10.7 — *The Griffin* 32 (February 1982): 3–4. 525 w
Brief review, announcing GC as a Readers' Subscription book club selection.

M10.8 — *Vancouver Province*, 9 May 1982
Brief review.

M10.9 — *Virginia Quarterly Review* 59 (Summer 1983): 86–7
Brief notice.

M10.10 Atkinson, David W. 'Northrop Frye: Another Landmark Work.' *Lethbridge Herald*, 1 May 1982, c8. 500 w
Judges the results of F's approach, which is to view the Bible as an imaginative unity, to be a 'remarkable accomplishment,' but thinks that he has ignored too much the modern scholarly approaches to Scripture and that he is 'irritatingly glib in his comparisons between Christianity and other world religions.'

M10.11 Ayre, John. 'Distilling the Font of Literature.' *Maclean's* 95 (5 April 1982): 56. 750 w
Places GC in the context of F's other books. Observes that F wants to affirm that 'the Bible is the essential code book of our thought processes, symbolism and mythology,' but that the book is theoretically complex, especially in the first half. Locates the strength of GC in the handbook of biblical symbolism developed in the second half. F's 'achievement is to strip the Bible of religious anxieties.'

M10.12 Balling, J.L. *Dansk Teologisk Tidsskrift* 47, no 1 (1984): 77–8. 250 w
Notes that F's view of the Bible is comprehensive, as it was for the older theologies. Although it does not speak of the Bible in a theological way, theologians will do well to show an interest in it.

M10.13 Barclay, Pat. 'Northrop Frye's Awe-inspiring Look at the Bible.' *Victoria Times Colonist* [BC], 19 June 1982, 34. 580 w
Gives a brief introduction to F's approach and to the main topics he examines.

M10.14 Bates, Ronald. 'A Literary Event of Major Scope.' *London Free Press* [Ontario], 10 April 1982, B9. 1600 w
Comments on F's strategic use of wit and irony as teaching devices and on the quality of bricolage both in the Bible and in F's approach to it.

M10.15 Baumgaertner, Jill P. *Christian Century* 99 (29 September 1982): 962–3. 800 w
Summarizes F's argument on narrative and imagery. 'F notices the minute and unusual and makes it relevant and thought-provoking.' Thinks that the two-part division of the book into the theoretical and the practical implies an unncessary separation.

M10.16 Becker, John E. 'The Word of God & the Work of Man.' *Worldview* 25 (September 1982): 5–8. 3870 w
Places the book in the context of F's views on Blake, the structure of literature, and, most important, his own vision of the universal task of

building a human community. Presents a concise but thorough account of F's understanding of the function of language in recreating a new society and of the distinction between the experience and the study of literature, the latter of which makes possible a shareable vision of the human community. Summarizes F's use of typology as a means for understanding patterns of narrative and imagery in the Bible. Argues that F's importance is in his helping us to see that without the imagination we inhabit a world of unreality and alientation.

M10.17 Bliven, Naomi. 'The Good Book.' *New Yorker* 58 (31 May 1982): 104–6. 1990 w
Gives a succinct digest of F's account of the nature of biblical language, and reviews F's argument about the three unifying techniques in the Bible (metaphor, narrative, typology) and about its power as kerygma.

M10.18 Bloomfield, Morton W. 'The Oldest Stories.' *Partisan Review* 50 (1983): 633–4. 400 w
Observes that while there is a similarity between F's approach and the rabbinical one (difficulties can be explained by reference to each other) there is also a difference (F emphasizes myth and typology at the expense of history).

M10.19 Bogdan, Deanne. 'From Stubborn Structure to Double Mirror: The Evolution of Northrop Frye's Theory of Literary Response in *The Great Code*.' Paper presented at the annual meeting of the South Atlantic Modern Language Association, Atlanta, Ga, 10 November 1984. 18 pp. Photoduplicated typescript
See L57.

M10.20 Borgman, Paul. *Christian Scholar's Review* 12, no 4 (1983): 360–3. 400 w
Compares GC with Amos Wilder's *Jesus' Parables and the War of Myths*. Calls attention to F's emphasis upon centripetal meaning and his exposition of the seven phases of revelation.

M10.21 Bouce, Paul-Gabriel. *Etudes Anglaises* 37, no 4 (1984): 449–50. 640 w
Gives a brief summary of F's purpose. Notes the double-mirror structure of the book. Thinks F's encyclopedic approach, as opposed to that of narrow professionalism, is to be admired. Observes that Blake's apocalyptic vision, which resolves ontological opposites, is always in the margin of the book.

M10.22 Brauner, David. 'In Man's Image.' *Jerusalem Post Magazine*, 7 January 1983, 13. 1050 w
Offers a brief summary of F's major theses. Claims that F is 'out of his element' because he lacks knowledge of the Hebrew language and Jewish tradition.

M10.23 Breslin, John B. 'The Gospel according to Frye.' *Book World* 12 (16 May 1982): 11, 14. 1400 w
Examines F's conception of types, and singles out for special comment his treatment of apocalypse. Says that the expanding vision of the ideal reader locates F firmly in the Protestant tradition.

M10.24 Briner, Lewis A. 'Divine Reading.' *The Common Reader*, August-September 1982, 1. 850 w.
Finds Part 2 of the book, especially the analysis of the seven phases of revelation, the most rewarding.

M10.25 Bronzwaer, W. et al. 'Recent Studies in Literary Theory – A Survey,' *Dutch Quarterly Review of Anglo-American Letters* 13 (1983/4): 300–19 [305–6]. 375 w
A brief glance at F's major assumptions about the mythological universe of the Bible, its teleological world-view, and its typological structure.

M10.26 Brown, Geoff. 'Deciphering *The Great Code*.' *Seed* [Univ of Toronto] 4 (January 1983): 3. 1000 w
Praises F's insights into the visionary qualities of the Bible, but believes that his treatment, if pushed too far, 'threatens a fundamental denial of what the Bible claims for itself' – a communication from God to man.

M10.27 Budd, Daniel. *Religious Humanism* 17 (Autumn 1983): 196–7. 650 w
Outlines F's approach to the Bible. Is concerned chiefly with the implications of this approach for Unitarians and religious humanists. Finds the most powerful part of the book to be in its coda.

M10.28 Burgess, Anthony. 'The First Jewish Novelists.' *Observer* [London], 6 June 1982, 31. 220 w
A brief outline of F's approach. Says that the book is 'assured, urbane, witty and full of remarkable insights ... It is a wise book.'

M10.29 Cahill, P. Joseph. 'Deciphering *The Great Code*.' *Dalhousie Review* 63 (Autumn 1983: 412–21. 4700 w
Summarizes F's views on the unity of the Bible, especially its typological unity and its imagery and style. Reflects on both the literary-critical and theological implication of F's conception of the Bible, calling attention to the similarities between his views and those of other literary and biblical critics. Hopes that F will develop his idea that the Bible contains a vision that can create community, showing how the power of such a vision can be assimilated and absorbed.

M10.30 — 'The Unity of the Bible.' *Biblica* 65, no 3 (1984): 404–11 3500 w
Reviews F's arguments about the typological, metaphorical, and stylistic characteristics of the Bible. Observes that F's thesis about the unity of the Bible means something different for Christians from what it means for Jews; that the Bible does not, contrary to what F claims, disdain history; and that it contains an existential and charismatic, as well as a poetic, vision. Hopes that F will clarify the relation between historical and literary criticism, between critical understanding and faith, and between the biblical and other religious visions.

M10.31 Caird, George. 'The Bible as Fiction.' *London Review of Books* 4 (17 November 1982): 16–17. 1250 w
Reviews F's arguments about the three phases of language and about typology as a form of biblical metaphor. Notes that despite 'the richness of Frye's treatment,' his use of the technical terms of criticism is ambiguous;

and that despite the ways in which biblical language enables us to see the vision of the Bible, that vision may be false.

M10.32 Cameron, J.M. 'A Good Read.' *New York Review of Books* 29 (15 April 1982): 28–31. Rpt in *Esprit* 9 (September 1982): 42–52, trans by Sylvie Courtine-Denamy. 5880 w

Sees the main idea in the book embodied in F's insistence that the Bible invites us to read it typologically. Believes that F has not adequately handled the question of the Bible's historicity. Still, *GC* 'is a magnificent book, a necessary recall to some fundamental principles of Biblical interpretation, and a collection of problems and questions of the first importance for critics, Biblical scholars, and the educated public in general ... F's architectonic power is ... astonishing.'

M10.33 C[ampion], N[ancy]. *Canadian Baptist* 9 (October 1982): 43
Brief review.

M10.34 Carroll, Robert P. *Scottish Journal of Theology* 37, no 2 (1984): 246–50. 2100 w
Provides a fairly succinct summary of the central issues treated in each of the eight chapters of this 'immensely readable and stimulating' book.

M10.35 Conradi, Peter. 'Master Myth.' *New Statesman* 103 (18 June 1982): 20–1. 480 w

Places *GC* in the context of F's total schematic framework and notes F's return to the issue of literal meaning. Finds that 'the polymathic scope' of the book 'makes it hard to focus.' It 'has an oracular tone and an eccentric unity. It abounds in small diagrams, wry asides, repetitions and discontinuities, loves to spawn arcane distinction, does not eschew the odd sermon.'

M10.36 Crossan, John Dominic. 'Literature and the Book.' *Commonweal* 109 (10 September 1982): 475–9. 1360 w

Places F's book in the context of modern biblical criticism: it is a part of one of the two main reactions to an exclusively historical interest in the Bible. Summarizes the argument of *GC*, finding that it hinges upon the chapters on typology. Concludes that the book lacks any real centre, and that what the study of the Bible requires is an emphasis not simply upon literature but upon history and religion as well.

M10.37 Delaney, Paul. 'The Letter and the Spirit.' *Saturday Night* 97 (May 1982): 55–6. 900 w

Sees *GC* as ideally suited to F's interest in literature as myth, his impersonal theory of literature, and his rejection of value-judgments. F 'has produced a remarkably learned, magnanimous, and inventive work,' yet he sometimes pushes his method too hard and brushes aside the immediate meanings of the text.

M10.38 DePinto, Basil. 'The Book of Life.' *America* 147 (28 August 1982): 96. 490 w
Praises *GC* for its attention to language and typology. 'There is scarcely anything in the book out of harmony with current, well-founded positions of biblical criticism.'

M10.39 Dudek, Louis. 'The Bible as Fugue: Themes and Variations,' *University of Toronto Quarterly* 52 (Winter 1982–3): 128–35. 3400 w

Comments on the ways in which F rejects the historical, cultural, and doctrinal approaches to the Bible, offering instead a view of the Bible that has its roots in nineteenth-century romanticism. Theologically, F is close to Schleiermacher, and his view of the significance of myth aligns him somewhat paradoxically with Bultmann, who claims that when the Bible is properly demythologized it reveals a meaning of universal reality. F 'has presented a secular and highly enlightened vision of reality – roughly Hegelian in character – as though it had evolved or always been present in the Judaeo-Christian tradition; it is a vision that really takes us beyond religion, since it is entirely free of any faith or doctrine as usually understood.'

M10.40 Edinborough, Arnold. 'The Books of Spring: Three Early Bloomers.' *Le Devoir*, 17 April 1982, 38. 630 w
Points to F's commentaries in Jonah and Job as examples of the insights he provides. *GC*, which 'probably will be Frye's greatest work,' forces one to go back to the Bible itself.

M10.41 Einbinder, Susan. 'Alter vs Frye: Which Bible?' *Prooftexts* 4 (September 1984): 301–8. 4000 w
Gives a detailed summary of the central arguments in each chapter. Compares F's approach with Robert Alter's in *The Art of Biblical Narrative*. Finds cultural anachronisms in *GC*, thinks F slights the cultic aspects of the Old Testament, and believes his theory of the U-shaped structure of the Biblical narrative does not fit well with the centre-oriented idea of sacred space. But finds that F's book with its insistent humanistic posture serves to help correct the prevailing currents of deconstruction.

M10.42 Evans, William R. *Best Sellers* 42 (June 1982): 112. 720 w
Offers brief comments in F's views on language, the wisdom literature, Jesus, and the power of verbal imagination in the Bible.

M10.43 Fixler, Michael. 'Myth and History.' *Commentary* 74 (August 1982): 76–80. 5000 w
After placing *GC* in the context of F's general theory of literature, turns to 'the real issue the book presents us with,' which is 'the Bible's status with respect to myth and history.' Contrasts F's typological approach, which makes historical concerns irrelevant, to that of modern biblical criticism: 'biblical myth and typology lead Frye into a kind of Platonic ... substitution of the greater reality of the mythic Idea the Bible incarnates for the lesser, almost negligible, accidental reality of whatever historical basis there is to the Bible.' Locates F's position within a non-realist and ahistorical movement in biblical criticism and theology, a movement that Fixler is somewhat anxious about: 'I for one am not certain literary criticism can provide answers to questions for which history still seems the arbiter ... history can exact fearful penalties if it is underestimated.'

M10.44 Fry, H. Paul. 'Northrop Frye's Myth of Concern.' *Yale Review* 72 (July 1983): 605–12. 3250 w
Seeks primarily to uncover the religious ground upon which *GC*, as well as

F's other works, rests. Believes that F's criticism 'reflects a poignant and rather old-fashioned crisis of modernity,' a crisis that he has tried to overcome by substituting the 'stubborn structure' of literature for that loss of sacred space that characterizes modernism. Concludes that throughout F's work there is too heavy a reliance on the concept of perfection: to aim at completing the cycle of romance and so to recover a lost paradise is to dismiss too easily the alienation and imperfection of life.

M10.45 Fulford, Robert. 'Frye Holds up the Bible to Us and Says: Thought Begins Here.' *Toronto Star*, 13 March 1982, F12. 1025 w

Places F's book in the context of his career as a critic and teacher. Emphasizes that F's real purpose is to suggest how the Bible 'provides the very structure of our minds.'

M10.46 Gervais, Marty. 'The Bible According to Norrie.' *Windsor Star*, 27 March 1982. 1480 w

Records some of F's responses in a telephone interview to questions about the Bible and about his own views on religion.

M10.47 Gillespie, Gerald. 'Bible Lessons: The Gospel According to Frye, Girard, Kermode, and Voeglin.' *Comparative Literature* 38 (Summer 1986): 289–97. 5220 w

Observes that F 'forcefully reinstates the widely-held Romantic view that literature is a continuation of mythmaking and that the Bible constitutes a "mythological universe," the supreme supertext of Western civilization.' Wonders whether or not F's argument simply re-enacts the celebration of a familiar cultural theme. Concludes that the Bible can be read as F reads it but that we should not fail to remember the non-Christian visions in Western literature as well as those versions of the Christian paradigm that get incorporated into larger imaginative bodies of thought.

M10.48 Globe, Alexander. 'Apocalypse Now.' *Canadian Literature* 97 (Summer 1983): 182–91. 3200 w

Gives a detailed summary of F's arguments in the separate sections of the book. Finds its quintessential insights in the chapters on typology and language. Examines especially the implications of the four imaginative levels F develops in the final chapter. Maintains that in the fourth level – the mode of vision framed in the language of love – F forges 'a new myth substituted for the biblical religions.' It is a vision 'radically Romantic (specifically Blakean) in the imaginative sense, subjectivist or idealist in the epistemological sense, totalitarian in the ideological sense, and neoplatonic, gnostic or eastern in the philosophical and religious sense.' Comments finally on the problems that GC raises for historical, non-idealist approaches to the Bible.

M10.49 Gold, Joseph. 'Biblical Symmetry: The Gospel According to Frye.' *Dalhousie Review* 63 (Autumn 1983): 408–11. 1900 w

Faults GC for being too Blakean, too Hegelian, and too visionary. Says that the book lacks attention to detail and, thus, falls outside the current trends of biblical literary criticism. Believes that F's expansive use of certain

key terms (eg, 'myth,' 'body,' and 'love') collapse the distinctions necessary for argument.

M10.50 — 'Review Essay.' *English Studies in Canada* 9 (December 1983): 487–98.
5500 w

Believes that in its efforts to blend theology and literary criticism F's book
fails. It is a 'mystical kind of pseudo-theological poetic vision-without-
poetry.' Finds that F's terminology is particularly confusing because too
expansive. Much of the review is devoted to faulting the book for what
Gold perceives as F's anti-Jewish sentiment.

M10.51 Gould, Allan M. 'Professor Publishes Second Masterpiece of a Glorious
Career.' *Thomson News Service*, 23 April 1982. 680 w. Appeared also with
the title '*The Great Code* a Second Masterpiece'

Gives a brief summary of F's views on the authorship of the Bible and
comments on the book's structure and its value.

M10.52 Grant, George. 'The Great Code.' *Globe and Mail*, 27 February 1982,
[Entertainment section], 17. 1500 w

Sees a conflict between F's Linnaean taxonomies ('the scientizing of literature') and his theological pronouncements, the latter of which show that
he is interpreting the Bible from the perspective of modern philosophy and
secularized Protestantism.

M10.53 Greenstein, Edward L. *Melton Journal* 16 (Spring-Summer 1983): 15, 24.
1100 w

Sees the strength of the book in F's making us 'appreciate the extent to
which metaphors and images are used and re-used in the Bible, the extent
to which even the Hebrew Bible rewrites itself.'

M10.54 Hamilton, A.C. 'The Bible as a Key to All Art.' *Whig-Standard Magazine*
[Kingston, Ont], 1 May 1982, 18. 2000 w

Outlines F's purpose and summarizes the book's content, with special
attention to his account of the three phases of language. Believes F's 'reading of the Bible will triumph over any shortcomings and errors Biblical
scholars may find in it because it is not based on reason, social anxiety or
prejudice but is the product of a fully imaginative response that is active
and informed.'

M10.55 Hellgardt, Ernst. *Germanistik* 24 (1983): 313–14. 260 w

Judges *GC* to be 'fully original' compared with the discussions of typology
in German and French criticism after 1945. F's finding an independent
position between the literalists and allegorists and between theological
criticism and traditionalism provides a fresh look at the Bible for the
twentieth-century reader.

M10.56 Helwig, Maggie. 'A Big Book on *The* Big Book.' *Arthur* [Trent Univ], April
1982. 450 w

Comments briefly on the book's general conception and approach.

M10.57 Hill, Edmund, O.P. *New Blackfriars* 64 (February 1983): 89–92. 2020 w

Gives two reasons why *GC* is valuable from a theological point of view.
First, it attacks the fundamentalist assumption that the language of the Bible

is demotic or descriptive; and second, it 'shows up the absurdity of the division, or even separation that has been allowed to develop between scriptural scholarship and dogmatic theology.'

M10.58 Hook, Janet. 'Anatomist of Criticism Confronts a "Huge, Sprawling, Tactless Book" – the Bible.' *Chronicle of Higher Education*, 27 October 1982, 19–20. 2780 w

Summarizes the book's major concerns and places its arguments in the context of F's other work, especially *AC*. Gives the initial reactions to the book by J.M. Cameron, Geoffrey Hartman, and others.

M10.59 Hopkins, Dewi. ' "A Glasse of Blessings." ' *Home* 37 (December 1983): 3–5, 12–14. 2300 w

Gives a general introduction to F's approach. Finds that he equivocates on the question of whether the Bible is true, which for the reviewer is regrettable.

M10.60 Horne, B[rian] L. *Heythrop Journal* 24 (1983): 432–3. 850 w

Finds the book 'a refreshing corrective to the excessive historicism of most of the work of modern biblical scholars,' but complains that F's method of identifying the imagery of the Bible leads to improprieties, that he emphasizes too much the unity of the Bible, and that his style 'obscures more than it reveals.'

M10.61 Jarret-Kerr, Martin. 'Word within a Word.' *Manchester Guardian* 126 (27 June 1982): 21. 250 w

Except for F's 'wise remarks about Bible-translation' and his concluding 'paean to freedom and love,' finds little in the book to recommend it.

M10.62 Jeffrey, David L. 'Encoding and the Reader's Text.' *University of Toronto Quarterly* 52 (Winter 1982–3): 135–41. 3700 w

Maintains that *GC* is closer to 'a treatise in hermeneutical theology' than to literary criticism, and observes that F's caveat that the book expresses his 'personal encounter' with the Bible pre-empts objective discussion of his claims. Goes on to argue, however, that F emphasizes typology at the expense of history. 'A biblical view of history appears to be essential for a reading of the biblical text.' F, however, neglects this view of history and the result is an interpretation that reflects his own subjectivity. A further problem is F's 'semantic and rhetorical sleight of hand,' which obfuscates the obvious.

M10.63 Johnson, Pegram, III. *Historical Magazine of the Protestant Episcopal Church* 52 (March 1983): 91–3. 950 w

Comments on F's understanding of biblical language and typology. Praises the breadth and depth of his application of the Western literary tradition to the study of the Bible.

M10.64 Johnston, Alexandra F. *Presbyterian Record* 106 (October 1982): 32–5. 1530 w

Consists largely of an outline of F's approach and a summary of the eight chapters.

M10.65 Kattan, Naïm. 'A Grand Passion.' *Books in Canada* 11 (June-July 1982): 12–14. Appears also as 'La Bible selon Northrop Frye' in *Le Devoir*, 12 June 1982, 17, 32. 1650 w

Sees *GC* as F's 'most important work' and also 'his most personal.'
Observes that for F the Bible, rather than the world of objects or the world
of imagination, is what explains 'the foundations of the religious mind.'
Gives a summary of F's attitudes about language, history, metaphor, and
myth as these relate to the Bible. Contrasts F's career to that of Malraux,
who found the secret of the world in art. For F 'the Word is both the
puzzle and the solution.'

M10.66 Kearney, Richard, SJ. *Studies* 72 (Summer 1983): 190–2. 1300 w
Calls *GC* 'a remarkable achievement, wide-ranging, eclectic, prolific, elegantly written and easily accessible to the non-specialized reader,' but it is
a book 'not without its faults.' Judges it to be too open-ended, quasi-
Hegelian, and indeterminate, and argues that it fails to distinguish clearly
between the socio-historical, mythological, and psychological levels of
human conditioning, thus ignoring fundamental questions.

M10.67 Kenner, Hugh. 'Imaginative Proclamation.' *New York Times Book Review* 87
(11 April 1982): 10–11, 28. 1350 w
Concentrates on F's beginning with the assumption of the Bible's unity
and on his explanation of literal meaning. Says that no one has shown with
'such cogent energy as Frye' that the Bible is 'our paradigm of all linguistic
working, all interpretative challenge.'

M10.68 Kermode, Frank. 'The Universe of Myth.' *New Republic* 186 (9 June 1982):
30–3. 2000 w
Believes that *GC* is a work 'of very great distinction,' but that its staying
power will depend more on the imaginative constructs it builds than on its
bringing to consciousness the assumptions lying behind the Bible. The
force of the book is therefore more figural than mimetic, less sceptical than
poetic. It constitutes F's 'own antitype of the Bible.' Kermode devotes
some space to summarizing F's position on biblical language, typology, and
the narrative phases, all of which are presented 'with the full force of F's
authority, and with all the old expressive power.'

M10.69 Kilpatrick, Ken. 'An Exciting List of Book Titles for the Fall.' *Spectator*, 22
August 1981, 46
Brief note.

M10.70 Kirss, Tiina. 'The Great Code: A Review Article.' *Crux: A Quarterly Journal
of Thought and Opinion* 19 (December 1983): 18–26. 6350 w
Gives a detailed summary of F's approach to his subject and of the book's
contents. Finds that *GC* provides a provocative new way to read the
Bible, but thinks that F is sometimes too cavalier about biblical scholarship,
that his emphasis on centripetal meaning too readily dismisses history as
a legitimate concern and elevates human recreation above divine creation,
and that his commitment to the principle of metaphorical identity collapses
the differences between such things as biblical vision and Eastern
consciousness.

M10.71 Knelman, Judith. 'The Great Code.' *The Graduate* [Univ of Toronto] 9 (May-
June 1982): 7–10. 2350 w
Feature story on F, written on the occasion of the publication of *GC*.

Comments on the inception, writing, and production of the book. Includes biographical anecdotes.

M10.72 Lee, Alvin. 'Towards a Language of Love and Freedom: Frye Deciphers the Great Code.' Paper presented as a symposium on *GC* at Emmanuel College, Univ of Toronto, 1 October 1982. 24 pp. Photoduplicated typescript. See L298.

M10.73 Levine, Herbert J. 'How Many Bibles?' *Georgia Review* 36 (Winter 1982): 900–4. 2200 w
Contrasts F's *GC* with Robert Alter's *The Art of Biblical Narrative*, books that exist 'in utterly incompatible universes of discourse.' The former is theoretical and deductive, and it points beyond history; the latter is empirical and inductive, and it points into history. Looks at the different ways these two critics treat the creation story in Genesis. Points to F's emphasis on the metaphorical identification between God and man and the community of vision in which individuality is of little importance.

M10.74 Loudon, John. *Parabola* 7 (August 1982): 104, 106, 108. 1600 w
Consists largely of a summary of the book. Believes that F errs in slighting the Bible's 'rootedness in actual historical events' and that the Bible cannot really be approached in F's cool dispassionate way.

M10.75 McConnell, Frank. *The Wilson Quarterly* 6 (Special Issue 1982): 138–9. 470 w
Describes briefly F's mythic approach to the Bible, which is said to be a welcome alternative to the widespread methods of contemporary criticism, which lack any intellectual and emotional response to literature.

M10.76 McDade, John, SJ. 'The Bible as Literature.' *The Month* 224 [15 ns] (September 1982): 320–1. 830 w
Reviews F's claims about the imaginative coherence of the Bible, and judges the book to be an excellent introduction to the Bible for both theologians and literary critics.

M10.77 Maddux, Percy. *Crossroads* [Winnipeg], 26 May 1982
Brief notice.

M10.78 Magesa, L. *African Ecclesial Review* 25 (April 1983): 128. 550 w
Says that F 'provides a very rewarding approach towards a basic understanding of the Bible,' especially the relation of its language to that of Western literature and to the oral tradition.

M10.79 Mandel, Eli. 'Tautology as Truth and Vision.' *Canadian Forum* 62 (September 1982): 30–1. 1580 w
Observes that for all of the arguments carried forth in *GC* and for all of the knowledge it embodies, it remains a prefatory book; that F's arguments about the unity of the Bible and syntactic, centrifugal meaning 'are not so much concerned to deny all allegorical meaning of the Bible as to cut off its historical roots'; that, similarly, F's conception of literal meaning and its relation to myth and metaphor is radically anti-historical; and that F's 'argument for the authority of vision and faith' is built upon the tautological structure of the double mirror.

M10.80 Manicom, David. 'Frye Finds *Code* in Bible Language.' *The Mike* [St Michael's College, Univ of Toronto], 16 March 1982, 8. 1000 w

Finds F's reflections on biblical language to be stronger than his speculations about the cultural influence and ultimate meaning of the Bible,
especially as presented at the end of each chapter. Believes the book's
principal accomplishment is F's account of the principles of imagery and
typology that arise out of metaphor.

M10.81 Martin, David. ' "Behold, I Make All Things New." ' *Times Higher Education Supplement*, 23 July 1982, 12. 2900 w

Sees GC as a structuralist, agnostic reading of the Bible. It is a book 'of rare
insight and intellectual beauty,' yet it is somewhat too loose in granting
the play of almost any meaning and too absolute in denying all demythologizing. Still, F's interpretation and the exegesis of believers 'arrive at
the same mode of understanding,' the principles for which Martin provides
general summaries.

M10.82 Martin, J.P. *Touchstone: Heritage and Theology in a New Age* 1 (May 1983): 42–3. 630 w

Contrasts F's approach to that of historical criticism. Judges his method to
pose 'new vistas for research, imagination and the fusion of paradigms
for Biblical study.'

M10.83 Medcalf, Stephen. 'A Blakean Bible.' *Listener* 108 (23 September 1982): 23. 1150 w

Sees F's vision of the Bible as 'detached from factuality.' Judges his thesis
about the phases of language to be 'generalised and slipshod,' and his
avoidance of the truth of the Bible 'impoverishes his book.' Still, F 'writes
marvelously,' especially on the notions of eternity and on his own beliefs,
even though his writing is closer to theology and poetry in these places
than it is to literary criticism.

M10.84 M[essic], P[enelope]. *Booklist* 78 (15 June 1982): 1350
Brief notice.

M10.85 Morgan, John Hanly. *Unitarian Universalist World*, 15 August 1982. 300 w
Brief review, summarizing F's idea of the biblical order of words.

M10.86 Moritz, A.F. 'The Great Code.' *Brick* 18 (Spring 1983): 5–7. 2900 w
Disagrees primarily with F's assumption that the Bible should be regarded
as a unified whole and with his attention simply to the literary dimension
of the Bible.

M10.87 Morley, Patricia. 'Vintage Northrop Frye: Worlds out of Words.' *Quill & Quire* 48 (May 1982): 35. 1000 w

Sees GC as a 'massive compendium of philosophy, theology, social theory
and aesthetics' that relies upon the Socratic method of argument.

M10.88 Newell, A.G. *Evangelical Quarterly* 57 (April 1985): 188–9. 740 w
Says that the book 'contains sparkling insights which shed light in places
where evangelicals rarely venture' but faults F for sometimes pontificating
and being too flippant. This last attitude 'must cast some doubt on Frye's
moral seriousness.'

M10.89 Nuttall, A.D. *Modern Language Review* 78 (October 1983): 882–3. 850 w
Gives a brief summary of F's thesis about the shape of the biblical narrative,
but worries about his lack of interest in fact and historicity.

M10.90 Pachet, Pierre. 'Comment lire la Bible quand on n'y croit pas.' *Quinzaine littéraire* 432 (1985): 20. 1030 w
Review of the French translation (A19g). Observes that the principal attraction of F's position is his ironic point of view, his democratic spirit, and his wide learning. Thinks that the book will be difficult for French readers but that reading it will be worth the effort. Regards F's treatment of the Bible as a literary text as minimizing the differences between canonical and non-canonical texts. Says that the great virtue of the book is that it makes one want to read the Bible and connect it with other literature.

M10.91 Phillips, E. Harrell. 'The Bible's Literary Framework.' *Jackson Sun* [Tennessee], 15 August 1982, 5B. 900 w
Sees *GC* as a 'provocative and helpful' dialectic that bridges the gap between literary and biblical critics, and places F's book in the context of the several kinds of biblical criticism. Summarizes F's chapters on language, typology, and myth.

M10.92 Poland, Lynn. 'The Secret Gospel of Northrop Frye.' *Journal of Religion* 64 (October 1984): 513–19. 2300 w
Places *GC* in the context of *AC* and shows how both, with their emphasis upon romance and myth, oppose themselves to New Critical theory and to the way it has influenced biblical studies. Finds a dual thrust running throughout the book. On the one hand, F anatomizes the Bible's myths and images, showing how they fit into the total 'order of words'; the Bible is a structurally unified work that provides for the properly distanced observer the code to Western culture. On the other hand, F engages the Bible, seeing it as a mysterious, visionary text that can transform the consciousness of its readers. Finds that F treats history, as he treats the relation of the imagination to human experience, ambiguously. But the ambiguity is resolved in F's theory of polysemous meaning. Concludes that *GC* 'properly belongs within the tradition of scriptural exegesis, of theological hermeneutics.' His reading of the Bible, while heretical, is not esoteric, for he intends, by showing that literature is religion, 'to make priests of us all.'

M10.93 Porter, Stanley E. *Journal of the Evangelical Theological Society* 27 (March 1984): 102–3. 980 w
Finds the book to be challenging and brilliant but is bothered by F's manipulation of the text, his anti-historical sentiments, his ambiguous theologizing, and his '*post hoc* mythic interpretations of various passages.'

M10.94 Pratt, William. *World Literature Today* 58 (Winter 1984): 172. 680 w
Gives a brief summary of F's approach and central claims. 'Frye's word is not the last word on the Bible, certainly, but it is one that is likely to prove lasting.'

M10.95 Preston, Richard J. 'The Spirit, the Code, and Critical Interpretation.' *Culture* [Canadian Ethnology Society] 2, no 2 (1982): 125–6. 900 w
Comments especially on the importance of *GC* for anthropologists, because of the clarity and scope of F's synthesis, his understanding of language

and myth, and the broad range of his inquiry into Western thought and imagination.

M10.96 Read, Stanley. 'Intellectual Giant Decodes the Bible.' *Vancouver Sun*, 21 May 1982, L29. 1080 w

Largely biographical information about F, along with some scattered quotations from the book.

M10.97 Richardson, Peter. 'Cracking the Great Code, or History is Bunk.' *Dalhousie Review* 63 (Autumn 1983): 400–7. 3700 w

Sees F's understanding of modern biblical criticism, especially the redaction and canonical critics and those working with social science methods, as limited. Maintains that F elevates theory at the expense of history; that such bias reflects the simplistic view of early-twentieth-century interpreters; that his assumptions about the causality of the Bible are not sustained by historical investigation; that his pattern of the seven phases of biblical narrative are close to dispensationalism; and that he errs in not looking first at the individual parts of the Bible before developing his generalized theory.

M10.98 Ridd, Carl. *Studies in Religion / Sciences religieuses* 11, no 4 (1982): 446–8. 1500 w

Chiefly a description of F's central purpose (to answer the question of the literal meaning of the Bible) and of his schema of the three phases of language in chapter 1. Sees the final chapter as proposing 'the most radical hermeneutic subversions': here F 'shows the kerygma operating to create the imagination that can imagine it, and that has imagined it.' Believes the greatest strength of GC is 'the synoptic power and lucidity' of the whole book.

M10.99 Robbins, Vernon K. *Quarterly Journal of Speech* 71 (August 1985): 383–6. 2600 w

Contrasts F's views on the metonymic and metaphoric functions of biblical language, his method of centrifugal analysis, and his emphasis on typology, with Robert Alter's approach in *The Art of Biblical Narrative*. Says that F's 'system is something of a merger of a demythologizing approach and a salvation history.' Points to F's insistence on the priority of metaphor to metonomy, and of myth to historical prose fiction, in the interpretation of the Bible.

M10.100 Robertson, Elizabeth. 'Supreme Fiction.' *English* 41 (Autumn 1982): 274–81. 3000 w

Sees Frye's book, along with Robert Alter's *The Art of Biblical Narrative*, as an important contribution of literary criticism to biblical scholarship, which has too long neglected the insights that literary critics might bring to the study of the Bible. Gives an overview of the schema of GC and calls special attention to F's discussion of myth.

M10.101 Robinson, Joseph. 'Bible Language.' *Church Times*, 10 September 1982, 6. 525 w

An appreciation of GC as 'one of those rare books that stimulate thought.'

Maintains that F gets beyond the 'objective' approaches to the Bible and shows us how language functions 'to open up to us the Bible as Bible.'

M10.102 Rodd, C.S. 'Talking Points from Books.' *Expository Times* 94 (October 1982): 1–3 [2–3]. 1000 w
Notes the similarity between F's view of the Bible and that of the 'canonical critics' among biblical scholars. Believes these scholars should take note of the book, even though its approach through imagination, its return to levels of interpretation (a re-introduction of allegory), and its insistence on the autonomy of the text (a flight from history) will seem dangerous to some and will not appeal to all.

M10.103 Rovit, Earl. *Library Journal* 107 (1 June 1982): 1097. 145 w
Brief review. Says the book is 'tightly but clearly argued' and 'almost endlessly provocative.'

M10.104 S[chell], R[ichard] D. *Spenser Newsletter* 13 (Fall 1982): 51–6. 2900 w
Sees GC as epistemologically prior to F's other books and as representing the fruits of his claims: that the Bible is the bedrock of all literary experience, that historically descriptive accounts of the Bible are insufficient, and that the metaphoric unity of narrative and image are prior to doctrine and abstract argument. Observes that despite F's wanting to distance himself from issues of belief, a strong apologetic, even evangelical, tone runs throughout; that the uniqueness of F's encounter with the Bible lies in his treatment of typology; and that 'the thrust of each chapter is towards a vision of the integration of all humanity in one universal creative imagination.'

M10.105 Schiller, Bill. 'The Bible: An Analysis.' *Windsor Star* [Ontario], 13 March 1982. 750 w
Brief overview of F's approach, along with a sampler of isolated insights.

M10.106 Schott, Webster. 'Bible, Codebook to Western Culture.' *Plain Dealer* [Cleveland, Ohio], 17 October 1982. 850 w
Emphasizes F's point that the Bible has seeded Western culture. GC 'may be one of the most provocative books ever written about the Bible. No one has ever stated so broadly the literary debt we owe to it.' Calls the book 'a work of staggering scholarship and dazzling insight.'

M10.107 Schwab, Gweneth B. *Christianity & Literature* 33 (Fall 1983): 87–9. 1200 w
Observes that GC embodies several different perspectives: rhetorical, psychological, socio-historical, and sacred. Sees the key to F's approach in his definition of the word 'literal.' Summarizes F's views on language, typology, imagery, and myth as they apply to the Bible. Calls GC 'a monument of literary criticism,' adding that it 'should be more significant in the history of the study of literature than Frye's *Anatomy of Criticism*.'

M10.108 Sheehan, John F.X., sj. 'An Appreciation of Northrop Frye's *The Great Code*.' *Renascence* 3 (Spring 1983): 203–16. 5000 w
Singles out a series of F's epigrams, ideas, and more or less isolated insights, and adds to these his own somewhat free-flowing and autobio-

graphical commentary. 'Northrop Frye may be the last educated man.
He has written a truly remarkable book. Its erudition is staggering.'

M10.109 Smith, Nicholas. *Review of English Studies* 142 (May 1985); 302–3. 670 w
Refers to GC as 'a final discovery or repetition of the meaning of all of [F's]
preceding texts ... a handbook which offers the key to the great code' of
his own work. Contrasts F's rhetoric of authority with the scepticism
of deconstruction, the self-referential views of language, and 'the laborious
elusiveness of contemporary critical strategies.'

M10.110 Smith, R.C. *Canadian Book Review Annual, 1982*, ed Dean Tudor and Ann
Tudor (Toronto: Simon & Pierre, 1983), 228–9. 560 w
Gives a summary of the book's contents. Says GC is 'a most interesting
and perceptive work and should be read by anyone interested in the
meaning of the Bible or its relationship to culture, life and thought.'

M10.111 Sparshott, Francis. *Philosophy and Literature* 6 (October 1982): 180–9. 4500 w
Argues that 'by academic standards' GC is 'an appallingly bad book.'
Believes that F has not argued convincingly that the Bible is the central
document informing Western culture. Disagrees with F's imaginative and
visionary conception of literature, preferring the nominalist view, and
faults F for both substituting 'critical construction for poetic particularity'
and confusing 'the functions of the critic and the minister of the gospel.'
Examines F's chief themes and finds that they all fall short in convincing
us that the Bible has uniquely determined our common literary vision or is
essential to our understanding of literature.

M10.112 Stern, Laurent. *Journal of Aesthetics and Art Criticism* 41 (Spring 1983): 340–3
3200 w
Compares F's approach with that of Robert Alter (in *The Art of Biblical Narrative*), maintaining that Alter will shed more light on a given biblical
text than F. Argues that when F does engage in 'literal reading' his interpretations illuminate concepts in literary criticism rather than biblical texts.
Cites in this regard F's reading of an episode in 1 Samuel and his view
about the focus of the Preacher's message in Ecclesiastes. Believes that F's
assumption about the unity of the Bible is illusory, for it brackets out
the contradictions and conflicts in the text. What F teaches us is not so
much about the Bible as about language, metaphor, and myth, about
the way the Bible has been understood, and about literary theory.

M10.113 Stiegman, Emero. 'Discovering the Bible.' *University of Toronto Quarterly* 52
(Winter 1982–3): 141–9. 3900 w
Judges F's achievement in GC to be 'immense' and thinks that he succeeds
in his central arguments about the way the Bible should be read, about
its influence upon our thinking, and about its 'appropriateness as a focus
and source of literary theory.' GC 'tells us what those who once knew
meant by speaking of the West as a Christian culture, making such meaning
available to those who deny in honest ignorance and to those who affirm
in less honest wistfulness.' Sees F's chief and prophetic proposal to be

his revision of the concept of 'literal' meaning. Centres much of his commentary, however, on his reservations about F's remarks on theology and history. Argues that *GC* does contain a theological position, F's demurrers notwithstanding; that his views on inspiration and on the relation between biblical and oriental thought are one-sided; and that his understanding of 'tradition' has not adequately taken account of current understanding of the term.

M10.114 Stock, R.D. *Spirituality Today* 35 (Fall 1983): 282–4. 510 w

Thinks that F is excellent on some matters, such as sin and repentance, but finds that his abstract theorizing blurs crucial distinctions. Suggests that such critics as T.S. Eliot, Dorothy Sayers, C.S. Lewis, and Rudolf Otto are better critics of the Bible because of the energy of their active belief.

M10.115 Stoneburner, Tony. *Anglican Theological Review* 66 (April 1984): 188–90. 1000 w

Complains that Frye is more interested in schemata than in illuminating biblical episodes and that this work lacks focus because he dismisses the historical character of biblical narrative.

M10.116 Swanston, Hamish F.G. 'Needs Encouragement.' *The Tablet* 236 (3 July 1982): 773–4. 975 w

Thinks F does not really sustain the claim about the imaginative coherence of the Bible. His thesis rather has to do with the liberating power of biblical language. Finds this thesis fanciful and unpersuasive and F's prose impenetrable and solipsistic.

M10.117 Takahashi, Yasunari. 'The Bible and Literary Criticism.' *Gakuto* 79 (September 1982): 8–11

In Japanese.

M10.118 Timson, Judith. *Chatelaine* 55 (May 1982): 6

Brief review.

M10.119 Tredell, Nicholas. 'Anatomy of Scripture.' *PN Review* 9, no 4 (1982): 80–1. 1440 w

Notes that F's book is not simply a commentary on the Bible but also 'an oblique commentary on Western culture and civilization, and an indirect statement of Frye's own broad, genial humanism.' Sees the last chapter as an ironic dissolving of the order that the previous chapters have established as characteristic of biblical rhetoric and structure: 'the great achievement' of the last chapter is the paradigm shift F makes 'from a centralized to a decentralized perspective,' which reveals the Bible's disunity along with its unity and illustrates that the Bible, like *GC* itself, 'is a work of anatomy and *bricolage*.'

M10.120 Trickett, Rachel. 'The Rhetoric of Revelation.' *TLS*, 2 July 1982, 712. 2000 w

Contrasts F's approach with Coleridge's: Coleridge is always relating the Bible to his own experience, whereas F claims neither belief nor disbelief, purporting to let the text speak for itself. Observes, however, that 'some of the most wise and striking insights F has to offer are, ultimately, about human experience … there are few critics today who, like Frye … can

touch so unerringly on the deepest concerns of the heart and the imagination.' Says that the initial chapter, on language, is the least successful
because it is based on assertion and inadequate evidence. Sees the basis of
F's approach in his belief that the primary function of literature is to
keep recreating the metaphorical phase of language, his equating myth and
story, and his opposition to demythologizing the Bible.

M10.121 Tucker, Mary Curtis. 'Shakespearean Comedy, *The Great Code,* and the
Myth of Deliverance.' Paper presented at the annual meeting of the South
Atlantic Modern Language Association, Atlanta, Ga, 10 November 1984.
11 pp. Photoduplicated typescript
See L527.

M10.122 Turner, Darrell. 'The Bible Is Also Literature.' *Anchor* [Fall River, Manitoba],
8 April 1983, 8. 1320 w
In an article on the recent attention being given to the literary criticism of
the Bible, glances briefly at GC.

M10.123 Ungaro, Joan. *Village Voice* 27 (20 April 1982): 41. 600 w
Provides a brief overview of F's central thesis ('myth and metaphor are the
true literal bases of the Bible; the Bible therefore requires a more complex
theory of meaning than do other books'), and calls attention to the
epigrammatic quality of F's prose.

M10.124 Wagner, Peter. *Quinquereme* 8, no 1 (1985): 93–5. 1200 w
Summarizes the book's chief themes. Believes that F has achieved what he
intended, but finds shortcomings in his restricting his examples to *belles-
lettres* and in the absence of a scholarly apparatus.

M10.125 Watt, Bill. *The Newspost,* 18 December 1982, 6. 325 w
Complains that the book is 'without any substance and is, at best, an
exercise … in nothing more than sophistry.'

M10.126 Weightman, John. 'The Word, with or without God?' *Times Educational
Supplement,* 17 September 1982, 30. 1900 w
Devotes most of the review to trying to uncover F's own religious stance in
order to explain why F attributes transcendental power and meaning to
imaginative structures. Is not convinced by F's main thesis, which is said
to involve a reconciliation between faith and doubt. F 'appears to add
just another idiosyncratic gloss to a text already over-encrusted with
dubious interpretation.'

M10.127 Wells, David A. 'German Studies: Medieval Literature.' *Year's Work in
Modern Language Studies,* ed Glanville Price and David A. Wells (London:
Modern Humanities Research Association 1983), 727–8. 250 w
A brief account of the organization of F's topics. Says that 'medievalists
will find encouragement and confirmation in particular from F's chapters
on typology, where his ability to stand back from a traditional methodology
and point to its wider literary and cultural significance reinforces our
understanding of the vital role of the Bible in the Western imagination.'

M10.128 Wheeler, Charles B. 'Professor Frye and the Bible.' *South Atlantic Quarterly*
82 (Spring 1983): 154–64. 5300 w

Is severely critical of F's assumptions, methods of argument, and conclusions. Claims that F's views on language are 'moonshine,' that his use
of myth is reductive, that his concept of typology is loose (in his phases of
revelation he has done 'nothing more than identify most of the standard
biblical literary genres'), that his chapter on imagery is more or less
conventional, and that his 'obsession with pattern-making' produces a text
that, however provocative and dazzling, is 'tiresomely exhibitionistic.'
Isolates several propositions that cause F to brush aside too easily the
relation of the Bible to the real world and to dismiss too readily biblical
scholarship. In short, finds that F is 'self-indulgent,' and that the imaginative vision of GC is 'claustrophobic.' F has turned the Bible 'into a transcendental metaliterary vade mecum for mad metaphorists.'

M10.129 Wiebe, Donald. 'The "Centripetal" Theology of *The Great Code.*' *Toronto
Journal of Theology* 1 (Spring 1985): 122–7
See L564.

M10.130 Willard, Thomas. *Arizona Quarterly* 38 (Autumn 1982): 280–3. 1600 w
Understands the original element in GC as F's treatment of typology, the
rhetorical device that 'lends the Bible's stories and symbols to re-creation.'
Outlines the view of typology set forth in GC as well as the typological
structure of the book itself. Sees the task F has set for himself as showing
that the shift from the order of the Word to the order of the Spirit does
not mark the end of Western culture. Thus, F's position is similar to that of
Joachim di Fiore. GC illustrates, following Blake's *Everlasting Gospel* and
Milton's 'The word of God in the heart,' that typology is 'the model of
modernism and revisionism in Western culture.'

M10.131 Williamson, Karina. *Notes & Queries* 31 (June 1984): 288. 600 w
Observes that F's book is just one of a flurry of recent studies of the Bible
by secular critics, all of them coming at a time when the notion of the
author-centred view of the text is crumbling. Comments briefly on the
categories of F's synthesizing approach. Believes it is possible 'to admire
and learn from the play of his dazzling critical intelligence even while
remaining sceptical of the system within which it operates.'

M10.132 Woodcock, George. 'Frye's Bible.' *University of Toronto Quarterly* 52 (Winter
1982–3). 149–54. 2500 w
Discusses GC in relation to its cultural context and to the general body of
F's work. Finds that it is linked to F's religious background, the English
dissenting tradition; that it is a typically Protestant book; and that its forbear
is Frazer's *Golden Bough.* Believes 'the Bible is an excellent subject for
Frye's kind of critical investigation' because it is a storehouse of myth, it
pays little attention to questions of authorship and the creative process, and
it is impossible to evaluate qualitatively, there being no aesthetic criteria
to apply to the whole. Says that for F the code or structure is the most
important thing in the Bible, and finds, therefore, an absence of empathy
in F's reading and no sense of the verbal beauty and historic power of
the Bible.

M10.133 Woodman, Ross. 'From the Belly of the Whale: Frye's "Personal Encounter." ' *Canadian Poetry* 10 (Spring-Summer 1982): 124–31. 4100 w
Stresses the authority of F's personal encounter with the Bible, which is to
be understood as an encounter with the myth of identity or metaphor.
Examines in some detail the implications of F's view of metaphor, the ultimate one being that it leads to an enlightened, open community of vision
whose informing principle is charity. Sees the moment of enlightenment in
F's vision of the Bible as similar to Paul's in 2 Corinthians 12. Looks also
at the strong revolutionary slant in this vision and suggests that GC could
have been written only by an English-Canadian Protestant. Goes on to
observe the connections between the social concerns in F's Blakean, Miltonic, and (in some respects) Arnoldian vision and his essays on Canadian
culture in *DG*.

M10.134 Wurtzel, Judy. 'Canadian Scholar Tries Different Interpretation.' *Richmond
News Leader*, 4 August 1982, 7. 650 w
Glances at F's approach to the Bible, especially his analyses of language
and typology. 'A personal, idiosyncratic, difficult, and exciting book' and
'an extraordinary piece of criticism.'

M10.135 Yamagata, Kazumi. *Eigo seinen* [*The Rising Generation*] 128 (December 1982):
36
In Japanese. Emphasizes the connection between biblical hermeneutics and
critical theory. Regards GC as the development of AC, and typology as
an effective way of viewing polysemantic reality as oneness.

M11 **The Modern Century** (*MC*) [A10]

M11.1 Anonymous. *Booklist* 64 (15 March 1968): 821
Brief notice.

M11.2 — *British Book News* 336 (August 1968): 634
Brief notice.

M11.3 — *Bulletin critique du livre français* 291 (March 1970), 283. 160 w
Brief review of the French translation (A10a). Sees the interest of the book
in the fact that F has gone beyond the analysis of literary works to examine critically most of the aspects of contemporary society.

M11.4 — *Chatelaine* 41 (March 1968): 6
Brief notice.

M11.5 — *Christian Century* 86 (4 June 1969): 786
Brief notice.

M11.6 — *Choice* 5 (September 1968): 760, 762
Brief notice.

M11.7 — *Kirkus Service* 35 (15 September 1967): 1172. 220 w
Comments generally on F's typical critical approach. Sees MC as offering 'a
genuinely sound and attractive summing up' of the twentieth century.

M11.8 — *Library Journal* 92 (1 October 1967): 3542–3
Brief notice.

M11.9 — *Publishers Weekly* 193 (12 February 1968): 86
Notice.

M11.10 — 'Short Shrift.' *Louisville Courier-Journal*, 17 March 1968, E6
Brief notice.

M11.11 — 'The Unborn Canada.' *Manas* 21 (21 February 1968): 3, 8. 1680 w
Isolates several of F's themes for special commentary: the idea of progress,
McLuhanism, and technology.

M11.12 — *Western Business & Industry*, Spring 1968, 57. 330 w
Lists some of F's themes and quotes brief passages from the concluding
chapter.

M11.13 B., R. 'Whidden Lectures.' *Saskatoon Star Phoenix*, 9 November 1967. 150 w
Brief review. *MC* 'presents a brilliant and, perhaps, sometimes bewildering
array of ideas and observations on our modern society.'

M11.14 Baragli, E. *La Civiltà Cattolica* 123, no 2 (1972): 515. 135 w
Brief review of the French translation (A10b).

M11.15 Bornstein, Stephen. 'Frye's Moral Attack on Modernism.' *Varsity* [Univ of
Toronto], 10 November 1967, 10. 1850 w
Understands F's central theme to consist 'essentially of the assertion of the
appalling hideousness of modern existence and the crucial role of the
arts in the regeneration of North American life' and his point of view to be
that of an 'enflamed moralist.' Sees running throughout F's analysis of
modern technological culture a commitment to religious humanism, volun-
tarism (improvement requires a change in the human will), and idealism.
F's emphasis on the arts as a means of reshaping modern mythology is
seen as an antidote to the technological determinism of McLuhan.

M11.16 Brigg, Peter. *Canadian Reader* 9, no 5 (1967): 8–9. 210 w
Gives a brief summary of the themes of F's three chapters. 'This book will
outlast the flash of its Centennial origins to become a guidebook for the
future of Canada.'

M11.17 Brittin, Norman A. *Southern Humanities Review* 3 (Winter 1969): 109–10.
520 w
Summarizes F's views on the alienation of man and woman in modern
society and on the ways in which the arts actively respond to their apprehensions and to the passivity of modern life.

M11.18 Capo, James A. 'McLuhan.' *Catholic World* 207 (1986): 137–8. 320 w
A brief review that summarizes F's views on technology, art, and leisure.
F's 'reflections should speak to all who suspect that life is more than
owning the latest car.'

M11.19 Cone, Edward T. *American Scholar* 37 (Summer 1968): 522
Brief notice, under the 'Recommended Summer Reading' heading. Says
The Modern Century offers 'a salutary antidote to creeping McLuhanism.'

M11.20 Daniells, Roy. *University of Toronto Quarterly* 37 (July 1968): 439–41. 800 w
Has misgivings about the way in which F's program for recreating society
is to come about. Sees F's argument in the last chapter as a masque of
reason that raises more questions than it answers.

M11.21 Dickstein, Morris. 'U. and Non-U.' *Partisan Review* 36 (Winter 1969): 153–6. 1600 w

Says MC 'is a work of high commitment, diagnostic and prescriptive rather than professorial, a tract for the times' that shows F moving from scholar to sage and engaging in the politics of culture. Judges F's politics to be that of 'an old-fashioned liberal humanist.' What F does offer is his Blakean faith in the will of individuals to change, but his program for an alliance between art and the universities remains too disinterested and abstract and too far removed from what is actually happening on campuses.

M11.22 Dubois, Pierre. *Revue philosophique* 164 (July-September 1974): 348–9. 330 w

Brief review that summarizes the three chapters.

M11.23 Dudek, Louis. 'The Kant of Criticism.' *Canadian Literature* 38 (Autumn 1968): 77–81. 1600 w

Finds the redeeming virtue of MC to be that it is more open and flexible than the Kantian system in AC. Says the book is 'brilliant' in its texture, wit, development, and ideas. Is most fascinated by the way in which F applies his method to 'the raw materials of life' rather than to literature. Is not convinced, finally, that F's Blakean myth of innocent vision, which he sets over against the modern myth of the tiger, is the saving myth for the modern age, and thinks that F's liberal humanism does not provide the kind of critique that both society and literature now need.

M11.24 Duffy, Dennis. 'The Too-Well-Tempered Critic.' *Tamarack Review* 46 (Winter 1968): 115–20. 1150 w

Believes that F's apprehensions about modern culture conceal as much as they reveal, that his understanding of contemporary life is deadeningly abstract, that he fails to engage in a genuine psycho-social critique of the modern world, and that his visionary solution in the last chapter is composed mostly of unconvincing maxims.

M11.25 Ethier-Blas, Jean. 'Un réalisme pessimiste.' *Le Devoir*, 18 January 1969, 14. 1250 w

Review of the French translation (A10a). Points to F's lack of interest in nationalistic themes in his study of the cultural order, but devotes most of the review to complaining that F has slighted the French-Canadian tradition.

M11.26 Evans, J.A.S. 'Books of the Month.' *Commentator* [Toronto] 12 (January 1968): 28

Brief notice.

M11.27 Flamm, Dudley. *Books Abroad* 42 (Summer 1968): 445–6. 650 w

Summarizes the three chapters. Judges the final chapter to be the weakest because of F's too heavy reliance on the arts to solve the modern spiritual crisis.

M11.28 Fulford, Robert. 'Northrop Frye: Where We Are Now.' *Toronto Star*, 13 January 1968, 34. 750 w

Notes that the core of F's argument is that the worn-out structure of modern society needs to be created anew. Judges MC to be 'one of the most distinguished books produced by a Canadian in any field in recent years.' F's 'personal sense of culture, so wide and so deep, has never been more directly displayed.'

M11.29 Hamilton, Alice. *Dalhousie Review* 47 (Winter 1967–8): 595, 597. 725 w
Provides a brief summary of the three chapters. Characterizes the book's argument as romantic insofar as F believes that the poets are the only ones who understand what we are and how we must act. Says that the problem with F's argument is that without some moral and rational criteria to judge the myths created by the imagination, we have no way to decide whether our commitments are right or wrong.

M11.30 — 'Man – His World and His Myths.' *Winnipeg Free Press*, 28 October 1967, 15. 950 w
Believes the first chapter is by far the strongest part of the book because of its acute analysis of contemporary individual and social ills. The last two chapters are more sporadic; and in finding in art an answer to the problems of the modern age, the book ends weakly. Thinks that F fails when he elevates the power of the imagination over moral and rational judgment.

M11.31 Hewett, A. Phillip. *Ferment*, March 1968, 23–4. 1050 w
Discusses primarily F's contention that the arts can provide an answer to the problems of passivity, propaganda, and technology in the modern world.

M11.32 Johnston, Alice. 'Myths of the Day.' *Montreal Gazette*, 7 October 1967. 25. 290 w
Brief review outlining F's central thesis. Sees the book itself as an example of creative art.

M11.33 Jones, Howard Mumford. *English Language Notes* 6 (March 1969): 230–5. 1950 w
Finds that F's views on urban life are sweeping generalizations that should be qualified by a more careful attention to the positive civic, social, and scientific achievements in the modern world. Thinks F's analysis of the twentieth century as a tragic, self-destructive age arises from 'the literary fallacy,' the fallacy that assumes the arts are the best interpreters of society. Says F has neglected to consider how medicine, science, business, and other products of rationality have improved the lot of modern humanity. The kind of new society F envisions is only 'a kind of genial (or congenial) open-ended pattern of anarchy put together by the disgruntled.'

M11.34 Kattan, Naïm. 'Littérature étrangère: notre siècle tel que le voit Northrop Frye.' *Liberté* 10 (March-April 1968): 39–41. 1200 w
Consists largely of a summary of the book's three chapters. Believes that F finally does not give an answer to the problems of the twentieth century. 'The book does give supplementary proof to the richness of his thought, but also to its limits.' 'By stressing only the great value of the imagination, Frye tends to minimize, and sometimes even to ignore, the power of things.'

M11.35 — 'Présentation de Northrop Frye ... ou l'anti-McLuhan.' *Le Devoir*,
23 November 1968, 11
See G9.

M11.36 L., S.G. 'Assessing Contemporary Culture.' *Muenster Prairie Messenger*,
13 July 1969. 250 w
Gives a brief listing of the topics F covers.

M11.37 Maddocks, Melvin. 'William Morris and the Utopia Game.' *Christian Science
Monitor*, 28 December 1967, 9. 200 w
Comments briefly on *MC*, placing F's vision in the context of various
utopian and dystopian visions. Review primarily devoted to a biography of
William Morris.

M11.38 O'Leary, Dillon. 'The Age through Its Art.' *Ottawa Journal*, 30 December
1967, 36. 750 w
Thinks F's central theme – that the modern century is, more than any
other, an age of anxiety and disillusionment – will not stand up under
critical scrutiny. History provides much evidence that these qualities
are a part of human fate. Although *MC* is 'a brilliant exercise in literary
criticism,' F's approach is too narrow, for it relies almost exclusively on
art as the yardstick by which to measure the present age.

M11.39 Poisson, Roch. 'Northrop Frye prône l'angoisse.' *Photo-Journal* 18
(27 August 1969): 46. 500 w
Review of the French translation (A10a). Sees F's extolling the intellectual
attitudes of doubt and anxiety as representing a particularly American
point of view. Says that F is to English Canada as Fernand Dumont is to
Quebec.

M11.40 Pontaut, Alain. 'Quand Northrop Frye se penche.' *La Presse* [Montreal] 84,
no 268 (16 November 1968): 25. 1250 w
Review of the French translation (A10a). Primarily a summary of F's thesis,
which is judged to be original, accessible, and clearly presented.

M11.41 Ricks, Christopher. 'Dead for a Docket.' *Listener* 79 (9 May 1968): 610–11.
150 w
Comments briefly on F's view of mythology, which is said to make everything in art come out as 'fresh and nourishing and homely' rather than
as 'old and enduring and alien.'

M11.42 Rosenbaum, S.P. 'Wit and Scope from a Mythic Mind.' *Globe Magazine*
[Toronto], 21 October 1967, 26. 540 w
Comments on F's rejection of McLuhan's determinism and on his broad
conception of mythology.

M11.43 Sayre, Robert. *College English* 30 (December 1968): 264–6. 1450 w
Places F's argument in the context of the crisis in the universities. Thinks F
comes close to answering the questions raised by the crisis because of
his fresh conceptual framework – the balance between detachment and
concern. Outlines F's views on the myth of concern and the difference
between open and closed mythologies.

M11.44 — 'Morality and the Intellectual.' *Middle Earth* 1, no 16 (1968): 10, 14

Same review as M11.43.

M11.45 Schiller, David. 'Critical Myth.' *Commentary* 46 (September 1968): 97–100.
2000 w
Examines *MC* in the context of *AC* and *EI*. Observes that *MC* is an example
of ethical criticism, which points toward the creation of a community of
human freedom. Believes, however, that F's 'description of the modern
situation ignores those political or historical facts which are the causes
and consequences of alienation and anxiety.' F's effort fails, finally, because
he has no vocabulary for political action and because he devalues politics.
His mythical mode of thought reduces him in the end to an ironic silence in
the face of the vision of the ideal city.

M11.46 Stackhouse, Reginald. 'On Books.' *Canadian Churchman* 95 (February 1968):
15. 430 w
A short summary of the central themes in *MC*.

M11.47 Wolverton, Charles. 'Progress – A Devastating Analysis of the Cultural
Message of Modern Society.' *Vancouver Province*, 10 June 1967. 640 w
Considers the implications of F's critique of the idea of progress for Canadian identity. F provides 'some evaluations and devaluations of the age
and his nation's place in it.'

M11.48 Z., A. 'Technology's Threat to Freedom Worries Leading Critic.' *Calgary
Albertan*, 24 February 1968. 590 w
Urges Canadians to take notice of the remedies F outlines for recreating a
sense of freedom in a technological age.

M12 **The Myth of Deliverance** (*MD*) [A21]

M12.1 Anonymous. *Choice* 19 (December 1982): 216
Brief notice.

M12.2 — *Choice* 20 (October 1983): 143
Brief notice.

M12.3 — *Whig-Standard Magazine* [Kingston, Ont], 15 October 1983
Brief notice.

M12.4 Ashley, L.R.N. *Bibliothèque d'Humanisme et Renaissance* 46, no 2 (1984):
433–4. 560 w
Says that although F's arguments about Shakespearean comedy are familiar
to readers of his other works, these lectures 'are as solid as those of the
same author's studies' of Shakespeare's tragedies.

M12.5 Baxter, John. *University of Toronto Quarterly* 53 (Summer 1984): 419–21.
880 w
Thinks that F's neat tripartite division of the reversals in the problem
comedies breaks down, especially in chapters 2 and 3. Believes that F
should have considered the principles of action and energy together,
for they (and their reversals) are both present in *Measure for Measure*. Says
that the mechanical symmetry of F's scheme is most apparent in the

third chapter: it is not at all clear that 'reality' is reversed in such plays as
Troilus and Cressida.

M12.6 Daniell, David. *Year's Work in English Studies* 64 (1983): 205–6. 350 w
Sees *MD* as a 'welcome appendix' to F's influential Shakespearean criticism.
Summarizes F's thesis about the different reversals in the problem comedies.

M12.7 Forst, Graham. 'Word-Centred.' *Canadian Literature* 102 (Fall 1984): 69–71.
770 w
Contrasts F's approach to Shakespeare's problem plays with that of E.M.W.
Tillyard: F's approach is to see the plays in relation to the conventions of
their comic structure rather than to measure them against some standard of
reality. Summarizes F's argument about the three kinds of reversals.
Judges his treatment of *Troilus and Cressida* to be handled especially well.

M12.8 French, William. 'Autumn Book Lists Laced with Enticing Titles.' *Globe and
Mail*, 27 July 1982
Brief notice.

M12.9 Kastan, David Scott. 'The Triumph of Comedy.' *TLS*, 17 February 1984,
163. 960 w
Observes that the argument of the book enacts the myth of deliverance it
seeks to define, 'reversing the critical fortunes of the problem plays to
permit the recognition of their secure plan within Frye's comic 'mythos.'' '
MD, therefore, embodies F's own 'constructive desire, and while it tells
us little about the particularities of Shakespeare's plays, it does reveal 'the
power of his visionary understanding of literature.'

M12.10 Knowles, Richard Paul. *English Studies in Canada* 11 (June 1985): 237–43.
2400 w
Finds the book to be both satisfying and frustrating. It is frustrating because
F devotes so little direct attention to the plays themselves, 'so cavalierly
dismisses readings of the plays that have proven convincing in the study
and on the stage,' and fails to develop carefully his arguments, which
are highly qualified at that. But if one accepts F's own assumptions and
method, the book is illuminating. Gives a rather detailed outline of F's
thesis in each of the three chapters. Thinks that the book does not measure
up finally to the best of F's Shakespearean criticism. Still, the fact that it
was written by F is enough to recommend it.

M12.11 O'Hara, Dan. *Criticism* 26 (Winter 1984): 91–5. 700 w
Finds that the book contributes nothing new either to F's ideas about
comedy or to Shakespearean scholarship. The tone, manner, and spirit of
the book, in fact, are 'souvenirs of a style of critical production no longer
available to us in the profession now,' and the book illustrates somewhat
poignantly how F's career and his own conventions as a writer are more
important in the production of his text than the particular value of its
arguments.

M12.12 Rose, Michael. *The Fulcrum* [Ottawa], 24 November 1983. 230 w
Judges F to have made no contribution 'either to a science of literature

properly understood or to the interpretation of texts.' Says that *MD* is 'distinctly unmemorable.'

M12.13 Siegel, Paul N. *English Language Notes* 22 (September 1984): 70–3. 1200 w
Reviews F's contribution to the study of Shakespearean comedy in 'The Argument of Comedy' (see D39), *AC*, and *NP*, in which F works like a comparative anatomist. These studies have left their imprint on subsequent discussion of the plays. But in *MD* 'the new insights ... are comparatively sparse and the old insights are not developed.' Believes that F 'did better with the problem comedies' in 'The Argument of Comedy' and *AC*.

M12.14 Speirs, Logan. 'The Myths and Visions of Northrop Frye.' *English Studies* 64, no 6 (1983): 518–23. 2650 w
Finds that F's method in *MD* is like that of his other books: he seeks to classify literary works according to their type. Believes that this procedure violates the reader's experience. Moreover, 'the "structures" that Frye groups round himself at any given moment are always more real to him than the literature he has read.' Glances at what F says in a number of his books in an effort to show that what he says about literature has no connection with the experience of literature.

M12.15 Wheeler, Richard P. 'An Affirmation of Literary Faith.' *Shakespeare Quarterly* 35 (Autumn 1984): 365–8. 2570 w
Finds the level of argument continuous with F's other criticism of Shakespearean comedies, though *MD* closes the gap between the voices of detachment and engagement found in *NP*. Discusses the correspondence F locates between the experience and the structure of the plays, reversal and recognition being the key structural elements in the myth of deliverance. Thinks F has not really confronted the thematic, structural, and affective qualities that have caused others to call Shakespeare's late plays 'problem comedies.' Does not find the kind of release and fulfilment that F finds in the conclusions of *Measure for Measure* and *All's Well That Ends Well*, but tends to agree that *Troilus and Cressida* does embody the theme of deliverance. Points to F's 'eloquent affirmation' about the relation between literature and life in his concluding remarks about *The Tempest*.

M13 Northrop Frye on Culture and Literature (*NFCL*) [A17]

M13.1 Adamowski, Tom. 'Plaster Toads in the Bush Garden.' *Books in Canada* 7 (June-July 1978): 18. 650 w
Believes that 'what makes this collection ... so appealing is that it allows one to see Frye turn history, anthropology, and psychology into imaginary gardens.' Is struck throughout by F's literary imperialism, which absolves such writers as Toynbee, Frazer, Jung, and Spengler from the requirements of truth, history, and brute facts.

M13.2 Anonymous. *ARTbibliographies MODERN* 11, no 1 (1980): 140
Brief notice.

M13.3 — *Book World* 10 (9 March 1980); 10
Brief notice.

M13.4 — *Choice* 15 (October 1978): 1035
Brief notice.

M13.5 — *Cultural Information Service*, 1 May 1978, 11. 225 w
Finds especially illuminating F's critiques of Frazer, Spengler, Eliade,
Cervantes, and Beckett. 'This impressive volume should give beleaguered
generalists confidence in their future within the humanities.'

M13.6 — *English Language Notes* 17 (September 1979); 28
Brief notice.

M13.7 — *Journal of Modern Literature* 7, no 4 (1979): 623
Brief notice.

M13.8 — *Queen's Quarterly* 85 (Spring 1978): 364. 160 w
'There is much of interest and value in the collection, both for those
interested in the development of Frye's thought and for those seeking
informed assessments' of such writers as Cassirer, Eliade, Toynbee,
Spengler, Jung, Coleridge, Beckett, and Hemingway.

M13.9 — *Sewanee Review* 88 (Summer 1980): lxxxii
Brief notice of the paperback edition.

M13.10 Barfoot, C.C. 'Current Literature: 1978.' *English Studies* 60 (December 1979);
790
Brief notice.

M13.11 Bates, Ronald. 'Centripetal Criticism.' *Journal of Canadian Fiction* 31–2 (1981):
227–30. 1350 w
Points to the centripetal nature of F's work (it always circles around the
same issues), gives an overview of the essays collected in the volume, and
praises the wit and elegance of F's style. 'This collection of reviews, with
the editor's lengthy, detailed Introduction, could be a way to the ideas of
one of the seminal thinkers of our day.'

M13.12 — 'New Anthology, TV Series Acknowledge Frye's Status.' *London Free
Press* [Ontario], 15 July 1978, B4. 425 w
A shorter version of M13.11. Says the book 'can serve as a good introduction
to the main concerns of Frye's work as critic and scholar.'

M13.13 Cain, William E. *South Carolina Review* 11 (November 1978): 123–5. 820 w
The book 'allows us to see Frye in his workshop, defining himself against
the other great system-builders and mythmakers (from Spengler to Toynbee) of modern times, and preparing the ground for his own system in the
Anatomy of Criticism.' Is not convinced that F has reconciled the opposing
claims that literature is both autonomous and socially relevant. Claims
that the danger of F's schemes is that they neglect literary differences and
'often ignore the experience of reading (and struggling with) specific texts.'

M13.14 Crowley, C.P. *University of Windsor Review* 14 (Spring-Summer 1979):
96–100. 1750 w
Sees the collection as forming 'an excellent cultural mirror' of the fifties
and as revealing F 'in the process of creating a critical point of view which

has been called the greatest global point of view in literature of any
literary thinker.' Points to a number of the writers F reviews – Boswell,
Pound, Wyndham Lewis, Toynbee, Spengler, Frazer, and Cassirer. Sees
the essay-reviews as having the qualities that have made F a great teacher:
'the precise summaries of subject matter, the sharp perceptions, the deep
respect for an author's work and motivation, are continually revealed
in clear and witty prose.'

M13.15 Dick, Bernard F. *World Literature Today* 52 (Autumn 1978): 697–8. 370 w
The volume 'complements the prevailing image of Frye the formidable
critic, for it presents him as a popularizer' – one who makes accessible such
writers as Jung, Cassirer, Coleridge, and Frazer. Says F writes with 'pris-
matic clarity' and displays his learning with grace.

M13.16 [Fulford, Robert] 'Midway.' *Canadian Reader* 20, no 3 (1979): [8]. 350 w
Says the collection makes conveniently available the pleasure of watching
F's mind in action. Also remarks on the difficulty of finding F's books
in Canadian bookstores.

M13.17 Gelley, Alexander. *Library Journal* 103 (August 1978): 1511
Brief notice.

M13.18 Gudas, Fabian. *Journal of Aesthetics and Art Criticism* 37 (Fall 1978): 106–7.
900 w
Gives a brief outline of the book's contents and summarizes the topics
covered in the introduction, but devotes most of his remarks to speculating
about the place of the review (and judicial criticism) in F's work as a
whole.

M13.19 Hesford, Walter A. *Christianity & Literature* 30 (Spring 1981): 104–6. 930 w
Maintains that these essays show F to be 'a romantic liberal who places
ultimate faith in the power of the imagination to transform self and society.'
Points to the essays that reveal F's long-standing interest in 'the deep
grammatical structure of the imagination.' Thinks these essays will be
engaging even to those who have not read the works under review. Sees
F's mind as more apocalyptic and gnostic than historical and Judaeo-
Christian.

M13.20 Hinden, Michael. *Journal of Aesthetic Education* 14 (April 1980): 105–7. 830 w
Says that the essays in part 1 cohere and drive toward synthesis, whereas
those in part 2 seem disconnected, even though they do reveal F's diversity.
Observes that the essays on Jung, Frazer, and Eliade in part 1 contain
the kernels for parts of *AC*. 'Frye remains entirely free of the temptation to
cannibalize his subjects' and his 'sense of history and difference is almost
as deep as his quest for archetypes and identity.'

M13.21 Kane, Sean. *University of Toronto Quarterly* 48 (Summer 1979): 431–3. 790 w
Sees the most striking aspect of the collection to be 'an absence of spatial
theorizing' and disagrees with the claim of the introduction that the essays
show the foundation of F's continuous vision: 'they are modest reflections
which pause with tact and commitment before often beautifully painted
subjects.' 'On balance, the pieces show the bookmanship of a man alert to

his cultural time and place, who is drawn to human oddity and genius with a humanism that is exemplary.'

M13.22 Lane, Lauriat. *English Studies in Canada* 7 (Spring 1981): 123–8. 2120 w
Examines primarily the issue of whether or not F's work is, as Gerald Graff and others have claimed, that of a visionary whose ideas 'deprive literature and criticism of any claim to referential truth to reality and hence ... of any epistemological or ethical authority.' Cites a number of places in these review essays to indicate that F's view of literature is not divorced from life and does contain a truth to reality. Thinks, however, that these examples, along with the claims of the introduction, will not satisfy readers such as Graff and will not really provide a sufficient philosophical foundation for the dialectic of F's myths of freedom and concern.

M13.23 Lindborg, Henry J. *Bookviews* 1 (June 1978): 77.
Brief review.

M13.24 Lodge, David. 'The Myth of Decline.' *New Statesman* 96 (29 September 1978): 412–13. 750 w
Says that 'there are not many critics whose 20-year-old book reviews one can read with pleasure and instruction, but Frye is an exception to most rules.' Sees the main interest of the collection as being a historical record of F's intellectual development and as showing that, in addition to being a formalist or structuralist, F is also a romantic-utopian.

M13.25 N[ew], W[illiam]. *Canadian Literature* 79 (Winter 1978): 132
Brief notice.

M13.26 New, W.H. *Journal of Commonwealth Literature* 15 (December 1980): 69
Brief notice.

M13.27 Paschall, Douglas. 'Continuity in Northrop Frye's Criticism.' *Sewanee Review* 88 (Winter 1980): 121–5. 2000 w
Compares and contrasts F's work with that of the French structuralists. Finds it difficult to assess F's insistence on the structures of literature and the necessity of a critical system to understand these structures, though concludes that F's categorizing does subordinate one's experience of particular literary works. Sees the collection of essays as demonstrating the continuity in F's principles and as suggesting his 'readiness to colonize at will, within the imperium of archetypal criticism, virtually any territory in his ken.'

M13.28 Perloff, Marjorie. *South Atlantic Bulletin* 44 (January 1979): 113–16. 2150 w
Contrasts F's work – 'probably the most impressive body of criticism written in English in our time' – with that of Harold Bloom, who excludes such poets as Eliot and Pound from among the 'strong poets,' and the deconstructionists, who view the literary text as a means for discussing the creation and decreation of meaning. Cites F's reviews of Pound and Valéry as illustrations of the way F's 'climbing and descent' are generously inclusive. Calls attention to F's interest in the primary texts, even where he is reviewing editions and translations, and to his 'astonishing power of assimilating a new body of poetry [such as René Char's] and clarifying

its mode of operation.' Thinks the introduction to the volume is too defensive and apologetic.

M13.29 Purcell, J.M. *Antigonish Review* 40 (Winter 1980): 110–13. 1380 w
Gives a brief overview of the contents of the book. Devotes most of the review to omissions he sees in the introduction, such as the "50's Engl.-dept. ethos' [sic].

M13.30 Schwartz, Sanford. 'Reconsidering Frye.' *Modern Philology* 78 (February 1981): 289–95. 3600 w
In a review devoted primarily to *Northrop Frye and Critical Method* (see K5), looks at F's debt to Frazer, Freud, Jung, and Spengler. Comments on how F, following these intellectual forbears, shifts 'the focus of literary studies from historical changes in the arts to the universal imaginative structures residing beneath them.'

M13.31 Wittreich, Joseph. 'Recent Studies in the English Renaissance.' *Studies in English Literature* 19 (Winter 1979): 145. 360 w
Believes that the essays in this collection illustrate the educative function of criticism, and, as 'an unfolding of Frye's education, they are, by extension, a revelation of the kind of education to which critics of Renaissance literature, ideally, might aspire.'

M14 Northrop Frye on Shakespeare (*NFS*) [A23]

M14.1 Adams, Robert Martin. 'New Bards for Old.' *New York Review of Books*, 6 November 1986, 50–4 [50–1]. 570 w
Finds that the book lacks the power of F's earlier work, that it is too colloquial, contains too much paraphrase, and is parochial and simplistic in its judgments. Says that unlike the ideas of Rymer and Dennis, which are strong and bad, F's are weak and bad.

M14.2 Anonymous. *Kirkus Reviews* 54 (15 September 1986): 1417. 325 w
Says that F 'retains an enthusiasm for and a refreshingly down-to-earth approach to material that seems to bring out the Polonius in many interpreters. No pontificating here, no overworked aphorisms; just lively, sensible, constantly stimulating insights."

M14.3 Baxter, John S. 'Northwind the Prophet: Critic as Hypocrite.' *Whig-Standard Magazine* [Kingston, Ont], 20 December 1986, 19–20
Approaches the review by reminiscing about F's classes at Victoria College, maintaining that the classroom is 'an important mirror of one aspect of a major critic's activity.' Says that F frequently distorts and contradicts Shakespeare's texts, as in *The Winter's Tale*, where F imposes his own primitive view of the seasonal cycles of nature onto the play. Wonders what persona, other than those of the actor (*hypoctita*) and the elegant stylist, lies beneath the performance of these lectures.

M14.4 Bemrose, John. 'The Joy of Shakespeare.' *Maclean's* 99 (6 October 1986): 86. 850 w
Finds that F's reader-response approach to Shakespeare's plays is quite

different from the formal elegance of his usual discussions of literary structure. Says that F makes Shakespeare's characters come alive and 'continuously expos[es] Shakespeare's own greatness.' Even though readers may
forget the details of F's arguments and observations, 'the memory of
his tireless curiosity and his respect for Shakespeare's art is enduring.'

M14.5 Boland, Eavan. 'Ben and Will.' *Irish Times*, 29 November 1986. 220 w
Prefers the spoken voice that comes through in these lectures to much of
F's other work, which is said to be 'difficult and abstruse.'

M14.6 Cowan, Bert. *Books in Canada* 15 (December 1986): 24. 380 w
Observes primarily that the speed with which the book moves along,
flinging its 'gems of thought into the air,' is a result of the original format
of the text – the undergraduate lecture. Praises the book's 'exemplary
economy,' but finds F's selection of the plays he discusses to be 'perhaps a
little skewed.'

M14.7 Craig, Paul. 'Many More Praise Shakespeare, Twain than Read Them.'
Times-Advocate [Escondido, Calif.], 10 November 1986.
Brief review.

M14.8 D'Evelyn, Thomas. 'Speaking of Shakespeare.' *Christian Science Monitor*,
25 February 1987, 19. 750 w
Calls attention to F's colloquial style and glances at his readings of *King
Lear*, *Measure for Measure*, *Antony and Cleopatra*, and *The Tempest*. Says that
F's 'reading of Shakespeare is a moral reading in the sense that it's pitched
against merely *moralistic* readings' and that F 'is a fascinating example of
the modern radical thinker finding his text in the classics.'

M14.9 Duffy, Dennis. 'A New Excitement with Shakespeare.' *Globe and Mail*,
4 October 1986, E21. 580 w
Praises F's wit, fluency, and insight, and says that the book will send the
reader back to Shakespeare 'with renewed excitement.' Calls attention
to the power in the shaping spirit of F's structural approach and to the
value in F's liberally educated intelligence, which flourishes throughout the
book.

M14.10 E., J. *Booklist*, 1 October 1986, 1832
Brief notice.

M14.11 Fuller, Edmund. 'A Celebration of Shakespeare.' *Wall Street Journal*,
4 November 1986, 32. 930 w
Regards *NFS* as 'the most accessible and sheerly enjoyable' of F's books.
Notes that F does not allow Shakespeare's poetic diction to deflect attention
from the action of the plays, and calls attention to F's non-ideological
stance toward Shakespeare. Reviews briefly F's treatment of Shakespeare's
comedies and romances.

M14.12 Greenblatt, Stephen. 'As They Like It.' *New Republic*, 10 November 1986,
42, 44–7. 900 w
Sees F's understanding of Shakespeare as closely tied to 'a transcendent
idea, an organizing principle, a prophetic vision of life.' Although the book
contains flashes of brilliance, it has none of 'the startling architectonic

power' of *AC*, *FT*, or *NP*. Notes that by elevating the poetic above the historical F has ignored the challenge of the new historicism: F seems to be 'magisterially indifferent to the theoretical turmoil of the past few years.'

M14.13 Haines, Charles. 'Breezing through Bard for a B Plus.' *Ottawa Citizen*, 7 February 1987. 1400 w

The review takes the form of an instructor's critical response to a student paper. Says that the 'paper' is stylistically a bit breezy though unpretentious, suffers from one serious misquotation, and includes some debatable interpretations.

M14.14 Hicks, Bob. 'Theater That's Worth Reading About.' *Oregonian* [Portland], 19 December 1986. 130 w

Calls F's essays 'sensible and illuminating': they remind us that Shakespeare was a practical playwright, and they set his plays in perspective.

M14.15 Homan, Sidney. 'Noted Shakespeare Scholar Opens His Classroom Door.' *Washington Times Magazine*, 19 January 1987. 900 w

Notes that the book reveals two of F's voices – that of the scholar bringing us 'interpretations new and refreshing' and that of the teacher well aware that Shakespeare's plays were written to be acted. Both voices make the book a 'very human and gratifying performance.'

M14.16 Howe, J.R. *Choice* 24 (January 1987): 760 185 w

Says that F gracefully shapes the basic issues of Shakespearean study 'into a key that unlocks the pleasure of the plays' and that these lectures are presented in a lively prose style.

M14.17 Klavan, Andrew. *Village Voice Literary Supplement* 50 (November 1986): 4. 350 w

Believes that F approaches his material 'diffusely, without an apparent coordinating vision.' Says that F's commentary on Shakespeare's plays is obvious and that, even though his knowledge of the plays is solid, his treatment of them is 'uninspired.'

M14.18 McCormick, Marion. 'Northrop Frye Takes Shakespeare's Measure.' *Montreal Gazette*, 11 October 1986. 800 w

Summarizes F's views on Shakespeare from the books introduction and glances briefly at F's treatment of *Hamlet*, *King Lear*, and *Antony and Cleopatra*. Says the book will instruct and delight the non-specialist.

M14.19 McFee, Michael. Typescript of a review presented on WUNC radio, Chapel Hill, NC, on 17 February 1987. 600 w

Summarizes F's thesis that *Hamlet* is a play for the nineteenth-century sensibility, *King Lear* for the twentieth, and *Antony and Cleopatra* for the twenty-first.

M14.20 Schoenbaum, S. 'Up the Wall with Hamlet.' *New York Times Book Review*, 30 November 1986, 15. 1800 w

Finds that F's lectures, although intended for undergraduates, have some sensible and wise observations for the expert, too. Thinks F's discussion of themes and images is especially good.

M15 **A Natural Perspective** (*NP*) [A7]

M15.1 Akrigg, G.P.V. 'Well-Spun Scheme.' *Canadian Literature* 27 (Winter 1966): 69–71. 900 w
Admires most 'the series of brilliant insights' F's work affords, but finds his obsession to categorize and to erect neat paradigms to be irritating. Says F's method causes him to twist Shakespeare's plays to fit his pre-established schemata. When F writes about such things as the relation of criticism to experience, enjoying Jonson, sentimentality, and Shakespeare's operatic way of handling themes he is stimulating, but one should be aware of 'the danger of listening too credulously to a seductive spinner of schemes.'

M15.2 Andrae, Irmgard. *Bücherei und Bildung* 18, nos 11–12 (1966): 925. 240 w
Brief summary of F's approach, which is said to be similar to that of E. Th. Sehrt in his essay, 'Wandlungen der Shakespeareschen Komödie.'

M15.3 Andrews, Alan. *Dalhousie Review* 46 (Spring 1966): 112–14. 570 w
Sees *NP* as a book that 'demands that we revise upward our assessment of Shakespearean comedy.' Is disappointed that, although F makes a gesture toward the theatrical approach to Shakespeare, he 'reverts to the category of structure' to explain the plays. Praises F's style and 'his profound engagement with his subject.'

M15.4 Anonymous. 'As They Like It.' *TLS*, 12 August 1965, 698. 600 w
Gives a clear summary of F's position on the self-contained structure of Shakespeare's comedies, their creating a unity of mood and an imaginative model of desire, and their non-allegorical effect. Believes F's position is 'beautifully built' but not above criticism. 'The most damaging counter-attack might be a neo-Bradleian one: an insistence that Shakespeare's comedies do frequently and inevitably remind us of humans behaving in a moral context.'

M15.5 — *Booklist* 61 (1 May 1965): 854
Brief notice.

M15.6 — *Choice* 2 (September 1965): 385
Brief notice.

M15.7 — *Quarterly Review* 303 (October 1965): 467. 150 w
Brief note that judges *NP* to be a dogmatic book that doesn't get much beyond 'academic pigeon-holing.'

M15.8 — *Ums Equipe* 5 (1967)
Brief notice of the German translation (A7a).

M15.9 — 'Why Comedy?' *The Economist* 216 (14 August 1965): 615. 600 w
Finds the book 'so unobtrusively well organised and so alluringly readable that its hard substance may actually be overlooked.' Summarizes F's structural approach to this substance. Thinks F is at his best when he concentrates on the theatrical nature of Shakespeare's comedies, and

praises the third chapter on the typical structure of the comedies as being especially 'brilliant.'

M15.10 A[rnold], A[erol]. *Personalist* 47 (Summer 1966): 430–3. 1150 w
Points to *NP* as continuing F's theory of comedy begun in *AC*. Finds F's arguments to be tendentious and says the book is filled with misreadings. Believes the book's failures are related to its virtues, 'for what interests one in Mr. Frye is his speculative daring': he dares to create a system, like Blake's. Thinks that this system arises from F's deep-felt need for the idea of rebirth, a need that Shakespeare himself did not have.

M15.11 Bache, William B. 'Two Essay/Reviews.' *Quartet* [West Lafayette, Ind] 11 (Summer 1966): 25–6. 550 w
Believes that although F ranges over Shakespearean comedy 'with much knowledge and with great urbanity' his elaborate theory is finally reductive because it fails to grapple in depth with the particular details of the plays.

M15.12 Barber, C.L. *Shakespeare Quarterly* 22 (Winter 1971): 68–70. 1350 w
Places *NP* in the context of F's larger purpose, which is not to prove a theory but to pursue a vision. Is distressed that in all of his writing about Shakespeare F never gets down to examining the details of individual Shakespearean plays and never turns his eye toward 'the mimesis of actualities.' Judges F to be finally a critic in the mould of Robert Burton and Sir Thomas Browne – one who spins out his own imaginative actions and 'high but half-inscrutable designs.' Even though these designs are F's speciality, *NP* is finally 'not very successful in his mode': so much of it is a restatement of what F has said elsewhere.

M15.13 Barrish, Jonas. *Studies in English Literature* 6 (Spring 1966): 362–4. 780 w
Believes that although F's relentless classifying tends to make one weary, his arguments 'do, in fact, allow for nuances within individual works, and so serve to sustain and enrich our remembered experience of the plays.' Sees *NP* as causing us to dig more deeply into the work. Summarizes the four chapters. Praises F's uncoercive approach: 'it does not aim to legislate our responses but to understand their multiplicity, discriminate them, and legitimize them.'

M15.14 Brower, Reuben A. 'Myth Making.' *Partisan Review* 33 (Winter 1966): 132–6. 1900 w
Sees F's strength in the cautionary statements he makes in the first two chapters, but thinks that when F says that Shakespeare had no values or principles beyond those of dramatic structure he runs the danger of leaving no place for significance at all. Believes that the analogies F finds between Shakespeare's plays and ritual lead to the conclusion that 'all plays are one universal Play, that there are no individual meanings, but only the Meaning.' Claims that the ritual analogies, once they have been located, lead nowhere and that the mythical forms F finds in the plays give one a 'sense of monotony and critical busy-work.'

M15.15 Bryant, J.A., Jr. *English Language Notes* 3 (December 1965): 134–6. 750 w
Summarizes F's argument about the difference between Ben Jonson's and

Shakespeare's plays. Says that while there will be objections to a number
of F's principles and claims, the objections should not 'diminish the
importance of this book,' because 'it describes accurately something essential about Shakespearean comedy' and is 'rich in incidental insights.'

M15.16 Buitenhuis, Peter. 'Northrop Frye's *Iliad*: the Alexander Lectures, 1965–66.'
Varsity Graduate 12 (June 1966): 2, 4–6, 8, 10, 98–100
See L71.

M15.17 Calve, Hans. *Englische Literaturbeobachtungen*, March 1967
Brief notice of the German translation (A7a).

M15.18 Carruth, Hayden. 'People in a Myth.' *Hudson Review* 18 (Winter 1965–6):
607. 1575 w
Sees F's emphasis on the conventional quality of Shakespeare's comedies
as pernicious because it leads to a split between art and experience,
between aesthetic and moral values. Although many of F's insights about
the comedies are 'genuinely enlightening,' he pushes his position too
far, with the result that he becomes ruled by his own system. F's Shakespeare ends up as a poet who 'had no aim in writing [the play] beyond the
creation of conventional structures.'

M15.19 Cogswell, Fred. 'Frye on Shakespeare.' *Fiddlehead* 65 (Summer 1965): 70.
180 w
Brief review that observes that the book is witty and ingenious but that it
is a 'rigid application' of the thesis contained in *AC*. The problem with
F's position is that it disregards value.

M15.20 Dodsworth, Martin. 'Hit or Myth.' *Manchester Guardian*, 18 June 1965, 8.
420 w
Brief review in which F is said to be most persuasive in arguing that
Shakespeare 'displays an operatic or balletic interest in the plot of his
comedies which is indulged at the expense of character-study.'

M15.21 Fuzier, Jean. 'Shakespeare et autour: Critique Shakespearienne.' *Les Langues
Modernes* 60 (1966): 212–15. 400 w
Complains that F is unable to see the connection between art and life, that
his approach to Shakespeare's plays from a 'middle distance' is the wrong
approach, and that the tone of his style wavers between the popular
talk and the academic dissertation.

M15.22 Hawkes, Terence. *Yale Review* 56 (Summer 1967): 563–5. 800 w
Thinks that 'despite their brilliance and energy, Frye's arguments tend to
lose their own hold on the "concrete" experience of the plays so quickly,
dissolving into abstractions whose goal seems to be symmetry rather
than sympathy.'

M15.23 Hugelmann, Hans. *Neue Bücherei* 3 (1967)
Brief notice of the German translation (A7a).

M15.24 Kermode, Frank. 'Deep Frye.' *New York Review of Books* 4 (22 April 1965):
10–12. Rpt in Kermode, *Continuities* (London: Routledge & Kegan Paul
1968), 116–21; partially rpt in *Contemporary Literary Criticism*, vol 24, ed
Sharon R. Gunton (Detroit: Gale Research 1983), 213–14. 2200 w

Provides a long introduction to F's general critical principles, for the issues they raise are present in *NP*. Says that in seeking to take Shakespeare's plays back to their mythical and ritual origins, or at least back to New Comedy, F is 'writing regressive criticism about plays he finds to be regressive.' In the process, one begins to lose sight of the difference among the plays. Says that 'what finally invalidates Frye' is the absence in his work of the reality principle. In general, accepts F's special insights but rejects his theoretical system.

M15.25 L[evin], H[arry]. *Comparative Literature* 17 (Summer 1965): 278–9. 1000 w
Believes that F's 'emphasis on the chthonic side of comedy may be acceptable as a counterpoise to the overintellectualization of many theorists.' Despite his a priori method and straining of terms, F is best in his outlining of the master-patterns in Shakespeare's plays, and his study extends and complements the work of C.L. Barber.

M15.26 Longford, Christine. 'Bottom's Dream.' *Irish Times*, 12 June 1965, 8. 900 w
A series of somewhat random remarks on Shakespeare's last plays. Glances briefly at F's approach. Disagrees that the last plays are the climax of Shakespeare as a poet.

M15.27 Maxwell, J.C. *Notes & Queries* 211 (April 1966): 152–5. 260 w
Thinks that 'much of the interest of the book lies in what it says about comedy and its assumptions.'

M15.28 Poirier, Michel. *Etudes anglaises* 19 (July-September 1966): 292. 300 w
Says that F's conversational and animated remarks are 'sometimes brilliant, sometimes digressive,' and that the book is 'remarkable for the frequency and soundness of the many analogies it establishes.' Is especially attracted to the second chapter on the objectivity of Shakespeare's plays as opposed to those of Jonson.

M15.29 Prouty, Charles Tyler. *University of Toronto Quarterly* 35 (July 1966): 405–7. 850 w
Has difficulty with the book because of F's shifting terms, his references to obscure plays Shakespeare is assumed to have known, and his errors of fact. Thinks that F offers a number of sane judgments, especially in chapter 2, but his effort 'to organize all of Shakespearean comedy in terms of ritual and myth' is too rigid a procedure.

M15.30 Rockas, Leo. *Criticism* 9 (Summer 1967): 298–301. 1460 w
Says that reviewers of *NP* such as Kermode and Brower (see M15.24 and M15.14) nod with approval at the insights of *NP*, but argues that this is to miss the point of what F is up to: what is at stake is whether criticism is discrete and analytic or whether it can also be synthetic. Proposes then to examine the book in terms of the structural theory of comedy. Observes that the book is an amplification of the theory of myths in *AC*, though F has introduced the additional character type, the *idiotes*, and· has revised his pairing of the four *mythoi*. Thinks F needs to justify these revisions better than he has done.

M15.31 Siegel, Paul N. *Shakespeare Studies*, 2, ed J. Leeds Barroll. (Cincinnati, Ohio:
Univ of Cincinnati 1966), 330–2. 1700 w
Believes that F's 'chart of Shakespearean comedy ... will be the basis for
more detailed maps' because of the 'immensely suggestive' ideas put forth
about such matters as the amoral clown, the power and harmony of
nature, the period of confusion and sexual licence, the irrational society at
the beginning of the plays and the discovery of identity at the end, and
the anti-comic themes and moods. Does quarrel, however, with the
blurring of distinctions that results from F's method: it can do 'violence to
a play by pushing it out of shape in fitting it into a system.' Says, too,
that F is sometimes 'cavalier with regard to other approaches and modes of
analysis.'

M15.32 Srigley, M.B. *Studia Neophilologica* 38, no 2 (1966): 375–8. 1700 w
Judges F to have 'performed a herculean task well and provocatively.'
Gives an overview of F's arguments in each of the four chapters. Thinks
that F's outline of the basic structure of Shakespeare's comedies is really
broad enough to encompass the tragedies, too, but says that occasional
disagreement with F's arguments 'in no way detracts from the value of this
pioneer work.'

M16 The Return of Eden (*RE*) [A8]

M16.1 Anonymous. *British Book News* 314 (October 1966): 772. 190 w
Brief review, summarizing F's central arguments.

M16.2 — *Yale Review* 55 (Spring 1966): XIV, XVIII. 675 w
Summarizes F's treatment of Milton's central concepts in *Paradise Lost*.
Judges F's Procrustean analyses and nominalism to diminish his arguments
but not to destroy them. 'The urbanity of his tone and the buoyancy of
his imagination always survive critical blindness, structural weakness, and
other momentary disasters, and they have helped to create a book delightful to read, eloquent, tonic, at times very wrong, and always interesting.'

M16.3 Barnes, W.J. *Queen's Quarterly* 73 (Autumn 1966): 455–7. 1140 w
Grants that there are many passages in *RE* that are 'brilliantly conceived
and well expressed,' but thinks the book as a whole is wrong-headed
about Milton and that F's writing is 'uncommonly bad.' Says F's chief fault
is his forcing Milton into a Protestant and Romantic mould, so that Milton
emerges as a 'kind of Blakean mystic.'

M16.4 Blondel, J. *Etudes anglaises* 19 (October-December 1966): 450–1. 500 w
Largely a summary of F's chief arguments.

M16.5 Broadbent, J.B. *English Language Notes* 4 (March 1967): 216–18. 700 w
Points to F's central argument about Milton's conception of spiritual liberty.
Thinks that F is sometimes too coy, too far removed from Milton's epic,
and too portentous for the poetry of spirituality.

M16.6 Cox, R. Gordon. *British Journal of Aesthetics* 7 (July 1967): 293–5. 1350 w

Lists and praises a series of F's incidental insights, but thinks the book
suffers from two basic problems. First, F presents his own views on
such issues as the presentation of God in *Paradise Lost* rather than trying
to capture Milton's views; and, second, F seems 'to make the reader's
appreciation in fact depend altogether upon his actually sharing Milton's
beliefs.' Wishes that F had paid more than perfunctory attention to Milton's style.

M16.7 Cruttwell, Patrick. 'New Miltonics.' *Hudson Review* 19 (Autumn 1966):
498–502. 2100 w
Divides the difficulties in reading *Paradise Lost* into four categories –
theological, cosmological, structural, and psychological – and examines F's
solution to each of them.

M16.8 Empson, William. 'An Anatomy of Taste.' *New Statesman* 72 (2 December
1966): 838. 425 w
Comments briefly on what he says is F's mistaken interpretation in seeing a
connection between the rebel angels in *Paradise Lost* and the error of Ham.
(The point is repeated from Empson's earlier review, M16.9).

M16.9 — 'Senator Milton.' *Listener* 76 (28 July 1966): 137. 800 w
Claims F makes Milton into the image of a rugged American. The book
makes 'improbable assertions,' and it is difficult to differentiate F's views
from Milton's. Is 'glad not to have to believe in the Milton of Professor
Frye and his individualist herd, as he would be a nasty character.'

M16.10 Fixler, Michael. *University of Toronto Quarterly* 35 (July 1966): 392–5. 1500 w
Summarizes F's exploration of the temporal and spatial patterns in *Paradise
Lost*, the discussion of which 'is so sensitively attached to Milton's poems
that more than any other general exposition it captures the baroque
complexity these patterns manifest.' Believes, however, that F stresses too
much the view of Milton as a revolutionary artist who wanted to discard
history and move toward the ultimate mystic beatitude of identity. Still, the
book 'has all the imaginative magnitude we have come to expect from [F].'

M16.11 Hamilton, Alice. *Dalhousie Review* 46 (Autumn 1966): 411, 413. 580 w
Says that the 'great value' of *RE* 'lies in its serious approach to Milton' and
that it deals ultimately with the difference between the real and the false.
States concisely F's thesis about the relation between liberty, virtue,
and heroism in Milton. The book is 'serious, witty, dignified, clear, concise,
moving with ease and assurance through difficult concepts, erudite but
not pedantic, disquietingly direct and forceful.'

M16.12 — 'Man – In Time and Eternity.' *Winnipeg Free Press*, 2 July 1966 [Leisure
Magazine section], 7. 600 w
Sees *RE* as 'a demanding and splendid book, a model of what scholarship
should be.' It is a book for people who want to confront the ultimate
problem of good and evil and who think it 'important to discuss such terms
as liberty and tyranny, lust and greed, power and apathy, despair and
distrust.'

M16.13 Lewalski, Barbara Kiefer. *College English* 27 (May 1966): 643–4. 730 w
Believes that 'the great merit of the book is that it illuminates the mythic
world, and therefore the structure, of Milton's two epic poems.' Thinks,
however, that F's exposition of the mythic world of the poem tends 'to
obscure the action of the poem itself' and that to identify Christ as the hero
of *Paradise Lost* is to obscure the central dramatic role played by Adam.

M16.14 Lievsay, John L. *South Atlantic Quarterly* 66 (Spring 1967): 260–3. 380 w
Gives a brief outline of the general plan of *RE*, which is said to be 'an
erudite and urbane blending of myth, allegory, and simple explication
of text.'

M16.15 Lobdell, David. 'Paradise Lost Viewed with Modern Outlook.' *Sherbrooke
Record*, 5 February 1966. 380 w
Sees the virtue of the book in F's having simplified the approach to Milton.
Says F's concluding words about the regaining of lost identity are 'perti-
nent to our time.'

M16.16 MacCaffrey, Isabel G. *Modern Language Quarterly* 27 (December 1966): 477–
80. 1450 w
Discusses chiefly the difficulty of keeping a balance between the concrete
drama of Milton's poem and the abstract theory used to interpret it.
Sometimes F's conceptual system takes on a life of its own and, in translating the poem, devours it. But when F is interpreting rather than translating, his commentary is 'largeminded, human, and balanced ... the product
of a magisterial intelligence.'

M16.17 Madsen, William G. *Criticism* 8 (Fall 1966): 389–94. 2700 w
Thinks that F's method, which relies on schematic diagrams both of the
action of *Paradise Lost* and of the four levels of existence in the poem,
causes him to distort Milton: '*Paradise Lost* does not possess the kind of
symmetry Frye attributes to it.' Discusses F's treatment of the theme of the
return of Eden. Agrees that the theme is true to the poem, but thinks it
should be developed at greater length. Judges F's emphasis on the centrality of the Garden symbol to be wrong 'because it omits the figure of
Christ.'

M16.18 Oras, Ants. 'Miltonic Themes.' *Sewanee Review* 77 (Winter 1969): 183–4.
430 w
Comments on the 'ease with which Frye conjures up large historical vistas
or complex thought structures' and on the many analogues he discovers
for *Paradise Lost*. Cites several of his 'brilliant' observations. Believes that he
over-emphasizes Milton's revolutionary character.

M16.19 P[atrick], J. M[ax]. *Seventeenth-Century News* 24 (Spring 1966): 1–2. 1060 w
Praises F's treatment of parody throughout the epic, his commentary
on Milton's view of the spiritual authority of the husband, and other insights. Thinks, however, that F's schematizations are imposed upon rather
than derived from the poem, and that the generic parallels F finds in
Milton (the colloquy, the Socratic dialogue, the symposium, the cyropedia,

the Jonsonian masque, etc.) are more confusing than illuminating. Recommends the book to sophisticated Miltonists but not to neophytes and general readers.

M16.20 Patrides, C.A. *Review of English Studies* 18 (August 1967): 330–32. 1100 w
Summarizes the theme around which each of the chapters revolves. Praises both the matter and the manner of the book, 'one of the finest introductions to *Paradise Lost*.' Says F has 'an unerring ability to distinguish the essential from the inessential and to phrase it forcefully, even memorably.'

M16.21 Rajan, B. *Alphabet* 11 [misnumbered as 8] (December 1965–March 1966): 74–5. 610 w
Characterizes F's approach as 'mytho-generic-structural.' Looks especially at his reading of the last books of *Paradise Lost*. F suggests 'that the paradise within is ... a natural stage in the evolution of the paradise myth.' Thinks that F sometimes wavers in his interpretation of the discrepancy between Milton's intentions and his performance.

M16.22 — 'Trepidation and Excitement.' *Canadian Literature* 28 (Spring 1966): 65–7. 1030 w
A somewhat fuller version of M16.21. Because of F's attack on historical criticism, this review includes a defence of the historical method, even though it is not excluded by F's 'approach nor the quality of his perceptiveness.'

M16.23 Ricks, Christopher. 'In Defense of Milton.' *New York Review of Books* 6 (9 June 1966): 27–8. 410 w
Thinks F places too much emphasis on Milton the revolutionary (he was conservative and traditional as well). Sees the book not as an example of F the myth critic but of F 'the expositor – patient, lucid, and deftly informative on a thousand topics.'

M16.24 Sirluck, Ernest. *Studies in English Literature: 1500–1900* 6 (Winter 1966): 187–8. 230 w
Says that F's commentary is distinguished by 'first, his power of retaining the living whole in his mind while he discusses the part, and secondly, his "wit," in the Renaissance sense of the discernment of underlying similarities in things apparently unlike each other.' Although F does not solve the problem of the discrepancy between the conceptual and dramatic aspects of *Paradise Lost*, he does enlarge our 'understanding of why Milton defied poetic fact in favor of "flat-footed honesty." '

M16.25 Summers, Joseph H. *JEGP* 66 (January 1967): 146–9. 1500 w
Says that 'few professional Miltonists ... would not gain valuable and fresh insights from a careful reading' of F, 'our most stimulating critic.' Registers complaints, however, against F's academic witticisms, the speed of his exposition, the mechanical nature of his abstract schemata, and a number of claims that are 'either mistaken in emphasis or just wrong.' Praises F's treatment of Milton's radicalism and individualism, his suggestions about the proper model of God, and his comments on reason and freedom and on the law and the gospel. Disagreements aside, what matters is

'that Milton's poems and Milton's vision of human liberty have kindled Frye's imagination and have caused him to write some marvellous passages.'

M17 **A Study of English Romanticism** (*SR*) [A11]

M17.1 Duffy, John J. *Modern Language Journal* 54 (February 1970): 131–2. 710 w
Devotes most of the review to summarizing F's definition of the romantic myth in the first chapter. Judges F's exposition of romanticism and its predecessors to be 'interestingly complete.'

M17.2 Hashiguchi, Minoru. 'Northrop Frye and Romanticism.' *Eigo seinen* [*The Rising Generation*] 116 (April 1970): 49
In Japanese.

M17.3 Lundin, John. *Studia Neophilologica* 43, no 2 (1971): 590–3. 1940 w
Summarizes F's argument about the romantic myth. Sees F's originality in the way he can manipulate the large elements in his schematic way of thinking. F 'challenges us by making us think in historical terms and by refusing to be limited by the usual categories of literature; above all because he is so well-equipped to pursue ritualized artistic forms through their evolution.' Praises the richness of F's allusions and reference. Thinks that his arguments are generally convincing if one accepts his premises. Reviews his chapters on Shelley, Keats, and Beddoes, the last of which is an original interpretation, even though F's 'fondness for generalizing sometimes leads him astray.' Judges F's primary strength to be the ability he has to visualize conceptual patterns.

M17.4 Woodman, Ross G. 'Literary Studies.' *University of Toronto Quarterly* 38 (July 1969): 371–3. 880 w
Sees one of the virtues in F's approach to literature to be his bringing neglected literary works, such as Beddoes's *Death's Jest-Book*, into focus. Devotes most of the review to considering F's treatment of Beddoes, who is for the first time integrated into a study of romanticism. Concludes that the 'same visionary power inherent in the conception of the poet as prophet is present also in Frye.'

M18 **The Secular Scripture** (*SeS*) [A15]

M18.1 Adams, Hazard. 'On Literary Criticism.' *New Republic* 75 (27 November 1976): 29–31 [30–1]
Brief notice.

M18.2 A[des], J[ohn] I. *Papers on Language and Literature* 14 (Summer 1978): 359–60. 430 w
Gives a brief summary of the book. Remarks that the astonishing breadth of F's reading would be intimidating 'were it not presented with such grace and wit.'

M18.3 Aldridge, A. Owen. *World Literature Today* 51 (Winter 1977): 167. 470 w

Comments briefly on F's archetypal and intrinsic approach to romance. Is not convinced by F's claim that the structure of the Bible provides the outline for Western mythology and worries about F's non-historical approach.

M18.4 Anonymous. *Choice* 13 (July-August 1976): 656
Brief notice.

M18.5 — *Christianity & Literature* 26 (Spring 1977): 56
A précis of the book, drawn from *MLA Abstracts*.

M18.6 — *The Griffin* 26 (February 1976): 9. 250 w
A brief overview of the book's aim.

M18.7 — *Milton Quarterly* 11 (March 1977): 25
Brief notice.

M18.8 — *New Yorker* 52 (26 April 1976): 147–8. 350 w
Brief overview of F's conception of romance. Says the book is an instructive and timely contribution, though how all the parts fit together is not clear.

M18.9 — *Yale Review* 66 (March 1977): XII–XIII. 540 w
Says that the book shows F's usual strengths and weaknesses. 'He writes cultural arguments rather than literary criticisms. He is more interested in what can be drawn together than in what can be discriminated, and he moves so rapidly as to make very difficult ascertaining whether his "wit" be true or false.'

M18.10 Blodgett, E.D. *Canadian Review of Comparative Literature* 4 (Fall 1977): 363–72. 4800 w
Maintains that F 'has magisterially invested both the mode and *mythos* of romance with virtually unassailable status.' Comments on a number of F's central assumptions and arguments: that the context for romance is its parallel relation to the Bible, that myth most clearly appears in romance and that realism is displaced romance, that the vertical structure of ascent and descent is a fundamental principle of romance, and that place is more important in romance than in other literary forms. Sees the book as 'a splendid demonstration of Frye's central argument that a knowledge of literature cannot pause over single works to the point where it prevents one from arriving at a state of "undiscriminating catholicity." '

M18.11 Bloom, Harold. 'Northrop Frye Exalting the Designs of Romance.' *New York Review of Books* 23 (18 April 1976): 21. Partially rpt in *Contemporary Literary Criticism*, vol 24, ed Sharon R. Gunton (Detroit: Gale Research 1983), 226–7. 1450 w
Places *SeS* in the context of *FS* and *AC*, the latter of which surpasses even Ruskin in its systematic and comprehensive vision of literature. Sees F as having provided the study of romance and romanticism with 'the fullest if not the most acute poetics that is currently available.' But judges *SeS* to be a disappointment largely because of its narrow scope. Is, however, still deeply moved by the optimistic and democratic element in F's work. Associates his true greatness with his being the 'legitimate heir of a Protestant and Romantic tradition that has dominated much of British and American literature, the tradition of the Inner Light.' Worries that F is

unable to explain what makes the archetype new in any particular work; that he therefore 'risks becoming the great homogenizer of literature'; and that, while F is the 'seer' of the joining of works together in the literary universe, he fails to account for the struggle of poetic wills to be free from their predecessors.

M18.12 Brennan, John P. *Clio* 6 (Fall 1976): 97–100. 1100 w
Summarizes F's distinctions between mythical and fabulous fictions and between secular and sacred scriptures. Says that the chapters on the narrative patterns and characters of romance delight because of F's wit and instruct because 'the ease of his allusions convinces the reader that there is something to be said for the concept of an imaginative universe.' Thinks the best chapters of *SeS* are those (2 and 6) that deal with the 'demand of the guardians of culture ... that our fictions exhibit "high seriousness," ' and in which F argues that the goal of humanistic education is remythologization. Says that one can complain about F's argumentative style, but that the book is richly textured and rewarding.

M18.13 Cismaru, Alfred. 'Hartman and Frye: American Criticism at Its Finest.' *National Forum* 60 (Fall 1980): 54–6. 580 w
Consists largely of a summary of the book.

M18.14 C[opeland], M.W. *Spenser Newsletter* 7 (Winter 1976): 1–6. 2300 w
Summarizes large sections of F's 'radical revision or reconsideration of the genre' of romance. Notes several parallels between F's work and Harold Bloom's theory of creation. Glances throughout at the implications of F's work for the study of Spenser.

M18.15 Daiches, David. 'The Roots of Fiction.' *TLS*, 5 November 1976, 1399. 2700 w
Gives a long summary of F's central theses and his characteristic method, which is to go beyond the individual literary work to larger verbal structures and eventually to the entire mythological universe. Observes that F is not concerned with making judgments about the relative quality of literary romances; rather, classifying them, he seeks to restore literary works to the tradition from which they have arisen. *SeS* is 'the work of a humane, original and genuinely inquiring mind.' More than a taxonomist, F 'is a man of wit and wisdom' who aims to place literature 'in the larger context of man's mental and imaginative needs and by so doing to show us how literature responds to those needs and in its response illuminates the human condition.'

M18.16 Dembo, L.S. *English Language Notes* 14 (December 1976): 151–4. 1350 w
Reviews F's purpose and his argument about the structural principle of displacement. Thinks F's schema for the heroes and themes of romance, while offering clear reference points, is neater and more coherent than actually exists in the literature F discusses. But whatever the shortcomings of F's generalizations, 'there is no denying that he is one of the great critical minds of the age.'

M18.17 Dickerson, Lynn. 'Enriching Life.' *Christian Century* 93 (26 March 1976): 522. 370 w
Gives a brief summary of F's thesis. Feels frustrated at the distinctions F

gives and then takes away, but says the book will be of interest to F
enthusiasts.

M8.18 Dobbs, Kildare. 'Northrop Frye Shines His Light on Popular Pulp.' *Peterborough Examiner* [Ont], 10 July 1976. 1000 w
A summary of F's map of the mythological universe of romance. Says *SeS*
is 'an extraordinarily profound and suggestive work ... one of those
books that teaches us how to read, and keeps striking echoes and reso-
nances from our own knowledge.'

M18.19 Feder, Lillian. 'The Traditions of Literature.' *Michigan Quarterly Review* 16
(Summer 1977): 350–5. 670 w
Says that although F's treatment of the *mythos* of romance is 'no more
convincing as a comprehensive critical scheme than are the mythoi of the
Anatomy,' F's analyses of motifs in particular romances is brilliant. Contrasts
F's view of fiction with Leavis's, observing that F believes the thought or
'reality' of literature is revealed only through structural conventions and
that his sense of the relation between tradition and innovation is a broad
one. Notes that F arrives independently at the idea, reiterated recently
by Harold Bloom, that poetic influence can involve misunderstanding.

M18.20 Fischer, Michael. 'The Legacy of English Romanticism: Northrop Frye and
William Blake.' *Blake: An Illustrated Quarterly* 11 (Spring 1978): 276–83.
5000 w
Ostensibly a review of *SeS* and *SM*, but devoted chiefly to clarifying the
moral role that Blake plays in the development of F's critical ideas and to
the question of aesthetic value that these ideas raise. Traces the influence
of Blake's epistemology, his view of the independence of art, and his
understanding of metaphor and the ends of art upon F's theory of literature. Argues that F's view of the imagination as a power for genuine
freedom raises the question of whether art does have the kind of socially
emancipating role F assigns it or whether he allows art 'to recede into
mere imagining.'

M18.21 Fulford, Robert. 'Scholar Finds That Romance Is Really a Secular Scripture.'
Toronto Star, 6 March 1976, F5. 950 w
Comments on F's view of popular literature, summarizes the book's thesis,
and praises F's prose style.

M18.22 F[uzier], J[ean]. *Cahiers Elisabethians* 11 (April 1977): 106–7. 620 w
Reviews F's purpose and thesis. Thinks that F is somewhat biased toward
the biblical, as opposed to the classical, influences on the Western mythological universe, but judges his general theory to be 'valid ... well-grounded,
and seminal.'

M18.23 Gans, Eric. 'Northrop Frye's Literary Anthropology.' *Diacritics* 8 (June
1978): 24–33. 5400 w
Begins by examining F's preference for the epic or narrative genre of
romance, but quickly turns to a critique of F's entire undertaking, which is
subjected to the 'absolute standard' of the human sciences. Sees F's
dismissal of evaluation as a particularly Anglo-American trait, placing him

in a tradition quite different from that of, say, Todorov. Says that F's
literal naturalism has prevented him from developing a proper view of
culture (his anthropology is essentially taxonomic), a proper understanding
of desire (he denies the disjunction between individual and communal
desire), and a proper understanding of the politics of literature (he is 'a
prisoner of the liberal-conservative cultural polemic'). Praises F for directing
our attention to the right issues but finds his cultural naturalism inadequate from the perspective of the human sciences as developed by European, especially French, thinkers.

M18.24 Gowda, H.H. Anniah. 'Stimulating to Read.' *Literary Half-Yearly* 18 (July
1977): 158–62. 1300 w
Chiefly a summary of F's arguments. Notes that his final words, which
refer to the end of speech as earning the right to silence, are 'very close to
Indian aesthetics.'

M18.25 Guaraldo, Enrico. *Tuttolibri* 4, nos 47–8 (23 December 1978): 15. 280 w
Looks briefly at F's treatment of the evolution of the genre and his view of
the human protagonist in romance forms.

M18.26 Halporn, James W. *Helios* 6 (Fall-Winter 1978–9): 84–94. 2000 w
Summarizes F's thesis about the difference between sacred and secular
scriptures and his definition of romance. Disagrees with F's view of myth,
finds that his definition of romance does not fit certain Greek stories
very well, and says that literary works resist the ease with which F places
them in categories. Feels therefore, 'curiously cheated' by the book, yet
grants that it 'is another stunning performance by Frye, whose ability to
connect so many disparate works, let alone remember them, puts us in
mind of a latter day Casaubon who has succeeded in finding the key to all
mythologies.'

M18.27 Hamilton, A.C. 'Northrop Frye and the Recovery of Myth.' *Queen's Quarterly* 85 (Spring 1978): 66–77. 5400 w
Places the book in the context of F's other work, especially *AC*. Sees *SeS* as
expanding, illuminating, and consolidating what F has written since
1957. Gives a detailed summary of each of the six chapters. Judges the
book to be 'a major event in modern English studies' because the genre of
romance belongs to F in the way tragedy belongs to Aristotle. Notes
that F concludes by affirming the older world-view of the sacred scripture,
and so remains puzzled at the end by F's attributing to romance a quality
similar to divine revelation, which earlier he had attributed to myth.

M18.28 Happel, Stephen. *Religious Studies Review* 3 (January 1977): 65–6. 200 w
Summarizes F's central thesis. Says F provides a 'helpful inventory of the
various structural elements of romance.' Finds that 'the pleasure of the
prose is often more persuasive than the cogency of the argument.'

M18.29 Herd, Eric W. *Germanistik* 22 (1981): 85–6. 220 w
Points to the bipartite structure of F's argument, a simplification that can
sometimes become irritating, and to the connection between this book
and F's earlier work.

M18.30 Hume, Kathryn. *Style* 11 (Spring 1977): 212–13. 750 w
        Notes that the thematic organization of the book 'avoids some of the
        problems of [F's] own former schemes.' Sees the strength of the book in its
        incidental insights and in the clarity of its arguments, its weaknesses in
        the 'insufficiently detailed' illustrations and in what sometimes 'seem
        methodologically irresponsible' comments.

M18.31 Hunter, J. Paul. 'Studies in Eighteenth-Century Fiction, 1976.' *Philological
        Quarterly* 56 (Fall 1977): 531–3. 1050 w
        Notes that F prefers the romance to the novel. Observes that if one grants
        F his premises, there is little to debate: his discussion is 'learned, symmet-
        rical, and persuasive – part of a larger Platonic, formalist, Anglican perspec-
        tive' that emphasizes timelessness, repetition, and cyclic movement.
        Grants that F's learning, sensitivity, scholarship, and wit enhance the act
        of criticism, but wants also to affirm ways of doing criticism that are
        less Platonic.

M18.32 Ireland, Jock. 'Secular Frye Examines Myths, Literature.' *Montreal Gazette*,
        29 May 1976, 50. 600 w
        Largely a series of quotations from the first chapter. Says that F's work is
        erudite, demanding, and aware of what literature can and cannot teach.

M18.33 Jeffrey, David K. *Southern Humanities Review* 13 (Summer 1978): 301. 550 w
        Gives a brief summary of F's thesis in *SeS*, which is judged to be his
        'most accessible book.'

M18.34 Jewinski, Ed. *Quill & Quire* 42 (April 1976): 41. 280 w
        Summarizes F's 'primarily theoretical' argument. Says it contains a series
        of complex and brilliant ideas about romance but is not easy reading.

M18.35 Johnston, Albert H. *Publishers Weekly* 209 (19 January 1976): 89
        Short review.

M18.36 Klimowsky, Ernst W. *Bibliographie zur Symbolik, Ikonographie, und Mythologie*,
        ed Manfred Lurker and Helmut Schneider (Baden-Baden: Verlag Valentin
        Koerner 1978), 53
        Brief notice.

M18.37 Kuczkowski, Richard. *Library Journal* 101 (1 April 1976): 901
        Brief review.

M18.38 Lawless, Greg. 'Rescuing Romance.' *Harvard Crimson*, 11 February 1976.
        1275 w
        Summarizes F's central argument. Finds the most interesting aspect of the
        book to be the theory of society F develops in relation to romance, a
        genre that is closer to the people than other forms. Comments on F's caveat
        against basing criticism on value-judgments. Maintains, however, that
        literature does have political consequences and that Marxists should be
        aware of the abuses of romance.

M18.39 Lindahl, Carl. *Journal of American Folklore* 92 (January-March 1979): 80–2.
        1210 w
        Sees *SeS* as F's finest, best-documented, most clearly focused, least dog-
        matic, and most valuable attempt 'to establish the folktale and its related

forms as genres worthy of esteem.' Calls the book 'intuitive rather than
scholarly'; and though F 'possesses a remarkable intuition,' 'he lacks the
all-important quality of self-discipline necessary for a synthesis of his
exciting ideas.' Still, *SeS* is 'a landmark book.' Refers to F as 'the Lévi-
Strauss of literary studies,' though F's schemes are much more flexible than
Lévi-Strauss's. 'Frye has opened the door for the long-awaited meeting
of folklore and literature on grounds congenial to both.'

M18.40 McMurtry, Larry. 'A Work of Critical Plums, Ripe for the Picking.'
Washington Post, 22 March 1976, B4. 630 w
Judges *SeS* to be 'the most sophisticated study of popular culture, considered on a world scale, that we have yet had.' Believes F is especially
brilliant on the themes of ascent and descent and the virginity of the
heroine and on the responsibility of readers to discover that the stories
in romances are ultimately about themselves.

M18.41 Moore, Mavor. 'He Restoreth My Soul.' *Canadian Forum* 56 (June-July 1976):
62–3. 1230 w
Thinks that *SeS* owes more to Jung than F is willing to admit, because F is
looking at literature 'through the binoculars of literature and psychology.'
Sees the book as 'unfailingly fascinating and refreshing' and 'couched
in the clearest, neatest, most unaffected prose since Bertrand Russell.'

M18.42 Nelson, William. *University of Toronto Quarterly* 46 (Summer 1977): 415–18.
1450 w
Summarizes F's central thesis about the structure of romance. Says 'the
persuasiveness of Frye's reconstruction of "the secular scripture" is enhanced by the wealth of his learning, the fertility of his imagination, and
the charm of his exposition.' Believes, however, that F's search for structure
and his dismissal of questions of belief neglect a great deal of what is
essential in literary works.

M18.43 Ogawa, Kazuo. 'The Structure of Romance.' *Gakuto* 73 (October 1976):
16–19
In Japanese.

M18.44 Payne, Michael. *College Literature* 6 (Winter 1979): 73–5. 280 w
Comments briefly on the importance of *SeS* for the renewed interest in
Spenser.

M18.45 Perosa, Sergio. 'Che cosa significa "narrare." ' *Corriere della sera* 104, no 62
(18 March 1979). 720 w
Review of the Italian translation (A15b). Thinks that although the translation
is a poor one, it will cause Italian readers to look again at F's other books
that have been translated into Italian. Comments on F's attention to the
roles that myth, fable, ritual, and the collective unconscious play in determining the narrative patterns in literature. Says the book provides a
synthesis of a vast and complex body of literature.

M18.46 Pfeiffer, K. Ludwig. *Anglia* 99, nos 1–2 (1981): 241–5. 1650 w
Places *SeS* in the context of *AC*. Says the main problem with this and F's
other works is his giving attention to structural relations only. He neglects

socio-cultural or functional relations. Too, his generic definitions are too loose, his levels of structure are too abstract, and the imaginary universe he creates is tautological.

M18.47 Sargent, Barbara Nelson. *Comparative Literature Studies* 15 (December 1978): 434–6. 1250 w
Thinks the first chapter is the most substantial of the six. Says that F's insights into romance are illuminating and brilliant and that the book is written 'in a style that is at all times graceful.' Finds, however, that his sweeping assertions have very little practical value for literary analysis and that some of the underlying similarities F locates may be only the 'critic's construct.'

M18.48 Takayanagi, Shunichi. 'Classics, Bible, and Secularization.' *Sophia* 26 (Summer 1977): 76–9. Rpt in Takayanagi *Seishinshi no nanka no Eibungaku* [*English Literature in the Context of Intellectual History*] (Tokyo: Nansosha 1977), 191–6.
In Japanese. Looks at the book in the context of the theme of secularization in literature. Reviewed along with *SM*.

M18.49 Watts, Harold M. *Modern Fiction Studies* 23 (Summer 1977): 307–10. 720 w
Compares F's vision of the hopes for our culture with those of two other critics, Leo Bersani and Murray Krieger. Examines chiefly F's effort to rescue the secular scripture of romance from having been overshadowed by the sacred scripture.

M18.50 Wood, Michael. 'A Fine Romance.' *New York Review of Books* 24 (14 April 1977): 33–5. 1950 w
Says that F's 'practice is usually more flexible than his theory,' but that the theory nevertheless does become more important for him than the reality of literary works. Observes that what F wants in literature is the completeness of a mythological universe rather than the imitation of reality. Is 'rather suspicious of Frye's seeing so much of the whole of literature and so little in the individual works he must pillage for his grander purpose,' but does 'recognize the community he evokes as the conclusion of his romance.' Praises, finally, F's effort to reclaim the ideal: 'if we didn't have pictures of transcendence, we should probably not remember why we want changes.'

M18.51 Yglesias, Luis Ellicott. 'Northrop Frye at Harvard.' *New Boston Review*, Fall 1976, 17. 1440 w
Looks at the book in the context of F's argument about the coherent structure of literature, and shows the relation of his central thesis to the realism-versus-romance debate.

M19 **Spiritus Mundi** (*SM*) [A16]

M19.1 Anonymous. *Book Forum* 3 (Winter 1977): 42, 44. 230 w
Refers to F as 'one of the most civilized and delightful scholar-teachers

publishing today,' one who posits a mythological universe against the discontinuity of intellectual faddism and anarchism.

M19.2 — *Booklist* 73 (March 1977): 983
Brief notice.

M19.3 — *Milton Quarterly* 12 (March 1978): 39. 290 w
Glances briefly at F's treatment of Milton in 'Agon and Logos' (D217) and
other essays.

M19.4 — *Virginia Quarterly Review* 53 (Summer 1977): 88
Brief notice.

M19.5 Ashley, Benedict M. *New Review of Books and Religion* 1 (May 1977): 20.
360 w
Thinks that F's observation that literary criticism interpenetrates other
disciplines is 'highly relevant to the study of religion and biblical hermeneutics.' Suggests that F is not familiar, however, with some of the current
theological interpretations of the Bible.

M19.6 Balfour, Ian. 'Can the Centre Hold? Northrop Frye and the Spirit of the
World.' *Essays on Canadian Writing* 7/8 (Fall 1977): 214–21. 3150 w
Offers a sketch of the individual essays in the book. Devotes most of the
review to examining the general theory of criticism F has developed in
AC and elsewhere, particularly its Blakean roots, its schematic character, its
celebration of romance, and its dependence on the paradigm of a centre.

M19.7 Beattie, Munro. 'Frye, in His Prime.' *Ottawa Citizen*, 2 April 1977, 34. 800 w
Believes F's way of doing criticism is 'an exhilarating game ... always
worthy of attention, and a godsend to teachers and students of a certain
bent.' Glances at F's social criticism, especially his views on the function of
the university in the face of contemporary radicalism.

M19.8 Bilan, R.P. 'Visionary Critic.' *Canadian Forum* 57 (June-July 1977): 38–9.
1800 w
Says *SM* reinforces his general experience in reading F: the expected
revelation never quite comes or comes only in cryptic ways. Observes that
F's social views are becoming more conservative, suggesting 'the possibility of a rather un-Blakean accommodation to society.' Glances at the
essays of practical criticism in this collection, and speculates about the
nature of F's religious beliefs.

M19.9 Bronzwaer, W. *Dutch Quarterly Review* 8 (1978): 318–20. 1050 w
Points to F's comments on the recent state of critical studies: his dissatisfaction with the New Criticism and his diagnosis and critique of the
anarchism of the New Left. Finds F's essay on the philosophical content of
Stevens's poetry to be especially impressive and somewhat of a relief,
'coming as it does after so many pages of what we have learned to recognize as Mr. Frye's characteristic mythological reading of literature.' The
relief, however, 'does not detract from the overpowering impression of
learning, wisdom and wit that the book as a whole leaves.' Although
F sometimes seems to say things too sweepingly, the book does fruitfully
elaborate certain topics in *AC*.

M19.10 Bruck, Peter. *Bibliographie zur Symbolik, Ikonographie, und Mythologie*, ed Manfred Lurker and Helmut Schneider (Baden-Baden: Verlag Valentin Koerner 1978), 53–4
Brief notice.

M19.11 Cain, William E. *South Carolina Review* 11 (November 1978): 123–5. 140 w
Brief critique that praises the essays on Spengler and Milton but judges the essays on education, the university, and research to be 'so detached, so grandly self-assured, that the reader feels almot no contact with the real pressures and tensions of these issues.'

M19.12 Cargas, Harry J. 'Canada's Distinguished Literature.' *St Louis Post-Dispatch*, 29 March 1977
Brief notice.

M19.13 Cismaru, Alfred. 'Hartman and Frye: American Criticism at Its Finest.' *National Forum* 60 (Fall 1980): 54–6. 590 w
Notes that the essays in part 1 are the theoretical platform from which the rest of the book springs. Comments especially on 'Expanding Eyes,' 'the most remarkable chapter in the second division.' Altogether, the book constitutes 'solid proof that neither structuralism nor axiology need limit the sources or the materials at the disposal of the critic.'

M19.14 C[opeland], M.W. *Spenser Newsletter* 8 (Fall 1977): 46–7. 680 w
Notes that this collection of essays provides 'the mental history of a literary critic' – a recording of F's views on the generic history of literature and on the relationship of literature to culture. Comments on the role of Spenserian poetry in the large vision of possibilities in F's social and educational universe.

M19.15 Eder, Doris. 'Spiritus Mundi.' *Denver Quarterly* 13 (Spring 1978): 81–5. 2700 w
Gives fairly detailed summaries of the essays on Blake, Yeats, and Stevens, which are said to be the most valuable things in this collection. Thinks that most of the other essays are 'pointless, dated, documents in the history of one critic's taste. They may be skimmed or skipped without loss.' Nevertheless, some of F's large ideas on such things as the loss of continuity, escapist literature, romance, the relationship between scientific and literary mythologies, and the primitive and civilized understanding of nature emerge repeatedly throughout the collection. Such ideas are interesting, though they are not the kind of well-researched, seminal work that *AC* is.

M19.16 Fischer, Michael. 'The Legacy of English Romanticism: Northrop Frye and William Blake.' *Blake: An Illustrated Quarterly* 11 (Spring 1978): 276–83
See M18.20.

M19.17 Gans, Eric. 'Northrop Frye's Literary Anthropology.' *Diacritics* 8 (June 1978): 24–33. 5400 w
See M18.23

M19.18 Halporn, James W. *Helios* 6 (Fall-Winter 1978–9): 84–94. 1750 w
Contrasts F's work with Trilling's, noting the kind of dialogue on the

relation between literature and life that issues from the contrast. Concentrates on the social, educational, and professional issues F raises in the first
section of *SM*. Observes that these opening essays 'reveal a deep disquiet'
about the role of the university in the modern world.

M19.19 Jewinski, Ed. *Quill & Quire* 43 (May 1977): 38–9
Frye's most 'important book since *Anatomy of Criticism*.' Sees the essays in
part 2 as containing 'Frye's most challenging and significant criticism of
recent years.'

M19.20 Keith, W.J. *Canadian Book Review Annual, 1983*, ed Dean Tudor and Ann
Tudor (Toronto: Simon & Pierre, 1984), 272–3. 290 w
Reviewed on the occasion of the paperback reissue. Believes the book
contains 'as clear an exposition of Frye's central idea – or vision' as one is
likely to encounter. Even if one disagrees with F's basic attitudes, this
'is an important production by Canada's most influential literary scholar.'

M19.21 Kuczkowski, Richard. *Library Journal* 101 (15 October 1976): 2177
Brief review.

M19.22 Lane, Lauriat. *English Studies in Canada* 4 (Winter 1978): 490–9. 3950 w
Sees the essays in *SM* as a 'convincing demonstration of the genuine contextualism that seems to be forming a larger and larger part of Frye's
work.' Shows in some detail how F's concerns in these essays are a continuous part of the overall critical project he developed in *AC* and elsewhere.
Looks especially at the attention F has devoted to Yeats over the years,
at his long-standing interest in Spengler, and at the seriousness of F's belief
that literature serves humanity through the mythologies it provides.

M19.23 Paschall, Douglas. 'Continuity in Northrop Frye's Criticism.' *Sewanee
Review* 88 (Winter 1980): 121–5. 2000 w
Notes the similarities and differences between F's criticism and that of the
French structuralists. Worries about whether or not F's insistence on
structure and system subordinates the reader's experience of particular
literary works. Notes that what F says about such writers as Frazer and
Spengler in 1975 is similar to his appropriation of their views in *NFCL*.
Sees the continuity of F's principles as having enabled him 'at best to enli-
ven and inform his readers as few other living critics have done.' His
insights exist in spite of the system, not because of it.

M19.24 Pausch, Holger A. *Canadian Review of Comparative Literature / Revue Canadienne de Littérature Comparée* 11 (June 1984): 283–4. 725 w
Catalogues the twelve essays in the book and gives a brief summary of
each. Finds F's method of criticism extremely conservative, his statements
often platitudinous, and his failure to cite secondary literature light-
handed.

M19.25 Rajan, B. *University of Toronto Quarterly* 47 (Summer 1978): 395–8. 1450 w
Is somewhat disappointed that these essays do not provide an unequivocal
demonstration that the structures of F's system work triumphantly, but
says that 'the disappointment of discovering this is by no means devastating: the essays do have the relationship offered by those characteristic

habits of understanding that have always distinguished the single mind behind them.' Provides an abstract of more than half of the essays. Notes that throughout F is fascinated 'by the relation of man to an otherness.'

M19.26 Sisk, John. 'Some Outstanding Books of the Year.' *Commonweal* 104 (27 May 1977): 346–7. 350 w
Looks briefly at the first and fifth essays, which 'are likely to be particularly welcome since their subject in great part is the mental history of one of our most important critics.'

M19.27 — *The Alternative: An American Spectator*, May 1977, 28. 870 w
A somewhat expanded version of M19.26. Says that 'the two autobiogra-phical essays alone ... make it clear that an attempt to distinguish be-tween literature and criticism at this level is to miss the point,' for 'no one who writes English prose as well as Frye does is writing anything but literature.'

M19.28 Spector, Robert D. *World Literature Today* 51 (Summer 1977): 505–6. 350 w
Sees these essays as an exception to most collections because they 'sub-stantiate a unified critical point of view.' F's consistent critical principle throughout is to recreate an author's text by studying its imagery and metaphors.

M19.29 Takayanagi, Shunichi. 'Classics, Bible, and Secularization.' *Sophia* 26 (Sum-mer 1977): 76–9. Rpt in Takayanagi, *Seishinshi no naka no Eibungaku* [*English Literature in the Context of Intellectual History*] (Tokyo: Nansosha 1977), 191–6.
In Japanese. Looks at the book in the context of the theme of seculariza-tion in literature.

M19.30 West, Thomas. *Journal of European Studies* 9 (September 1979): 208–10. 870 w
Provides an abstract of each of the twelve essays. Says the basic problem is how to evaluate F's vision of the mythological structure of culture. Thinks F has not clarified what significance a knowledge of this structure has for our lives and whether the movement from the particular to the general context is both a means and an end. Characterizes F's philosophy as 'a kind of Myth-Idealism wherein the significance of human activity lies in its imaginative expression of the essential Myth-Idea,' but wonders whether the activity or the Myth-Idea has ultimate significance. Thinks F's work has little to offer the initiated reader of literature, yet finds his map of the literary universe convincing.

M19.31 Wood, Michael. 'A Fine Romance.' *New York Review of Books* 24 (14 April 1977): 33–5 [34]. 300 w
Is particularly attracted to F's essays on Yeats and on charms and riddles. Says the essays display F's 'prodigious learning as well as his usual intellectual agility' but that they bring him perilously close to elevating intellectual schemes over reality.

M19.32 Woodcock, George. 'One of the Great Canadian Gurus, Frye Still Provokes.' *Globe and Mail*, 19 January 1977, 13. 1140 w
Regards *SM* as an exemplary collection of essays, more important in some ways than his academic books with their formal architecture. Sees these

essays as revealing F the public critic, a mediator in the tradition of Hazlitt
and Wilde. Believes that F's survival value results from his projecting a
true philosophy of life.

M20 **The Stubborn Structure** (*StS*) [A12]

M20.1 Anonymous. *Christian Century* 87 (18 November 1970): 1385
Brief notice.
M20.2 — *Virginia Quarterly Review* 47 (Summer 1971): cxii
Brief review.
M20.3 — *Yale Review* 60 (March 1971): VI, X, XIV. 1250 W
Distinguishes between those essays in *StS* that are necessary and those
that are important. The essays in the first part of the book are necessary
because they address fundamental human questions with assurance and
humour. Does not find F's discussion of the myth of concern particularly
illuminating. Finds the essay on romanticism to be the best applied criticism in the book: it suggests 'both great mastery and receptivity to a power
"below/All thoughts." '
M20.4 Aranguren, Jose Luis L. 'La critica mitopoetica.' *Triunfo*, 3 November 1973
Looks at F's general system and its structuralist foundations, noting
that F presents a rhetoric of mythology similar to Todorov's grammar of
poetic expression and Lévi-Strauss's structural mythology. Devotes most of
the review to F's understanding of social mythology and to the paradox
involved in his call for both detachment and engagement.
M20.5 Brown, Merle. 'Critical Theory.' *Contemporary Literature* 15 (Winter 1974):
131–40. 1900 W
Criticizes F's separation of knowledge and judgment and says that the
opponents F argues against are straw men: 'Frye never argues against any
position that a thinking person could consider to be his own.' Maintains
that even though F does sometimes talk about the overlap of such categories as engagement and detachment, he makes only 'minimal concessions
to overlapping.' Contrasts F's views with those of Frederic Jameson.
Concedes that in 'The Instruments of Mental Production' and 'The Knowledge of Good and Evil' F does offer a proper social vision of the synthesis
of self and other.
M20.6 Colombo, John Robert. 'Polished Performance by a Canadian Essayist.'
Toronto Star [Book section], 20 May 1971, 65. 450 W
Observes that what these essays have in common is their clarity of style,
range of reference, and treatment of the ideas that have informed F's other
books. Thinks that F's 'Conclusion' to *Literary History of Canada* 'offers
seminal insights that will keep literary scholars busy for decades.'
M20.7 Cox, C.B. 'What Tales Should Tell.' *Sunday Telegraph* [London], 17 January
1971. 440 W
Calls attention primarily to F's revolutionary understanding of education.
M20.8 Daiches, David. *Review of English Studies* 22 (November 1971): 522–5. 1330 W

Reviews F's characteristic method of literary study, which is to move 'outwards from the work under consideration to illuminate it by placing it with other works that employ the same kind of myth, and inwards to interpret its structure and meaning with reference to the general mytho-poeic area to which it belongs.' Considers the outward movement to be more conspicuous, especially in the more theoretical essays, even though a writer's individuality is frequently lost in the process. Remains puzzled by F's views on value-judgments. Characterizes F's mind as wide-ranging, original, civilized, provocative, seminal, and humane. Notes that he is a cultural historian as well as a literary critic, and glances at his 'perceptively tolerant' essay on Canadian literature.

M20.9 Donoghue, Denis. 'Doing as the Greeks.' *Listener* 85 (21 January 1971): 88. 520 w

Thinks that the justification of F's method is in the illuminating perceptions it produces, as in his essay on Dickens. Finds an altogether new element in F's work to be his belief that the universities embody the real social and moral authority of our age, a belief that strikes Donoghue 'as nonsense, or at least as ... extraordinarily innocent.'

M20.10 Flamm, Dudley. *Books Abroad* 45 (Summer 1971): 524. 450 w

Points chiefly to the social vision that emerges from these essays: they reveal 'the kind of commitment to the exploration of literary study and its relation to society that only a person with a legitimate social concern could have.'

M20.11 Frankel, Anne. 'Literature and Society.' *New Society* 15 (3 December 1970): 1010–11. 500 w

Looks chiefly at F's views on the social function of literature. Objects to his preferring ideal and eternal values to the moral commitments of the group to which one belongs. Thinks F gives 'a better testimony to the real value of literature' in the essays in practical criticism in the second half of the book.

M20.12 Fry, A.J. *Neophilologus* 55 (October 1971): 466–7. 700 w

Thinks F's work is crippled because his interpretative system, which is detached from literary experience, is a reductive orthodoxy. Says that F's commitment to his system 'produces a great deal of comparative religion, intellectual history and circular reasoning but hardly any literary criticism.'

M20.13 Furbank, P.N. 'Northrop Frye: The Uses of Criticism.' *Mosaic* 3 (Summer 1972): 179–84. 2750 w

Says F's system of criticism, as developed in *AC*, arouses admiration and wonder, but doubts that the system has any real critical value beyond classification for its own sake. Quarrels with F's position on value-judg-ments and his views on teaching criticism rather than literature. Concedes that F writes luminously about the social role of the critic and the ends of the humanities. Finds the essay on Dickens to be convincing, but con-cludes that the essay on romanticism employs an external approach, taking us away from individual literary works.

M20.14 Goetsch, Paul. *Die neueren Sprachen* 72 (March 1973): 172–3. 380 w
Sees the essays in this book as a supplement to *AC*. Thinks F's method
comes through best in his genre studies of Dickens and utopian literature.
Says that F's explanations are offered mainly as a brilliant justification
of his own theories but they are also valuable for anyone interested in
literary didacticism.

M20.15 Gonzalo, Angel Capellán. *Filologia Moderna*, November 1971–February 1972,
132–4. 1200 w
Largely a summary of the book. Says that although the essays lack a
unified theme, *StS* does embody a unified critical method and a consistent
point of view.

M20.16 — *Sin Nombre* [San Juan, PR] 2, no 2 (1971): 90–2
Same as M20.15.

M20.17 Hashiguchi, Minoru. *Eigo seinen* [*The Rising Generation*] 117 (April 1971): 50
In Japanese. Brief review that points to F's humanistic commitment despite
his rejection of value-judgments as the basis for literary study.

M20.18 Hough, Graham. 'Panoptic Vision.' *Spectator* 225 (5 December 1970): 733–4.
880 w
See *StS* as a set of footnotes to *FS* and *AC*, though the vision in these essays
is not quite as bright as in the originals. What motivates all of F's work
is not the spirit of taxonomy, 'but the sense of a great closely articulated
organic whole; and his earlier and more substantial work is not an aid
to academic study but an imaginative construction in its own right.' Finds
F's faith in the university as the 'real society' implausible. Nevertheless,
F is 'the most original and stimulating critic of our time,' and *StS* contains
vestiges of his earlier brilliance.

M20.19 Jackson, Wallace. *South Atlantic Quarterly* 70 (Summer 1971), 418–20. 900 w
Argues that because these essays are redactions or extensions of earlier
work they do not really form a book, and that 'the inspiration behind the
work is remarkably egocentric, since its greatest value is to document
the mind's own search for new openings.' Says the essays in the first part
are an 'exercise in humanistic sagacity,' but they exist at the periphery
of F's thought. The 'book is important only because Frye is important.'

M20.20 Lewis, Roger C. *Dalhousie Review* 51 (Spring 1971): 109–13. 1870 w
Says that the unity in this collection 'derives from the awesome comprehensiveness of Frye's mind' and that its central concept, treated in the
opening essays of each section, is utopia. Summarizes the arguments of
these two essays, 'The Instruments of Mental Production' and 'Varieties of
Literary Utopias.' Notes the two essays on Blake give evidence of some
common ground between F and McLuhan. Judges F to be an ideal critic
when he is at his best – 'when the austere intensity of his prose complements the clarity and power of his insight.' But his essays on romanticism
and Canadian literature illustrate that he is not always at his best.

M20.21 Poto, Daniele. 'La struttura ostinata.' *La fiera letteraria*, 10 October 1976.
430 w

Review of the Italian translation (A12e). Says that because of F's originality and openness he is different from the fashionable ideological critics. Compares F to Roland Barthes: they both offer new perspectives and both move away from the fragmentation of specialized, disciplinary scholarship.

M20.22 Puffmore, Henry. 'Philistines, Unite.' *Bookseller*, 21 November 1970, 2427. 215 w

Comments briefly on the opposing reviews of the book by Raymond Williams (M20.31) and Stephen Vizinczey (M20.30).

M20.23 Ray, William Ernest. 'On Frye and Peckham: A Review Essay.' *Southern Humanities Review* 8 (Winter 1974): 85–92 [85–8, 92]. 1670 w

Compares and contrasts F's work to that of Morse Peckham in *The Triumph of Romanticism*, noting that F has moved toward a concern with the social and ethical functions of literature. Sees the two parts of the book as 'linked both by the terms and principles brought over from the *Anatomy* and by the Arnoldian dialectic of present and potential society.' Provides an abstract of each of the essays except the final one.

M20.24 Ross, Malcolm. 'Northrop Frye.' *University of Toronto Quarterly* 41 (Winter 1972): 170–3. 1500 w

Says that whatever one reads in this collection, 'one is conscious of being in the presence of a scrupulous and discriminating intelligence exercised unfailingly with a concern which never twists into anxiety and with a detachment which never declines into indifference.' Sees F primarily as a 'salvationist,' one who affirms 'the redemptive power of literature *for* life.' Traces this affirmation through several of the essays in the collection.

M20.25 Sacca, Antonio. 'Due lezioni di umanesimo.' *L'Osservatore Romano*, 5 May 1977. 490 w

Review of the Italian translation (A12e). Looks at the book primarily as embodying a great sense of unity between classical and biblical culture and the present. Notes that F is fundamentally a humanist, who tries to avoid ideological preconceptions.

M20.26 Sage, Lorna. 'Aesthetic Democracy?' *New Statesman* 80 (18 December 1970): 844–5. 900 w

Wishes that F's literary democracy were more open to divergent mythologies, such as social realism.

M20.27 Sanders, Scott. 'Literature as Entrance/Literature as Exit.' *Cambridge Review* 92 (7 May 1971): 177–8. 1450 w

Argues against the radical separation F makes between ordinary life and ideal vision, a separation that 'tends, like Eliot's reactionary utopia, to discourage creativity in the present,' sets up a false division between culture and history, and leads to a schizophrenic existence. Likens F's vision of culture to a 'proxy theology,' which sees salvation as a kind of utopian, imaginative escape from ordinary society.

M20.28 Sibaldi, Igor A. 'Northrop Frye: il mythos della critica.' *Uomini e libri* 12, no 60 (1976): 50. 330 w

Review of the Italian translation (A12e). Comments briefly on the connection between *AC* and *StS*: in *AC* F was the high priest of a new structuralist religion; in *StS* he is a refined gourmet cook. Says that F still remains a great humanistic rhetorician.

M20.29 Thomas, Gilbert. *English* 20 (Summer 1971): 62–3. 285 w
Looks briefly at F's central thesis about the social function of literature, which is said to be presented 'persuasively and with quiet humour.'

M20.30 Vizinczey, Stephen. 'Reading and Literature: The Rules of the Game.' *The Times* [London], 12 November 1970, 14. 1125 w
Contrasts F's approach to literature with that of Lukács ('the two most important critics of our time'): Lukács sees literature as a reflection of social reality, whereas F sees it as revealing the power of the imagination. The two aesthetic systems, though opposed, complement each other. Says F is not so much a critic as a philosopher of literature, whose work is important for the general reader.

M20.31 Williams, Raymond. 'A Power to Fight.' *Guardian*, 12 November 1970, 9. 830 w
Finds F to be 'one of the four or five people, in contemporary cultural studies, who need to be faced, because of the solidity and influence of their work,' but sees in his work a familiar enemy – an intellectual tradition that places little weight upon contemporary experience, elevates abstraction, and is simply another form of Arnold's claim that poetry will save us.

M20.32 Woodcock, George. 'Criticism and Other Arts.' *Canadian Literature* 49 (Summer 1971): 3–7 [3–5]. 1050 w
Distinguishes between the academic critic and the public critic. (The first three paragraphs of this review repeat the first three of M2.26). Sees the essays in *StS* as examples of an academic, detached criticism, which, for all its elegance and ingenuity, is too far removed from the realities of life to be of much interest.

M20.33 Yura, Kimiyoshi. 'A Solid Foundation.' *Gakuto* 68 (January 1971): 36–9
In Japanese.

M21 **T.S. Eliot** (*TSE*) [A5]

M21.1 Anonymous. 'Nine Writers and Their Critics.' *TLS*, 12 July 1963, 511
Brief notice.

M21.2 — *Quarterly Review* 301 (July 1963): 365–6
Brief notice.

M21.3 Beattie, Munro. 'A Wickedly Witty Essay on Eliot in New Series.' *Ottawa Citizen*, 18 May 1963, 14. 320 w
Thinks 'the matching-up of the greatest of living poets with the most erudite and acute of living critics' has produced a dismaying result, chiefly because in F's mapping out of analogues and image structures Eliot's poems get lost. Says that the unseasoned reader should avoid the book; what it provides the seasoned reader is another glimpse of F's learning, intelligence, and wit.

M21.4 Blissett, William. 'Literary Studies.' *University of Toronto Quarterly* 33 (July 1964): 401–8. 1070 w
Says that the book possesses the virtues of all of F's work: 'it is strong in relating image to concept, it is well-organized and well-paced, and it does not flatter or insult its subject.' Notes that F has learned from Eliot a sense of tradition and that the book is 'marked by a sort of tension between progressivism and conservatism.' Cites several of F's witty attacks on Eliot that miss the mark: 'Eliot's words were better weighed than his critic's.'

M21.5 Cook, Eleanor, and Ramsay Cook. *Canadian Annual Review for 1963*, ed John Saywell (Toronto: Univ of Toronto Press 1964), 457
Brief note. Reviewed along with *EI, FI,* and *WTC.*

M21.6 Mandel, Eli W. 'The Language of Humanity: Three Books by Northrop Frye.' *Tamarack Review* 29 (Autumn 1963): 82–9. 3400 w
Places *TSE* in the context of F's other, purely critical works that relate to the study of literature as a whole and that are distinguished from his social and cultural criticism. Shows that F's way of understanding Eliot is to separate his social and historical studies from his poetic and critical work. 'Frye is prepared to grant Eliot his majority but only on Frye's terms, that is, in so far as Eliot's thought and imagery form a consistent unit in the deployment of an imaginative vision of innocence and experience.'

M21.7 Nott, Kathleen. 'Old Masters.' *The Spectator* 211 (5 July 1963): 24. 450 w
Sees F as engaged in both evaluative criticism (in the early part of the book) and critical analysis. Says that F's 'own natural method is a remarkable combination of structural insight and allusive aptness ... an inductive, indeed, Artistotelian method, which results in both richness and incisiveness.'

M21.8 P., H.B. *The Living Church*, 23 August 1981
Brief notice.

M21.9 Ricks, Christopher. 'Yes I Said.' *New Statesman* 66 (16 August 1963): 198–9. 130 w
Finds F to be good on Eliot's prose. 'In a tiny space he manages both to describe justly and to disagree by means of witty inflections.' On Eliot's poetry, F does less well.

M21.10 Thomas, Gilbert. 'Aspects of Genius.' *Poetry Review* 54 (Winter 1963–4): 326, 328. 200 w
Judges the book to be a 'lucid guide' to Eliot, showing 'learning, insight, and balance.' Summarizes F's judgments about Eliot's view of culture and tradition.

M21.11 Watt, F.W. 'The Critic's Critic.' *Canadian Literature* 19 (Winter 1964): 51–4. 1600 w
Says the book is 'a penetrating and abundantly rewarding study.' Provides an overview of F's reaction to Eliot's historical myth of decline and notes his endorsement of Eliot's contribution to critical theory (the order of words). Observes that F's treatment of Eliot's poetry seeks 'to establish the

geography of Eliot's total imaginative world.' Concludes by characterizing
the book not as an 'elementary handbook' (F's phrase) but as 'a critic's
manual, an outline of a creed, a declaration of principle and a demonstration of their practice ... [and a] conversation about the meaning and
value of literature.'

M21.12 West, Paul. 'Turning New Leaves (1).' *Canadian Forum* 43 (December 1963):
207–8. 310 w
See F's last chapter as the 'most original,' and praises F's tactful interpretation of *Ash Wednesday*. Calls the book a 'magisterial study.'

M21.13 Winship, G.P. *Bristol Herald-Courier* (Va), 17 May 1981. 320 w
Calls F's study a handy introduction that 'clearly maps out the intellectual
paths to follow' in reading Eliot's poems.

M22 The Well-Tempered Critic (*WTC*) [A6]

M22.1 Anonymous. *Booklist* 59 (June 1963): 808
Brief notice.

M22.2 — 'Il Metodo di Frye.' *Il Lavoro*, 20 August 1974. 175 w
Review of the Italian translation (A6b). Briefly summarizes the three
chapters.

M22.3 — *Virginia Quarterly Review* 39 (Autumn 1963): cxxvi. 160 w
Says the most valuable new contribution by F is his classification of the
three primary rhythms of speech.

M22.4 — *Yale Review* 52 (Summer 1963): xx, xxii. 600 w
Gives a concise summary of each of the three chapters and shows how
they fit together as a unit. Sees the book as having more value for those
familiar with *AC* than for the general reader. Notes that in the last chapter
F's solution to the issue of poetry and belief is quite different from that
of such theorists as W.K. Wimsatt, Jr, F's autonomous literary universe
containing the world of belief and action rather than escaping it.

M22.5 Beattie, Munro. 'Critic Sees New Things in Familiar Writings.' *Ottawa
Citizen*, 22 June 1963, 16. 690 w
Points to F's interest in theoretical criticism, and says that his contribution
to critical theory has had a 'sweeping influence on the teaching of English.'
Singles out for special comment the distinction F makes between prose
and ordinary speech because of the insights it provides for teachers of
composition.

M22.6 Blissett, William. 'Literary Studies.' *University of Toronto Quarterly* 33 (July
1964): 401–8 [407–8]. 530 w
Calls attention to the 'verbal felicities' found throughout the book. Con-
fesses to having some difficulty following the schematic diagram of F's
complex taxonomy of high, middle, and low styles.

M22.7 Cairns, A.T.J. *Canadian Book Review Annual, 1983*, ed Dean Tudor and Ann
Tudor (Toronto: Simon & Pierre 1984), 273. 400 w

Reviewed on the occasion of the Canadian reissue of the book, which 'welcomes rereading' after twenty years.

M22.8 Carena, Carlo. 'Alla scuola di un critico ben temperato.' *La Stampa* [Turin] 14 June 1974. 550 w
Review of the Italian translation (A6b). Glances briefly at *WTC* in a review devoted primarily to *EI*.

M22.9 Casati, Franco. 'Critica e cultura.' *Il Giornale di Vicenza*, 29 August 1974. 700 w
Review of the Italian translation (A6b). Lists some of F's central themes and points out that he is sensitive to both substance and form. Says his essays are like Pound's in the scope of what they undertake: they range from the study of rhetoric to the morality of writing. Looks at F's critique of the way literature is commonly taught in the university.

M22.10 Cook, Eleanor, and Ramsay Cook. *Canadian Annual Review for 1963*, ed John Saywell (Toronto: Univ of Toronto Press 1964), 457
Brief note.

M22.11 Elliott, George P. 'Variations on a Theme by Frye.' *Hudson Review* 16 (Autumn 1963): 467–70. 1800 w
Refers to F as 'the Blake of criticism,' a brilliant system builder whose books are difficult to synthesize once they have been read. Says *WTC* is 'worth a hundred critical studies, better put together but illuminating hardly anything.' Sets down the main idea that reading the book stimulated – that unless we learn to use language well our culture is doomed – and devotes most of the review to a homily to English teachers based on this idea.

M22.12 Engelborghs, Maurits. 'Recent Kritisch Werk.' *De Zeven Kunsten* 7 (19 September 1967): 4

M22.13 Griffin, Lloyd W. *Library Journal* 88 (1 April 1963): 1527
Brief summary of F's classification of literary styles.

M22.14 Hallie, Philip. 'The Master Builder.' *Partisan Review* 31 (Fall 1964): 650–1, 653–8. 2600 w
Sees *WTC* as an important book, but devotes most of this review to a critique of F's critical system in *AC*.

M22.15 Kibel, Alvin C. 'Academic Circles.' *Kenyon Review* 26 (Spring 1964): 416–22. 1600 w
Places the arguments of the book in the context of F's views in *AC*, which are seen as adumbrations of New Critical doctrines. Thinks F's schema in *WTC* do not 'convey anything of the immediate presence of the object he is studying'; instead he is pointing to certain systematic relations that are unverifiable and unrelated to literary experience. In short, F is part of a critical ethos that wants to methodize literary study.

M22.16 Mandel, Eli W. 'The Language of Humanity: Three Books by Northrop Frye.' *Tamarack Review* 29 (Autumn 1963): 82–9. 3400 w
Sees *WTC* as F's answer to the paradox of how criticism can be both detached from commitment and engaged in belief and action, an answer that involves a distinction between literary and other kinds of writing,

as well as a distinction between 'the language of the ego and the language of a genuine self.' F seeks to show that some uses of language enslave us and some make us free. Believes that for F the 'ethical and participating aim' of literature is fulfilled, finally, in the social ideals of the community, which constitute culture.

M22.17 Ostroff, Anthony. *Quarterly Journal of Speech* 49 (December 1963): 457–8. 590 w

Judges that F's book will be of most value to teachers: 'the categories and relationships he establishes are extremely useful.' Summarizes F's central arguments about style, which are said to provide 'an integrated view of verbal expression and its relation to literary expression.'

M22.18 Rovit, Earl. 'The Need for Engagement.' *Shenandoah* 14 (Summer 1963): 62–5. 1030 w

Explicates the triple pun in the book's title. Believes that F withdraws too much from the existential engagement with literature. Pays tribute to his usefulness as a scholar ('my own possibilities for insight and involvement are enhanced and enlarged by his efforts'), but finds his model of the literary critic to be far too Apollonian.

M22.19 Smith, A.J.M. 'The Critic's Task: Frye's Latest Work.' *Canadian Literature* 20 (Spring 1964): 6–14. 3560 w

Recapitulates in detail the arguments of each of the three chapters. Says that although the framework of the book is expository, its technique is that of a philosophical poem, organized in such a way as to make it a unified work of art. Observes that the tone of the first chapter is set by satire and controlled indignation; that of the second by rational argument, complemented by aphoristic *tour de force*; and that of the third by a tight organization that moves to a metaphysical climax.

M22.20 Stillwell, Robert L. *Books Abroad* 38 (Spring 1964): 186. 270 w

Brief review that judges the book to be marked by 'hard thought and abiding intelligence.'

M22.21 Walsh, Chad. 'Clearing Away a Multitude of Literary Confusions.' *Chicago Tribune Magazine of Books*, 7 April 1963, 2. 400 w

Gives a brief summary of F's exposition of style and praises the book for its own elegant and precise style and for its power to clarify.

M22.22 Weisinger, Herbert. 'Victories in a Lost War.' *New Leader* 46 (13 May 1963): 18–19. 410 w

Sees F's work as belonging to a new generation of scholar-critics who understand their methods and purposes as analogous to those of science yet who also defend the traditional moral function of literature.

N

Dissertations and Theses

N1 Ahmad, Iqbal. 'Northrop Frye's Theoretical Criticism.' PH D dissertation, York Univ 1974
A study of F's influence and his relationship to modern criticism, his idea of a scientific critical theory, his conception of archetypes, and his understanding of the language of poetry and of value-judgments.

N2 Aitken, Johan L. 'Children's Literature in the Light of Northrop Frye's Theory.' PH D dissertation, Univ of Toronto 1975. 291 pp
Maintains in chapter 1 that F's educational and literary theory forms a sound basis for the teaching of literature. Chapter 2 outlines the central principles of F's theories of modes, symbols, and myths. Chapter 3 examines the relationship between F's theories and children's literature and applies these theories to the study of myths, legendary heroes, fairy-tales, and nursery rhymes and stories.

N3 Antczak, Janice. 'The Mythos of a New Romance: A Critical Analysis of Science Fiction for Children as Informed by the Literary Theory of Northrop Frye.' DLS dissertation, Columbia Univ 1979. 362 pp
Investigates the imagery of science fiction in light of F's theory of imagery. Discovers a pattern here that conforms to that of F's romantic mode. Also finds that characterization and setting in science fiction are typically romantic and that the archetypal quests in romance and science fiction are structurally the same.

N4 Barrett, Jeannine Allison. 'Frye and Jung: Mirrored Harmonies: A Jungian Explication of Northrop Frye's *Anatomy of Criticism*.' PH D dissertation, New York Univ 1978. 480 pp
Discovers in the archetypal cosmology of Jung a mirror of the archetypal concepts in *AC*. Concludes that the whole of literature and criticism has its

roots in a universal pattern of cosmic opposition. Part 1 provides a handbook to ten key concepts in *AC*, and part 2 is a companion handbook to Jung's ideas about archetypal cosmology. Part 3 brings the contents of the two handbooks together through a series of analogies. Part 4 shows briefly how the original concepts, now reconstructed, have theoretical and practical value.

N5 Barton, Henry Alfred. 'A Study of the Interrelations among Criticism, Literature, and Literary Education in the Thought of Northrop Frye.' ED D dissertation, Harvard Univ 1972
An explication of F's 'theory of literature, construed both as a theory of what he calls the "formal causes" of literature and as a theory of the literary imagination' and of 'his ideas on the place of literature in the structure of formal education, especially as these ideas are shaped by his theory of literature.'

N6 Bennee, Florence Ethel. 'Selected Applications of Frye's Academic Criticism in the Senior High School Years.' ED D dissertation, Columbia Univ 1971.
259 pp
Seeks to determine whether the synoptic vision in F's *AC* can help to unify literary study in the high school. Analyses F's theories of modes, symbols, myths, and genres, as well as his assumptions about historical, archetypal, and thematic contexts, concluding that his work can be coherently applied to literary experience.

N7 Bogdan, Deanne Gail. 'Instruction and Delight: Northrop Frye and the Educational Value of Literature.' PH D dissertation, Univ of Toronto 1980.
544 pp
Examines F's contribution to the problem of the educational value of literature. Finds his solution to the problem in his own quest-myth at the anagogic level of literature. Gives detailed attention to F's theories of criticism and response, his idea of comic structure, his understanding of the spatial projection of reality, his notion of desire, his view of comedy and romance, his use of musical analogies, and his concept of form. Uses these fundamental principles in F's work to show how he resolves the Platonic paradox of the relation between art and ethics.

N8 Breucha, Susanne. 'Ordnung und Einheit der Literatur in Tradition und Mythos: Eine Studie der Literaturkritischen Schriften von T.S. Eliot und Northrop Frye.' Doctoral dissertation, Univ of Freiburg 1967
An analysis of F's concept of literature as a total order of words and of myth as the chief structural principle of literature. Finds the concepts of F's system to be internally incoherent, and questions the validity of the system itself.

N9 Celli, John Paul. 'The Uses of the Term "Archetype" in Contemporary Literary Criticism.' PH D dissertation, Kansas State Univ 1974. 239 pp
Studies the meaning of 'archtetype' in critical theories as the term is used by F (a literary category), Jung (a psychological category), and other critics who lie between these two poles. Observes that for F 'archetype' means

simply a recurrent unit of literary structure, either large (eg, plot) or small (eg, image). Believes that more is to be gained from F's theory than from Jung's because it encourages induction from literary observation.

N10 DeMaria, Robert, Jr. 'Critical Worlds: A View of Literary Criticism as an Artistic and Literary Form.' PH D dissertation, Rutgers Univ 1975. 234 pp
Devotes one chapter to F. Claims that 'Frye's critical world embodies its literary predilections not only because it is essentially "romantic" and comic in form but also because its originality is a profound conventionality ... To understand the nature of Frye's critical world as a reordering and elaboration of critical conventions is to see his criticism as about criticism.'

N11 Denham, Robert D. 'Northrop Frye's Criticism: Theory and Practice.' PH D dissertation, Univ of Chicago 1972. 403 pp
Revised and published as K5.

N12 Eskey, David Ellsworth. 'A Preface to the Study of Literary Style.' PH D dissertation, Univ of Pittsburgh 1969. 184 pp
Examines the chief ideas about style in the works of F and Chomsky and seeks to provide a synthesis of their ideas. Concludes that their theories coalesce naturally within a larger generative theory of mind.

N13 Feder, Herbert. 'The Place of Literature in Moral Education: An Examination of the Moral Aspects of Literature, Their Significance for Aesthetic Value, and Their Influence on Moral Development.' PH D dissertation, Univ of Toronto 1977
Chapters 3 and 4 examine, respectively, the relation between literature and morality in F's critical theory and F's view of the function of literature in moral education.

N14 Fekete, John A. 'John Crowe Ransom, Northrop Frye, and Marshall McLuhan: A Theoretical Critique of Some Aspects of North American Critical Theory.' Doctoral dissertation, Cambridge Univ 1971
Material on F published as L151.

N15 Fischer, Michael. 'The Triumph of Romanticism over Classicism in Modern Literary Theory: A Reconsideration.' PH D dissertation, Northwestern Univ 1975. 304 pp
'Chapters Three and Four show that the continuity between Coleridge's thought and the views of such later critics as Matthew Arnold, T.S. Eliot, and Northrop Frye lies in their shared unclassical unwillingness to release literature from accountability to rationally known truth.'

N16 Flynn, Elizabeth Ann. 'Feminist Critical Theory: Three Models.' PH D dissertation, Ohio State Univ 1977. 187 pp
Chapter 3 examines F's conception of archetypal criticism and formulates an archetypal feminist criticism.

N17 Gosman, Michael T. 'The Concepts of Literary Form as Represented in Three Modern Theories.' PH D dissertation, Catholic Univ of America 1971. 440 pp
An analysis of F's theory of form (along with the theories of Kenneth Burke and La Drière). Looks at F's handling of semantic problems and the

way he specifies literary form. Sees his theory of form as one of cosmic process: it is primarily 'spiritual,' but has anthropological and psychological dimensions.

N18 Govitrikar, Vishwas P. 'Literary Theory: The State of the Art.' PH D dissertation, Univ of Pennsylvania 1975. 222 pp
Chapter 2 examines both the theoretical and methodological statements and the implicit assumptions of F.

N19 Hamm, Minon Auda. 'Anatomy of the Center: An Application of Some Concepts of Northrop Frye.' PH D dissertation, George Peabody College for Teachers 1975. 276 pp
A study of F's idea that there is a centre to the imaginative experience of literature. Applies this concept to the study of four literary works in an effort to demonstrate its soundness.

N20 Loveday, S.C.H. 'Northrop Frye: Aspects of the Anatomy.' M PHIL dissertation, Oxford Univ 1978
Compares F's understanding of the imagination to Jung's 'collective unconscious,' and relates both of these to structural anthropology.

N21 Marquis, Paul Anthony. 'A Comparison of the Theories of Symbol in the Writing of Northrop Frye and George Whalley.' MA thesis, Queen's Univ 1980
Compares the elementary, mythic, and anagogic phases of symbolism as presented in the criticism of F and Whalley. Shows how F perceives symbolic design by 'standing back' from the literary work and perceiving a larger social construct and a vision of humanity as a whole, which is different from Whalley's interest in the imaginative appeal that symbols of individual works have for one's personal vision.

N22 Masteller, Richard Nevin. 'The Concrete Universal and *Anatomy of Criticism*.' MA thesis, Univ of Virginia 1968
'This paper examines how Frye, or one of his ideal "synoptic" critics, attempts to solve the paradox of the concrete universal.'

N23 Mugerauer, Robert William. 'The Autonomy of Literature: Toward the Reconciliation of the Intrinsic and Extrinsic Dimensions with Special Reference to the Work of Northrop Frye and Yvor Winters.' PH D dissertation, Univ of Texas at Austin 1973. 282 pp
Sees F's position on literary autonomy as representative of the modern commitment to intrinsic meaning and value. Examines three aspects of literary autonomy: an organic pattern of motifs, a formal structure of images incorporating nature as content, and a literary universe where individual works are related to the whole of literature.

N24 Rahme, Mary Hursey. 'The Invisible Medium: Criticism and the Language of Literature.' PH D dissertation, Wayne State Univ 1969. 528 pp
A study of style that draws upon the works of F, among others, to support an analysis of 'metalanguage' and 'fictionality.'

N25 Ray, William Ernest. 'Northrop Frye and the Development of Literary Criticism.' MA thesis, Univ of North Carolina 1967

Shows the connection between *FS* and *AC* and seeks to answer detractors of the latter by diagramming the development from the first book to the second – a development that is seen as logical, coherent, and brilliantly elaborative.

N26 Rodi, Dolores Suzanne Bissell. 'A Study of the Contributions of Carl Jung and James Frazer and Their Followers to the Hero Archetype with Suggestions for Teaching Literature.' PH D dissertation, Univ of Texas at Austin 1977. 304 pp
Argues that F, as one of the followers of Jung and Frazer, gives primacy in his interpretation and analysis of literature to Jung's psychological hero patterns and to Frazer's ritual patterns.

N27 Rodríguez, Julían. 'Enseñanza de la literatura comparada desde temprana edad hasta la universidad: pautas generales en su estudio y enseñanza a través de los principios estructurales de la teoría de Northrop Frye y maneras posibles de su aplicabilidad.' PH D dissertation, Univ Autonoma de Barcelona 1982. 340 pp
Part 1 outlines the basic principles of F's theory of literary structure. Part 2 illustrates through a variety of examples and techniques how the theory can be applied in the schools, from kindergarten through high school.

N28 — 'Introduccion a Northrop Frye.' MA thesis, Univ Autonoma de Barcelona 1980
Seeks to map out the global overview of F's criticism in order to interest Spanish scholars in his work.

N29 Salusinszky, Imre. 'The Neo-Romantic Imagination in North American Criticism and Poetry since 1945; with Particular Reference to the Criticism of Northrop Frye, Its Influence, and Its Relation to the Work and Influence of Wallace Stevens.' PH D thesis, Oxford Univ 1982
Devotes separate chapters to *AC*, to F's writings on Blake, Shakespeare, and Milton, to his view of the imagination, and to his influence on later critics, especially Hazard Adams and Harold Bloom. In a number of places, quotes from personal interviews with F.

N30 Searle, Leroy Frank. 'Basic Concepts in Literary Criticism: Some Controversial Instances.' PH D dissertation, Univ of Iowa 1970. 285 pp
Looks at the controversies surrounding *AC* as exemplary of the problem of concept formation in literary criticism. Sees F's attempt to account for all valid critical procedures as finally unsatisfactory, claiming that F confuses the contexts of theoretical explanation and critical description. Also examines F's ideas about criticism as scientific and as conceptually autonomous.

N31 Sloan, Glenna Davis. 'The Practice of Literary Criticism in the Elementary School as Informed by the Literary and Educational Theory of Northrop Frye.' ED D dissertation, Columbia Univ 1972
Revised and published as L475.

N32 Sparks, Elisa Kay. 'Sons of the Fathers: Critics of Romanticism and Romantic Critics.' PH D dissertation, Indiana Univ 1979. 599 pp
Investigates the assumptions underlying the critical theories of Arnold,

Eliot, Frye, and Bloom in order to illustrate the evolution of critical attitudes toward romanticism: 'Whereas Arnold and Eliot see Romanticism as offering a perniciously immature and individualistic vision of the universe, Frye and Bloom apotheosize the Romantic imagination as a quasi-religious faculty whose liberation perspective can restore man's sacred communion with the universe.' Still, the four critics share the same critical principles: they differ only in their judgment about the Romantics.

N33 Stanley, Lorraine Walton. 'Evaluation and Interpretation: A Discussion of Three Theories (Propounded by Frye, Krieger, and Hirsch).' MA thesis, Univ of Virginia 1974
Examines the issue of 'implicit evaluation and interpretation ... and explicit evaluation prior to or as a result of interpretation.' On F, see pp 2–8, 18, 19, 23.

N34 Stewart, Helen J. 'Northrop Frye's Theory of Imagination: A Study of the Theory in the Context of the Work of Bert Case Diltz and Ontario Secondary School English, 1952–1962.' PH D thesis, Univ of Toronto 1985
Looks at F's theory of education in the context of secondary school English in Toronto during the 1950s. Argues that F's theory offers a better model for teaching English than those offered by the reigning educational philosophies in Ontario from the 1950s to the present, particularly the philosophy of Bert Case Diltz. Maintains that F's views, unlike those of Diltz, offer a way of looking at literature that is sequential, structured, and coherent.

N35 Teeuwissen, Walter J. 'The *Anatomy of Criticism*: An Overview.' PH D dissertation, Univ of Michigan 1973. 220 pp
Looks at *AC* from four perspectives: as science, as a formal imitation of science, as a total vision of culture that contains but is not limited to science, and as a parody of science. Also examines the relationships among these several perspectives. Includes a survey of the criticism of *AC*.

N36 Tucker, Mary Curtis. 'Toward a Theory of Shakespearean Comedy: A Study of the Contributions of Northrop Frye.' PH D dissertation, Emory Univ 1963. 245 pp
'Primarily an attempt to explicate within the framework of Frye's larger theory those concepts which seem to be important in Frye's approach to Shakespearean comedy.' Devotes separate chapters to F's larger theory, his theory of comedy, his practical criticism of Shakespearean comedy, three separate essays on individual comedies, and an analysis and assessment of F's approach. Includes an appendix of thirteen diagrams illustrating the schematic nature of F's thought.

N37 Verma, Rajiva. 'Concepts of Myth and Ritual, and Criticism of Shakespeare.' PH D dissertation, Univ of Warwick 1972
Maintains that F's Shakespearean criticism breaks very little new ground, but that it is interesting nonetheless because of the way it fits into F's own system and reiterates the themes of more traditional myth and ritual critics 'with far greater theoretical awareness than they were capable of.'

N38 Webster, William B. 'Meaning and Significance: The Limits of Archetypal Interpretation.' PH D dissertation, Stanford Univ 1972. 255 pp
Sees F and some of his followers as representing one of the two main schools of literary typology. Argues that the school associated with Jung, Freud, and the Cambridge Hellenists assumes the existence of a correlation between literary types and the human psyche or culture, while the school associated with F does not.

N39 Welsh, James. '*Melos* and *Opsis*.' PH D dissertation, Univ of Pittsburgh 1970. 276 pp
Examines the Aristotelian terms F uses in the Fourth Essay of *AC* to distinguish the three radicals of presentation: *melos*, *lexis*, and *opsis*. Expands on F's suggestions, analysing the radical forms of the lyric as they appear in both primitive and sophisticated poetry.

O

Bibliographies

01 Denham, Robert D. *Northrop Frye: An Enumerative Bibliography*. Metuchen,
   NJ: Scarecrow Press 1974. 142 pp. Scarecrow Author Bibliography no 14
   Contains a listing of F's writings from October 1935 to June 1973 (306 en-
   tries), an annotated list of secondary sources (129 entries), and a list of
   reviews of F's books (348 entries). Includes title and name indexes.
   Reviews:
   Anon. *Reference Services Review* 2 (July 1974): 28
   A[ppenzell], A[nthony] (pseudonym for George Woodcock). 'Frye Enumer-
      ated.' *Canadian Literature* 61 (Summer 1974): 128
   Lochhead, Douglas. 'Letters in Canada.' *Univ of Toronto Quarterly* 44
      (Summer 1975): 413–15 [414]
   Olevnik, Peter P. *Library Journal*, 15 June 1974, 1691
   Ray, William E. *Southern Humanities Review* 9 (Fall 1975): 445–6
02 — 'Northrop Frye: A Supplementary Bibliography.' *Canadian Library Journal*
   34 (June 1977): 181–97
   A supplement to 01. Lists 28 primary and 103 secondary items, the latter
   of which are annotated.
03 — 'Northrop Frye Bibliography: An Addendum.' *Canadian Library Journal*
   34 (August 1977): 301–2
   Adds four primary and thirteen secondary entries to 02. The secondary
   entries are annotated.
04 — *Northrop Frye: A Supplementary Bibliography*. Emory, Va: Iron Mountain
   Press 1979. 67 pp
   A supplement to 01. Contains 56 primary and 201 (annotated) secondary
   entries.
05 — *Northrop Frye's Books, 1947–1978: A Descriptive Catalogue*. Emory, Va: Iron
   Mountain Press 1979. 14 pp

A catalogue of 59 of the various editions and translations of F's books, including edited volumes, exhibited at the Frederick Thrasher Kelly Library, Emory & Henry College, March 1979.

06 Grant, John E. 'A Checklist of Writings by and about Northrop Frye.' *Northrop Frye in Modern Criticism*, ed Murray Krieger (New York: Columbia Univ Press 1966), 146–78

A listing of primary and secondary sources through 1965. Includes separate sections on books, contributions to books, periodical articles, review articles, speeches, other writings, forthcoming publications, and editorships. Under secondary sources, lists biographical notices, reviews and discussions of F's books, and adaptations of his ideas. Contains 161 items written by F and 179 secondary items.

07 Hartley, Brian T. 'Northrop Frye and the Bible: An Interim Report, 1975–1984.' Unpublished typescript. 18 pp

A annotated overview of F's literary criticism of the Bible.

08 Hoy, Helen. *Modern English-Canadian Prose: A Guide to Information Sources* (Detroit: Gale Research 1983), 468–85

Lists 162 primary and secondary sources from 1940 to 1980, plus the reviews of F's books through *CR*.

09 Priestley, F.E.L. *The Humanities in Canada* (Toronto: Univ of Toronto Press 1964), 143–5

Lists more than 70 of F's books and essays written between 1941 and 1963.

P

Miscellaneous: News Stories, Biographical Notices, Letters, Anecdotes, etc

P1 Anonymous. 'Awards.' *Quill & Quire* 44 (July 1978): 6
Notice about F's winning the Royal Bank Award.

P2 — 'Banfield No Racist, Professor Says.' *Toronto Star*, 8 April 1974, C3
News story about F's response to the sds's having prevented Univ of
Pennsylvania professor Edward Banfield from speaking at the Univ of
Toronto, claiming he was a racist. F places the issue in the context of
academic freedom.

P3 — 'Canada a Model for All Nations?' *Moncton Times*, 13 March 1981
News story, based on an interview, on the occasion of F's address in the
Imperial Review series, Sackville, NB, March 1981. F responds to questions
on bilingualism, regional culture, the Americanization of Canada, and
Quebec separatism.

P4 — 'Canadian Author Prefers Simple Name.' *Peterborough Examiner* [Ontario],
30 August 1981, 38. This wire-service story appeared also in other Canadian newspapers.
Brief feature story of F's unassuming personality and disavowal of disciples.

P5 — 'Una conversazione di Northrop Frye all'Accademia Olimpica.' *Il Gazzet-
tino* [Vicenza], 18 May 1979
An announcement of F's lecture in Vicenza, Italy, on *The Tempest*. Lists the
Italian translations of F's books, briefly describes his approach to literature,
and mentions his witty style.

P6 — ' "Find Your Speed" N. Frye Advises Amateur Authors.' *Varsity* [Univ
of Toronto], 11 February 1938, 1
News story about F's address to the Univ of Toronto Press Club, 10
February 1938, in which he stressed the rhythm and simplicity necessary
for good writing and cited Joyce as a writer who progressed from the

straightforward short story to the masterful experiment in style and thought in *Ulysses*.

P7 — 'Frye Discusses English Satire.' *Varsity* [Univ of Toronto], 18 February 1943, 1
On F's lecture at Victoria College about the history and present state of satire.

P8 — 'Frye, H. Northrop.' *Who's Who in Canada: 1966–68*, ed Hugh Fraser et al (Toronto: International Press 1969), 418. And in subsequent editions
Lists biographical data.

P9 — 'Frye, Herman Northrop.' *An Illustrated Guide to the Canadian Establishment* (London: Methuen 1983), 285–6
Brief biographical sketch.

P10 — 'Frye, (Herman) Northrop.' *Current Biography Yearbook, 1983*, ed Charles Moritz (New York: Wilson 1984,) 136–9
Gives biographical data along with comments on the central themes of F's books.

P11 — 'Frye Praises Undergraduate Art Work.' *Varsity* [Univ of Toronto], 12 February 1943, 1
On F's critique of the Undergraduate Art Exhibit, Univ of Toronto.

P12 — 'Historians Are Awarded Canada Council Medals.' *Sarnia Observer*, 12 December 1967, 7
Wire-service story on F's having received the Canada Council Medal for outstanding achievement in the humanities.

P13 — 'Honored Company.' *Time* [Canadian edition], 29 March 1971, 8
On F's having been awarded one of the three Molson Prizes for 1971.

P14 — 'How Men Think.' *Manas* 5 (12 January 1972): 1–2, 7
In an editorial about how people might humanize their lives, draws upon F's ideas in *StS* about the nature of science and the myth of concern. Agrees with F's critical evaluation of science and sees value in his understanding of the way people think.

P15 — 'McLuhan's Message a Lasting One, Associates Say.' *Toronto Star*, 1 January 1981, A9
News account of tributes by F and others paid to McLuhan after his death.

P16 — 'Michener Invests 10 into Highest Rank of Order of Canada.' *Toronto Star*, 26 October 1972, 52. The same wire-service story appeared in *Ottawa Citizen*, 26 October 1972, 36, and a different story about the same event appeared in *Ottawa Journal*, 26 October 1972.
News story about F's having become a companion of the Order of Canada in ceremonies in Ottawa, 25 October 1972.

P17 — 'Modern Literature Club Hears Banned Novel Discussed.' *The Silhouette* [McMaster Univ], 10 November 1939
About F's address on *Ulysses* to the Modern Literature Club.

P18 — 'Newsline.' *Vic Report* 11 (Summer 1983): 10
A report on the special 'Frye Evening' held 12 April 1983, in the Victoria

College Chapel and attended by some two hundred alumni, students, and staff. Frye spoke on the topic 'The View from Here' (see I159).

P19 'Northrop Frye.' *Canadian Writers*, ed Guy Sylvestre et al. Rev ed (Toronto: Ryerson 1966), 52–3
Gives a sketch of F's career.

P20 — 'Northrop Frye.' *Contemporary Authors* 5–6, ed James M. Ethridge (Detroit: Gale Research 1963), 170
Biographical sketch.

P21 — 'Northrop Frye.' *Toronto Star*, 28 April 1962, 67
A sketch of F's career and reputation as a critic and teacher.

P22 — 'Northrop Frye.' *Varsity Graduate* 7 (June 1959): 78–9
Biographical note about F after he was appointed principal of Victoria College.

P23 — 'Northrop Frye.' *Writers' Union of Canada: A Directory of Members*, ed Ted Whittaker (Toronto: Writers' Union of Canada 1981), 84–6
A biographical and bibliographical sketch.

P24 — 'Northrop Frye: The Better to See.' *University of Toronto Graduate* 6 (Winter 1979): 4
An account of one of F's undergraduate classes. Quotes F on the subject of teaching: 'There is a danger of becoming a personality in your own right and taking over from the author you're teaching.' 'I'd rather teach undergraduates than graduates, because graduates should be in a position to teach themselves.' Gives opinions from three students about F as a teacher.

P25 — 'Northrop Frye Sees Culture as Society's Savior.' *Toronto Star*, 19 September 1978, A3
A news story about F's speech (D245) given on the occasion of his receiving the Royal Bank Award. Quotes several paragraphs from the speech.

P26 — 'Northrop Frye Wins $50,000 Award.' *Montreal Star*, 19 May 1978, B2
Wire-service story on F's receiving the Royal Bank Award. Gives a brief sketch of his career.

P27 — ' "Once I Was an Agnostic" Testifies Young Minister.' *Toronto Star*, 13 June 1936, 19, 21
New story on the report given by F and nine other young men to the United Church Conference meeting about their religious experiences. Reported F: 'I have had no mystic experience to relate. I have had no thrilling emotions, and I cannot name the date of my conversion.'

P28 — 'Poet and Critic.' *Saturday Night* 65 (13 December 1949): 8
Editorial comment on F's essay, 'The Function of Criticism at the Present Time' (D37).

P29 — 'Pomp, Pageantry ... Principal.' *The Strand* [Victoria College, Univ of Toronto], 28 October 1959
About the performance of the Gate House delegation at the installation of F as principal of Victoria College.

P30 — 'The "Popular Mythology." ' *Manas* 5 (12 January 1972): 4

Draws upon F's understanding of popular mythology to argue that we 'need to look again at "mythic" thinking, without assuming it to be necessarily "childish" or "primitive," but as representative of the kind of thinking men do when they take action in relation to the issues and decisions of their lives.'

P31 — 'Le prix de la Banque royale est décerné à Northrop Frye.' *Le Devoir*, 19 May 1978, 8
On F's having been chosen as the recipient of the 1978 Royal Bank Award.

P32 — 'Professor H. Northrop Frye.' *Canadian Library Association Bulletin* 10 (July 1953): 18–19
Brief sketch of F's career.

P33 — 'Royal Bank Award for Frye.' *Financial Post*, 3 June 1978, 9
About the Royal Bank's having chosen F, 'Canada's greatest living scholar,' to receive its award for 1978.

P34 — 'Royal Bank Award to Northrop Frye.' *Interest*, July/August 1978, 1
On F's being named recipient of the Royal Bank Award for 1978. Comments on F's influence as a scholar, teacher, and critic.

P35 — 'Royal Honors for Frye.' *Quill & Quire* 44 (October 1978): 1
An account of F's winning the Royal Bank Award. Lists some of the guests attending the banquet and quotes from F's address (D245).

P36 — 'Says Canadian Culture Lacks National Basis.' *Varsity* [Univ of Toronto], 15 January 1943
A report on F's speech, 'The Relation of Canadian Literature to Canadian Art,' presented to the Fine Art Club, 14 January 1943.

P37 — 'Socialism, Democracy Compatible – H.N. Frye Tells Vic CCFers.' *Varsity* [Univ of Toronto], 2 February 1950, 1
On F's address, 'Liberalism and Laissez-Faire,' presented to the CCF Club of Victoria College, 1 February 1950.

P38 — 'Television Censorship Not the Answer: Frye.' *Whig-Standard* [Kingston, Ont], 27 August 1975, 45
New story summarizing F's address to the CRTC's symposium on television violence (see D237).

P39 — ' "La tempesta" di Shakespeare commentata da Northrop Frye.' *Il Giornale di Vicenza*, 18 May 1979, 5
News story announcing F's lecture on *The Tempest* at the Olympic Academy in Vicenza. Gives a brief introduction to F and his work.

P40 — *Vic Report* 7 (Fall 1978–9): 2
An announcement of F's appointment as chancellor of Victoria Univ. Includes a sketch of his career as a scholar, teacher, and critic.

P41 — 'With Varsity Fund as His Silent Partner, a Student Puts Northrop Frye on Film.' *University of Toronto News* 2 (February 1970): 1
Brief photo-story about Jon Slan's setting out 'to capture Dr Frye's intellect – his thoughts and scholarship – on film' (see H18).

P42 Atwood, Margaret. 'Fifties Vic.' *CEA Critic* 42 (November 1979): 19–22.
Reflects on life as a student at Victoria College in the 1950s. Comments on

the undergraduates' attitude toward F ('He was an *eminence gris* [sic]'
and on his influence upon her own work as a writer.

P43 Ayre, John. 'Frye, Herman Northrop.' *Canadian Encyclopedia*, vol 2 (Edmonton: Hurtig 1985), 701
Points to the roots of F's literary theory, which combines a visionary
poetics with a disciplined study of conventional literary forms.

P44 — 'Northrop Frye in New York City.' *Graduate* [Univ of Toronto] 7 (January-
February 1980): 6–8
An account of F's giving the Leland B. Jacobs lecture at Columbia Univ on
26 October 1979 (see C8). Gives an abstract of the lecture and describes
the reception that followed. Comments on F's extensive schedule of lectures, the textbook series *Literature: Uses of the Imagination* (B14) for which F
was supervisory editor, and his Italian lecture tour in 1979.

P45 Baker, J. 'Poets of Their Time.' *TLS*, 10 September 1964, 845
A letter to the editor defending F's reading of the imagery in Keats's 'To
Autumn' and 'Ode to a Nightingale,' a reading that was questioned by the
TLS reviewer of *Romanticism Reconsidered*.

P46 Baxter, C.F.N. 'Northrop Frye.' *Globe and Mail*, 28 March 1972, 7
Replies to David Enn's critique of F's letter on the Wright Commission
report (see F87 and P73).

P47 Bell, Stewart. 'Students' Welcome on the Occasion of the Installation of
Principal Northrop Frye.' *Acta Victoriana* 84 (December 1959): 13
Student congratulatory message.

P48 Birney, Earle. *Spreading Time: Remarks on Canadian Writing and Writers, Book
1: 1904–1949* (Montreal: Véhicule Press 1980), 27
Remarks on the arguments presented by F in a 1933 Victoria College
debate.

P49 Birtch, George W. 'Personal Anecdote.' *CEA Critic* 42 (November 1979): 43
Brief reminiscence about an amusing incident when F was a student at
Emmanuel College.

P50 Bladen, Vincent W. 'Three Sons of the University.' *Varsity Graduate* 8
(January 1960): 3–6 [4–5]
A sketch of F's career.

P51 Bogdan, Deanne. 'Introduction to Northrop Frye.' *Indirections* 6 (Winter
1981): 1–2
An introduction of F as the keynote speaker for the Ontario Council of
Teachers of English Conference, 30 October 1980. For F's address, 'The
Beginning of the Word,' see D269.

P52 Borovilos, John. 'Response.' *Indirections* 6 (Winter 1981): 15
A brief message of appreciation to F for his keynote speech, 'The Beginning
of the Word' (D269), presented to the Ontario Council of Teachers of
English.

P53 Boyle, Harry J. 'Personal Anecdote.' *CEA Critic* 42 (January 1980): 19
Brief reminiscence about F's work on the Canadian Radio-television and
Telecommunications Commission, especially his ability to detect preten-

tiousness in broadcast applicants. Boyle was a fellow member of the commission.

P54 Braithwaite, Dennis. 'Nothing to Fear but Frye Itself.' *Toronto Star*, 8 April 1976, E17
Review of 'Journey without Arrival' (see H44).

P55 Brown, J.A. 'The Toronto Literary Mafia: Is Robert Fulford Next in Line?' *Canadian Review* 1 (June-July 1974): 5–7
An attack on F and other Canadian writers who are said to be in control of the Toronto literary establishment.

P56 Campbell, Ronald. 'Personal Anecdote.' *CEA Critic* 42 (November 1979): 36
Gives a brief account of the course in the Typology of the Bible that F has taught at Victoria College for some forty years. Speaks of its popularity over the years and of the way, even with more than three hundred students, F still conducts it as a seminar.

P57 Colombo, John Robert. 'Canadian Writers the Worst.' *Varsity* [Univ of Toronto], 27 February 1959, 1
About a lecture by F on Canadian literature presented at Hart House, Univ of Toronto, on 26 February 1959

P58 — ed. *Colombo's Canadian Quotations* (Edmonton: Hurtig 1974), 207–8
Reprints brief selections from *FS, EI, MC,* 'America: True or False?' (D188), *StS,* and *BG.*

P59 — 'Frye, Northrop.' *Colombo's Canadian References* (Toronto: Oxford Univ Press 1976), 197
Brief biographical sketch.

P60 Conarroe, Joel. 'Editor's Column.' *PMLA* 95 (January 1980): 3–4 [3]
Comments on how PMLA contributors have tended regularly to pay homage to F's work.

P61 Conway, Jill. 'Personal Anecdote.' *CEA Critic* 42 (January 1980): 48. Excerpted from 'Higher Education in an Unsteady State,' *Harvard Graduate Society Newsletter,* May 1979, 4
Observes that the person most responsible for helping Canadians understand the issues in the debate about the place of French Canada in the Canadian union has been F. Attributes F's understanding of the issue to 'a lifetime of commitment to humanistic study.'

P62 Corbeil, Carol. 'Recordings Offer Frye Lectures.' *Globe and Mail*, 25 March 1982, E8
About the release of the video series, 'The Bible and Literature: A Personal View from Northrop Frye' (H51).

P63 Cornell, Pamela. 'The Formal Art of Teaching: Northrop Frye: The Better to See.' *University of Toronto Graduate* 6 (Winter 1979): 4
A description of F's teaching practices.

P64 Cosgrove, Gillian. 'Plain Mr. Frye Condemned To Be Lonely.' *Toronto Star*, 7 August 1980, F1
One in a series of feature stories on people who possess what we desire most. Includes remarks by F's colleagues and former students on his

imposing intellect, as well as F's own comments on his reputation ('profoundly embarrassing'; 'a ball and chain that you drag around after you'). Gives an anecdotal sketch of F's life, and comments on the social detachment F has chosen in order 'to write books on impossible subjects.'

P65 Coughlin, Ellen K. 'Assigning the Blame for the Bleak Job Market.' *Chronicle of Higher Education*, 10 January 1977, 3
Brief report on selected remarks from F's 1976 MLA presidential address (D238) about unemployment among younger members of the profession and about the need for organized action to solve the problem.

P66 Deacon, W.A. 'Irving Layton Roasts Frye.' *Globe and Mail*, 13 April 1963
Reports on Layton's attack on F as representing the tendency of the academic in Canada to become more influential than the poet, Layton claiming that 'the university, and culture generally, are the worst enemies of creativity.'

P67 DeMille, C.W. Letter to the Editor. *Canadian Forum* 28 (April 1947): 18
Comments on F's unsigned editorial, 'So Many Lost Weekends' (F34). Speaks about the 'grave dangers attending to use of alcoholic beverages.'

P68 Donaldsen, Susan. 'Traditional Frye.' *Queen's Journal*, 26 November 1982, 18
News story on a lecture, 'The Imaginative World and Its Environment,' presented by F at Queen's University on 18 November 1982.

P69 Dudek, Louis. 'Northrop Frye Opposes "the Anti-intellectual Norm." ' *Montreal Gazette*, 31 May 1980, 101
An account of the tribute to F at the 1980 conference of the Association of Canadian University Teachers of English, Univ of Quebec. Summarizes F's banquet address.

P70 Edgar, Pelham. 'Northrop Frye.' *Across My Path*, ed Northrop Frye (Toronto: Ryerson 1952), 83–9
Gives an account of his relationship with F as a student at Victoria College; recounts, with the help of a letter from F, the history of F's interest in Blake; and comments on F's understanding of Blake in *FS*.

P71 Edinborough, Arnold. 'Canadian Riddles: "Who Are We?" and "Where Is Here?" ' *Financial Post*, 3 April 1976, 42
A review of 'Journey without Arrival,' the CBC television program in which F sets forth his views on Canada (see H44).

P72 — 'Frye, Pirandello and the Identification of Truth.' *Financial Post*, 17 January 1981, 20
On F's speech given to the American Association for the Advancement of Science (D264). Quotes several paragraphs about illusion and reality from the address.

P73 Enns, David. 'The Wright Report.' *Globe and Mail*, 23 March 1972, 7.
Reply to F's letter on the Wright Commission report (see F87, P46, P94, P112, and P129).

P74 Fetherling, Doug. 'A Publishing Pantheon.' *The Canadian*, 4 October 1975, 3
In an article on the people who 'affect the books of English Canada,'

Fetherling says of F: 'The undisputed dean of Canadian critics, he's equally important as a critic of criticism and a critic of literature. His influence here and in the rest of the English-speaking world is hard to measure but difficult to overestimate. With his interest in myth and symbolism in literature, he has influenced such writers as Dennis Lee and Margaret Atwood. Our only Pantheon critic.'

P75 Finlayson, Judith. 'The Fearful Shyness of Northrop Frye.' *Quest*, September 1978, 26–30
A feature story, based on an interview, on F's academic and personal life.

P76 Fisher, Douglas. 'On an Evening of Frydolatry.' *Toronto Telegram*, 25 January 1971
News column occasioned by Fisher's having attended An Evening with Northrop Frye at the University of Toronto, a program that included the viewing of Jon Slan's film, *Fearful Symmetry* (H18). Fisher reflects on the reasons F is not as well-known in Canada as Frank Underhill and Marshall McLuhan and recalls his experience as a student of F. Concludes that F is 'the one person of authentic genius' he is certain about.

P77 — 'The Symbol of an Era.' *Toronto Star*, 7 January 1981, 11
Reminisces about F and McLuhan during the late 1940s, when Fisher was a student at the University of Toronto.

P78 Fleming, Allan. 'The Books I Enjoyed Most in 1968.' *Financial Post*, 7 December 1968, 41
Lists F's *MC* as one of the three books in his list of those most enjoyed.

P79 Forsey, Eugene. Letter to the Editor. *Globe and Mail*, 10 October 1981, 7
Corrects an error in Adele Freedman's article, 'The Burden of Being Northrop Frye' (P80).

P80 Freedman, Adele. 'The Burden of Being Northrop Frye.' *Globe and Mail*, 3 October 1981, E1
A feature story, occasioned by F's having completed *GC*. Contains anecdotes about F's teaching and a brief biography. Quotes F, apparently from an interview, on his reasons for writing *GC*, on structuralism, and on the rootlessness of modern society. For P.J.M. Robertson's reply to Freedman's article, see P137.

P81 French, William. 'Frye the Conqueror Wows Them in Italy.' *Globe and Mail*, 14 June 1979, 15
An account of the 1979 lecture tour of Italy where F 'spoke to capacity audiences in Milan, Florence, Venice, Rome and other cities and was welcomed as an intellectual celebrity.'

P82 Fritz, Aileen. 'Lazy Author at Vic.' *Varsity* [Univ of Toronto], 2 November 1949, 1
Biographical profile, based on an interview.

P83 Fulford, Robert. 'Carve It on Our Tombstone.' *Saturday Night* 86 (March 1971): 7
Thinks that F's remark in *BG* about having grown up living in 'a state of more or less amiable apartheid' represents Canadian opinion about English/

French relations in a microcosm. Argues, however, that there is no such thing as 'amiable apartheid.'

P84 — 'Northrop Frye: A Life Spent Trying to Make Everything Fit.' *Toronto Star*, 29 January 1983, H5
Announces F's lecture at the opening of the Art Gallery of Ontario Symposium on Blake (6 February 1983). Surveys F's lifelong interest in Blake and recalls the reaction to *FS* by three reviewers.

P85 Garfield, Eugene. 'Is Information Retrieval in the Arts and Humanities Inherently Different from That in Science? The Effect that ISI's Citation Index for the Arts and Humanities Is Expected to Have on Future Scholarship.' *Library Quarterly* 50 (1980): 40–57.
Garfield's tables show that in a 1977–8 review of more than 950 journals F and Roland Barthes were the most frequently cited living writers in the arts and humanities. F ranks among those who are not living only behind Marx, Aristotle, Shakespeare, Lenin, Freud, and Plato. See also Garfield's citation data in *Current Contents*, 10 July 1978, 5–17; 11 September 1978, 5–11; and 6 August 1979, 5–10. The last of these articles, entitled 'Most-Cited Authors in the Arts and Humanities, 1977–1978,' is rpt in *Essays of an Information Scientist* 4 (Philadelphia: ISI Press 1981), 238–43.

P86 Godfrey, E.R. 'Personal Anecdote.' *CEA Critic* 42 (November 1979): 6
Brief description by one of F's colleagues at Toronto about F's 'physical trademarks.' Recalls their conservations from the 1930s.

P87 Gould, Allan M. 'Chatelaine's Celebrity ID.' *Chatelaine* 56 (November 1982): 43
F replies to a series of questions about hobbies, habits, favorite composers, current issues, and the like.

P88 Gustafson, Ralph. 'Correspondence.' *Canadian Forum* 23 (March 1944): 287
Replies to F's brief review of *A Little Anthology of Canadian Poets*, edited by Gustafson, in which F had wished for a statement of the editor's intention and principles of selection (see E21). Gustafson says that poetry needs no such statement.

P89 Hale, Barrie. 'Canadian Culture Goes to Washington: Starring Margaret Trudeau, Northrop Frye, and the Paintings of Jack Bush.' *The Canadian*, 7 May 1977, 8–10
On the opening ceremonies of the Symposium on Twentieth-Century Canadian Culture in Washington, DC, for which F was the keynote speaker. Notes that F departed from his printed text to present a more informal talk.

P90 Hamlin, Cyrus. 'Acta Feature: Literary Studies Programme.' *Acta Victoriana* 105 (Fall 1980): 53–61
Comments, in an interview, on F's role in helping to establish the graduate program in Comparative Literature at the University of Toronto, and on the 'incredible' fact that the English departments at Toronto and other universities have been little influenced by F's educational ideas.

P91 Harron, Don. 'Personal Anecdote.' *CEA Critic* 42 (November 1979): 17

Brief recollection by a former student about F's incisive comments on one of his papers.

P92 [Hillman, Serrell]. 'Letters: Critics' Choice.' *Time* [Canadian edition], 13 October 1967, 19–20
A brief account of F's status as a critic. Includes some biographical data. Quotes Claude Bissell as saying that F is 'the most distinguished literary critic living today.'

P93 Hirano, Keiichi. 'Frye, Northrop.' *The Kenkyu-sha Dictionary of English and American Literature.* 3rd ed, ed Takeshi Saito. Kenkyu-sha 1985
Biographical essay. In Japanese.

P94 Horn, Michiel. 'Northrop Frye.' *Globe and Mail*, 28 March 1972, 7
Replies to David Enn's critique (P73) of F's letter about the Wright Commission report (see F87).

P95 Howarth, Dorothy. 'Professor of English Abhors Horses, Tales of $5 "Millionaires." ' *Toronto Telegram*, 25 March 1950, 39
Feature story on F, primarily biographical.

P96 Hyman, Ralph. 'Gallery of Canadians: Draws a Bead on Blither.' *Globe and Mail*, 16 July 1960.
Brief biographical sketch.

P97 Johnston, George. 'A Celebration of Northrop Frye.' *The ACUTE Newsletter*, June 1980, 5–7
A thirty-stanza poem that reviews F's life and achievement, read on the occasion of F's becoming an honorary member of the Association of Canadian University Teachers of English.

P98 Jones, Frank. 'To Frye Fame Is No Fortune.' *Toronto Star*, 28 May 1978, D7
A story based on an interview in which F answers questions about such things as money, fame, and his reading and writing habits.

P99 Jones, Joseph, and Johanna Jones. 'Northrop Frye.' *Authors and Areas of Canada* (Austin, Tex: Steck-Vaughan 1970), 22–3.
Brief overview of F's work and professional career.

P100 Kappell, Jean, and Beverley Geary. 'Soap Tales Cling to Classic Plots.' *Dayton Daily News*, 15 December 1971, 25
F responds to questions about the working formula and stock characters in soap operas and traces their roots to classical literature and melodrama.

P101 Kirby, Blaik. 'Frye: Seeking the Canadian Rainbow's End.' *Globe and Mail*, 6 April 1976, 15
A review of 'Journey without Arrival' (H44).

P102 Klinck, Carl F. 'Personal Anecdote.' *CEA Critic* 42 (January 1980): 31
Brief reminiscence about F's role in encouraging the study of Canadian literature and about the importance that his theory of Canadianism had in the *Literary History of Canada*, which Klinck edited and for which F wrote the conclusion (see D154 and D233).

P103 Knelman, Judith. 'Experiment in Electronic Publishing Takes Frye from Stone Tablets to Computer Terminals.' *University of Toronto Bulletin*, 22 February 1982, 5

On F's use of the word processor to prepare his manusript for *GC*.

P104 — 'Scholars from across North America Contribute to *Festschrift* for Frye.' *University of Toronto Bulletin*, 11 April 1983, 5
An announcement of the publication of *Centre and Labyrinth* (K4).

P105 Knelman, Martin. 'Frye Makes His Film Debut.' *Globe and Mail*, 8 August 1970, 25
A review of *Fearful Symmetry: Northrop Frye Looks at the World*, a film produced by Jon Slan (see H18).

P106 Knight, Norm. 'Re Canadian Culture.' *Acta Victoriana* 57 (April 1933): 33–8
A review of a Victoria College student debate on the development of a distinctly Canadian culture. F, speaking for the opposition, is given credit for defeating the resolution.

P107 Krentz, Arthur. 'The Christian Tradition and Shaping of World Viewpoint.' *Leader-Post* [Regina, Sask], 27 March 1982, E17
Reports on F's 1982 Luther Lecture at the University of Regina, 'The Reformation in Mythology: The Christian Tradition and the Romantic Movement in Literature.'

P108 Lawless, Greg. 'The Myth of Northrop Frye.' *Harvard Crimson*, 7 April 1975, 3
An introduction to F's work on the occasion of his delivering the 1975 Norton Lectures at Harvard, later published as *SeS*.

P109 Layton, Irving. 'Am I Cheering to Empty Bleachers?' *Globe and Mail*, 25 April 1981, 7
Criticizes the Canadian press for not covering F's 1979 'triumphal tour' of Italy, where his lecture on Castiglione 'won standing ovations for its originality and brilliance.'

P110 — 'The Excessively Quiet Groves.' *Cerberus: Poems by Louis Dudek, Irving Layton, and Raymond Souster* (Toronto: Contact Press 1952), 55
Layton's lampoon on F. The poem in full: 'I said: Mr. Butchevo Phrye / Make no mistake, / I'm the reincarnation / Of William Blake. / But alas: Mr. Butchevo Phrye / was born to pry / Among old bones / And cemetery stones.'

P111 Lee, Rohama. Letter to the Editor. *Canadian Forum* 23 (April 1943): 17
Criticizes F's knowledge of 'music in the movies' in his article with that title (D16).

P112 Lennon, J.H. 'Northrop Frye.' *Globe and Mail*, 25 March 1972, 7
A reply to letters by F and David Enns (F87 and P73) on the Wright Report.

P113 Lindon, Mathieu. 'La Bible en duty Frye.' *Liberation*, 21 November 1984, 28–9
Gives a sketch of F's career, commenting on the importance of *FS*, *AC*, and *GC*. Based on an interview with F.

P114 Lochinvar. 'The Monocle: Debating Parliament.' *Acta Victoriana* 56 (October–November 1931): 35

An account of a Victoria College student debate in which F was one of the speakers for the opposition party, which won by four votes.

P115 MacDonald, Jeanine. 'Students and the Numbers Game.' *Victoria Reports* 14 (April 1964): 24–5
Summary of an address by F to the Victoria College Alumnae Association, 19 March 1964, on the problems facing the modern university and on the proper relationship between the university and society.

P116 MacKenzie, N.A.M. Letter to the Editor. *Canadian Forum* 33 (August 1953): 113, 115
A reply to F's editorial, 'Regina vs the World' (F56). Claims that Britain is far from declining as a world power.

P117 McMahon, Kevin. 'Scholar Keeps His Overflow Audience Breathless.' *St Catharines Standard*, 30 November 1984
A news story about F's lecture, 'The Authority of Literature,' presented at Brock Univ, St Catharines, Ont, 29 November 1984.

P118 Matas, Robert. 'Canada's World Image Is at Risk, Scholars Warn.' *Globe and Mail*, 3 February 1984, 4
News story about F and others expressing concern at a news conference about Canada's 'reluctance to provide adequate support for research in the humanities and social sciences.'

P119 Mauchan, David. 'Canadian Writer Isn't Concerned His Books Are Not Bestsellers.' *Leader-Post* [Regina, Sask], 6 March 1982
News story in connection with F's presenting the Luther Lecture at the University of Regina, March 1982.

P120 Mickleburgh, Bruce. 'The Canadian Key to a Chinese Door.' *Globe and Mail*, 9 September 1982
Story about a group of students at Wuhan Teachers' College, Wuhan, China, who wrote F on his seventieth birthday saying how much they had learned from studying *EI*. Says that F's approach provided the key to the students' understanding of different literary forms.

P121 Miller, Jeff. 'Elysium's Lap.' *Books in Canada* 12 (May 1983): 5–6
Recounts a humorous experience from F's course in Literary Symbolism.

P122 Moore, Arthur B.B. 'Personal Anecdote.' *CEA Critic* 42 (January 1980): 25
Brief recollection by the chancellor of the University of Toronto of an incident in which the authority of F's name, raised in the course of a heated discussion, was sufficient to close off the argument.

P123 — *Victoria Reports* 9 (April 1959): 5
An announcement that F will succeed Dr Harold Bennett as principal of Victoria College.

P124 M[oore], K[atherine]. 'The Installation of the Principal.' *Victoria Reports* 9 (November 1959): 4–5
On F's installation as the principal of Victoria College. Reports on the pro- ceedings and on F's address (C2).

P125 Newman, Christina. 'The Best Years of My Life and Other Lies.' *Maclean's*, January 1972, 32, 56, 38 [32, 56]

Comments briefly on F's influence as a teacher on Victoria College students in the 1950s.

P126 Newman, Peter C. 'In the Beginning Was the Word, and Now the Word Is with Frye.' *Maclean's*, 5 April 1982, 3
An editorial, occasioned by the publication of *GC*, which praises F for his attention to the question of 'the Canadian identity.'

P127 Nudell, Rosalyn. 'Canada Needs "Ghosts" to Bring Tradition Alive.' *Winnipeg Free Press*, 1 November 1978, 59
News story about F's delivering the Sidney Warhaft Lecture. 'Courtiers without Courts: Some Comments on Renaissance Education,' at the University of Manitoba.

P128 O'Malley, Martin. 'Northrop Frye's Life as a Literary Legend.' *United Church Observer* 47 (January 1984): 38–41
Feature story, based on an interview, in which F describes the 'epiphanic' experiences that lie behind much of his writing and responds to questions about *GC* and about his relation to the United Church.

P129 Orton, J.E. 'Northrop Frye.' *Globe and Mail*, 25 March 1972, 7
A reply to F's letter on the Wright Report (F87).

P130 Parent, Mgr A.M. 'Pierre Chauveau Medal: Northrop Frye.' *Proceedings of the Royal Society of Canada*, 4th series, 8 (1970): 18–19
Biographical sketch, read on the occasion of F's receiving the Pierre Chauveau Medal.

P131 Parker, Patricia. 'Crossing Boundaries.' *Vic Report* 14 (Winter 1985–6): 15
Comments briefly on F's role in helping to establish the Graduate Centre for Comparative Literature and the program in Literary Studies at the University of Toronto.

P132 Parnes, Pearl. 'Campus Profile: Prof Northrop Frye.' *Varsity* [Univ of Toronto], 21 February 1952, 4
Feature story on F, primarily biographical. Reports on F's early schooling and on his studies at the Univ of Toronto.

P133 Reaney, James. Editorial. *Alphabet* 6 (June 1963): 6, 73–6 [73–5]
Reacts to Irving Layton's claim that Canadian intellectuals 'lack colour and drama, lack boldness and vigour.' Cites F's work, along with that of Sapir, Cochrane, Innis, and McLuhan, to illustrate the contrary.

P134 Reeves, John. 'A Reeves Gallery: 2.' *Books in Canada* 8 (May 1979): 10–12 [11–12]. Rpt in *Canadian Fiction Magazine* 34–35 (1980): [94], as part of 'John Reeves' Literary Portraits.' This photographic section of *CFM* was also issued as a special supplement.
Brief comment on his effort to capture F's shyness in his photos. Portrait included.

P135 Richmond, John. 'Frye Translation Launched.' *Montreal Star*, 14 November 1969, 15
News story about a reception given in F's honour on the occasion of the French translation of *EI*. Quotes F on French-Canadian culture and politics and on Confederation.

P136 Ripley, Gordon, and Anne V. Mercer. 'Frye, Northrop.' *Who's Who in Canadian Literature 1983–1984* (Toronto: Reference Press 1983), 115
Brief biographical note, along with a list of F's books.

P137 Robertson, P.J.M. 'Is the Experience of Judgment an Activity like Vacuuming?' *Globe and Mail*, 10 October 1981, 7
A letter to the editor in regard to Adele Freedman's article, 'The Burden of Being Northrop Frye' (P80), particularly to a statement she makes about F's views on value-judgments.

P138 Robson, John M. 'Tribute to H.N. Frye.' *The ACUTE Newsletter*, June 1980, 3–5
A witty, anecdotal tribute, given on the occasion of F's becoming an honorary member of the Association of Canadian University Teachers of English.

P139 Schachter, Harvey. 'Let Quebec Go: Professor.' *Toronto Star*, 3 March 1977, B5
News story, based on an interview, in which F outlines his views on the separatist movement in Quebec.

P140 Schaefer, William D. 'Editor's Column.' *PMLA* 92 (May 1977): 379–80
An introduction to F's 'Presidential Address' to the Modern Language Association (see D238). Comments on F's being 'eminently quotable,' his treatment of professional topics, his wit, and his dedication to literary scholarship.

P141 Schwartz, Joseph, et al. '*CCL* Book Award Citation.' *Christianity & Literature* 32 (Spring 1983): 3
A citation acknowledging F's *GC* as the 1982 winner of the Book Award given by the Conference on Christianity and Literature.

P142 Shenker, Israel. 'A Literary Gathering on a Professional Level: What Does It All Mean?' *New York Times*, 29 December 1976, 27
Juxtaposes quotations from F's 1976 Modern Language Association presidential address (D238) with vignettes from the MLA's annual meeting.

P143 Shields, Roy. 'And Now, TV's Own Northrop Frye.' *Starweek Magazine*, 19–26 June 1982, 68
About the video series, 'The Bible and Literature: A Personal View from Northrop Frye' (H51).

P144 Sinclair, D.A. Letter to the Editor. *Canadian Forum* 25 (October 1945): 166
A response to part 1 of F's article, 'A Liberal Education' (D22). Finds portions of F's argument difficult to follow, particularly his definition of the ideal type of person the educational program he proposes is designed to produce.

P145 Slopen, Beverley. ' "Code" Sales Surprise Booksellers.' *Sunday Star* [Toronto], 2 May 1982, F11
News story about the brisk sales of *GC* and about the video series, 'The Bible and Literature: A Personal View from Northrop Frye' (H51).

P146 — 'Frye on Creation.' *Quill & Quire* 46 (March 1980): 12
A brief acount of F's Larkin-Stuart lectures at the Univ of Toronto in

January and February 1980, later published as CR. Summarizes the themes of the lectures.

P147 Snider, Joel. 'Academic Clash of the Titans – and May the Best Mind Win.' Globe and Mail, 3 July 1982, F2
Sees the differences between F and McLuhan as constituting 'the agenda of cultural debate in this country for the foreseeable future.' Examines briefly their different responses to the mass media and their different conceptions of the role of the teacher.

P148 Stoffman, Daniel. 'Media Built René's Image.' Toronto Star, 17 October 1977, A2
News story that quotes portions of F's remarks to the closing session of a conference on the future of confederation. The 'built-in flunkeyism' of the news media, according to F, has elevated René Lévesque as the only Canadian leader with a genuine vision. Reports F's urging the media to become more analytical and critical. For the text of F's remarks, 'A Summary of the Options Conference,' see D241.

P149 Story, Norah. 'Frye, Northrop.' Oxford Companion to Canadian History and Literature (Toronto: Oxford Univ Press 1967), 300
Brief account of F's life and career.

P150 Strong, Joanne. 'The Informal Northrop Frye.' Globe and Mail, 26 February 1983, 18
Story, based on an interview, in which F comments on the problems that come with being well-known and on the future of the universities. Includes a biographical sketch.

P151 Stroup, Thomas B. 'Introduction.' The Humanities and the Understanding of Reality, ed Thomas B. Stroup (Lexington: Univ of Kentucky Press 1966), v–xi [v–x]
Places the argument of F's lecture, 'Speculation and Concern' (D166), in the context of the other lectures given as a part of the Conference on the Humanities, University of Kentucky, 22–3 October 1965.

P152 Sutherland, Douglas. 'Ham and Frye Defend the Liberal Arts.' Varsity [Univ of Toronto], 26 January 1979, 3
News story about a discussion by F and University of Toronto president James Ham of the role of the liberal arts in times of economic recession.

P153 S[utherland], R[onald]. 'Frye, Herman Northrop.' Cassell's Encyclopedia of World Literature 3, rev and enlarged ed, ed S.H. Steinberg (New York: Morrow 1973), 504
Biographical sketch.

P154 Swail, David. 'Dennis Lee: A Poet's Progress at Mid-Career.' Vic Report 12 (Fall 1983): 6–10 [10]
An interview in which Lee reports that F was one of the two professors at Victoria College 'who made the most distinct intellectual impression' on him.

P155 Taylor, Charles. 'Choice and Master Spirit: Fame Is Pursuing Northrop Frye.' Maclean's 91 (6 March 1978): 36b–36d

An anecdotal portrait of F, written on the occasion of the projected (though never produced) television series featuring F on the great heroes of literature. Speaks about F's life as a student, teacher, and writer, his influence on Canadian writers, his commitment to Canada and his political sympathies, and his personal shyness.

P156 Tegelberg, Henning. 'Frye Labels Universities' Critics as Malicious, Stupid.' *Kitchener-Waterloo Record*, 27 May 1972, 3
New story summarizing F's convocation address at the University of Waterloo, 'Universities and the Deluge of Cant' (D212).

P157 Thomas, Clara. 'A Tribute to Northrop Frye.' *The ACUTE Newsletter*, June 1980, 1–2
Pays tribute to F for his championing 'the living and continuing' heritage of literature, for his teaching and writing about Canadian authors, and for his generosity of spirit. Thomas's remarks were made on the occasion of F's becoming an honorary member of the Association of Canadian University Teachers of English.

P158 Thompson, Robert G. Letter to the Editor. *Canadian Forum* 27 (May 1947): 41
A reply to F's editorial, 'So Many Lost Weekends' (F34). Maintains that people do not become alcoholics because of 'psychological maladjustments, or economic insecurity,' as claimed in F's editorial.

P159 Toombs, Farrell, et al. 'The Way It's Going to Be.' Audiotape in the CBC Radio Archives, Toronto. CBC reference no 680101-5. Broadcast on 1 January 1968.
The first part of this broadcast includes an excerpt from *MC* on the myth of progress. The panelists (Farrell Toombs, Kildare Dobbs, Wilfred Pelletier, and Dalton Camp) agree that society's source of anxiety is a feeling of alienation accelerated by the amount of information we are fed.

P160 Tovell, Vincent. 'Personal Anecdote.' *CEA Critic* 42 (November 1979): 11
Brief recollection, by the producer of F's CBC television program, 'Journey without Arrival' (H44), of the way F skilfully timed his narration during the production of the program.

P161 Traynor, Tim. 'Two Views of Canadian Literature: An Angry Poet, A Master Critic.' *Interpreter* [Univ of Western Ontario], 1 April 1963
Two news stories. The first reports on Irving Layton's attack on F as a clever academic who has had a pernicious influence on creative writers. The second summarizes an address F gave in London, Ont, on modern and Canadian literature.

P162 Underhill, F.H. 'Lorne Pierce Medal: Northrop Frye.' *Proceedings of the Royal Society of Canada*, 3rd series, 52 (1958): 44–5
A sketch of F's achievement as a scholar and critic, read on the occasion of F's receiving the Lorne Pierce Medal.

P163 Urquhart, Rupert N. 'Technology Answers.' *Technology Digest*, November 1972, 10–11
A reply to F's address, 'Universities and the Deluge of Cant' (D212). Seeks

to supplement F's analysis of higher education, and advocates applying scientific methods to solve the problems of education.

P164 Velkley, Richard. 'Critic Northrop Frye Livens Up CBTA.' *Telluride Newsletter* [Cornell Univ], May 1968, 8
Brief account of F's seminars on Shakespeare when he was a visiting lecturer at Cornell.

P165 Veroni, Clive. 'Frye: Timely Installation Speech.' *The Strand* [Victoria College, Univ of Toronto] 21 (25 October 1978): 4
An account of F's speech given on the occasion of his installation as chancellor of Victoria University.

P166 Vienneau, David. 'Northrop Frye Wins $50,000 Award.' *Toronto Star*, 19 May 1978, A3
News story on F's receiving the Royal Bank Award.

P167 Whittaker, Herbert. 'Frye Compares Victorian Woman with Today's Adolescent.' *Globe and Mail*, 2 August 1971, 15
A news story about F's lecture, 'The Philanderer and Shaw as Social Critic,' presented at the Eighth Annual Seminar of the Shaw Festival.

P168 Wolfe, Roy I. Letter to the Editor. *Canadian Forum* 22 (February 1943): 330–1
Takes issue with F's statement in 'Music in the Movies' (D16) that 'the incidental music [in the movies] has kept pace with [the movies proper] only just enough not to be completely incongruous.'

P169 Woodhouse, A.S.P. 'Vignette LXIII.' *PMLA* 76 (May 1961): i
Sketch of F's scholarly and teaching career.

P170 World, Margaret. 'Profs Away.' *Acta Victoriana*, November 1951, 11–12
An account, based on an interview, of F's study at Harvard during the year he received a Guggenheim fellowship and his summer teaching at the University of Washington.

P171 Wyers, Hugh. '$50,000 Award.' *Canadian Banker and ICB Review* 85 (July–August 1978): 25–6
Notice about F's being the fourteenth Canadian to receive the Royal Bank Award.

P172 Young, Dudley. 'The Deep Wood's Woven Shade.' *PN Review* 5, no 1 (1977): 65–6
A letter to the editor in reply to Gerald Lindrop's 'Generating the Universe through Analogy: The Criticism of Northrop Frye' (L306). Argues that F is a structuralist, trying to do for Western literature what Lévi-Strauss has tried to do for American mythology. 'Both men believe that the imagination has a knowable structure, which informs its expressions.' Believes that the knowledge gained from F's criticism helps one to rise above imperfect existence and 'to participate "ideally" in the fully human.' Thinks Lindrop underestimates F's wit. Sees F's large project to be a theological search for the 'white radiance' of the Incarnation, a project that modernism should have made possible.

Appendix
A Chronological Listing of Entry Numbers for Books and Essays about Frye's Criticism (Sections K and L)

1945 L397
1947 L504
1949 L505
1950 L219
1953 L96, L128
1954 L42, L411
1955 L106
1957 L572
1958 L131
1959 L4, L284, L338, L573
1960 L416
1961 L272, L529
1962 L208, L415, L444, L570
1963 L210, L268, L320, L485, L506, L550
1964 L31, L43, L162, L169, L203, L218, L233, L281, L309, L481
1965 L26, L44, L64, L139, L242, L267, L289, L299, L326, L418, L516, L547
1966 K8, L71, L81, L165, L212, L215, L235, L282, L334, L364, L380, L533, L543, L571
1967 L50, L85, L87, L90, L125, L145, L174, L221, L277, L303, L435, L530
1968 L67, L76, L93, L111, L135, L138, L144, L189, L196, L207, L230, L232, L236, L280, L286, L287, L292, L296, L378, L453, L496, L534, L574
1969 K7, L6, L22, L75, L84, L136, L140, L167, L243, L243, L250, L279, L285, L331, L342, L354, L363, L369, L382, L384, L396, L412, L452, L461, L470, L487, L494, L583
1970 L1, L10, L17, L35, L37, L80, L88, L94, L97, L142, L166, L194, L216, L255, L323, L359, L362, L374, L402, L438, L486, L500, L517, L551, L576, L586
1971 K2, L8, L100, L160, L161, L172, L184, L188, L234, L244, L262, L271, L310,

L314, L336, L339, L341, L344, L375, L381, L456, L469, L471, L499, L518, L549, L565, L566, L585

1972 L19, L45, L46, L74, L91, L107, L119, L154, L170, L199, L227, L249, L273, L293, L294, L301, L307, L312, L367, L394, L395, L427, L428, L434, L463, L474, L480, L563

1973 L18, L27, L30, L89, L92, L113, L182, L204, L217, L258, L318, L352, L398, L405, L408, L410, L422, L433, L445, L451, L464, L466, L468, L476, L478, L508, L515, L519, L531, L545, L554, L557, L561, L562, L579, L587

1974 L32, L48, L49, L103, L105, L115, L137, L251, L263, L264, L291, L304, L379, L443, L454, L458, L460, L462, L488, L495, L536, L538, L546, L560, L568, L577

1975 L5, L23, L25, L55, L56, L99, L116, L120, L127, L164, L176, L185, L195, L202, L247, L297, L302, L426, L446, L447, L457, L475, L535, L537, L540

1976 L12, L14, L41, L52, L70, L104, L121, L150, L163, L187, L229, 245, L246, L253, L259, L276, L283, L288, L332, L346, L366, L383, L389, L429, L441, L449, L459, L541, L548, L580

1977 L13, L24, L53, L65, L118, L132, L151, L157, L179, L237, L239, L252, L260, L274, L306, L333, L355, L360, L361, L387, L388, L390, L430, L510, L553, L555

1978 K5, L34, L39, L72, L78, L79, L86, L110, L117, L130, L153, L159, L168, L190, L220, L228, L278, L290, L295, L300, L328, L343, L345, L348, L350, L421, L455, L482, L491, L552, L567

1979 K6, L38, L83, L102, L109, L114, L193, L198, L205, L241, L254, L305, L308, L311, L316, L319, L324, L340, L356, L358, L370, L376, L399, L401, L420, L424, L448, L477, L483, L507, L513, L514, L524

1980 L3, L9, L11, L20, L36, L40, L66, L69, L82, L147, L148, L152, L156, L214, L223, L256, L257, L275, L368, L417, L493, L498, L511, L521, L525, L532, L581, L584, L588

1981 L16, L59, L77, L122, L181, L191, L192, L224, L225, L248, L329, L349, L351, L371, L400, L403, L413, L414, L439, L442, L450, L473, L509, L523, L539, L542, L556, L575, L582

1982 L28, L47, L51, L58, L61, L68, L101, L129, L171, L175, L200, L265, L269, L270, L298, L313, L321, L327, L353, L365, L404, L406, L497, L503, L526, L559

1983 K4, L7, L73, L124, L133, L134, L146, L178, L197, L201, L206, L209, L213, L222, L330, L337, L357, L373, L377, L385, L391, L419, L425, L432, L467, L479, L484, L489, L501, L502, L578

1984 L15, L21, L57, L62, L63, L95, L98, L112, L123, L149, L180, L211, L238, L315, L325, L335, L407, L437, L492, L512, L520, L522, L527, L528

1985 K3, L2, L60, L143, L155, L158, L173, L177, L186, L226, L231, L240, L266, L317, L322, L347, L372, L409, L423, L431, L436, L440, L472, L544, L564, L569

1986 L29, L108, L126, L141, L183, L465, L490

Name and Subject Index

This index lists the names of authors and editors, and it includes selected subjects. The entry for a given writer lists reference numbers for both author and subject.

Title Index

This index includes the titles of both primary and secondary sources, titles of books reviewed by Frye, and titles referred to in the annotations. The name in parentheses is that of the author or editor. If the title is not followed by a name, Frye is the author or editor. Interviews and recordings have been treated as primary sources.